Handbook of Research on the Global Impacts and Roles of Immersive Media

Jacquelyn Ford Morie
All These Worlds, LLC, USA

Kate McCallum
Bridge Arts Media, USA & Vortex Immersion Media, USA

A volume in the Advances in Media,
Entertainment, and the Arts (AMEA) Book Series

Published in the United States of America by
> IGI Global
> Information Science Reference (an imprint of IGI Global)
> 701 E. Chocolate Avenue
> Hershey PA, USA 17033
> Tel: 717-533-8845
> Fax: 717-533-8661
> E-mail: cust@igi-global.com
> Web site: http://www.igi-global.com

Library of Congress Cataloging-in-Publication Data

Names: Morie, Jacquelyn Ford, 1950- editor. | McCallum, Kate, 1956- editor.

Title: Handbook of research on the global impacts and roles of immersive
  media / Jacquelyn Ford Morie and Kate McCallum, editors.
Description: Hershey, PA : Information Science Reference, [2020] | Includes
  bibliographical references and index. | Summary: """This book explores
  the global impacts and roles of immersive media"--Provided by
  publisher"-- Provided by publisher.
Identifiers: LCCN 2019039304 (print) | LCCN 2019039305 (ebook) | ISBN
  9781799824336 (hardcover) | ISBN 9781799824343 (ebook)
Subjects: LCSH: Virtual reality--Social aspects. | Interactive
  multimedia--Social aspects.
Classification: LCC HM851 .H348635 2020 (print) | LCC HM851 (ebook) | DDC
  006.7--dc23
LC record available at https://lccn.loc.gov/2019039304
LC ebook record available at https://lccn.loc.gov/2019039305

This book is published in the IGI Global book series Advances in Media, Entertainment, and the Arts (AMEA) (ISSN: 2475-6814; eISSN: 2475-6830)

British Cataloguing in Publication Data
A Cataloguing in Publication record for this book is available from the British Library.

For electronic access to this publication, please contact: eresources@igi-global.com.

Advances in Media, Entertainment, and the Arts (AMEA) Book Series

Giuseppe Amoruso
Politecnico di Milano, Italy

ISSN:2475-6814
EISSN:2475-6830

MISSION

Throughout time, technical and artistic cultures have integrated creative expression and innovation into industrial and craft processes. Art, entertainment and the media have provided means for societal self-expression and for economic and technical growth through creative processes.

The **Advances in Media, Entertainment, and the Arts (AMEA)** book series aims to explore current academic research in the field of artistic and design methodologies, applied arts, music, film, television, and news industries, as well as popular culture. Encompassing titles which focus on the latest research surrounding different design areas, services and strategies for communication and social innovation, cultural heritage, digital and print media, journalism, data visualization, gaming, design representation, television and film, as well as both the fine applied and performing arts, the AMEA book series is ideally suited for researchers, students, cultural theorists, and media professionals.

COVERAGE

- Visual Computing
- Fine Arts
- Design Tools
- New Media Art
- Print Media
- Products, Strategies and Services
- Humanities Design
- Traditional Arts
- Environmental Design
- Digital Heritage

IGI Global is currently accepting manuscripts for publication within this series. To submit a proposal for a volume in this series, please contact our Acquisition Editors at Acquisitions@igi-global.com or visit: http://www.igi-global.com/publish/.

Titles in this Series

https://www.igi-global.com/book-series/advances-media-entertainment-arts/102257

Handbook of Research on Combating Threats to Media Freedom and JournalistSafety
Sadia Jamil (Khalifa University, UAE)
Information Science Reference • © 2020 • 408pp • H/C (ISBN: 9781799812982) • US $265.00

Deconstructing Images of the Global South Through Media Representations and Communication
Floribert Patrick C. Endong (University of Calabar, Nigeria)
Information Science Reference • © 2020 • 469pp • H/C (ISBN: 9781522598213) • US $195.00

Handbook of Research on Multidisciplinary Approaches to Literacy in the Digital Age
Nurdan Oncel Taskiran (Istanbul Medipol University, Turkey)
Information Science Reference • © 2020 • 405pp • H/C (ISBN: 9781799815341) • US $265.00

International Perspectives on Feminism and Sexism in the Film Industry
Gülşah Sarı (University of Bolu Abant Izzet Baysal, Turkey) and Derya Çetin (University of Bolu Abant Izzet Baysal, Turkey)
Information Science Reference • © 2020 • 277pp • H/C (ISBN: 9781799817741) • US $195.00

Handbook of Research on the Global Impact of Media on Migration Issues
Nelson Okorie (Covenant University, Nigeria) Babatunde Raphael Ojebuyi (University of Ibadan, Nigeria) and Juliet Wambui Macharia (Karatina University, Kenya)
Information Science Reference • © 2020 • 392pp • H/C (ISBN: 9781799802105) • US $280.00

Media and Its Role in Protecting the Rights of Children in Africa
Olusola Oyero (Covenant University, Nigeria)
Information Science Reference • © 2020 • 368pp • H/C (ISBN: 9781799803294) • US $195.00

Gender and Diversity Representation in Mass Media
Gülşah Sarı (Bolu Abant Izzet Baysal University, Turkey)
Information Science Reference • © 2020 • 338pp • H/C (ISBN: 9781799801283) • US $195.00

Handbook of Research on Deception, Fake News, and Misinformation Online
Innocent E. Chiluwa (Covenant University, Nigeria) and Sergei A. Samoilenko (George Mason University, USA)
Information Science Reference • © 2019 • 651pp • H/C (ISBN: 9781522585350) • US $295.00

701 East Chocolate Avenue, Hershey, PA 17033, USA
Tel: 717-533-8845 x100 • Fax: 717-533-8661
E-Mail: cust@igi-global.com • www.igi-global.com

List of Contributors

Aguilera, Julieta Cristina / *Independent Researcher, USA* 416
Amirsadeghi, Leila / *MESH, USA* 284
Daut, Michael / *Independent Researcher, USA* 237
Francis, Kelley M. / *Independent Researcher, USA* 79
Heller, Christina / *Metastage, USA* 158
Hurst, Brian Seth / *StoryTech Immersive, USA* 221
Kantor, Jessica / *Independent Researcher, USA* 142
Lantz, Edward / *Vortex Immersion Media, USA* 314
Leonard, Brett / *Studio Lightship, USA* 200
Malicki-Sanchez, Keram / *Constant Change Media Group, Inc., USA* 10
McCallum, Kate M. / *Bridge Arts Media, LLC, USA & Vortex Immersion Media, USA* 453
Morie, Jacquelyn F. / *All These Worlds, LLC, USA* 348
Panos, Gregory Peter / *Persona Foundation Founder, USA* 37
Phillips, Audri / *Robot Prayers, USA* 123
Remann, Micky / *Fulldome Festival Foundation, Germany* 79
Ricci, Linda / *Decahedralist Consulting, USA* 393
Scott-Stevenson, Julia / *University of the West of England, UK* 1
Si, Mei / *Rensselaer Polytechnic Institute, USA* 59
Wang, Shaojung Sharon / *Institute of Marketing Communication, National Sun Yat-sen
    University, Taiwan* 371
Weston, Eve / *Exelauno, USA* 176, 264
Weyers-Lucci, Dorote / *Institute of Transpersonal Psychology, Sofia University, USA* 430
Wilson-Brown, Saskia / *The Institute for Art and Olfaction, USA* 109
Zheng, Li / *Shandong University of Arts, China & Rensselaer Polytechnic Institute, USA* 59

Table of Contents

Foreword xvii

Preface xxi

Acknowledgment xxviii

Section 1
Immersive Media and Experience: Philosophy and Research

Chapter 1
Virtual Futures: A Manifesto for Immersive Experiences 1
  Julia Scott-Stevenson, University of the West of England, UK

Chapter 2
Out of Our Minds: Ontology and Embodied Media in a Post-Human Paradigm 10
  Keram Malicki-Sanchez, Constant Change Media Group, Inc., USA

Chapter 3
Humans Enter the Age of Avatarism 37
  Gregory Peter Panos, Persona Foundation Founder, USA

Chapter 4
Narrative Strategies in VR Movies, Traditional Movies, and Digital Games 59
  Li Zheng, Shandong University of Arts, China & Rensselaer Polytechnic Institute, USA
  Mei Si, Rensselaer Polytechnic Institute, USA

Chapter 5
Towards a Fulldome Manifesto: Tour d'Horizon for the Immersive-Inclined 79
  Micky Remann, Fulldome Festival Foundation, Germany
  Kelley M. Francis, Independent Researcher, USA

Chapter 6
Smell Is All Around Us: History, Meaning, and (Immersive!) Applications for Scent 109
  Saskia Wilson-Brown, The Institute for Art and Olfaction, USA

Chapter 7

The Intersections of Creativity, Technology, and the Mind: How This Applies to Immersive Projects... 123
Audri Phillips, Robot Prayers, USA

Section 2
Immersive Media and Experience: Production and Creation

Chapter 8
Discovering a Language of Stories in Immersive Storytelling: An Essential First Step 142
Jessica Kantor, Independent Researcher, USA

Chapter 9
Bringing the Human Dimension to Virtual Experience 158
Christina Heller, Metastage, USA

Chapter 10
Case Study of The BizNest: The World's First Immersive Sitcom... 176
Eve Weston, Exelauno, USA

Chapter 11
Virtual eXperience as a Mass Market Phenomenon: Spatial Computing and the World Building Challenge 200
Brett Leonard, Studio Lightship, USA

Chapter 12
Cinematic Virtual Reality: Inside the Story... 221
Brian Seth Hurst, StoryTech Immersive, USA

Chapter 13
Immersive Storytelling: Leveraging the Benefits and Avoiding the Pitfalls of Immersive Media in Domes 237
Michael Daut, Independent Researcher, USA

Chapter 14
POV in XR: How We Experience, Discuss, and Create the Virtual World....................................... 264
Eve Weston, Exelauno, USA

Chapter 15
Location-Based Entertainment: How Immersive Technology Can Make Us More Human 284
Leila Amirsadeghi, MESH, USA

Chapter 16
Immersion Domes: Next-Generation Arts and Entertainment Venues... 314
Edward Lantz, Vortex Immersion Media, USA

Section 3
Immersive Media and the Human Experience: Wider Implications From Entertainment to Beyond

Chapter 17
The Promises and Challenges of Immersive Education.. 348
Jacquelyn F. Morie, All These Worlds, LLC, USA

Chapter 18
Spatial Immersion and Human Interaction: Comparing Cross-Generational Experiences of
Pokémon GO Play 371
*Shaojung Sharon Wang, Institute of Marketing Communication, National Sun Yat-sen
University, Taiwan*

Chapter 19
Immersive Media and Branding: How Being a Brand Will Change and Expand in the Age of True
Immersion 393
Linda Ricci, Decahedralist Consulting, USA

Chapter 20
Immersive Media, Scientific Visualization, and Global Umwelt.. 416
Julieta Cristina Aguilera, Independent Researcher, USA

Chapter 21
Virtual Reality as a Tool for Mental Health and Conscious Living and Death: Immersive
Contemplative Approaches to Existential Anxieties... 430
Dorote Weyers-Lucci, Institute of Transpersonal Psychology, Sofia University, USA

Chapter 22
Immersive Experience: Convergence, Storyworlds, and the Power for Social Impact...................... 453
Kate M. McCallum, Bridge Arts Media, LLC, USA & Vortex Immersion Media, USA

Compilation of References 485

About the Contributors 527

Index.. 535

Detailed Table of Contents

Foreword xvii

Preface xxi

Acknowledgment xxviii

Section 1
Immersive Media and Experience: Philosophy and Research

Chapter 1
Virtual Futures: A Manifesto for Immersive Experiences 1
    Julia Scott-Stevenson, University of the West of England, UK

In this chapter, the author explores how immersive media experiences might lend themselves to examinations of pathways to a preferred future. After surveying a number of immersive media projects—some that have dealt with environmental and social issues and some on broader topics—the author identifies a number of affordances of the form. These affordances are crafted into a 'virtual futures manifesto', or a set of guidelines for the commissioning and creation of such works. The manifesto points include 1) stage an encounter; 2) be wild: bewilderment is powerful; 3) move from being to doing; 4) embody the future; and 5) care: the participants matter. It is hoped that immersive media experiences that consider these points may assist audiences in imagining pathways to preferred futures.

Chapter 2
Out of Our Minds: Ontology and Embodied Media in a Post-Human Paradigm 10
    Keram Malicki-Sanchez, Constant Change Media Group, Inc., USA

With the exponential development rate of technology at the start of the 21st century, humanity faces data that it alone cannot process without the aid of even more technology. As we move into a post-human era, how can immersive, spatialized, and embodied media assist us in comprehending the effects of these agents, and reconsider our past conclusions? These are media that can communicate new perspectives or run complex simulations tirelessly. They can provide the scaffolding to test our analytical reasoning and process to potentially escape our cognitive biases, develop greater plasticity, or even test new forms of embodiment. We must also consider how they can be manipulated and weaponized, and the rights of our future digital selves, as we become subsumed by data. This chapter explores ontology and embodied media in a post-human paradigm.

Chapter 3

Humans Enter the Age of Avatarism 37

Gregory Peter Panos, Persona Foundation Founder, USA

The internet, social networks, emerging virtual/augmented/mixed reality technology platforms and portals are beginning to utilize and display interactive, spatially relative, three-dimensional versions of objects, persons, and environments. The human need to document and archive one's form, behavior, beliefs, experiences, and wishes is an inherent need and desire of our species to preserve and tell their unique life stories. An ability to track and/or capture human movement, expression, environment, and experience with technology designed to acquire hand gestures, body and facial tracking inputs, as well as speech will play an important role in the life documentation process. The eventual goal will be for humankind to interact with, and be remembered as, autonomous virtual agents beyond the scope of physical life, providing "virtual immortality" to any and all that adopt the capability as it evolves in our culture, and with the machines and applications that we utilize. This chapter explores the age of avatarism.

Chapter 4

Narrative Strategies in VR Movies, Traditional Movies, and Digital Games 59

Li Zheng, Shandong University of Arts, China & Rensselaer Polytechnic Institute, USA
Mei Si, Rensselaer Polytechnic Institute, USA

Virtual reality (VR) movies have gained tremendous attention in recent years, with an increasing amount of experimentations and explorations from researchers and practitioners with various backgrounds. Many VR movies are aimed at providing the audience with a narrative experience, just as in traditional film and digital games. VR movies are a relatively new art form. The audience's experiences in VR movies share many common properties with traditional film and narrative games. On the other hand, VR movies offer a unique way for the audience to view and interact with the content, which differentiates it from other visual and narrative-based digital experiences. In this chapter, the authors review the narrative techniques used in movies and narrative games and present a survey and analysis of whether the techniques can or have been applied to VR movies.

Chapter 5

Towards a Fulldome Manifesto: Tour d'Horizon for the Immersive-Inclined 79

Micky Remann, Fulldome Festival Foundation, Germany
Kelley M. Francis, Independent Researcher, USA

The time for a Fulldome Manifesto has come because fulldome as an immersive, surround, communal medium is happening now. It comes as a vast vessel and in new form, with deep changes in the production and perception of 360-degree media. Within seconds, and without changing seat or body, one can switch from visiting a church, mosque, synagogue, or temple to being lured onto The Red Light District on a custom, generative, real-time responsive, science-fiction planet. Fulldome's mere scale can provoke profound wonder and interconnectedness and encapsulate the intersection of all media disciplines, unlike any other multimedia vessels humans have built so far. Like the membrane of a cell, fulldome houses the cross mingling of desires, projections, and technological abilities. In Tour d'Horizon For The Immersive Inclined, authors venture Towards a Fulldome Manifesto—exploring fulldome as a medium, venue, and genre while pointing to its promise for the advancement of immersive media.

Chapter 6

Smell Is All Around Us: History, Meaning, and (Immersive!) Applications for Scent 109

    Saskia Wilson-Brown, The Institute for Art and Olfaction, USA

While much of today's immersive media claims to be "multi-sensory," in actuality most such works have only audio and visual sensory cues. Scent, a powerful human modality that helps us to understand and derive meaning from the world, is often overlooked. However, scent in the service of art has a long and rich history, especially looking back to its ancient uses in establishing power, mystery, or memorability within religious or political domains. Early attempts at incorporating scent into artistic performances were not well received, perhaps due to inadequate technology of the time. Today a renaissance of olfactory art points to broader acceptance and appreciation of scent in artistic productions. Many artists are taking on the mantle of scent today, and the authors look forward to its increasing application in many forms of immersive media.

Chapter 7

The Intersections of Creativity, Technology, and the Mind: How This Applies to Immersive Projects.. 123

    Audri Phillips, Robot Prayers, USA

This chapter examines the relationships between technology, the human mind, and creativity. The chapter cannot possibly cover the whole spectrum of the aforementioned; nonetheless, it covers highlights that especially apply to new immersive technologies. The nature of creativity, creativity studies, the tools, languages, and technology used to promote creativity are discussed. The part that the mind and the senses—particularly vision—play in immersive media technology, as well as robotics, artificial intelligence (AI), computer vision, and motion capture are also discussed. The immersive transmedia project Robot Prayers is offered as a case study of the application of creativity and technology working hand in hand.

Section 2
Immersive Media and Experience: Production and Creation

Chapter 8

Discovering a Language of Stories in Immersive Storytelling: An Essential First Step 142

    Jessica Kantor, Independent Researcher, USA

In this chapter, the author explores storytelling in immersive media along with a systematic way of utilizing other forms of media to inform choices in these new techniques. The author argues that storytelling, as a human instinct, shows up in all forms of media as they emerge and that we are now at the beginning step on a long road of discovery. The chapter goes on to explore traditional forms of storytelling for the stage and screen to see how those mediums can inform emerging immersive media. Examples are presented of early immersive media that have achieved more or less success in telling a story.

Chapter 9

Bringing the Human Dimension to Virtual Experience 158

    Christina Heller, Metastage, USA

Immersive media can be achieved through many types of production techniques, each designed to achieve a specific purpose. This chapter describes Metastage, a volumetric capture studio aligned with Microsoft, that is being used by a wide range of creators to produce their groundbreaking immersive works. The common element in these works is the desire to bring realistic human representation to the productions. In addition to interviews with select practitioners, this chapter also describes techniques and best practices for high end volumetric capture.

Chapter 10
Case Study of The BizNest: The World's First Immersive Sitcom.. 176
    Eve Weston, Exelauno, USA

The immersive medium of extended reality presents plentiful opportunities to invent and reinvent. Some of these opportunities are technical, some are creative, and some are a mix. One of the agreed upon areas in this new medium that has been in need of invention and reinvention is storytelling. This chapter presents a case study of the world's first immersive sitcom produced by Exelauno, explaining how it came about and why it promises to open up a new avenue of storytelling for virtual and extended reality. It will share insights gained through the process of creating the series. And it will cover revelations gained at all stages—from rehearsals through post-production—about narrative, directing, comedy, and more in the context of this new immersive world.

Chapter 11
Virtual eXperience as a Mass Market Phenomenon: Spatial Computing and the World Building
Challenge 200
    Brett Leonard, Studio Lightship, USA

The focus of this chapter is twofold: How do we create immersive work that incorporates the best of our traditional media knowledge into this new realm? and How do we take new forms of immersive media to mass market? This chapter also covers the process of creating an innovative immersive new wave, independent cinema that incorporates a feature-length film done in multiple media formats with immersion at the core. Activating our own creative imaginations and unleashing participants and empowering them with this technology is the only positive route ahead into the future of immersive media.

Chapter 12
Cinematic Virtual Reality: Inside the Story.. 221
    Brian Seth Hurst, StoryTech Immersive, USA

This chapter presents a case study of the groundbreaking PBS digital studies cinematic VR film My Brother's Keeper. It covers all aspects of cinematic VR from conception and writing for the medium to ensuring the technology serves the story, filming, and postproduction. The piece set a bar for innovation in cinematic VR as the first production to combine 360- and 180-degree stereoscopic image capture to forward story and character interaction, the first to use true slow-motion 120 frames-per-second in VR and the first to establish intimacy with camera movement and close-ups, among other innovations. Six key videos are discussed, illustrating and demonstrating the principles of filmmaking innovation articulated in the chapter, as well as insights from behind the scenes interviews with the directors, producers, cast, and technologists talk about the making of the piece.

Chapter 13

Immersive Storytelling: Leveraging the Benefits and Avoiding the Pitfalls of Immersive Media in Domes 237

Michael Daut, Independent Researcher, USA

This chapter compares and contrasts the development of traditional cinema and fulldome cinema, describing the way their origins shaped not only their current success and potential as unique cinematic mediums, but also how their cinematic languages developed. There is a vastly different approach to storytelling that filmmakers must understand when creating shows for immersive digital dome theaters versus the approach they would take to tell stories in a traditional film. This chapter identifies key differences between cinema and fulldome and provides a primer for immersive storytelling on the dome from understanding the technology to understanding how most effectively to use the strengths of fulldome while avoiding its weaknesses. Ultimately, this discussion is designed to help creative artists become more effective immersive filmmakers for the fulldome canvas.

Chapter 14

POV in XR: How We Experience, Discuss, and Create the Virtual World 264

Eve Weston, Exelauno, USA

This chapter will introduce and explain the applications of a taxonomy for discussing point of view (POV) in XR. The simple designations of first, second, and third person that are used to categorize books, movies, and video games don't cover all the options and combinations available in immersive media. Accordingly, XR requires a new taxonomy that will allow for clear communication about content and experiences. This chapter will do three things: (1) present the four main POV tiers: narrative, visual, effectual, and experiential; (2) address less common tiers and how they might be incorporated and acknowledged in future XR experiences; and (3) show the taxonomy in action by using it to describe contemporary XR content.

Chapter 15

Location-Based Entertainment: How Immersive Technology Can Make Us More Human 284

Leila Amirsadeghi, MESH, USA

This chapter goes on a journey through time, highlighting key milestones, present-day realities, and future possibilities in the unbounded world of location-based entertainment (LBE). It explores the constant human desire for connection and play and looks at the role immersive entertainment has played in getting us out of the house, thus encouraging social interaction and mental stimulation in the most unconventional of ways. The chapter explores the impact that this growing industry will have on the (traditional) entertainment, retail, hospitality, art and education spheres, and touches on the history and background of venues and players (old and new), demonstrating diversity, creativity, and inimitability in execution. By taking a look at the power of immersive storytelling, the authors touch on the future of location-based entertainment and its ability to inspire ideas, conversation, and community.

Chapter 16
Immersion Domes: Next-Generation Arts and Entertainment Venues..314
    Edward Lantz, Vortex Immersion Media, USA

Large-scale immersion domes are specialized embodiments of spatial augmented reality allowing large groups to be immersed in real-time animated or cinematic virtual worlds with strong sense-of-presence. Also called fulldome theaters, these spaces currently serve as giant screen cinemas, planetariums, themed entertainment attractions, and immersive classrooms. This chapter presents case studies for emerging applications of digital domes, reviews dome theater design basics, and suggests that these venues are on track to become mainstream arts and entertainment centers delivering global impact at scale. Standard venue designs will be necessary to realize the full potential of an immersive media arts and entertainment distribution network. This chapter provides rationale for standardization of immersion domes for multi-use events spaces, immersive cinemas, and live performing arts theaters.

Section 3
Immersive Media and the Human Experience: Wider Implications From Entertainment to Beyond

Chapter 17
The Promises and Challenges of Immersive Education...348
    Jacquelyn F. Morie, All These Worlds, LLC, USA

This chapter covers immersive media as an educational tool, from its origins as a simulation training device for military applications to more recent examples of how it is being used in education and training today. Educational immersive media provides firsthand experiential learning opportunities. Educational theorists have supported the use of experiential learning as an effective approach even before the current development of digital applications, and these ideas are mentioned briefly. A continuum of immersion is discussed to include several approaches from low cost to high-end simulation. The chapter provides several examples of the ways today's immersive education is being utilized. Benefits as well as challenges and issues of this approach are outlined. A call for future research concludes the chapter.

Chapter 18
Spatial Immersion and Human Interaction: Comparing Cross-Generational Experiences of
Pokémon GO Play..371
    Shaojung Sharon Wang, Institute of Marketing Communication, National Sun Yat-sen
    University, Taiwan

This study investigated how Pokémon GO play may integrate players' gaming experiences and physical environments to facilitate spatial-human immersions in psychologically meaningful ways. Two age groups that represent generational players were further compared. A survey of 1031 players found that co-presence was positively associated with game enjoyment and game involvement, and nostalgia was positively associated with game enjoyment. The mediation effect of nostalgia on game involvement through game enjoyment was significant and game involvement completely mediated the relationship between game enjoyment and place attachment. In the 35 years and older age group, the direct effect of nostalgia on game involvement and the indirect effect of nostalgia on game involvement through game enjoyment were both significant. Theoretical implications on linking spatial relationships and the process of movement in the immersive AR environment and connecting the media experiences from one's formative youth period to the world of technological advances are elaborated.

Chapter 19

Immersive Media and Branding: How Being a Brand Will Change and Expand in the Age of True
Immersion 393
Linda Ricci, Decahedralist Consulting, USA

This chapter explores the impact immersive technologies—augmented reality and virtual reality—will have on consumer branding and business in the near- and longer-term future. Weaving multiple use cases and examples throughout, the author discusses the next phase of experiential marketing: how immersive branding will develop as spatial computing becomes more mainstream, and how brands can start thinking about how they can leverage the technology. The author examines the rise of virtual influencers, how they will affect social media marketing—and how artificial intelligence will ultimately enable true one-to-one interaction with customers through virtual avatars. Finally, the author discusses risks, rules, and recommendations for how to successfully proceed as a brand curious about how to best harness the technologies.

Chapter 20

Immersive Media, Scientific Visualization, and Global Umwelt.. 416
Julieta Cristina Aguilera, Independent Researcher, USA

This chapter deals with the global implications of immersive media: First, it considers how the concept of the umwelt can be used to address the extension of sensory motor capabilities of the human body. Next, it discusses what the implications are when the concept of the human umwelt is applied to scientific visualization in astronomy, which scales space and time to present data. Then, these scientific visualizations are discussed in the context of planetarium domes and what it means to collectively experience an immersive environment based on large scale data. As a case study, the final section articulates what this entails for the understanding of the effects of collective human interactions with our planetary environment at this stage of climate change.

Chapter 21

Virtual Reality as a Tool for Mental Health and Conscious Living and Death: Immersive
Contemplative Approaches to Existential Anxieties.. 430
Dorote Weyers-Lucci, Institute of Transpersonal Psychology, Sofia University, USA

In this chapter, the authors look at the possibilities of impact of VR in the mental health and wellness area through the lens of contemplative practices and immersive experiences. The area of existential anxieties is often stigmatized or difficult to address directly. Death is the most transformative journey possible but may not be viewed this way. Immersive experiences designed to encourage and allow for non-dual experiences can support this transition. They are difficult to design since non-dual experiences by their very nature are both deeply personal and yet totally impersonal at the same time. Yet, the authors examine how existential anxieties are the perfect framework for a non-dual experience. The wellness app StarflightVR serves as an explorative tool. We mention a past study in this area, which revealed that it is possible to mitigate depression by addressing anxiety on a daily basis through this immersive contemplative VR experience. The authors build on this study with existential fear mitigation examined through an online workshop experience and StarflightVR.

Chapter 22

Immersive Experience: Convergence, Storyworlds, and the Power for Social Impact.........................453
Kate M. McCallum, Bridge Arts Media, LLC, USA & Vortex Immersion Media, USA

This chapter examines the evolution of trends in the arts, storytelling, and immersive media, along with the emerging awareness, expansion, and deliberate application of social impact entertainment (SIE). The author discusses how the ideas and concepts of transmedia, convergence, and storyworld-building have now expanded beyond academic theory into more organic commercial and artistic applications. The focus is on how this approach relates to extending intellectual properties and stories into immersive media platforms and beyond. Additionally, the author presents several case studies and examples of emerging arts and media formats to support what we might expect to experience in the near future.

Compilation of References 485

About the Contributors 527

Index...535

Foreword

The year was 1989. Paula Abdul, Gloria Estefan, Chicago, Janet Jackson, Bette Midler and Milli Vanilli were on top of the charts. Film sequels of *Lethal Weapon, Ghostbusters, Back to the Future, Indiana Jones,* and *Karate Kid* launched. *The Simpsons* premiered. The Berlin Wall came down. Microsoft launched Office Suite with Spreadsheet, Word Processor, Database and Presentation Software. A proposal memorandum was submitted to CERN which would go on to become the World Wide Web. Intel released a series of microprocessors that opened the way for the next generation of much more powerful PC's. The first GPS satellite was put into orbit.

In 1989, Jacki Morie first walked into the University of Central Florida's Institute for Simulation and Training (IST) Virtual Reality Group in the Visual Systems Lab. While there Jacki worked with Army Research Institute (ARI) scientists Witmer and Singer (who developed the Presence and Immersive Tendencies Questionnaires which were used extensively in early VR studies). Jacki's work for ARI contributed to their VR-centered perceptual and navigational studies. She also worked on other projects resulting in breakthroughs that still impact virtual reality today, including programming and modeling for advanced image generators, like those used for the SIMNET networked tank simulators. This led to her helping create the SIMNET database in 1991 for the Battle of 73 Easting recreation, the largest expanse of virtual territory ever made for a simulator at that time. She built the entire digital city of Kuwait, as well as checking the huge digital landmasses and oil fields for errors.

Also, while at IST she also pioneered the concept of creating emotionally evocative VR, at a time when many offerings were simple and factual. With her partner, Mike Goslin, she created the VR experience called *Virtopia*, which had eight specially crafted VR worlds, each designed to elicit different emotional responses. *Virtopia* was the first ever VR to be showcased at a film festival: it was shown at the Florida Film Festival in Orlando in 1992 and again in a more advanced form in 1993. Today we see virtual reality and impressive immersive media installations at the most prestigious film festivals including the New Frontier at the Sundance Film Festival, Tribeca Immersive at the Tribeca Film Festival, Cannes XR at the Cannes Film Festival, and Venice VR at the Venice Biennale.

Morie also worked with an after-hour group of undergrad and high school students called the *Toy Scouts*, who were sponsored by Dr. Michael Moshell (Head of the Visual Systems Lab) and co-led by Florida grad student Dan Mapes (inventor of the VR gloves that eventually were marketed by FakeSpace Lab). The Toy Scouts made full bodied immersive VR games that were shown at the 1994 and 1995 SIGGRAPH conferences. Today large companies, content creators, and start-ups highlight VR and AR at SIGGRAPH and conferences ranging from CES to SXSW to I/ITSEC (The Interservice/ Industry Training, Simulation and Education Conference) to IAAPA (The International Association of Amusement Parks and Attractions) to Educause, a non-profit whose mission is "to advance higher education through the use of information technology.

During this same time period, Kate McCallum worked at NBCUniversal Studios and Paramount Studios for over 20 years specializing in television and feature film development and production alongside some of the world's top storytellers on iconic TV series such as *Miami Vice, Law and Order, The Marshall, Charles in Charge,* and *Equalizer.* Since then she has been Vice President of Programming for The Harmony Channel which was launched on Comcast On Demand, has produced 240 episodes of *Vidblogger Nation* for Comcast On Demand, and through the company she founded, Bridge Arts Media LLC, she consults, and has written white papers, presented talks, and in 2013 she designed and programmed the *TransVergence Summit* addressing transmedia storytelling and future trends in media technologies. Today, nearly all Hollywood film, television studios, and theme parks experiment with storytelling using immersive media, VR, and AR to launch their new productions, engage and immerse audiences in new worlds, and provide once-in-a-lifetime experiences and drive deep connections to their universes in the way only immersive media can.

Morie went on to help found the University of Southern California's Institute for Creative Technologies (ICT), where she continued her research into techniques that could predictably result in more evocative VR environments. Her work during this time included the invention of a scent collar for subtle VR smells and an infrasonic floor to elicit a visceral, though unheard, emotional response. Today we find VR, AR and Immersive Computing training, labs, and majors at universities including: Yale University, University of North Carolina, University of Hong Kong, Full Sail University, and so many more. And we find scent and aroma play an important part in location-based entertainment experiences such as The Void's *Ghostbuster's* experience or Marshmallow Laser Feast's *Ocean of Air.*

Today, Jacki continues to develop ground-breaking VR content with clients and partners including the U.S. Army, NASA and XPRIZE, as well as teaches the next generation of students the necessary tools and knowledge to take the reins, make their own mark, and continue to drive this important industry forward.

Since 2010, Kate has been a producer and creative consultant with Vortex Immersion Media and worked with founder Ed Lantz to launch the Vortex Innovation Lab and *AIR: Artist In Residence* program at Los Angeles-based The Vortex Dome. She has developed and produced 360 fulldome immersive/VR and interactive content and live performances such as *Migrations*, an immersive arts+music concert with visual artist, Audri Phillips, *Deep, Deeper and Deepest* art+music concert series with musician Steve Roach and Phillips, and *Melting Rainbows* arts+music performance art piece with artist Aaron Axelrod. She is currently distributing and producing a follow-up to *Mesmerica 360*, one of the most successful fulldome shows to be released to date in both the live and fulldome cinema version with musician James Hood. Kate recently produced a mixed-media VR installation project for a museum in Grand Rapids, Michigan for The Fetzer Foundation. As a producer in various traditional 360 and VR, she brings a unique understanding of blending the best of traditional media with the new super powers of immersive media such as presence, interactivity and immersion.

Kate has also been very active in the Producers Guild of America and served six years on the board of the PGA New Media Council (PGA NMC), three years on the PGA National Board, and she still serves on the PGA Education Committee. Kate and other members of the PGA NMC contributed their experience and passion towards creating and producing educational events for fellow members such as *Transmedia Storytelling*, *VR 360 Deep Dive: From Production to Post*, *Producing for Fulldome* (at the Griffith Observatory), and she helped create and co-present a PGA NMC series called *Special Venue Deep Dive* which featured events and talks with the founders at immersive venues such as Dreamscapes,

The Void, Two Bit Circus, and Hologate. Kate also spearheaded the creation of the PGA Social Impact Entertainment (SIE) Task Force which was launched after an initial event called *Producing Social Impact Entertainment* with Hollywood Health & Society at the University of Southern California.

The combined experience of early stage tech and ground-breaking content and storytelling provides a great marriage of intertwining industries and makes Jacki and Kate the perfect guides to take us on a deep journey into immersive media.

THIS BOOK IS FOR YOU

Jacki and Kate conduct us on a journey covering a wide range of topics through their hand-selected chapters by distinguished authors. These topics prepare us, educate us, inspire us and empower us to create the future together. The material ranges from philosophical to practical, and from broad to specific case studies. Chapters cover what the future will look like, the role of the individual, storytelling paradigms, practical production guidelines and business cases, as well as the impact on society, brands, mental health, and potential for positive social impact.

While the immersive media and virtual reality industries are not new today, there are still broad challenges to tackle before they become adopted by enterprise and consumers in mass numbers. It is the positive impact that immersive media brings to use cases such as training, healthcare, product development, architecture, engineering and construction, location based entertainment, and consumers' ability to connect, learn, communicate, and exist in new universes that will drive widespread adoption, along with technological breakthroughs, perhaps some even made by readers of this book. Large companies, start-ups, content creators from backgrounds spanning game development, engineering, film, television and music production, immersive theater, design, healthcare, government, and more are bringing this imagination, enthusiasm, tenacity, magic, and passion for this industry to make new discoveries, content, technologies, ultimately generating a new computing world.

This book is recommended reading for anyone interested in learning about the history of the industry, how to create and produce your own projects, and how to develop a business in immersion. Students, educators, professionals, hobbyists, and more will gain a deeper understanding of immersive media by immersing themselves in this book.

At a time when technological change is happening faster than ever, and when representative voices are sorely needed to build this next wave in computing, Jacki and Kate are uniquely suited to guide our path through this exciting new medium, as genuine pioneers in the field with a mix of research, academic, practical, production purview, and experience. They were involved as this immersive media was fledgling, only available in research and military labs, and continue to be at the forefront today as immersive media, while still in a nascent state, begins to make its way into common lexicon, finds its footing and develops into an important and vital industry—the true next wave in computing.

Joanna Popper
HP, USA

Joanna Popper *is a Hollywood and Silicon Valley media executive. She is HP's Global Head of Virtual Reality for Location Based Entertainment. Prior she was EVP of Media & Marketing at Singularity University, and VP Marketing at NBCUniversal. Joanna developed a TV show in partnership with NBC and Singularity University for a new TV series on technology and innovation. Joanna has been a leader in creating an inclusive and representative environment for women and other underrepresented groups. Joanna was selected as "50 Women Can Change the World in Media and Entertainment," "Top Women in Media: Game Changers," "Top Women in Media: Industry Leaders," "Digital It List," "101 Women Leading the VR Industry," and is on the Coalition for the Women in XR Fund. She is a sought after international speaker for media and technology. Instagram/ Twitter @JoannaPopper. LinkedIn http://linkedin.com/in/joannapopper.*

Preface

At the beginning of the 21st century, we are encountering an accelerating media revolution much like the cinema experienced at its birth in the early 20th Century. Just over 100 years later, new forms of media, creation tools, storytelling, and narrative methods are expanding beyond the frame and moving us from being just passive viewers to active participants. The media now surrounds and immerses us in ways film or television never could through the mechanism of "embodiment." With embodiment we can finally put our full sensory agency to bear on experiences that were once the sole domain of physical, factual, and lived reality. Reality itself has morphed into something that now incorporates those encounters in which we can have full control, ones that can recreate the past, bring to life our fantastic imaginations, and affect the health, well-being, and even spiritual dimensions of people in ways heretofore unimaginable.

These evolving, immersive media forms include: Virtual Reality (VR), Augmented Reality (AR), Mixed Reality (XR), fulldome, holographic characters, projection mapping, and mixed experimental combinations of old and new, live performances, and generated media. These new platforms, increasingly connected by the Internet, offer both the creators and the audiences brand new frontiers to explore.

This book positions itself firmly at the intersection of five distinct and critical groups: the technology developers and manufacturers (both business and academic); the organizers, trade associations, and participants of information-based networking events; the creatives and content creators; the distributors who get new ideas and projects out into the world; and of course—the audiences—for whom this work must have resonance and meaning.

The chapters explore the foundations and practices happening now that will have crucial global impacts in the near, as well as distant, future. The power to create new realities has placed at us at a momentous crossroads where the frame has been replaced by full spatial and immersive experiences—a paradigm shift that will carry us into the coming centuries.

TARGET AUDIENCES

In addition to the interest of a general audience those who are expected to benefit from this book include: academics, educators and researchers; directors, producers and visual effects artists; content creators, designers and immersive equipment makers; festival directors, production companies, consultants, writers and journalists; industry executives, students, and lifelong learners everywhere.

ORGANIZATION OF THE BOOK

The book is arranged in 22 chapters covering topics that will appeal to diverse types of readers. From philosophical to practical, these chapters provide glimpses into the broad trajectories of immersive media. It is organized into three sections, listed below, followed by their included chapters:

Section 1: Immersive Media and Experiences – Philosophy and Research

This section includes chapters concerning philosophical and research-oriented topics. Historical backgrounds are introduced, as are ways of being in—and dealing with—virtual experiences, storytelling, narrative strategies, and expansive sensory inputs. These subjects all help support new understandings of immersive media and its potential for human experience. Rounding out the section is a discussion about the intersections of creativity, technology and the mind, and how these connections can influence the ways in which we think.

Chapter 1. Virtual Futures: A Manifesto for Immersive Experiences

In this chapter, the author posits a set of critical and basic guidelines for the creation of immersive works and how these immersive experiences might assist in developing scenarios for a more evolved future. The manifesto explores the affordances of new media creations and offers a set of key guidelines and points that every practitioner should consider when building immersive experiences.

Chapter 2. Out of Our Minds: Ontology and Embodied Media in a Post-Human Paradigm

The author, the founder of a well-regarded VR/AR conference, dives deeply into the new perspectives proffered by embodied media and its impact on human evolution, and ponders these questions: How can immersive, spatialized and embodied media assist us in comprehending the effects of these agents, and reconsider our past? How can this media be manipulated and weaponized, and what are the rights of our future digital selves, as we become subsumed by data?

Chapter 3. Humans Enter the Age of Avatarism

This chapter details how we as humans can and will enter these new immersive perspectives via the constructs of our personal avatars. The author examines existing technologies that are giving us the ability to recreate our personas in a multiplicity of ways and postulates the possibilities for archiving ourselves digitally to be able to be remembered beyond the scope of physical life, providing a form of "virtual immortality" to any and all that utilize these capabilities as they evolve.

Chapter 4. Narrative Strategies in VR Movies, Traditional Movies, and Digital Games

In this chapter, the authors review the narrative techniques used in movies and narrative games and present a survey and analysis of how these techniques have been applied to immersive media. Through exploration of how traditional narratives are changing, they position these advancements alongside new virtual storytelling forms and analyze the differences from the audience's perspective and experience. They argue that VR movies offer unique audience interactions, which differentiates them from other narrative-based digital experiences.

Chapter 5. Towards a Fulldome Manifesto: Tour d'Horizon for the Immersive-Inclined

This 'manifesto' provides insights and delves deep into the world of fulldome from archetypal planetariums to visions of these venues in the future. Founder and executive director of one of the world's foremost fulldome festivals, and his co-author, an immersive producer, share insights from hands-on experience of this powerful spatial format, and the types of 360 content and immersive experiences that have been created for the fulldome space. This chapter explores fulldome as a medium, venue, and genre while pointing to its promise for the advancement of immersive media.

Chapter 6. Smell Is All Around Us: History, Meaning, and (Immersive!) Applications for Scent

This chapter explores the concept of scent as an integral aspect of immersion and immersive media. The author provides a number of examples of its use from history, including an early 20th Century performance that utilized scent as a method to enhance the meaning inherent in the presentation. Scent in the domain of modern media is surveyed, from early experiments in film to its use in current technological and immersive means of communication and entertainment such as theme park offerings and virtual reality. Finally, some thoughts are presented for why and how a person might work with scent, from the technological aspects to context and meaning.

Chapter 7. The Intersections of Creativity, Technology, and the Mind

The author, a digital visual artist with a background in fine art and painting, and with extensive experience in visual effects and animation, offers a philosophical approach to producing content for fulldome and immersive platforms. The nature of creativity, creativity studies, the tools, languages, and technology used to promote creativity are discussed. The parts that the mind and the senses—particularly vision—play in immersive media technology, as well as robotics, artificial Intelligence (AI), computer vision, and motion capture are discussed. The immersive transmedia project, *Robot Prayers*, is offered as an example of the application of creativity and technology working hand in hand.

Section 2: Immersive Media and Experience – Production and Creation

This section places us center stage in the production domain. Various case studies and real-world experiences familiarize us with the background, approach, and creation of some of today's most innovative immersive works that keep the best of traditional media while testing the boundaries of the new. Detailed discussions of specific immersive techniques and venues of the future finish off this section.

Chapter 8. Discovering a Language of Stories in Immersive Storytelling: An Essential First Step

This chapter looks to traditional forms of storytelling from stage and screen to see how those expressions and techniques can inform emerging immersive media. Storytelling, as a human instinct, shows up in all forms of media as they emerge, and we are now at the beginning steps of a long road of discovery. The chapter goes on to explore how techniques from mise en scène can serve to inform immersive media. The author also presents her work, *Ashes,* as an example of an immersive 360 video that incorporates many of these methods.

Chapter 9. Bringing the Human Dimension to Virtual Experience

This chapter delves into and details the most advanced methods to capture human performances for virtual experiences. The author describes *Metastage,* the Microsoft Company's volumetric capture studio being used by a wide range of creators to produce their groundbreaking immersive works. This chapter also includes interviews with top practitioners and thought leaders in the immersive space, and additionally describes techniques and best practices for high-end volumetric human capture.

Chapter 10. Case Study of the BizNest: The World's First Immersive Sitcom

This chapter presents a case study of the world's first immersive sitcom produced by Exelauno, explaining how it came about and why it promises to open up a new avenue of storytelling for virtual and extended reality. The author and creator shares information gained through the entire production process; from pitching to rehearsals through post-production. Additional insights about narrative, directing, comedy and more are presented in the context of this new immersive world.

Chapter 11. Virtual eXperience as a Mass Market Phenomenon: Spatial Computing and the World Building Challenge

The focus of this chapter is two-fold: how do we create immersive work that incorporates the best of our traditional media knowledge into this new realm, and how do we take new forms of immersive media to mass markets. In this chapter, the author, a seasoned director and creator, also covers the process of creating *Hollywood Rooftop,* an innovative *Immersive New Wave,* independent cinema that incorporates a feature-length film done in multiple media formats with immersion at the core.

Chapter 12. Cinematic Virtual Reality: Inside the Story

This chapter presents a case study of the groundbreaking PBS cinematic VR film *My Brother's Keeper* from the perspective of the producer and creator. It covers all aspects of cinematic VR from conception and writing for the medium, to ensuring the technology serves the story, to filming, and postproduction. The piece set a bar for innovation in cinematic VR using techniques such as combining 360 and 180-degree stereoscopic image to capture story and character interaction, use of true slow-motion 120 frames-per-second in VR, and ways to establish intimacy with camera movement and close-ups.

Chapter 13. Immersive Storytelling: Leveraging the Benefits and Avoiding the Pitfalls of Immersive Media in Domes

This author/practitioner provides insights into the language of the fulldome immersive storytelling. As a producer of fulldome content, he examines the different ways to approach storytelling that filmmakers must understand when creating shows for immersive digital dome theaters versus the approach they would take to tell stories in a traditional film. This chapter identifies key differences between cinema and fulldome and provides a primer for immersive storytelling on the dome, from understanding the technology to understanding how most effectively to use the strengths of fulldome while avoiding its weaknesses.

Chapter 14. POV in XR: How We Experience, Discuss, and Create the Virtual World

This chapter introduces and puts forth a detailed taxonomy for discussing points of view (POVs) in immersive media. This proposed taxonomy may facilitate clearer communication about the possible POVs that immersive content and experiences can incorporate. The four main POV tiers presented include narrative, visual, effectual and experiential. As well, less-common categories are presented with an eye to how they might be incorporated and acknowledged in future XR experiences. Finally, distinct media examples are given that illustrate the POV tiers.

Chapter 15. Location-Based Entertainment: How Immersive Technology Can Make Us More Human

Location-Based Entertainment (LBE) venues are destinations that can facilitate social interaction within the experience of immersive media, and they are becoming more and more popular with audiences of all ages. The author explores the impact that this growing industry is having on (traditional) entertainment, retail, hospitality, art and education spheres. She includes a history and background of venues and players (old and new), and explores the future of LBEs of many forms, as well as their ability to inspire new ideas, and enhance conversation and community.

Chapter 16. Immersion Domes: Next-Generation Arts and Entertainment Venues

The author, a fulldome professional designer and executive producer, reviews a range of technical considerations and design recommendations for digital dome theater venues. This chapter presents case studies for emerging applications of digital domes, reviews dome theater design basics and suggests that these venues are on track to become mainstream arts and entertainment centers delivering global impact at scale. This chapter provides rationale for standardization of immersion domes for multi-use events spaces, immersive cinemas, and live performing arts theaters.

Section 3: Immersive Media and the Human Experience – Wider Implications From Entertainment to Beyond

Here we explore the broader influences where immersive media has started to make significant inroads. From education, social connections, and scientific visualization, to health consequences, branding and social betterment, we are already starting to see the positive effects these new media forms are having now and will have as they evolve into the future.

Chapter 17. The Promises and Challenges of Immersive Education

The original underlying principle driving the development of early immersive media was its recognized usefulness as a training mechanism. From the early days of the United States military's funding and research, to NASA's rapid advancement of immersive technologies in the 1980s, we have now arrived at a place where many people can access and benefit from these technologies. The author covers the medium's training history as well as providing numerous examples of education-based applications today. The possibilities for a paradigm shift in education engendered by immersive media are also explored.

Chapter 18. Spatial Immersion and Human Interaction: Comparing Cross-Generational Experiences of Pokémon GO Play

This study investigated how playing the Augmented Reality game *Pokémon GO* could facilitate spatial–human immersions in psychologically meaningful ways. Over 1,000 participants in two age groups that represented different generational players were compared. Social relationships, nostalgia and place attachment were all investigated as part of the study. Co-presence led to increased game enjoyment as did both nostalgia and place-related game involvement. Theoretical implications consider technology as a variable that can have profound implications on co-presence and human interaction, two important factors of immersion.

Chapter 19. Immersive Media and Branding: How Being a Brand Will Change and Expand in the Age of True Immersion

In this chapter, the author examines the rise of immersive media for branding, business and experiential marketing. She also covers the increasing use of virtual influencers, how they will affect social media marketing, and how artificial intelligence might ultimately enable true one-to-one interaction with customers through virtual avatars. Finally, the author discusses risks, rules and recommendations for those companies and individuals curious about how to best harness new immersive technologies.

Chapter 20. Immersive Media, Scientific Visualization, and Global Umwelt

This chapter looks at the potential for immersive media to facilitate a better global understanding of how we, as humans, are connected to other life forms as well as to our home planet. Virtual Reality and other synthetic experiences accommodate human senses and actions, making space a deeper construct that supports and informs the human umwelt. The author explores how the unique affordances of immersive media can be applied to scientific visualization in astronomy, allowing space and time to be scaled to dimensions that facilitate increased human understanding of our place in the universe.

Chapter 21. Virtual Reality as a Tool for Mental Health and Conscious Living and Death: Immersive Contemplative Approaches to Existential Anxieties

In this chapter the author looks at the possible impacts VR might have in mental health and wellness domains. A deep practitioner of contemplative practices and immersive experiences, the author presents a case study of the wellness app *StarflightVR,* which serves as an explorative tool that can mitigate depression by addressing anxiety on a daily basis through an immersive contemplative VR experience. The chapter includes extensive research and references to state of the art uses of immersive applications for both brain and body health.

Chapter 22. Immersive Media, Convergence, Storyworlds, and the Power for Social Impact

The chapter probes the immersive media's potential for social impact. The author, a multimedia producer and creator, presents an approach towards understanding immersive media technologies, platforms, and experiences in light of storyworld-building and transmedia strategy design. Included in this strategic approach is consideration of Social Impact Entertainment (SIE) in the development of immersive projects. Additionally, examples of emerging arts and media formats and future trends are presented.

CONCLUSION

With the continued expansion of media beyond the traditional frame, content creators, storytellers, technologists, performers, artists, educators, and health practitioners are inventing and working in new immersive forms in marvelous and diverse ways. They share a common passion: crafting new media experiences to see how they can influence and shape our world for the better. It is our hope that this book will serve as an enlightening overview to inform new as well as established practitioners about important projects, techniques, and best practices that can bring the power of immersive media into the future it is meant to forge. The authors—wizards in their own rights—are using their magic wands at an unprecedented pace and sharing their discoveries with the world. May they inspire you to do the same.

   A magic wand—like any technology—is nothing until it is picked up and used.

Jacquelyn Ford Morie
All These Worlds, LLC, USA

Kate McCallum
Bridge Arts Media, USA & Vortex Immersion Media, USA

Acknowledgment

The editors would like to acknowledge the help of all the people involved in this project and, more specifically, to the authors and reviewers that took part in the review process. Without their support, this book would not have become a reality.

First, the editors would like to thank each one of the authors for their unique contributions and voices. It is an honor to have each of you included. Our sincere gratitude to you all for contributing your time and expertise to the making of this book.

Second, the editors wish to acknowledge the valuable contributions of the reviewers regarding the improvement of quality, coherence, and content presentation of chapters. Many of the authors also served as reviewers; we highly appreciate their double task. Those include Kelley Francis, Ed Lantz, Audri Phillips, Michael Daut, Linda Ricci, Jessica Kantor and Julieta Cristina Aguilera Rodríguez. Our additional reviewers include: Heather Renee Barker, Mike Baron, Edd Dawson, Nick DiMartino, Ryan Gill, Jill Gurr, Josh Hayes, Robyn Janz, Randal Kleiser, Mark Laisure, Philip Lelyveld, Joanna Lewis, Lisa Padilla, Anna Marie Piersimoni, David Polinchok, Allen Smith, Pamela Smith, Marc Spraragen, Lori H. Swartz, and Ruth West.

A special thank you and acknowledgement to Joanna Popper, Global Head of Virtual Reality for Location Based Entertainment at HP who contributed the Foreward.

Additional acknowledgements are due to Mark Laisure, CEO of Vortex Immersion Media and team, Stacey Quakenbush and Jamesen Re for their continued encouragement, several members of the Producers Guild of America New Media Council board who have been especially supportive include: Dina Benadon, Stacy Burstin, John Canning, Jeanette DePatie, Steve Ecclesine, James Fino, Emily Barclay Ford, Gregg Katano, Dan Halperin, John Heinsen, Jenni Ogden, Chris Pfaff, Alison Savitch, Brian Seth Hurst, and Chris Thomes. Thank you to Kate Folb of Hollywood, Health & Society at USC, who has been an inspiration and supporter, and to the PGA Social Impact Entertainment Task Force members: Kia Kiso, Anne Marie Gillen, Will Nix, Megan Mascena, Rebecca Graham Forde, and Robert Rippberger. Also, Tobias Demi of *Producing Impact*, Kathy Eldon of Creative Visions Foundation, The Skoll Center for Social Impact at USC, Jerome Glenn and The Millennium Project, James Hood, Bennett Freed, Michael Saul, Jon Cotton, Brianna Amore and the *Mesmerica* team, Winter Lazerus, Jahna and Michael Perricone, Elizabeth Yochim, Eve (Tiff) Randol, Amrita Sen, Anthony Marinelli, Aaron Axelrod, Sokamba, Kristin Petrovich of Createasphere, Michael Mansouri, Russell Bishop, Bruce Fetzer and the Fetzer Institute, Gordon Kurowski - Professor at Cal Arts, Brent Young of Super78, Los Angeles

Acknowledgment

Center Studios, Studio School, Eva Bitar, Citywide Filming Coordinator and Industry Liaison - City of Los Angeles, SOC, IMERSA, GSCA, SIGGRAPH, and IPS.

Thank you to Ed Lantz for the introduction to the magic of fulldomes and Madison Rubin for daily inspiration.

A special thanks to Richard Cray, virtual performer extraordinaire, Taylor Freeman of Axon Park and most especially Robbie Smith for continued optimism, reassurance and faith that we would indeed help change the world.

Jacquelyn F. Morie
All These Worlds, LLC, USA

Kate McCallum
Bridge Arts Media, USA & Vortex Immersion Media, USA

Section 1
Immersive Media and Experience: Philosophy and Research

Chapter 1
Virtual Futures:
A Manifesto for Immersive Experiences

Julia Scott-Stevenson
University of the West of England, UK

ABSTRACT

In this chapter, the author explores how immersive media experiences might lend themselves to examinations of pathways to a preferred future. After surveying a number of immersive media projects—some that have dealt with environmental and social issues and some on broader topics—the author identifies a number of affordances of the form. These affordances are crafted into a 'virtual futures manifesto', or a set of guidelines for the commissioning and creation of such works. The manifesto points include 1) stage an encounter; 2) be wild: bewilderment is powerful; 3) move from being to doing; 4) embody the future; and 5) care: the participants matter. It is hoped that immersive media experiences that consider these points may assist audiences in imagining pathways to preferred futures.

INTRODUCTION

There is significant hyperbole around immersive media technologies, for instance relating to claims around empathy, behavioral change and bias reduction. In parallel, a commonly heard concern is that digital media technologies distract us, take us out of the 'here and now'—affixing our attention to a mobile phone perhaps, or isolating us behind a head mounted display.

Notwithstanding these fraught debates, it seems clear that one of the affordances of immersive media, and virtual reality (VR) in particular, is the creation of a sense of presence, of 'being there.' So why take a user out of the 'here and now' and attempt to situate her somewhere else? One reason is to take her somewhere she cannot otherwise go. Some creators use it to visit someone or something lost or past (see for instance *Vestige VR* (2018), about the creator's late husband, or historical pieces like *Immersive Histories: Dam Busters* (2018)) or to venture inside another's mind (*Manic VR*, 2018). Some explore future worlds (*Biidaaban: First Light*, 2018), or visit remote places that demonstrate the impacts of the anthropocene (*Sanctuaries of Silence*, 2018). Many future narratives, though, across multiple screen

DOI: 10.4018/978-1-7998-2433-6.ch001

media forms, tend to be dystopian in flavor. Here, my focus is on what might be termed preferred futures—what is a future we *want* to get to? What is the world we want to make?

To investigate this idea further, I devised the following research question:

Might there be possibilities within immersive media for creating shared experiences that imagine pathways towards a preferred future?

I undertook a survey of existing media works across VR/AR/immersive experiences, and began to identify a number of themes. Rapidly I realized that, in fact, what I was developing was a manifesto—in other words, a set of guiding principles for the development of immersive projects. These principles are particularly relevant for those that want to explore preferred futures, but are likely useful for those making other kinds of stories as well. In writing an immersion manifesto, I'm in the esteemed company of Kat Cizek (2016) and Janet H. Murray (2016), whose earlier manifestos also propose approaches to immersive media, but are more focused on VR and its relationship with film; while this manifesto explores a broader category of immersive media and responds to more recent works.

VIRTUAL FUTURES MANIFESTO

Stage an Encounter

See Also: Connection, conversation

I had a wonderful, transcendent experience in *The Collider* (2018), an immersive installation by creative duo Anagram, in its showing at IDFA DocLab in Amsterdam. In *The Collider*, two participants enter 'the machine'—a connecting series of tiny rooms—via separate doors, while wearing headphones relaying a voiceover track. I entered one door, and undertook a series of actions as instructed by the voice, then moved into a second room, donned a VR headset, and then my fellow participant entered and used the hand controllers to guide what I was seeing. We went on to undertake a series of sensory interactions in very close quarters.[1]

The most intriguing part of the experience was the curated encounter with another person, whom I had not met until that moment. In this way, the work differed from many immersive experiences that attempt to create a sense of embodiment of another. There are a number of ethical conundrums apparent in claiming to develop empathy by enabling the user to walk in another's shoes, as while we might have the feeling that we are experiencing another's existence, we cannot really or fully know their lived experience (Nash, 2018). With an encounter, the user is not trying to *be* someone else; she is instead going to meet them for a while. Most of the immersive experiences that led to this understanding enabled an encounter with another human being—but perhaps we could have an encounter with ourselves? Or possibly even an encounter with the natural world?

Following a conversation with my boss, Professor Mandy Rose, I borrowed the idea of encounter from the philosopher Levinas. Levinas (1969) noted that an ethical encounter with another recognizes their infinity—that is, the complexity of that person, and an understanding that we will never fully know their entirety. Levinas also noted that in representing others, we run the risk of instead totalizing them—of suggesting that the incomplete picture we present is, in fact, all there is to them. Consider, for instance, stories of people with disabilities. It can often be the case that the story of their disability is presented as the only story they have, ignoring the individual's great complexity of being and of experience. So by crafting an encounter with another, instead of attempting to represent another or to have the user 'be' another, I hope that immersive experiences move us towards an opportunity to understand the infinity of whom we encounter.[2]

Finally, I also wonder if expanding the idea of encounter to specifically include conversation—allowing the user to speak back to the person they encounter—might be even more transformative. There are a number of questions around whether one can truly have an encounter with a simulation of a person that are beyond the scope of this manifesto, but would be ripe for future exploration particularly in the age of artificial intelligence.[3]

BE WILD: BEWILDERMENT IS POWERFUL

See Also: Joy, awe

It is clear that the planet and its inhabitants are in fairly dire straits, facing the current and impending impacts of human-induced climate change. There is a case to be made that the situation is so desperate that the only route is to shock people out of complacency, and anything less is not enough (Wallace-Wells, 2019). On the other hand, there is a risk that viewers will simply switch off from relentless difficult stories because it all just seems so overwhelming and intractable. Imagining the future is clearly a fraught business.

I wonder, though, if the unique affordances of immersive media (the feeling of presence, for instance), might offer us a way forward. If we can see/touch/hear/interact with the things we love about the world now, are we better able to envisage a way to protect them in the future?

Kevin Berger (2018) writes about a conversation he had with novelist Richard Powers, who brings up an essay by Lewis Thomas from the 80s, 'On Matters of Doubt'. Powers points to Thomas' reminder that bewilderment, in essence, means partaking in a state of being wild. So rather than the more common usage of a feeling of confusion or bamboozlement, it is a reminder of our animal state and our existence within a vast and complex system. Demonstrating a connection with the natural world has a long history in storytelling. Consider, for instance, the many Shakespearian characters that wander into the woods to soliloquize and better connect with their thoughts.

At CPH:DOX (Copenhagen Documentary Film Festival) in 2019, I experienced a VR work called *Re-Animated* (2018). The piece is about the now extinct ō'ō bird of Hawaii, and uses 3D scans of the forests of the island of Kaua'i. The viewer is placed within an animated forest environment; however, it is not a fully faithful representation of the Hawaiian forest. There are additional layers of illustration, animation and sound, such as silver glittering streamers fluttering through the air, and rendered segments of the ō'ō skeleton loom above. The effect offers a sense of magic and awe, and indeed bewilderment of the kind described here.

This notion of bewilderment is useful for environmental narratives, but it can apply in other narrative forms relating to connection too. Games designer Jane Friedhoff is onto something similar when she says she looks for catharsis over education in her games. Friedhoff (2018) says she instead wants to create joy, while still pointing to a desired world. She defines joy as containing a number of elements: a capacity for action, a sense of feeling seen and heard, a feeling of being part of a larger whole, an ability to envision a new and better world, and something that cannot be fully explained or quantified. With this approach, she is advocating a move away from the extractive model of storytelling where we look from the outside and peer in at someone else who is different from us. Instead, it is about a joyful connection with a shared community. She says, "I can make mosh pits for my friends." I think this sense of catharsis that Friedhoff is talking about is bewilderment by another name. We connect with others and are reminded of our position within a complex, majestic system.

MOVE FROM BEING TO DOING

See Also: Agency, interaction, control

I have lost count of the number of (usually) nonfiction 360-degree film experiences in which I have wondered why I am wearing a headset, and whether I am gaining anything more than I would by seeing the same piece on a flat screen. The creation of a feeling of presence can be enough for certain stories, but for many, there needs to be a next step of some level of interaction. It is a fine balance though, as the interaction needs to have some meaningful purpose to it.

Homestay VR (2018) is an animated VR story by Paisley Smith and the Canadian National Film Board. In it, the user explores a computer generated and rendered Japanese garden while listening to Smith's voiceover tell the tragic story of Taro, a Japanese student who did a home-stay with Smith's family. Sparkling red leaves flutter around the user, and the user is encouraged to reach out and collect them. While I thought the leaves were lovely, I was initially uncertain how they related to the story, or specifically, how my catching them was relevant. But later I heard Smith speak about the work, and she said, "Sometimes giving you something to do helps you stay in the present" (Smith, 2018). Smith has neatly encapsulated here the problem I noted above with some VR work—a lack of apparent necessity for being in 360 degrees, and identified an important first step to encouraging a feeling of connection.

How do we go from *being* in the present, though, to having an *impact* on it? I would suggest that interactivity can lead to a feeling of agency (some level of control) in the participant, only when the interaction has some meaning to the story. Janet H Murray, in her seminal 1997 book *Hamlet on the Holodeck*, calls this participating in the 'Active Creation of Belief.' We have to put in enough work to help continue the illusion, but not so much that the effort pulls us back out.

While at CPH:DOX, the Copenhagen festival I mentioned above, I experienced not one, but two VR works about the Hawaiian ō'ō bird. Coincidentally, a second had been produced on the same topic at the same time—this one titled *Songbird* (2018). The piece places the participant in a hand-painted rendering of the Hawaiian forest, with a distinct visual style. The audio track is made up of two voices: a female narrator's voiceover, interspersed with recorded narrative from a male ornithologist who travelled to Hawaii in the 1970s and saw the ō'ō. No one had seen an ō'ō for years, and it was assumed to be extinct—as he explains in voiceover, this ornithologist likely spotted the last surviving member of the species. Inside the VR piece, I shared the sense of awe related by the ornithologist in seeing the bird alight on a nearby branch. As he described fumbling for a tape recorder to capture the call of the bird, the narrator asked me to look to my hand, where I discovered the visual representation of the VR hand controller had now become a tape recorder. Her voice exhorted me to press the record button quickly, to ensure I too was capturing the call. As I did so, animated bubbles representing the call emanated from the bird and flowed into the tape recorder. As the bird flew away, the narrator then directed me to check that I had correctly captured the bird's call, as the ornithologist described his own hurried attempts to rewind his tape and confirm whether he too had captured the final ō'ō's song. As I hit the play button on my controller, the bird's call rang out and I was momentarily relieved, in tandem with the ornithologist who related his own similar relief. But then, of course, the ō'ō bird returns—it had heard the call, a sound it had presumably not heard for a long time, and believed that a fellow of its species was nearby.

This is a heartbreaking, climactic moment in the VR piece. Suddenly, my simple act of recording and playing back the bird's call has marked me as complicit in its loss. I have taunted the final, solitary bird, and in doing so I stand in for all humans and our destructive actions that have decimated the bird's habitat. My finger on the controller connects me in a corporeal way to this narrative of destruction, and highlights that it is human action that is implicated.

EMBODY THE FUTURE

Also: Bodies, voices

I love the work of Lynette Walworth, Australian filmmaker and VR maker, and *Collisions* (2017) is one of my favorite VR pieces. Exploring her latest work, *Awavena* (2018), at IDFA DocLab late last year, I enjoyed the storytelling and was awed by the stunning CGI design of the forest. But at 35 minutes long it made me feel incredibly nauseous, and I was constantly aware of the heaviness of the headset and of each tiny pixel in my view. I regularly had to close my eyes to attempt a self-reset. If I could have stood up from my chair and walked around, I might have been able to better ignore some of the distractions of the technology.

Manifesto point number four, on using embodiment, is closely linked to the previous point on agency. By being able to take some control—in a physical, bodily way—over the experience, perhaps the participant invests in a more complete way, or in a substantively different way? I want to be careful, though, not to suggest that engagement in a story or media form is only possible through movement, as of course there are countless traditional-screen films and documentaries that deeply and effectively engage the audience. Perhaps the key difference here is using the unique sense of presence and the consequent opportunity for embodiment as a conduit to a different kind of engagement. Or maybe it is simpler than that—perhaps by providing someone an opportunity to move or speak, they realize that they *can* move and speak. If this is the case, might it be possible to connect this awareness of capability for action to social and environmental impact narratives?

Intriguingly, many of the immersive projects I have experienced over the past year that have engaged the body beyond the eyes and ears have been, to some extent, based on voice. *VVVR* (2018), *Make Noise* (2018), *Injustice* (2018), *Terminal 3* (2018), *The Collider* (2018); all have called on the user to speak. *Make Noise,* by May Abdalla, is a wonderful example of curating this interaction in such a way that the participant knows precisely what is required of them. A VR piece about the suffrage movement, *Make Noise* gives suggestions for what kind and level of noise one should make, and later, particular words one should speak (or shout) as a specific act towards smashing visible barriers within the VR environment. This removes much of the self-consciousness often associated with audience participation, which can come from a fear of doing the 'wrong' thing.

When done well, the embodied immersive experience can also create joy and catharsis. *VVVR* is a two-person VR experience in which the participant sits on the floor, facing another participant, and makes any sounds they like with their voice. The sounds are visualized in shapes and colors streaming from their mouth, and the results can also be seen emanating from the other participant seated opposite. The creators, Ray McClure and Casey McGonagle, spoke at Open City Documentary Festival Expanded Realities Symposium in London in 2018, and McClure noted that he was overjoyed to watch a five-year-old child paired with an eighty-year-old person in the experience. He heard them howl and laugh, and described them as being "reduced to the same thing" (McClure & McGonagle, 2018). He went on, "there's a moment when you see them break through" (into the unselfconscious mode of just being there).

The joyfulness in *VVVR* comes from several things—the sharing of the experience with the other person (the encounter), the recognition of and connection with our animal nature (bewilderment), and the feeling of making ridiculous noises and speaking ourselves present (agency and embodiment). And while I have focused here on voice, there are plenty of other projects that explore different sensory approaches to embodiment. For movement/walking see *It Must Have Been Dark By Then* (2017) and *Pilgrim* (2018), for touch see *Micro-utopia: The imaginary potential of home* (2018), for taste see *Leaked Recipes* (2018) and *Frankenstein AI* (2018) and for smell see *Munduruku: The Fight to Defend the Heart of the Amazon* (2017).

CARE: THE PARTICIPANTS MATTER

At IDFA DocLab in November 2018, Steye Hallema presented *The Social Sorting Experiment* (2018), which was a fun, hilarious and slightly disconcerting experience. Forty-eight people were invited to stand on squares on a grid marked on the floor, and follow instructions on the screens of their smartphones to either move positions or to rate their grid neighbors in various ways. To participate, though, we first had to visit a URL on our phones' browsers, the landing page of which asked us to accept a data disclaimer along the lines of 'we have the right to use this data in any way we see fit.' I paused, my finger hovering over the assent button, as I wondered what data they meant. The data I enter into the browser? Every other page currently open in my browser too? Anything at all on my phone? Eventually I gritted my teeth and clicked 'yes,' comforting myself that 'this is art' and temporarily subscribing to the convenient view that artistic intent meant the creators were not planning to sell my data to shady advertisers or election engineers. One woman standing in the grid, however, put her hand up and objected, loudly. I was envious of her conviction, but it did mean that she could not participate.

By care, I mean care for the participant in two ways. Firstly, through respect for their privacy and data—as creators make yet more personalized experiences and collect ever more data on how each version unfolds (and think here beyond immersion about things like streaming service algorithms, for instance), it is vital that we maintain an ethical eye on how and why this data is stored and used.

Secondly, I mean care as consideration of participant experience, all the way from the introduction to and the exiting of the experience, as well as the moments afterwards. For me, one very simple test of whether an experience has considered this is whether I have somewhere safe to put my bag. If I am going to be experiencing a room scale VR piece, the sense of immersion is ruined if I have a constant urge to peek outside the headset and check that no one is stealing my belongings.[4] Care in this sense also means considering the viewer's response to the content. If the story is distressing or unsettling it can take some time for the viewer to decompress or rebalance afterwards, and being thrust straight back into a busy festival hall might not be appropriate. Ensuring they have an opportunity to reorient themselves is important.

Putting The Manifesto To Use

Most of the immersive projects I have discussed here include some of the manifesto points, but generally not all of them. It may be that some points will be applicable to a work, and some will not (although I think care is fairly non-negotiable). I do think that if we want to create immersive works that envisage a way towards a preferred future, then these points are going to offer some assistance (and they will hopefully assist even for projects aimed at something quite different). All the manifesto points are also closely intertwined, so it is less a checklist and more a Venn diagram.

Returning to my earlier comments about the precarious state of the world—the journey forward will not be easy, but I believe there is value in taking an optimistic approach and that we can *do* something by imagining the future through looking for the positive. The cultural landscape here is not completely empty; think of films like 2013's *Her,* starring Joaquin Phoenix and Scarlett Johanssen. The film presents a future city in which everyone walks to work rather than zooming around in the standard issue future vision of gleaming space pods (but yes, intimacy is also in danger of extinction—I'm looking for small wins here).

Biidaaban: First Light (2018) is also an intriguing example—in this VR project's future vision, nature has reasserted supremacy over the city of Toronto, yet local indigenous tribes have since flourished, as it is they who hold the knowledge necessary for survival.

This manifesto is, purposefully, technology-agnostic. A project that enables encounter, bewilderment, agency, embodiment and care will lend itself to a range of forms, across augmented reality, projection, installation, VR, a combination of these and more. My humble hope is that creators can use this manifesto to inform the development of amazing projects that will each connect us a little bit more with the way forward, and commissioners and funders can use it as a way-finding tool when considering what projects to champion and support. Ultimately, I hope the resulting immersive projects can help us illuminate those very necessary paths toward the future we want to create.

ACKNOWLEDGMENT

This research was supported by the South West Creative Technology Network [https://swctn.org.uk/]. An earlier version of this chapter appeared online in *Immerse* in March 2019, at https://immerse.news/virtual-futures-a-manifesto-for-immersive-experiences-ffb9d3980f0f

REFERENCES

Abdalla, M. (2018). *Make Noise* [interactive VR installation]. United Kingdom.

Abdalla, M., & Rose, A. (2018). *The Collider* [interactive VR installation]. United Kingdom.

Alchemy, V. R. (2017). *Munduruku: The fight to defend the heart of the Amazon* [interactive VR installation]. Retrieved from http://alchemyvr.com/productions/munduruku/

All Seeing Eye. (2018). *Immersive Histories: Dam Busters* [VR installation]. Retrieved from http://allseeingeye.co/projects/immersive-histories-dam-busters/

Anagram. (n.d.). Retrieved from http://weareanagram.co.uk/project/the-collider/

Berger, K. (2018). We Are All Bewildered Machines. *The Nautilus*. Retrieved from http://nautil.us/issue/66/clockwork/we-are-all-bewildered-machines

Bertin, K. (2018). *Manic VR* [VR installation]. Retrieved from http://kalinabertin.com/manic-vr/

Bradbury, A. (2018). *Vestige VR* [interactive VR]. Retrieved from http://vestige-vr.com/

Cizek, K. (2016). Towards a VR Manifesto. *Immerse*. Retrieved from https://immerse.news/towards-a-vr-manifesto-b97aca901192

Friedhoff, J. (2018). *Playful Possibilities*. Talk presented at Eyeo Festival. Retrieved from https://vimeo.com/287093861

Greenwell, L., Jones, A., Panetta, F., Oppermann, H., Kranot, U., Andersen, M., & von Bubnoff, A. (2018). *Songbird* [interactive VR]. Retrieved from https://www.theguardian.com/technology/video/2018/jul/30/songbird-a-virtual-moment-of-extinction-in-hawaii-360-video

Hallema, S. (2018). *The Social Sorting Experiment* [interactive performance]. The Smartphone Orchestra. Retrieved from https://www.doclab.org/2018/the-social-sorting-experiment/

Hutchinson, L. (2018) *Pilgrim* [interactive augmented audio walk]. Retrieved from https://www.doclab.org/2018/pilgrim/

Ivens, G. (2018). *Leaked Recipes* [interactive installation/performance]. Retrieved from https://www.doclab.org/2018/leaked-recipes/

Jackson, L., & Borrett, M. (2018). *Biidaaban: First Light* [VR installation]. Canada: Jam3 & National Film Board of Canada. Retrieved from https://www.nfb.ca/interactive/biidaaban_first_light/

Jonze, S. (Dir.) (2013). *Her* [motion picture]. United States: Warner Bros.

Kalpana. (2017). *Injustice* [interactive VR]. Retrieved from http://www.etc.cmu.edu/projects/kalpana/

Kudsk Steensen, J. (2018). *Re-Animated* [interactive VR - 15 min]. Retrieved from https://cphdox.dk/en/programme/film/?id=1207

Levinas, E. (1969). *Totality and Infinity: An Essay on Exteriority* (A. Lingis, Trans.). Pittsburgh, PA: Duquesne University Press.

Loften, A., & Vaughan-Lee, E. (2018). *Sanctuaries of Silence* [VR experience]. Go Project Films. Retrieved from https://sanctuariesofsilence.com/

Malik, A. J. (2017). *Terminal 3* [interactive augmented reality experience]. United States: RYOT. Retrieved from https://www.tribecafilm.com/filmguide/terminal-3-2018

McClure, R., & McGonagle, C. (2018). *Spotlight talk*. Expanded Realities Symposium—Open City Documentary Festival, London, UK.

McClure, R., & McGonagle, C. (2018). *VVVR* [interactive VR installation]. Retrieved from https://plusfour.io/vvvr/

Murray, J. H. (1997). *Hamlet on the Holodeck: The Future of Narrative in Cyberspace*. New York: The Free Press.

Murray, J. H. (2016). Not a Film and Not an Empathy Machine. *Immerse*. Retrieved from https://immerse.news/not-a-film-and-not-an-empathy-machine-48b63b0eda93

Nash, K. (2018). Virtual reality witness: Exploring the ethics of mediated presence. *Studies in Documentary Film*, *12*(2), 119–131. doi:10.1080/17503280.2017.1340796

Smith, P. (2018). *Homestay VR* [animated VR]. National Film Board of Canada. Retrieved from https://www.jam3.com/work/#homestay-vr

Smith, P. (2018). *Spotlight talk*. Expanded Realities Symposium—Open City Documentary Festival, London, UK.

Speakman, D. (2017). *It Must Have Been Dark By Then* [interactive augmented audio walk]. Retrieved from http://duncanspeakman.net/darkbythen/

Wallace-Wells, D. (2019). Time to Panic. *The New York Times*. Retrieved from https://www.nytimes.com/2019/02/16/opinion/sunday/fear-panic-climate-change-warming.html

Wallworth, L. (2017). *Collisions* [interactive VR]. Retrieved from http://www.collisionsvr.com/

Wallworth, L. (2018). *Awavena* [interactive VR]. Retrieved from http://www.awavenavr.com/

Weiler, L. (2018) *Frankenstein AI* [interactive installation/experience]. Columbia University Digital Storytelling Lab. Retrieved from http://frankenstein.ai/

ENDNOTES

[1] You can read more about my experience in *The Collider* in Scott-Stevenson, J. (2019) "This is the Story of the Space Between People…" *Immerse,* https://immerse.news/this-is-the-story-of-the-space-between-people-f99a953e31f2.

[2] Freya Wright-Brough has also explored Levinas in relation to digital refugee narratives during her PhD at Queensland University of Technology.

[3] These questions were addressed by Silke Arnold-de Simine at the Heritage Empath symposium, December 4, 2018, in Bristol, United Kingdom.

[4] For a more thorough take on viewer concerns while in VR, see McIntosh, V. (2018) "I always feel like somebody's watching me", *Medium*, Dec 16, https://medium.com/@veritymcintosh/i-always-feel-like-somebodys-watching-me-d50f2db2694b.

Chapter 2
Out of Our Minds:
Ontology and Embodied Media in a Post-Human Paradigm

Keram Malicki-Sanchez
Constant Change Media Group, Inc., USA

ABSTRACT

With the exponential development rate of technology at the start of the 21st century, humanity faces data that it alone cannot process without the aid of even more technology. As we move into a post-human era, how can immersive, spatialized, and embodied media assist us in comprehending the effects of these agents, and reconsider our past conclusions? These are media that can communicate new perspectives or run complex simulations tirelessly. They can provide the scaffolding to test our analytical reasoning and process to potentially escape our cognitive biases, develop greater plasticity, or even test new forms of embodiment. We must also consider how they can be manipulated and weaponized, and the rights of our future digital selves, as we become subsumed by data. This chapter explores ontology and embodied media in a post-human paradigm.

INTRODUCTION

"Immersive," "spatialized," and "embodied" media—where the participant feels to be inside of the experience rather than an external viewer observing action within a frame, generally terms not limited to but that are interchangeable for the study of the technologies more colloquially known as Virtual Reality (VR) and Augmented Reality (AR), and sometimes Extended Reality (XR), creates a head-scratching and exhilarating nexus of participation and observation, action and reaction, dread and awe. For many, its myriad "launches" into the public sphere have often proven underwhelming, frustrating, or lacking longevity or long-range utility. Extended inquiry into the media from a philosophical layer, and a very quick list of small victories and failures, may foster new discussion around what is missing and what is possible.

DOI: 10.4018/978-1-7998-2433-6.ch002

What are the ultimate effects of these media beyond the mere novelty or industrial application? What is their stuff of dreams that can bring us a deeper understanding of our yearning for the truth and our place and potential within it?

This chapter will explore how these new spatialized media can provide the mental scaffolding to create an expanded line of inquiry and understanding of our consensus reality and what is beyond the sensorium through which we process it. Coverage will include essentialism, social relativism, scientific process, ritual, and ethics from the pursuit of knowledge to the posthumous legal rights of digital ghosts.

What can we achieve through the affordances of the models provided, and how we can use immersive media as powerful epistemological, phenomenological, and ontological tools to discover the qualities not addressed by mathematics, physics, marketing and diversions? What is the warping power of art, love, and objects typically relegated to being outside of consciousness?

How can we use new spatialized digital media—immersive media—to explore the concepts of metaphysics, ontological materialism and quantum indeterminacy? Will these media take us closer to a simulated universe, or help us to escape one?

We will look at the opportunities for how these media can lead to short term and immediately actionable positive gains, including examining the efforts of several doctors, researchers and developers working with sick children and hospitals who are exploiting cognitive limits to override endemic pain responses. What we are truly exploring here, however, is the idea that the mind can transcend matters of the body and in so doing betrays how it is also capable of creating for us a reality that is wholly our own.

Further, we will explore the matter of ethics, aesthetics and legalities around volumetric effigies— three-dimensional digital likenesses. In a paradigm where our bodies can be captured at scale in photo-realistic detail, what are our post-mortem rights?

The Space Between

Ontology is the study of what fundamentally exists in the world and how those things relate to each other (Löfgren, 2019). If we contrast "ontological materialism" and "scientific monism" (John Locke, David Hume, Martin Heidegger), versus "ontological idealism" and "religious dualism" (René Descartes, George Berkeley, Immanuel Kant, simulation hypothesists), we see a critical divide in approach. Do we examine things for their own existence outside of human-centrism? Or do we align with the notion that nothing exists until observed (by [human] consciousness)? How can the new immersive media afford us new vantage points to get beyond these dueling frameworks? Circa 1929, a peak time for epistemological revolution, Alfred Whitehead (1929) introduced a "process philosophy" to escape the rigid approaches that had been deployed before, and favored instead constant change and the need to modulate in step with inevitable and unforeseeable transformations in context, innovation and understanding.

Ninety years later, we must prepare for unexpected accelerations and leaps in innovation and development that lead to futures we could not have imagined. For example, at every advancement on the road to the so-called Singularity,[1] we will see giant leaps that will displace the expected continuum and compound the next quantum leap forward. By the end of the 21st Century, the exponential acceleration of technological advancement may bring us to the brink of human capacity to contain it, leaving its creators to merely wonder at the residual output of artificial intelligence and deep learning processes, and surrender to the fact that there was simply no precedent upon which to rely, be it aesthetical, scientific or cognitive.[2] In fact, when social media company Facebook developed two chatbots to converse with one another, they rapidly developed their own shorthand language and the company shut it down so they could include a failsafe—a "fixed supervised model" to make the output comprehensible to humans (LaFrance, 2017).

In 1994, the Internet was about to become a graphically-oriented publically available technology, emerging from various constituent programs like Veronica, Lynx, Gopher, and Archie. It had been only seven years since Jaron Lanier had adopted the phrase "virtual reality" from sci-fi author Damien Broderick's book *The Judas Mandala* (1982) and turned the Nintendo power glove into a locomotive controller for these digital proxies for space that we could wrap around our faces and hands.

This was about the same time that Michael Heim wrote *The Metaphysics of Virtual Reality* (1993), describing how "an ontological shift, (is) more than a change in how humans see things; it is a change in the world under our feet, in the whole context in which our knowledge and awareness are rooted." (Heim, 1993). Only five years later a rather formalized new branch of philosophy called Speculative Realism (and its derivative Object Oriented Philosophy) would rise that put pressure on centuries of human-centric inquiry about the nature of being and asked what about the rest of the stuff out in the cosmos? When Ivan Sutherland and his team created the Sword of Damocles for DARPA in the 1960s they did not call it Virtual Reality. Now in 2019, we have a technology that is decidedly different from that of earlier VR and yet it comes with all the baggage and onus of the term that made it most famous.

In the same way that spatialized and embodied media are tempered by the notion of being transported to other virtual worlds (where the implication is that they are less real than the "real" world), our perception of truth, consciousness and reality are tempered by a legacy of philosophical inquiry akin to a first-person exploration game. This paradigm is being challenged by a school of philosophy that some might trace back to Martin Heidegger (who, it is important to note, was a member of the Nazi party and whose written works must be handled with care) who challenged the ability of a thinking subject to think outside of itself when considering objective truth. The school of Object Oriented Ontology that arose in 1999 through Graham Harman rejected the Cartesian/Kantian "anthropocentric" view that requires the human consciousness at the center of existence, and instead equalized the existence of non-consciousness at the same level of significance as human consciousness.

Roy Wood Sellars' *Empiricism and the Philosophy of Mind* (1956) argued that we cannot have knowledge independent of the conceptual processes that create our sense of reality. Others agree. University of California, Irvine (UCI) cognitive scientist Donald Hoffman describes "that people may be perceiving the world as they need it to be, rather than as it really is," making the case in his books and lectures that evolution made us see in a very particular way to survive. For example, the way that we perceive a train accentuates its velocity and direction over the totality of its parts. In computer simulation experiments he conducted with his students, creatures that demonstrated more literal perception went extinct sooner (Hoffman, 2019). In an interview with UCI School of social sciences he observes:

If you look back into history, we thought Earth was center of the universe. We burned people at the stake for contradicting something we believed so deeply to be true. It's very hard to let go. And that was just a warm up. If we've mistaken our perceptions for the truth, our entire perception of spacetime and physical objects is misleading. This is just our interface. (In Ashbach, 2019)

And on the PBS program *The Brain*, Dr. David Eagleman states:

In the outside world there is no color, no sound, no smell. These are all constructions of the brain. Instead there is electromagnetic radiation, air compression waves, and aromatic molecules, all of which are interpreted by the brain as color, sound and smell. (Eagleman, 2015)

The Anthropic Principle is the notion that if no life was possible then there would be no consciousness to observe it, thus it would not be known. The new school is algorithmic—moving into position new formulae that feed on our behavioral patterns, before they surprise us with their solutions (interpretations.) Of course once Artificial Intelligence (AI) is successful in producing its programmed objective, it can then tirelessly repeat and iterate on processes that would simply be out of range for human lifespans. Once it can operate at a more robust, and mature level, however, it will map for us levels of inquiry that would otherwise be very difficult for we humans to extrapolate alone.

The new resultant spaces provided a glimpse at an alien output, which like the universe itself, is indifferent to our feelings. Observing it from behind glass, without falling prey to associative human mental mapping techniques, is obscenely difficult at first. Immersive media, however, could grant us access and practice in new modalities of witnessing such processes and escape our outmoded processes of sense-making.

While some may suppose that this "out of mind" exercise is akin to transcendental meditation (and perhaps it is), here we consider it without need to tie its value or meaning back to the self-centering human gaze (and all of its derivatives).

Let's explore a basic example for how a sense of place and the plausibility of a scenario to a human mind can also afford the possibility and observational vantage point of not existing in that space:

An example of this is the 360-degree video piece *Strangers with Patrick Watson,* a performance of Canadian music artist Patrick Watson captured by spherical video pioneers Felix & Paul (2015). In it, you are like a ghost in the center of the room, observing a jazz band playing in the round. On one side of the room is a dog. Normally, in consensus reality, such a dog would react, perhaps with a raised eyebrow or a sniff of the air, if observed by us. But here the dog is unaware of being observed: the nature of the spherical omni-directional camera eye allows us to view the dog without its knowing. As a result, many observers admitted to watching the dog in fascination, rather than paying attention to the live musical human performers in the room.

This very simple example of a world that exists, unfazed by human presence of consciousness, while placing our sensory receptors within its midst, affords us a metaphorical view of object-oriented ontology, in contrast to the idea of quantum indeterminacy (or "QI") that informs much of 20th Century philosophy and physics, and subsequently the simulation hypothesis, that posits we are living in a massive artificial simulation created by higher level intelligence, or "ancestors."

Perhaps what the new media lacks is substantial criticism. In *The Critic as Artist,* Oscar Wilde (1925) wrote that a civilization's culture can best be understood through the voices of its critics. Here by critics we do not mean "reviews" or "breakdowns" or "constructive criticism" or "market analysis", but rather in the manner that Wilde described—a sort of catalyst for evolution: "The tendency of creation is to repeat itself. It is to the critical instinct that we owe each new school that springs up" (p. 12). Wilde goes on to underscore that the critic is not so much in search of some fallacy of objectivity, but rather reveling in the inescapable subjectivity of the reception of a work:

Yes: it has been…that the proper aim of Criticism is to see the object as in itself it really is. But this is a very serious error, and takes no cognizance of Criticism's most perfect form, which is in its essence purely subjective, and seeks to reveal its own secret and not the secret of another. For the highest Criticism deals with art not as expressive but as impressive purely. (Wilde, 1925. p. 18)

Our meta-analysis will survey some of the ways in which immersive, embodied and spatialized media can explore this process and afford us new, and actionable insights.

Why do we seek to escape our reality, or pierce its veil to discover the great beyond? Are the new immersive technologies we are developing at a parabolic pace a signifier that we wish to seek further for answers to our pains and problems, that we are returning to mysticism to mitigate the anxiety from an age filled with uncertain outcomes for the human race, and all life on Earth, for that matter? Alternatively, are they a cycle being reborn, converging upon a singularity/pandemic simulation that proves, as Nick Bostrom (2003) postulates, that if we can create a believable and indistinguishable simulation, then we are already living in one?

MESSAGE IN A BOTTLE

In the 1977 film *Star Wars*, a pair of derelict droids finds their way through a series of unbelievable coincidences (or tremendous serendipity), to end up before a young man who works on a farm. As he is fiddling with a stuck mechanical part that he is trying to remove in order to fix one of the droids, in this case, the dome-shaped so-called "R2D2," he triggers the playback of a holographic transmission—the figure of a woman in white robes—clearly caught in the middle of great peril. "This is our most desperate hour," she pleads, "Help me Obi Wan Kenobi, you're our only hope."

The way that three-dimensional, projected harbinger is depicted includes the scrolling scan-lines intrinsic in the cathode ray tube television monitors of the time in which the film was made. For decades this visual pattern was used to convey over-the-air transmission. Then came digital media and dispensed with this visual trope almost overnight. What matters here is the idea that an entire civilization's fate hangs in the balance, wavering on the brink of collapse at the hands of an evil empire—in this case quite literally "The Empire"—and whose salvation can only come through this diminutive holographic message. Now the S.O.S, the message in a bottle, could have been delivered on parchment, or via radio waves or carved into the wall of a prison cell using a small stone, but it is the volumetric nature of the avatar that makes it so much more pressing and compelling, as though the Princess Leia was almost there, in the room, and the enormous distance between her representation and her reality is crushing.

It is difficult not to feel the same sense of rising desperation in the year 2020, where the scientific community (that hasn't been corrupted by corporate lobby groups) is shouting from the rooftops of inundated high-rises that the world, that the creatures living in the Anthropocene age, the age of humans, are in tremendous peril. The author can't help but wonder if whatever succeeds it, whether it be in a hundred or ten thousand or a hundred thousand years hence, will discover, from the very final edge of this collapse, a similar, volumetric relic, eyes darting left and right for danger, as it embeds its pleas for salvation from a galaxy far, far away. Such contemplation begs the question: how will we represent ourselves? What would we ask for? And from whom or what?

Will we embed this message into robots? Into code? How will it re-trigger and be received? Will our methods seem as quaint as a gold-plated record/data disc, like the Golden Record sent with the 1977 Voyager spacecraft that carried sound and pictures to depict life on Earth,[3] in hopes that some alien disc jockey might pick it up and unravel the "great works of man?" What then?

What if, instead, we could represent our lives and experience the way that the ancient city of Pompeii, tragically and almost instantaneously sealed preserved by volcanic rock and ash in AD 79, revealed its configuration and trappings to us 1,900 years later? Or the famed Tyrannosaurus Rex whose soft tissue was preserved after 68 million years, due to iron in its body, before it was fossilized, revealing collagen similar to that of birds (O'Keeffe, 2013).

What data could we capture, with sufficient foresight that could impart, rather than a codified, abstract language etched into an igneous plank like the Rosetta stone, a spatialized, embodied, articulated, interactive, and dynamic depiction of our reality? We can only speculate how such encapsulated memorials or emissaries might be powered or activated in the far future, but for the purposes of our investigation, we will concern ourselves more with what such media could impart.

CITIZEN OBJECT

On an intestacy (when a person has died without a will) and the deceased has no close next of kin, a creditor or distant (possibly unknown) relative, or perhaps the deceased's lawyer, may apply to be the executor. When this happens this executor is sent to organize and dispose, auction or sell the remaining items in the person's estate. They are tasked with sorting through a lifetime of tchotchkes and keepsakes, journals, sundry unfinished affairs, receipts, clothes, and love letters, most of which were there to create a feeling for the owner: a state of mind, a motivation or rumination. Most items will be thrown away. But their essence, their emotional imbuement remains.

In his book *How Pleasure Works: The New Science of Why We Like What We Like*, Paul Bloom (2011) discusses how a form of essentialism runs throughout our culture, or perhaps instinct, wherein we imbue a metaphysical value to tangible items, enhanced by those who touched them. Our grandmother's sweater is more precious than a new one bought off the rack. Is the value of a T-shirt worn by a Hollywood celebrity worth more before or after their sweat has been washed out of it?

Consider the difference between a 1980s "Teddy Ruxpin" or "Furby" animatronic doll, and simply using sensors, motors and networked components to animate a century old teddy bear passed down through generations of children. Is this undead object merely a patchwork of matted fur, cotton and stiches, or is there something else to the antiquated and emotionally ingrained object? Does animating it technologically add or subtract from its imbued meaning?

The 2018 documentary *How Radio Isn't Done,* remembers and, in its own odd way, celebrates Don Joyce, a member of the band Negativland, who collected analogue tape cartridges of sound collages and combined them live on the radio at Berkeley for over thirty years. When he died, his other band members mailed his cremated ashes out with every record sold to fans. Then they sampled each of his analogue cassettes—thick, rich, pastiches of contemporary and pulp culture detritus—that he used to express complex ideas about perception, media manipulation and how audio enters us like a series of complex and modulated waves. This overtakes us and incites emotions, and we are embodying those frequencies and their intertextuality. Bandmate Marc Hosler, busy stuffing padded manila envelopes of

Joyce's remains, opines: "He scoped out an aesthetic and a tradition and workflow and series of basic aesthetic rules that could outlive him, and he didn't want it to stop." (Worsley, 2017)

Joyce drew parallels between his style of "musique concrete" and pop art (Warhol, Lichtenstein, Hockney) usurping the most familiar, oversaturated, targeted sensory attacks of the mundane and blowing them up in search of meaning, or perhaps just to see. What is fascinating in the case of Joyce and the members of Negativland who survived him is this essentialism—that his ashes somehow carried his intention and value, and yes also the fatalism of their approach—shipping it out with material goods like a postcard from a souvenir shop. This is a self-conscious act that belies the plasticity that Negativland espoused and encouraged its followers to do the same.

Taken together, or perhaps in more stark relief, we can see that between Hoffman's idea of visual-consciousness constructs that evolve for the betterment of our odds at survival, Bloom's idea of essence within objects, and the psychogeography of virtual spaces, we see a model of consciousness and its relationship to imagined or virtual space in all aspects of our gestalt.

Brian Lonsway argues that the manufactured spaces we create—for example historical dioramas, theme parks, or shopping malls are authentic. "They fashion themselves after other environments not to imitate them, but rather to reconstruct or re-contextualize them in new [authentic ways]" (Lonsway, 2016).

MIND OVER REALITY

In her essay *Dancing With the Virtual Dervish: Virtual Bodies*, Diane J. Gromala, with Yoav Sharir (1996), writes about how she transcends her intense and chronic pain:

I have had to develop two basic strategies to deal with my various physical alterations: pain, and increased volume on perception. The first strategy was to develop an ability to reach a transcendent or disembodied state at will, related perhaps to the experience of a dervish. The second strategy was to develop a sensual or erotic response to pain, embracing an enjoyment of eros and thanatos. These strategies represent less a denial of my body than a reconfigured inhabitation. (Gromala & Sharir, 1996. p. 281)

By examining how we rely so heavily on anthropocentric ontology, and consider OOO (Object Oriented Ontology), by exploring with Donald Hoffman and Dr. Eagleman how we craft each our own version of reality, then we can begin to soften its edges and mold it better to suit our needs and odds for survival in new paradigms more involved with the mind than with escaping predators in the wild.

Virtual Reality now has a rich and lengthy history of use in transforming the experience of physical and psychological pain. Perhaps one of the most well-known examples of using Virtual Reality to assist the mind to sublimate the body's pain is David Patterson and Hunter Hoffman's *SnowWorld* (2000)—a whimsical, but simultaneously completely serious study and implementation of a virtual wintery world used to aid burn victims.

Dr. Walter Greenleaf at Stanford, and Dr. Stephane Bouchard (Klinger, et al., 2005) at McGill have similarly used cognitive behavioral therapy (CBT), exposure therapy, reframing and somatosensory tracking devices for those with phobias, social anxiety, nervous disorders and mental disease for over two and a half decades. Greenleaf's work extends into addiction recovery, putting the user into predicaments where they decline offers of substances to which they are addicted.

USC professor and researcher Alberto "Skip" Rizzo aids veterans with post-traumatic stress disorder and panic attacks (Rizzo, et al., 2009). Rizzo's *Bravemind* system (2016) affords clinicians realtime transformation, stimulation and immersion tools to create psycho-emotional triggers while observing and responding to the effects of such exposure on the patients.

Further to the method of psychological exposure treatment, there is also the sleight of hand or re-direction of mitigating pain or anxiety for physical visits to hospital. At the Division of Hematology, Oncology and BMT (bone marrow transplant) at Nationwide Children's Hospital in Ohio, Jeremy Patterson, has created an in-clinic, distraction treatment for young hemophiliac patients (Dunn et al., 2018). Patterson and his team have deployed this treatment via wireless VR headsets to mitigate the anxiety of receiving a needle for IV during pediatric hemophilia care. In the at-home version, children can build out the persistent fantasy world they interacted with at the hospital. The experience at home is set up to require a return to hospital to advance, or have the full experience again, in order to keep the hospital session new and engaging for each visit.

A similar approach by Dr. Hillel Maresky with collaborator and software developer Shachar Weis and their company VRAL, unveiled *Emma Rye*[4] at the VRTO conference in Toronto in June 2019. *Emma Rye* is a fear mitigation solution in VR for children and adults who require an MRI (Bojic, 2019). "How big is the Problem? 459 pediatric hospitals around the globe, 5.4 million MRI scans each year, 25% or 1.4 million children need sedation. It is estimated that 14 children per year never wake up," Maresky said during his presentation. *Emma Rye* not only redirects attention but also gamifies the experience, immersing patients in a vivid virtual environment that simulates a real MRI scan in Virtual Reality with true proportions, sounds and motion. VR offers a gentle, kid-friendly, and technologically advanced pediatric biofeedback mechanism to relax and train the child to lie still in the MRI gantry. The young patient is welcomed by the eponymous fairy avatar Emma Rye, and uses an algorithm to reflect back to the child various biofeedback including their heart rate while gently encouraging them that everything will work out just fine. The child and their fairy friend can collect more fairy dust the longer the child stays still. It follows that by not using sedation, risk of death or complications arising from anesthesia are eliminated, wait times are radically reduced and improved imaging leads to important secondary outcomes.

This displacement of self, while still holding space in the mind for the parallel reality is something we will explore in more depth in the next section.

OUT OF BODY EXPERIENCES

What would it mean to explore new embodiments for human minds? The octopus, which split off into its own evolutionary path from that which led to homo sapiens some 400 million years ago (Montgomery, 2016), uses a distributed, versus central, nervous system that means that its various tentacles can make decisions without input from the brain. Astrobiology researchers Dominic Michel Sivitilli and David H Gire (2019) describe how the octopus outsources a large part of the computation necessary to support its complex cognition, allowing it to parallel process massive amounts of information from its densely innervated suckers to coordinate the infinite degrees of freedom of its multiple arms.

Can embodied media further advance our understanding of such alternative forms of distributed neuronal intelligence? One might begin to wonder about the true value of the specific corporeal manifestation we inhabit? Was it designed expressly to work in tandem with our brains and the mind-activity that arises therein? What happens when we deviate from this construct? Not merely by degrees, such having an amputation or being born as a conjoined twin, or with an extremely rare skin disease that turns our hands into tree-like[5], but rather when we are given a tail or wings or a beak or tentacles? Or perhaps appendages not yet seen in nature; extension derived from machine intelligence feeding on alien datasets?

In his research on the qualia that arose from body transfer experiments in Virtual Reality, Mel Slater, who researches the field of body ownership illusions as studied in cognitive neuroscience determined that it was not so much about synchrony in head or digit movement but first-person placement in the body of the other. In one study 24 males were placed into an experiment where they observed a woman stroking a girl's hair for a few moments, before striking her across the face repeatedly (Slater et al., 2010). Some were in the third person, others had been, at one point, placed into the first person experience of the girl's body and could observe themselves in the mirror. Furthermore, some of them had agency to turn their head, others had their sight tracked with a series of previously recorded head turns. The team determined ultimately that "bottom-up perceptual mechanisms can temporarily override top down knowledge resulting in a radical illusion of body transfer ownership." Body ownership, is not necessarily interchangeable here with self-recognition.

Kent Bye, who has recorded over 1,100 interviews with immersive industry experts in his *Voices of VR* podcasts, has pointed out that these public and social VR spaces, within which we can mask ourselves, (in some cases, in others we present as ourselves as innocuous digital versions) also allow us to test the reaction of our behavior in a community environment/mediated virtual reality.

On one episode of Bye's podcast (Haskes, Ho, Bye, 2019), he interviewed Sarah Haskhes of Radix Motion, a neuroscientist whose platform called MEU was designed to experience asynchronous alternative embodiments, be it an octopus or to have a tail, that allow us to move outside of our mental framework constraints. Her development partner Matthew Hoe points out that with 2D social media we have skipped a step—where "Likes" are numbered—but we are missing the expression of a smile, and the nuance of human response. Their asynchronous platform is designed to exchange small recorded gestures between remote people, deploying "unique synesthesia algorithms to connect movement and heartbeat to avatars, visuals, music and haptic vibrations." By capturing nuanced body movements, gestures, or actions—perhaps a dance move or a secret handshake, but represented in abstraction, they may delve to the essential element of that gesture that is relatable to the receiving party. In their design they attempt to forego the more nefarious dopamine-triggering model deployed by many social media sites, mobile games and casinos, and instead rely on surprise and curiosity to foster plasticity.

In 2017, at the VRTO conference, Phillip Rosedale, creator of *Second Life* and *High Fidelity*, both multi-user worlds (the latter in VR), described how a hand gesture or head movement can be as uniquely identifiable as a fingerprint and that not only does this have meaning on a relational level, but on a security level.

MY FRIENDS ARE TOYS, I MADE THEM[6]

Companies like New Zealand's Soul Machines and Quantum Capture out of Toronto (who began making realistic human models for AAA game companies like Ubisoft), have iterated into the world of photorealistic digital humans, starting from their vast array of cameras to capture their subjects into models made up of tens of millions of polygons before being reduced down to more practically optimized version (Malicki-Sanchez, 2017). These alluring barely-out-of-the-uncanny valley supermodel avatars may be the next "influencers"—tireless, never worse for wear, always twinging their lower eyelid just so, in such a way as to subtly convey that they understand you. And likely they do, far better than your own family, as they are powered by the algorithms that observe our daily habits online and via social media, our movements and buying habits, mined like so much raw ore for a hyper-dimensional monument to our intrinsic desires.

In fact, in 2018, a "virtual influencer" named 'Lil Miquela,' already gained over a million Instagram followers. She was eventually traced back to the Brud agency out of Los Angeles, which caused a real head-scratcher for the Federal Trade Commission that had imposed rules for traditional human influencers to disclose their affiliations. But what happened if the influencer itself was just a digital homunculus (Katz, 2018)?

This leads us to the story of "Deepfakes" and the implications when the avatar is not only photorealistic but bears an indistinguishable resemblance to a "real" person, living or dead?

What is Truth in This age

We are now in the era of "Deepfakes," where thousands of images of a person are fed to an AI to create an increasingly indistinguishable digital clone. Our very personages can be reanimated and exploited without or beyond our consent, possibly even by bad actors. What was once a laborious and not always successful machine learning process that took many hours to process, has become remarkably simpler within only a couple of years. Deepfakes, a product of a method using Generative Adversarial Networks (GANs) that pit two AI processes against each other to discern between artificial and "real-world" sources (Wiggers, 2019), have been used for fascinating and whimsical applications like bringing to life portraits of historical figures or to replace one thing in a video or photograph with another. It is astonishing to see the Mona Lisa (Daley, 2019), Albert Einstein and the *Girl with The Pearl Earring* come to life like the portraits in Disney's *Haunted Mansion* theme park ride, all of which have been posted to social media in 2019. In May of 2019, researchers from Samsung's A.I. Center in Moscow and Skolkovo Institute of Science and Technology demonstrated their highly optimized "few shot learning" technique to create the animated images in far less time and even in real time (Johnson, 2019). The Deepfakes Lab has been busy face-swapping actors, replacing entire scenes or even film-length performances, and have made these software technologies freely available via their GitHub repository.[7]

In 2019, Deepfake artists began proliferating on the internet—one such artist "ctrl shift face" made international headlines with his collections of incredible smooth and sometimes subtle face transfers. One such video involved comedian Bill Hader speaking on a late-night talk show, and when he began to do his impression of Tom Cruise or Seth Rogan, his face almost indistinguishably become that of the actor he was impersonating (Libby, 2019).

The blog *Collider* posts a weekly Youtube series called "Deepfake Theater" using soundalike actors doing impressions of such famous personalities as George Lucas (performed by actor Josh Robert Thompson and deepfaked by Frank Lucatuorto), Harrison Ford and Leonardo DiCaprio, whom the deep-faked Lucas claims he has used to digital replace Hayden Christensen in all of the *Star Wars* prequels in what may be one of the most mind-bendingly stretched-thin exploitations of the provisions of satire and fair use wrapped in a meta-critique seen in popular contemporary media (Collider, 2019). These videos do not declare their appropriation of these personas except to title themselves "Deepfake." This alone, is all the audience is given to parse what speakers are real and complicit and which are being puppeteered. Of course, the more they do it, the more the process and its act becomes normalized.

The author finds it worthy of note that the general reaction at first, was one of fear and even revulsion—concern for the future of humanity. Within two years, however, it was little more than curiosity used to create a new form of comedic impersonation on the shareable web. There remain, however, real causes for concern insofar as privacy and rights, as we will explore below, but also it is a new dawn of enormous creativity and possibility. The ironic notion that not being able to trust what we see, however, is quite telling.

There may be some grim implications for a society that believes what it perceives as objective reality, one that is so easily conceived that photographs and videos (even in this age of manipulation) can be taken as fact. The era of believing what you see is now a century in the rear view mirror. But here we argue that this is nothing less than the Platonic shadows flickering on the walls of the cave. It doesn't end at the visual evidence, either. Voice can just as easily now be emulated. Adobe Systems Inc. raised concerns with its Voco software that uses machine learning to understand the phonemes and timbre of a person's voice and then synthesizes their speech from text in a manner that is almost auditorily indistinguishable (BBC, 2016).

Chinese search giant Baidu can make a copy of your voice for further speech synthesis by listening to just a minute of your voice over a phone (Gent, 2018). The implications of that should be chilling to anyone who still uses their voice to talk to others online. Real-time puppeteering of talking avatars whose sight and sound is indistinguishable from the real person they reference is only the beginning of a world that will eventually have a one to one copy of its actual spatial geography. In other words, countless versions of people that you know may soon populate such alternate digital dimensions, and there are presently no regulations to stop them. The ability to identify such fakes forensically is already a top priority for the Pentagon—the United States Department of Defense headquarters. (O'Sullivan & Donie, 2019).

By 2019, Chinese developers FaceUnity offered a commercialized B2B service to video-animate any human face photo-realistically from a single image, enhanced by their Dynamic Portraits, Face Transfer and Expression Recognition technology or as their website claims, "After transfer, the new face can synch with your expression in real-time. The expression is natural and realistic just like a real-life Face Off" (Phase Core Technology). The result is that a local news anchor, could submit a headshot and then give the nightly news on camera, though she never left her house, never uttered a word, and no set was ever built of light ever plugged in. To the observer, however, her 2D doppelganger described the events of the day on television.

Deepfakes, though, are not the origin of such appropriation of the public image in new media: "holographic" performances, often using something not unlike Pepper's Ghost illusion (projecting a seemingly dimensional personage through a translucent surface set at an angle so as not to be reflective) have been used to cash in on the likeness of famous musicians (Tupac Shakur, Michael Jackson, Old Dirty Bastard, Frank Zappa), famous Hollywood icons and historical figures for decades. It may be that the fidelity and complexity of such representations, though, is what society finds most troubling.

In the 2013 film *The Congress*—based on Stanisław Lem's novel *The Futurological Congress* (Folman, 2013)—actress Robin Wright, (playing herself in a perfectly post-modern-self-referential satire), is pressured by her agent (Harvey Keitel) to forego bad future decisions about her career and be captured volumetrically so that her avatar can be used in films forever, preserving her in her youth. The catch? She must never act in the flesh again. She is most reticent about her personage appearing in some of the trashier genres, like pulp sci-fi or sexploitation comedies, and of course she is assured that this will never happen. Without spoiling the end of the movie, one can assume how such assurances play out.

The idea of parents being exploited posthumously for financial gain is marked with controversy. Robyn Astaire, the 46-years junior widow of the legendary dancer and star of cinema is vilified for her exploitation of his image. Astaire's son defends her in the context of protecting his image: "I'm behind Robyn 100%. I think my father knew how people exploited personalities [after their death], and he didn't want that to happen to him. Protecting him is Robyn's job" (Lacher, 1997). Perhaps this has more to do with the vast gray area where posthumous right of the reanimation of an historic effigy are not designated. She argues: "It's a moral issue with me," she says. "I see some of these older, well-known actors struggling along, not knowing where their rent is going to come from. Their pictures are being shown every day, and once in a while people will use an excerpt and the person who created it gets absolutely nothing."

Ahmet Zappa, enterprising son of the late legendary composer and rock guitarist Frank Zappa, worked with a company called Eyellusion to create a "holographic" performance of his father, that would tour with some of his still-living bandmates and cash in on the ongoing fanbase that spends hundreds of thousands of dollars on licensed merchandise and music to the Zappa Estate (Rathbone, 2019). Zappa's longtime guitarist and collaborator Adrian Belew refused to participate in the tour. "I will not be playing Zappa music in the foreseeable future in any situation," he wrote in a Facebook post. "This whole thing is far too caustic and divisive" (Belew, 2017). Whether it was the matter of digital exhumation of his once and longtime musical collaborator, or the bitter in-fighting that the ethical and financial turmoil this tour created, it is a challenge that is arising again and again. Fans express their delight and also sadness that while his presence is felt, he is also known to be deceased (Grow, 2017).

Financial protections are in place for those who have privately taken up the cause, but for whose benefit? When should an historic likeness be considered fair use? This is terra incognita, yet as the technology advances, must be addressed. The powerful screen actors' union SAG-AFTRA fought for protection of its members, and of course beyond the moral dilemmas such technologies pose, the financial implications are unimaginable to the entertainment industry. Yet it found resistance at its front doorstep from other organizations wanting to protect free speech and free enterprise. As Eriq Gardner wrote in *The Hollywood Reporter:*

SAG-AFTRA says it's now critical that performers have the ability to control how their likenesses are used to construct digital performances. The MPAA, while somewhat sympathetic to the scourge of deepfakes, maintains that a broadly worded statute could interfere with the ability of filmmakers to tell stories about and inspired by real people and events. (Gardner, 2019)

He goes on to report how on June 19th, in a "historic legislative session" in New York, over 300 bills were passed but the one pertaining to publicity and privacy rights was presented for the second time. It would, Gardner describes legally bar:

Unauthorized use of a digital replica to create sexually explicit material in an expressive audiovisual work, extended the protection of one's likeness past death, and even created a registry whereby the heirs of famous people could document their official control over their dead relative's name and image. (Gardner, 2019, para. 2)

For the second time, the bill was bypassed.

But in the same article Loyola School law professor Jennifer Rothman, submits an incredibly prescient argument that "such rights alienable could end up backfiring...if a celebrity declared bankruptcy, then her creditors could take ownership of her publicity rights. Similarly, ex-spouses could take an ownership interest in a person's identity when assets of the marriage are split. Moreover, she points out that the legacies of the past will be perpetuated even if (and perhaps especially if) artists and personalities have the voluntary right to do so. Rothman cautioned:

Allowing the free transferability proposed in this bill will place at risk aspiring actors, musicians and models, who are all particularly vulnerable to signing away their rights of publicity for a chance of getting representation, or a record deal, or doing a photoshoot. (ibid. para. 8)

As we have seen in the case of Robyn Astaire and Ahmet Zappa, this is already past-tense.

Facebook—a social media portal with over 3 billion human users globally as of 2019, will soon have more profiles for deceased persons than living by early as 2060 (Dunham, 2017). Should all representations of these people, who may not have a digital will, cease immediately, or, because of the nature of the EULA in regards to user-generated content, are their images property of Facebook? In the event that Facebook, which owns Oculus, one of the pioneering commercial VR companies and that has invested billions of dollars into immersive media, choose to animate such images that it owns, perhaps using a deepfake algorithm, for a model that can then be extruded into 3D dimensions and activated, where does the line get drawn?

By the end of 2019, Facebook removed over 900 accounts from its platform and Instagram product that were being used to champion U.S. President Donald Trump using shallowfake and GAN-generated photographs of people that do not exist. The accounts, associated with a digital news outlet calling itself "The BL" that was connected to *Epoch Times*—a conservative media group with a strong history of backing the president. (Martineau, 2019). An infinite number of such artificially created but credible human faces can be found at a website like thispersondoesnotexist.com based on the work of (Karras et al., 2019), and NVIDIA, building on the work of former Google Brain research scientist Ian Goodfellow – inventor of GANs.

In fact, in 2019 Professor Parham Aarabi (ECE) and his team of researchers presented a new stereoscopic deepfake technique for VR at IEEE International Workshop on Multimedia Signal Processing in Kuala Lumpur, Malaysia. (Irving, 2019) When we can forego all of the expensive capture and render a person living or dead in real time using these deep learning methods and output them in volume within VR then we are in a new phenomenological domain for anything from roleplay, to identity theft, to supernatural visitation.

Of course the provenance and ownership of identity could and may likely be stored on the blockchain, creating a nearly immutable record of title or its transfer. The verdict is out on whether this will ultimately be a benefit or hazard. That assumes, that such ownership is recorded (and this may soon be inescapable). But what happens when it does not? When we have, as we saw above, an intestacy?

To whom will these algorithms vend their wares when the bodies are all gone—these bodies that carry these chemical reactions with analogue patterns? On the other hand, we must also be careful not to put out the fire of this revolution. Legal and ethical concerns intact, there can also powerful beneficial applications for the capture of digital humans and their spaces.

VR developer Lucas Rizotto (Rizzotto, 2019) attempted to find a ray of sunshine in terms of the application of such technology in his article "Why Deepfakes Will Change Advertising Forever." Towards the end he speculates that a drug addict might benefit from seeing themselves recast, via GANs in a better life—looking healthy clean, and I certainly can align with this notion: that the tools could be there for new forms of cognitive behavioral therapy. But once the tech is commonplace, and we have removed its gravity, will such effects maintain their impact? What other positive applications might we previsualize?

WALK A MILE IN THE SHOES I LEAVE BEHIND?

Consider future forms of embodiment from a different angle: what is the experience of entering another individual's public face? In other words, what would it be like to enter into the body of Marilyn Monroe, Beyoncé, or Kim Kardashian, or a disabled elderly man, or a young boy wandering into a crowded and somewhat scary street? Could this walking a mile in another's shoes teach us about ourselves and others?

While the author rejects the term "empathy machine,"[8] in this thought experiment we are discussing using Deepfakes, volumetric capture and voice match synthesis to literally personify another person in a way that is visually and aurally indistinguishable (to others) from the original.

At the time of this writing, the author is at an age where many of his friends' parents are dying. The so-called "Boomer" generation is turning gray, and tens of millions them will enter their most senior years by 2030 (Knickman, 2002).

Despite the tremendous strain this will put on the already volatile and gravely structured American healthcare system, a positive note is the Boomers' willingness to adopt new and improved technologies when they become available as methods for care (Barr, 2014). In fact, the impact of this vast generation moving into their golden years may force the healthcare system into radical transformation, and immersive technologies can be subsumed into that deluge of change. How can the transformational and transportive nature of immersive media be able to assist in this passage?

It is not only the burden of managing health that we must consider, but the potential to lose much of the knowledge, experience and wisdom of those who have gone before. How will immersive media enable those who remain alive to have access to the stories and histories of those who have passed on? What lessons, stories, and expressions can be captured and communicated? Immersive media, with its unique interactive grammar, is able to convey much in a short, interactive form, in a manner that long form cinema may not.

In a talk at Moses Znaimer's 2017 *ideacity* Conference in Toronto, the author discussed the matter of humans and anomalies, and ghosts in machines, and how capturing these effigies of my grandparents, these photorealistic spatialized, dimensional 1:1 holograms, immediately made apparent their ethical implications (Malicki-Sanchez, 2017). That story follows.

Paco was in love with Victoria—his wife of 67 years. I knew she was growing exceedingly weak, and, in those last ten months before she passed, I approached my friends at Quantum Capture for a special assignment. Morgan Young, Craig Alguire and company, would bring in my grandparents, capture them separately and together, holding hands, a kiss, and then render a static, high resolution, three-dimensional effigy. Morgan and his team handled the material with true care and affection. Morgan even placed them in a gentle, off-the-shelf pastoral setting (by all appearances in the English countryside where I am sure they had never been) and sent the author a Dropbox link to the Unreal file.

Paco and Victoria subsequently died within two years of their volumetric capture. We activated the digital volumetric memorial once, grateful for the work, and then archived it. A year later, the author still hasn't had the heart to ask his mother, their eldest daughter, if she wants to visit them in VR.

While we were certain that the decision to have the grandparents captured in their final days was the right thing to do, it still raises issues such as how do we spend time capturing the world as it is today for future generations, and where and how do we store all this data, and for how long? Indefinitely? What is our obligation to preserve these avatars and locations? Who decides what is important?

What will the experiences for future minds that immersive media and these digital remains say about us? These trace patterns, will they carry the outline of our organic and unpredictable and chemical reactions? Or will they, as Douglas Rushkoff (Rushkoff, 2019) puts it: by virtue of sales marketing algorithms, shave off the messy bits, and leave only the algorithmic targeting data behind as their legacy?[9]

PSYCHOGEOGRAPHY AND THE ESSENCE OF ABANDONED PLACES

Volumetric capture is of course not limited to humans and objects but extends to spaces and all that they contain. There is also interest in psychogeography and the phenomenology of spaces. What if the Nuremberg rally had been captured in 360 8K stereoscopic videos? What about the Beatles' first concert in America? Or the streets of New York City in 1910 captured with immersive techniques?

As an example, in Toronto in 2019 the Cadillac Lounge was closing down after 25 years. This huge bar served as an ad hoc community center for many in the lower income neighborhood that had managed until only recently to thwart gentrification. The most notable thing about the venue, besides its two stages, huge outdoor backyard patio, and completely asymmetrical layout, was the barrage of textiles and colors: from red sparkly vinyl couches to leopard print bar stools, Elvis memorabilia and a country music jukebox. Considering that the space would close down forever after the owner, Sam Grosso stated his desire to spend time with his young children, it became acutely clear that it held countless memories in its walls: a true kaleidoscopic pastiche of culture. The custom neon signs, the velvet curtains, the actual Cadillac car, sawed in half and stuck to the wall above the entrance doors, would all be destroyed and transformed into a condominium. These sorts of spaces, some might argue, carry their own essential legacy.

Laser scanners, photogrammetry and volumetric capture tools could be deployed at various levels of resolution (anything as simple as a phone with a depth sensor to a millimeter precision LIDAR/laser scanner) to capture and store that for all time. Such combinations of mesh and texture from locations now gone, will be of tremendous value to future generations, who might wonder what old Toronto was like or what dive bars were like, or what the neighborhood was like or what the very Cadillac Lounge that daddy used to operate was like? From a cultural anthropological perspective, the value is immense. Already research and development being done to synchronize the gathering of images and angles necessary to expedite and enhance such captures by groups of people. Our concern may fall into the question of how to capture the essence of a place, along with its textures and geometry? How can we capture the mood, the smell, the temperature, the squeak of the vinyl seat covers or the graffiti scratched into a barstool with a pen-knife?

Such a volumetric model could easily and quickly be imported as an .obj three-dimensional model file into any variety of VR or even AR platforms for further exploration or population of virtual immersive citizens.

What will happen when we have multitudes of such abandoned spaces, details as relics from a culture no longer alive? How can we best capture the essential nature of the mise en scène rather than merely render it as a low quality texture map or a provisional low poly mesh?

Are we so myopic as to not foresee that the world we live in today will appear utterly quaint half a decade hence? A domicile is the story of a life lived therein. Linear narrative cannot be done or do justice to the cross-hatching perambulations of the many lives and motives that cross the floor of a house of any size. Immersive media is about existing within a setting and what we can experience, infer, or leave in it by virtue of our manifestation therein.

PUMP UP THE VOLUME

What happens when not only the people, but also the entire world and all of the things in it are captured in volume, and space? Inspired by David Gelernter's 1991 book *Mirror Worlds: or the Day Software Puts the Universe in a Shoebox* (Gelernter, 1992), Kevin Kelly, founding editor of WIRED magazine describes a near future where "every place and thing in the real world—every street, lamppost, building, and room—will have its full-size digital twin" (Kelly, 2019).

Optical technologies like photography and video are becoming interactively dimensional. Three-dimensional photos now carry depth information and normal maps (Hedman et al., 2017). Six DoF video allows us to observe video playback on all six axes: up/down, left/right, forward and back. Light field capture technology—a technique for capturing structured light that viewers later observe from any angle—allows us to invoke the original array of photons from the original space and maneuver and manipulate them as actions and desires dictate (Overbeck et al., 2017). This recreated light is no different to the eye than that moment at which it was first captured. Jules Urbach, CEO of OTOY, a platform for doing extremely high end graphic processing in the "cloud," said that by 2030, the world would start to see buildings covered in large-scale emissive lightfield projection panels—the sort that are almost indistinguishable to the eye from the real thing.[10]

The hybrid of optical and computer generated graphics will soon plaster the planet, or perhaps a better way to put it, is that it will echo it—until it forks off into its own dimensions with their own reasoning.

One of the most interesting notions posited from such a parallel dimension is the notion that time is decoupled from consensus reality; in other words, in a mirror-world we could rewind back to a certain capture point (something already possible with Google Streetview and Maps), and also forward to the possible entropic or renovated future of any place. Magic Leap, an Augmented Reality (AR) company determined to use this technology to enhance our experiences with our world, describes the future as having layers, where some of these layers might be more alluring, or addictive (or profitable, beguiling, enjoyable, populated?) than others.

Never have we seen such agency over the creation of these imagined realities that can affect us in direct, embodied, spatialized manner. We are not the chorus or the audience, we are the experience now, and the better we understand it, the more we can harness it to take us into places that we once only relegated to the domain of dreams.

Imverse Technology enables game studios to create voxel-driven real-time photorealistic volumetric capture systems for first person experiences in online multiplayer games. Meanwhile Facebook Reality Labs jockeyed for position with metric telepresence—the Princess Leia holographic communication fantasy in the crosshairs, and when ready, available to Facebook over 3 billion users.[11]

And yet, perhaps there is a value to not being literal in our virtual-dimensional embodiment; the pursuit of realism may be far less important for a compelling construct than other factors.

In his book *Flatland: A Romance of Many Dimensions*, Edwin Abbott (Abbott, 1884) describes how it may be impossible for two-dimensional beings to perceive or comprehend a third dimension of existence, fourth dimensional beings to perceive a fifth or sixth dimension or beyond. It may be equally hard to imagine in the other direction. In 2019, James Scargill, a physicist at the University of California, wrote a paper demonstrating how life could live in a uniquely 2+1 dimension, flying in the face of the established assumption that life requires a three-dimensional universe (Scargill, 2019).

Liquid computing, is a way of manipulating data through biological engineering, a method that could store and retrieve enormous amounts of data in an amorphous and/or 3D printed medium. Successful experiments have been done to retrieve photographic data from such a process (Miodownik, 2019).

What other forms of embodiment could we imagine and assume through immersive media when our newest scientific revelations outpace our wildest imaginings?

These concepts undermine the anthropic argument for cosmologists and philosophers, who may need to find another reason why the universe takes the form it does. An interesting discovery to make in the new age of "spatial computing." Similarly, we must be cautious in using contemporary events to forge our mental models of the cosmos, as they are heavily tainted by our provinciality.

World of Warcraft, *EverQuest*, *Second Life* and *Uru Diaspora* were massively multi-player online worlds that offered a persistent place to which you could return at any time, revisiting and resuming adventures with your friends in the same geographic spaces that you left behind. Even when the original commercial servers shut down for worlds like these, communities that have arisen therein might have developed strong social meshes capable of migrating to new virtual locations—what Celia Pearce recognized as "digital refugees" (Pearce, 2011).

What is the implication of a mirror world or Metaverse that is persistent and iterated by every human that passes through it? What happens when we move these into the embodied, spatialized realms of immersive technologies? How different than the real world that we live in is this idea of a consensus alternate reality where all of its citizens are traversing the same territory on the same clock and regarding each other from their subjective placements, but able to return to an immutable timeline, shared by all? Presuming we can ward off an autocratic master controller, it would very much require the dynamics and characteristics of a world that makes sense to human consciousness.

From a cultural anthropological perspective, these so-called virtual spaces will one day serve as the ultimate record of our zeitgeist, not only by virtue of clues we cannot yet forecast for our lack of critical distance, but also for the way in which they belie our evolutionary perceptual biases.

If we are trapped in a simulation created by higher dimensional beings, how do we stop the ride and get out? Or better yet, like Jim Carrey in the 1998 film *The Truman Show*, who discovers his entire existence is a game show inside of a dome, how do we escape through the doorway in the sky to the outside world of truer truths, one wonders if ultimately he made the right choice.

We see this tension in managing two parallel realities: the uncompromising complex nature of the consensus reality and the idealized internal vision of daydreams in the film *Brazil* (Gilliam, 1985) which Ben Wheeler summarized perfectly:

The film centers on the struggles of protagonist Sam Lowry (Jonathon Pryce), a cog in the impersonal machinery of the bureaucracy that governs Brazil's society who desires anonymity within consensus reality, but in his dreams is a winged warrior fighting noble battles with symbolic adversaries. Sam finds he is increasingly unable to successfully reconcile or differentiate these paradoxical existences as they begin to bleed into one another throughout the film. (Wheeler, 2005)

By the end of the film Lowry, who has expressed his outrage through the delusion (or is it real) of a rebel force spearheaded by Henry Tuttle is effectively lobotomized and catatonic. With VR not only do we have a proxy for the experience of human consciousness, but we have repeatability upon which we can really investigate and revisit such daydreams of our mind-palaces at will.

INSIDE OUT

In the examination of what is required to move outside of one's persistent and consensual space-time continuum, we look at both the Place Illusion (believing you are in a place), and the Plausibility Illusion, (belief that what is happening is actually taking place), as described by Mel Slater (Slater, 2009). One key concept Slater makes the case for is that in both Place and Plausibility Illusions, the person inside of the immersive experience is aware that neither of these is also true. In other words, they have the mental elasticity to hold the idea of both the consensus reality and the illusory reality (and its events) in parallel.

Humans have the ability of imagining detailed future scenarios that present varying outcomes from which they select a general course of action. What can immersive media help us to understand about the processes of human cognition and decision making?

What if we were to run a hypothetical experiment of putting the reader on the moon in VR. There she is, bouncing along in the soft silt of space dust, gleaming back at the big blue marble of Earth. After some 30 seconds in the head-mounted display, she is somewhat physically convinced of the lower gravity, the vacuum of space, the condensation of her breath within her space helmet.

Then we take this VR experience off of her face and stick it on a cat.

Would the cat have no idea what was going on, why was it now in a place where it wasn't seconds before? Though we share our respective visceral and sensory cues of the empirical reality in our intrinsic, evolutionarily developed ways, the VR experience that represents only what is sufficient to be convincing to a human, would seem utterly alien and practically meaningless to a cat. Or would it? Would the cat understand that it is not, in fact on the cat-moon, (or human-moon) but in fact in a simulation of it, while still being physically in the rent-controlled beige apartment where it was moments before?

Though it's difficult with the current data to know the veracity of this fact, since we aren't cats and aren't quite sure how to get a subjective answer from a cat, let alone from chickens (Andrew, E 2019), could the experiences that we have tuned and iterated to best serve humans also someday serve as a sort of fossil record of the homo sapiens' perceptual construct. What could VR created by Neanderthals have taught us about their world and perception of it?

Deploying Virtual Reality for free-moving animals can also teach us much about not only about emotion transmission, but also spatial cognition. A system called FreemoVR designed and studied by Prof. Dr. Andrew Straw and his colleague Prof. Dr. Kristin Tessmar-Raible in a joint venture study, created a variety of immersive environments for tiny creatures that ranged from mice to zebrafish to fruit flies to that test how convinced the creatures were and how they reacted to different perceptual cues (Figure 1).

Figure 1. It may be difficult to visualize how Virtual Reality for fruit flies might appear, so here is an example
Credit: IMP/IMBA Graphics Department, https://strawlab.org/freemovr

For example, the mouse tended to align with shallower appearing areas than those that might indicate heights (Straw & Tessmar-Raible, 2017).

In fact, before Ivan Sutherland's Sword of Damocles precursor to the contemporary Virtual Reality headset, Canadian psychologist Donald Hebb was doing research about how humans and animals might understand one another's emotions. He was concerned with getting around the problem of anthropomorphizing their responses. In his landmark 1946 paper: "Emotion in man and animal: an analysis of the intuitive processes of recognition," he ultimately concluded that:

There is no fundamental difference in recognition of emotion in man and animals. The "ultimate criteria of the various emotions are found in distinctions of overt behavior (Hebb, 1946).

In his research he also determined that rats that were placed in more stimulating environments, rather than drab, unimpressive ones, exhibited far greater resourcefulness and facility maneuvering through mazes, the implication being that vacuous, orthogonal surroundings, dull the cognitive abilities of sentient beings (Ellard, 2015).

CONCLUSION: IS THAT ALL THERE IS? THEN LET'S KEEP DANCING...

Will the AR and VR that we make be messy? Or will it be clean? Will it be dirty and fearless or will it be sterile, safe and institutionally sanctioned? What will these works say about us and what will they leave behind?

It is the author's belief that in exploring these new complex media we do not rest on our laurels, or epistemological paradigms in examining—or even worse reinforcing—approaches that have deluded us in the past. Bold new choices can and must be made so that we can leverage these tools to escape our holding patterns, those things that keep us in dark trenches.

We need critics to create a purview so that future generations can understand the methodologies and intentions of the experimenters of our time.

In a paper titled "Experimental test of local observer independence," (M. Proietti et al., 2019) researchers at Heriot-Watt University in Edinburgh used a quantum computer for a state-of-the-art six-photon experiment to expand upon physicist Eugene Wigner's work in 1961 to argue that there is no objective or empirical reality, and that this may be provable outside of an anthropocentric bracketing by way of quantum mechanics, which would allow for the OOO argument in a whole new way.

I once read an article, perhaps it was in *Scientific American*, about the imperative for creation to procreate. Scientists concluded that the nature of consciousness is not, as we have so long assumed, to procreate, but rather to revel in its own gaudy excess; in other words, besieged by the very mental mapping ability that was made to save it, one that is exploited at every turn for manipulation, it may do best to reclaim its dominion over the imagined dimensions and revel in it the splendors of its evolutionary perceptual illusions, a kaleidoscopic wonder that, in combination with the Anthropocene, data-infested era, has outpaced its biological utility.

After making a grand tour through provocation, paranoia, eroticism and subterfuge, Kubrick's protagonists in the film *Eyes Wide Shut* (Kubrick, 1999) wind up shopping for toys with their daughter. The final words that Nicole Kidman whispers into Tom Cruise's ear (a meta relationship in real and theatrical life in every way)—the final words in a film ever made by Kubrick, may be the most important whispered words of all.

Maybe, I think we should be grateful

Grateful that we've managed to survive through all of our adventures

Whether they were real or only a dream. - Nicole Kidman in Eyes Wide Shut[12]

"And so the picture becomes more wonderful to us than it really is, and reveals to us a secret of which, in truth, it knows nothing." (Oscar Wilde, 1925)

ACKNOWLEDGMENT

Thanks to Kent Bye, Dr. Hillel Maresky, Jeremy Patterson, Douglas Rushkoff, Memo Akten, Matthew Johnson, Robin Fry, Marika Woyzbun, Audri Phillips, Paul Darvasi, Jesse Damiani, Elvira Sanchez de Malicki, Marek Malicki, Stephanie Greenall, Scott Montgomery for information, feedback and conversations provided while writing this chapter and to editors Jacki Morie and Kate McCallum.

REFERENCES

Andrew, E. (2019). These Virtual Reality Headsets Make Farmed Chickens Believe They Roam Free. *IFLScience*. Retrieved from https://www.iflscience.com/plants-and-animals/these-virtual-reality-headsets-make-farmed-chickens-believe-they-roam-free/

Ashbach, H. (2019). *The case against reality: School of Social Sciences: UCI Social Sciences. Interview with D. Hoffman*. Retrieved from https://www.socsci.uci.edu/newsevents/news/2019/2019-07-22-hoffman-reality.php

Barr, P. (2014). Baby Boomers Will Transform Health Care as They Age. *Hospitals & Health Networks, 14*. Retrieved from https://www.hhnmag.com/articles/5298-Boomers-Will-Transform-Health-Care-as-They-Age

Belew, A. (2017, September 24). Retrieved July 3, 2019, from https://www.facebook.com/AdrianBelew/posts/10150895474944995

Bloom, P. (2011). *The New Science of Why We Like What We Like*. W. W. Norton & Company.

Bojic, Z. (2019). Come fly with MRI. Spotlight Quality and Safety. *SickKids Diagnostic Imaging, 3*(1), 2-3. Retrieved from https://www.researchgate.net/publication/334249355_Come_fly_with_MRI_Spotlight_Quality_and_Safety_SickKids_Diagnostic_Imaging_Toronto_Ontario

Bostrom, N. (2003). Are We Living in a Computer Simulation? *The Philosophical Quarterly, 53*(211), 243–255. doi:10.1111/1467-9213.00309

Broderick, D. (1982). *The Judas Mandala*. New York: Pocket Books.

Daley, J. (2019). 'Mona Lisa' Comes to Life in Computer-Generated 'Living Portrait.' *Smithsonian Institution*. Retrieved from www.smithsonianmag.com/smart-news/mona-lisa-comes-life-computer-generated-living-portrait-180972296/

Debord, G. (1955). Introduction to a Critique of Urban Geography. *Les Lèvres Nues, 6*, 23–27.

Dunham, E. (2017). Facebook of the Dead. *What if*. Retrieved from what-if.xkcd.com/69/

Dunn, A., Patterson, J. F., Biega, C., Grishchenko, A., Luna, J., Stanek, J. R., & Strouse, R. (2018). A Novel Clinician-Orchestrated Virtual Reality Platform for Distraction During Pediatric Intravenous Procedures in Children with Hemophilia: A Randomized Clinical Trial (Preprint). JMIR Serious Games, 7(1).

Ellard, C. (2015). *Places of the heart: The psychogeography of everyday life*. New York: Bellevue Literary Press.

Gardner, E. (2019). Deepfakes Pose Increasing Legal and Ethical Issues for Hollywood. *Hollywood Reporter*. Retrieved from https://www.hollywoodreporter.com/thr-esq/deepfakes-pose-increasing-legal-ethical-issues-hollywood-1222978

Gelernter, D. (1992). *Mirror worlds - or the day software puts the universe in a shoebox: how it will happen and what it will mean*. Oxford, UK: Oxford University Press.

Gent, E. (2018, February). Baidu can clone your voice after hearing just a minute of audio. *New Scientist, 26*. Retrieved from https://www.newscientist.com/article/2162177-baidu-can-clone-your-voice-after-hearing-just-a-minute-of-audio/

Gilliam, T. (Director), & Gilliam, T., Stoppard, T., & McKeown, C. (Writers). (1985). *Brazil* [Motion picture]. US/UK: 20th Century Fox.

Glanz, K., Rizzo, A., & Graap, K. (2003). Virtual reality for psychotherapy: Current reality and future possibilities. *Psychotherapy (Chicago, Ill.), 40*(1-2), 55–67. doi:10.1037/0033-3204.40.1-2.55

Gromala, D. J., & Sharir, Y. (1996). Dancing with the virtual dervish: virtual bodies. In M. A. Moser & D. MacLeod (Eds.), *Immersed in technology* (pp. 281–285). Cambridge, MA: MIT Press.

Grow, K. (2017). Frank Zappa Hologram to Perform with Steve Vai, Ex-Mothers of Invention. *Rolling Stone*. Retrieved from https://www.rollingstone.com/music/music-news/frank-zappa-hologram-to-perform-with-steve-vai-ex-mothers-of-invention-199881/

Hashkes, S., Ho, M., & Bye, K. (2019, June 23). #780: Invoking Psychedelic Embodiment Experiences in VR. *Voices of VR Podcast*. Retrieved from https://voicesofvr.com/780-invoking-psychedelic-embodiment-experiences-vr-radix-motion-meu/

Hebb, D. O. (1946). Emotion in man and animal: An analysis of the intuitive processes of recognition. *Psychological Review, 53*(2), 88–106. doi:10.1037/h0063033 PMID:21023321

Hedman, P., Alsisan, S., Szeliski, R., & Kopf, J. (2017). Casual 3D photography. *ACM Transactions on Graphics, 36*(6), 234. doi:10.1145/3130800.3130828

Heim, M. (1993). *The metaphysics of virtual reality*. New York: Oxford University Press.

Hoffman, H. G., Patterson, D. R., & Carrougher, G. J. (2000, September 16). Use of virtual reality for adjunctive treatment of adult burn pain during physical therapy: A controlled study. *The Clinical Journal of Pain, 16*(3), 244–250. doi:10.1097/00002508-200009000-00010 PMID:11014398

Irving, T. (2019). From quality control to deepfakes: How one U of T Engineering team is advancing VR technology. *University of Toronto Engineering News*. Retrieved October 3, 2019, from https://news.engineering.utoronto.ca/from-quality-control-to-deepfakes-how-one-u-of-t-engineering-team-is-advancing-vr-technology/

Johnson, K. (2019, May 23). *Samsung's AI animates paintings and photos without 3D modeling*. Retrieved August 20, 2019, from https://venturebeat.com/2019/05/22/samsungs-ai-animates-paintings-and-photos-without-3d-modeling/

Karras, T., Laine, S., Aittala, M., Hellsten, J., Lehtinen, J., & Aila, T. (2019). *Analyzing and Improving the Image Quality of StyleGAN*. arXiv preprint arXiv:1912.04958

Katz, M. (2018). CGI 'Influencers' Like Lil Miquela Are About to Flood Your Feeds. *Wired*. Retrieved from www.wired.com/story/lil-miquela-digital-humans/

Kelly, K. (2019). AR Will Spark the Next Big Tech Platform—call It Mirrorworld. *Wired*. Retrieved from https://www.wired.com/story/mirrorworld-ar-next-big-tech-platform/

Klinger, E., Bouchard, S., Légeron, P., Roy, S., Lauer, F., Chemin, I., & Nugues, P. (2005). *CyberPsychology & Behavior*. Preprint. doi:10.1089/cpb.2005.8.76

Klinger, E., Bouchard, S., Légeron, P., Roy, S., Lauer, F., Chemin, I., & Nugues, P. (2005). Virtual reality therapy versus cognitive behavior therapy for social phobia: A preliminary controlled study. *Cyberpsychology & Behavior*, 8(1), 76–88. doi:10.1089/cpb.2005.8.76 PMID:15738695

Knickman, J. R., & Snell, E. K. (2002). The 2030 problem: Caring for aging baby boomers. *Health Services Research*, 37(4), 849–884. doi:10.1034/j.1600-0560.2002.56.x PMID:12236388

Kubrick, S. (Director). (1999). *Eyes Wide Shut* [Motion Picture]. UK: Stanley Kubrick Productions. Distributed by Warner Bros.

Lacher, I. (1997). Fred Is Her Co-Pilot. *Los Angeles Times*. Retrieved from www.latimes.com/archives/la-xpm-1997-aug-17-ca-23118-story.html

LaFrance, A. (2017). An Artificial Intelligence Developed Its Own Non-Human Language. *Atlantic (Boston, Mass.)*, 21. Retrieved from https://www.theatlantic.com/technology/archive/2017/06/artificial-intelligence-develops-its-own-non-human-language/530436/

Libby, K. (2019). This Bill Hader Deepfake Video Is Amazing. It's Also Terrifying for Our Future. *Popular Mechanics*. Retrieved from https://www.popularmechanics.com/technology/security/a28691128/deepfake-technology/

Löfgren, K. (2013). *What is ontology? Introduction to the word and the concept*. Talk given in Sweden. Retrieved from https://youtu.be/XTsaZWzVJ4c

Lonsway, B. (2016). Complicated Agency. In S. A. Lukas (Ed.), *A reader in themed and immersive spaces* (pp. 239–248). Pittsburgh, PA: Carnegie Mellon/ETC Press.

Malicki-Sanchez, K. (2017). *Virtual Reality: ideacity 2017*. Retrieved from https://ideacity.ca/video/keram-malicki-sanchez-virtual-reality-toronto/

Martineau, P. (2019). Facebook Removes Accounts With AI-Generated Profile Photos. *Wired*. Retrieved from https://www.wired.com/story/facebook-removes-accounts-ai-generated-photos/

Miodownik, M. (2019). *Liquid Rules: The delightful and dangerous substances that flow through our lives*. Rancho Cucamonga, CA: Houghton Mifflin Harcourt.

Montgomery, S. (2016). *The soul of an octopus: A surprising exploration into the wonder of consciousness*. New York: Atria Paperback.

NASA. (n. d.). *The Golden Record*. Retrieved from voyager.jpl.nasa.gov/golden-record/

(n.d.). InBauder, H., & Engel-Di Mauro, S. (Eds.), *Critical Geographies. A Collection of Readings. Praxis (e)*. Press.

News, B. B. C. (2016). Adobe Voco 'Photoshop-for-voice' causes concern. *BBC News*. Retrieved from https://www.bbc.com/news/technology-37899902

O'Keeffe, H. (2013). Mystery of preserved T Rex tissue solved: High levels of iron in dinosaur's body kept it intact. *Daily Mail*. Retrieved from https://www.dailymail.co.uk/news/article-2515769/How-T-Rex-tissue-preserved-68million-years.html

O'Sullivan, D. (2019). When seeing is no longer believing: Inside the Pentagon's race against Deepfake videos. *CNN Business*. Retrieved from https://www.cnn.com/videos/business/2019/01/28/deepfakes-interactive-social-cut-orig.cnn

Oculus. (2015). *Strangers with Patrick Watson*. Felix and Paul Studios, Developers.

Overbeck, R. S., Erickson, D., Evangelakos, D., Pharr, M., & Debevec, P. (2018). A system for acquiring, processing, and rendering panoramic light field stills for virtual reality. *ACM Transactions on Graphics*, *37*(6), 197. doi:10.1145/3272127.3275031

Pearce, C. (2011). *Communities of Play: Emergent Cultures in Multiplayer Games and Virtual Worlds*. Boston, MA: MIT Press.

Phase Core Technology. (n.d.). *Professional avatar and beauty solutions*. Retrieved August 20, 2019, from http://faceunity.com/#/faceswipe

Proietti, M., Pickston, A., Graffitti, F., Barrow, P., Kundys, D., Branciard, C., ... Fedrizzi, A. (2019). Experimental test of local observer independence. *Science Advances*, *5*(9), eaaw9832. doi:10.1126ciadv.aaw9832 PMID:31555731

Rathbone, O. (2019). Ahmet Zappa And Eyellusion Talk The Bizarre World Of Frank Zappa. *UDiscover Music*. Retrieved from www.udiscovermusic.com/stories/ahmet-zappa-bizarre-world-frank-interview

Reid, J. (2014, March 26). *The power of animism: John Reid at TEDxQueenstown* [Video]. Retrieved from https://www.youtube.com/watch?v=lmhFRarkw8E

Rizzo, A., Reger, G., Gahm, G., Difede, J., & Rothbaum, B. O. (2009). Virtual reality exposure therapy for combat-related PTSD. In *Post-traumatic stress disorder* (pp. 375–399). Humana Press. doi:10.1007/978-1-60327-329-9_18

Rizzotto, L. (2019). Why Deepfakes Will Change Advertising Forever. *Medium*. Retrieved from https://medium.com/futurepi/why-deepfakes-will-change-advertising-forever-2949ec3f87ee

Rushkoff, D. (2019). *Team Human*. New York: W. W. Norton & Co.

Scargill, J. H. C. (2019). *Can Life Exist in 2+1 Dimensions?* arXiv preprint arXiv:1906.05336

Sellars, W. (2003). *Empiricism and the philosophy of mind*. Cambridge, MA: Harvard University Press.

Sharir, Y., & Gromala, D. J. (1997). Dancing with the Virtual Dervish: Virtual Bodies. In M. A. Moser & D. MacLeod (Eds.), *Immersed in technology: Art and virtual environments* (pp. 281–286). Cambridge, MA: MIT.

Sivitilli, D., & Gire, D. H. (2019). *Researchers model how octopus arms make decisions*. Retrieved from https://phys.org/news/2019-06-octopus-arms-decisions.html

Slater, M. (2009). Place Illusion and Plausibility Can Lead to Realistic Behaviour in Immersive Virtual Environments. *Philosophical Transactions of the Royal Society of London. Series B, Biological Sciences*, *364*(1535), 3549–3557. doi:10.1098/rstb.2009.0138 PMID:19884149

Slater, M., Spanlang, B., Sanchez-Vives, M. V., & Blanke, O. (2010). First Person Experience of Body Transfer in Virtual Reality. *PLoS One*, *5*(5), e10564. doi:10.1371/journal.pone.0010564 PMID:20485681

Stowers, J. R., Hofbauer, M., Bastien, R., Griessner, J., Higgins, P., Farooqui, S., ... Straw, A. D. (2017). Virtual reality for freely moving animals. *Nature Methods*, *14*(10), 995–1002. doi:10.1038/nmeth.4399 PMID:28825703

Videos, C. (2019, December 12), *Leonardo DiCaprio as Anakin Skywalker in the Star Wars Saga - Deepfake Theater* [Video File]. Retrieved from https://www.youtube.com/watch?v=pVW6cdpEirU

Waldrop, M. M. (2018). Free Agents. *Science*, *360*(6385), 144–147. doi:10.1126cience.360.6385.144 PMID:29650655

Wheeler, B. (2005). Reality is What You Can Get Away With: Fantastic Imaginings, Rebellion and Control in Terry Gilliam's Brazil. Critical Survey, (17), 95-108.

White, C. (2014). *The science delusion: Asking the big questions in a culture of easy answers*. Brooklyn, NY: Melville House.

Whitehead, A. N. (1929). *Process and reality: An essay in cosmology: Gifford lectures delivered in the University of Edinburg during the session 1927-1928*. New York: Macmillian Company.

Wiggers, K. (2019). Generative adversarial networks: What GANs are and how they've evolved. *Venture Beat*. Retrieved from https://venturebeat.com/2019/12/26/gan-generative-adversarial-network-explainer-ai-machine-learning/

Wilde, O., & Wilde, O. (1925). *The writings of Oscar Wilde. Intentions*. New York: Wells.

Worsley, R. (Producer, Director). (2017). *How Radio Isn't Done* [Motion Picture]. USA: Independent.

Yirka, B. (2019). Researcher shows physics suggests life could exist in a 2-D universe. *PhysOrg*. Retrieved from https://phys.org/news/2019-06-physics-life-d-universe.html

KEY TERMS AND DEFINITIONS

Ambisonics: A spherical audio format; rather than mere left and right stereo, this technique captures audio in 360 degrees.

Animism: The belief that all things have a spiritual essence and character.

Anthropocentrism: Interpreting or regarding the world in terms of human values and experiences.

Chatbots: A digital avatar, text, or speech program that uses machine learning and artificial intelligence to respond to questions and conduct conversations around specific subjects in a meaningful way.

Deepfakes: A machine learning process that uses visual data about a face to mutate, modulate or transpose onto another actor. The cumulative effect is that the target object appears to be the source object, while using the target's expressions.

Essentialism: In the Platonic sense, the idea that all things carry attributes that identify their nature and form.

Generative Adversarial Networks (GANs): An artificial intelligence process that includes a "generator" that produces samples, and a "discriminator" that differentiates between computer-generated samples and samples derived from "real-world" sources.

Light-Field Capture: A data-intensive approach for capturing all light data in a space.

Phenomenology: A philosophical approach initialized by Edmund Husserl to study the perception of events and how consciousness corresponds to it.

Psychogeography: An examination of how constructed environment affects mood and emotion.

Simulation Hypothesis: The argument that the nature of reality is an artificial construct created and operated by a computer.

Virtual Assistants: Digital avatars that reliably answer queries to assist an end-user.

Volumetric Effigy: A digitally captured, three-dimensional, photographic model representing the likeness of a person, living or deceased.

Walking Simulator: A colloquialism for a genre of videogame that involves exploration more than completing any goal in particular.

ENDNOTES

[1]   The Singularity is sometimes viewed positively and sometimes as the total collapse of humanity and even in some cases, all of creation, when technology reaches a critical mass and outpaces the ability for biological entities to counter its effects. The positive view is that we can upload our consciousness to the cloud and live forever, the direst scenario is that artificial intelligence turns the universe into grey goo.

[2]   Hence the Roy Batty quote; we will scarce be able to parse, let alone utilize, most of what our post-human agents deliver to us, unless we handicap them so as to make their output understandable to us.

[3]   *NASA*, NASA, voyager.jpl.nasa.gov/golden-record/. retrieved July 6th, 2019.

[4]   Find more information on the MRI sedation substitute at at www.emmarye.com

[5]   Sugam Pokharel and AJ Willingham, (Updated 9:33 AM ET, Tue January 10, 2017) CNN "Bangladesh's 'Tree man' has his hands back.

6   A mantra spoken by the character JF Sebastian in the film Blade Runner – Sebastian is the brilliant creator of the advance, bio-like bodies used for the Nexus 6 humanoids. In his personal workshop a horrific mélange of animated toys and life-sized dolls belie his more personal experiments.

7   Iperov. (2019, June 27). Iperov/DeepFaceLab. Retrieved from https://github.com/iperov/Deep-FaceLab

8   Chris Milk, an early developer of narrative VR content coined the phrase Empathy Machine to espouse the transportive nature of the medium and its ability to transfer an experience from one person to another in a uniquely embodied manner. The other sides with Paul Bloom around the dangers of taking empathy to always mean a sympathetic or ultimately positive transformation is the result of such understanding.

9   This phrase was used verbally by Douglas Rushkoff in Los Angeles in early May 2019 at an event the author attended, but is also stated in Rushkoff, D. (2019). Team Human. W W Norton & Co. Section 43: "section 43: "raw material for digital processing or labor to be extracted and repackaged." and section 44: "We are all just numbers: the quantified self. Like a music recording that can be reduced to code and stored in a file, the quantified human can also be reduced to bits, replicated infinitely, uploaded to the cloud, or installed in a robot. But only the metrics we choose to follow are recorded and translated. Those we don't value, or don't even know about, aren't brought forward into the new model."

10   Jules Urbach shared this opinion at the Intel Create SIGGRAPH reception at the Conga Room, Los Angeles, July 30th, 2019.

11   Yaser Sheikh from Facebook Reality Labs discussed Metric Telepresence at SIGGRAPH 2019.

12   Interesting to consider the meaning of "Eyes Wide Shut" when speaking about Virtual Reality where one has one's eyes wide open, yet is blind to anything going on beyond the headset.

Chapter 3
Humans Enter the Age of Avatarism

Gregory Peter Panos
Persona Foundation Founder, USA

ABSTRACT

The internet, social networks, emerging virtual/augmented/mixed reality technology platforms and portals are beginning to utilize and display interactive, spatially relative, three-dimensional versions of objects, persons, and environments. The human need to document and archive one's form, behavior, beliefs, experiences, and wishes is an inherent need and desire of our species to preserve and tell their unique life stories. An ability to track and/or capture human movement, expression, environment, and experience with technology designed to acquire hand gestures, body and facial tracking inputs, as well as speech will play an important role in the life documentation process. The eventual goal will be for humankind to interact with, and be remembered as, autonomous virtual agents beyond the scope of physical life, providing "virtual immortality" to any and all that adopt the capability as it evolves in our culture, and with the machines and applications that we utilize. This chapter explores the age of avatarism.

INTRODUCTION

The age of virtual humans has arrived. After decades of technological evolution, key pieces have fallen into place and human life on earth is now being born into the virtual universe of us, what we can call the *Age of Avatarism*, where we are integrated with our avatars, or virtual personas.

Within a decade, any person alive on Earth will never have known a world where believable virtual humans didn't exist. Human simulation technology will pervade all aspects of human life, and virtual agents will evolve to efficiently mitigate complex interactions with trust, authenticity, empathy and intelligence for all living persons.

Believable human simulation will become the standard way to express one's self and interact with the coming blend of physical and virtual reality. One will be able to use a normal representation: an approved or validated version, or perhaps a custom "crafted" version that shows some specific aspect of one's self. These simulations will contain the best and most salient aspects of our selves, not only

DOI: 10.4018/978-1-7998-2433-6.ch003

the visage, but behaviors, and more unique characteristics of our individual human attributes. We have a built-in preference for human-like interaction. Our evolutionary wiring is optimized and naturally acclimated toward conversational language, facial expression and emotional perception, and these will all be contained in our digital representations in the rapidly approaching future.

Conversations and consultations with virtual medical practitioners, officials, institutions, entertainment systems, social networks, spiritual figures, and the virtual constructs of ones we know and love, will be the primary manner with which humans will communicate, interact with, and document the lives they are living.

The goals of this chapter are to introduce some vocabulary with which to present these persona concepts, describe the work that has been going on in the domain of virtual representations over the past decades, including how personas are captured, and the many ways in which such constructs are being and will be used. Finally, the chapter closes with some predictions about the future in which our digital selves are common.

BACKGROUND

Naming Conventions For Human Simulation Constructs

As any important development or aspect of, history, culture or technology begins to appear, it becomes necessary to name and describe its relevance, meaning and future. The field of human simulation is a broad area of study and will continue to require further definition using common, easy to understand language.

A variety of example attempts to describe aspects of human simulation have already been defined and are being used. Certain words have gained traction and are easily recognizable, others less so. Figure 1 shows a chart that attempts to illustrate some of the more commonly used word fragments and the resulting combinations that have the potential to simplify understanding and discussion related to the field.

The word **Avatar** tops the chart, as it has become the most widely adopted word to describe a human simulated construct, although now the word is not specifically anthropomorphic in meaning. Today an Avatar can take any form to represent a person. Some of the other familiar terms in the chart have more specific intentions or meanings that most English-speaking people can associate with aspects of human simulation, however, we do not, as yet, have specific, universal understandings of these terms.

Rather than adherence to any specific word, this chapter will remain general in discussing the art, science and philosophy of human simulation. The author's personal choice would be to use the word "construct" in most cases, although, it is not listed on the chart and seldom appears in literature and presentations. It is for this reason the word is less likely to be confused or constrained to any specific context, so that it can serve as a valuable device, and thus it will be used freely in this regard within the remainder of the text.

Figure 1. Some of the vocabulary surrounding human simulation
Source: Greg Panos

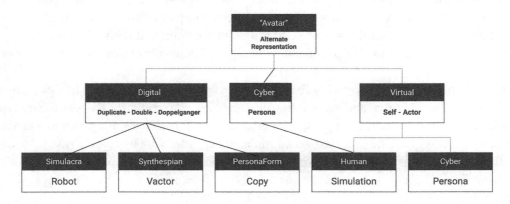

POTENTIAL USE CASES FOR BELIEVABLE HUMAN SIMULATION

The human need to document and archive one's form, behavior, beliefs, experiences, and wishes, is ages old and serves to support how we live, discover, understand and materialize our identities. From carved stone to cave paintings to personal diaries, many forms aligned with specific time epochs have been utilized to capture and convey the essence of a human's existence beyond their actual life span. This will continue to be a part of our virtual representations moving into the future. A few brief potential examples follow.

Physical Healthmap (Body Plan)

Virtual human simulation constructs will be used to build a time-variant healthmap of vital test results sensor data, and health history. Such a detailed, interactive data set, fully referenced and aligned with a personalized 3D human model, will assist in the complex and difficult task of understanding what is required to diagnose, treat and manage one's health and wellness over time. More clarity, transparency and certainty will be a major benefit in having a personal health map of this nature.

Your Personal Actor (Agent)

One's personal construct can be used to perform, entertain, advocate and express personal, creative endeavors in service to education, invention, original thought, life-storytelling, acting, singing, personality, and philosophy. All aspects of what we do as humans can be augmented, extended or enhanced with digital constructs, allowing us to be more places and perform more activities with less overhead and human wear and tear.

Your Eternal Record (Soul's Story)

One's human simulation "construct" could also be used as a personal life container to deposit one's life experiences, thoughts, likes, loves, hopes and dreams to represent you and the life you lived, and be passed on for posterity. Living persons may even be expected to gradually, voluntarily and purposefully contribute toward, and thoughtfully assemble, throughout the course of their life, enough information to allow their virtual persona to continue to authentically and believably simulate themselves once they no longer physically exist.

A personal virtual agent can ostensibly live beyond the scope of one's physical life, providing a form of "virtual immortality" for each and every living human being who regularly access life-archiving tools during their corporeal existence. As a person's memories and experiences are gathered, organized and preserved, those archives will be accessed via a simulated construct with believable fidelity to one's self, allowing future generations to know and experience those whose record has been conserved in this way.

One's need for, and occupation with, the task of whole life experience archiving, may actually come to be thought of, and characterized as, a person's essential "Soul."

These are a few simple examples. Many more will emerge as the technologies to enable more faithful constructs are perfected.

Next this chapter will explore some of the key motivators over human history in the quest to build, evolve and continue to perfect human simulation.

THE PRACTICAL EVOLUTION OF HUMAN SIMULATION TECHNOLOGY

Since the beginning of time, humankind has endeavored to record and represent our physical existence. Some of the earliest cave paintings discovered illustrate man's need to memorialize their lives, adventures and stories, with novel techniques created to depict images on the surfaces of caves.

As time progressed, more innovative techniques to capture our "selves" have emerged. From earliest paintings and sculpture, humans have rapidly adopted salient technologies to better represent their life stories and histories.

The long march of technology has been, in part, a quest to advance visual imagery. Each step up this visualization ladder has been accompanied by attempts to better represent human faces, figures and actions. Portraits, pictures, home movies, videos and today's "selfies" have evolved to fulfill a universal desire to memorializes our human lives with the ever widening, available technology of the day. From the early development and use of stable color pigments, black and white, and then color photography with light sensitive chemicals, holography enable by lasers, motion picture film to bring moving images to life and onto video, computer-generated imagery, real-time imaging, 3D animation, numerous 3D scanning methods, volumetric capture, and eventually, synthetic artificial image generation by machine learning, these are all part of this progression of techniques to create ever more realistic constructs of ourselves.

Early examples of human simulation began can be traced back to the early 1970s, when computer graphics graduate student Fred Parke completed his dissertation at the University of Utah on the topic of modeling and animating human faces (Parke, 1972). These techniques were of interest to the Hollywood film industry for a number of reasons. By the mid-1970s, the advances coming out of the graphics researchers at Utah starting to appear in feature films. In the film *Futureworld* (1976) some of the footage showing humans being created in a lab was actually work from the university research at Utah, including an animation of the hand of Ed Catmull (later to become head of the animation studio Pixar) and a parametric facial animation from Parke's thesis work. The next film to incorporate digital humans was the 1981 film *Looker*, where a fully (tediously) hand-digitized version of the actress Susan Dey's body makes a starring role. By 2002, director Andrew Niccol's comedy *S1m0ne*, continued in the vein of noteworthy examples of human digitization/simulation work used creatively as plot devices to tell a comedic story of a non-existent virtual actress.

A more recent, and specifically relevant, example of human digitization was utilized in film *The Congress* (2013) where the USC Light Stage System was featured as a plot element used to illustrate how an actress (played by Robin Wright) was convinced to create a virtual model of herself, ostensibly to allow her to continue her career.[1]

Today many films use character scanning in some form or another. Sometimes it is to place the actor's face on a stunt double that performs dangerous actions. A growing trend is to scan all actors in case the body data is needed, as Lucasfilm recently did for its main *Star Wars* cast members (Evans, 2018).

THE PROCESS, TECHNOLOGY AND METHODS OF "HUMAN VIRTUALIZATION"

The commensurate research and development that contributed to the availability of the computer generated imagery tools, methods, and technology required to innovate the field of virtual human simulation, began to flourish at universities, laboratories, and corporations throughout the world during the 1980s and 1990s. Sharing of innovation and discoveries in published papers, articles and disclosures at events, conferences, and expositions, rapidly accelerated the adoption and growth of the field. The defense industry made a large contribution toward the advancement and cost reduction necessary to bring computer image generation technology to the masses (National Academy Press, 1999).

Let's take a look at some of the key elements in the evolution of human simulation technology. Some of the essential tasks necessary in building a human 3D model are described in the sections that follow.

Modeling A 3D Human

The earliest method to create a 3D database of a human model was to "digitize" points along a 2D surface (from illustrations laid onto a "2D Digitizing Tablet") with a magnetic stylus to manually gather the points into a data file using a connected computer and program. Points taken from illustrations drawn from different points of view (POV) were combined to create a 3D database file, which was utilized to build and render a faceted or solid computer generated image of the object or subject. This time-consuming, labor-intensive method had incremental advancements to become more efficient, however, even newer technologies automated and replaced the process acquisition tasks performed by hand.

A **3D Digitizing Rig**, consisting of a number of mechanically connected, counter-weighted arms, terminating at a tracked stylus point, were next in line to digitize, small 3D objects. However, to create human models, a head or body cast would need to be crafted and used to gather points along its surface. These rigs were largely useless to acquire surface data from a living person, without casting a model first. Also, time and labor intensive operation limited their use.

As soon as non-contact laser-based measurement became practical, hand-held and then automated, mechanically scanned, surface imaging/laser measurement sensors eventually replaced physical "brute-

Figure 2. Mechanical, non-contact laser scanner and seated 3D scanner array
Source: Greg Panos

force" 2D to 3D digitization methods to rapidly and accurately acquire human face and body form data (Figure 2).

As light-based human body/facial scanners evolved, the experience of "being digitized" became more natural, even enjoyable, as a less obtrusive task for those involved. More recent advancements in human acquisition technology have migrated toward fully digital data gathering systems that no longer contain motors, moving parts or require the subject to move in a specific way.

These configurations consist of multi-camera sensor arrays networked together. An often-employed example is the Light Stage system, developed by Dr. Paul Debevec and his team at the University of Southern California's Institute for Creative Technologies (ICT) and subsequently advanced at Google, Inc. It is a complex "fullerene" shaped structure, with many camera/lighting/sensor units pointed inward at the human subject.

Body Shape Data Capture

When an expert tailor performs a fitting to provide a customer with the best looking clothes, they are using years of experience with others (and their fittings), knowledge of clothing behavior, material comfort, and the motion of the cloth on the body under typical conditions. Of course, each fitting must be subject to a series of constraints as to the type and purpose of the clothes to be worn. A bride might require a different fit than a groom, with extra material and certain areas tighter or looser than others. Astronauts must be fitted with specialized materials that must be measured and cut to order to enable motion without damaging their protective suit while performing and professional tasks in harsh environments.

Historically, manual measurements were taken by hand with measuring tape and numbers were called out and recorded onto a paper form during the measuring process. Although time consuming, this process had cultural value through the respectful interaction with a human expert, providing a social opportunity, often involving humor, friendship, and a communal discussion of ideas and wishes in service toward an intended vision and outcome for the garment and the person wearing it.

And so, our practical history and experience is a valuable resource to inform subsequent, innovative development and the advancement of working with body shapes. This experience and culture must circumscribe the goals and intentions of any technology to assist body measurement, recording and data processing as we move into the future.

Innovation hasn't yet replaced this personalized, hands-on, person-to person "fitting experience." Rather, customers are offered variations of a style, fabric, sizing, color, pattern or pre-cut, customized fit, in hope of selecting a correct garment, often through the process of elimination. Although, a customer might begin with a good sense of their sizing and metrics, the process requires the trying on of clothes at a retail establishment or, ordering garments online, and the time and inefficient rejection required to advance toward a satisfactory sale.

Also, typical trying-on methods do not lend well toward factoring in a second opinion by others who need to see the fashion and fitting take place, or to discuss with the customer their impressions without their being physically present. Other concerns, perhaps related to modesty, privacy and convenience also might complicate the process of sharing. The potential for social engagement and participatory enjoyment of having the experience of trying on various fashions with others to assist and commune, bring a level of meaning absent when alone or in isolation.

Other industries, such as motion picture special effects, human factors, design, medical, artistic and other research initiatives have pioneered most of the new innovations in technology that we see today. Chief among the more commonly used techniques is a method of 3D modeling called *photogrammetry*. A series of photographs are taken, either manually or automated, around an object or person, and these images are submitted to a computer program. The program then processes the assembly of images taken from the different points of view that have been gathered. A resulting 3D model is generated of the subject, which also contains the visible color and texture details from the images, and aligns them onto the model's surface.

Photogrammetric tools, when properly used, can create very accurate, detailed 3D models. They are, by their nature, extremely compute intensive, time-consuming and require many rules and constraints in their use. The data obtained with this method, however, is considered to be a "gold standard" in efforts to derive 3D data from real world, physical, static subject matter.

Another key development in the field of 3D object generation has been the adoption of specialized 3D depth-sensing camera technologies. These novel imaging devices utilize projected visual or infrared dot patterns, when projected onto an object and gathered by the sensor are capable of calculating exact distances along an object's surface.

Many 3D human body and facial capture solutions have emerged to use combinations of various sensor packages, some systems having many sensors configured into geometric arrays, moving scanners, mirrors, and innovative methods to capture, scan and calculate accurate, fully color, high resolution, textured models.

The development of and integration of advanced sensors and system has been refined toward the creation of specialized "Facial Capture" and expression sampling and recording devices, which will be covered next.

Facial And Expression Capture

Each of us is not only composed of our physical shape, but also exist as the collective manifestation of our specific human facial expressions. Sampling, identification and cataloging of human facial expressions is an extremely important part of the human archiving and re-simulation process. Through our smiles, frowns, winks, and numerous other more subtle facial representations, we convey recognizable and specifically identifiable characteristics that make real our existence to other humans.

Those that know/have met us, each have a biologically organized memory area, which evolved to specifically process and store facial recognition information. The process of recording each of one's discrete expressions is evolving rapidly with a variety of important results.

Facial sampling technology—which can rapidly and accurately capture a person's facial shape, bone structure, muscle behavior and expressions—has been steadily evolving. Early facial 3D scanning systems used stationary, visible light camera rigs designed to record multiple, static photos from different points of view (POV). The series of images were then processed, using photogrammetry to derive 3D, color textured models. Eventually, specialized depth-cameras were added to facial capture rigs. These sensors could observe and derive surface height point data directly, at the time a subject was scanned. This additional depth information, helped increase surface accuracy, computation time to build a model in post-processing and other optimizations of the capture process.

There are two flavors of depth camera modules, one type utilizes **Structured Light** and the other uses **Time-of-Flight (ToF)**. Both depth sensor designs have various advantages of accuracy, operational efficiency, power requirements, cost, and functional parameters that inform their selection for different uses. Efficiencies in component innovation, mass manufacturing, and speed of computation required to use them, have brought large cost savings, making adoption for applications in human simulation a realistic option.

The Structured Light technique uses a specialized visible light pattern projected onto a subject, while a visible light camera photographs the face (overlaid by pattern). The subject must be still, however, the pattern can be static or quickly shifted in different directions while being recorded. The resulting camera image and/or rapid video sequence is then analyzed to determine surface height information derived from the observed position and/or behavior of the overlaid pattern. This method is inexpensive, rapid, accurate and from a subject's point of view can be considered to be experientially interesting or even entertaining.

The Time-of-Flight-based facial capture system uses an infrared depth sensor designed to scan invisible points of light onto a subject and measure the time required for each point to return to the sensor. Prior to modern-day solid-state, ultra-high-speed photonic sensor availability, the physics and computational complexity involved to accomplish this rapid, accurate measurement technique was impractical, expensive, and unpredictable. For facial capture the ToF Depth Sensor also includes a visible light camera that acquires color surface information, which is aligned and assigned to each measured point. This allows for the creation of a color **Point Cloud** 3D data construct that can be processed in many different ways to build a 3D facial model (Figures 3).

Other, simplified facial capture techniques exist with varying results in capture time, accuracy and the need for a subject to move in a specific, constrained way while being captured. A stereoscopic camera pair, or a single monoscopic camera can be used with a technique described as **Structure from Motion,** which records a short video sequence of the subject turning their head along an axis. The video frames are then processed to extrapolate a 3D color-textured facial/head model. For simple applications, the

Figure 3. Structured light facial (a) and time-of-flight facial (b) capture session
Source: Greg Panos

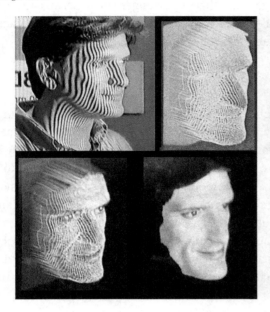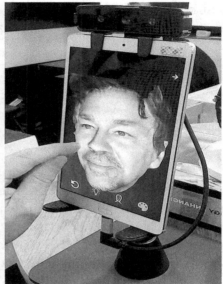

results are minimally acceptable for many applications where high-resolution and depth accuracy are not required.

Recent, state-of-the-art facial capture solutions have taken a turn away from the need for depth sensors, stereoscopic cameras, subject movement requirements, static physical rigs or markers, to more sophisticated techniques such as computer vision-based Machine Learning to assist in the capture process.

Machine Learning, and artificial intelligence methods, have begun to utilize the enormous corpus of human facial images obtained via computer vision to learn to produce bone/muscle-structure enabled, colored, textured, lighting accurate, 3D facial models from a source: camera, sensor, or image. These advancements are rapidly replacing most of the techniques described above, and are suited well toward applications that can use human facial information, such as virtual make-up, animoji visual tricks, and more recently facial insertion/replacement in what is called **Deep Fakery.**

The main drawback in the use of computer vision and machine learning methods is the necessity to upload a source image to the cloud, so a processing application can access, add to and compare the image to extremely large facial image databases. These "learning corpus" repositories are often amassed without specific permission from each of the people whose images are added to the database.

Another constraint is the absolute need for powerful, expensive computational cloud computing systems needed to create a resulting 3D model from a submitted facial image. And yet, much progress has been made in the simplification of algorithms and computational needs. The improvement of consumer-grade computational performance has continued to rise exponentially, year over year (according to Moore's Law.)[2] Soon, local, non-cloud-based solutions using a typical personal computer will be all that is needed to accomplish these tasks.

Recent critique of the machine vision/learning approach to facial simulation has begun to center around privacy issues, unauthorized facial image data sharing arrangements, permission gaps, and potential misuse scenarios. Many actual and real threats have been demonstrated and the absence of sensible safeguards and user controls, concerns are rapidly escalating.

Body Motion Capture

When it comes to the realistic perception and believability of a human simulation, when animated, a subject's movement, posture and gestures must be recognizable, obvious and familiar to another person who knows them. The ways in which we move, walk, run, skip, sit down, get up, jump, standby idly, and a variety of other body positions and motions, are important to record, catalog and index into a robust human simulation database. It is for this reason that body motion capture is an important element in the data-gathering process in the creation of a human simulation of a living person, especially for an athlete, actor or physical performer, or whenever motion is a necessary component of the use case.

The technological evolution of body motion capture began with simple 2D based body-joint position digitization, gathered frame-by-frame from films and written down as numbers on a list in X and Y positions along a graph (Badler, 1975). Data had to be manually by hand inputted into a file or translated to become useful.

Mechanical systems were next, with systems that utilized frames and armatures attached to a person with various means of adhesion. The human joint position points on the frames were attached to "encoder" devices consisting of magnetometric, optical, electrical resistor, inductor coil, or strain gauge rotational or linear measurement devices designed to transmit movement data to a recording device, data logger or computer.

Evolving beyond the "brute-force" hand digitization of frames and clunky armature-based solutions, the emergence of Magnetic Field Tracking Motion Capture systems developed. These utilized AC or DC magnetic field sources and detector arrays affixed to a wearable suit or strapped onto a person's limbs, hands, feet, head, neck, etc. The signal generated by the magnetic coils were synchronized and pulsed in a variety of ways that generated fast, real-time, accurate motion and skeletal data that could directly animate a computer generated character as well as stream the data into a file for later processing, cleanup, and application.

More current, present day optical motion capture systems are in wide use in industrial and entertainment applications. These fixed-position, multi-camera array, infrared marker-based tracking systems require a subject to wear retro-reflective objects (dots, bands or patterns) on their clothing to be tracked. Hybrid systems are evolving to integrate, not only infrared markers, but also visible fiducial markers that can be seen by visible light camera arrays that are used to capture and process motion data with machine vision, learning and deep data analysis.

Today, state-of-the-art systems are being demonstrated which use a single, monoscopic, low-resolution camera, without the need for markers. They function by using machine-learning image analysis and a trained large data corpus to analyze, compare and intuit the actual body motion with increasing accuracy, simplicity and robustness for a variety of applications in computer vision.

The capture, processing and usage of body motion data does not necessarily confer an ability to accurately model a human body shape. Where approximate, simple human shapes will suffice, a human body shape can be extrapolated from motion data using newer computer vision and machine learning techniques, however, shape date is a by-product of the motion acquisition process and is not directly

Figure 4. Charles martinet performing Mario
Source: Greg Panos

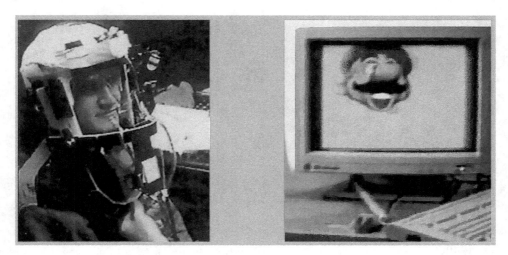

measured. This free body shape date might be useful for many casual applications, however, accurate body shape data is far more complex to obtain in detail, and requires specialized, hardware, scanning methods, and post processing.

Real-Time Facial Performance Capture

One of the earliest manifestations of real-time, facial capture/expression sampling technology utilized a helmet with physical actuators, usually linear or radial (potentiometric or magnetic) encoder components anchored to a helmet, worn by a "performer." The actor, euphemistically referred to as a **Vactor,** would glue small, rigid cables to specific points on their face that were attached to the encoders situated about the helmet. The system generated digital electronic numbers in real-time to an off-body processor, which recorded and streamed data to another computer system designed to render a 3D facial model and animate it accordingly.

Hollywood make-up artist, Rick Lazzarini, was first to implement this design commercially to track human movement, live into a computer for real-time **Performance Animation**. He built a variety of custom, modular configurations for clients and his systems were subsequently referred to as a **Waldo**, a word originally taken from a Robert Heinlein science fiction story: *Waldo and Magic Co.* (1950).

Rick was the first to provide hand controllers used to puppeteer Jim Henson's *Muppet* characters, for Jim's computer animation projects, and live performance events (Sturman, 1998). Eventually, Rick engineered a helmet-based facial capture solution for one of the first real-time, performance animation studios and consultants, SimGraphics Engineering. The system was bulky, not particularly comfortable for long periods of time, however, it was accurate, and fast enough, to be used for live performance by a small number of traditional stage and television actors brave enough to try a new twist in their craft.

Actor Charles Martinet was hired by Nintendo to bring their virtual *Mario the Plumber* character to life at their trade show events (1990). Charles literally became the "man behind the curtain," hidden from view, wired up, laughing, singing, joking with people he could see and interact with on a monitor being fed from under a giant video wall projection of his zany, larger-than-life real-time, computer animated

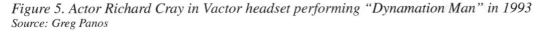

Figure 5. Actor Richard Cray in Vactor headset performing "Dynamation Man" in 1993
Source: Greg Panos

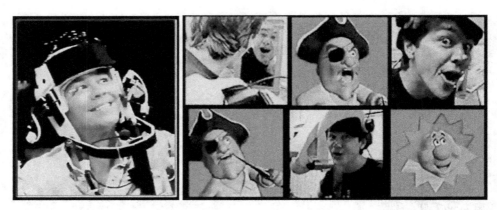

Mario. It was really quite a spectacle to see and his work always drew a huge crowd into Nintendo's booth (Earnshaw and Vince 1995, p. 261).

Charles also volunteered in a groundbreaking experiment developed by SimGraphics (based on their "Mario in Real Time" or MiRT System to entertain sick children in hospitals. A small camera set up in the child's room, usually at their bedside, was used to send their interaction to Charles (or another "VActor") in a remote location, where their characters were displayed on a TV monitor in the child's room (See Figure 4). Children interacted with the virtual character, bringing laughter, joy and a welcome distraction from their therapy and challenging conditions. This work inspired director Steven Spielberg to create the Starbright Foundation in 1991with the goal to find and use emerging multimedia technology to help ill children cope with their challenges.

Broadway veteran actor/singer Richard Cray performed "Dynamation Man" to demonstrate Sim-Graphics Engineering's "VActor Performer" solution at Silicon Graphics' SIGGRAPH 1993 booth, to the delight of conference attendees. Richard recants his waking up after a brief snooze-break to the face of actor Danny DeVito, lurking backstage, to see the system in action, catching him off-guard and with complete surprise.

Richard's performance was the first time an actor performed an operatic solo in real-time as a computer generated character to a live audience, much to the annoyance to the occupants of nearby booth exhibits. Richard went one to utilize a newer, optical facial capture system (Figure 5), also developed by SimGraphics, to perform *A Musical Performance Animation* (1994). He also created his own *Performance Animation* home page, the first online link repository (for actors and performers) to find, learn, research, and discover the history, technology, and companies/products available to those with creative interest in the newly emerging field (prior to current search engines like Google). This led to the creation of the **Performance Animation Society** (PAS), the first bird-of-feather, special interest group for the acting/performing community to attend, learn and launch experimental activities and projects utilizing this new, groundbreaking technology as a legitimate craft for storytelling and entertainment. The PAS had local chapters in Los Angeles, San Francisco, New York and Tokyo and conducted a number of meetings/events for years.

Facial Motion Capture Today

More commonly used, recent facial expression capture rigs designed to record real-time performance utilize small, light-weight, low-power infrared camera(s) attached to small boom anchored to a head-strap. The user wears tiny, retro-reflective, infrared markers that have been carefully positioned on specific areas of their face, in plain view of the camera aimed at their facial center. As the user emotes, recites lines and performs expressions, the camera input streams into a computer, which processes the information rapidly, often in real-time. This process is often referred to as "performance capture" and when used to animate a virtual avatar in real-time, like a puppet head, can be referred to as *Performance Animation.*

The technique might appear as an encumbrance to the wearer, however, tests have indicated that any discomfort or interference with the natural evolution and sampling of expression events is negligible. Once a number of expressions are elicited and sampled, the recordings are analyzed by the computer and reduced to digital motion representations of the various points on the face that were involved in the creation of each expression.

A previously acquired 3D model (of the person's head and face), which is typically a static facial capture system, can then be spatially registered to the captured expression points from their performance and the data is re-calibrated (targeted) for alignment, association and storage into a time-tagged data file. Think of it as a facial recorder that simplifies the essential nature of one's expressions, and reduces the complexity down to a manageable piece of information designed to puppeteer or re-simulate a related facial model.

Human Personality Encoding

Capturing the human personality, with all of its soul and secrets, is currently the most difficult problem to solve in service to the completion of any adequate, believable human simulation effort.

The future might include direct brain interfacing to gather data from a human nervous system, however, the delicate and transitory construct that we call the mind, and the elusive, debated existence of the soul may never be in reach of our scanners and elaborate sampling systems. Thus, we must depend on voluntary reporting of things we believe to be specific to us, that which we know. Our memories of our life experiences, choices we've made, feelings of our love, hate, pain, happiness, etc. is the information that really makes us who we are, not just to ourselves, but to those others that took the time to get to know us as we lived, as real human spirits in the physical world.

The creation of a comprehensive personality profile designed to acquire data about our favorite things: colors, music, art, places, people, songs, books, movies, TV shows, fictional characters, etc., could be utilized effectively, depending on our willingness to log or journal these criteria. Things we did not like, experiences we wanted to have, people we wanted to love or be loved by, jobs we had, lost, never got, accidents, feeling of loss, and on and on and on, are all topics about which a subject could be interviewed by an automated online system or kiosk, and might hopefully—with truth—answer many life-defining questions.

A sizable corpus of personal responses could provide enough data to allow us to create a fairly crude psychological personality simulation. As technologies evolve, and our understanding of human psychology progresses, we will improve the data-gathering process to include more valuable and significant information that can help us insure fidelity and realism into human simulations of our own making.

Our present day interaction with social media and online repositories, where we choose to store our photos, videos, thoughts, arguments, daily reports, family and friend related engagements, etc. would be considered the low-hanging fruit for an automated personal information seeking apparatus. Data gathering behavior is already in place and running at full speed, in service to the providers of these platforms. However, their motivations are mostly to keep one engaged and to determine what exactly can be advertised to you, and if successful, sold to you, the user. Every aspect of platform interaction is mined, profiled, horded, tagged, ranked and sometimes, but not always, anonymized. Our devices silent listen to our environment, waiting for questions, commands, eavesdropping on our conversations with others, reading our email, leering at us through our connected cameras, media devices and through security devices designed to protect and inform us. The personal data gathered in service to our wants and needs is the price of convenience.

And so, the task to create an authentic, believable construct that represents oneself has literally solved itself. We no longer need to thoughtfully consider our dreams, ideas, and experiences in a manner that must be voluntarily articulated in a form that will insure our personal human simulation construct will reliably represent us while we are alive or when we pass on.

The Process And Reasoning Of Human Simulation

We've suggested that the simulation of a human being would begin with the deliberate gathering and assembly of all physically available data of a person. The acquisition of life defining personality information is another key task that can be automatically collected through social media, etc. and intentionally supplemented, to a large degree through regular, frequent voluntary submission. And, finally, an artificial intelligence model could be used to create a realistic, responsive, believable simulation of the person sampled.

Once created, a subject would presumably interact with their personal simulation to calibrate, edit and augment its underlying personality construct and fine-tune its responses to behave with greater fidelity, more accurately and true-to-form. This complex process, which all of us do, is an unconscious effort that we take for granted in real life. As we ask why we'd even try to duplicate ourselves in this way, it is our belief that the simulation of real people is a valuable and worthwhile task. It should be easy, natural, meaningful and accepted as a step forward in our intellectual and personal spiritual evolution.

Technology is typically applied toward specific application needs that are involved with our work, entertainment and physical environment management. Very little of our great new technology has been used to document, understand and to celebrate the human condition, existence and form, thus far. And yet, there is evidence that our need to document our lives with greater fidelity is increasing. This true not only in an ongoing social media personal storytelling context (Humphreys, 2018), but also in preserving evidence that may be about to disappear, as shown in the Shoah Foundation Project (Lindberg, 2019). Video camcorders of the past evolved with features that could allow the user to input metadata, such as location, time and date, which is now done automatically. Some early marketing materials (since lost to time) allowed for text to be added to user programmable fields like a recording title (e. g. birthday) or the age of the subject being recorded. This was done, presumably, because companies wanted to encourage parents to document the development of their children (and sell more expensive cameras). Today there is a ton of metadata gathered for a specific recording. We can expect this type of data gathering to continue to expand as avatars are captured and used.

As technology improves, people will take full advantage of the documentation process and willingly create archives of their experiences. In the near future, 3D data recordings of their physical self and casual avatar creation, along with 3D dimensional volumetric video/holoportation (a type of real-time, human capture technology for transmission to a distant location) will be our next communication medium and eventually, the benefits of fully autonomous, self-simulation will become a standard way of life on planet earth.

Entertainment

As has been shown with examples like Nintendo's *Mario* described earlier, cartoon characters have been successfully animated in real-time using advanced motion capture and real-time computer graphics technology. Many of the characters developed are anthropomorphic in nature; however, many have not been developed from real human data or to emulate a real human performer.

Many of our celebrities and famous figures will be the first to take advantage of the opportunity to create digital versions of themselves. Many already are (Giardina, 2017). Rising interest in the future uses of Virtual Actors will create new opportunities for creative expression and many actor-performers will wish to refine and to license their virtual likeness for use in a variety of interactive venues and film/TV special effects.

All this comes with many challenging legal issues. Law Professor, Dr. Joseph Beard, at St. John's University Law School, was the most prolific legal scholar in the area of the rights of Virtual Actors, authoring at least a dozen key papers and articles (1993, 1997, 1999, 2000, 2001, 2003, 2004). His groundbreaking works include topics such as challenges for intellectual property laws, use of trademarks, copyrights and patents in this domain, who owns publicity and usage rights, and how to deal with unauthorized uses of one's digital data. Current laws have a long way to go to catch up to these issues.

Motion Picture Special Effects

The demand for ever-more dazzling special effects in the stories being told by our creative talent is insatiable. Motion pictures from as far back as the previously mentioned *Looker* (1981) have used the 3D human digitizing process as a tool to create exciting new transformational effects. The use of innovative technologies in these applications has been limited to the exact requirements of the story and director. Few tools have evolved out of their use for any other purpose or commercial development. Hollywood is very protective about their effects technologies and they often discard their developments from one project to the next, often to insure that the next creative challenge will exceed previous efforts and force a fresher look. But the use of Virtual Actors, even if proprietary, is well established in Hollywood films now. Overlapping with the issues in the entertainment section above are new concerns such as aging and "de-aging" movie actors (Houghton, 2019), as well as using digital technologies to complete a film even if a main actor dies during the film's making (Bui, 2019).

Medicine And Prosthetics

Human forms, of both body and head, have been digitized in three dimensions to assist in the development of prosthetics, as an aid to surgical procedures, and to assist in physical therapeutic treatments in a variety of ways (Koutny et al., 2012). As 3D computer graphics technology is increasingly utilized in the medical environment, new and valuable uses for 3D data of human internal structures and diagnostic data overlay will continue to evolve (LeClerc, 2012) (Lerch et al. 2007). Medical education, clinical training, and patient consultation have been some of the early applications for human simulation technology. The age of the "Virtual Patient" is just now beginning to make sense commercially, Better understanding of complex, lengthy traditional printed diagnostic results and therapeutic information display will become a staple instrument in future health, wellness and treatment management (Rizzo et al., 2011).

Computer-Human Interface

A number of research efforts have been under way to enhance the interface between computer systems and their human user counterparts. The field of *Human Centered Computing* is just now evolving, as what many believe, will be the predominant way that we, as a person, will work with the increasingly more complex systems. Digitized human voice synthesizers, facial animations with moving lips and eyes, and speech recognition are key areas being focused on through research and development efforts. Use of 3D digitized human databases to represent intelligent agent interfaces is being introduced daily. While none are yet in place, computer systems that look and act like familiar humans will become the de facto operating system of our future. They will provide a less threatening, more interesting, entertaining and easier to use way of interacting with our computers. Right now even the most advanced examples of these are primarily chat bots—or simple AI-enables cartoon-like avatars, but they should gain sophistication as the technology progresses (Gentsch, 2019).

Clothing Design

3D human form digitizing has been used on occasion to create carefully fitted clothing. This concept will evolve further when the clothing design process becomes further automated and designers begin to accept the advantages that this fast, accurate human form digitizing technology can provide them in their work (Reid et al, 2020).

Amazon has been quietly acquiring key companies in its effort to augment its position in fashion sales. They believe that 3D measurement capability (i.e. scanning) added to their devices (Echo Fit), will allow customers to better try, select and order fashions that will better satisfy their needs for fit, feel and fashion, minimizing the trial and error involved in wasteful returns, delay, damaged goods, and the subsequent environmental impact of inefficient service (Miley, 2018).

Fitness Training

Fitness services are beginning to roll out 3D human-form-based digitization, display, and targeted advice solutions. Expert systems utilizing one's regularly acquired 3D body scan data are already optimizing customer's workout regimens, diet plan, and other wellness-based advice with rapid, accurate visual monitoring. For example, companies such as Styku (styku.com), Naked (nakedlabs.com), and Fit3D (fit3D.com) offer in-gym or even at-home body scanner systems that not only capture but also analyze measurements over time to support clients' fitness goals. A recent online site listed the 16 best 3D body scanners of 2019 (Lansard, 2019) and more are certainly coming. As economies of scale, ease of use and word of mouth demonstrate a clear advantage in a human simulation-centered approach, this will rank among the most widespread uses for this technology.

Missing Persons and Security Identification

Research has shown spectacular results in the area of documenting the human form, face and body in the field of missing persons and security identification. Application of 2D, still image based predictive aging is being used to identify missing children and to find known criminals (Haridy, 2017). 3D databases of humans can more effectively be used to create even more accurate descriptions of those persons that have aged and/or changed their appearance. Rapid and cost effective results can be created more easily and automatically with 3D sampling, manipulation and display. Privacy issues aside, it is inevitable that institutions responsible to protect a population will not hesitate to attempt to gather, share, access and process vast databases of living persons for a multitude of difficult to solve tasks with uncertain outcomes that, if solved, insure our collective safety (Abate et al., 2007).

FUTURE APPLICATIONS

A personal human simulation construct can and will be an important instrument in one's life to self-calibrate. Humans will be able to maintain a reference point into their own appearance, personality and behavior from particular moments in their life. The use of this reference can be very valuable in rehabilitative therapy, recovering from an addiction, abuse or bad experience, for example. People often forget how they became who they are, and a reference simulation could help trace back and presumably give clarity to their present reality alone or with guided therapy.

Grief and the loss of a loved one is one of the most emotionally, and sometimes physically, devastating experiences that a person can go through. We all, eventually, must deal with these experiences, up to and including the inevitable loss of our own self to death. If one were to have access to a human simulation of a loved one that has been lost, there could be a substantial emotional cushion that could be used to comfort one from the pain of separation and/or the reality of their loss. The use of their simulation could allow for a more gradual resolution and personal encounter to occur, thus softening the difficulty. Loss syndrome is a well-documented condition that many suffer, usually due to accident, early terminal disease or disaster. Anything that could help one integrate and transcend this pain of loss, could be extremely valuable toward maintaining the delicate balance of happiness and misery that we are all at risk to experience in life. Such posthumous access to a loved one may well be possible within a few decades, and will raise new questions about how we view such constructs. For example, a recent publication asks where the line between simulated and authentic sentience lies, and should we be able to or even want to tell the difference if it brings us some positive effect (Leaver, 2019)

Children could experience their lost grandparents or older ancestors with greater fidelity, perhaps enhancing their own sense of self, heritage, ancestry and culture. Parents could re-experience the joy of their children who have since grown, moved away and centered their lives around others or have been lost. All who contemplate the many benefits that human simulation could provide agree it is a goal worthy of pursuing.

Ultimately, the value of access to human simulations will have to be determined by each of us in our own time and for our own reasons.

CONCLUSION

The process of human simulation will continue to evolve into mankind's future, but our need to begin the documentation process of real people is already taking place. As we have moved from text to talk, to 2D images, 2D video, 3D data, 3D video, volumetric, virtual and augmented reality, and holographic experience, our journey is just now becoming clear, and our destiny evolves.

The general public with their own elderly, terminally ill and new young are the ones that have a vast and important need for human archiving. The value of this process and its benefits will become deeply ingrained into our society, hopefully to fulfill a common spiritual need that each of us share, to adequately preserve our sacred existence, our one and only journey through the gift of life.

ACKNOWLEDGMENT

All images used in the chapter are courtesy of the author.

REFERENCES

Abate, A. F., Nappi, M., Riccio, D., & Sabatino, G. (2007). 2D and 3D face recognition: A survey. *Pattern Recognition Letters*, *28*(14), 1885–1906. doi:10.1016/j.patrec.2006.12.018

Badler, N. I. (1975). *Temporal Scene Analysis: Conceptual Descriptions of Object Movements* (PhD Thesis). Retrieved from https://repository.upenn.edu/cgi/viewcontent.cgi?article=1247&context=hms

Beard, J. J. (1993). Casting Call at Forest Lawn: The Digital Resurrection of Deceased Entertainers-A 21st Century Challenge for Intellectual Property Law. *J. Copyright Soc'y USA*, *41*, 19.

Beard, J. J. (1997). Will the Reel, er, Real Bill Clinton Please Stand Up-The Unauthorized Use of the President's Image-A New Contact. *Sport. Ent. & Sports Law*, *15*, 3.

Beard, J. J. (1999). Fresh Flowers for Forest Lawn: Amendment of the California Post-Mortem Right of Publicity Statute. *Ent. & Sports Law*, *17*, 1.

Beard, J. J. (2000). Digital Replicas of Celebrities: Copyright, Trademark, and Right of Publicity Issues. *UALR L. Rev*, *23*, 197.

Beard, J. J. (2001). Clones, bones and twilight zones: Protecting the digital persona of the quick, the dead and the imaginary. *J. Copyright Soc'y USA*, *49*, 441.

Beard, J. J. (2003). Virtual Kiddie Porn: A Real Crime-An Analysis of the PROTECT Act. *Ent. & Sports Law.*, *21*, 3.

Beard, J. J. (2003). Is Virtual Kiddie Porn a Crime. *Ent. & Sports Law*, *21*, 1.

Beard, J. J. (2004). Everything old is new again: Dickens to digital. *Loy. LAL REV*, *38*, 19.

Bode, L. (2007). 'Grave Robbing' or 'Career Comeback'? On the Digital Resurrection of Dead Screen Stars. *History of Stardom Reconsidered*, 36-40.

Bui, H.-T. (2019). De-Aging Technology and Fully CGI Characters "Raises Some Serious Issues," Andy Serkis Says. *Slashfilm*. Retrieved from https://www.slashfilm.com/digital-actors-de-aging-tech-andy-serkis

Earnshaw, R., & Vince, J. A. (1995). *Computer Graphics: Developments in Virtual Environments*. Academic Press.

Evans, N. (2018). Lucasfilm Actually Scans All of Its Lead Actors for Later Use. *CinemaBlend*. Retrieved from https://www.cinemablend.com/news/2400072/lucasfilm-actually-scans-all-of-its-lead-actors-for-later-use

Gentsch, P. (2019). Conversational AI: How (Chat) Bots Will Reshape the Digital Experience. In *AI in Marketing, Sales and Service* (pp. 81–125). Cham: Palgrave Macmillan. doi:10.1007/978-3-319-89957-2_4

Giardina, C. (2017) How Artificial Intelligence Will Make Digital Humans Hollywood's New Stars August 25, 2017. *The Hollywood Reporter*. Retrieved from https://www.hollywoodreporter.com/behind-screen/how-artificial-intelligence-will-make-digital-humans-hollywoods-new-stars-1031553

Haridy, R. (2017). New face-aging technique could help locate missing persons. *New Atlas*. Retrieved from https://newatlas.com/facial-aging-software-missing-persons/50051/

Heinlein, R. (1950). *Waldo and Magic, Inc*. Doubleday.

Houghton, R. (2019). Will Smith clone movie Gemini Man praised as "breathtaking" in first reactions. *DigitalSpy*. Retrieved from https://www.digitalspy.com/movies/a29117708/will-smith-clone-movie-gemini-man-first-reactions-ang-lee/

Humphreys, L. (2018). *The Qualified Self: Social Media and the Accounting of Everyday Life*. The MIT Press. doi:10.7551/mitpress/9990.001.0001

Koutny, D., Palousek, D., Koutecky, T., Zatocilova, A., Rosicky, J., & Janda, M. (2012). 3D digitalization of the human body for use in orthotics and prosthetics. In Proceedings of World Academy of Science, Engineering and Technology (No. 72, p. 1628). World Academy of Science, Engineering and Technology (WASET).

Lansard, M. (2019). The 16 Best 3D Body Scanners in 2019. *Aniwaa*. Retrieved from https://www.aniwaa.com/best-3d-body-scanners/

Leaver, T. (2019). Posthumous Performance and Digital Resurrection: From Science Fiction to Startups. In T. Kohn, M. Gibbs, B. Nansen, & L. van Ryn (Eds.), *Residues of Death: Disposal Refigured*. London: Routledge. doi:10.4324/9780429456404-7

Leclerc, F. (2012). 3D Scanning for Post-Mastectomy Custom Breast Prosthesis. *Medical Design Briefs*. Retrieved from medicaldesignbriefs.com/component/content/article/mdb/tech-briefs/15287

Lerch, T., MacGillivray, M., & Domina, T. (2007). 3D Laser Scanning: A Model of multidisciplinary research. *Journal of Textile and Apparel. Technology and Management*, 5(4), 1–8.

Lindberg, E. (2019). Personal stories of surviving the Holocaust unveiled at powerful art exhibition. *USC News*. Retrieved from https://news.usc.edu/160806/holocaust-survivors-art-exhibition-usc-shoah-foundation-fisher-museum

Miley, J. (2018). Amazon Wants to Scan Your Body So You'll Never Return Your Online Shopping Again. *Interesting Engineering*. Retrieved from https://interestingengineering.com/amazon-wants-to-scan-your-body-so-youll-never-return-your-online-shopping-again

National Academy Press. (1999). Funding a Revolution: Government Support for Computing Research. Committee on Innovations in Computing and Communications: Lessons from History. Washington, DC: Author.

North, D. (2005). Virtual Actors, Spectacle and Special Effects: Kung Fu Meets 'All That CGI Bullshit.' *The Matrix Trilogy: Cyberpunk Reloaded*, 48-61.

Parke, F. (1972). Computer generated animation of faces. *Proceedings of the ACM Annual Conference*, *1*, 451–457. 10.1145/800193.569955

Reid, L. F., Vignali, G., Barker, K., Chrimes, C., & Vieira, R. (2020). Three-dimensional Body Scanning in Sustainable Product Development: An exploration of the use of body scanning in the production and consumption of female apparel. In *Technology-Driven Sustainability* (pp. 173–194). Cham: Palgrave Macmillan. doi:10.1007/978-3-030-15483-7_10

Rizzo, A. A., Lange, B., Buckwalter, J. G., Forbell, E., Kim, J., Sagae, K., & Parsons, T. (2011). *An intelligent virtual human system for providing healthcare information and support*. Madigan Army Medical Center. doi:10.1515/IJDHD.2011.046

Sturman, D. J. (1998). Computer Puppetry. *IEEE Computer Graphics and Applications*, *18*(1), 38–45. doi:10.1109/38.637269

Tidy, J., & Aarabi, P. (2010). Visual modeling of faces for security applications. *Government Security News*. Retrieved from https://www.gsnmagazine.com/node/20213?c=cbrne_detection

Volino, P., Thalmann, N. M., Jianhua, S., & Thalmann, D. (1996). An evolving system for simulating clothes on virtual actors. *IEEE Computer Graphics and Applications*, *16*(5), 42–51. doi:10.1109/38.536274

Westmas, R. (2018). *This AI-Assisted Aging Software Looks Spookily Realistic*. Retrieved from https://curiosity.com/topics/this-ai-assisted-aging-software-looks-spookily-realistic-curiosity/

Williamson, C. (2018). "An Escape Into Reality": Computers, Special Effects, and the Haunting Optics of Westworld (1973). *Imaginations: Journal of Cross-Cultural Image Studies*, *9*(1), 19–39.

KEY TERMS AND DEFINITIONS

3D Digitizing Rig: A graphics input system that records x, y and z coordinates of a real object. Contact is made with various points on the object's surface by a light sensor, sound sensor, robotic instrument, or pen.

Avatarism: A term that characterizes the recent manifestation of technology applications applied to the creation and usage of personal virtual representations for various purposes.

Construct: In the context of this chapter, a "construct" can be interpreted as a virtual embodiment (or representation/imitation of a person or thing. Also referred to in this context as "simulacra", avatar and many other terms. See https://en.wikipedia.org/wiki/Construct for disambiguation.

Deep Fakery (aka Deep Fake): A portmanteau of "deep learning" and "fake" (coined in 2017) is a technique for human image synthesis based on artificial intelligence and machine learning. The combination and superimposition of existing images and videos onto source images or videos using a technique known as generative adversarial network (GAN). Deep fakes have been used to create illicit, simulated celebrity pornographic videos and more recently are being used to create fake news and malicious hoaxes, easily spread on social media sites (https://en.wikipedia.org/wiki/Deepfake).

Depth-Sensing Camera: A camera which is able to determine accurate distance (range) information in addition to visual information using a variety of technologies.

Fiducial Markers: An object, image or printed pattern, when placed in the field of view of an imaging system, a fiducial can be used as a point of reference or a measure to determine a position, often within a sequence of elapsed time. See: https://en.wikipedia.org/wiki/Fiducial_marker.

Healthmap: A detailed, interactive data set, fully referenced and aligned with a personalized 3D human model.

Holographic Recordings: Captured video sequences, usually of a person's performance obtained by the use of volumetric capture, depth camera acquisition, or other methods. A holographic recording, one created and edited, can be seen from any angle or perspective and re-positioned with an area of 3D space as viewed in virtual/augmented reality or through 2D stereographic video on a flat screen.

Holoportation: A type of real-time, 3D human capture technology that allows a visual re-creation of people to be compressed, transmitted and reconstructed at a remote location for live, immediate, interpersonal communication and engagement.

Machine Learning: The scientific study of algorithms and statistical models that computer systems use to perform a specific task without using explicit instructions, relying on patterns and inference instead. Seen as a subset of artificial intelligence, machine learning algorithms build a mathematical model based on sample data, known as "training data", in order to make predictions or decisions without being explicitly programmed to perform a task (https://en.wikipedia.org/wiki/Machine_learning).

Performance Animation: Control and creation of an animated virtual character in real-time with the use digitally tracked body and facial action by a performer, puppeteer, or actor.

Point Cloud: A set of data points in space, generally produced by 3D scanners and used to represent 3D objects in visualization, animation, rendering and 3D manufacturing applications (https://en.wikipedia.org/wiki/Point_cloud).

Structure From Motion: A range imaging technique used to estimate the 3D form / structure of an object or scene. A camera (or the object) must be moving during a video captured clip and the resulting video frames are output as 2D images for photogrammetric processing (by computer) resulting in the creation of a 3D point cloud representation of an object / scene captured. The generated output is then topologized into a suitable 3D format for use in simulation, re-construction using 3D printing and for many other applications including the creation of 3D topological maps, 3D model building and for ground plane detection required to perform augmented reality (AR) spatial anchoring from an observed scene (https://en.wikipedia.org/wiki/Structure_from_motion).

Structured Light: A process of projecting a known pattern (often grids / horizontal bars) on to a scene that deform when striking surfaces, allows vision systems (cameras) to calculate depth and surface information of objects in view. 3D scanners can utilize invisible (often infrared) structured light, without visible detection, as a reliable, accurate way to create 3D objects and measure distances in an observed scene (https://en.wikipedia.org/wiki/Structured_light).

Time-of-Flight: A technique used to measure the time taken by an invisible, infrared light pulse to travel from an emitter to a subject and return to a detector (sensor). This information can be used to establish a method to measure approximate distance to many points on the surface of a target object.

Vactor: A virtual actor, first coined and subsequently trademarked by SimGraphic Engineering in the early 1990's to describe a proprietary computer system which allows a live, human performer to control a real-time computer-generated character or construct for entertainment and other applications.

Volumetric Video: A video technique that captures a 3D spatial volume in real-time, such as a location or human performance. The acquired 3D data that can be viewed on flat screens as well as using 3D Displays and VR goggles. The main, compelling feature of this technique is the ability for a viewer (or audience) to navigate and change their point-of-view when observing or exploring the generated capture volume. Various methods such as photogrammetry, 3D depth camera arrays and multi-point visible light video camera arrays are used to generate a volumetric video database.

Waldo: A device used by an actor that translated the motion of the face to control a generated character. A word taken from a Robert Heinlein science fiction story: *Waldo and Magic, Inc.* (1950) about a handicapped man who uses remote manipulators to interact with things he cannot physically.

ENDNOTES

[1]   Views of the Lightstage can be seen in the trailer for The Congress at https://www.youtube.com/watch?v=1rNSTizOsws

[2]   https://www.britannica.com/technology/Moores-law

Chapter 4
Narrative Strategies in VR Movies, Traditional Movies, and Digital Games

Li Zheng
Shandong University of Arts, China & Rensselaer Polytechnic Institute, USA

Mei Si
iD https://orcid.org/0000-0001-8642-8806
Rensselaer Polytechnic Institute, USA

ABSTRACT

Virtual reality (VR) movies have gained tremendous attention in recent years, with an increasing amount of experimentations and explorations from researchers and practitioners with various backgrounds. Many VR movies are aimed at providing the audience with a narrative experience, just as in traditional film and digital games. VR movies are a relatively new art form. The audience's experiences in VR movies share many common properties with traditional film and narrative games. On the other hand, VR movies offer a unique way for the audience to view and interact with the content, which differentiates it from other visual and narrative-based digital experiences. In this chapter, the authors review the narrative techniques used in movies and narrative games and present a survey and analysis of whether the techniques can or have been applied to VR movies.

INTRODUCTION

Virtual reality (VR) technologies have developed rapidly in recent years. Devices for creating virtual reality, such as head-mounted stereoscopic displays and motion sensors, have been widely used in entertainment, pedagogical, and assistive technology applications. In particular, the emergence and development of VR technologies provide artists, designers, and researchers with new tools to create highly immersive narrative art. VR has been used to provide a unique form of visual narrative experience—the virtual reality (VR) movie.

DOI: 10.4018/978-1-7998-2433-6.ch004

Figure 1. Screen shot from age of sail.
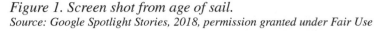
Source: Google Spotlight Stories, 2018, permission granted under Fair Use

Age of Sail (Figure 1), which was nominated for the Venice Award for Best Virtual Reality, is a good example of a VR movie (*Age of Sail,* 2018). It tells the story about an old sailor named William Avery who is drifting in the North Atlantic. On his way, he saves a little girl, who later lights up new hope in his life. Another example is *Pearl,* which was nominated for the Oscar Award for Best Animated Short Film category. This six-minute short film tells a story about personal growth—how a father and his daughter spent a happy time together in an old car (*Pearl*, 2017). Both *Age of Sail* and *Pearl* were produced by Google Spotlight Stories—Google's story experience platform for VR movies. Both films have a strong narrative component. Although they share similar narrative and artistic characteristics as traditional movies, the fact that the audience can choose their viewing angles provides a hugely different experience.

Firebird Series: The Unfinished is a VR movie that won the 2017 VRCORE Award for Best Film category (*Firebird Series: The Unfinished*, 2017). In this VR movie, the audience is put in a museum dedicated to the mighty sculptor Auguste. On the night before the grand opening, the statues become alive and whisper about Auguste's love story with Camille. This is a VR film that integrates interaction and narration skillfully. The audience can feel the charm of the story, and at the same time—the development of the story through their own choice and interaction.

Henry tells the story of a cute hedgehog who constantly seeks friendship. This work becomes the first Emmy-winning virtual reality movie in the United States (Henry, 2015). In this VR movie, the audience is free to visit Henry's living space and bedroom downstairs, and a restaurant upstairs. Additionally, in order to establish emotional bonds with the audience, Henry sometimes turns his big, watery eyes to look directly at the audience.

As we can see, in most VR movies, the audience or user needs to move the story forward through their own choices and interactions. Even when they cannot affect how the story develops, the user has control over their own viewpoint, and can experience the story from different perspectives and locations. For example, *Duet* was nominated for the *Oscar for Best Animated Short* in 2014. It tells stories about how a boy and a girl grow up together and fall in love (*Duet*, 2014). Every time the two characters pass by each other, the audience needs to make a choice: viewing the next segment of the content from the boy's perspective or from the girl's perspective. Thus, the audience is both viewing a movie and helping decide how the movie is shown.

Storytelling has been the focus of many entertainment experiences. As VR movies gain popularity, the authors believe it is time to study how storytelling in VR movies is related to, or different from storytelling in traditional movies and digital games. In this chapter, we want to explore the space of storytelling techniques that can be used in VR movies by first looking at how storytelling is used in traditional movies and narrative games.

BACKGROUND

Narrative Structure in Traditional Films

The theories and classification methods developed for the analysis of film structure can provide a good reference point for the analysis of narrative structures in VR movies. Andre Bazin emphasizes the connection between film and reality (Bazin, 2004). He proposed the principle of authenticity—that film creators should preserve the authenticity of the object, the authenticity of time and space, and the authenticity of the narrative structure of the events. In particular, he emphasizes the meaning and expressiveness of a single shot, and believes that films should use real-time flow, and real depth of reality. This authenticity is more convincing in a single shot. Later generations summarized his theory as "Full-length Shot Theory." (A Full-length shot is a shooting technique which is relative to the splicing shooting method. The term "Full-length shot" neither refers to the appearance, or the long focal length of the photographic lens, nor the distance between the photographic lens and the photographic object, but to the time between the starting point and the closing point of the shooting, that is—the length of the film clips.)

Montage is a popular technique in film editing in which a series of short shots are edited into a sequence to condense space, time, and information. In contemporary films, the application of a full-length shot is often endowed with the profound meaning of a realism spirit, such as in the film *Birdman* (2014). In this film, the director describes the real world in great detail and tries to express "A thing is a thing, not what is said of that thing." Bazin did not completely disagree with using montages, however, he did mention that montage is a secondary means of film expression. Bazin emphasizes the meaning, and expressiveness of a single shot, and opposes using montage to cut, arrange, and assemble shots at will, because it will destroy the ambiguity and polysemy of shots, and destroy the unity of time and space (Bazin, 2004).

The issue of long shots versus montage is controversial, with observers taking sides. Jean Mitry elaborated in his works that they are two different forms of montage effect (Mitry, 2000). In some films, many shots only show a single scenario in isolation. Therefore, the way to combine two scenarios is by connecting two shots (namely, narrow montage). In the film segments where one is a continuation of the other either spatially and temporally, two scenarios are linked either by lens shift (the second scenario is introduced after the first one), or by simply showing them simultaneously on the screen. Mitry's view on montage is clearly more open than Bazin's. The authors believe that both theories provide valuable inspirations and directions for the creation of VR movies. Jean Mitry's interpretation of generalized montage provides a theoretical basis for the shot connection and transformation in VR films. The realistic expressiveness view from Bazin's theory can be applied to full-length shot is suitable VR films.

The study on traditional film narratives typically looks at films from the perspectives of time and space. Furthermore, the process of changing time and space is considered an important narrative skill for filmmaking. In this regard, Keith Cohen expounds that the dynamic narrative space and the infinite potential of time transfiguration are two basic characteristics of film narrative (Keith, 1979). Time transfiguration in films is easy to be detected. Similarly, spatial deformation can be regarded as a residual effect of montage as the linearity of negative time. The authors believe the transfiguration of narrative time will also become a focus of research on VR film.

With regard to specific narration techniques, F. Dick Bernard summarized common narrative methods for films in his monograph, such as dramatic prologue, flashback, pre-narrative, and perspective (narrative in the first or third person) (Bernard, 2009). These theories are the basis of the later systematic film theories, and also the early form of VR movies narrative strategy theories.

Instead of looking at the techniques for handling a particular task, e.g. scene switch, the theory of narrative structure looks at the overall narrative structure of the films. X. J. Li divides narrative structures of films into five categories: causal linear structure, loop nested structure, composite block structure, interwoven contrast structure, and dreamlike polyphony structure (Li, 2000). Later, Liu reduces the causal linear structure and the interwoven contrast structure to a linear structure, and the loop nested structure and composite block structure to non-linear structure (Liu, 2011, p. 18).

Interactive Narrative in Games

In the process of game development, and especially for narrative games, a large number of film pictures and sound techniques are used for reference to improve the narrative ability and effect of games rapidly. For example, Mads Haahr discussed how to apply visual displays techniques to assist storytelling by obscuration, distorting the view, mediation, picture perspective, and disruption (Haahr, 2018). Other game narrative researchers have tried to classify game narratives based on the narrative structures of films.

Calbee divides the narrative structures of games into linear and non-linear narrative structures. Further, the linear narrative structure is divided into linear order, linear flashback, and linear narration interspersed structures. The non-linear narrative structure is divided into single perspective with multiple clues, multiple perspectives, chaotic narrative, multiple space-time, nested structure, loop structure, and repetitive narrative structures (Calbee, 2019).

Game narrative structures have also been classified according to the characteristics of the infinite space-narrative ability of game. Josiah Lebowitz and Chris Klug divide the narrative structures of games into fully traditional stories, interactive traditional stories, multiple-ending stories, branching path stories, open-ended stories, and fully player-driven stories, which are adopted by numerous games (Lebowitz and Klug, 2011). The branching path stories structure is an extended version of the multiple-ending stories structure. Fully player-driven stories share many characteristics with open-ended stories. Therefore, the authors believe Lebowitz and Klug's theory can be summarized into three types of narrative structures: fully traditional stories, branching path stories, and fully player-driven stories. Matteo Sciutteri, who has many years of experience in game design, has different views on this popular way of classifying narrative structure (Sciutteri, 2018). Similar to Calbee, he divides game narrative structures into linear and non-linear structures, wherein the linear mode is similar to that of fully traditional stories (i.e., a single ending, a single clue and an obvious causal relationship). His view on the non-linear mode emphasizes the point that existing branch narratives are not really non-linear. He argued in the non-linear mode all the activities of players should have an effect on the game. The effect may be delayed and not immediately related, and may occur in different ways, i.e. as the "Butterfly Effect" of the real world. We agree with Sciutteri's view on non-linear narratives, and believe this will be supported by Artificial Intelligence (AI) technology in the future.

Narrative Theory of VR Films

Haahr pointed out that the VR concept developed in the 1990s has begun reappearing in people's lives in new ways such as consumer grade head-mounted displays (e.g., Oculus Rift and PlayStation VR), and featured with new narrative application forms in recent years (Haahr, 2015). Mirjam Vosmeer and Ben Schouten (2014) pointed out that since Facebook acquired Oculus Rift in March 2014, VR has started to attract global attention. Instead of facing the screen, the audience can experience the movie or game from a 360-degree perspective in VR.

For building the VR movies, the immersive media producers have two choices in general: building within a game or animation engine, or using a 360-degree camera system for shooting. Unless the camera is mounted to a movable object, such as a moving ship, the audiences can't move in space while looking around when they watch from a fixed camera angle. Moreover, the camera is not a part of the story, rather it simply records the scenes like a fly in space. Sometimes, the camera movement is included in the design of the VR film, and the users can interact through camera movements. For example, when a user zooms in on a something like a bug, the bug can act as if it knows it is being watched and therefore move away quickly.

C. J. Mu pointed out that the narrative structure of VR movies has changed from the traditional linear narrative structure to tree structure, network structure, parallel structure, instant generation structure, and other non-linear structures (Mu, 2018, p.181). The diversification of structures presents further possibilities—VR movies. In addition, immersion includes emotional immersion, spatial immersion, and psychological immersion. How to protect the immersion and fluency of the story from interaction? Mu mentioned that utilizing the intervals between events in storytelling is a promising solution to the possible contradiction between immersion and interactivity. For example, looking around the surroundings after the narrative and before the interaction is an effective means of transition between the narrative and the interaction.

Regarding the editing and lens transformation of VR movies, Li states that the editing of VR movies is closer to the editing and the switching of scenes in the Georges Méliès period in the history of movies (Li, 2018, p.4) than the current Hollywood three-shot method. The Hollywood three-shot method of storyboard narrative style, positive editing, and negative editing will be replaced by the way of left and right head turning. On the other hand, some shots that look similar to full-length shots are in fact resulted from editing. Simple special effect conversion can adopt traditional fade-in, fade-out, superimposition, wipe, and other methods.

RELEVANCE OF EXISTING NARRATIVE THEORIES TO VR MOVIES

The relationship among narrations of traditional movies, video games, and VR movies is the premise of studying the narrative strategies of VR movies. Narrative characteristics of traditional movies are often based on montage and narrative contents. In traditional movies, screenwriters, directors, and photographers play a decisive role in the narration of the story. The sequence of shots received by the audience is all decided upon by these artists. However, VR movies have given audiences the right to watch movies on their own initiative, and the artist's control over the story has decreased. Since audiences have the right to actively choose the viewing angle, and are completely immersed in the virtual world—at least visually, this brand-new viewing mode is essentially different from the traditional viewing mode. Although this artistic form is derived in some ways from traditional movies, VR technology enables such films to have interactive characteristics such as; participation, active exploration, and interaction which expand the options beyond traditional movies. At the same time, these new characteristics have certain similarities with electronic games.

With the increasing commercial creation of VR movies, video games and movies tend to merge with each other. On the one hand, in the process of conducting a large number of commercial experiments on VR movies, researchers are able to learn from the relatively mature interactive narrative mode of games. On the other hand, VR movies can and should also develop their own unique narrative mode. From another perspective, narrative games have gradually become mainstream in game development. For example, *Heavy Rain*, issued by Quantic Dream may be a precursor to such integration (*Heavy Rain, 2010*). The game tells a story of revenge, and players need to observe the whole process from four angles. The story has a complete plot, well-reasoned branching logic, and profound connotation. Moreover, the final outcome varies depending on the player's choices and goal completion progresses. The story of *Heavy Rain* also produces plot conflict similar to that of the classic and ground-breaking film, *Rashomon*, with profound insight about human nature (*Rashomon*, 1950). Although it is only developed in a game form, we believe *Heavy Rain* may embody the embryonic form of some interactive movies in the future because it suggests a promising certain development trend of interactive movies.

In the industry, there is often a distinction between VR movies and VR games. We believe because both have interactive and narrative characteristics, they are essentially similar. We anticipate the two terms will be combined into one in the future. In this chapter, the authors will use "VR film" to refer to both VR movies and VR games.

NARRATIVE CHARACTERISTICS OF VR FILMS

At this date in 2020, VR creation is still in exploratory stages. Based on technical characteristics and limitations, works created in recent years show many distinct features in all aspects, such as alternative forms of narrative, spatial sound positioning, and interactive design, compared to traditional films. So, what are the content creation characteristics of VR film as a new media? This chapter analyses and summarizes the creative characteristics of VR films from four aspects: spatial density of VR videos, narrative guidance of VR films, narrative rhythm, and interactive design.

Spatial Density of VR Videos

Traditional films usually use linear narrative, connecting the shots in logical or artistic fixed order. The audience can only see the picture in the frame in that order, and their visual space is limited. Even if the film is about two events happening at the same time, traditional films are narrated sequentially. In fact, in the real world, many events, big or small, often occur at the same time. The information contained in a visual space is very rich. The influence of events on each other is also three-dimensional, reticulated, and intertwined. Compared with traditional films, VR films cancel the viewing frame, and the audience can see from anywhere within the space. Therefore, virtual scenes have become an important factor that directly affects the subjective experience of the viewers. Secondly, because the surrounding visual displays used in VR films, there are more content in the environment for the users to visually explore. While this is one of the intended features of VR films, this type of visual exploration may actually reduce the initiative of exploring the interactions from the players. In addition, VR film's presentation mode is not suitable for frequent switching of scenes. Thus, generally, there tends to be no more than three scenes in a VR short film.

At present, use of a single scene is the featured mode of most VR short films. Using this mode requires rich and well-structured scene design, and the space created in the VR movies will be similar to a theatrical stage with a sense of reality and immersion. For example, the animated short film *Henry*, which won an award during the 68th Emmy Awards, was created by Oculus Studio, within the company Facebook (*Henry,* 2015). It tells a story about a little hedgehog (Henry) who longs for friends but is isolated because of his sharp spines. At the beginning of the short film, the audience is placed in the living room of the hedgehog's tree house home. Downstairs there is the hedgehog's bedroom, and the audience should to walk to see it. The living room is connected by a small staircase to the attic, which is a small study. The hedgehog (Henry) is making a cake in the kitchen. The details in the scene enrich the environment language for the narration of the short film. Audiences can walk, watch, and reach out to "touch." The audiences' observation and exploration of the environment is merged with the story of the film to form a three-dimensional narrative, and together constitute the length of the film.

Another example is *Fresh Out*, the second VR animated short film of Sandman Studio (2018), which was entered into the VR competition unit of Venice International Film Festival in 2018. In *Fresh Out*, the audience can not only look at the three main characters, but also look around and explore the novel underground scenes. There are all kinds of strange rocks, permeable air at the roots of the plants, and there are also couriers (the winged insects). In this work, the audience can truly experience the feeling of being underground.

Narrative Guidance of VR Films

In traditional films, professional directors can often manipulate the audience's point of view. They not only choose what to show the audience, but also determine the direction the audience looks and exactly what the audience/viewer sees. In VR films, audiences have a choice to watch scenes freely, looking wherever they wish, which brings great challenges to the creators. As the audience enters the virtual world, it is strange but novel. On the one hand, the creator needs to let the audience understand the plot, and on the other hand, they cannot interfere too much with the audience's freedom to explore the environment. The use of obvious "signals" to guide the audience's vision has become the focus of the creator's design. Generally, depending on the plot, the way to guide the audience to follow the plot differs depending on the plot. Common ways include:

Mobile Object and Light on the Stage

When the audiences enter the VR film, they can be attracted by a moving object and follow it into the content of the story. For example, in *Windy Day*, the red hat of the little mouse is right in front of the audience, capturing their attention (*Windy Day,* 2013). The audience would most likely follow the movements of the red hat that caught their attention.

In traditional stage plays, the use of a spotlight is an effective way to guide the audience's attention. Similarly, this approach can also be used in VR films. In the short animation film *Buggy Night*, several insects move in grass in a dark night. The director uses stagelights to follow the insects' movements (*Buggy Night,* 2016). The attention of the audience is easily attracted to follow the stage lights, and the insects that are moving in the light beam.

Figure 2. Screen shot from windy day
Source: Google Spotlight, 2013, permission granted under Fair Use

Sound Guidance

VR films have utilized methods of combining visual elements and sound technology to help direct the audience's attention. Taking *Duet,* for instance, the music is only turned on when the player's attention is focused on the main character. When the player looks somewhere else, the music becomes weaker. The sound designer and composer, Scot Stafford, used the technique of playing different levels of music at the same time. By picking different pictures, the audience can decide sight decide which soundtrack of music gets played stronger or louder. In *Lost,* the audience can hear deafening footsteps in the dark forest, and the sound grows louder as the footsteps approach, and then a robot appears.

Narrative Rhythm

When a narrator tells a story, it is important to form a narrative rhythm. For VR films, slowing down is an important way to adapt to the audience's exploration behaviors. In traditional films, the sense of space is weak, but the director has more power to control the time. In VR films, the sense of space has been ***

enhanced a lot, but the director's control over time cannot be as accurate as in traditional films. In traditional films, the opening is often a fast-paced detonation of the first plot node to pull the audience's attention into the plot. This method is hard to use in VR films because it is "too fast" for the audience. At the beginning of VR films, the audience has been suddenly moved to a new environment. When the audience is still looking around and checking on the details of the rendered objects in a scene, showing an important plot will fight for the audience's attention and is not a good idea. Therefore, the creators should slow down the tempo of VR film, narrate at the right time, and leave the audience time to adapt to the new environment. *Henry* and *Lost* both spend 40 seconds to let the audience to familiarize themselves with the new environment by perceiving the location, time, and other features of the environment. This period of free-flowing time is also a golden opportunity for the audience to actively self-discover, explore, and self-create.

The narrative rhythm of VR films should be based on the content of the films. *Pearl*, a masterpiece of the Google Spotlight project team, tells a story about the history of an old car that skillfully uses language with relaxed music to keep the tone of the film warm and romantic. *Rain or Shine* (Figure 3) tells a story of a girl who receives a pair of sunglasses that will bring rain when they are worn (*Rain or Shine,* 2016). The short film has bright colors and pleasant content. This short film uses the full-length shot that is commonly used in VR films, and the audience needs to follow the girl's movement to the end of the film. Similarly, *Windy Day* also used full-length shots. These short films both have fast and

slow in rhythm, and with music, so that the audience's vision can follow the movement of the protagonist with the rhythm of the music.

Interactive Design

Participation or agency is an important factor that distinguishes VR films from traditional ones. Designers can choose to allow the audience to participate in the story, or they can choose to prevent the audience from doing so. When audience participation is supported, the story either can be carried forward easily or with a certain degree of challenge. The challenge of the story in a VR film is similar to the narrative advancement within a video game. Challenges and setbacks are fundamental sources of playability in video games. In the process of carrying forward a story, designers will set challenges for the audience, which when at an appropriate level, allows the audience to experience more pleasure and increase the playability of the game. In the VR short film *Buggy Night* (by Google Spotlight Stories), bugs hide in the grass. They react when the user focuses his/her attention on them. As another example, in *Lost* (by Oculus Story Studio), the small firefly Fi, which appears at the beginning, leaves when the audience is moving close to look at it. This interaction is the creator's response to the audience's "presence."

There can also be interactions where the audience is asked to complete a task. For example, *Firebird: The Unfinished* (Figure 4) by InnerspaceVR from France, which received the *2017 VRCORE Awards Best Film and Television Award*, tells a story of a sculptor and his female student completing their work together. In this story, the sculptors use their lifelong enthusiasm and diligence to create and give life and soul to the sculpture. The audience participates in the sculpture creation three times during the VR film: the first attempt to make a sculpture, perfecting a sculpture, and completing Rodin and the final unfinished work of the female student. In the process of watching the film, the audience can participate and appreciates the role's persistent emotion and awe for art. In this VR film, the three instances of interaction for the participant do not interrupt the coherence of linear narrative, but rather enhance the understanding of the plot and the feelings of the main character.

From the perspective of plot advancement, many VR films give the audience full control for forwarding the story, i.e. the story will not move forward without the audience's interaction. In *Henry*, for example, little Henry starts busily preparing birthday cakes, the main part of the story won't unfold unless the audiences' eyes are only focused on where the Henry is standing. Similarly, in *Windy Day* and *Rain or shine*, the story can only continue when the audience's eyes keep on looking at the main character.

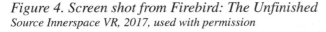

Figure 4. Screen shot from Firebird: The Unfinished
Source Innerspace VR, 2017, used with permission

Comparative Analysis on Traditional Film Narrative Methods and VR Film Narration

Traditional films have rich practical experience, forming a large number of systematic theories of narrative structure and narrative technique. According to the narrative structure classification defined by Li, the commonly used narrative methods are as follows: causal linear structure, contrast linear structure, recollection narrative, block structure, fragmentary mode, repetitive mode, and nested structure. The application status and potential of these narrative modes in VR films are analyzed in the sections that follow by combining with the narrative characteristics of VR films (Li, 2000).

Causal Linear Structure

Events in the film usually follow the order of time and have obvious causal relationship. A story typically consists of four parts: beginning, development, climax, and ending. Time shows a single direction, and the story of the film develops and ends with the passage of time. This is a common narrative method used in traditional films, and Hollywood's heroic films are mostly of this type, such as the *Transformers* (2007).

Similarly, linear narrative is often used in VR films. For example, in the film *Henry*, the director uses the traditional linear narrative to tell the story of Henry, a lonely hedgehog, preparing for his birthday party and turning a balloon doll into a dancing partner when the candle is blown out. As the little hedgehog accidentally pierces one of the balloon dolls, the other balloon dolls stay away from him due to fear of being pierced. In the end, the little hedgehog, with the help of the balloon dolls, finds a friend in a little turtle. In this film, the narration is smooth, rhythmic, and effective, and the task of narration is completed in a relatively short time. In *Rain or Shine*, the girl receives a pair of eyeglasses sent by express delivery, which cause it to rain when she wears them. So, after repeated attempts by the girl, she masters this magical ability of controlling the rain. These examples show that linear narration, as in traditional films, can be an effective narrative method for VR films.

Contrast Linear Structure

Contrast linear structure usually has two or more narrative clues, which are typically the main clue and the secondary clue. The events in different clues have distinct characteristics and interwoven contrast. What the narrator emphasizes is typically not the rise and fall of the main story line, but the dramatic conflicts formed through interwoven contrasts. It is characterized by making full use of time and space to organize the plot of the story, and to show the story of multiple characters and multiple clues in a limited time window on the screen. For example, *Crash* (2004) uses 113 minutes to tell a story of 36 hours, during which events between groups of characters take place. The films that are representative of this narrative mode include: *Babel* (2006), *Lock, Stock and Two Smoking Barrels* (1998), and *Crash* (2004) which won the 78th *Oscar Award for Best Picture* in 2006.

This technique can bring the audience additional perspectives and a broader view of the world. The impact of this technique in VR films, could create an immersion experience for the audiences that feels as if they are "in" different worlds. However, this narrative method is seldom used in current VR films, and the main reason is that players need to switch between different scenes to enter different story lines, which increases the difficulty of creation.

Recollection Narrative

In recollection narrative, the story is carried out in an interweaving fashion, based on the memory of the protagonist, the non-protagonist, or the cross-narration of reality. This technique is often used in classical films, such as *Titanic* (1997) and *Citizen Kane* (1941).

Recollection narrative has been used in several VR films. For example, *Pearl* is a typical example of recollection narrative. At the beginning of the film, the protagonist walks into an old car that he has abandoned and recalls the wonderful times he spent in it. As with the narrative of film and game, recollection narrative is mostly used in story to show a sense of history to strengthen the audience's understanding of what happened in the past.

Fragmentary Narrative

Fragmentary narrative does not advance the process of events in the order of cause and effect but rather narrates events from different angles and levels to enhance the profound meaning of events. The process of viewing a film is like completing a "jigsaw puzzle," for example, as illustrated in the film *Memento* (2000). The film tells the story of the protagonist who, after being attacked by a gangster, looks for one of the gangsters but with only a short memory. In the complex relationship between characters, the story uses multiple clues to review the truth and arouse the audience's interest in suspense.

This narrative method is also embodied in the game *Heavy Rain*. Players play different roles, see things happen and end from different perspectives. This narrative method can be applied to VR films. Moreover, this fragmentary narrative structure has great potential in driving audiences to interact with the film.

Repetitive Linear Narrative

For repetitive linear narrative, the whole film has a repetitive time point in time from which each story starts again, such as in *Run Lola Run* (1998), *Hero* (2002), *Black Mirror: Bandersnatch* (2018), an interactive television show. The rewind technique is borrowed from TV "catchup" intros that serve to position the audience inside the narrative. The advantages of repetitive linear narrative in films are not obvious, but they are very suitable for VR films. Because the audience will develop a sense of identity as a traveler first arriving in a strange city with the repeated scenes in the film, they will feel intimacy with the origin of his/her departure or the scenic spots that they pass through repeatedly.

Block Narrative

Block narrative refers to a series of sub-stories that are not obviously related to each other but yet form an overall story of the film. In this mode, these disparate stories are often grouped together by a clue or element, for example, as in *Dr. Strangelove* (1964) and *2001: A Space Odyssey* (1968). The application of such narrative method is used relatively widely in VR films. The block narrative mode is similar to the narrative technique often applied to introduce different spaces in a game, i.e., different locations are related to the same task or cues. Similarly, the space in VR films is infinitely large, and the audience can "watch" different stories in different location. At the same time, the audience can either accomplish a "task" or experience the philosophical and metaphorical truth conveyed by the director's stories.

Nested Narrative

The narrative of films with nested narratives are like Matryoshka dolls, interlocking layers one by one and forming a nested structure step by step. For this mode, the typical film is *Inception* (2010). This narrative technique is seldom used in films, but the effect it brings to the audience is very powerful. VR films have certain advantages in using nested narrative. Because the audience is the controlling their role in VR work, the director can switch the environment by directing the audience's sight or attention. Compared to traditional films, we believe the participants will have a better chance of understanding the nested narrative within VR films.

Full-Length Shot and Montage

In addition to the narrative structures described above, full-length shots and montage are two other key narrative methods of traditional films that also can be used in VR films.

In traditional films, shots are indispensable for telling stories. The sequence of the shots should be arranged as the sequence for telling the story that the audience can accept. In order to switch among different scenes, different time, and different events, the shots need to be bridged.

The director of the film *Birdman* (87th *Oscar Best Picture Award* in 2015), Alejandro González Iñárritu, abandoned complicated film editing and multi-line narration. Instead, he applied the full-length shot technique. The whole film is composed of ten odd, seamless, full-length shots. Some of the shots even last up to 15 minutes. In order to realize a seamless connection, he used large amplitude shots moving at the time of each scene switch to lock on an object (person or thing) that belongs to both scenes. For example, focusing on a flowerpot on a terrace is used to accomplish a switch from indoors to outdoors. He applied this technique multiple times in the film. With this technique, an intermediate cease time point could be created for the staff and the actors. Such full-length shots have similar viewing angles when brought to audiences in VR action.

In virtual reality, the filmic frame does not exist requiring other techniques to be applied to direct the viewer's attention. In the animated movie *Windy Day*, the red hat guides the view of the audience from the beginning of the story to the end. The director shows the story by simulating full-length shots. There are two main approaches applied to bridge shots in the film (mainly for scene transitions). In the first approach, scenes are changed while they are outside of the audience's views by attracting the attention of the audience to the main character. For example, the little mouse chases the hat and the forest changes to be exuberant. Then, the mouse enters the tree hole following the hat, and the scene moves inside of the tree hole. When the little mouse chases the hat and leaves the hole, the scene switches to the outside of the tree hole and changes to a snowy environment. In the second approach, the transition happens right in front of the audience. The transition is typically switching the scene from sky to ground or from ground to sky, and is realized through a gradual change of the background light between black and white.

Montage, as an important narrative technique of film, helps tell many wonderful stories, both in the movies and in narrative games. In *Her Story*, the best narrative game of The Game Awards 2015, a police data bank is placed on an old computer desk, and the user is able to view various video fragments through searching the computer, and can see a self-statement of a criminal suspect (*Her Story,* 2015). There is no correct order for how the videos should be connected. Different players will have different hypotheses and conclusions by seeing the clues in different sequences. Thus, *Her Story* is a suspenseful story that completely hands over its narrative power to the players. Such a design realizes the narrative effect of the film that relies on the montage technique, but allows for showing different stories. The players become narrators as well. Just as montage has been successfully applied to narrative games, it also is used in VR works, giving the right to choose the narrative order of the story to the players to form a range of different stories.

Comparative Analysis on Game Narrative Methods and VR Film Narration

As stated and explored in this chapter, the interactive basic narrative of games is similar to that of VR films. After decades of development and the golden age of action games, chess, and card games—narrative games have gradually become the focus of game development. Games can influence and stimulate the audiences' emotions to bring the audience into the game. Game narrative can thereby achieve effective integration with the work, and its techniques can be adapted to the creation of VR films. Considering narrative games is an effective way to draw lessons from the mature techniques of games and analyze their applicability, non-applicability, and potential effect on VR works.

According to Lebowitz and Klug's division of narrative structure of games, the narrative of games can be roughly divided into: fully traditional stories, player-driven narrative, and branching path stories. According to this division, the narrative of game is compared with that of VR (Lebowitz and Klug, 2011).

Fully Traditional Stories

Fully traditional stories, also called linear narrative, are based on traditional storytelling. In this mode, the main plot itself is basically unchangeable; no matter how many times the player repeats the experience, the plot is the same. However, beyond the important story scenes, players can have a certain degree of freedom to interact with the game. Similar to linear films, fully traditional stories have the characteristics of unity of time and space, single ending, single clue, and strong causality. The mode focusing on logical integrity, coherent plot, and linear narrative is the most common and the most acceptable narrative structure for players. As long as the narrative structure serves a single main line, it can also be regarded as a linear narrative, even if it contains flashbacks and narration interspersed with flashbacks. The game *God of War* uses a typical linear narrative structure (*God of War*, 2018). The background story features Kratos, who after losing his favorite family, began to challenge the Greek gods and succeeded in revenging them. So far, three series of this title, using linear narrative structure plot, have been published. The mode is simple and easy to understand, and belongs to the traditional narrative way.

Linear flashback is also a type of linear narrative. *Uncharted 2: Among Thieves* is about Nathan Drake, the protagonist, who searched for more than a dozen cargo ships that were missing more than 700 years ago (*Uncharted 2: Among Thieves* 2009). As the plot develops, he finds the real preserve that Marco Polo found in Tibet, Shangri-La. The story employs the narrative structure of flashback. It creates a small climax at the beginning of the story, which helps to catch the attention of players. Many VR films use flashbacks. For example, the film *Easter Rising: The Voice of Rebel* tells a story of the war that took place in Dublin in 1916 in a flashback fashion (*Easter Rising: The Voice of Rebel*,2017). At the beginning of the story, a man sitting in front of a campfire plays a tape and takes the audience into the age of war everywhere.

Pearl also adopted a typical linear flashback structure. At the beginning of the film, the protagonist walks into an old car he has abandoned and recalls the good times he spent in it. Similar to the narrative of films and games, flashback is mostly used in stories with a sense of historical hierarchy, so as to highlight the independence of the event and strengthen the audiences' understanding of it.

Linear narration interspersed with flashbacks is the method of inserting a related story or recollection when narrating the main line of the story to depict an event or person more deeply and to supplement the main story line. In *Call of Duty: Modern Warfare* (2019), "Remastered" is a reminiscent level, and Lieutenant Price recounts the assassination of Zakayev in Chernobyl 15 years ago with Captain McMillan. In this story, Lieutenant Price's infiltrating memories are used to portray this brave and wise soldier, which is one of the classic episodes of narration interspersed with flashbacks in the history of games. There are few examples of successful use of linear narration interspersed with flashbacks in the latest VR films, including *Firebird: The Unfinished* (France). The film begins one night when the curator of the sculptor's Auguste memorial makes his final tour before the exhibition, and suddenly there is a heavy rain outside. Then the statues on display seem to move and pray for help to complete the masterpiece, which is unfinished. The narrator said it might be an illusion because of the rainstorm, or it's the appearance of Auguste's soul. Then, the film tells the story of the sculptor and his female student, which paves the way for the audience to finish the sculptural works and enhances the sense of substitution.

Player-Driven Narrative

Usually, there is no main plot in player-driven narrative. So, how does the creator show a story? The story is typically created by the players' interaction with the game within the scope of the game rules given by the system, instead of by plots prearranged by designers. The simplest example is chess and card games, such as *Go*. Chess and card games do not contain a story by their designs, but the players can write their own stories about interacting in the game.

A representation of a player-driven narrative is *The Sims (2000)*. In this game, players are required to create and manage a person's life. At first, *The Sims* had no plot, no goals, and no winning conditions. However, players could set goals for themselves in the game, for example, building a house, forming a family, and keeping a pet dog. These are goals that are not recognized by the system. Because of this, some people think *The Sims* is not a real game, but an interactive experience.

All the steps that take place in the game can be called the story of the game. However, two seemingly opposite narrative types—embedded narrative and sudden narrative—can exist in the same game. For example, the massively multiplayer online games (MMOS) usually contain a large number of world tasks,

Figure 5. Multiple-branch cross narration in hunters and robbers

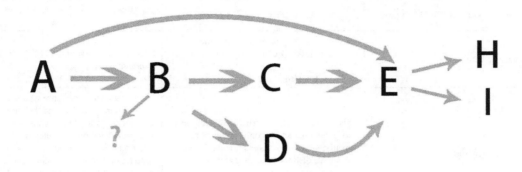

plot-related tasks, and various additional tasks. Once these tasks are completed, the game will become a completely player-driven story in which players can explore the world freely. This kind of player-driven narrative approach is particularly suitable for VR films. In VR films, players are completely immersed and free to move, and they are more willing to spend time to familiarize themselves with and explore this magical world or strange environment. Currently, many VR films use the narrative mode of combining embedded narrative and sudden narrative, such as *The Little Prince* VR (2018), in which the players' task completion behaviors and autonomous activities coexist.

Branching Path Stories

Branching path stories lie between player-driven narrative and fully traditional stories. This is a scenario in which the player can choose to design the space. The narrative structure looks like a network. Players can have multiple versions of stories and endings, as branching path stories insert multiple decision points throughout the narrative, allowing players to make a series of choices during the game. In branching narrative, some plots have little influence on the outcome of the story, but some decisions in branches can make it deviate to the other direction. Usually there are multiple endings in a branch path story. Players can reach these endings from different paths. So, players have more freedom and control compared with linear stories. Because of the combination of well-structured stories and player agency, branching stories are very popular. For example, *The Witcher 3: Wild Hunt* (2015) is a typical multi-branch scenario game. In this game, every task the player does will affect the fate of non-player characters in the game as well as the next branch task.

An example of the cross narrative of multiple branches from *Hunters and Robber*, the story made by the authors (Figure 5).

The story includes the following main plots: The story starts by a hunter who has just started his own journey (A). When he arrives at the forest, he meets a robber who is trying to rob the hunter. The hunter raises his shotgun and aims at the robber. The robber petitions to let him go (B). The hunter shows sympathy to the robber and lets him go (C). Another choice of the player: The hunter still chooses to kill him regardless of the petition of the robber (D). The hunter continues to move forward and reaches a small town (E). The player selecting C meets the robber once again, who it turns out, was looking after his ill mother. He was forced to rob because he had no money to buy medicine (H). The player selecting D meets an old woman looking after her son. According to her description, her son has the

Table 1. Comparative analysis on film narrative methods and VR film applicability

Structures/Methods of Film Narrative	Characteristics and Cases	Applicability Analysis and Cases in VR Films
Causal Linear Structure	Narrate according to the normal time pattern and the sequence of events *Example:* *Captain America: Civil War*	Common narrative methods in VR films *Example: Henry*
Contrast Linear Structure	This kind of narrative structure usually has two (main clue and secondary) or more narrative clues. The events related different clues have distinct characteristics and interweaved contrast. *Example: Crash*	The immersion experience of audiences will be more prominent as they are "in" a different world. At the same time, it also provides more abundant narrative techniques for the creators. But the application is rare. It's mainly because the switching of scenes increases the difficulty of content creation. No representative example at the time of writing
Recollection narrative	Narrate the reality and memory crosswise according to the memory of the protagonist and the non-protagonist. *Example: Citizen Kane*	Recollection narrative has high applicability and can strengthen the audience's understanding of events. *Example: Pearl, Easter Rising: The Voice of Rebel*
Fragmentary Narrative	The process of events is not advanced in the order of cause and effect, but narrated from different angles and different levels. *Example: Memento*	Fragmentary Narrative has great potential in stimulating the interaction between audiences and the film. No representative example at the time of writing
Block Narrative	Block Narrative refers to a series of stories that are not obviously related to each other, forming the overall story of the film. *Example: Dr. Strangelove*	In VR films, audiences can "watch" different parts of the story in different spaces or accomplish common "tasks" as the space is enlarged infinitely. No representative example at the time of writing
Repetitive Linear Narration	Every story in the film starts again from a repetitive time point. *Example:Run Lola Run*	For VR films, the audiences immersed in the film will have a sense of identity to the repeated scenes in the film. No representative example at the time of writing
Stratified Narration	The narrative structure is interlinked, forming a nested structure step by step. *Example:Inception*	Compared with traditional films, the audience is one of the "roles" in VR films, and it is easier to understand the nested narrative. No representative example at the time of writing
Full-length shot	Express the authenticity of space, reach the natural transformation of space in the shots, and realize the connection between the whole and the parts. *Example: Birdman*	Full-length shot can help tracking central figures and events, and connect different scenes and time changes. *Example: Windy Day*
Montage	Complete the narrative by using the sequence of shot splicing. *Example: Her Story*	Montage is suitable for VR films, and the right to choose the narrative sequence can be given to the audience, so as to form different stories. No representative example at the time of writing

Table 2. Comparative analysis on game narrative methods and VR film applicability

Narrative Method of Game	Characteristics and Cases	Applicability Analysis and Cases in VR Films
Fully Traditional Stories	Strong causality, single logic and coherent plots. *Example: God of War*	This narrative method can be easily accepted by players. *Example: Rain or shine*
Linear Flashback	Guide narration, highlight the independence of events and strengthen understanding of the events . *Example: Uncharted 2: Among Thieves*	It is easily accepted. *Example: Pearl,* *Easter Rising:The Voice of Rebel*
Linear Narration interspersed with Flashbacks	Deep characterization of a person or event to supplement the main line. *Example: Call of Duty: Modern Warfare*	This narrative method helps to develop the narrative. *Example: Firebird: The Unfinished*
Player-Driven Narrative	Players create their own stories based on the rules of the game. *Example: The Sims*	Freedom-driven action is suitable for players to explore the environment in VR films. *Example: The Little Prince VR*
Branching Path Stories	It allows players to make a series of choices during the game, change or influence the outcome. *Example: The Witcher 3: Wild Hunt.*	Branching lines creates high production costs, and therefore is rarely applied. No representative example at the time of writing

same appearance as the robber. The old women asked the hunter: "Do you see my son?" (I). This is the mainline of the story. Of course, the player can also jump from A to E directly. However, then he would miss the plot of meeting the robber in the middle and reach the small town directly.

Evidently, based on the mode interactive narrative can allow, players can decide the outcome of the story or even the plot. New branches can be opened up and new ideas can be created at any node. As a result, the multiple versions and optionality of the story are welcomed by both creators and audiences. Although the stories of branching path are commonly applied in games, there is a substantial problem in building them—the cost. This problem can be particularly prominent in VR films. A new story branch means that the art, programming, and sound requirements will grow geometrically, so the cost is prohibitive for existing small VR film production teams.

CONCLUSION

Table 1 and Table 2 summarize the authors' views on the applicability of film narrative methods and game narrative methods in VR films:

As we can see from Table 1 and Table 2, many narrative structures and methods used in films and games have been applied to VR films, including causal linear narrative structure, repetitive narrative structure, full-length shot, fully traditional stories of games, linear flashback, linear narration interspersed with flashbacks, and player-driven narrative. Some narrative methods, i.e. fragmentary narrative, repetitive narrative, and nested narrative are more suitable for VR films than movies. These methods have great potential in the future VR film creation. There are also narrative methods, including contrast linear structure, block narrative and branching path stories, need to be used cautiously in VR films due to the potential high production cost.

For a long time to come, VR film creators and researchers will continue to pay attention to narrative techniques that have been used in the past, as well as creating new ones derived from them. By analyzing the techniques and narrative methods of traditional films and games, the creators of VR films can choose or invent suitable narrative structures and methods according to the needs of their own stories and within the interactive affordances in immersive VR. In doing so, they will most certainly broaden their creative ideas and narrative repertoires.

REFERENCES

Alejandro, G. I. (Producer & Director). (2006). *Babel* [Motion Picture]. United States: Paramount Pictures & France: Mars Distribution.

Alejandro, G. I. (Producer & Director). (2014). *Birdman* [Motion Picture]. United States: Fox Searchlight Pictures.

Barlow, S. (2015). *Her Story* [Computer software]. Sam Barlow.

Bazin, A. (2004). *What is Cinema* (2nd ed., Vol. 1). Berkeley, CA: University of California Press.

BBC Media Applications Technologies Ltd. (2017). *Easter Rising: The Voice of Rebel* [Video file]. Retrieved from https://www.youtube.com/watch?v=Nyc2F3evi-Y

Bernard, F. D. (2009). *Anatomy of Film* (6th ed.). New York, NY: St. Martins Press.

Calbee. (2019). *Talking about the Narrative Structure Design of Games*. Retrieved from https://indienova. com/indie-game-development/narrative-structure-design-of-game/

Call of Duty: Modern Warfare. (2019). [Computer software]. Activision Publishing, Inc.

Christopher, N. (Producer & Director), & Emma, T. (Producer) (2010). *Inception* [Motion Picture]. United States: Warner Bros Pictures.

Cohen, K. (1979). *Film and Fiction: The Dynamics of Exchange* (1st ed.). New Haven, CT: Yale University Press.

Don, C., Paul, H., Mark, R. H., Bobby, M., Cathy, S., & Bob, Y. (Producer) & Paul, H. (Director). (2004), *Crash* [Motion Picture]. United States: Lionsgate Films.

God of War. (2018). [Computer software]. SIE.

Google Spotlight Stories. (2013). *Windy Day* [Video file]. Retrieved from https://www.youtube.com/watch?v=VG4FlT7c-AY

Google Spotlight Stories. (2014). *Duet* [Video file]. Retrieved from https://www.youtube.com/watch?v=x0Y35XLBY8A

Google Spotlight Stories. (2016a). *Buggy Night* [Video file]. Retrieved from https://www.youtube.com/watch?v=sk8hm7DXD5w

Google Spotlight Stories. (2016b). *Rain or Shine* [Video file]. Retrieved from https://www.youtube.com/watch?v=QXF7uGfopnY

Google Spotlight Stories. (2017). *Pearl* [Video file]. Retrieved from https://www.youtube.com/watch?v=WqCH4DNQBUA

Google Spotlight Stories. (2018). *Age of Sail* [Video file]. Retrieved from https://www.youtube.com/watch?v=TH3HOcRayC8

Haahr, M. (2015). Everting the Holodeck: Games and Storytelling in physical Space. In H. Koenitz, G. Ferri, M. Haahr, D. Sezen, & I. T. Sezen (Eds.), *Interactive digital narrative: History, Theory and Practice* (pp. 212–226). Oxfordshire, UK: Routledge Co. doi:10.4324/9781315769189-17

Haahr, M. (2018). Playing with Vision: Sight and Seeing as Narrative and Game Mechanics in Survival Horror. *11th International Conference on Interactive Digital Storytelling. ICIDS 2018*, 11318, 193-205. 10.1007/978-3-030-04028-4_20

Heavy Rain. (2010). [Computer software]. SCE.

Innerspace, V. R. (2017). *Firebird: The Unfinished* [Video file]. Retrieved from https://www.youtube.com/watch?v=2QPMbkQEOks

James, C. (Producer & Director), & Jon, L. (Producer). (1997). *Titanic* [Motion Picture]. United States: Paramount Pictures & 20th Century Fox Film.

Keith, C. (1979). *Film and fiction: The dynamics of exchange* (1st ed.). New Haven, CT: Yale University Press.

Lebowitz, J., & Klug, C. (2011). *Interactive storytelling for video games*. Waltham, MA: Focal Press.

Li, J. L. (2018). Challenges and Revolutions of VR Film Narration. *Advanced Motion Picture Technology, 12/2018*, 4–7.

Li, X. J. (2000). Film Narratology: Theories and Examples, Beijing, China: China Film Press.

Liu, F. (2011). Analysis on the Narrative Structure of Films: Linear and Non-linear. *Movie Literature, 15/2011*, 18–19.

Lorenzo, B., Tom, D., Don, M., & Ian, B. (Producer), & Michael, B. & Travis, K. (Director). (2007). *Transformers* [Motion Picture]. United States: DreamWorks Pictures & Paramount Pictures.

Matthew, V. (Producer), & Guy, R. (Director). (1998). *Lock, Stock and Two Smoking Barrels* [Motion Picture]. United Kingdom & United States: Gramercy Pictures.

Minoru, J. (Producer), & Akira, K. (Director). (1950). *Rashomon* [Motion Picture]. Japan: Daiei Film.

Mitry, J. (2000). *The Aesthetics and Psychology of the Cinema*. Bloomington, IN: Indiana University Press.

Mu, C. J. (2018). A Research on Storytelling of Interactive Documentary: Towards a New Storytelling Theory Model. *11th International Conference on Interactive Digital Storytelling. ICIDS 2018*, 11318, 181-184. 10.1007/978-3-030-04028-4_18

Oculus Story Studio. (2015). *Henry* [Video file]. Retrieved from https://www.youtube.com/watch?v=IUY2yI5F16U

Oculus Story Studio. (2016). *Lost* [Video file]. Retrieved from https://www.youtube.com/watch?v=_gk-cLuAGzLw

Orson, W. (Producer & Director). (1941). *Citizen Kane* [Motion Picture]. United States: RKO Radio Pictures.

Red Accent Studios. (2017). *Little Prince VR* [Video file]. Retrieved from https://www.youtube.com/watch?v=k7qoZOpJRLU

Russell, M. (Producer), & David, S. (Director). (2018). *Black Mirror: Bandersnatch* [Motion Picture]. Netflix, Inc.

Sciutteri, M. (2018). Interactive Storytelling: Non-Linear. Retrieved from https://gamedevelopment.tutsplus.com/articles/interactive-storytelling-part-2--cms-30273

Stanley, K. (Producer & Director). (1964). *Dr. Strangelove* [Motion Picture]. United States: Columbia Pictures.

Stanley, K. (Producer & Director). (1968). *2001: A Space Odyssey* [Motion Picture]. United States: MGM.

Stefan, A. (Producer), & Tom, T. (Director). (1998). *Run Lola Run* [Motion Picture]. Germany: Prokino Filmverleih.

Studio, S. (2018). *Fresh Out* [Video file]. Retrieved from https://www.with.in/watch/fresh-out

Suzanne, T., & Jennifer, T. (Producer), & Christopher, N. (Director). (2000). *Memento* [Motion Picture]. United States: Newmarket Films.

The Sims. (2000). [Computer software]. Electronic Arts.

The Witcher 3: Wild Hunt. (2015). [Computer software]. CD Projekt Red.

Uncharted 2: Among Thieves. (2009). [Computer software]. SCE.

Vosmeer, M., & Schouten, B. (2014). Interactive Cinema: Engagement and Interaction. *7th International Conference on Interactive Digital Storytelling. ICIDS 2014*, 8832, 140-147.

Zhen, Y. Z. (Producer), & Yi, M. Z. (Director). (2002). *Hero* [Motion Picture]. China: Beijing New Picture Film Co.

Chapter 5
Towards a Fulldome Manifesto:
Tour d'Horizon for the Immersive-Inclined

Micky Remann
Fulldome Festival Foundation, Germany

Kelley M. Francis
Independent Researcher, USA

ABSTRACT

The time for a Fulldome Manifesto has come because fulldome as an immersive, surround, communal medium is happening now. It comes as a vast vessel and in new form, with deep changes in the production and perception of 360-degree media. Within seconds, and without changing seat or body, one can switch from visiting a church, mosque, synagogue, or temple to being lured onto The Red Light District on a custom, generative, real-time responsive, science-fiction planet. Fulldome's mere scale can provoke profound wonder and interconnectedness and encapsulate the intersection of all media disciplines, unlike any other multimedia vessels humans have built so far. Like the membrane of a cell, fulldome houses the cross mingling of desires, projections, and technological abilities. In Tour d'Horizon For The Immersive Inclined, authors venture Towards a Fulldome Manifesto—exploring fulldome as a medium, venue, and genre while pointing to its promise for the advancement of immersive media.

INTRODUCTION

With media expanding from square screen to the world around us, a vivid projected multimedia arena has found a way to immerse us not only in worlds out beyond in deep space, but also in our own inner worlds. Technological evolution has caught up with this spherical, multisensory venue to emerge as a medium, and soon one to host humans as they transcend perception, time, space, and habitats of consciousness.

The dome in the 21st century is associated with sober science visualization, psychedelic experimentation, future-city dreaming, planetariums, Burning Man, and Las Vegas-scale entertainment. This medium has emerged as an interdisciplinary hotbed for DIY culture, citizen science, technologists, futurists, and free-thinking storytellers, cultivated in science centers and planetariums among star-gazers.

DOI: 10.4018/978-1-7998-2433-6.ch005

Figure 1. Immersive dome experiences are bubbles of indefinite opportunity
Source: Photo by Torsten Hemke / Fulldome Festival Foundation

This piece has been written as a *Manifesto* underway; "Towards" indicates that we explore core building blocks of the fulldome medium, which shape where we are with the medium in contemporary times and what is on the near horizon. Being delivered as a *"Manifesto in the making"* allows for the switching of viewpoints from generalist to practical, from radical to informative, at times inspirational, sometimes satirical—and with the accompaniment of anecdotal evidence from the authors' experience.

The growth of such a medium is perpetual and ongoing (Figure 1). Here the authors cull from history to cast an evolution of the captured image from cave paintings, to imprinting images deep within the psyche of an audience by pairing tech with technique. Enjoy this tour of the discipline coupled with a tour of the mind, as small and large-scale fulldome experiences are used to paint a vision for how this medium is finding its way into a community near you; and how visioneers are engineering their use for profound impact.

Picture was taken at the Jena FullDome Festival, with artist Alexander Stephan experimenting with 3D effects for fulldome shows.

Why is diving deep into the world of fulldome an Alice-in-Wonderland-esque eye and mind-opening endeavor?

This burgeoning medium invites future butterflies to come out from cocooning. Giants and giant-themed entertainment domes are to soon hit mainstream accessibility. Wellness domes, which cure wear and fatigue, aren't far away either. From petite single-user experiences projected inches from an individual's eyes, to massive gatherings hosting thousands under one sphere, from 360-degree projected macro-mites or mega-structure vessels embracing the multitudes, immersive dome experiences are bubbles of indefinite opportunity! Mix in some healthy utopian pragmatism and this piece is a testament to its evolution!

A SMALL SPARK IN THE MIND LEAPS TO A GIANT SPARKLE ON THE DOME

… and a giant sparkle on the dome leaps to the mind. Immersion in the dome can be as poetic as "a sight, an emotion … this wave in the mind, long before it makes words to fit it,"[1] which, according to Virginia Woolf (1931), is how consciousness shall be defined. Or it can be to gross scale what lurks at the opposite end of subtlety—say, a maximalist extravaganza? The experience has inevitable, if not enormous, repercussions for our self-image as individuals or groups of individuals. When dome and mind become undistanced, as is common in a relevant fulldome exposure, a third space is revealed in the overlaps of the mind-field and the dome-field, inviting us to question the semi-illusionary nature of our reality constructs and to participate with media differently. Innovatively. The authors believe in the importance of the evolution of high-quality amazement domes, of 360-degree meditation temples, immersive theatres, sound palaces, and multisensory amphibious amphitheaters into which we can dive. Although not categorically rejecting the art of cheap thrills, they do believe in the transformational capability of these omnidirectional, multiperspective capsules for physiological participation and community engagement. For an experience to be deemed immersive, it must tickle the senses and captivate the imagination! Simply surrounding the population with environments of triviality doesn't live up to the uplifting potential of the dome, so a rise in narrative and engagement is in order. Shallow is an enemy to wonderful, and masterful experiential storytelling is imperative for immersion that satisfies.

This age of the *Avant-Immersive* accommodates concerts, cinema, floating experiences, and other gravity defying art forms. Iconoclasts of all disciplines borrow inspiration from the world around them, celebrating the fulldome medium as an intersection that houses the cross-mingling of vision, projections, and technological abilities.

Once interactive dome-to-dome networks are interlinked globally—which the authors propose to be an ambitious but only semi-utopian endeavor—the trajectory of where this Manifesto propels us will reveal itself before your very 360-degree eyes!

HISTORY'S FANFARE

It's time to proclaim what this leap from flat world to surround-world multimedia-transition is all about. As a "manifesto" is always a proposal under construction, so is the 360-degree theatre and the promise it holds. Fulldome theaters may enlarge or shrink any perception within the mind to surround-scale. Whatever is inside one's head can be externalized as a fulldome show in perfect proportion, projected on the cave-like canvas of the dome-skull. People already exercising a vivid imagination who feel at home inside their skull are likely to also feel at home in the dome where they can be teleported to castles in the air, or be alongside mermaids underwater, or even choose alternative environments with an ecology of their own selection.

If the movers and shakers of the past were asked to raise their voices towards the paradigm shift brought by immersive fulldome media, what would they say?

The philosopher Immanuel Kant in a variation of his famous 1784 treatise *might* have proclaimed:

"What is fulldome? Fulldome is mankind's emergence from the self-incurred restriction of their field of view."[2]

Karl Marx, ridiculing conservative suspicions, might have rewritten the opening of his 1848 Communist Manifesto to warn that "a specter is haunting the world—the specter of a communist spherical revolution."[3]

When Walter Gropius founded the famous art school *Bauhaus* in Weimar in 1919, he might have pondered "the ultimate aim of all visual art is the complete building of the fulldome theatre!"[4]

Closer to the present, R. Buckminster Fuller, in his 1961 speech *The Architect as World Planner*, could have supported Gropius by proposing a world plan for fulldome architecture, postulating that this" .... will unquestionably be world news of the first order, and not only world news, but news that men all around the Earth have waited for."[5]

Shifting focus from building to content, Bauhaus teacher Oskar Schlemmer might have proclaimed in his Manifesto for the first Bauhaus exhibition in Weimar in 1923, with only slight variation to the original:

We, [the creators of fulldome content], become the bearers of responsibility and the conscience of the whole world. An idealism of activity that embraces, penetrates, and unites art, science, and technology [that will] construct the 'art-edifice' of Man, which is but an allegory of the cosmic system. Today we can do no more than ponder the total plan, lay the foundations, and prepare the building stones. We exist! We have the will! We are producing![6]

Schlemmer's fanfare echoes and heralds the concept of the *Gesamtkunstwerk*, which challenges our capacity to not only handle new technological tools but also grasp their significance mentally, esthetically, and socially. The challenge becomes more urgent today as people are on the brink of an iconic shift from frame to sphere, with consequences to our efforts to make sense of it. It is a time of liberated images, of expanded mind, expanded cosmos, and expanded cinema, which prophets like Gene Youngblood have seen coming for some time:

When we say expanded cinema, we actually mean expanded consciousness. Expanded cinema does not mean computer films, video phosphors, atomic light, or spherical projections. Expanded cinema isn't a movie at all: like life's a process of becoming, man's ongoing historical drive to manifest his conscious-ness outside of his mind, is in front of his eyes. (Youngblood, 1970, p. #)[7]

FRAMELESS FRENZY

The "building stones" for a Fulldome Manifesto have gathered in modernity, but are not exclusively bound to the recent past. In fact, prehistory has a lot to offer in terms of immersive art experience, as expressed in an editorial addressing the delegates of an international gathering, the Jena FullDome Festival:

Remember the Paleolithic era? That's when we artists and audiences alike were surrounded by works of visual wonder. Half crawling, half dancing through cavernous spaces, we were ready to lose our sense of direction while being lured to and by strange and beautiful sights and sounds: stars, birds, bees, and buffaloes above and below, to the right and to the left, all alive in a ghostly manner. The age of immersive paintings in rough and dripping caves was the primordial heyday of frameless frenzy! Then came the dark ages. This was a time of caged images—a time of broadening distance between vision and viewer: the frame age! Today, media consumers and producers are still hypnotized by the frame, believing that fat rectangular screens are a primary legitimate format for visual display of any kind. Part of the hypno-sis is a failure in discovering the change that has come with 360-degree immersive spaces, from digital Planetariums to fulldome theatres and the integration of virtual reality devices. This news won't be kept in the dark for long; 360-degree audio visual entertainment is a fertile medium for discovery beyond old restrictions. The producers and creators of fulldome experiences are ready to break the frame. The shift happens and that's why we celebrate Frameless Frenzy![8]

A problem with any new medium is that it cannot be described or understood by the means of the old medium that it evolved out of; it exists beyond what it was. What is performed across a theatre stage is not the same as what is revealed in a movie. Fulldome, the next step in this evolution, has become a paradigm-shifting medium of its own. Fulldome challenges the silver screen like Galileo challenged the dogma of his time.

Despite uncharted boundaries of play in this new frontier, the aspiring fulldome producer must not do away with the skills learned from filmmaking and other disciplines: they are helpful tools up a spiraling ladder in designing a fully-immersive fulldome experience.

Paleolithic cave paintings offer a most instructive model to the art of fulldome choreography. Only in glossy coffee table books or coffee table iPads do Paleolithic cave paintings look like they were designed to fit rectangular viewing devices. In the interplay of light and shadow among the physical world, some figures in the cave space may look familiar and benign, others threatening and nasty, but all of them seem to be alive in a ghostlike manner, and—wow—they are all around you when projected in the dome! Surround cave paintings can only best be viewed in surround-video, especially when delivered along with an enticingly eerie, spatially-deceptive audio accompaniment! A haunting of the senses inside and out … teleportation to a distant time and a distant place. What more could a producer do? Contemporary fulldome producers tip their hats to you, spiritual elders of prehistoric immersive performance art!

FROM CAVE TO KANDINSKY

Not quite as far back in history as the Neolithic past, and not quite as far into the future as the multi-sensory multimedia fulldome theatre, the authors find kindred spirits in our temporal neighborhood.

As far back in recorded history as one can travel, it is apparent that humans have had an interest in discovering and rediscovering themselves among spatialized surroundings in reality, as so in art. When the world's first planetarium with accurate, hemispheric star projection was installed in Jena in 1924 on the Zeiss factory roof, it immediately attracted the attention of Walter Gropius and Lászlo Moholy-Nagy, teachers of the time at The Bauhaus Art School in nearby Weimar, Germany. Together with the architect Adolf Meyer and Bauhaus students, they were among its first visitors and vehemently discussed the implications of the star projection system for their own projects.[9] Moholy-Nagy's later work for Erwin Piscator and his arena stage, as well as his Light-Space Modulator, seemed to be just as much influenced by the Jena Planetarium as Gropius's Total Theatre project conceived for Piscator. Other Bauhaus teachers and artists like Oskar Schlemmer and Wassili Kandinsky pursued similar ideas during their time at the Bauhaus.

Kandinsky described his visionary artist's dream as a "synthetic work in space, together with the building … For many years I have been looking for a way to enable the spectator to 'take a walk' in the picture, to force him with self-abandonment into the picture."[10] Is it a premonition of a fulldome artist who came ahead of his time? "Taking a walk in the picture with self-abandonment" sounds like a benign constituent toward a Fulldome Manifesto.

360-DEGREE HAPPINESS

Fulldome art is not an alien intrusion into an otherwise true and real world. All of reality is surround; all sensory input is immersive! The recognition that our field of view allows us to see only a 180-degree segment of our surroundings does not stop sensations from coming at us from all directions. The center of our perception is always located in the round. The world is always full circle, not portioned to the rectangle in front of a room, or wherever display for visual representation happens to be used. Sensory input may be choreographed in bursts—with fluctuations, soft edges, depth of field, and subtle differentiations and combinations that merge and celebrate the *"surroundness"* of a non-pigeonholed medium.[11]

Olfactory perception can't isolate one flat sheet of perfume from the next in shared space; diffusion expands spherically.

To give another example, sounds bellowing from square speakers echo outwardly, organically crawling across space like spherical emanations, which if visualized, would look like wobbly, vibrating ghosts. There is hardly a better place to popularize the visualization of the physical properties of music, or any kind of sound vibration, than the dome. New digital planetariums are bound to have spatial audio systems installed to allow acoustic events to move freely through three-dimensional space, driven by the intention of their acoustic choreographers, as visual events do.[12] Sound waves only appear to be flat when represented as two-dimensional oscillograph curves, and they themselves are part of the fulldome creators' palette in crafting multisensory input for a spherically-choreographed, spatially-curated acoustic experience.

Why simplify the natural 360-degree symphonies of senses when humans have the means to display and excite them with contemporary technology? Humans can create media environments all around us, just like in the real world—binding fiction with environmental realism. Inside our own minds? In massive spaces? Converge the two! This is a supreme tool for actualizing the imagination, integrating physical with imagined worlds, and teleporting environments from place to place—or teleporting people from place to place within them.

This effort towards a Manifesto would miss its point were it not to promote the inalienable right to the pursuit of happiness in 360 degrees, because the human field of vision is never flat, square, or rectangular. People must ascertain their human birthright to media in the round! People undoubtedly exist in a multi-dimensional, multi-directional world, and media, art, and storytelling have finally caught up to overlap here in virtual planes, and even into deeper planes of the human psyche and neurology.

To refer to a fulldome audience member as a "viewer" would be a gross misnomer; one is not simply a "viewer" in this environment which weaves together spatial acoustic impressions, multisensory exposure, and physical engagement. The full enjoyment of fulldome requires the birth of a new tribe united in, and dedicated to, the pursuit of 360-degree happiness. Media mavens call members of this tribe *Immersivists!* Enjoying their glorious *Immersivevistas*!

JANUS 2.0

Musing about the full-scale multisensory curation of experience in these 360-degree pixel-spaces does not mean to neglect a most significant role of what most of us consider the king of sensory input—the visual domain. The bad news: because of their limited field of view, humans are almost short of the faculties to best enjoy the maximum potential of these maximalist immersive arenas. There is someone who seems better equipped to enjoy fulldome shows than most of us—the Roman god Janus! Tradition-

Figure 2. The double headed Janus is fulldome's celebrated patron saint

ally depicted as a handsome double-faced, double-bearded god, he is able to view front and rear, past and future (or any other polar opposites), simultaneously. In classical Roman mythology, Janus's unique abilities qualified him to be the guardian of transitions, doors, and gateways.

People in the fulldome community have learned that Janus has assumed a more down-to-Earth role recently, having been elevated from the status of a metaphorical deity of the past to a sought-after award statue of today. Janus revisited is an encouraging model of one person's ability to integrate more views than the one in their own body, without splitting personalities or getting lost in contradictions. Imagining Janus's everyday experience of a 360-degree hemispheric projection panorama makes him a helpful guide to lead us out of the flat media hypnosis and into multimedia multidimensions. Those under the influence of flat media hypnosis—a condition that will soon be diagnosed as *Janus deficiency syndrome*—suffer familiar symptoms of being glued to seats and sofas with stiffened necks while staring at flat-world screens in boxes, victims to settling for square media, equipped with only one straight pair of headlight eyes. What does it take for mankind to *emerge from the self-incurred restriction of their field of view,* as we have paraphrased Kant's motto"… to transcend the monotony of mono-directionality, and migrate to the realm of omnidirectional immersion?" Are humans cursed by our biological status quo to remain as we are? How do people open their sensory receptors to absorb and enjoy live 360-degree rocket science and music visualization events? Shall people put their hope in becoming hybrids, synergizing our conventional senses with multi-eyed *Homo Deus* robots in order to optomechanically widen the doors of our perception? Is that what the proposed Janus 2.0 deity wants to help us achieve?

Picture taken at an award ceremony with Janus impersonator, together with Venus, companion deity in the Roman Pantheon.

Recognizing that an outstanding fulldome production needs a worthy award, the Jena FullDome Festival (founded in 2007), commissioned the god Janus to act as the patron saint for the fulldome community. Artist Cosima Goepfer was commissioned to create a Janus statue (which, for good reason, may have a slight resemblance to Oscar from Hollywood), with Janus's chiseled gaze looking in two directions. As of today, 60 Fulldome producers from around the world have been awarded a JANUS from the Fulldome

Figure 3. Ralph Heinson, happy winner of a Janus-Award honoring excellence in science visualization
Source: Photo by Torsten Hemke / Fulldome Festival Foundation

Festival, in recognition of excellence of their fulldome films and contributions to propelling the medium forward. What will we see from pioneers in the near-future? (Figure 2 and Figure 3)

EYE-SPHERE VS. EAR-SPHERE

Janus, the patron saint of Fulldome, reminds us of the simple fact that while humans are not equipped to *see* in 360 degrees like Janus, they are privileged to *hear* in 360 degrees, as mentioned in the 360-degree happiness section. Our ears can locate where a sound is coming from without looking in that direction. Natural sound, like natural hearing, is always surround and not stereo or 5.1. When people open their eyes, half of the visible world around us, although never lost, is invisible to our view. When they close their eyes, they are still able to hear the full range of the audible world. The discrepancy between the range of the eye-sphere and the ear-sphere should not be lamented, but creatively incorporated in holistic productions. Fulldome shows at their best skillfully orchestrate the medium's assets by guiding the audience's attention around the virtual real estate of the structure to follow the narrative and skillfully introduce action (Figure 4). As dances take place and are witnessed in a seamless sphere, they lure us to no longer just *sit around* like museum statues, but to *walk around*, to explore, to tango, and to *move* to other times and spaces—a literal mov(e)ie!

Figure 4. Guiding the audience's attention around the virtual real estate of the structure. Tunnel effects are popular in the dome. This one by Jordanian immersion designer Mohammad Jaradat. (Credits: Mohammad Jaradat / Fulldome Festival Foundation)
Jaradat. Source: Photo by Mohammad Jaradat / Fulldome Festival Foundation

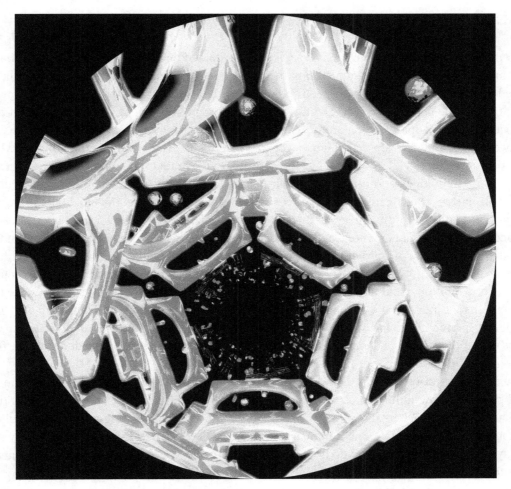

SICK BAGS

Robert Sawallisch, a former student of Media Art and Design at *Bauhaus University*, created a massively psychedelic, experimental fulldome show he called *Raumschwindel* (spatial vertigo). His ambition was to pioneer to extreme limits, the aspect of physiological disorientation some people experience in a fulldome show. For the *Raumschwindel* premiere at the Jena FullDome Festival in 2009, he humorously equipped the audience with specially designed "sick bags" for "your personal safety," as the audience sat back to enjoy the spins and turns and patterns and motion of his intentionally exaggerated and dizzying production. Vertigo can be elicited intentionally (and at times accidently) as another tool on the fulldome producers palette of multi-sensory cues for immersive storytelling. It may not be a business model for eternity, but the irony worked. People loved the show, (no one felt nauseous enough to need the safety sick bags), and *Raumschwindel* became a great success, winning its creator Robert Sawallisch both international awards and eventually landing him a full time career with a German Planetarium.

VERTIGO

There is no denying that fulldome media may catapult the audience to the edge of perception, across and beyond their comfort zones, intensifying the experience of being almost violently absorbed by, or immersed in, an interdimensional voyage, a show, a story, or a space, be it real or fictitious in a way that can be jarring to the nervous system. The difficulty, if not impossibility, of distancing oneself from the experience can make people quite uncomfortable, with or without a "sick bag" at-hand. Being overwhelmed is not always desirable, and drawing a line between where the confines of ego-self ends, and where immersion begins, is not trivial. Some believe the decision to make that transition should remain with the authority of the individual, and not be dictated by directors with estranged manipulative tendencies.

Walter Gropius optimistically and ambiguously propagates overcoming the old dualistic world view: "the 'I' as the antithesis of the universe is fading and the concept of a new world unity … is emerging in its place."[13] However, not everyone in the audience may be prepared to experience such grand cosmic unity in their individual confines at the spur of the moment. A fusion between audience and fulldome may happen unexpectedly in these spaces, where media climbs into the mind and fires along neurotransmitters, having emotional and physiological effect of the immersive kind. Or by design: Since the field of view engulfs an individual's peripheral vision, it tricks human perception neurologically. This is a physiological interconnectedness with the dome, and along with skillfully crafted content narration, deepened sense of interconnectedness, and/or a barrage of curated emotions, can be drawn from the audience intentionally.

There's still a question as to the effect of various spectrums of light, therefore video, on the impressions of people in how light particles travel through, and may affect, our neurological faculties. The medium amplifies sensory intake and is not as gentle on the eyes and faculties as say, passively gazing out of your window right now. The dome environment and technology involved in immersive experiences play trickery on the brain and body in ways that continue to be explored (and experimented with).

Consider this notion regarding the people's intake of film, moving at a speed of 24 frames per second. Jonathan Lahay Dronsfield remarks in regards to Hitchcock's film *Vertigo*, "It has been argued that the speed of film is such that its images are 'too immediate' to allow for thinking. (...) We find sensation being opposed to thought."[14] People's attention span and sensitivities mentioned in this section must be carefully considered in designing fulldome storyworlds. It is common for an audience to disconnect from the media when they are alienated by the content or simply dislike it. However, when the technology behind an experience is so overpowering that people cannot extract themselves from it, the art of cinema storytelling is lost to "flexing" technology. Hitchcock made *Vertigo* not only a theme, but also a tool in the art of visual storytelling. As a creator he used technology and illusion to provoke evocative reactions in the audience, also considering intentional discomfort as a building block to the film, along with: pacing, darkness, motion, movement, temperature, spectrum, and space. The same toolbox is available to directors of immersion too, except that their effects are heightened in the dome as if seen through a magnifying glass.

Figure 5. Undergoing a phase of adaptive acceleration for the sake of sanity; particles fly as guests of the IX Symposium, 2015, lounge about in their desired posture about modular bean-bag seating
Source: Captured by photographer Sebastien Roy

SPEED OF MIND

The tradition of rationalism has cultivated a mode of thinking which sometimes has a hard time catching up with the speed of film, let alone with the immediacy and sense of presence that comes with immersion in fulldome surround media. Vertigo, or the fear of vertigo, may arise when an overprotective ego-self tries to close the wagons around its fortified persona. However, in view of the fast digital world humans live in, one might speculate, if not argue, that people's mental processes may have to undergo a phase of adaptive acceleration for the sake of sanity. If that's the ride humans are on—and the authors will watch closely—then one optimistically hopes that such pacing will nudge the *conditio humana* towards a modality of deepened integration of body-mind-intellect, in order that thought and sensation no longer drift apart uncomfortably in different directions at different speeds, and that, when bathing in immersive projections, the rhythm of consciousness and the rhyme of media technology will synchronize in a *Pas de Deux* of healthy co-evolution, as opposed to feeling overwhelmed by a forced and maximal disruption (Figure 5).

FROM STILL TO SURROUND

As much as *Towards a Fulldome Manifesto* authors like to invite readers to indulge in musings of futuristic trajectories, there's also a need to honor the historical roots from which new art forms like fulldome draw their nourishment, before they manifest milestones in their own immersive right. Here is a micro-tour through the evolution of fulldome cinema from still to surround—and beyond.

Imagine the ponderings of a pre-teen youth of the Paleolithic era living among caves and carnage, sitting beside the surface of a pond: "how does water trap the image of the full moon and night sky in its reflection?" She may ponder. "How could I capture image of lilies and trees projected into the water too?" If the fragments of light are trapped on the smallest pieces of the water's surface and form a picture, then how to translate little pieces of light and color to something else?

From the early creative pangs of humans, to photographs, and now as humanity enters into a realm of holographics and surround-media, humans have developed technology to create and recreate the worlds around us. We observe. We trap. We project. We've come to 'map' our three-dimensional environments entirely with little pixels of light to represent other places and provoke a shared sense of wonder among audiences to teleport them there.

Can readers imagine the sensation of seeing the image of a living thing duplicated to cerebral fiction for the first time without first experiencing it? Imagine the extraordinary wonder in witnessing a still image frozen in material or translated to paintings on stone for the first time; what is common-place now, would have been extraordinary to this Paleolithic-teen.

Once images were imprinted to film through the impression of light, scientists went to work at perfecting what realism they could capture with the technological support of a camera, while artists and thought leaders continued to probe and poke into new uses and hypothesized applications.

Man Ray did away with the camera all together undergoing material and medium experimentation in similar curiosity to the likes of artists such as Pablo Picasso. Now known as "photograms," Man Ray referred to his works as Rayographs and would place physical objects directly on the surface of a light sensitive material.[15] Exposure to light would create the image cascading from the stack of three-dimensional objects. A kind of sculpture-photograph, deconstructing the tools perceived to be needed to take a picture.

Experimentation and manipulation of two-dimensional images lead to the discovery in a human's ability to create moving illusions: films! Imagine before this, that man had no way of moving still life objects into fantastical animation; magic realism to those without knowledge of its medium: cinema!

Modes in storytelling as well as technology continue to evolve from there (Figure 6).

FROM MARCEL DUCHAMP TO CLASSICAL HOLLYWOOD

On the subject of spheres, consider Marcel Duchamp's surreal short *Anemic Cinema*, 1926. Circular shapes of black and white are animated in what the artist refers to as "Rotoreliefs." These stark circular movements are spliced with rolling images of text in the round, engraved with *suggestive* notions in French. The audience traverses between vertigo-inducing spatial color planes and these spirals of text, which cause introspection and sultry interpretation. One uses a different part of the brain to view and take-in one set of frames from the next. *Anemic Cinema* lives as a piece created with the intention for

Figure 6. The evolution of fulldome cinema from still to surround—and beyond; VJ University hosts a Blendy Dome workshop at The Fort Collins Museum of Discovery
Source: Pictured here are fulldome creators Kelley Francis and Axel Cuevas Santamaria.

its audience to watch and ponder and to affect not only the eyes, but also the psyche and introspection of its audience.

The provocation of a physiological response in response to moving visual art was a discovery towards contemporary fulldome. Such discovery continues!

With discovery of how visual media enter human biology, let's migrate into how visual media may call people to climb out of their own perception and engage with their physical surroundings for engagement with surround-cinema: recall the technological breakthrough of sound?

In the time of Classical Hollywood, budgets weren't spared to push technological discovery if it led to the enhancement of the entertainment of cinema: ticket sales drove breakthroughs. Experimentation led to "talkies;" movies that could capture and project sound. What a technological breakthrough! To capture and project sound paired with film, wow! Now, one could not only read and watch films, but hear the actors and be *immersed* in their private conversation, as if they were in the halls of the decadent Hollywood stages or standing beside the characters themselves.

FROM BUSBY BERKELEY TO THE SPHERICAL SCREEN

Busby Berkeley is known as one of the great choreographers who incorporated illusion in the time that talkies came about: illusions like that of Duchamp's *Anemic Cinema*. In the classic film *42nd Street*, grand stages hosted acutely choreographed women adorned in smart costumes, where they took to dance and interlocked with each other, moving in spherical patterns which were captured as psychedelic moving pictures by cranes from above: a bird's-eye view of hundreds of ladies poised as spherical moving shapes.

In the famous kickline: the camera's presence is made aware to the audience. No longer a mystery, Berkeley gives the technological device personality as the audience becomes aware of its point of view while traveling through the gaping legs of Hollywood's most lovely dames of the day.

The Jena Fulldome Festival in Jena, Germany, is a 360-degree spherical screen festival and the first of its kind. A hotbed for experimentation, and the development of 360 filmmakers' skills, and the medium in general, this festival housed and houses the forefront most examples of creative, artistic and performative fulldome art and entertainment. Creators of all creeds, ages, and professions have submitted fulldome movies for the consideration of a carefully selected panel of international Jena Fulldome Festival jury members to watch and judge who shall go home with the honorable *Janus Award*. Fulldome cinema enthusiasts from around the world gather to watch, engage, immerse, and enjoy independent fulldome movies while intermingling in one of the longest-standing planetariums still in operation today.

In 2015, the festival awarded Masashige Iida, a Japanese artist, "Best Use of Innovative Production Technologies," for his 15-minute piece *Fermentation*. Imagine those Busby Berkeley aerial crane shots again, although this time IIida brought the audience in the dome into his choreographed piece— like Berkeley did with his characteristic camera's point of view. The audience member's perspective moved along like the camera itself moving above and around the dancers—near and far—but in this case the "viewer" is surrounded by those dancers in projected physical space. The audience is the camera—and moves among and within the choreography, darting between limbs and from bird's-eye view to side-by-side perspective—a perspective that is part of the choreography.

Had chairs not been in the way, the audience could have moved and grooved, blending in with the performance by embodying it. Fulldome is the closest way to get into something without really being there.

FROM VIRTUAL GALAXIES TO RADICALLY INCLUSIVE VENUES

All experiences of art and entertainment lend themselves to fulldome. The range in application is extraordinary. From hand-painting plexiglass domes, to custom-generated virtual environments integrating artificial intelligence (AI), these vessels accommodate a wide variety of use and material application.

Thanks to recent evolutions in multimedia, this medium has great range for inception: tactile elements or virtual galaxies are a causeway to 360-degree immersive experiences through fulldome theatres, causeways for beings to come together in physical and virtual space, in the round, as civilizations have gathered for thousands of years around new ideas. It lends itself across hybrid-mediums as a structure to house projects that range in storytelling across a wide array of possible multi-integrated platforms.-

I think it's okay to move ahead and incorporate technology as long as you have the foundation, and I think as Navajo people; that's part of our strengths. If you look through our history, one of the reasons why I think Navajos have prospered more than a lot of other tribes are our abilities to adapt and grab

Figure 7. The fulldome venue is a technological yurt inhabited by tribal neighbors, strangers, and creators all ready for interaction with inner and outer worlds
Source: Screenshot from Diana Suyerbayeva's fulldome film "Kyiz ui," named after the Kazakhstan style of a yurt in central Asia. (Photo by: Diana Suyerbayeva / Fulldome Festival Foundation).

things from other cultures and we just kind of twist it and make it our own, and it becomes Navajo. (Benally, 2014)

This passage is a quote taken from Navajo artist Bert Benally about his piece, *Pull of the Moon,* as part of the *Temporary Installations Made for the Environment* (*TIME*) in Coyote Canyon, New Mexico—a collection of land performances in 2014. Thanks to the fulldome format being in the round, Benally told curator Eileen Braziel: "Now we can tell our stories the way our culture does—in cycles."

Domes are radically inclusive venues. One may be alone in a dome, but these are not lonesome vessels: the fulldome venue is a technological yurt inhabited by tribal neighbors, strangers, and creators all ready for interaction with inner and outer worlds, in waking or dream states (and all those in-between) (Figure 7).

FROM STAR NURSERIES TO PLANETARIUMS

The combination of nonfiction and fantasy has been coming together in planetariums, since observatories came into existence. Fantastical stories and myths from indigenous, Greek and Roman folklore are told around the sphere in tandem, where science is busy mapping the cosmos. This spherical venue is host to reproductions of the smallest known of atomic particles, to the greatest expanse in our known universe.

Planetariums have been the nurseries for the cultivation of dome-based alternative media. Those that open their doors to new creators have contributed to the cultivation of an emerging media. Planetarium Hamburg has hosted live rock concerts under the dome, where they project music from the live performance inside to thousands sitting in the garden lawn around the venue outdoors under open skies. Attendance reflects it's a worthwhile endeavor to keep star-gazers engaged in their ongoing programming.

Science has been engaging artists since the birth of Rock and Roll. In 1965, The Lowell Observatory commissioned illustrator Patricia Bridges to draw geological observations of the moon, which were used in mapping the Apollo 11 Lunar Landing.

The Fort Collins Museum of Discovery (FCMoD) has opened its doors to fulldome creators through the likes of their digital dome manager, Ben Gondrez. Gondrez has been hosting *Domelab*, a meetup that is open to any new or veteran fulldome cinematographers at the Otterbox Digital Dome Theater at FCMoD. *Domelab* is gearing up for their 93rd meetup. Other 360-degree media meetup groups have begun to form and cultivate the medium in this way internationally, and now exist in most cities around the world interconnected through the World Wide Web of resource.

IMERSA is a global gathering of artists and industry folk who come together around the subject of immersive media each year. In a *TV-Dome* interview, Dan Neafus explains what motivated him and the IMERSA-team to found the organization: " … enthusiasm for the fulldome world is primarily about connecting audiences with the technology. It's very important that we are aware of what the audience is experiencing in digital theatre, and that we journey with them to take them to places that are exciting and wonderful, and have them leaving with a different perspective of space or earth or science. The intrigue for me is to improve that process with the evolving technology and ideas, and to leverage our assets, to see in which way we can share the knowledge between each other in the community and get better experiences for our audiences … That's the spirit in which IMERSA was founded." (Figure 8)

SAT, or the Société des Arts Technologiques (Society for Arts and Technology), built the *SAT Stratosphere*, one of the first permanent fulldomes with a contemporary media server solely dedicated to the arts. This space has sponsored and hosted artists from around the world to cultivate works that can only be actualized in spherical pixel spaces.

Take *Résonances Boréales*: videographer Dominque St-Amant and pianist Roman Zavada hauled gear and an upright piano to a remote place in Canada to film aurora borealis using 360-degree camerawork. Following a stunning 360-degree capture of the emerald lights, Zavada has since toured with the spherical video piece to domes around the world and performed alongside the visuals by playing piano live with the invigoration to convey the impression he's carried with him from that first venture into the wilderness. *Résonances Boréales* is a piece that couldn't live in any other medium and convey the scale and emotion it does as a surrounding fulldome, spatially-projected and emotionally-evocative piece.

SAT also hosts the *IX Symposium*, which has become a leading global gathering for immersive producers and fulldome cultivation, located in one of the worlds greatest creative cities, Montreal. It's in part thanks to gatherings like these and the *Fulldome Festival* that so many international fulldome and

Figure 8. Dan Neafus is interviewed by Micky Remann in an innovative 360-degree TV-Dome TV network: Salve.tv
Source: Photo by Salve.tv / Fulldome Festival Foundation

aspiring fulldome cinematographers exist around the world, ever-contributing to the spherical multimedia revolution!

At SAT's IX Symposium in 2018 there was one particular performance that opened the floodgate for the emergence of "Choose Your Own Dome Ventures." Seats had been cleared in the dome. Guests had to choose where to move and find themselves. Many gathered around a map, projected downwards to the floor. A tall shaft, which appeared to be formed of crystal, stood as a marker on the map. Audience members could pick up and move the marker form place to place on this two-dimensional atlas, and in direct affect the 360-degree projected landscape surrounding the audience would shift into live action footage of the newly selected destination. The 360-degree surround footage was shot on video at existing locations for scenes to populate the fictional map, and then manipulated for artistic intentions. The audience was literally choosing their own environmental visual adventure.

Domes have long been a celebrated shape among planetarium communities. Now the Planetariums that are opening their doors and their missions to encompass the arts are finding increased engagement with the public, an increased passion for astronomy, and climbing numbers in attendance. With resources like *Domelab* and FDDB; *The Full-Dome Database*, creators and producers are finding each other and coming together more freely than before, to preview and share news and works. It's only a matter of time before anyone yet to experience the exhilaration of a fulldome piece that makes their belly roll and their emotions soar, finds themselves laid back and suspended into a fulldome venture right in their own neighborhood.

Figure 9. "It's a mistake to simply view the dome as a curved screen"
Source: Photo by Warik Lawrance, Melbourne Planetarium

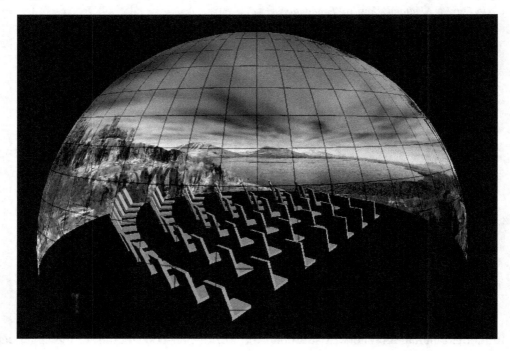

Figure 10. "Imagine the dome as a device to transport the audience to new worlds"
Source: Photo by: Warik Lawrance, Melbourne Planetarium

FROM TOFU TO MELBOURNE

Having assembled the diverse building blocks of current fulldome affairs, it's time to ask for the common denominator, i.e. for a definition of the *Game of Domes*. Here comes the first: Fulldome is like Tofu—it has no taste of its own but it will take on any flavor you add to, or project upon it. Or this: Content in the dome is similar to content in a lucid dream, and vice versa. Any idea in someone's head, however vague or wonderful, can be displayed in everybody else's dome, provided the producers have the skills, funds, creativity, and technology to design the experience realistically.

Another definition is coming in from Melbourne, Australia. "It's a mistake to simply view the dome as a curved screen. Imagine the dome as a device to transport the audience to new worlds,"[16] proclaims Warik Lawrance, director of the Melbourne Planetarium, when asked to describe the function of fulldome in the emergence of digital 360-degree immersive art (Figure 9 and Figure 10).

The question runs deeper: if immersive technology allows you to emit what imagery is in your mind onto the dome, will your head, after you have emptied it out onto the dome, eventually be free of it? Will your mind then be like a clear and peaceful lotus pond, unrippled by daily rubbish, suffering, and distress? This utopian trajectory would surely and immersively beam you toward a state of enlightened "tofuness," should ingredients from the 360-degree fulldome creators' toolkit come together in sweet and delectable immersive achievement. There is no reason why a dome should not transform itself into an ashram for deep, futuristic meditation.

On the dystopian side: the dome is but a huge echo chamber that reflects and reinforces *ad nauseam*.

Undoubtedly, some people can culminate vivid immersive worlds together with imagination alone. Why then go to the dome theatre with stories and states in your head? When building immersive installations in the three-dimensional world, a piece is more than simply surrounding the audience with pixels. The two-dimensional pages of a good book can already elicit emotion and engulf the reader into imagined scenes, feelings, and other worlds *immersively*.

"If we create technologies that interface better with parts of our own ecology, with parts of our own nature, we enhance our lives," says fulldome artist Mileece (Mok, 2014).

Mileece is a sound artist, programmer, and environmental designer who was selected as a resident artist at the London School of Economics Innovation Center, where she began an exciting ecological endeavor to interconnect various domes housing microclimates of living plants. This artist creates living soundscapes generated by the plants themselves, where people can sit in and among their inter-communication.

Mileece connects electrodes to the leaves of living plants to migrate the current emitting off of them (bio-emissions) into an amplifier. The analog input is drawn into the amplifier where it turns into binary code. From there the software she's developed takes that data and animates it into sound. She houses these musical plantscapes in geodesic domes, and has been interconnecting them as part of *The Weaver Project*. Sounds from a biodome in the Amazon can be played to lull their American counterparts into tranquility.

Yes, there are incredible fulldome shows about the outer world, about planets and stars, and journeys across the galaxy, into a black hole and out again. There is also much adventure in scanning the horizons of our inner worlds. The shape of the dome resembles a skull. The dome is a hemispheric canvas able to display the stories that go on in the mind, as convincingly as showing what goes on in the asteroid belt. Domes are a transcendent venue at the intersection of what we can explore in the mind, and what our mind can explore through what we envision.

CRAWLING INTO THE HEAD—AND OUT

The space explorer's quest to travel to faraway star systems is mirrored by the mind explorer's wish to give genuine accounts from inner world adventures. In this passage, Ed Lantz joins us to call for using these giant screen environments to share introspection with each other:

Another possible storytelling device is to depict archetypes representing the character's inner conflict or imagination. In other words, we would crawl in the character's head. The immersive display allows room for the simultaneous depiction of our external reality and our inner archetypes, memories, and internal imaging. (Lance, 1995)[17]

Crawling into the character's head is one thing, but what if there's no escape? Does this sound impossible?

What if immersion is not a matter of choice, but an issue of mental health? In her media art and design master thesis, Jing Augusto-Wuethrich portrays the inner world of a person suffering from schizophrenia by means of an animated fulldome documentary. She explains why and how:

The purpose of the film was not to portray a very in-depth technical documentary about schizophrenia. It was aimed at understanding a person who is suffering from it based on her narrated experience. (Augusto-Wuethrich, 2018)[18]

In that film, the protagonist herself is never shown. Only her voice is heard, where she describes her experiences and hallucinations when she is in the schizophrenic state. The audience getting to know her through the real audio recording and the animation of the artist illustrating her visions in a fulldome film, lures onlookers into sharing the subjective experience of psychosis, without identifying with it. Jing Augusto-Wuethrich proceeds to elaborate on the concept, where she not only makes use of surround projection with fulldome, but also of the spatial audio system for 360-degree sound:

The priority, at this given situation of the project, is the impact of the audio narrative of her mental experience rather than how I can invent it. Of course, the role of the filmmaker is to transmute her narrative into visuals through animation, which is as close as possible to the description of her mental reality. (...) e.g. the voices that she hears, the sound coming from hallucinatory images etc. (...). (Augusto-Wuethrich, 2018)

Her visualization concept reveals a lot about the strategies and technical precision necessary to use the fulldome space in an adequate way. It's worth looking into how Jing Augusto-Wuethrich goes into the details of her project:

To emphasize the difference between the TV or cinema and the dome-based viewing experience, a flat rectangular screen occupying a small portion of the dome was used as an establishing shot that depicts the typical viewing we are accustomed to. It would then zoom in to the head of the protagonist until the camera is situated inside the head. This segue brings the viewer into the dome environment 'where all the mental events would happen.' At this point, the visualization is conceptualized under the premises that:

Figure 11. Crawling inside the head of a schizophrenic; screenshot from Jing Augusto-Wuethrich's award winning fulldome film "S is for Episode"
Source: *Photo by Jing Augusto-Wuethrich / Fulldome Festival Foundation*

Everything is in the head.

The protagonist is not seen.

The camera represents the protagonist.

The protagonist's voice emanates from a now absent body.

In effect, all these conditions equate to the viewers experiencing the mental event as narrated by the main character. (Augusto-Wuethrich, 2018)

Needless to say, this concept of embracing subjectivity relied exclusively on the protagonist's version of reality. There was no scientist present to expound upon what schizophrenia really is (Figure 11).

Jing Augusto-Wuethrich's animated documentary *S is for Episode* won the JANUS Award for Best Student Film in the 2019 Jena FullDome Festival.

The dome is a communal and community space, inhabited by strange people and interactive microbes you have never met before, but now have the privilege to encounter as if they are neighbors. You may be lonely in the dome, but you are never alone in the dome. It's the space where the Kantian notion of self-incurred restriction of mankind's field of view is lifted for good, the ultimate Bauhaus art and science cathedral of Gropius's programmatic vision (Gropius, 1919: p. 3). It even accommodates some of Marx's communist specters, along with some super intelligent animals committed to creating content that strengthens a new global conscience, as Oskar Schlemmer suggested (Ibid. p.4: *We exist! We have the will! We are producing!)*

If the loneliness of an inflated ego-mind is the question that bothers head, dome, and world, then a shift toward a benign multisensory multiperspectivism in a shared conceptually and emotionally open immersive environment is the answer!

What fulldome contributes towards that shift is that you can exit an immersive show in the same body you entered it, yet leave the venue with a different mindset, with experiential sensations of the inner world of others—humans, animals, plants or planets—thus getting to know something that outgrows the mental confines of the self with its limited perceptions and notoriously under-complex mix of presumption and prejudice.

The simplest summary is this: to leave a fulldome show, one has absorbed the multisensory onslaught of a spherical pixel world and the ideas, inspirations, and tracing left behind of being suspended between entertainment and introspection, between external space and introspective imagination. Now isn't that some good news?

AN URGENT CALL FOR A REDEFINITION OF DOME SEATING

Now to some worse news. There is something sadly unsatisfying when sitting in the dome for a long time in today's day and age. What, may you inquire, is cause for this pain in the neck? Chairs!

We have reached the year 2019, depicted as "the future" in popular sci-fi film *Blade Runner* (1982), and the beanbag still reigns supreme as the world's best omni-directional seating device. This is a call for Janus-minded engineers to please come out of the closet! It is also a plea for planetariums and new venues to consider mobile, modular non-square seating. Or no seating at all.

Most seating arrangements in planetariums and dome theaters have a regretful tendency to reintroduce the limitation of the field of vision that the 360-degree projection technology has overcome. As long as the seats more or less force you to direct your attention in only one direction and omit the rest of the dome space, the notion of sitting as humans know it must be reexamined. There is an urgent demand to design new devices for adequate placement of the aspiring Immersivist's body, so that the beauty of visual or auditory activity that spreads out across the huge hemispheric canvas can actually be perceived without incurring a stiff neck, or worse kinds of damage that call for physiotherapy.

The enthusiastic "wow-effect" so typical among fulldome neophytes usually ends with the acknowledgement of utter pain in those parts of the body that are not designed to experience immersive dome shows on uncomfortable chairs.

The issue has become a source of many complaints and a subject matter of another master thesis worth citing: *Dome without Chairs*, by Mohammad Jaradat, an interior designer who turned to a career in media art and design (Jaradat, 2017). In his chapter on "Description of Methods, Process, and Materials," he gets right to the point:

The research examines the difference between the conventional Fulldome seating and the Fulldome without traditional seating.

The hypothetical expectations that are examined are:

- That, while conventional Fulldome with seating limits its user. Fulldome without traditional seating gives its user an opportunity to interact with the space.
- That, Fulldome without seating gives the user a better view of the dome by granting him or her the freedom to enjoy the screening from various perspectives.
- That, since users' points of interest differ from person to person, Fulldome without seating allows users to choose their preferred points of interest.
- That, Fulldome without seating makes the user feel more immersed in the show.[19]

The true gift of fulldome media is that it can make you believe that you neither need to stand, sit, or walk on firm ground, nor are dependent on the existence of firm ground at all. The experience may leave you suspended in mid air, or mid water, exposed to a negligible amount of gravity. If floating and hovering in space is the virtual reality of the experience, then any kind of orthodox seating is quite a literal "pain in the neck" to immersive enjoyment.

FLOATING IS THE NEW SEATING

If at the heart of the matter questions arise like: what is the appropriate technology to let the fulldome medium rise and shine? What is the framework for good content, what are the tools for teaching, learning, and promoting excellence in fulldome production? What kind of myth-making and myth-marketing is needed to attract people to the fulldome theatres of the future, and how will they differ from what people might think they will be? Then, in a radical examination of all the above factors, one might come to the conclusion that the fulldome theatre of the future has no seating or floor, but is built above a pool filled with water! Warm, body-temperature saltwater, to be exact—since it allows the audience to float effortlessly and comfortably on their backs while looking up and around at the projections displayed on a giant, semi-transparent, shimmering cupola. Not only does this arrangement solve the bothersome seating problem, it is also the most natural way to make all of the fulldome projection visible to human eyes at one glance—submerged. All of a sudden, our 180-degree field of view is no longer an impediment but the exact measure to grasp the show in the hemispheric projection dome that covers the pool. Watching the show is as easy as floating and stretching out freely in a condition of buoyancy. Looking around is equivalent to moving around with a body that recognizes its weightlessness, feeling like an astronaut in space or a dolphin in the sea. All of a sudden, it dawns on the aspiring *immersivist*s why *immersion* is borrowed from the Latin *immersio*, meaning *diving into*. All of a sudden, this is no longer a metaphorical abstraction but an accurate *terminus technicus* describing the fact that the presence of water in the dome is as real as the sense of diving into it.

Figure 12. "Floating is the new Seating." Visitors to Liquid Sound Spa listening to underwater music. Soon with fulldome projection above?
Source: Photo by Ortwin Klipp / Liquid Sound

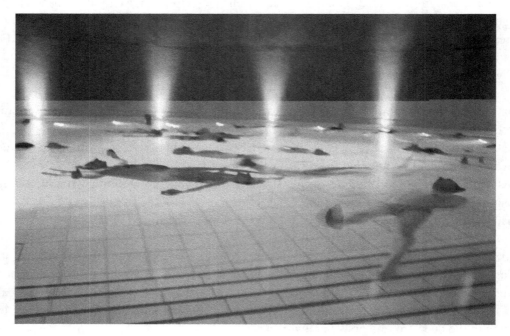

To quote the punchline of a dinner presentation held at the IMERSA Summit in Denver, Colorado: "Immersion, true immersion, is only complete when people get really wet!" [20]

But what about the sound in a warm saltwater floatation dome? Fortunately, that issue has been solved before the first water-filled fulldome opera house will open its doors and locker rooms to the public. With the *Liquid Sound* system, any audio signal can be brought to the water environment in high quality. Listening to sound underwater, ears submerged, is as immersive as can be. Here is a suggestion of why and how the fusion of fulldome and *Liquid Sound* shall be the next step in the evolution of immersive venues (Figure 12).

To sum up the game changer concept in telegram style:

Spherical fulldome projection above the warm saltwater pools

Audiovisual immersion; suspension in 360-degree media art

Optimal seating-adjustment flexibility for ultimate vista-gazing

Shared VR experiences in the water (without clumsy gadgets)

Curation of content for visual teleportation; Inspirational with a mix of natural or abstract scenes, stars, clouds, water worlds, voyages to meditation temples (or extraterrestrial red light districts), fantasy fractals, redwood forests and anything else creators craft into spherical delight!

ROCKET SCIENCE

Excerpt from *'Immersion' kommt von Eintauchen"* (immersion comes from diving-in) by Micky Remann, translated into English for *Toward a Fulldome Manifesto*:

Earth is the cradle of humanity, but one cannot live in a cradle forever." Inspired by this thought, we dare ask: If the Planetarium is the cradle of fulldome, will it remain the only venue for immersion? What other forms of a 'real' exploration into virtual experiences are possible? When immersion dissolves the coordinates of the physical environment, merging perceptions with artificial creations, then it's simply a matter of time that the realm of fulldome merges with the realm of Liquid Sound.

People in a Liquid Sound pool, half dancing, half dreaming to underwater music, yearn to see real dome-like imagery when they look up to the ceiling. Underwater sound, combined with hemispheric projection above the water, will offer a new kind of experience for audiences in the multi-sensory immersion pool. Such an installation will also challenge producers to create adequate content for such exquisite venues. (Remann, 2006. P. 105-106.) [21]

INTERACTIVE DISTANCE PROXIMITY

What seemed like a far-fetched dream only a few years ago has become a reality: fulldome shows are no longer limited to playback mode. They can be created and mixed live in real time. Plug a computer into the media server and watch how your content is immediately displayed and adapted to the dome over any multi-channel projection system. Interactive games, real-time applications, and presentations find their way into the dome with high resolution and almost zero latency.

While interactivity inside one dome may not be an unfamiliar concept based on what people know from popular VJ shows and festivals, the idea of dome-to-dome communication, and interactivity between many immersive theatres and audiences, is still in its infancy and gaining momentum.

Speckled around the globe are domes and planetariums. Some are grand, some are small, and many have a lot in common, but mostly these planetariums operate unconnected from each other.

What if leading planetariums teamed up to highlight a network of insight and inspiration? A global web of venues with amazing shows to share, and true stories to tell?

Staging immersive, interactive celebrations across all borders and time zones is an opportunity for planetariums to emphasize their mission, at the same time promoting their potential with the use of new technologies. The experiences they offer are stunning, unique, and specific to dome theatres, and not available otherwise (Figure 13).

Humans will not have to wait long for simultaneous performances of immersive programming among circuits of domes sharing media coverage around the world. With immersive 360-degree projection systems now established in leading planetariums, it's an exciting time to showcase how entertaining the alternation of astronomy with avant-garde art and other engaging programming can be! The dome theatre is the place to witness the paradigm shift from the flat, rectangular screen to a world of immersive, interactive, surrounding media experiences. This shift is not only redefining contemporary media art, live performance, and science education, but also offering a chance to redefine the mindset in which the human race perceives its place on this global sphere, and how it may engage to shape its landscape.

Figure 13. The audience is taken on a visual journey with sensations of movement through shape and space at the IX Symposium at SAT in Montreal; captured by photographer in 2015

TOWARDS A CONCLUSION

Although the notion of a comprehensive conclusion somehow belies our promise of an ongoing work in progress for this *Tour d'Horizon cum Manifesto*, the authors (Figure 14) still have to end somewhere. So, here we go!

ACKNOWLEDGMENT

All images used in the chapter are courtesy of the authors.

Figure 14. Authors Micky Remann and Kelley Francis moderating a FullDome Festival gala night
Source: *photo by Michael Schomann / Fulldome Festival Foundation*

REFERENCES

Aaronson, X. (2014). The Exquisite Sounds of Plants. *Motherboard, Soundbuilders*. Retrieved from www.vice.com/en_us/article/4x3nmb/the-exquisite-sounds-of-plants

Boréales, R. (2019). *Résonances Boréales*. Retrieved from www.resonancesboreales.com

Conrads, U., & Bullock, M. (1975). *Programs and Manifestoes on 20th-Century Architecture*. Boston: MIT Press.

Dronsfield, J. L. (2018). Immediacy. In *Immersion - Design - Art: Revisited*. Marburg, Germany: Buechner Verlag.

FullDome Festival. (2015). *Program Brochure of the 10th FullDome Festival*. Program Brochure of the 10th FullDome Festival.

Gropius, W. (1935). *Die Neue Architektur Und Das Bauhaus. Grundzüge Und Entwicklung Einer Konzeption*. Faber & Faber.

Kruse, J. (2006). Architektur Aus Dem Geist Der Projektion: Das Zeiss-Planetarium. Wissen in Bewegung. 80 Jahre Zeiss-Planetarium Jena, 51-78.

Mok, K. (2014). Sonic artist derives captivating "organic electronic" sounds from plants. *Treehugger webite*. Retrieved from https://www.treehugger.com/culture/organic-electronic-sounds-from-plants-sonic-artist-mileece.html

Navajo, T. I. M. E. (Temporary Installations Made for the Environment) 2014 Inaugural Biennale. (2014). *New Mexico Arts*. Retrieved from www.nmarts.org/Navajo-Time-Pull-of-the-Moon.html

Poling, C. V. (1986). *Kandinski's Teaching at the Bauhaus*. New York: Rizzoli.

Popova, M. (2014). A Wave in the Mind: Virginia Wolf on Writing and Consciousness. *Brainpickings*. Retrieved from www.brainpickings.org/2014/10/23/virginia-woolf-a-wave-in-the-mind

Symposium, I. X. (2001). Excerpt Medica. *Stratosphere Dome*. Retrieved from ix.sat.qc.ca

The Communist Manifesto. (n.d.). Retrieved from en.wikipedia.org/wiki/The_Communist_Manifesto

Wolf, V. (1931). *The Waves*. London: Hogarth Press.

Youngblood, G. (1970). *Expanded Cinema*. Boston: P. Dutton & Co.

KEY TERMS AND DEFINITIONS

Artificial Intelligence: Computer science dealing with the simulation and development of intelligent behavior in computers.

Avant-Immersive: Forefront experimentation towards discovery in the medium of immersive art and media.

Fulldome: Fulldome refers to immersive dome-based video projection environments. The dome, horizontal or tilted, is filled with real-time or pre-rendered computer animations; live capture images, and/or composited environments among other integrated medias.

Fulldome Festival: A 360-degree cinema, art, live performance, and/or entertainment gathering.

Generative Systems: Generative systems are technologies with the overall capacity to produce un-prompted change driven by input.

Immersive: Story, experience, and instillations that invigorate the mind and immerse an audience or audience member in their experience.

Immersive Theatre: Theater that immerses audiences within the performance itself.

Real-Time Computing: A real-time system is one which controls an environment by receiving data, processing that data, and returning the results sufficiently and quickly enough to affect the environment within milliseconds and without latency (the measure of the time delay experienced by a multimedia system).

ENDNOTES

1   "A Wave in the Mind: Virginia Wolff on Writing and Consciousness," Brain Pickings, https://www.brainpickings.org/2014/10/23/virginia-woolf-a-wave-in-the-mind/

2   The original question in Kant's essay *What is Enlightenment?* is answered by himself as: *Enlightenment is man's emergence from his self-incurred immaturity* (Unmuendigkeit in German). See https://en.wikipedia.org/wiki/Answering_the_Question:_What_is_Enlightenment%3F

3   Marx's original wording: *A spectre is haunting Europe — the spectre of communism.* See https://en.wikipedia.org/wiki/The_Communist_Manifesto
It might be added that a contemporary fulldome activist-artist, Pedro Zaz, has a presentation on the theme of SPHERICAL REVOLUTION, see https://www.somos-arts.org/spherical-revolution-padro-zaz/ Pedro Zaz also elaborates the concept of DOMECRAZY, as in a talk at the *Frameless Forum* of the 13th. Jena FullDome Festival, May 2014, documented at https://www.fddb.org/news/the-domecrazy-talk-by-pedro-zaz/?fbclid=IwAR2QT_dQTLeRlT3QdEJTltPQ3E1lTXHEX-V3fTQOxvfVNugo1wgeZPh7m6Xg

4   For the original wording of Gropius's Bauhaus Manifesto, see "Walter Gropius: Programme of the Staatliches Bauhaus in Weimar" in *Programs and Manifestoes on 20th-Century Architecture*, ed. Ulrich Conrads, MIT Press, Cambridge, Massachusetts, 1971, p. 49. Changes to the original are set *in italics*. See also: https://bauhausmanifesto.com/

5   R. Buckminster Fuller, "The Architect as World Planner," in *Programs and Manifestoes on 20th-Century Architecture,* ed. Ulrich Conrads, MIT Press, Cambridge, Massachusetts, 1971, p. 180. Fuller was addressing the London Congress of the International Union of Architects in 1961.

6   Oskar Schlemmer, "Manifesto for the first Bauhaus Exhibition," *Programs and Manifestoes on 20th-Century Architecture*, ed. Ulrich Conrads, MIT Press, Cambridge, Massachusetts, 1971, p. 70. Minor changes to the original set *in italics*.

7   Gene Youngblood: *Expanded Cinema.* New York, P. Dutton & Co., Inc., 1970. Preface.

8   Program brochure of the 10th FullDome Festival, Jena, May 2015. Editorial by Micky Remann and Kelley Francis: "Frameless Frenzy at the 10th FullDome Festival, " www.fulldome-festival.de

9   Joachim Kruse, "Architektur aus dem Geist der Projektion," in *Wissen in Bewegung. 80 Jahre Zeiss-Planetarium Jena*, ed. Ernst Abbe Stiftung, Jena, 2006, p. 64.

10   Quotation from Clark V. Poling, "Kandinski: Unterricht am Bauhaus," Mannheim, 2002, p. 38. Translation of the German original by the author.

11   Or should it be *surroundity*?

12   The field of spatialized sound, and the principle of wave-formed synthesis, deserve their own manifesto. For an overview of see https://www.idmt.fraunhofer.de/en/institute/projects-products/spatialsound-wave.html

13   *Walter Gropius: Die neue Architektur und das Bauhaus*. First published by Faber & Faber, London, 1935. Quoted from: *Neue Bauhausbücher*, ed. Hans W. Wingler, Berlin, Gebr. Mann Verlag 2003, p. 28.

14   Jonathan Lahey Dronsfield: *Immediacy. In: Immersion - Design - Art:Revisited*. Ed. Lars C. Grabbe, Patrick Rupert-Krause, Norbert M. Schmitz, Marburg, Buechner Verlag 2018, p. 182.

15   See the definition and an example of a Rayogram at The Metropolitan Museum of Art site: https://www.metmuseum.org/art/collection/search/265487

16   Quoted in: Janus 2.0 – God of Fulldome, by Micky Remann. In: Jahrbuch Immersiver Medien 2012. Ed. Institut fuer Immersive Medien im Auftrag des Fachbereichs Medien der Fachhochschule Kiel 2013, p. 95

17   Ed Lantz: Spherical Image Representation and Display: A new Paradigm for Computer Graphics. Siggraph Course no. 2 - Graphic Design and Production for Hemispheric Projection. 1995

18   Jing Augusto Wuethrich: *S is for Episode. Animated Documentary in Full Dome Theatre.* Master thesis Fakultaet Kunst und Gestaltung der Bauhaus-Universitaet Weimar, 2018.

19   Mohammad Jaradat: Fulldome without Chairs. A 360 Degree Animation Project. Bauhaus-Universitaet Weimar, 2017

20   Presented and pronounced by Micky Remann at the IMERSA-summit gala dinner in the Denver Museum of Natural History, Denver, Colorado, February 16th. 2013. By its own mission statement, *IMERSA fosters the growing interest in digital fulldome cinema, immersive entertainment, performance art and virtual experiences through its Summits and activities.* https://www.imersa.org

21   Freely adapted and translated from the original article in German by Micky Remann: *'Immersion' kommt von Eintauchen.* In: Jahrbuch Immersiver Medien 2008-2009. Ed. Eduard Thomas im Auftrag des Fachbereichs Medien der Fachhochschule Kiel, 2009, p. 105-106.

Chapter 6
Smell Is All Around Us:
History, Meaning, and (Immersive!) Applications for Scent

Saskia Wilson-Brown

The Institute for Art and Olfaction, USA

ABSTRACT

While much of today's immersive media claims to be "multi-sensory," in actuality most such works have only audio and visual sensory cues. Scent, a powerful human modality that helps us to understand and derive meaning from the world, is often overlooked. However, scent in the service of art has a long and rich history, especially looking back to its ancient uses in establishing power, mystery, or memorability within religious or political domains. Early attempts at incorporating scent into artistic performances were not well received, perhaps due to inadequate technology of the time. Today a renaissance of olfactory art points to broader acceptance and appreciation of scent in artistic productions. Many artists are taking on the mantle of scent today, and the authors look forward to its increasing application in many forms of immersive media.

INTRODUCTION

This chapter explores the concept of scent as an integral aspect of immersion and immersive media. It starts with a number of examples of its use from history, including an early 20th Century scented performance—an entertainment the public was not ready for—as a method to enhance the meaning inherent in the presentation. Memorable personalities throughout history have employed scent as a defining part of their being and power. This leads us to examine scent and the meanings that it can embody, and then to how the invention of synthetic scents fundamentally changed our relationship to this powerful aspect of our lives. Examples of scent used as artistic expression are also presented, especially the creation of perfumes as a fine art form. Scent in the domain of modern media is surveyed, from early experiments in film to its use in current technological and immersive means of communication and entertainment such as theme park offerings to virtual, augmented and mixed realities (VR, AR, XR). Finally, some

DOI: 10.4018/978-1-7998-2433-6.ch006

thoughts are presented for why and how a person might work with scent, from the technological aspects to context and meaning.

A SCENT PERFORMANCE

When Sadakichi Hartmann took the stage in 1902 to present his 'A Trip to Japan in Sixteen Minutes' (Hartmann, 1913), the New York audience—heretofore enjoying a high-spirited program of music and novelty acts—was talkative, opinionated, and most likely inebriated. They had no time or patience for Hartmann and his delicate aromatic experience. His scents—disseminated by his "Hartmann Perfumator" timed to the tune of a tinkly piano—fared no better. Within a matter of minutes Hartmann found himself shakily slinking off stage, amidst a rowdy chorus of enthusiastic boos and (we imagine) ribald cries of "this stinks!"

A thinker, artist and lover of perfume, Hartmann struggled with a dual heritage in a time where that wasn't the norm. His Japanese mother died when he was a baby and his German father, with whom he had a difficult relationship, summarily brought him to Germany. By the time he was a teenager, now living in America, Japan was as foreign to him as it would be to any other German-raised boy, and yet there was the incontrovertible proof of his heritage, looking out at him every morning from the mirror.

When he conceived of "A Trip to Japan in Sixteen Minutes," one can guess that he hoped to explore his Japanese self from the outside-in. His performance was perhaps as much a voyage of discovery for himself as it was intended to be for his audience. It is no wonder, then, that he chose to accompany his music, his large fans and cheesecloth "perfumator," his *Japonesque* assistants (the program stated: "the Meredith Sisters as the Japanese twin Geisha Girls" (Bradstreet, [2016]), and his fictional narrative of a *grand voyage,* with that most immersive and personal of mediums: scent. Scent, he believed, would render the voyage in vivid strokes. Without it, the experience would be meaningless.[1]

Scent and Meaning

When you study history, you find that the most brilliant characters—the ones that come down to us in high definition—tend to share some common attributes: a keen understanding of human psychology, an uncanny ability to get their way, excellent communication skills, and in many cases, a clever understanding of how spectacle can enhance power. Many of them also understood that scent was an important component of spectacle. It is not by chance that Emperor Constantine expected his processions to be scented, that Napoleon practically bathed in Eau de Cologne, that Fidel Castro surrounded himself with an aromatic cloud of cigar smoke. Scent has almost always accompanied great efforts of conversion along with great efforts of cultural shift—most often led by the great efforts of a charismatic, and often aromatic leader.

It is no surprise then many would-be powerful people intentionally utilized scent to enhance their performances, be it on the vaudeville stages of turn of 20th century New York or on the cultural stages of palaces, reception rooms and regal barges. The history of perfume is stuffed with real-life perfumed performers, a veritable litany of the who's who of geo-political power players.

Some examples among many: Emperor Nero (reputedly) accompanied his feasts with roomfuls of rose. Secret trap doors in the roof would unleash the flowers' petals on his guests from above, while doves dipped in rose oil would be sent careening through the banquet halls, their flapping wings disseminating the aroma to all corners (Johnson & Ryan, 2005; Faraone, 1999). Cleopatra was reported to have perfumed her sails so strongly that her subjects could smell her cortège coming up the Nile (one guesses that this gave them the requisite time to spruce up their temples before her visit).

The list continues. Louis XIV was veritably obsessed with perfume, in particular with the scent of orange blossom. As a sign of favor, he would give his courtiers orange trees, and his power was expressed both in his dress, his ritual, and the aromas he had broadcast through the hallways of Versailles in custom-made *cassolettes*, scent disseminators for incense or potpourri dripping with gold and enamel (Lewis, 1997). The 18th century French courts that followed, certainly, were so perfumed that Louis XV's court became derisively known as "La Cour Parfumée"—the perfumed court. Later, Marie Antoinette's lover Axel de Fersen noted the excess of scent in French high society, and exclaimed in disgust about "the bizarre odor of the salons of this country!"

Indeed, it was scent that (allegedly) helped to blow Marie Antoinette's cover as she tried to flee France in disguise during the Revolution (de Feydeau, 2006). The country's suffering people had long associated beautiful perfume with unchecked power. An unexpectedly pleasant smell led to suspicion, and ultimately served to be one of the sources of her downfall. Only the truly powerful could smell so good: à la guillotine!

There is certainly much mythology within the history of perfume, and it is often hard to separate urban legend from fact. The message is nonetheless clear: ruling classes have throughout time inexorably been linked with pleasant smells, and with perfume. We see this even to this day, with brands like *The Fragrance Kitchen* (founded by Kuwaiti royal Sheikh Majed Al-Sabah) and *Amouage* (founded by the Sultan of Oman Qaboos Bin Said and Prince Sayyid Hamad bin Hamoud al bu Said to preserve Omani traditions of perfumery). Throughout time, then, scent has communicated meaning, and what it has also often communicated is power.

Just as importantly, however, scent has been used to communicate meaning in another equally powerful and influential sphere: religion. The history of religion is rife with aroma. From the incense in ancient Japanese temples, to the sandalwood paste used in Hindu rituals; from the musk and saffron floors of the Islamic conception of paradise to the budget-busting aromatics commissioned for early Christian churches in 4th century Constantinople. And let's not forget the scented associations between the Greek Goddess Aphrodite and the smells of rose, the ocean, and the burnt offerings of myrrh; scents handily serving not just to pacify, flatter and describe the goddess, but also to instigate desire (eros) or love (philia), whence the concept of aroma as "aphrodisiac."

There is a formula for the scent of God in the Old Testament, a combination of materials like myrrh, and cinnamon (Sirach Ecclesiasticus 24: 15). Even the Prophet Muhammad was said to be shiny with aromatic oils, so that his followers could smell him as he walked the streets of Mecca. The theatre of belief, like the theatre of power, is heavily enhanced by scent. For the converted, scent conveys faith, scent signifies worship, and scent communicates the presence of god.

Finally, scent has conveyed something else through time: illness and good health. When the plague hit Medieval Europe, many believe that malodors (what 19th century city-dwellers later called "miasmas") were at the root of the disease. And so scent was used as a ward against illness, carried around in small metal balls known as pomanders for the wealthy, or as simple aromatic vinegar-imbued sponges for the poor. Good scent, then, communicated (and encouraged) health. Bad scent was a sign of (or invited) illness. One might note that this tradition of beliefs continues to this day in aromatherapy.

Shifting Meanings

These liturgical, powerful and healthful associations with scent became more fractured and complex in the 19th and 20th centuries. The increasing availability of synthetic materials made perfumes less expensive, easier to make in large quantities, and therefore allowed more people to consume scent.

When the German and French chemists A. Vogel and Nicholas Guibourt independently isolated a particularly aromatic molecule in 1820, they unwittingly sowed the seeds that would eventually lead to our current multi-national, technology-driven fragrance and flavors industry. Guibourt named this molecule "coumarine." English chemist William Henry Perkin later synthesized the pair's aromatic discovery. Coumarin thus became the first synthetic aromatic molecule, and perfumers took note. The genius perfumer Aimé Guerlain applied it in a perfume called *Jicky* in 1889, and in so-doing, launched a march towards commercialization that continues to this day.

Over the course of the 20th century, increasing development of synthetic aromatics allowed perfumes to be created in larger quantities, for lower cost, and reaching more people. After World War II, a shift in the global western power base from Europe to North America meant a lucrative new market for European perfume companies (look to the history of Chanel No. 5 for a wonderful illustration of this). With these new markets, the perfume industry took steam. Marketing strategies complicated the perception of perfume, with traditional understandings of scent ditched in favor of lucrative and increasingly individualized sales pitches. No longer were there a relatively small number of perfume formulas designed for denizens of royal courts, or a handful of aromatics associated with the gods and goddesses through time. Over the course of the 20th century, a staggering amount of perfume options were developed and put to market. These were increasingly individualized, marketed to young debutantes, sophisticated women about town, outdoorswomen, dandies, family men, businessmen, hippies, power-women, grunge kids, teeny-boppers and so, so, so many more.

And so, with these complicated new trade structures, democratic marketing messages and less wealthy consumers, the multiplicitous meanings of scent became even further fractured. Perfume, itself, became a dizzying series of symbols, in turn representing femininity, masculinity, wealth, poverty, the status of a woman's morals, mood, environment, season, fashion, and everything else you can imagine. In gaining so many meanings, the component aromatics of scent, in many ways, lost meaning entirely.

Olfactory Art

With the advent of more accessible materials also came the first forays into a field that later would come to be known as "olfactory art." At the very dawn of the 20th century, we see that Sadakichi Hartmann was not only a pivotal figure in the history of scent, but was also working with scent in a moment where the meaning of scent in society was beginning to change. And yet, traditional symbolic associations (beauty, power, health, worship, etc.) still carried sway, and he was the inheritor of a long line of implicit social agreement as to how scent could be used as a tool for communication.

Sadakichi was attempting to communicate with scent in a distinctly modern way, where aromas had personal and specific symbolic meaning, associated strongly with his own particular dreams, perceptions and memories. Although increased experimentation with scent in the 19th century had led to creative and technological advances, including coumarin and a notable attempt at a scent piano such as the "Octophone" (Septimus Piesse, 1857), there was, at the time, no obvious precedent for what Hartmann was attempting. But that was all to change: Hartmann was a harbinger of what became what we can only call a "growth industry" in artmaking.

The 20th century ushered in a wealth of artistic work with scent (where scent was used to convey conceptual meaning in the context of a fine arts practice), and many of these works served to tweak and eventually dismantle the perceptions and associations of meaning with scent.

Marcel Duchamp's 'Belle Haleine' (1921) played with femininity, masculinity through a mass-marketed perfume object. Piero Manzoni's 'Merda d'Artista' (1961) proposed his excrement as art piece, and in so-doing served to elevate the material—and its implied scent—or at the very least re-contextualize its meaning. Fluxus artist Takako Saito's 'Spice Chess' in 1972 elevated scented objects to even further conceptual levels, assigning new meanings (a given scent now meant "queen," or "king," or "pawn") and even strategy to understand our own interpretations of scent.

Scent really started to come into its own as a contemporary form of art with the dawn of pop culture (and the synchronous interest in mass market products). The spiritual father of pop culture, Andy Warhol, had a deep interest in scent, famously making the correlation between perfume and "tak[ing] up more space."

This burgeoning attention to scent as creative tool was cemented in 1978 when a Belgian artist penned a smell manifesto called "The Thrill of Working with Odors" (Bleus, 1978). Guy Bleus' missive was by all accounts not very widely received, but it nevertheless marks a point of cultural change, marking a moment in an already fracturing narrative. Indeed, scent was becoming increasingly used to communicate and express abstract ideas in the creative sphere. Signifier of the presence of god and demonstration of power this is not.

As Bleus himself stated it: "using authentic scents [...] could mean an enrichment since a new medium and unexplored form of communication would be introduced" (ibid.)—and he was right.

There are many artists taking on the mantle of scent today, trading ideas and applications in tight knit groups on Facebook and other online forums, and meeting face to face at occasional exhibitions ('Belle Haleine' at Museum Tinguely, Basel in 2015 to 'Perfume: A Sensory Journey' at Somerset House in London in 2017) and conferences (like the annual Experimental Scent Summit, produced by the Institute for Art and Olfaction in collaboration with Berlin's Smell Lab). Notable among them are of course their contemporary pioneers: Sissel Tolaas, Peter de Cupere, Anicka Yi, Maki Ueda, Oswaldo Macia, Boris Raux, Klara Ravat, and so many more. Increasing efforts to organize and bring visibility to these olfactory artists are underway, centered largely through public-facing groups like the loose-knit social practice collective clustered under the banner of The Institute for Art and Olfaction in the United States, Nez Magazine in France, the efforts of Claus Noppeney in Switzerland and Ashraf Osman in Lebanon, Caro Verbeek's Odorama program at Mediamatic in the Netherlands, Perfume Playground in Australia, A Library of Olfactiove Material in Glasgow, and Smell Lab in Berlin, amongst others. Although the practices are diverse, most of these artists and organizations are actively and frenetically exploring and attempting to codify how working with scent can convey new meanings, be it social, emotional, historic or even data-driven.

The increasingly fractured significance we apply to scent means that when our personal experiences, memories and preferences are expressed in smell, they are often done so through an uneasy combination of assumptions. "Timeless" meanings like "Frankincense smells holy!" are assumed to be general understandings, and specific individual perspectives ("The smell of chocolate cake reminds me of my childhood summers in the south of Vietnam") are assumed to be relatable.

Thus, a young trans woman in Atlanta can perceive the smell of rose as a meaningful signifier of her feminine identity while a Somali scholar in Dubai can concurrently ascribe to it the symbolic meaning of traditional hospitality. An elder from a Canadian First Peoples tribe can understand sage in the context of medicine and healing, while an affluent banker in Hong Kong can understand it as a luxury object in the form of a refreshing room spray.

The meaning of any given smell is heterogeneous: as Derrida would have it with language, so it is with scent. Traditional understandings, fragmented as they already are amongst cultures and epoch, are further splintered with every personal memory, micro-niche, trend, marketing pitch, and emotional analysis. In our globalized world everyone can see or experience everything, and everything means something to everybody. What this means for people working with scent is that, in fact, nothing means *one* thing to everybody (at least not without a hefty dose of contextual information). In other words, aromatic materials have no consistent meaning. And therein lies the very primary problem when working with scent.

Scent in Film

When compared to the output of other forms of olfactory art in the 20th century, scent has come up as a communication tool a surprisingly small amount in time-based mediums like film, taking place mostly in bursts of frenetic energy put forth by movie producers-cum-showmen.

Efforts to scent narrative had taken place on at least two notable instances (Sadakichi Hartmann's in 1902 and an aromatic dissemination at a 1923 music revue), but when Leonardo Bonzi teamed up with Walter Reade to add scent to a screening of Carlo Lizzani's documenatry *Behind the Great Wall*, they produced the first in a rogue's gallery of uneasy attempts to aromatize film. Their *AromaRama*-enhanced screening in 1950 went off middlingly, with *The New York Times* disparaging its very purpose. "Check off the novel experience as precisely what we've labeled it—a stunt," film critic Bosley Crowther sniffed. "The artistic benefit of it is here demonstrated to be nil" (Crowther, 1959).

Their failure didn't discourage the director-technologist duo of Jack Cardiff and Hans Laube, who premiered their *Smell-O-Vision* system the following year with *Scent of Mystery*. Where Crowther's review of *Behind the Great Wall* stated that the filmmaking was excellent but that the scent merely served to "confuse the atmosphere," in this case he felt that both the filmmaking *and* the scent were poor. As he put it: "It is an artless, loose-jointed 'chase' picture [...]. And whatever novel stimulation it might afford with the projection of smells appears to be dubious and dependent upon the noses of the individual viewers and the smell-projector's whims" (Crowther, 1960).

Perhaps poor Mr. Crowther wasn't a fan of smell. Nevertheless, *Scent of Mystery* had the benefit of having a more robust scent dissemination system. Laub's *Smell-O-Vision* apparatus placed little tubes on the back of every seat, so the scent—at the very least—was intelligible. Another advance was that *Scent of Mystery* had been written with scent in mind. Scent was a both a critical aspect of the story (the scent of a mysterious woman) and provided clues to the plot. A scene where Peter Lorre appears to drink coffee was paired with the scent of alcohol for comedic effect, and a tobacco smell was broadcast at a crucial moment in order to clue the audience in to the presence of a murderer.

Alas, it didn't work. According to Crowther: "[…] we do not advise the viewer to depend upon these clues, or the alleged clues from the perfume of his victim. They are—shall we say—indistinct" (ibid.).

Scented screenings were largely left aside until 1980, when John Waters produced a scratch-and-sniff card in support of *Polyester*, a visceral smell-fest that the Variety review called a "cheap gimmick" (Variety Staff, 1980). But that, of course, was the point. This was John Waters, after all: in failing to charm the critics, his effort was all the more successful. Certainly, the scents were intelligible, and had the added benefit of being opt-in. The audience could smell them—or not—depending on their sensitivities and desires. And with included smells such as flatulence and skunk, this was a very important component, indeed.

These nascent efforts at including scent in film have been minimal and problematic when compared to equivalent yet more successful efforts in contemporary art. This distinction can be ascribed in large part to technology. The scents-in-the-air-ducts approach in the *AromaRama* system and the individualized tubes in the *Smell-O-Vision* system both produced technically unreliable results. Scratch-and-sniff cards, on the other hand, worked well, but broke the filmic moment with large instructional cues on screen followed by frenetic scratching from the audience. For John Waters—a director who good-naturedly but very consciously plays with kitsch, camp, and audience reaction—this attention break-down proved no problem. One hesitates, however, to imagine it working in the context of a drama, a tragedy, or an action movie.

The failure can also be ascribed to the development and treatment of the scent elements. With the exception of *Scent of Mystery*, the smells were added on later as a marketing idea. In that way they were not fully actualized into the story, as conceived by the creative stakeholders at the beginning of the project's conception.

In such a precise medium as film, timing, tone and timbre need to be impeccably delivered. It relies also on an attentive but passive audience. Until recently, the technology available to disseminate scent hasn't matched the technology required by the medium, and so a scented screening required colossal efforts in tech development alone, or costly add-ons like scratch-and-sniff cards. Most filmmakers would have been hard-pressed to allocate the budget and time to harnessing the scent flow in a large theater or find themselves willing to interrupt their audience's attention. It is no wonder, then, that most 20th century filmmakers chose not to take on the challenge of adding aroma to their storytelling.

Contemporary Scenting

More recent efforts to combine scent with moving image show promise for the possibility for scent in narrative media. They do this in two ways: by solving the precision issue in audience scent dissemination, and by paying proper attention to the scents themselves.

Disney California Adventure's *Soarin'* (premiered 2001) and Universal Studios' *Shrek 4-D* (premiered 2003) both deliver perfectly calibrated scent cues, timed impeccably with the visual narrative without breaking the audience's admittedly already fractured attention. Both, also, are delivered in custom-built theatres. In Disney's case the experience feels more like a ride than a movie: the chairs soar above the ground and wind is pushed through your hair through in-seat air vents. In Universal's case the experience comes complete with mechanically-moving chairs, haptic triggers, and temperature cues. Nevertheless, they work well as immersive storytelling experiences, and scent serves to add a sincere and unexpected element of subtle magic.

Outside the big budget worlds of amusement parks, independent perfumers, storytellers and unclassifiable creative people are also tinkering with using scent in narrative. In 2009 perfumer Christophe Laudamiel and writer/director Matthew Stewart presented *Green Aria: A ScentOpera* at the Guggenheim in New York. This thirty-minute performance based on a libretto loosely exploring technology and nature boldly placed scent front and center of importance. At the beginning of the opera, Laudamiel's 35 scents were introduced one by one as narrative protagonists, much like opera stars would be on a stage. Scent was given the same creative and narrative value as composers Nico Muhly and Valgeir Sigursson's score.

The performance was a success. *The New York Times* called it "beguiling" (Tommasini, 2009), and *The New Scientist* called it "impressive to say the least" (Gefter, 2009). This was possible not only because of personalized tweaks in the dissemination technology, but also because of the level of attention given to the performance of the molecules. It succeeded where others had failed because of the thought put into the scent compositions.

For dissemination, the team used a system similar to Hans Laube's *Smell-O-Vision*. Fed by a central control module, the apparatus ended with individualized pipes feeding a "scent microphone" installed on every seat. Crucially, these "microphones" were adjustable, allowing the audience to move them according to their comfort levels. In addition, Laudamiel used his background as a chemist to hone in on how the scent performed in time and space; how long it took each scent to reach the audience in each individual tube. This allowed for a more precise timing of scent to music. In addition to that, Laudamiel—who is a highly talented and well-trained perfumer—spent almost two years on scent development. Each and every one of the 35 scents was thoughtful, worked, conceptual and decidedly unique.

Laudamiel and Stewart showed that critical success was possible when using smell in story. Their legacy is clear: this independent effort at olfactory narrative inspired cross-genre artists, filmmakers, and storytellers to increasingly explore the potential for scent in both contemporary art (as we have seen), but also in story-reliant time-based media. Thus we saw—subsequent to *Green Aria*—an explosion of cross-modal activity: in 2013, the Institute for Art and Olfaction re-staged Sadakichi Hartmann's failed *Trip to Japan* at the Hammer Museum, a contemporary art institution in Los Angeles. Up-to-date technology and an art museum context meant that the week-long installation-cum-performance skirted the challenges faced by Hartmann, and it was a sold out success. In 2014, Dutch group Polymorf created an immersive installation called *Famous Deaths* where attendees were invited to slide themselves into mortuary coolers containing the sounds and scents of four celebrities' last moments. They toured this immersive and cross-genre art installation at film festivals around the world. More firmly placing herself in the AR, VR and XR world(s), storyteller and technologist Grace Boyle founded a group called The Feelies, which utilizes all our senses in the service of story, with a strong attention to scent. Her celebrated *Munduruku* (produced in collaboration with Greenpeace and Alchemy VR) was released in 2017. The VR film features a narrative of six scents that combine with haptic cues and infrasonics to enhance the story of a fight to save the heart of the Amazon. She succeeded: *Munduruku* won awards at Sheffield Doc/Fest, Raindance Film Festival, and the Future of Storytelling in New York.

So what is different about these newer efforts to incorporate scent into narrative? As we have seen, it might have something to do the incremental developments in the dissemination technologies. It might also have to do with the fact that scent was a creative consideration from the very beginning of story development and treated with care as a narrative device.

However, the largest part of their success surely lies in the shifting relationship between story and audience. Whereas *AromaRama* and *Smell-O-Vision* counted on the goodwill of a passive spectator to submit to the additional stimulus, culture has since changed—as has the conception of the audience's role. Contemporary experiences reach audiences (or should we call them participants?) who are already primed for clues and cues, their bodies moving through space and their hands reaching out for story elements. Enhanced storytelling experiences are therefore ready for added stimulus, and scent can be a subtle signal that compels further curiosity from an already active mind. One imagines that John Waters understood this coming shift when he chose to produce his scent narrative through a mechanism that encouraged personal choice.

Our contemporary audiences are prepared and ready to receive the implied meanings that scent can bring, and our storytelling technologies rely increasingly on these active, engaged audience. Thus, the feasibility of working with scent becomes increasingly apparent. Its future success now largely relies on newer, smaller, and more affordable technologies.

TECHNOLOGY

As the technology powering moving images has developed and evolved over the turn of the 20th and 21st Century, so too has the tech powering scent. Indeed, the will to work with scent compels a need for newer and better scent dissemination technology. Hartmann was content to use large fans and cheesecloth to disseminate his scents, but newer storytellers are more concerned with the potentially magical effects of unexpected and hidden scent technology and—as we have seen—the audience's agency. Theatricality thus increasingly gives way to invisibility and choice, and the uncanny results of a subtle scent surprise.

This is nowhere more apparent than in the VR/AR/XR, or immersive spaces.

Jacquelyn Ford Morie has pioneered the technology for seamless scent dissemination in VR experiences with her Scent Collar, which has been in stages of development and production since 2004 (with a patent registered in 2009). The scent collar's purpose is to precision-time scent dissemination in virtual narratives, triggered by actions and intersections in the virtual space. This allows VR storytellers to add a higher degree of embodied reality to the virtual experience. While this is a potentially important tool for storytellers, the tech also shines when used in social applications such as training (particularly for high-stress jobs that contain highly unpleasant odors). The military, for instance, has made use of scent collar in their VR scenarios, bettering prepare the soldiers for the noxious and potentially debilitating smells that they might encounter on a battlefield.

The running order of technology development with scent includes increasing efforts to produce smaller and smaller automated scent dissemination devices with more and more personalized applications. So in cell phone technology, so in scent. The oPhone, released by David Edwards in 2014, is an example of such an effort. Using a digital interface to trigger smells from far away, the oPhone emits scent through a receiver (Walikainen, 2014). Much like a telephone, the system allows a person to send an aromatic experience to a friend in another location, provided that the friend has the requisite aromatic components.

Meanwhile, German theatre producer Wolfgang Georgsdorf had been working on theatrical dissemination systems, hoping to fix some of the issues of propagating scent into large spaces. His "Smeller 2.0" takes the form of an impressively aesthetic room-sized apparatus that allowed precision timing on scent dissemination without personalized apparatus (the tube-to-seat method used in *Smell-O-Vision* and *Green Aria*, for example). In 2017 he premiered his Smeller 2.0 in a three-month long festival of scent he called *Osmodrama*, where the capacity of the machine was demonstrated through performances in a multi-functional and constantly evolving space (Thaddeus-Johns, 2019). In addition to being precisely timed, this scent disseminator could be installed in any theatre, dance hall or nightclub. He thus removed the physical bind between scent dissemination and fixed seats, creating an easily-adoptable model for any theatre, anywhere.

There are plenty more experiments going on. Examples include walk-in scent pods with scent cues supplementing a linear aural and visual narrative, countless variations on Morie's Scent Collar, and environmental explorations in museum-like environments where scent cues trigger new meanings. Getty Villa produces occasional scent-objects that serve to supplement the didactic texts in their museum. Most recently, The Color Factory incorporated scent triggers in their newest public space in Houston, which opened in October 2019.

Technological development of course comes with its own set of issues. As many people remind one another within the scent world, there is no RGB of scent. Each molecule is unique unto itself, and each accord (a combination of molecules to make an aromatic impression) requires very specific building blocks. In order to get an endless amount of scent possibilities, then, you need an even more endless amount of molecules. This serves to hamper the effort to minimize technology size and cost. Easily surmounted with a system of pods (as used in the oPhone and Scent Collars), this nonetheless means that digitizing scent—truly—is not possible with how we understand scent today.

Nevertheless, the technology developed by Morie, Edwards, Georgsdorf and others is still relatively new, and it is moving quickly. If this progress continues, scent in immersive experiences—both virtual and in real life (IRL)—will soon be standard fare.

WHY WORK WITH SCENT

Working with scent in a public setting can be complex and rewarding. The complications relate to how the public perceives the scents and the challenges of scent dissemination technology. The rewards, on the other hand, come with the magical moment when a smell hits its target, and the audience gasps with recognition and pleasure. It's a visceral click.

Although we would like to think that scents carry specific signifiers that everyone can relate to, the application of meaning to a particular scent, in truth, can be quite complex. As an example, common knowledge has it that lavender is soothing. And for the most part it is, simply because it's a popular ingredient featured in a lot of scented products that are advertised as calming. Consider, however, that the soothing effects are often received in controlled opt-in contexts: the application of a lotion, a spritz on your linen before bedtime, an aromatic pump in a healer's office. If you had had the misfortune of being the victim of some violence in a lavender field, you would find the smell anything but soothing. This presents an obvious problem when you're trying to communicate a concept through scent to a large and inherently varied group of people (barring, of course, fecal and rotten smells, which can indeed have notably consistent perceptual results. Disgust seems to be the common denominator).

The good news is that context is everything, and storytellers are nothing if not context creators. In more passive experiences of scent—for instance when sitting in a theatre—a scent can be heavily underlined and cued by music and visual inputs. However, this tends to work best with a sort of linear parallel: red for the smell of cinnamon, orange for the smell of orange, yellow for the smell of lemon, etc. Abstraction or mixed signals complicate this one-to-one relationship. If someone is shown an oily brown color and fed jarring music while smelling a molecule called hexenol-cis-3, the perception might be focused on the tang of gasoline. Shown the color green, suddenly the scent becomes—indubitably—fresh grass. This can be very fun to play with, of course, but can also mean that the joke is sometimes lost on the audience.

In a 2017 screening of *The Scent of Mystery* in a 600 seat theatre in Los Angeles, the production team had the opportunity to put this to the test with the scent gag that replaced the visual cue of coffee with the smell of alcohol. Half the audience got coffee, and half got alcohol. The overwhelming result was that the half that got alcohol (a good strong cognac) didn't get the joke. People simply didn't perceive the smell strongly enough as alcohol to override their more developed visual input telling them it was the coffee. Perhaps they had never smelled cognac before. More likely, the one-to-one relationship intended between what they *thought* they smelled and what they *definitely* saw was too tenuous. They didn't have the confidence in their olfactory perception to believe that they had perceived a joke. Or, possibly, they simply couldn't smell cognac when their eyes saw coffee.

Another issue when working with the public is that of people's diverse smell sensitivity. Often for biological reasons such as advanced age, trauma, or selective anosmia, some people simply don't smell as well as others. Conversely, other people are extremely sensitive to smell. Although allergies are rare, and mostly caused by direct skin contact with an undiluted aromatic, a good portion of an unprepared audience will often register discomfort when exposed to large amounts of scent, no matter how delicate and thoughtful the dissemination. It becomes a question of adequately preparing the audience, or—perhaps more crucially— providing them with the option to control the experience, or to opt out altogether.

For these reasons, working with scent requires excellent preparation, adherence to safety guidelines, a lot of test runs, and making an effort to predict your audience. Is this an audience that is accustomed to smelling? Is this an audience that might err on the side of chemophobia (most often manifested as a general dislike of "synthetic" molecules)? One thing is for sure: propagating scent to a group of yoga teachers will be a different experience than propagating a scent to a group of chefs, a set of Canadians will be different than a set of Cubans. Cultural references vary, further compounding the issues we've already seen around divergent personal meanings.

FINAL THOUGHTS: WHITHER ARE YE, SCENT

With the shifting meanings, the hyper-personal symbolic associations, and the challenges artists face corralling and controlling molecules, working with scent in the context of immersive applications can be challenging. Be it some variation of virtual reality, augmented reality, digital or real-life storyworlds, or simple installations at any scale, it can be hard to control and often hard to predict how people will react. However, when it works, it's uncanny, it's effective, and often it can allow even the most jaded of audiences to feel something memorable.

Moreover, the concerns people face about alienation and anomie, often placed squarely on the shoulders of increasingly digital experiences, are nicely solved by the decidedly non-digital act of smelling. Scent can therefore also serve to re-embody digital experience. From a narrative perspective, it has the possibility of playing with our understanding of our virtual environments.

The technology is still developing, although hindered by minimal scientific research and incremental technological advances. One can nevertheless imagine a future where the technology will support widespread adoption of scent as a communication tool. Scent disseminators are getting smaller, are less expensive, and have increased capacity for customizable aromatic output. Perhaps one day we will see a theatre chain where scent dissemination with countless aromatic possibilities will come as standard format, scent as a feature in every VR headset or AR experience, or scent curation as vital as visual curation in every museum.

In the fall of 2019, Frederik Duerinck—one part of the team behind the Dutch group responsible for *Famous Deaths* (Polymorf)—launched the world's first storefront devoted to Artificial Intelligence-created scents: *Algorithmic Perfumery*.[2] Although the technology behind the AI capacities is so complex that it is practically unreplicable at this stage (at least for us mere mortals), the tool now exists for anyone to walk in, pay their money, and create an unimaginable variation of perfumes for an unimaginable variation of people. The focus here is on perfume–as–product, but the applications are staggering. With the launch of AI perfume creation, Duerink has also in one fell swoop removed another problem: access to perfumers, and to aromatic materials. We're beginning to see part of the solution manifesting, in front of our very eyes.

If a comparative effort were to be put into the development of scent dissemination devices—if the existing work being done would find the requisite support to be seen through—we would soon have the other part of the puzzle resolved. Then, we could leave the tech and the access problems behind, and focus on the hardest part: the meaning, the context, the story and—of course—the careful crafting and selection of the scents themselves. It will be up to the creative people, storytellers, curators and artists to design better experiences and more meaningful interactions. Only when scent is fully harnessed as a communication tool, will our immersive experiences truly be immersive.

Let's get to work!

REFERENCES

Bleus, G. (1978). *The Thrill of Working with Odours, A Smell Manifesto* [Mail Art Archive]. Retrieved from http://www.mailart.be/thrill.html

Bradstreet, C. (2016). A Trip to Japan in Sixteen Minutes: Sadakichi Hartmann's Perfume Concert and the Aesthetics of Scent. In P. di Bello & G. Koureas (Eds.), *Art, History and the Senses: 1830 to the Present*. Oxfordshire, UK: Routledge, Taylor & Francis Group.

Crowther, B. (1959, Dec. 10). Smells of China; Behind Great Wall Uses AromaRama. *The New York Times*.

Crowther, B. (1960, Feb. 9). Screen: Olfactory Debut: Scent of Mystery Opens at Warner. *The New York Times*.

de Feydeau, E. (2006). A Scented Palace (J. Lizop, Trans.). London, UK: I.B. Tauris & Co., Ltd.

Faraone, C. A. (1999). *Ancient Greek Love Magic*. Boston, MA: Harvard University Press.

Gefter, A. (2009). Green Aria: An opera for your nose. *New Scientist, 5*. Retrieved from https://www.newscientist.com/article/dn17236-green-aria-an-opera-for-your-nose/

Hartmann, S. (1913, July). In Perfume Land. *Forum, 50*(1), I-1.

Johnson, M., & Ryan, T. (2005). *Sexuality in Greek and Roman Society and Literature*. London, UK: Routledge.

Lewis, W. H. (1997). *The Splendid Century: Life in the France of Louis XIV*. Long Grove, IL: Waveland Press Inc.

Septimus Piesse, G. W. (1857). The Art of Perfumery And Methods of Obtaining the Odors of Plants. Philadelphia: Lindsay and Blakiston.

Thaddeus-Johns, J. (2019). Welcome to the Cinema of Smells, where Movies are a Different Kind of Cheesy. *The Outline*. Retrieved from https://theoutline.com/post/7044/wolfgang-georgsdorf-the-smeller-osmodrama

Tommasini, A. (2009, June 1). Opera to Sniff at: A Score Offers Uncommon Scents. *The New York Times*.

Variety Staff. (1980, Dec. 31). Polyester [film review]. *Variety*.

Walikainen, D. (2014, Feb. 11). Scents that are Sent: oPhone Delivers Aromas. *Michigan Tec News*. Retrieved from https://www.mtu.edu/news/stories/2014/february/scents-sent-ophone-delivers-aromas.html

ADDITIONAL READING

Burr, C. (2006). Smellbound. *The New York Times*. Retrieved from https://www.nytimes.com/2006/11/19/magazine/19style_perfume.t.html

Henshaw, V., McLean, K., Medway, D., Perkins, C., & Warnaby, G. (Eds.). (2018). *Designing with Smell: Practices, Techniques and Challenges*. Oxfordshire, UK: Routledge, Taylor & Francis Group.

Legro, M. (2013). A Trip to Japan in Sixteen Minutes. *Believer Magazine*. Retrieved from https://believermag.com/a-trip-to-japan-in-sixteen-minutes/

Osman, A. (2013). *Olfactory Art*. Postgraduate Programme in Curating; Institute for Cultural Studies in the Arts. Zürcher Hochschule der Künste.

Stewart, S. (2007). *Cosmetics and Perfumes in the Roman World*. Gloucestershire, UK: Tempus.

Thompson, C. J. S. (2006). *Perfumes of Ancient Roman Times*. Whitefish, MN: Kessinger Publishing, LLC.

KEY TERMS AND DEFINITIONS

Accord: A combination of molecules combined to make an aromatic impression.

Anosmia: Also known as smell blindness, anosmia means the inability to detect certain or all smells.

Chemophobia: Originally a term to describe a dislike or fear of any chemicals, it has now come to also mean a dislike of synthetic scent materials, or scents in a closed environmental setting that may incur a reaction in some people.

Synthetic: The term synthetic refers to any chemical, including scents, that was created by humans in a laboratory. It is contrasted with materials derived from a naturally occurring source.

ENDNOTES

[1]   To see the archives of Hartmann's manuscripts, the interested can visit https://oac.cdlib.org/findaid/ark:/13030/tf7s2007q4/entire_text/

[2]   To see more about this effort, see the *Algorithmic Perfumery website at* https://algorithmicperfumery.com/

Chapter 7
The Intersections of Creativity, Technology, and the Mind:
How This Applies to Immersive Projects

Audri Phillips
Robot Prayers, USA

ABSTRACT

This chapter examines the relationships between technology, the human mind, and creativity. The chapter cannot possibly cover the whole spectrum of the aforementioned; nonetheless, it covers highlights that especially apply to new immersive technologies. The nature of creativity, creativity studies, the tools, languages, and technology used to promote creativity are discussed. The part that the mind and the senses—particularly vision—play in immersive media technology, as well as robotics, artificial intelligence (AI), computer vision, and motion capture are also discussed. The immersive transmedia project Robot Prayers is offered as a case study of the application of creativity and technology working hand in hand.

INTRODUCTION

As a child, I read a book a day and had no fear of growing old. I reasoned I would always be able to pick up a book, and escape to another reality. I wish I had the same surety now!

Mankind has a desire, or perhaps an instinct, for experiencing other lives, environments, and realities. This drive or instinct may be at the core of our imagination. Did it contribute to the development of our creativity? When did humanity start exhibiting this peculiarity? Do other animals have this same desire? When did mankind develop this urge to escape to other realities? Was it early on when sitting around a campfire telling stories about adventures on a hunt? Was it earlier during the era of the cave paintings? Was it because we were transported by awe when confronted with the beauty of nature?

We developed words, languages, visuals, sounds, coding, which became, and are, our vehicles for communication, discovery, invention, expression, and escaping to other realms.

Did our creativity and technology arise first as survival tools?

DOI: 10.4018/978-1-7998-2433-6.ch007

Each new development of human technology has been an exercise in mankind's creativity. These new technologies have not only trained our brains to take in information in new ways, but perhaps have also expanded our brain's abilities by creating new perceptions of time and space.

The historic path is long and full of examples of mankind's creativity alongside technology. This path includes humanity's attempts to explore different environments, and live other lives through performances, plays, books, movies, immersive realities—interactive and not—and of course the coming interactions with virtual beings.

The creative project *Robot Prayers,* the case study in this chapter, is an immersive media project designed to express itself in many formats such as virtual reality (VR)/augmented reality (AR), and fulldome shows. The project, and the robots in *Robot Prayers*, are a prime example of the intersection of creativity, the mind, and technology. In a project that is on the cutting edge, the pipeline the includes hardware and software is a big part of the creative process and will be discussed in this chapter.

Technology influences our creative output, our minds create our technology, and how our minds process and takes in information influence both. This chapter examines the complicated relationship between the three, while admitting there is still much to be learned. Questions are raised, and hopefully more questions will occur to the reader leading to a further desire to explore the subject. Questions can be the directions to truth.

WHAT IS CREATIVITY

Michael Grybko, neuroscience research scientist and engineer from the Department of Psychology at the University of Washington defines creativity this way:

In science, we define 'creativity' as an idea that is novel, good, and useful. It's a little broader than the Oxford Dictionary's definition, where it's just the ability to create, because that doesn't really say much. You can create something and it's not very useful or it just won't work well. (Grybko, 2016)

Another definition of "creativity" from the *Cambridge Academic Content Dictionary* states that creativity is: "the ability to produce original and unusual ideas, or to make something new or imaginative."

THE CREATIVE PROCESS

There have been many studies and theories on creativity and the brain. Creativity doesn't happen in any one region of the brain. Most theories boil down to the fact that creativity depends first on being open to a free flow of thoughts, and secondly on a lack of inhibition. Finally, executive reasoning and logic, are employed to decide which of the creative ideas and thoughts can be useful.

John Baer in his book *Domain Specificity of Creativity* (2016), and Mark A. Runco in his book *Divergent Thinking and Creative Potential Creativity* (2013), talk about creativity, and also about creativity tests for divergent thinking and convergent thinking. Neuroscientists define three types of creative thought: convergent thinking, divergent thinking, and intuition. Convergent thinking is the process of figuring out a concrete solution to an idea. IQ tests generally involve convergent thinking. Tests that have only one answer require convergent thinking. Convergent thinking helps us find the best possible solution to a problem. Ambiguity unwanted. One test for convergent thinking is called the "Remote Associates Test" (RAT) (Mednick, 1968) A typical RAT item would give you three words and ask you to think of a word (or words) that links all three together. You are finding the connections between the words, which may have no obvious connection.

Divergent thinking starts with one takeoff point and from that you come up with numerous ideas. With divergent thinking, you are brainstorming many different ideas to solve a problem. Divergent thinking is free flowing, where convergent thinking is more systematic and logical. Divergent thinking is especially useful for creating many different solutions to a problem.

There is also a divergent thinking test. It is called the "Torrance Test of Creativity" (Torrance, 1977). In the Torrance Test you are given a problem, and a timeframe within which you come up with as many solutions as possible.

An intuition is when we understand something right away without conscious reasoning. It can be an instinctive feeling. Understanding how creativity works in the human brain is also a possible road map to creating AI that helps us with our problem solving, and creative solutions using the tools and technology we advance with. How do you create free association in a machine ... in AI? How do we encourage free association in our own brains to know how to apply that to a machine?

This random meeting of ideas that humans are capable of is the spark of true creativity. It is one of the powers of a poem or immersive experience, not directing but empowering the mind to make the abstract and random connections that would not happen with an enforced linear story.

Immersive media is ideal for creating an environment, and an expansive experiential experience to be explored, where free thoughts are encouraged. Participants can make their own discoveries. The fourth wall is removed, and the individual viewer is a participant. The mind is opened up to its own creativity.

THE CREATIVE FLOW

The word "flow" has become a very popular way now to describe what the word "Zen" means—living in the moment—and it is a critical part of the creative process. The best flow states promote awe. This awe is a form of escape to a timeless moment. In a state of flow creative people can bring in many disparate thoughts and find a connection between them.

Alan Watts (1915-1973), was a philosopher and a studier of comparative religions and Asian philosophies, which he interpreted for Western audiences. Watts often talked about Zen states (Watts, 1936) and the mysterious nature of creativity (Watts, 1995).

There have been many proponents of the notion that the altered state achieved through hallucinogens serves as an aid to creativity. Albert Hoffman (1906-2008) discovered lysergic acid (LSD). There are numerous quotes from him about the mystic qualities of LSD and the wonderful visions he saw when using it. He created paintings and poetry inspired by his use of LSD (Hagenback & Wertmüller 2013).

Creative people often start projects by gathering together many thoughts, ideas, sparks and memories in various ways, and then slowly narrow this database down to create something meaningful. It is a process, much like a painter who has the initial idea, and uses the process of painting itself to allow something new and unexpected to emerge.

THE LANGUAGE OF CREATIVITY

Our languages have been around for thousands of years and contain knowledge that we may not be consciously aware of. Each language embeds the culture and knowledge of many generations. Our language is the framework from which and by which we perceive things. As such it forms the base of our thought processes and our creativity. For example, some cultures have only one word for snow, while it is often mentioned that in the Eskimo language there are 50 different words for snow. The words we use to describe our creative technology, especially immersive technologies, are numerous and increasing at a fast pace. There are so many terms being tried out to describe essentially the same things—almost a new one every week! Who really knows or understands the differences between the terms augmented reality, mixed reality, spatial computing, and XR?

The words we use may have developed initially from metaphors, from a concrete word that had one meaning and gained more as it was used. Researchers Lakoff and Johnson (1980) explore this idea in depth in their book, *Metaphors We Live By*. The word *face* most likely initially just referred to the actual physical anatomy of a face. A connection was made to the idea, or act of a person turning their face towards something. Then the word face took on more meanings, such as being the front of something, or something is aimed toward something else, such as an object, a person, or an idea. Metaphors such as, "We face up to something," and "Face the music" came about.

Feeling is another interesting word. The English language has given *feeling* two meanings. It recognizes that not only are feelings related to our emotions, but our body as well. Often when we have strong emotions, feelings, we feel them in our body. This may be one way we know we are alive. We feel and we know we are alive. This is a reason why using haptics are so important to include to mixed reality projects.

Another word example is *vision*. It connotes both a physical sense, and also an imaginative conception or anticipation, a dream. The French word for vision—*vue*—seems to also have this double meaning. One can wonder how many other languages besides English contains more than one meaning for the word vision.

A vision lights up our minds. To create a powerful immersive experience, we need to know what our dreams are, what our visions are. When you bring up the word vision you have to start talking about light. There are similarities now to the Renaissance where artists and scientists were not so far apart in their study of the universe. The study of light has always been central to artists and scientists, now and then.

In an 1890 book I have handed down from my grandfather, *The Theory of Light* by Thomas Preston, is this definition of Optics:

The Science of Optics is a branch of natural philosophy which treats of the nature of light and vision. In its domain we meet with a multiple of experiments of exquisite beauty, and investigations which afford ample scope for all the refinements of modern mathematical analysis. (Preston, 1890)

The mathematics and science of light is central in much of our immersive technology. Starting with photography and film, it is now vital to 3D computer rendering programs, and most recently—to the development of lightfield technology.

METAPHORS, A TOOL OF CREATIVITY

Metaphors are a powerful tool for creating and encouraging free association. Artists and writers have found metaphors to be extremely important in their work. They help convey the ideas and meanings in the work, the theme, and storylines. They are used in the many of the stories found in *Robot Prayers*. Metaphors give work an abstract quality. It is the difference between telling someone the sky is blue and showing someone the sky. They can add depth to our work. We use them in our storytelling, in our visual representations, our poetry, and our everyday speech.

Moby Dick is one big whale-sized metaphor (Melville, 1902). The animation of a bird flying upwards is a metaphor for freedom or escape. The making and understanding of metaphors falls into all three categories of creative thought. Your search for a metaphor is wide ranging, but you want to narrow it down to something very specific. You understand a metaphor right away without having to logically break its meaning down. Metaphors are a doorway to beyond what is right in front of us, the obvious. To use another metaphor, they are a shot across the bow. They rattle your cage. They pry open your mind. Metaphors state that something is something else, create a likeness, or analogy between ideas and objects. The pendulum swings both ways. A metaphor can be representative or symbolic of something else. Feather your nest. Are the virtual worlds we create metaphors for the real world?

In creating the stories and themes of *Robot Prayers* (Figure 1), metaphors have been important. For example; all of the creatures and robot characters can be thought of as stand-ins for mankind. *Robot Prayers,* as in every creative project, first the concept, themes, and stories, must be developed but with one important caveat—the concepts, themes and stories are designed to take advantage of what immersive media is best for, creating experiential experiences which will allow participants to make their own discoveries, rather than directing them with strict linear storylines.

It is designed to allow the participants in the project as well as the audience to ponder questions and explore possible answers. Questions such as; Are we physical machines trying to create machines in our image? What was that biblical phrase...? What are the ethics we should be employing in AI? Without getting into the whole question of is there a spirit and a soul, *Robot Prayers* asks how does creativity play into the question of consciousness? As we watch the characters in *Robot Prayers* strive to solve these questions and go on their adventures, we can ask, what is the point of life, and how does one fulfill one's potential and creativity versus merely surviving?

THE MIND

The brain analyzes the sensory information it receives, but our brain also creates its own states independent of what the senses are taking in i.e. be it drug-induced or dreaming. The brain can create temporal illusions which distort time, slowing it down, speeding it up, or changing the order of events. All play a part in creativity and are used and mimicked in immersive works.

The brain also colors everything it takes in. To paraphrase Immanuel Kant, a well-known philosopher from the 18th century, we cannot directly experience anything, or have knowledge of things in themselves because our perception of reality is filtered through the internal structures of our mind (Kant, 2018). If we are to agree with Kant, then science is really the study of how the human mind works, and how it perceives the surrounding universe.

Figure 1. Performance of Robot Prayers in The Vortex Dome. dancer Edward Fury
Source: Image courtesy of Kate McCallum.

We can even go as far as to say our minds create our reality. But if there is a connection between all people then perhaps there is a consensus on the reality we are creating, and the reality created is not just in one individual mind.

FOOLING OUR BRAINS TO CREATE AN IMMERSIVE REALITY

To paraphrase, Ray Kurzweil, inventor and futurist now at Google, speaking at a TED talk (Kurzweil, 2009), "We can now see with brain scanning how our brain creates our thoughts, and how our thoughts form our brain."

To create an immersive reality that is believable we must understand how our brains work, how they take in and process data from the real world, and how the data that is taken in is organized, stored and prioritized. It has been discovered that the closer we come to fooling our brains—our senses, vision, hearing, taste, smell, and feel—through techniques like haptics and mimicking the human vestibular system, the closer we come to creating an immersive reality that is believable to us. When we make unreal things totally believable to our minds—are they then real? Is what we see in an HMD as real as everything else if our mind is perceiving it as such? This is not a new idea. Even a *Star Trek* episode from the 1960's by Gene Roddenberry had a badly injured star ship captain being given a new, totally believable imaginary reality by aliens on another planet that existed only in his brain, something we would refer to as a *virtual reality*. The feeling of being actually present in a non-physical world is known as a feeling of *presence*.

TECHNOLOGY IN CONCERT WITH THE MIND: TIME AND SCALE

When one talks about creativity intersecting with technology one must include the workings of the human mind in the conversation. How does creativity play into the question of consciousness and time? The human imagination envisions the past, present, and the future sometimes simultaneously.

The mind does not work in a linear fashion—the past, present, and future blend together, and memories and ideas almost randomly are drawn from different parts of the brain. There is a subjective experience of time's passage. The expression, "A watched kettle never boils," is an expression that sums it up. Call it the simple theory of relativity. Time passes slower for a child because each experience is new. The brain is processing new information for the first time. For an adult, the time between Monday to Friday can seem to pass in the blink of an eye. It is previously stored and processed information that doesn't have to be stored again. So, time is subjective, or it can be called psychological time. The perception of time is linked to memory.

Personal space is now merging with virtual space. Immersive media has widened and changed the expression of space in our cultural media. In our society now we have a much less consistent portrayal of space, just as editing is no longer linear. Images can be splashed across our vision in paintings and on screen with variety of ways to portray space. We are learning to look all around a scene, be it in a VR HMD or by using our fingers to roll about an image on a tablet. Our media has changed how space is illustrated and understood, and this says something important about the culture. The depiction of space has been expressed differently by different cultures over time. For example, in early European medieval religious paintings, distance was portrayed by how high up something was in the painting. The iconography was what was important. There was no attempt at a true perspective. That, of course, came later in the Renaissance. In Daoist and Buddhist philosophies there is the concept of nothingness, emptiness or the void, which has influenced the compositional portrayal of space in Chinese paintings over the centuries. Our understanding of space is very much a construct of our time and our media.

In a similar manner, the technology of the microscope has influenced our perception of space, and scale, and in doing so greatly influenced our creativity. Robert Hooke, who lived in the 17th Century, was a true polymath, combining art and science. He is credited with the discovery of cell in 1665 using a compound microscope that had been invented by Hans Janssen and his son in 1595. Hooke also drew beautiful drawings of insects, defining their anatomy and other tiny natural structures in his famous book, *Micrographia* (original published in 1665). Today microscopes are greatly advanced; we have optical microscopes, electron microscopes and scanning probe microscopes. With a transmission electron microscope, we can even see nanoparticles and atoms (Lewis, 2013).

Because of this, artists today can see previously unseen structures and movement from the cellular level on down, which adds to the vocabulary from which they can draw. Some of the robot designs and environments I designed for *Robot Prayers* are influenced by this close-up look at the world. What in our everyday lives can compete with a close-up of an ant or microbe for the inspiration to design an alien creature or environment?

HOW WE PROCESS TIME AND SPACE

Albert Einstein famously said (1952), "Time is relative." And this is borne out in our modern lives. Compare how humans processed time and distance as we went from walking to flying in an airplane, and now to spaceship travel (Waugh, 1999). The advent of photography gave us a different vision of the world enabling us to capture moments to hold onto. How is our culture and understanding of our place being changed by technology allowing us to explore and get images of the vast outer space within which we are but a speck?

At the start of filmmaking, movies were shown in a master view as if the audience was watching the stage in a play. There was an attempt to imitate real time. The passage of time is now portrayed in different ways; past, present, and future are mixed, and time can be compressed, skipped, or slowed down.

People are now accustomed to fast, sophisticated editing using many types of shots and cuts that emphasize different perspectives and points of view. We are now creating immersive media with different frame rates and editing styles. [Ed. Note: See Chapter by Brett Leonard that dives deeper into this topic.]

IVR has introduced a new relationship, which has been formed of the relationship of the audience to the content. The audience is also now a participant in a 360 degree environment, creating an experiential experience. The fourth wall has now been removed, resulting in changing our perceptions.

It has also been found that the sense of time can be changed by how many frames per second are being projected. A special effects artist, Douglas Trumbull, on landmark films such as; *2001: A Space Odyssey* and *Blade Runner*, created a cinematic process in the late 70s called "Showscan," and was the first to project film at 60 frames per second. People who were used to watching a film at 24 frames per second often come out of a Showscan movie thinking it was twice as long as the actual time of the movie (Zyber, 2012). Was it because their brains were taking in more frames per second then before and they were still estimating time based on the 24 frames per second rate? There are many theories as to how changing frame rates affect our sense of time and reality (McGregor, 2016). The brain can be trained to accept new things. People today seeing films at 60 frames per second now do not necessarily experience that doubling of time, or do they? New kinds of editing are being developed for immersive media because the old ways are no longer relevant. For example, fast cuts, popular in today's films, do not work in VR as well as a more continuous editing style.

THE SENSE OF SIGHT

While all senses are involved with making a believable immersive reality, vision is particularly important. Human brain development evolved in concert with the development of the sense of sight. At least half of the brain is involved with vision. The brain processes a visual much faster than it does a word. According to research done by neuroscientists it takes only 13 milliseconds to process an image versus 400 milliseconds to read and understand a word (Trafton, 2014). Visuals can have immediate entry into our unconsciousness. Marketers have always been aware of this: that the mind understands, makes sense of, and can create or pick up a story from even a short, abstract visual animation.

The eye is part of the central nervous system and is actually brain tissue. The tools used to create visual content are formulated on how our sight works. For centuries, artists had been exploring compositional rules, maybe not fully aware that these rules were based on how the brain processes what it sees. We are always trying to make sense of what we see, and then organize it into something coherent for us.

Our minds organize what we see for our survival, and to make sense of chaos. Many of the interesting facts in this section can be found in more detail in Stephen Palmer's *Vision Science: From Photons to Phenomenology* (Palmer, 1999).

The brain makes sense of the patterns, separating the predators from the shadows. Things of like shape or color are grouped together, and a black object separated out from other objects will become a focal point, i.e. a black shape in a white field. A human face will always attract attention first. The use of light and shadow can provide an organizing factor for the mind. When a mind cannot find an organizing principal, chaos is perceived.

The offset between our two eyes gives us stereoscopic vision. The brain calculates this difference between the two images to obtain and understand depth data. Brightness (the perceived illumination) and color are treated separately by the brain. The human eye is more sensitive to differences in lightness than in color. The eyes actually have separate color versus black and white detectors (cones vs. rods). The perception of color is both physical and psychological and seems to be somewhat based on relative differences (Albers 1963). Our eyes are much more sensitive to changes in dark tones than to similar changes in light tones, nor does the eye respond linearly to light. The human eye is most sensitive to the middle range values. The response of the eye to light isn't absolute. It is relative to the surrounding intensities.

Perception of shape and form are more based on brightness than color. As the eye moves it constantly readjusts its exposure by adjusting the iris which adjusts the size of the pupil. The lenses of eyes change shape to focus at the correct depth for whatever object they are currently looking at. Currently, most VR headsets can only focus at one distance, usually a fixed focus at two meters. For people, the field of view is the number of degrees of visual angle while the eyes are being held steady fixating on one point. The field of view human eye is capable of is 180-degree forward facing horizontal arc. The vertical would be more like 135 degrees, depth perception only covers about 14 degrees. We are always trying to increase the field of view of an HMD to match that.

Eyes are our input sensors in the world, and now they are our digital ones. Using our eyes to act not only as recipients of input, but also to serve as controllers is being tried in immersive experiences. For example, in an HMD with eye tracking incorporated, your gaze can indicate what it is you want to interact with (Dickson, 2017). However, it is still much more reliable to have our head positioning be the controller rather than our stare., in other words, where we are looking or facing, which is more stable than the saccadic and rapid movements of our eyes themselves.

The highest color vision and shape/form perception are concentrated in the center of the field. There is a small depression or dimple in the middle of the retina at the back of our eye, called the fovea. This is where visual acuity is highest. The center of the field of vision is focused in this region, where retinal cones are particularly concentrated. It is called the fixation point. The fixation point for each eye directly stimulates the fovea of the retina. This is important in terms of what we call foveated rendering, where only that portion of the image that is taken in by the fovea is rendered in full quality. Imagery outside of that area can be rendered with far less resolution. Foveated rendering is very useful for decreasing the amount of overall pixels in the scene having to be drawn, thus saving processing power for rendering, which can then be applied to higher frame rates and far greater resolutions where the viewer is gazing. This is obviously very attractive for the new immersive technologies as this makes it possible to come closer to natural human vision levels. For VR headset technology, this is becoming increasingly more important as one element to achieve total immersion (Boger, 2018).

TECHNOLOGY AND ARTIFICIAL INTELLIGENCE

The current trend of AI developers is to create an architecture that emulates the human mind, that is both software and hardware working together. Artificial Intelligence (AI) encompasses both machine learning and deep learning and attempts to get machines to learn for themselves. One of the most interesting things happening in AI is the development of neural networks which emulate the way the human mind is structured, designed to classify information the same way the human brain does. It is a system of hardware and software designed to be like the operation of neurons and their many connections in the human brain.

A good example of a company facilitating AI is Nvidia, with architecture and software that is built for AI. Nvidia got an early start ahead of other companies with a GPU chip which was designed for graphics and computer games. They can process a large amount of data swiftly, a lot of it being visuals. Intel is now developing its own GPU chip. AI deep learning algorithms also require a lot of computational power for learning information directly from the data of images, texts, and signals. GPUs can take a matrix of pixels and apply the same operation to them all whereas a standard CPU processes one operation at a time. Because of the parallel computing power of the GPU chip and its further development Nvidia was able to position itself as a leader in artificial intelligence chips. Intel known for its CPU, not to be left behind, they are now also developing a GPU chip and software.

Using AI Virtual beings designed to emulate people, act and look like us are being added into our immersive technology.

TECHNOLOGY INFLUENCES CREATIVITY

The tools and media used influence creativity: they can limit or open up creative possibilities. Using paint and a paintbrush will influence results as much as a software package might. A brush lends itself to making certain kinds of strokes. Paint creates a certain type of surface. Most digital artists can recognize when a game was created in Unreal Engine or Unity. How often have you seen an image and known the Photoshop filter that was used to create it? On the other hand, new tools give us previously unknown speed with which to create content not imagined before. For example, when designing by in putting data an unexpected visual may be output, influencing the next design decision. Fast access to formerly unknown information and results enables random new associations, introducing chance. Copies and duplicates can be made. It is said that the painter Picasso would stop a painting at a certain point and have his assistance make copies of it so that he could then try taking the painting in different directions. Even some tools in the Adobe Creative Suite are starting to or will soon be employing AI. Adobe is now offering Adobe Sensei for machine learning and AI across the board to enhance its products. A simple example of machine learning is a computer being taught how to recognize and discern the differences between objects. This is useful for a search through a data base of millions of stock images such as Adobe has. The computer might also be further trained to recognize abstract concepts to aid in finding the requested image. In addition, perhaps the computer has the profile and record of past actions of the person seeking the image to aid it in finding the best image. So now the question to ask is how much will the use of AI in our tools start to influence and shape creativity? People are already externally augmented with all the computers, smartphones, etc. they use. What happens to creativity with this increase in augmentation, the explosion of virtual beings? The development of software and hardware a digital artist must learn to use is already expanding exponentially.

For years I have jokingly said, "Learn all the software and then you die." I finally made a T-shirt for myself that says this.

COMPUTER VISION AND CAPTURING DEPTH

The development of "computer vision" is not surprising. Ultimately, computer vision is an attempt to enable computers to see the same way we do – in full 3D surround format—critical to today's immersive technologies. Computer vision gives the ability to track movement, to measure depth, create a color image, map out a location in 3D as well as creating interactivity with devices like the Microsoft Kinect or Intel's RealSense cameras.

There are a number of elements encompassed in computer vision. Depth information is a vital part of volumetric filmmaking, light fields, light stages, and photogrammetry. These elements of computer vision, scanning (mapping the environment), measuring depth, tracking, finding the RGB values can be found together in one device or separately in different devices. The way of the future is for all to be enabled in one device. Different technologies and techniques to get and display this information are used. Light fields—a mathematical technique that can describe the amount of light that flows all around us in space—is one of the technologies. While currently the most computationally intensive of all, is perhaps the way of the future, and will help fundamentally change the way we create environments and map the world.

Computer vision is also central in robotics, (perhaps mankind's attempt to create something in our own image), security, health, and self-driving cars. Self-driving cars and robots that need to navigate the environment must use computer vision. Computer vision for them includes machine learning and even the deep learning of artificial intelligence to recognize, differentiate and track objects of importance in the world.

Techniques used for scanning and depth-mapping are important features in cameras, smartphones, VR, facial recognition, scene and environment scanning, location information, AR and mixed reality. Facial recognition, which uses artificial intelligence, is becoming an important feature that it is being added to many new apps and cameras including some VR cameras.

To create models of the world and environments, lasers, as well as the electromagnetic wave spectrum (which includes visible light, infrared, X-rays, ultraviolet, and gamma rays for scanning, mapping, measuring) are being used. For example, you can build a model of the world around you with the depth, stereo, location and RGB information from the sensors and cameras on your smartphone. Often in smartphones stereo depth mapping is accomplished by using two sensors or cameras because stereo depth information is gained in a similar way to how eyes work.

Another technique to get depth information is to project a pattern of infrared light onto a scene, then the depth is calculated by evaluating the discrepancies in the pattern due to the distortion on the 3D environment and objects.

Generally, the basic principle used in recovering 3D depth information is the triangulation principle. Triangulation in computer vision is used to determine the location of a point in space. It can be gotten based on the projection onto two or more objects.

In active vision techniques, the object, the light, and the sensor create a triangle. In passive stereo vision techniques, the object and two sensors are used (Beltran & Basañez, 2014). Techniques of controlled sources of structured energy like a scanning laser source, or a projected pattern of light, and a detector-like A camera are called the active group. A laser range scanner belongs to this group. An active source moves around an object to scan the entire surface of an object.

LiDAR (Light Detection and Ranging) systems use active sensors, which emit energy to illuminate the target object (Corrigan, 2019). A pulsed laser, invisible to the human eye, is sent to the object and the reflected pulse is received back. The distance is calculated from the return time and wavelength of the laser. Rapid scanning of the target area, point by point with laser pulses, makes it possible to create a depth map of the scene. LIDAR sensors, are popular in self-driving cars being developed now, or for mapping terrain from above as mapping can be done even when there is a dense covering of trees.

In passive stereo vision techniques, two cameras are used, creating a triangle between the object and two sensors. Structured light is a combination of a single camera, and a single projector, and the projector projects a pattern. The way the pattern is deformed when striking the surface is what how the depth and surface information of the objects is calculated. The camera and the projector make a stereo system, and no second camera is needed. The Microsoft Kinect uses structured light.

Around 2000, a new class of active sensors emerged based on the Time of Flight (ToF principle).

Based on the principal of pulsed light sources in a ToF camera, the time offset between a signal sent out by the emitter and when it arrives back at the sensor is calculated. A short infrared light pulse is emitted by the 3D depth sensors and each pixel of the camera sensor measures the return time. More detailed information about techniques to capture depth information can be found in (Meyers, 2018).

THE *ROBOT PRAYERS* PROJECT

Robots: An Intersection of Mind, Creativity and Technology

The word *robot* was first used in a play by Czech writer Karel Capek published in 1920. In the Czech language the word robot came from the word for slaves. In 1942 Isaac Asimov first used the word robot in print in his science fiction short story *Runabout*. (Asimov, 1942)

In this same story Isaac Asimov introduced his Three Laws of Robotics. They were:

1. A robot may not injure a human being or, through inaction, allow a human being to come to harm.
2. A robot must obey the orders given it by human beings except where such orders would conflict with the First Law.
3. A robot must protect its own existence as long as such protection does not conflict with the First or Second Laws.

Robots of the Past

Pinocchio, an early inspiration for the project *Robot Payers*, is a wooden puppet that could be thought of as a robot. He wanted to become a real boy. Like some of the characters in *Robot Prayers*, Pinocchio went on a journey of discovery during which he had to master aspects of his character to pass tests and become real.

The notion of intelligent robots, or thinking mechanical machines, has actually been around since ancient days in mythology (Friedman, 2011). For example, in Greek mythology Hephaestus the Greek god of fire crafted automatons, golden robot-like statues called to be his servants. The statues could think and speak. He also made two mechanical immortal guard dogs from gold. He created Talos, a gigantic bronze warrior to protect the island of Crete. Talos was interesting because Hephaestus gave him a single internal artery through which was poured the life fluid of the gods. He could be thought of as perhaps the first vision of a cybernetic organism. To the ancient Greeks was Talos a hybrid between the gods and man? In the mythology Talos desired to become human, but this was thwarted by Medea who tricked him and drained the god's life fluid out of him. Like Hal in the movie *2001*—he didn't want to be turned off.

What is the test to see if something is alive? We know that everything that is alive wants to survive or knows it can die. The smallest ant will flee from the descending foot. I was joking with some friends that if a machine was alive it would protest being unplugged, having its power turned off. They suggested I call it the "Audri Test," an upgrade or addition to the Turing Test.

In a project such as *Robot Prayers* that is on the cutting edge of technology, the pipeline that includes hardware and software to be used is a big part of the creative process. These elements will influence the final project in terms of look and sound. Since *Robot Prayers* will be produced in many different formats an array of software will be used. The software most used for the project include; Autodesk Maya, Autodesk Motion Builder, TouchDesigner, Unreal Engine, Xfrog, the Adobe Suite, and Handbrake. Other technologies used are; photogrammetry, projection mapping (on the fulldome, performers and virtual sets) motion capture, volumetric rendering, and interactivity.

If a team is working on a project it is usually desirable that they use the same software, otherwise ways of converting files from one software to another must be found. Because it is a project to be done in different mixed reality formats, the same assets can be used for all of them if shot with different lens shaders. It is also important to consider the hardware, the rendering time, the file formats, and resolution.

Photogrammetry

Photogrammetry is a technique for creating mesh or point cloud models, from environments, people and objects. It is a photographic technique which uses multiple photographs taken from around the subject. It was a technique we used to create the computer graphic (CG) models for *Robot Prayers* (Figure 2).

Motion Capture

Dance and dancing robots play a big part in performances of *Robot Prayers*, making motion capture, or mocap, right for the project. Motion capture records realistic movement from a human and is especially useful for complex and subtle movements. It can also enhance the speed and capabilities of the character animator by giving them a more advanced starting point. There are many ways of studying movement and animators who have studied dance have said that it has improved their ability as animators. In the *Robot Prayers* project the mocap movement captured from the dancers will be merged into CG characters, the various robots. For the live performance sections, the motion of the performers will be captured in real time and put into the animation of the projected CG robots.

Figure 2. CG robots from Robot Prayers representing our future augmented selves
Source: Image courtesy of author

The idea of motion capture is not new (Dent, 2014). In some sense it can be said that forms of motion capture have been around for a while. In the late 19th century, Eadweard Muybridge used stop motion photography to study and capture the movements of people and animals. Each photo captured a split second of the movement (Muybridge, 1955). Besides being an inspiration for motion pictures opening up a new field of creative possibilities and endeavors it also led to Max Fleischer inventing the rotoscope a piece of projection equipment used for rotoscoping in 1914 (Skwigly, 2004). The rotoscope was used to project frames of live action film onto a surface so that animators could trace over them capturing the movement in each frame. This technique was used to give cartoons realistic and smooth movement. The copied frames could either serve as animation reference or used more directly, for example inked onto an animation cell. Max Fleisher first used the technique to create three short cartoon animation called *Koko the Clown*. He then opened up Fleischer Studios which created *Betty Boop* and *Popeye*, two early cartoon animation characters. It was also used in the Walt Disney Studios, where it was used as a base for the animators who would then exaggerate the characters. Rotoscoping has been used to mix drawn animation and live action film together in many films in the past, examples are *Star Wars* where it was used to remove wires and create glowing effects for the light sabers. In *Mary Poppins* it was used to aid in compositing, putting in the birds.

Rotoscoping has since gone digital in the early 1990s being used especially in the VFX industry. There are many rotoscoping programs available to be used on computers, but they still take painstaking work on the part of the roto artists.

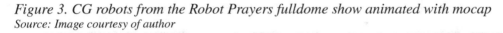

Figure 3. CG robots from the Robot Prayers fulldome show animated with mocap
Source: Image courtesy of author

Motion capture is just another step forward from the rotoscoping. Now with motion capture full body movements, as well as subtle facial motion and precise hand and finger animation, can all be captured and applied to CG rigged mesh characters (Figure 3).

The technologies for motion capture are always evolving. Currently there are a number of companies employing different methods for motion tracking.

Tracking

Tracking is an inseparable part of motion capture. Many of the technologies used for tracking in motion capture are also used in all forms of computer vision, such as different depth mapping techniques. The major categories of tracking used in mocap are, optical tracking, electromagnetic tracking acoustic tracking, and mechanical tracking. Optical tracking uses light to measure the objects orientation and position and acoustic tracking uses electronic sound waves to do the same. Mechanical tracking establishes a connection between the target and a fixed reference point. Electromagnetic tracking measures magnetic fields.

Tracking is also a useful tool for creating interactivity during a live performance.

For example, in a live performance of *Robot Prayers* there are dancers onstage whose movements are not only controlling the movements of the on-screen CG characters but also creating effects such as animating objects or throwing light beams from one robot to another (Figure 4). To do this both the Intel RealSense Camera and the Microsoft Kinect have been used. The tracking information is feed and programmed into the proper nodes in the program TouchDesigner by Derivative. The point cloud and depth information provided is also used to create volumetric renders not only for characters but for effects such as turning the characters into particles.

Figure 4. CG robot in a fulldome animation being controlled by movement of performers

FUTURE RESEARCH DIRECTIONS

What effect is the use of technology having on our perceptions of time and space, and the structure of our minds? What effect is it having on our creativity, our culture, our consciousness? The development of artificial intelligence is largely modeled after the workings of the human mind. With the continued development of deep learning and machines programming themselves will the intelligence and thinking of a machine continue to bear any resemblance to the human mind? It can be said we are already augmented by the technology we use, such as computers and smartphones. Advanced hearing aids are already put inside our ears, what will happen if for example computer chips are put into our brains? At some point the ethics of AI needs to be examined as well as the effect artificial intelligence is having on our culture, perceptions of the world and the working of our minds. How do we encourage and support creativity?

It may be that we continue to expand the possibilities by creating new works with these technologies, like *Robot Prayers*. Such works bring us into the possibilities of the immersive future. Like Asimov's short stories (1942) unleashing modern automaton in the form of robots into the world, our new, inventive immersive works will evoke new ways of thinking and being creative, keeping the endless dance of technology and creativity moving forward.

CONCLUSION

The tools of and nature of creativity, the mind, consciousness, human perceptions and new technology, as applied to our immersive projects have been discussed in this chapter. The immersive media project *Robot Prayers* has been described, which leads us to robots, perhaps the perfect intersection of creativity, the mind and technology.

Creativity, the human mind, and technology are inseparable from one another. Creativity is influenced and shaped by the technology used and technology is a creation of the human mind.

Our technology tools lead our creativity in directions we might not have gone in otherwise. The challenge is now to understand how and how much of our creativity and culture is being influenced by technology and when that is desired and when it is not. It must be recognized that the answers will be subjective.

REFERENCES

Albers, J. (1963). *Interaction of Color*. New Haven, CT: Yale University Press.

Asimov, I. (1942). *Runabout. Astounding Science Fiction Magazine*.

Baer, J. (2016). *Domain Specificity of Creativity*. Amsterdam: Elsevier Academic Press.

Beltran, D., & Basañez, L. (2014). A comparison between active and passive 3d vision sensors: Bumblebeexb3 and Microsoft Kinect. In *Proceedings of Robot2013: First Iberian Robotics Conference* (pp. 725-734). Springer.

Boger, Y. (2018). Understanding Pixel Density & Retinal Resolution, and Why It's Important for AR/VR Headsets. *Road to VR*. Retrieved from https://www.roadtovr.com/understanding-pixel-density-retinal-resolution-and-why-its-important-for-vr-and-ar-headsets/

Cambridge English Dictionary. (n.d.). *Creativity*. Retrieved from https://dictionary.cambridge.org/dictionary/english/creativity?q=creativity

Collodi, D., & Brundage, F. (1924). *Pinocchio*. Mineola, NY: Saalfield Publishing Company.

Corrigan, F. (2019). *Flash Lidar Time of Flight (ToF) Camera Sensors On Drones And 10 Terrific Uses*. Retrieved from https://www.dronezon.com/learn-about-drones-quadcopters/best-uses-for-time-of-flight-tof-camera-depth-sensor-technology-in-drones-or-ground-based/

Dent, S. (2014). *What you need to know about 3D motion capture*. Retrieved from https://www.engadget.com/2014/07/14/motion-capture-explainer/

Dickson, B. (2017). *Unlocking the potential of eye tracking technology*. Retrieved from https://techcrunch.com/2017/02/19/unlocking-the-potential-of-eye-tracking-technology/

Einstein, A. (1952). *Relativity: Relativity. The special and the general theory*. New York: Crown Publishers.

Friedman, J. (2011). *Robots Through History*. Rosen Central.

Grybko, M. (2016). *Quote from Podcast and blog by Damien Farnworth.* Retrieved from https://www.copyblogger.com/define-creativity/

Hagenback, D., & Wertmüller, L. (2013). *Mystic Chemist: The Life of Albert Hofmann and His Discovery of LSD.* Santa Fe, NM: Synergetic Press.

Kant, I. (2018). *Critique of Pure Reason* (J. M. Meiklejohn, Trans.). Mineola, NY: Dover Publications. (Original work published 1781)

Kurzweil, R. (2009). Get ready for hybrid thinking. *Ted Talk.* Retrieved from https://www.ted.com/talks/ray_kurzweil_get_ready_for_hybrid_thinking

Lakoff, G., & Johnson, M. (1980). *Metaphors We Live By.* Chicago: University of Chicago Press.

Lewis, T. (2013). Incredible Technology: How to Explore the Microscopic World. *Live Science.* Retrieved from https://www.livescience.com/38470-how-to-explore-microscopic-world.html

McGregor, L. (2016). The Surprisingly Fascinating World of Frame Rates. *The Beat.* Retrieved from https://www.premiumbeat.com/blog/advanced-look-into-frame-rates/

Mednick, S. A. (1968). The Remote Associates Test. *The Journal of Creative Behavior*, 2(3), 213–214. doi:10.1002/j.2162-6057.1968.tb00104.x

Melville, H. (1902). *Moby Dick.* New York: Charles Scribner's Sons.

Meyers, S. (2018). Capturing depth: Structured light, Time-of-Flight, and the Future of 3D Imaging. *Android Authority Features.* Retrieved from https://www.androidauthority.com/structured-light-3d-imaging-870016/

Muybridge, E. (1955). *Eadweard Muybridge: The Human Figure in Motion.* New York: Dover.

Palmer, S. E. (1999). *Vision science: Photons to Phenomenology.* Boston: MIT press.

Preston, T. (1890). *The Theory of Light.* London: Macmillan and Co.

Runco, M. (2013). *Divergent Thinking and Creative Potential Creativity.* New York: Hampton Press.

Skwigly. (2004). The Rotoscope of Max Fleischer. *Skwigly Online Animation Magazine.* Retrieved from https://www.skwigly.co.uk/the-rotoscope-of-max-fleischer/

Torrance, E. P. (1977). *Creativity in the Classroom; What Research Says to the Teacher.* National Education Association.

Trafton, A. (2014). In the Blink of an Eye. *MIT News.* Retrieved from http://news.mit.edu/2014/in-the-blink-of-an-eye-0116

Watts, A. (1936). *The Spirit of Zen: A Way of Life, Work and Art in the Far East.* New York: E. P. Dutton and Co.

Watts, A. (1995). *Om: On Creative Meditations.* Anaheim, CA: Creative Press.

Waugh, A. (1999). *Time.* Terra Alta, WV: Headline Books.

Zyber, J. (2012). Douglas Trumbull May Have This Frame Rate Thing Figured Out. *High Def Digest: The Bonus View.* Retrieved from https://www.highdefdigest.com/blog/douglas-trumbull-showscan-digital/

Section 2
Immersive Media and Experience: Production and Creation

Chapter 8
Discovering a Language of Stories in Immersive Storytelling:
An Essential First Step

Jessica Kantor
Independent Researcher, USA

ABSTRACT

In this chapter, the author explores storytelling in immersive media along with a systematic way of utilizing other forms of media to inform choices in these new techniques. The author argues that storytelling, as a human instinct, shows up in all forms of media as they emerge and that we are now at the beginning step on a long road of discovery. The chapter goes on to explore traditional forms of storytelling for the stage and screen to see how those mediums can inform emerging immersive media. Examples are presented of early immersive media that have achieved more or less success in telling a story.

INTRODUCTION

Stories still exist in immersive media (Virtual Reality, Augmented Reality, and 360 videos). Only their presentation has evolved from story*telling* to story *experiencing*. The author discovered this by diving into immersive storytelling and creating 360 video experiences. As a former dancer who then worked in cinematic film and television, the author's approach to telling immersive stories started from a natural place of blocking or exploring how a person might move through a world in order to guide future participants through an experience. The author's experience spurred the concept of using the traditional aspects of mise en scené, the French term of where to place on stage, but reinterpreting them for immersive mediums, focusing first on 360 video experiences, and then moving on to virtual reality with full agency, and finally augmented reality.

DOI: 10.4018/978-1-7998-2433-6.ch008

The goal of this chapter, based on the author's practice, is to suggest a systematic approach for telling compelling stories across media that will uniformly evoke a language anyone can use to tell their desired story best.

BACKGROUND

Immersive media defined here as a general term encompassing 360 videos, Virtual Reality, and Augmented Reality. Each of these is on the spectrum of what is also called Mixed Reality. This spectrum offers the user different levels of immersion, agency, and interactivity. The author defines agency as the ability for the user to exist and take action in the virtual world as they can within the real world.

360 video is a live-action or animated video where the person experiencing the video (user, viewer or participant) puts on a head-mounted display (HMD) to immersive their self in the world with three degrees of freedom (DoF). Those three degrees allow the user to look around left and right, or up and down, but they cannot move forward or back within the virtual 360-degree world. Interactivity can exist in 360 videos by utilizing the participant's gaze, voice, or with remote control. It is possible to view a 360 video through a browser or by utilizing a mobile device as a magic window. However, for this chapter, the author refers solely to the experience as delivered through an HMD.

Full Virtual Reality is a live-action or animated experience where the user has six degrees of freedom in an HMD. The user has full agency to move throughout all spatial aspects of the virtual world. The creator of the experience defines the level of agency. In most experiences, the user will have an avatar representing their character in the virtual world, whether it be just hands or a full-body, and with this persona, the user interacts with the surrounding environment.

Augmented Reality (AR) refers to digital assets layered on or atop a real-world physical environment. The user has full agency in the physical world while the AR overlays digital or video elements for viewing and potential interaction. Augment Reality can be experienced via the magic window of a mobile device or with a special see-through HMD or display device that allows simultaneous viewing of real-world and virtual elements.

Some critics have suggested that authentic storytelling is not possible in immersive media, but the author takes the opposite position—believing that storytelling is an innate human experience, in line with the thinking of anthropologist Yuval Harari who says:

The real difference between us and chimpanzees is the mysterious glue that enables millions of humans to cooperate effectively. This mysterious glue is made of stories, not genes. We cooperate effectively with strangers because we believe in things like gods, nations, money and human rights. Yet none of these things exists outside the stories that people invent and tell one another. (Harari, 2017)

Like Yuval Harari's beliefs, the natural disposition of humans is to buy into a collective fiction that only exists as ideas. These ideas create a shared belief system that centers around stories. This concept is essential to creating stories in immersive media as well as for the communication between humans. They push storytelling beyond entertainment as they also underpin so many aspects of human life on earth. For example, scientist Laura Osburn uses storytelling for design practices in the real-world.

Storytelling is a central part of our human experience. We tell ourselves and others stories about who we are, what we do, and why we do it. Being an expert in the use of storytelling for decision-making means understanding how people use stories to make strategic decisions on any number of things, from determining the boundaries of one's social community to deciding what energy designs should be developed for a building. (Osburn, 2017)

These theories for world-building in the real-world also apply to the creation of immersive worlds. They support learning how and why a person creates their own story to make decisions and choices, and how such stories can help propel a person through the created space in a meaningful way. This line of thinking is the foundation for building a language of the story within immersive media. Whether it is the intention or not, humans are at the center of immersive media, and stories are critical to their existence. Therefore, discovering techniques that will build a consistent language for the user will be essential for the human adoption of the technology, as without story, the user loses their humanity.

Since a human in a natural storyteller, the immersive experience can take advantage of this fact. Even with a lack of direction or established storyline, the participant will create their own story in an immersive space. Now, that means the participant might not experience the world as the creator had intended, but more as they see fit. A simple example is the story of the sidewalk. As a worldbuilding tool, it seems pretty straightforward: the sidewalk informs a person is it safe to walk on it whereas, by comparison, the street has objects moving at speeds that could be harmful to the human. The sidewalk limits the infinite possibilities of walking anywhere and narrows it down to a path with two directions. People, for the most part, will tend to walk on such a provided path, though a few may take the risk of walking elsewhere, like in the road. However, that is only a single variable, and one can calculate additional variables for divergent thinkers. In today's world, there are stories around the usage of sidewalks. Starting with the poem by Shel Silverstein, *Where the Sidewalk Ends* (2004):

There is a place where the sidewalk ends

And before the street begins,

And there the grass grows soft and white,

And there the sun burns crimson bright,

And there the moon-bird rests from his flight

To cool in the peppermint wind.

Let us leave this place where the smoke blows black

And the dark street winds and bends.

Past the pits where the asphalt flowers grow

We shall walk with a walk that is measured and slow,

And watch where the chalk-white arrows go

To the place where the sidewalk ends.

Yes we'll walk with a walk that is measured and slow,

And we'll go where the chalk-white arrows go,

For the children, they mark, and the children, they know

The place where the sidewalk ends.

This poem, from the World War II era, is loosely interpreted as a plea to not create sidewalks in streets and neighborhoods that do not want visitors. Anastasia Loukaitou-Sideris, an expert in urban planning at the University of California Los Angeles, says the perception of sidewalks goes back to the Shel Silverstein days.

There is this perception that if we have sidewalks, we are going to bring people who do not belong to our neighborhoods. (Loukaitou-Sideris, 2018)

In the context of worldbuilding and human's proclivity to create a story, people have given a poem about a simple sidewalk a more profound implication. This concept showcases how humans can add a layer of drama on a mundane object, and thereby cause complete shifts in culture. This innate human instinct causes us to more deeply examine the language presented to form a story that makes some sense to us. Just as with stories we tell from the real world, or the simple words of a poem, current forms of immersive media are experimenting with how the same concepts can evoke stories within the experience of a virtual space.

PAST, PRESENT, AND FUTURE

Storytelling originates with our ancestors' retelling events around a campfire, marking essential people and events through ancient hieroglyphics, and even the desired outcomes called forth by primitive cave drawings that date back over 30,000 years. We also observe how most human's first storytelling episodes occur spontaneously in early childhood. These examples hint at how communication in many forms is facilitated and enhanced by storytelling. Studies have found benefits from being a good storyteller, resulting in better livelihood, companionship, and reproduction. These illustrations showcase how important storytelling is and has been to humans through the ages, and how it can support humans in leading a productive life (Smith et al., 2017).

Why Create a Language of Storytelling?

The goal of creating a language of storytelling is to provide an experience where the technology falls away and becomes transparent. Think about reading a book. When the story is engrossing, the reader forgets they are turning pages. The mechanisms by which they are experiencing the story fall away due to the story itself. The elements the author uses depends on words, sentence structure, and pacing, as well as characters' development and plot.

Scientists have tested a fiction feeling hypothesis where they had users reading passages from the Harry Potter books while connected to an MRI machine to look into what their brains are doing. They found that the brain was particularly engaged when the author presented vivid descriptions of emotion, inducing empathy in the reader (Hsu et al., 2014).

The question is, how does one achieve such transcendence in literature? It seems to be a mix of mastery of language but also building a world, compelling characters, and a story that's well-structured and interesting. Studying each of these ideas and discussing how they come to bring life off the page is essentially the mise-en-scène concept in cinema. Each aspect is a piece of building a story. These different choices made by the creator bring the story to life. When put together the elements of mise en scène are the language of storytelling, and if done well will transport the user to be completely present in the experience.

Similar to reading, when a person experiences a well-crafted story, they get lost in it, and the mechanism of telling it falls away. Watching a play, a movie or a television show can be as equally an engrossing experience as reading a great book. At first, television seems like a very passive activity. However, a recent trend, that of binging watching eight to ten hours of television in one go is in itself proof that the medium can transport and thoroughly immerse and captivate that user.

If a person can sit in a theatre, their living room or with a book in hand and be transported to another world, fully engaged in a story, why does it seem that we have not achieved this in the new medium of virtual reality, which we call *immersive*? We might expect it is because each of the other mentioned media has techniques developed over the years, and these have built upon the human tendency to tell stories. There has been much time to refine how these forms of media to engross their audiences fully. Television will celebrate its one-hundredth birthday in 2027, and its golden age of storytelling is just upon us now in 2019. The medium film is even older, and its techniques have reached a very high level of engagement and maturity.

With immersive media, only a small handful of artists have begun experimenting with the unique possibilities for storytelling. The technology is in desperate need for us to crack this code as it is the key to its mass adoption. The first step is to look at ideas from different forms of earlier storytelling to reinterpret them and bring what is germane from them into this new medium. The goal is not to forget the learnings but reapplying it smartly while developing additional ways to tell compelling stories.

Exploring Theater

Dance was a precursor to theatre; from 800-600 BCE, dramatic dance that included imitation of animals, gymnastics and rhythms was first performed (Howard, 2016). Then came the addition of more sounds, and the inclusion of things like costumes and masks to make the performance more spectacular. Similarly, there was a tradition of oral storytelling that created myths and developed characters that evolved into Greek Theatre around 600-400 BCE.

This evolution of exposition is similar to the development of a child. Beginning with movement and rhythm, cries and laughter, as a child grows, they develop rudimentary language before they spontaneously start telling stories. It is a unique formula the author applied to her work in immersive media derived from the earliest forms of exposition both in the macrocosm of society and microcosm of a single person.

Immersive theatre dates back to the Middle Ages with a call and response. The players would call out something and expect the audience to answer. Immersive theater is also known as site-specific or participatory theater, a form that takes audiences to all kinds of places, both physical and emotional (Halls, 2018). A recent example of a near-legendary immersive theater production, often referenced by storytellers in immersive media is *Sleep No More* (King, 2018). It is a site-specific retelling of *Macbeth*. Audience members enter and receive a mask, and then are taken into an elevator and let out on one of the multiple floors within the performance space. The location is designed as a hotel and becomes a character in and of itself. Once they arrive on their floor, the audience is free to roam and explore where ever they please. Performers appear, and audience members are encouraged to follow them, but it remains up to each audience member if they do that or not. The entire story plays out simultaneously across multi-floors, making it impossible to see every moment of the play in one go. Therefore, every audience member's experience is unique, with infinite possibilities of how to engage with the experience.

Sleep No More is an exciting blueprint for immersive media, creating a world with a performance that happens for the user to witness as they choose. Every time they enter the story world, the user remains free to discover new aspects of the world and performance. One would think that this sort of experience lacks direction. However, the opposite is true. Every detail of this world is meticulously designed giving clues to the story and essence of the world. The performances are directed and blocked in space. Even the interactions with the users are preplanned. The user's reaction is what gives a spontaneous feeling. This example creates a clear distinction between direction and agency. With a lack of direction, there would be no experience, and with a lack of user agency, the experience would be received similarly by each person in the audience. However, here we have meticulous direction and free agency interwoven to create an immersive experience that has had audiences coming back for over seven years.

Compare the ideas behind *Sleep No More* with the recent Oscar-winning Virtual Reality piece *Carne y Arena* by Alejandro Iñárritu. While the feat of making a VR piece of this scale is commendable and celebrated, this work is a political statement to raise awareness. It positions the participant as a fellow sufferer (Raessens, 2019). We can look at such works not only with a critical eye, we can learn from each work for its contribution to our collective understanding and knowledge or how to make works that truly affect us. Such a critical approach enables us all to continue to push the medium forward.

The sign on the wall one sees while entering the exhibition for *Carne y Arena* indicates that due to the format of Virtual Reality, each participant acts as director, choosing their movement and how they wish to experience this world. While this statement has an element of truth, it is somewhat misinformed. A VR experience should be directed subtly, through a variety of techniques that guide the participant while allowing them the freedom of their agency. Understanding the uniqueness of user agency and creator direction is essential. That sign, however, could have been used to help the participant learn about their agency to help them make the most of their experience.

In the exhibition, a single participant enters a holding area, designed to emulate where migrants wait to be processed. It is a fully designed space. Next, they invite the participant into a big open room where they put on a headset and experience what it feels like to cross the American/Mexican border. When exiting this part of the experience, there is a beautiful multi-media exhibition that introduces the participant to the people who crossed the border with them. If the creator of this work had taken more ownership in their direction in several ways, the experience could have been exponentially more impactful and immersive. The first way could be to introduce the participant to the other characters at the start, thus setting them up for an emotional payoff in the headset and the development of a stronger sense of empathy because they have already been made aware of them. Another method could involve direct interaction between the participant and the police, adding more tension, thrill, and dramatic involvement. Those two elements, empathy, and thrill create immersion in literature and theater, and they could have enhanced the potential for *Carne y Arena* to achieve that state where a participant loses themselves in the experience and forgets the mechanism of delivery.

For the author's point of view, because her agency in the experience was not defined, most of the time in the headset was concerned more with the technology itself rather than becoming emotionally engaged with the story at hand. Though this work is one of the most acclaimed Virtual Reality experiences to date, in retrospect, we can see that were several missed opportunities for expanding the storytelling potential of immersive media. Hopefully, the creator, as well as others in the immersive community, have learned valuable lessons from this work and will apply these lessons to future works. Working in these early days, with no formal language of a story inside the Virtual Reality arena is a challenge we all face until we collectively create that new language.

Another example of Immersive Theater that has a more linear story is *The Willows* by Just Fix It Productions (Rylaf, 2018). In this experience, the audience is told to meet at a parking lot off-site. The group of 12 is picked up in a van and taken to an old Hollywood mansion. A butler greets the group and invites them into the sitting area for a drink. The guest receives drinks are encouraged to roam the house where members of the dysfunctional family are getting ready for a dinner party. This moment helps define the group's agency while introducing them to the characters of the play. Next, the guest participates in a family meal where the characters introduce the reason for the dinner party. Different audience members are taken away for a unique one-on-one experiences, and then after dinner, the group is split up into three groups of four. The characters reveal that an audience member is a target and they are trying to discern which one until a final scene culminates in choosing the sacrifice while everyone else is quickly ushered back out to the van with one audience member left behind. After some time, the missing guest reappears and joins the group in the parking lot. In this story, every audience member participates in the same plot while every audience member also has a unique experience. The balance between agency and direction is different from *Sleep No More* creating a different outcome. Understanding those two ingredients are vital to the language of story experiences.

Learning from Film and Television: Mise en Scène

Moving pictures first emerged in the late 1880s. Like the mediums that went before, it took time until the moving pictures told stories. That they were called moving pictures was in context to the most similar and popular medium at the time, the photograph—the still picture. Moreover, an early form of moving pictures was called 'Actualities' a genre where the camera filmed snippets of real events a minute or two long for playback to an audience (Sklar, 2019). Very quickly in the early 1900s music, sound effects and narration were added to these single-shot stories, and an industry was born. Georges Méliès is credited as the first storyteller in the medium, creating sequences and stop motion animations. Méliès made 500 films from 1863 to 1913 and though pushing the medium forward, were mainly filmed stage plays.

Current immersive media creators are experimenting in ways similar to the pioneering filmmakers, but perhaps have overlooked some of their pioneers from the earliest waves of VR experimentation that happened in the 1980s and 1990s. We are actually in the second wave of VR development, yet for many recent immersive media creators, those early works were ignored or not accessible, and there was a tendency for some to start from a clean slate as if it was the first time the medium existed. The focus for this second wave of virtual reality seems to focus on two bottom lines: selling headsets and gear, and encouraging mass consumption. The technology has been driven in no small measure by companies with financial implications and vested interests. This financial motive is driving the technology forward before the creators have the time to experiment with the story. In (House, 2016) Werner Herzog explains:

The strange thing here is that normally, in the history of culture, we have new stories and narrations and then we start to develop a tool. Or we have visions of wondrous new architecture—like, let's say, the museum in Bilbao, or the opera house in Sydney—and technology makes it possible to fulfill these dreams. So, you have the content first, and then the technology follows suit. In this case, we do have a technology, but we don't have any clear idea how to fill it with content.

Like Méliès, there were some in this second wave of Virtual Reality who started to experiment deeply with the medium. One of those people is Jessica Brillhart, formerly principal filmmaker at Google. Jessica utilized her access to new tech to experiment and invent different ways to edit, position characters, and tell stories. She published her findings for others to utilize in their work. Jessica created her innovative immersive work before landing a position in 2019 as the Director of the Mixed Reality Lab at the University of Southern California's Institute for Creative Technologies (ICT) (Damiani, 2019). Bringing Jessica, a creative storyteller, onboard at the ICT positions the institute to move from technology development into the start of building a unified language of story in immersive media.

Just as Ms. Brillhart brought her filmmaking skills to bear on new techniques for immersive media, the author similarly has utilized her background in dance to create new approaches to building story language in the 360-video space. The use of dance thinking has provided an appealing way to test different techniques and effects for camera placement, guiding a user, distance from the camera, sound, worldbuilding, and editing. Each of these is an aspect of mise-en-scène, the choices a director makes to best tell their story in the medium of choice. This concept has been used in theatre in addressing each element of the production, including the scenery, lighting, and performance. For cinema, the term was then adapted to mean placing on the screen and can now mean everything from theater plus framing of the camera (Moura, 2016).

This term can now be adapted further for immersive media, allowing it to mean placing in the world or setting (as opposed to on the stage or the screen). Mise-en-scène applied to immersive techniques also requires the essential aspects of agency and interactivity to be considered. How involved or passive will the user be in experiencing their story? There is no right or wrong answer; only a choice a director needs to make when designing their experience.

It is also essential to understand how much of the story needs to actually be written before interpreting and directing the story for interaction. Put another way; the first question that should be asked when suggesting a story for immersive media, should be "Why VR?" A more specific version of this question is why is VR the best way to tell *this* story? To answer these questions, the creator needs to have an understanding of what it means to interpret the story in immersive media. Every story can be appropriate for immersive media, but the way the story reveals itself to the user will be unique and feel very different. This choice is similar to deciding when to use film or television. Why tell a story in one or the other? For a film, it should be a self-contained story with a beginning, middle, and end. For television, it can be an ongoing world with hours and hours of plot and character development. Some stories are also better experienced in a big screen cinema with surround sound and an audience, while others work better on a smaller screen with different pacing and less social experience. What makes an experience best suited for immersive media? In short, it might be location or world, and telling a story across the real or virtual world where the location itself is a character and place is at the center of the story.

Adapting Mise en Scène to Immersive Media

Once a creator has deemed the story suitable for immersive media, it is time to explore the many facets of mise en scène that can adapt to this new media format. These aspects include performance, production design as worldbuilding, sound design, lighting, editing/pacing, and agency. These are not everything that may emerge as the new storytelling language of immerse media is developing, but they are all important ones to consider. We will next explore these in some detail.

Performance

Performance is quite different between the stage and the screen. Many actors trained for theater need to learn the subtly of cinema and vice versa, cinema performers can sometimes fall flat on stage. At its core, a performer learns the story, the world, and the character. They discover the driving factors for the character, along with their inner and outer obstacles to create a dynamic performance. The actor must choose how to best express these characteristics for the specific medium and director. Each production has a very different tone, from quirky comedy to understated drama demanding a different expression of the character's qualities. Performers are at their largest on stage in order to reach the last row of the audience. In contrast, cinema has close-ups that allow performers to be their most subtle. Performance and gesture change depending on how it is received, recorded, or shown.

There are many kinds of performances in immersive media, from real people to motion capture, voice-over, and animation. Actors can be captured during a live performance in 360 video, or as a hologram (volumetric capture) for virtual and augmented reality. With 360 videos, the elements seem similar to the film, as a lens is capturing the performer. Unlike cinema, the idea of close-up changes the actor is performing in a world where the camera is the user. An actor can use the subtly of cinema when they are close and yet might need the scope of theater when they are further away. They have the choice still of breaking the fourth wall and talking directly to the audience, in immersive media's case, it can feel like the performer is talking directly to them as if they are the only person in the room.

The performer can have a larger purpose than being *in* the story, perhaps serving as a guide throughout the world. For example, the performers in the immersive play, *Sleep No More,* are meant to be so captivating that the audience follows them to their next interaction. The performers can acknowledge the audience or not, or even prompt them to take action in an interactive story. In virtual and augmented reality, an actor's performance can be challenging. For instance, if an actor does not have a proper eye line when being volumetrically captured on a sound stage, it can feel like they are talking to a void, especially when the user is free to roam away from them. When capturing a performer for real-time animation, the performance tends to be in layers, from the way they move, speak, and interact, each aspect is captured separately and then brought together in a game engine.

An example of layering this technology is an experience called *Greenland Melting* created by Nonny de La Pena, Catherine Upin, Rany Aronson-Rath, and Julia Cort, which won best immersive experience at Venice Film Festival in 2017. The documentary experience was created for PBS' *Frontline* show. *Greenland Melting* merged live performance with immersive environments to create a very innovative documentary experience. The captured volumetric performances of the scientists added an element of excitement, though ultimately these did not add to the immersion as the scientists were each looking into a void. If they had been talking to someone, perhaps a travel companion for the participant, the scientists could have directed their performance to a person, making it feel more grounded and connected. Despite this shortcoming, this film takes a bold step forward, even acknowledging the fact that using this technology to drive performance is at its very beginnings.

Production Design as Worldbuilding

Scenic design did not start in theatre until the 1600s with the first person receiving the credit being Robert Edward Jones for the 1915 stage production of *The Man Who Married a Dumb Wife*. For the stage, production or scenic design includes all the visual elements on the stage except the costumes. The overarching guideline for this aspect is that the design should express the mood and spirit of the play.[1]

In film the title *Production Designer* was first coined for William Cameron Menzies for his work on the film *Gone with the Wind* (1939) and the extraordinary way his work affected the look of the film. Different film genres call for the different stylization of the story's world, eventually leading to genres across films. The work of a production designer starts with a script, and they contribute based on what the story dictates. Art direction and production design can actually overlap, with production design being the more inclusive term.[2]

The production designer oversees every aspect of the story's world, which includes everything from the furniture to the artwork on the walls, to props and sets. The production designer can make a city street look like it is in a different era, whether past or future. In the film, the design is limited to the frame. Depending on the lens the camera is using, the design can be on a small or more significant area but only includes the elements inside the frame, perfectly crafted to tell the story best. However, with 360-video and virtual reality, the production design encompasses the entire world. The production designer becomes essential in creating or building the world of the story. In video games, the world designer creates an environment for the game. Similarly, the production designer becomes a world designer, with the consideration of how the elements of the world best help a user experience the story. With augmented reality, the designer focuses on 3D elements and how they place the elements within the real world and how a user might interact with the element.

The production design in immersive media immediately grounds the user in the story. In an instant, it will inform the user of era, tone, and genre. The story starts at that moment, whether it is the discovery of a digital element in a real-world environment or virtual world. That sense of place in itself embeds with the story. The author plays with a sense of place as a character in her short 360-video, *Ashes* (2016). The experience takes place at a beach and shows three memories tied to a single location. Where a man and a woman fall in love on the user's left, that same couple suffer a loss directly in front of the user, and to the user's right, the woman returns to mourn—moving forward and backward in time, giving the user an experience of the tryptic of memories tied to a single place (Figure 1).

Figure 1. A scene from the author's VR work, ashes
Source: Image courtesy of the author

Sound Design

Sound design in theater stayed relatively the same until 1930 when the recording industry took off. This revolutionized recorded sound in both film and theater. Before that time, any sound effect or music was created and performed live. Previously, movies were silent or sometimes had a live pianist or set of musicians playing along (Kushins, 2016).

The first film with sound was *The Jazz Singer* in 1927. Since that time, the evolution of sound design has progressed rapidly. It was not until *Star Wars* (1977) in the 1970s when George Lucas took the sound from mono, a single spear to work with Dolby to create 4-channel stereo. Dolby continued to innovate creating 5.1 sound in 1991, where the sound come from front left, center and right plus forward and behind and then 7.1 surround sound in 2010 adding two additional speakers in the back. In 2012, Dolby created the Atmos system, which allows a sound designer to place sounds anywhere around a space.[3]

Along with Dolby, immersive media has pushed other companies to create sounds in space-spatialized sounds—as they are crucial to the immersion and storytelling. Imagine having music come from a record player or radio and getting louder as you get closer. Sounds emanating from specific objects help trick the brain to feeling that the world is real—everything from the sound of high heels tapping on the floor to the sound of a refrigerator opening to the buzz and hum of an air conditioner. Each sound has a specific place or object to situate it within the world.

Google Spotlights Stories created a short-animated story called *Pearl*, which won an Emmy in 2017 for *Outstanding Innovation in Interactive Storytelling*. The father/daughter story takes place in a car where the sound is used to ground the user. Lead sound designer, Jamey Scott placed the sounds very specifically while mixing it with the music and soundtrack, keeping the user completely emotionally engaged in the story.

Film uses music in addition to sound effects as a tool to add emotion into a story. In immersive media, it becomes difficult to place music without grounding it in the world from something such as a music player. The sound designer has to play with ensuring its subtle enough not to distract the user.

Many spaces in the real world incorporate music, sometimes from ceiling speakers at a volume as to not distract from the tasks at hand. The effective sound design in immersive media follows that pattern.

Sound can also be a tool to direct the user's gaze. A loud crash or a doorbell can compel a user to look in the direction of the sound. If a person is running towards a person in real life, they would like to look before the person reaches them hearing the footsteps fast approaching. Many sounds explicitly placed in an immersive environment can compel a user to look for the source of that sound. This use of sound works across all types of immersive media, typically when experienced with headphones.

Lighting

In the 1700s lighting design was a manual affair with candles and chandeliers on pully systems along with the snuffer who was in charge of keeping the wicks shorts and transitioning the theater from light to dark. In the late 1800s with the advent of gaslighting, elaborate, centralized systems were created to create a gas table, the early beginning of the modern switchboard. At the turn of the 20th Century is when incandescent lights were invented and lighting systems to advance the telling of the story appeared, including spotlights. In the mid-20th Century projection and special effects began to appear in stage performances (Trip et al., 2015).

Methods of using light helped draw the audience to a specific performer or moment with technology advancement increasing the usage of light for storytelling. In film, lighting is necessary in order for the film to be processed. Early film stock called for stronger lights and this affected the look and lighting style in the late-1920s to early-1930s. The German expressionists then used even more contrast and shadow. As technology in the film industry evolved, fewer lights were needed, and new techniques emerged that can drive a wide range of the look, feel, and genre of a story. In addition to location and production design, the way a film or TV show is lit can instantly reveal much about the genre. For example, low contrast is typically used for comedy while higher contrast might typically be the style for horror or thriller films.

Practical lights are those that appear as if the light source is coming from within the storyworld, while other lights, such as high-key or ambient fill out the frame. In more recent cinema, natural lighting has become a trend. Many filmmakers have a specific look to their films that's consistent, like Wes Anderson whose films are graphic, full of color and light and are typically odd comedies, where as someone like Nicolas Winding Refn uses high-contrast and neon lights bleeding against fog to add tension to his dark thrillers.

In immersive media, light can do more than create mood and look. Light can be an essential tool to drive gaze. A beautiful film that uses light and the lack thereof to drive the story is *Dear Angelica*, directed by Saschka Unseld. In this short virtual reality narrative, the illustrations come to life in story, driving gaze and slowly drawing the viewers immersion deeper into the world. When it premiered, it was one of the more successful usages of the medium that heightened the user's emotion and thus their immersion into the story.

Editing / Pacing

One of the distinct differences in storytelling between theater and film is editing. In theater, the story takes place on a stage, and techniques used to move the play across time and location include changing sets, adjusting lighting, and even spoken words. In film, the viewer is moved from location to the point of view through editing of the film sequences. A story can move across countries, decades, and rooms in less time than a blink of an eye. Another filmic technique is the use of cross-cutting to create a narrative. The filmmaker Edwin S. Porter could cut between two elements, say a woman screaming in a house on fire and a scene with fire engines, and the audience would piece together what was happening to form a narrative. Porter's *A Great Train Robbery* in 1903 was the first realistic narrative and one of the first box office successes. This film inspired investors and thus ushered in the advent of theaters to view films (Sklar et al., 2019). It was the craft of filmmaking that drove technology to serve better and project it.

The technology of editing continued to evolve as the techniques and desires to drive the art of film forward expanded. Editors explored different techniques to drive tone, the telling of a story, and the pace of a film. Quick cuts work for action, and slower pacing works for drama and stories that need room for performances to drive the narrative. Over more than 100 years, the editing and placing of frames have changed how stories are created and received in filmmaking. Consistent techniques are used across a film to tell stories best, jump thru time, move between scenes, and drive the story forward while keeping the viewer emotionally engaged in the story. From match cuts that match imagery from one scene to the next to orient the viewer visually, jump cut which abruptly jumps in time to create tension and disorientation to cutting on an action that effortlessly moves the viewer from one scene to the next. Countless cutting techniques been used and perfected over thousands of film and television sequences. It took time and experimentation to find cuts that help the story rather than confuse the viewer. For example, in film and television, there is the 180-degree rule where cutting conversation to ensure the two people talking are looking at each other. This rule was created to combat the problem of filming in a three-dimensional space and having it remain correct when translated to a two-dimensional screen.

In immersive media, these rules do not always make sense, since the environment is a three-dimensional space being re-experienced in a virtual three-dimensional space. There have been a few techniques that carry over from traditional cinema, with many more techniques that will be determined for successful use over time. For example, in certain instances, a match cut helps move people between worlds while staying grounded and oriented. Cutting on the action is also a useful tool but needs to make sense within the story to keep the user grounded. The author played with cutting on action extensively in her VR *Dance Project* films and experimented with using the same action while changing worlds to see how it might work to move between spaces in a single immersive experience. These films experiment with jump-cutting as well. Some viewers have loved the use of cutting, while others felt they were jarring. Montages have proven to disorient the view across worlds, and building a conversation is still a question. Camera placement will significantly affect the edit. Whether it is a camera in the game engine or a real environment, capturing the world in specific relation to the subjects will change how the edit will work. It will take many more years of experimentation across creators and stories to find a consistent use of edits that will create an intuitive, emotional response from the audience.

Agency

Unique to immersive media is the user's agency. In theater, everyone watches the same stage; in and the director will use techniques to direct the gaze within the theater's frame, but it is tough to miss the intended story in a theater. Similarly, in film and television, there is a single location for the viewer to gaze. In each of these mediums, stories have pushed technological advancements. Yet, all three of these mediums ask the viewer to sit and watch passively.

In a type of theater called *No Proscenium Theater*, it is a narrative structure without a stage where the viewer in within the story surrounding them. Video games, too, are a mechanism where the users' interactions drive the story. Both these storytelling mechanisms utilize the audience or player's agency to experience the story. How can this be translated into immersive media, and what are the different forms of storytelling that can drive the story? That is the question creators are trying to answer with each experience. Immersive media needs to find its form that it is a little bit of all of these mediums but also a unique and new medium in and of itself.

Different levels of agency can be given to a user, from simple gaze and turning their head, to moving in space, to touching an object. The creator's responsibility is to explain the user's level of agency within their story and ensure the user has a reason for that agency. If a user can touch objects, the creator must ensure those objects can help drive the story, determining the proper interactivity to make the agency pay off. If the user can look around the creator needs to ensure there is a reason to look, determining they discover something. The integration of plot, pacing, character, sound, light, and agency allows a compelling, immersive story to come to life.

There are many layers to stories, in cinema and television, usually an A, B and C story. The A story is the critical driver of the plot, while the B and C stories are essential to the world. In immersive media, the world and the agency help drive the story, and the creator can use this to develop the A, B, and C stories. The author has not yet seen this sort of layered storytelling in immersive media, but that is not to say it does not exist. The mechanisms of consuming immersive media are still limited, usually at film festivals and specific events. Though the author believes that when a creator does master layered and compelling storytelling, it will be hard to miss, as it will likely be the first blockbuster in immersive media.

These are just a few of the areas vital to discovering a new language of storytelling in the immersive space. However, the expectation to fully realize this in a short period without massive amounts of experimentation will remain a challenge. It took film and television a 100 years or more to discover their unique voices. VR may not be allowed the luxury of that type of time frame. The need to drive revenue and audiences to keep business may hamper storytelling language development in immersive media. There is a difference between NASA and SpaceX. NASA is exploring the future of space while SpaceX is taking what has been discovered and commoditizing it. Both are important, but if immersive media does not encourage exploration, there will never be a need for commoditization, or it will ultimately fail.

SOLUTIONS AND RECOMMENDATIONS

The most important ways to drive the emergence of story language in immersive media are experimentation, learning, and sharing. History shows us that it took time to perfect storytelling across theater, film, and television, but it also shaped a constant multi-billion dollar a year industry. It will take the VR industry slowing down, finding a way to self-sustain before it can grow to a similar size. Even further, the stories need to be told across the entire immersive world, not just in the entertainment domain.

The use of a story in worldbuilding will drive this next computing paradigm. It will be more important than ever to use storytellers across every business, use case and domain.

The companies building the technology are so hungry for mass adoption they are taking short cuts, thinking that any highly sought-after story or property can take on an immersive form and like magic, it will attract users. That might be true, but it probably will not keep them. Just like putting lipstick on a pig does not make it more attractive. There is a need for experimentation amongst the many, and not just the privileged few. For that to truly take place, there needs to be an economic incentive for those experiments to happen.

The more people from diverse backgrounds are incentivized to experiment in this space, the more quickly the rules and the language of stories will be discovered. It will take thousands of attempts before one will hit it beyond the fanatics and reach deeply into all humans, all of whom need stories, and not just cool technology.

REFERENCES

Cummins, E. (2018). *The surprising politics of Sidewalks*. Retrieved from https://www.popsci.com/politics-versus-sidewalks/

Damiani, J. (2019). Jessica Brillhart Named Director of USCICT Mixed Reality Lab (Exclusive). *Forbes*. Retrieved from https://www.forbes.com/sites/jessedamiani/2019/06/25/jessica-brillhart-named-director-of-usc-ict-mixed-reality-lab-exclusive/#65bb01a07cb2

Halls, A. (2018). *A Brief History of Immersive Theater*. Retrieved from https://www.postandcourier.com/spoleto/a-brief-history-of-immersive-theater/article_baf19760-637c-11e8-b8ad-3b7339b572ac.html

Harari, Y. N. (2017). *Power and Imagination*. Retrieved from https://www.ynharari.com/topic/power-and-imagination/

House, P. (2016). *Werner Herzog Talks Virtual Reality*. Retrieved from https://www.newyorker.com/tech/annals-of-technology/werner-herzog-talks-virtual-reality

Howard, A. (2016). *A Short History of Ancient Theatre*. Retrieved from https://www.newhistorian.com/2016/09/19/short-history-ancient-theatre/

Hsu, C. T., Conrad, M., & Jacobs, A. M. (2014). Fiction feelings in Harry Potter: Haemodynamic response in the mid cingulate cortex correlates with immersive reading experience. *Neuroreport*, *25*(17), 1356–1361. doi:10.1097/WNR.0000000000000272 PMID:25304498

King, D. (2018). *Spend A Night at The McKittrick Hotel, A Damned Good Spot*. Retrieved from https://www.forbes.com/sites/darrynking/2018/07/19/spend-a-night-at-the-mckittrick-hotel-a-damned-good-spot/#7d5e04df126d

Kushins, J. (2016). *A brief history of sound in cinema*. Retrieved from https://www.popularmechanics.com/culture/movies/a19566/a-brief-history-of-sound-in-cinema/

Moura, G. (2016). *Mise-En-Scène*. Retrieved from http://www.elementsofcinema.com/directing/mise-en-scene-in-films/

Osburn, L. (2017). *Storytelling, Central to Human Experience*. Retrieved from https://500womenscientists.org/updates/2017/7/31/storytelling-human-experience

Raessens, J. (2019). Virtually Present, Physically Invisible: Alejandro G. Iñárritu's Mixed Reality Installation Carne y Arena. *Television & New Media*, *20*(6), 634–648. doi:10.1177/1527476419857696

Rylaf, J. B. (2018). House of Secrets: A Night With 'The Willows' (REVIEW). *Noproscenium.* Retrieved from https://noproscenium.com/house-of-secrets-a-night-with-the-willows-review-a3e13bc3e0e1

Silverstein, S. (2004). *Where the sidewalk ends: the poems & drawings of Shel Silverstein.* New York: Harper Collins.

SklarR.CookD. (2019). *Edwin S. Porter.* Retrieved from https://www.britannica.com/biography/Edwin-S-Porter

Sklar, R., & Cook, D. A. (2019). *History of the Motion Picture.* Retrieved from https://www.britannica.com/art/history-of-the-motion-picture

Smith, D., Schlaepfer, P., Major, K., Dyble, M., Page, A. E., Thompson, J., . . . Migliano, A. B. (2017). Cooperation and the evolution of hunter gatherer storytelling. *Nature Communications, 8,* 1853. Retrieved from https://www.nature.com/articles/s41467-017-02036-8

Trip, H. M., & Gillette, J. M. (2015). *Stagecraft.* Retrieved from https://www.britannica.com/art/stagecraft

ENDNOTES

[1] Holmes, R., Dufford, S., Bay, H., Gillette, M. J. et al. (2015). *Stagecraft: Theatre.* Retrieved from https://www.britannica.com/art/stagecraft

[2] Production Design. Schirmer Encyclopedia of Film. Retrieved July 17, 2019, from Encyclopedia. com: https://www.encyclopedia.com/arts/encyclopedias-almanacs-transcripts-and-maps/production-design

[3] See more about Atmos at https://www.dolby.com/us/en/brands/dolby-atmos.html

Chapter 9
Bringing the Human Dimension to Virtual Experience

Christina Heller
Metastage, USA

ABSTRACT

Immersive media can be achieved through many types of production techniques, each designed to achieve a specific purpose. This chapter describes Metastage, a volumetric capture studio aligned with Microsoft, that is being used by a wide range of creators to produce their groundbreaking immersive works. The common element in these works is the desire to bring realistic human representation to the productions. In addition to interviews with select practitioners, this chapter also describes techniques and best practices for high end volumetric capture.

INTRODUCTION

Breaking Free From The Frame

There are many of us (such as those authors featured in this book) who believe the next digital media platform will be immersive, free from the constraints of the flat frame. Say goodbye to hunching over a laptop or straining to read a smartphone, and hello to spatial computing and immersive technology, where we stand up tall, move freely in our spaces, and summon digital assets that more accurately reflect the world around us—a vivid user experience, full of depth and physical presence. As someone who has spearheaded two companies in XR (and at risk of sounding like a 'Silicon Valley' parody), the author's hope is that immersive technology will bring us closer—physically and psychically—than ever before. The Internet brought the world into our living rooms, but then it locked us behind screens while we marveled at our new tools and toys. Perhaps this era of "tech neck" and digital isolation is just our generation's burden to bear while we usher in the full potential of immersive cyberspace.[1]

DOI: 10.4018/978-1-7998-2433-6.ch009

The Internet, in tandem with TV, provided such an amazing shift in our perceptions of, and interactions with, the world that *screen time* in the 21st Century dominates our existence. And who could blame us for succumbing? In the past, one's social interactions were limited by physically close neighbors and one's immediate social networks. Now we are literally connected to the entire world.

We've made willing (and sometimes begrudging) tradeoffs for the connected screen. We love our smartphones, tablets, and laptops. We love our Spotify and Netflix and GPS and Sonos and Amazon and Lyft and Airbnb and Postmates and… the list goes on and on.

But if we are honest with ourselves, we know that we've lost something in the process, something important. We now must go out of our way to seek what used to be the norm: things like face-to-face human interactions, the thrill of exploring real environments, and the subsequent surprises that these interactions can bring. In a world of flat screens with primarily text and image-based communication, we've lost a large measure of fundamental human stuff. How do we reconcile the human, physical world with the new forms of connectedness that the Internet and our screens provide?

This is where AR and VR come into play. They are the positive disrupters to today's flat screen mode of interacting. Social VR allows multiple participants to inhabit the same virtual environment simultaneously. WebXR (the evolving immersively configured web-based browser) promises to transform the way we browse, from flat to fully dimensional. And volumetric video, which this chapter explores, will provide the means to bring real people and real performances into those worlds, changing our relationships to our media in evolutionary and exciting ways. There is no going back.

Volumetric Capture

The focus for this chapter is volumetric capture, sometimes called holographic capture, or volumetric video. The author is currently the CEO of Metastage, a company based in Los Angeles, CA, which specializes in this particular emerging creative technology. Metastage has helped pioneer a number of groundbreaking early projects and applications. Volumetric capture (*volcap* for short) allows a person to experience digital captures of real people and authentic performances in an immersive environment, permitting them to move around freely in this space, with what our industry calls six degrees of freedom, or DoF.[2] These performances are recorded from every possible angle on a special stage using multiple video cameras and customized software to capture and render an authentic, fully 3D asset. This technique provides the closest thing to the true experience of what transpired live. Picture a human hologram from any science fiction movie such as the holographic librarian in the film *The Time Machine* (2002). Today this can actually be realized: A fully three dimensional, authentic representation of what was captured that can be experienced in full dimensions after the original event.

Volumetric capture often gets confused with motion capture (or mocap), a process of recording an actor's motions that has been used in films from *The Polar Express* (2004) to *Avatar* (2009). Motion capture is the technique of recording movements digitally from multiple cameras, so that the motion can be reapplied to digital characters after the fact. An actor can have their full body tracked and recorded, or simply the movements of their face, which is called performance tracking. The goal of mocap is a realistic animated character without having an animator doing tedious handwork. To the layman, a volumetric stage might look similar to a mocap stage, as both volcap and mocap involve actors being captured by a surrounding array of cameras. Each method produces a huge amount of data, requires specific hardware and software, and produces a 3D asset. However, there are key differences between the two approaches in both the production process and final output.

In motion capture, for the most part, actors are required to wear tracking suits with markers, and when capturing facial performance capture, tiny marker dots all over the face (though recent techniques can work without markers). These markers generate data via the software that corresponds the marker locations to each targeted body part through time, thus tracking the movements of the body and/or face. Then this movement data can be applied to other assets such as a cartoon character or an actor's digital stunt double.

By contrast, in volumetric capture, no special suits are needed. The subject or performer simply goes out onto the center of the capture stage in their regular clothes or a costume, without trackers or applied markers. The capture takes place in real time, as the person goes through their actions. This data then goes through a render step, and what comes off the render farm is production ready, no additional animation needed. You have a totally authentic representation of what transpired live.

A Typical Day at Metastage

It's day two of shooting a new internal initiative at Metastage. Brent, the performer, stands in the center of the green 8-foot circular stage surrounded by 106 cameras. "What song do you want to do dance to?" I ask. "Teach Me How to Dougie," he says without hesitation.

The goal of today's Metastage sessions is to scan a set of stock actors to be used in the background of game engine environments. Developers will be able to license these stock captures at an affordable rate to help bring more life to their game or XR experiences. To accomplish this the Metastage team will volumetrically capture a diverse set of people in a series of common "background" activities, such as:

- Talking while standing
- Listening while standing
- Talking while sitting
- Listening while sitting
- Thinking
- Presenting
- and for the party scenes that are bound to be created—Dancing.

Over the course of four days, twenty actors visit us with their own wardrobe options, and a simple set of acting instructions. I am surprised and delighted to see each performer bring a totally different attitude to the same acting cues. It turns out that, "stand and look around like you are waiting for someone" can be interpreted in more ways than one might expect!

But in every session, the dancing sequence is by far the most fun for the performers and for the capture crew. By encouraging these diverse actors to be themselves, and by allowing them to pick a song that speaks to them, we can capture a small piece of their authentic selves—the real Brent, not actor Brent. These people, standing in the background of future XR experiences, will be real and authentic expressions of the humans we were lucky enough to scan.

People are imperfect, compelling and mysterious. It's why we can watch the same play over and over if it's done with different performers. Each person—on the stage and in real life—brings their own unique combination of nature and nurture, personality and performance to this exact moment in time. They bring that individual humanity to their craft, and inspire a sense of seeing something new, never seen quite like this before.

Figure 1. A shot of metastage

In an era where digitizing actors is becoming more and more common, and since volcap is often confused with mocap, some performers may be resistant to the idea of a computer generated version of themselves. Volumetric capture might also confused with high resolution face scanning technology, which allows actors to play younger versions of themselves, or perhaps allows actors to even become animated versions of themselves. This scanning process has already caused ambivalence in the acting community as it becomes increasingly adopted as a Hollywood production practice.

However, volumetric capture is nothing to fear. It is simply capturing what transpired on the stage in full 3D (unlike traditional video or film), and it is intended to present that performance with as much integrity as possible. Volcap attempts to create and preserve the closest thing to the actual physical performance that has ever existed. In that sense, volumetric capture is the real person's seat at the virtual table.

BACKGROUND

The volumetric capture studio at Metastage consists of 106 cameras: 53 RGB and 53 Infrareds (Figure 1). The RGB cameras capture the visual data, and the infrared cameras create the point cloud, the 3D figure upon which that visual data is placed. Like a globe facing inward, these cameras surround the performer. Those who have been captured at Metastage have reported feeling both a sense of isolation (alone on the stage) and also a feeling of being 'seen' (knowing you are being filmed from every angle).

We are emphatic about testing. For almost every shoot, we dedicate a day to trying anything we may have questions about, whether that is hair, makeup, wardrobe, choreography, or props. We then process those results and review as a group to evaluate if there are any issues or changes that need to be made.

Figure 2. The metastage technical team

On every shoot, there is standard production crew: a production manager to coordinate, hair and makeup artists, and production assistants. We also have a wardrobe technician who makes sure the clothing will capture correctly. This is such an important job that we require someone who is focused on that completely. The technical team consists of a capture technician, audio team, and processing specialist (Figure 2). The capture tech uses specialized software to control all the cameras simultaneously. When we are ready to roll, the capture tech syncs with the director, audio team and talent to make sure everyone is coordinated. Audio starts recording. The capture tech starts recording. Once they are "speeding" (i.e. recording), the director calls action.

Once we're rolling, the shoot runs similar to a traditional framed production. The director can do multiple takes to get the performance they desire. A script supervisor keeps detailed notes on their select and safety shots. Throughout the day, the processing specialist renders short clips to make sure everything is coming out correctly, and again, we review internally and then with the creative team.

After the shoot wraps, the director is sent the timecoded reference videos of their select and safety shots for review. They can evaluate the performance again. Once they have decided on their best takes, they send our team the time code and frame ranges for their final selections. We then process based of these time codes. Processing times vary, though we typically deliver the final volumetric assets within one to two weeks. Faster processing is possible, and the technology to do so is evolving rapidly to the point where volume no longer presents the same challenges, and projects can be turned around more quickly. The final captures are delivered in two file formats: .mp4 containers that are compressed and ready to integrate into the game engine, and the full size .obj and .png sequences in case our client wants to do their own VFX. They can then be returned to us for re-encoding to the .mp4 container, which maintains the quality of the capture at tiny file sizes that are easy for distribution.

We are now at a point where the question has changed from "Can we do it?" to "What should we do with it?" And most importantly: "Where does this new video technology serve the commercial market and humanity as the whole?"

CONVERSATIONS WITH KEY PRACTITIONERS

To bring more perspectives into this snapshot of volumetric capture in 2019/2020, I conducted interviews with three key industry practitioners who represent different facets of the landscape.

Each has contributed in significant ways to this emerging medium. They have dedicated themselves to the technical and creative challenges of volumetric capture, and lend their thoughts on its challenges, opportunities, and significance in the legacy of photographic and cinematic history. These experts included Steve Sullivan, the General Manager of Microsoft's Mixed Reality Capture Studio efforts, James George, CEO of the company Scatter, which is on the forefront of new forms of immersive storytelling, and Asad J. Malik, who has created critically acclaimed immersive works that are both interactive, and also evocative examples of this new medium.

Surpassing the Uncanny Valley: Steve Sullivan

Coined by Professor Masahiro Mori in the 1970s, the term uncanny valley was initially used in the robotics industry (Mori, MacDorman & Kageki, 2012). Professor Mori determined that the more human-like the robots began to appear, the more people increasingly started to bond with the robot, but only until a certain point. Once the robot reached a certain threshold of "realness," the positive feelings tended to turn into revulsion. Besides robots, this phenomenon was also shown in early digital humans used in films, such as the aforementioned *Polar Express* film. Actor Tom Hanks was mocapped for the film, and even though his acting is award-winning, the motion capture of the time could not give a fully realistic or high enough resolution sampling of his movements. That film character left people feeling something was missing (Wilkins, 2015). Even the advanced photorealistic rendering techniques of that time could not overcome what was perceived by viewers to be missing with the motion capture. It was firmly situated in the uncanny valley. The was due to the fact that even though the entity was highly realistic, it still lacked something essential that we, as humans were specifically attuned to. Subtle movements, especially in individual body language or micro-expressions were not captured in enough detail for humans to believe they were being made by an actual human. (Page-Kirby, 2015).

But once a robot or digital actor surpasses this uncanny valley of realness, it then graduates to the highest degree of positive association and empathy, generating a genuine human-to-human connection. Apparently the gulf of the uncanny valley spans the spectrum from "barely human" to "fully human," and you are better off creating something that falls more towards the barely human category than achieving a near miss of fully human to avoid the uncanny valley. The big question is: How does a production get past this uncanny valley to where people feel a positive association? Techniques such as are utilized at Metastage are some of the ways this can happen.

Metastage works with the Microsoft Mixed Reality Capture technology system developed as part of Microsoft's Mixed Reality Capture Studios (MRCS). With its sophisticated pipeline, this studio is now considered a leader in premium volumetric capture software. However, when Microsoft researchers started to develop this work, they stumbled onto their volumetric process almost accidentally, as this was not their intended initial research direction. Now, with dedicated effort covering the past decade, the research has evolved to allow moving past the uncanny valley into the "fully human" threshold. A secondary goal for the researchers was to ensure the captured material could be widely distributed and enjoyed on every day devices people could access. How were they able to do this?

Steve Sullivan, the general manager of the Microsoft MRCS, explains the conception and evolution of the volumetric capture technology.

The original concept was trying to capture personal memories from multiple Kinect devices.[3] The researchers set up an array of [Kinects], went for it, and the quality just wasn't there. It was essentially an incubator startup project. The pivot went to, let's forget about Kinects in particular. We think this kind of content could be really interesting. Let's do it with cameras and stereo techniques. So we switched over to multiple cameras.

They then started increasing the camera count based on what people were responding to and what needed to be captured. They adjusted their process with a tremendous amount of feedback, the goal being believability of the final holographic content and also production practicality. The capture volume was originally too small to capture a full-sized person. They needed more for the kind of content most people would need to create or that people wanted to experience.

Sullivan states:

We went from a very small capture volume to the current 8 feet, and it really stabilized there—106 cameras in a certain configuration of 8 feet—that has been the sweet spot for quite a long time.

Building a technology stack that was high quality but also viable for average productions meant overcoming a number of challenges.

First it was just getting good point cloud," Sullivan recalls, "The basic foundation for the rest of the hologram is the capture quality, and so we balanced the speed of processing, speed of implementation, maintenance... all these factors... and landed with an algorithm called "patch match.

After implementing variations on that algorithm, they were able to get the quality to the acceptable standard.

We messed with point clouds early on. Definitely considered voxel grids, point clouds, all kinds of representations, but we found in the things that people were asking us to do for the devices we wanted to play on, to get the compression ratios we needed, meshes were going to be much more flexible, so we stuck with that path.

A mesh-based system presents its own challenges. A "mesh" is a broad net of polygons that's derived from a point cloud and serves as a framework for the visual information and textures. The wireframe mesh, texture map, and UV atlas are the elements that make up the complete virtual representation of the person. Essentially It tells the software where to place the eyelids, the buttons on the jacket, along with all the visual information to make a person look like a person.

Picture the old Paint By Numbers: The mesh is the figure on the paper, the texture atlas is the paint, and the UV map is the numbers. And since these figures are moving, you will have many unique meshes and UV Maps to create the dynamic, moving figure, kind of like taking your Paint by Numbers art and turning it into a flip book. Therefore 30 frames per second would translate into 30 pages in the flip book if you were using a unique mesh for every frame.

Sullivan and the MRCS team needed to make the meshes and UV maps as clean as possible, or the holograms would have visual anomalies, pieces that might stick out in certain areas and simply don't look correct.

The mesh cleanup took a great deal of concentrated effort. He describes:

Once you've got the cleaned up mesh, if there's a different mesh every frame, it's hard to work with, and really heavy, so we put probably two years of effort into our tracking technology to stabilize it between keyframes.

To keep with the flip book analogy, if we shoot at 30 fps, without keyframing it translates to a different mesh for each frame—30 meshes for just one second of content. Since ease of distribution was one of the targets of the process, having all that data made the final processed content too "heavy"—too large to distribute in a commercially viable way. The MCRS keyframing technology taught the software to keep just one mesh for as long as it possibly could before it was forced to change meshes and UV maps. With this technique there were a lesser number of meshes in the overall product, and the deliverable could be compressed to an astoundingly small file size.

Finally, the content needed to be delivered on consumer devices. All this R&D coincided with the development of the Hololens, Microsoft's flagship augmented reality headset. Volumetric capture being a natural fit for the Hololens, MRSC was tasked with getting its holographic content into a standard delivery codec (a compression-decompression algorithm for data) that could ideally translate to other consumer devices.

We went from research project in a startup group incubator over to the Hololens program at the end of 2013, and that's when we really focused on making it work for Hololens." Their mandate was to make it work over wi-fi with a low power computer device. "And that drove a lot of our engineering for the next couple of years, which has been very useful since then, of course. It got us into a form factor that could be consumed everywhere.

He describes the .mp4 container codec, which is the format in which the processed volumetric content is delivered, along with the full size .obj and .png sequences. These compressed .mp4 containers come with plugins for the Unity and Unreal game engines, which allow the game systems to properly read and decode the .mp4 volumetric files and display them as they are meant to be displayed.

We figured if it was a known file type, and we will have no friction in moving this stuff around as long as our decoder can recognize that our geometry is in there.

As for the MRCS roadmap, Sullivan is looking at ways to increase flexibility for creators and the asset's versatility, saying, "We get very consistent requests and always have for reanimation and relighting," as well as tools for editing and interactivity."

With companies like Dimension Studios (London) and Metastage (Los Angeles) licensing the MRCS technology for commercial use, what was once an R&D project has become a product in the market, the beginning of a long time vision of Sullivan and the MRCS team.

The next year is all about commercial adoption and value—what do people want to use this for? Making sure it's truly useful, frictionless access on any platform that people care about, engaging creators, making sure they understand what the medium is.

We hope that capture becomes a commodity. There's no secret sauce in getting these point clouds and meshes, it's really about how people use them, and how people value them. We've seen plenty of indication from people that they want these holograms for their own personal preservation and memories, but to do that you need the consumption ecosystem. You need to share the hologram with grandma. You need to come back to your hologram from last year and look at them together. I'm as confident about that, because it doesn't rely on VR or AR or any of these other waves. It has it's own value.

When asked about cinematic volumetric capture, and using these performances for storytelling purposes, Sullivan says that the creative language and best practices around for that have yet to be established.

It's been a very recurrent point from the earliest days that when you capture volumetric, people think volumetric cinema and storytelling. Next generation of movies. It has not played out that way. We haven't been able to crack the nut yet of how to direct point of view, cutting, all the standard creative tools that we use in our current narrative, and I'd be really intrigued to see where that goes. Because I think people understand that there is some potential there that they want to be a part of and engage with, but we just haven't gotten there yet.

Next Generation of Storytelling: James George

James George, the CEO of the New York City-based company Scatter,[4] is paving the way for the next generation of movies to which Sullivan refers. By way of introduction, it would be hard to put Scatter or James George in one box. Having pioneered award-winning content while simultaneously publishing their core product, Depthkit, they have taken the road less traveled toward technical IP while also pursuing content creation. You don't usually see software companies with Emmys under their belt.

That ethos of software innovation in the service of creative storytelling is at the heart of Scatter's process. Standout immersive projects include the 2012 interactive documentary *CLOUDS* (Co-Directed by George and Jonathan Minard), the 2017 Emmy award-winning *Zero Days VR* (Directed by Scatter Co-Founder Yasmin Elayat), and the 2017 *Blackout* (Directed by Scatter Co-Founder Alexander Porter, and Co-Directed by Elayat), which premiered at the Tribeca Film Festival.

George states:

We don't see ourselves as a traditional studio. If we were a traditional studio, we would be focused on just our titles and keep the tools and workflows we use private or proprietary. Instead we see that by releasing our tools as software products, ensuring that they are accessible, easy to use, and ensuring they can be used globally from day one, because we use distributed low cost hardware. This way we are able to foster a community of creators who are using the same tools. Our users are then in a creative dialogue with us, and all of our projects feed off of one another. That creative community is the thing that really motivates me, and its part of the mission of Scatter.

Rather than comparing volumetric capture to other performance capture technology, he looks to other live action mediums as roadmaps for this next evolution in reality capture:

I think what makes volumetric different from previous motion capture technologies is the sense of verisimilitude. Volumetric is inheriting more from film and theater than it is from videogames.

Let's look at the creators who are working in the volumetric medium today. Most of them have backgrounds coming from visual storytelling in live action, or theatrical production, and that's because the lens through which they see the world for creation comes from an impetus to draw from the canvas that is the reality we live in. When a filmmaker becomes enamored with an actor, or a documentary filmmaker becomes enamored with a story that's unfolding in the real world, their instinct is to bring their camera into that space, or bring that person in front of their camera and capture who they are, what they are… capture the reality that they represent and then craft that into a story by shaping the image through filmmaking and editing.

That impulse of drawing from the world is the same underlying impulse that brings many creators to the volumetric medium, except that volumetric has this added layer of interactivity—which speaks to our generation's needs as storytellers to tell stories that are immersive and participatory. Essentially, volumetric is a collision of filmmaking with the spatial dimension.

For those that are coming from a background of mocap for videogames and looking to volumetric as a way to continue their work they will run up against some of the medium's limitations that are also inherent to its value.

Videogames rely a lot on the interactive mechanics interactions to facilitate the storytelling: interactive mechanics first, and gameplay first. Therefore, characters in games need to be highly dynamic puppets or modeled representations that respond to player's actions. Dynamic interactions are very difficult to do in volumetric at this stage of the volumetric medium.

The sacrifice a creator makes for the verisimilitude of reality capture is to lose the dynamics that you can get with videogames characters, where you can change those characters' actions on the fly. This means the type of experiences you create have to play to the strengths of the medium today, and that's a whole new creative grammar. The pure hybrid of the two will someday be possible and it's easy to imagine a Westworld-esque world where it's photorealistic and fully participatory, but that's still science fiction.

Figure 3. A scene from the 2017 immersive work "Blackout"

George and his team at Scatter used some of the volumetric limitations to their advantage in the creation of *Blackout*, their 2017 and ongoing immersive project. *Blackout* takes place in a New York City subway where as a viewer you hear the stories of the humans sharing the public transit with you.

George was looking for a story he could tell with Depthkit's full body capture. He was also looking for something that would work within the constraints of their reality capture tools at the time, which are that the people are real and they look like themselves, but once in a virtual world you can't interact with them, you can't say anything to them, and they don't follow your gaze.

From a creative point of view we're like, well, when you're on the subway, it's actually really normal for people to ignore you, so what if you were on a subway as an observer, and could actually float through that space and learn about all the people who were there. If you've ever visited New York or lived in a city, there's this amazing cross sectional diversity that exists there, that's so visible on public transit. Even if you're in your bubble elsewhere, you get a taste of the diversity of the city when you're in these public areas. It always evokes this curiosity about who people are, you want to know their stories. So we actually make that fantasy real manifest that people watching fantasy in our experience.

They worked with a documentary casting director to find unique stories throughout the city, such as an African-American Trump supporter, or a man who used *Blackout* as a vehicle to come out to his community as being HIV positive (Figure 3).

George says the goal was:

… finding these really raw, gut-wrenching or surprising stories that people don't always share, but you know people have locked away in their life experiences. We sought out the stories that make our subjects' identities very complex, beyond not what meets the eye. We brought them into experience this project as a participatory project, so that when we premiered it at Tribeca Film Festival, we would bring them

into the capture stage, capture them in the full volumetric 3D Depthkit, and then put them on the train the next day.

Participants would come back the next day to see themselves and hear their stories, along with others on the train, up to 15 virtual passenger people at the same time.

Beyond narrative and storytelling, George is pleasantly surprised to find that creators from other fields are also finding value in volumetric capture.

If you need to educate a workforce or create simulations for trauma therapy, for example, do something in that realm, access to video productions' talent can be more accessible and affordable than 3D design talent, and especially if you have a subject matter or domain expert that you would otherwise have to take to a mocap stage or model. You can just film that person and put them in the experience… The industry's growth in these enterprise sectors is great for us because we continue to focus on developing the creative entertainment and artwork that is Scatter's main fingerprint, and regardless of what industry you're in, you'll be looking to our artistic experiences in XR as an example of how the way to learn what volumetric filmmaking mechanics that can work for communication. You can then use Depthkit to apply those techniques to your own story and needs.

Interactivity in Volumetric: Asad J. Malik

Having used both Depthkit and Microsoft technologies in his critically acclaimed immersive experiences, creative Asad J. Malik, founder of media company 1IRC,[5] is challenging the perceived limitations of volumetric. Malik debuted on the festival circuit with *Terminal 3* (2018), an interactive augmented reality experience that put viewers in the shoes of a person experiencing a racially motivated airport interrogation. The piece, created with DepthKit, premiered at the 2018 Tribeca Film Festival, and put the 20-year-old director on the map of rising auteurs in this emerging medium.

He followed *Terminal 3* with his Sundance entry *A Jester's Tale* (2019). *A Jester's Tale* is a surrealist experience wherein the viewer has to prove he or she is not a robot within a narrative involving a young boy, rats, and a "Rat Queen" played by social media star and musician, Poppy. To execute his vision, he built interactivity into the narrative. Viewers engage in a one-on-one experience with the holographically captured performers. Different viewer decisions, made by voice commands, affect the narrative outcome of the story, and create a customized experience along the way. All of the performances, which involved multiple characters interacting, were captured at Metastage in Los Angeles (Figure 4). An Augmented Reality (AR) first of its kind, *A Jester's Tale* was premiered in 2019 on the just-released Magic Leap headset.

Malik says:

Volumetric is really important to me. We live in this time of 'fake news' right now, with conversations about what is simulated, or what is completely created out of nothing. Compare this (simulated experience) to photographic evidence, or volumetrically captured content.

It's really interesting to me to capture authentic human presence. The actor is there. Take them as they are, rather than create something completely synthetic. There have been all these theories about what it means to capture essence. As soon as photos emerged, the first conversations that people were having

Figure 4. At the Metastage shoot for A Jester's Tale

were about how [photography] immortalizes dead people. Some of the most popular forms of photos at the start were pictures of dead people—brushed up, with makeup on, in their nicest clothes—their final immortal piece of photography. And there's been this whole conversation: Does this photo capture this person's true essence?

Malik cites French literary theorist Roland Barthes and his book *Camera Lucida* (1981) as a big inspiration:

Barthes talks about when his mother died, he couldn't find a single photo of her that really captured her essence. They all captured part of her, but no photo really captured her. Until he found a photo that did. And it was just this photo that captured a particular angle, and it just worked, somehow the mom's essence really came through.

I think volumetric is really interesting, because it's all the photos that can be captured from all the angles of the person. An essence exists somewhere. The viewer becomes a new observer once again. And then photography [of the volumetric] is a separate thing—You can actually take photos of the photos. All the trajectories, working on top of that history.

Malik creates stories using his own branching narrative techniques that work to layer in a level of interactivity within an established narrative structure.

With branching narratives my technique usually is to give the viewer agency on a micro level. On a macro level there's still a dramatic arc.

He counters this structure to that of something like the 2018 *Black Mirror's* Choose-Your-Own-Adventure episode *Bandersnatch* (Roettgers, 2018), where the viewer

… hits all these walls where you go a certain direction and it doesn't work so you have to go back. That never happens in our pieces. It's really important for us that you just feel like you're in it, making decisions, things are happening, and they constantly happen until you reach a certain climax. We build it so there is a dramatic arc, and all the choices are micro.

This creative structure not only ensures that particular aspects of the user experience happen to each visitor but is also used to time dramatic elements.

We want to make sure you hit certain points of importance. With Terminal 3, I used a lot of sticky notes with all kinds of detailed lines. With A Jester's Tale it was more about writing a dramatic script. We don't want the transitions to feel too gimmicky… [We want to ensure] that it matters what you say, and it affects things.

Because premium volumetric technology is expensive, Malik had to be very discerning with his script. Questions with customized responses needed to be carefully maneuvered, or else he would need to capture and process an infinite number of responses from the performers to accommodate the story. For instance, in *A Jester's Tale*, a child asks you who read you bedtime stories growing up. Depending on your answer, the child responds with either "Oh, he did?" or "Oh, she did?" or, "Oh, they did?" resulting in only three possible responses as opposed to many more.

In order to execute this technically, artificial intelligence software was used for making sure the right responses were triggered by the viewers' interactions. They also used VFX tools to track the actor's gaze to the viewer, creating the illusion of eye contact and thus creating more realism to the viewers' participation in the narrative.

Techniques for production to create a seamless interactive narrative are also evolving. Malik and the Metastage team had to try and direct the actors back to the same position at the end of the takes. Neutral poses were recorded to have on hand for decision moments.

I use volumetric capture for interactive…so if anyone is going to say that it's interactive it's going to be me. He goes on to say that motion capture has a lot of aspects that make it effective for interactive storytelling but that, "for me, the real capture is important enough that I will force the interactivity on top of it. And with these couple of things I have mentioned, I think that you could totally have an interactive volumetric experience."

BEST PRACTICES FOR VOLUMETRIC CAPTURE

Not all volumetric systems are the same, and thus the limitations will vary depending on what system you are using. The following limitations are for the Metastage technology system. Other volumetric companies will have similar and likely more complicated limitations. Success in this new medium requires a fresh approach to production, so in the spirit of that, here are things that a burgeoning volumetric professional should keep in mind.

- **Total Capture Space:** All actions must take place inside of an 8' diameter circle. This means creative problem solving for any creative content that involves walking a greater traveling distance than 8' around the virtual space, or if more than three characters are engaging with each other.

- **Thin Items:** The software is looking for geometry to create a mesh. Anything in the capture volume that is too thin—strands of hair, glasses, and certain props—makes it difficult for the system to create the correct geometry. With hair for example, the software will mistake the thin strands of hair as geometry that belongs with the chin or collar of the clothing, and thus begin attaching the mesh of the hair to the other incorrect items. The result is that the capture fails to meet the integrity test, an in-house term used to assess how correct the geometry appears. If it looks "crunchy" or not smooth, or otherwise incorrect, then it fails the integrity test. If the mesh has been correctly calculated, then it will pass the test. Integrity failures can be especially noticeable around the face. If a performer wears glasses, for example, the software will warp the frames to the temples of the person, creating an unauthentic capture. In some cases, like with glasses, the only solution is to capture the subject without them and add them later with Visual Effects (VFX) in a post-processing pass.

- **Wardrobe:** Certain clothing items, especially items that are thin, such as stiletto heels or the fringe on a jacket, will not *solve*, which is a term used to indicate the correct calculation of the geometry mesh. One will run into the same issues that happen with glasses. In addition, shiny or reflective items are extremely difficult to capture, so if a person to be scanned comes in with such items, we will suggest other wardrobe options or use dulling spray to remove the shine.

- **Props:** Some props solve, and others do not, especially ones with complex surfaces or challenging surface characteristics. Sometimes the only approach is to create a test capture to find out. If the item does not solve correctly due to size, specific details, or reflective surface, the crew will need to create a fabricated substitution, which can either be clipped out or replaced with VFX in post. There is increasing use of motion capture systems used in tandem with volumetric systems to help with tracking fast moving props. In addition, moving props can be a problem as the rapid movement causes issues for the software solver.

- **Choreography:** This issue can be framed around the issues in capturing moving geometry. It is especially challenging if two characters are choreographed together. Say they come together to engage in an embrace—at that point the system will have trouble understanding that these are two distinct entities that should maintain their individual meshes. As a result, if two characters are coming close, once their forms get within a certain distance of one another, the software will begin to see these two items as a single one and start combining their meshes, which we call a "globbing effect." If the movements are quick enough, the globbing effect will be harder to notice, but in a slow dance, for instance, one will need to be conscious of dancer positioning to ensure a high quality capture without globbing.

- **Occlusion:** There are also issues of involving camera occlusion, which is when one object hides parts of another from one or more cameras, resulting in missing data for a part of an object or person. This can often happen when bringing multiple figures into the capture volume. It is important to make sure enough cameras are getting enough data from the right angles so that the textures and meshes resolve with integrity.

For those looking to build volumetrically-friendly production materials where they can achieve a top quality result with minimal VFX work, we offer this quick list of practices that will make the process easier both during and in post production:

1. Subject(s) should be ideally standing (not required but easiest on the post-production process).
2. All key movement must happen in an 8' diameter circle.
3. Cast actors with short haircuts or style longer hair into updos.
4. Wardrobe should be form-fitting, tidy, avoiding dark colors, green, or white. While we can capture dark and white colors, they tend to create added complications in processing.
5. Shiny or reflective objects should be eliminated or minimized.
6. Thin objects should not be used in a volcap shoot.

With these items taken into consideration, most major technical complications can be avoided. The crew can then focus on getting the best performances possible from the people and actors on the stage.

TV and film actors rely on editing their strongest takes together to create a performance. Volumetric editing is possible, and the tools around doing so are evolving, however the best practice will always be an un-edited seamless performance. Film actors are also used to being captured (filmed) in extreme close-up, so often their performances will entail evocative facial expressions but not necessarily full body language. And yet, for the volumetric medium, strong physical presence, which includes using the whole body to show emotion, translates best. Creating narratives that are immersive and free from the frame in full dimensional space brings the nature of the physical performance more in line with the craft of live acting for plays or theater than for TV or film. So, while it helps to have experience in both types of performance (facial acting for close-ups and full body acting), using the full body as an expressive tool is even more important for volumetric captures.

CONCLUSION

Achieving Moonshots

Creating work with emerging and ever-evolving technologies has much in common with a business startup endeavor. It can be challenging and frustrating at times. One is working with tools that were either designed for another medium, meant for different use cases, or simply experimental and not fully formed. Reaching a desired solution often requires hacking together combinations of different software and hardware products, and inventing the necessary process in real time! And yet, no matter how arduous the process or how groundbreaking the execution, critics will be quick to point out the flaws in a finished product. Even so, most practitioners would say the reward, in the end, is worth the struggle. Making that key breakthrough, creating something that has never been seen before, or witnessing the look of astonishment on the face of a participant is a satisfying reward that nearly everyone working in this field would say justifies the commitment and the hard work.

The good news is that the tools are getting better. The work is getting easier. With each hard sacrifice of our predecessor pioneers, we can focus more on making the technology work for our creative visions. We can break free from the limits of the frame to educate, entertain and inspire each other with a presence more akin to physical reality, which is still the best interface the world has to offer.

ACKNOWLEDGMENT

All images used in the chapter are courtesy of the author.

REFERENCES

Barthes, R. (1981). *Camera Lucida: Reflections on photography*. New York: Hill and Wang.

Cameron, J. (Producer and Director). (2009). *Avatar* [Motion Picture]. United States: 20th Century Fox & Lightstorm Entertainment.

Mori, M., MacDorman, K. F., & Kageki, N. (2012). The uncanny valley: The original essay by Masahiro Mori. IEEE Spectrum, 98-100.

Page-Kirby, K. (2015). 'he D Train' isn't actually about trains. But these 5 movies are. *Nearly done final edits*. Retrieved from https://www.washingtonpost.com/express/wp/2015/05/07/the-d-train-isnt-actually-about-trains-but-these-5-movies-are/

Parkes, W. F., & Valdes, D. (Producers), & Wells, S. (Director). (2002). *The Time Machine* [Motion Picture]. United States: Dreamworks Pictures.

Roettgers, J. (2018). Netflix Takes Interactive Storytelling to the Next Level With 'Black Mirror: Bandersnatch. *Variety*. Retrieved from https://variety.com/2018/digital/news/netflix-black-mirror-bandersnatch-interactive-1203096171/

Wilkins, C. (2015). *Let's Talk About: The Polar Express*. Retrieved from http://laurawilkens.com/thoughts/2015/12/14/lets-talk-about-the-polar-express

Zemekis, R., Starky, S., & Geotzman, G. &Teitler, W. (Producers) & Zemekis, R. (Producer). (2004). *The Polar Express* [Motion Picture]. United States: Warner Brothers.

KEY TERMS AND DEFINITIONS

Codec: Compression and decompression programs that make data smaller so it can transfer more efficiently and quickly.

Globbing: An internal term used at Metastage to indicate when two objects lose their integrity and their geometry is no longer perceived as separate.

Integrity Test: This is when an observer determines that the capture data looks correct from all viewpoints.

Keyframing: An animation term that refers to a frame that indicates the start and end of an action.

Solve: When the system correctly calculates the geometry mesh so that it looks like the object that was captured.

Visual Effects (VFX): This term includes any special effects that are added to filmed scenes after primary shooting, in the post-production phase.

ENDNOTES

1   Cyberspace is a term coined by science fiction author William Gibson in his novels and short stories from the early 1980s. It is a term often used to indicate a coming shared immersive virtual space that people can co-inhabit.

2   Degrees of Freedom, or DoF refers to motion forwards and back, up and down and rotational right and left—six degrees in all.

3   A Kinect is a computer vision device developed at Microsoft to be used in place of controllers for their XBOX game systems. It followed on and perfected pioneering work by a number of companies exploring this territory during the 2000s. The basic technology involves a depth-sensing camera, along with other camera sensors that can support the tracking of a user's body motions in real time, mapping those motions to a function such as selection of an object or menu item in a program. More about the development of the Kinect can be found here: https://www.businessinsider.com/the-story-behind-microsofts-hot-selling-kinect-2011-1#a-small-incubation-team-figured-out-the-challenges-2

4   https://scatter.nyc/

5   https://1ric.com/

Chapter 10
Case Study of The BizNest:
The World's First Immersive Sitcom

Eve Weston
https://orcid.org/0000-0002-8841-5491
Exelauno, USA

ABSTRACT

The immersive medium of extended reality presents plentiful opportunities to invent and reinvent. Some of these opportunities are technical, some are creative, and some are a mix. One of the agreed upon areas in this new medium that has been in need of invention and reinvention is storytelling. This chapter presents a case study of the world's first immersive sitcom produced by Exelauno, explaining how it came about and why it promises to open up a new avenue of storytelling for virtual and extended reality. It will share insights gained through the process of creating the series. And it will cover revelations gained at all stages—from rehearsals through post-production—about narrative, directing, comedy, and more in the context of this new immersive world.

INTRODUCTION

The immersive medium of extended reality (XR) presents plentiful opportunities to invent and reinvent. Some of these opportunities are technical, some are creative and some are a mix. One of the agreed upon areas in this new medium that has been in need of invention and reinvention is storytelling. Stanford Professor Jeremy Bailenson, in his excellent book on virtual reality, *Experience On Demand* (2018), devotes a whole chapter to what he calls "stories in the round." He covers various solutions and approaches that he's gathered from talking to everyone from Brett Leonard, the director of *Lawnmower Man* (1992) to James Cameron's VFX guru for *Avatar*. And yet, there is one genre his chapter does not consider and one format unaddressed: that of comedic VR. To be fair, when his book was published in January 2018, this specific genre didn't yet exist. In 2017, when the Facebook VR content team heard about plans for the first 360VR sitcom, they said, "Good luck. No one knows how to do comedy in VR." By 2019, while viewing *The BizNest*, Oculus employees were laughing—not at the idea—but at the immersive show itself. (It's a comedy, so that's a good thing!) This chapter presents a case study

DOI: 10.4018/978-1-7998-2433-6.ch010

of the world's first immersive sitcom produced by Exelauno, explaining how it came about and why it promises to open up a new avenue of storytelling for virtual and extended reality. It will share insights gained through the process of creating the series. And it will cover revelations gained at all stages—from rehearsals through post-production—about narrative, directing, comedy and more—in the context of this new immersive world.

THE SHOW: AN IMMERSIVE EXPERIENCE

Imagine if instead of just watching the television show *Friends* (1994-2004) or *The Office* (2005-2013), you could be *in* it, sitting inside the iconic Central Perk coffee house in 1990s Manhattan or at a desk next to Jim, salesman and office prankster, at the Dunder Mifflin paper company. Well, that describes *The BizNest*. It is the world's first 360VR immersive sitcom, and it is set in a co-working space where YOU, the viewer, are a member, surrounded by freelancers and entrepreneurs who are working, socializing, flirting, antagonizing, and navigating the modern work-life balancing act.[1] This series is a thoroughly enjoyable entertainment experience and also a brand new, replicable format for storytelling in an immersive medium. In the same way that the multi-camera television format led to the Golden Age of Television Comedy, the narrative and directorial format pioneered and presented by *The BizNest* has the potential to create a similar legacy.

An abbreviated synopsis of the immersive experience follows:

The commute is a cinch. You put on an Oculus Go, or any other VR headset, and are transported to The BizNest co-working space, where you can look around and take in your desk and coworkers. Your fellow "BizNesters" approach with questions, problems and commentary, and you experience a level of engagement that makes you feel part of this community.

Today, one-hit wonder novelist Donna shows up for the first time, needing a quiet place to work. Life-hacker Tim forgot his wallet and can't afford lunch. Science writer Kate has a meltdown on account of her unspoken attraction to Tim. Fashion designer Rebecca puts her brother Uri on the spot when she's late for a big meeting. And your co-worker Sadie won't stop bothering you about all that tax stuff you need to do for your LLC. It's just another day at The BizNest and you're in the middle of the action.

After witnessing how the day plays out, you're left with a feeling of happiness, and a desire to spend more time with these charming, quirky characters.

The BizNest set out to fully utilize 360 degrees, situate the viewer in a believable world and pioneer spatial storytelling, redefining sitcom conventions for a new medium. The result is an immersive, real-time experience with multiple interwoven stories—more than TV—and a rich storytelling environment. Now, how did it come to be?

GETTING THE SHOW OFF THE GROUND

With a solid story, vision and pitch, Eve Weston, the executive producer of *The BizNest,* sought out 360 and VR companies in hopes of finding someone interested in producing the show. At that time, in 2016, not many folks were creating 360VR narrative. And—as little narrative as there was—there was even less comedy. Since there was no clear infrastructure for getting pitches to the right people—and no clear sense of who the right people were—she found combining Google and LinkedIn searches, paired with attending conferences and panels, proved to be most helpful. And because there was no clear precedent for how to do a show like this, a lot of options were on the table. This is particularly plain to see in the second paragraph of this excerpt from an early pitch document for *The BizNest*:

On Tone & Approach

Inspired by classics such as Cheers and The Office, The BizNest shares the experiences of the "every(wo) man" millennial, for whom working out of a co-working space is as normal as shoulder pads were in the 1980s. As such, the tone and aesthetic should be grounded and relatable; The BizNest could be a co-working space in your city; it could be the co-working space you work from tomorrow. And you'd find it entertaining to work alongside these charismatic characters.

The set of The BizNest, whether it's a location, a built-set, or a digitally rendered space, should present itself to the viewer as a continuous, contiguous space. The format of the show will blend sitcom structure with immersive theatre. In addition to plot-driven "scenes" that will play out in the space—not restricted to any frame—additional comedic and character-driven content will round out the world. Some actions will relate to plot in the episode, some will relate to plot in other episodes (think How I Met Your Mother's early introduction of the goat and the yellow umbrella), and some will be standalone moments.

Simple, largely single-set workplace comedies have proven to transition well, with Cheers being television's version of radio's Duffy's Tavern and The Office leaping across the pond. The BizNest is well-positioned to succeed as a pioneering virtual reality narrative experience.

Pitching

In December 2016, Weston spoke with Jim Migdal, Vice President of Business Development at Lytro, an American company founded in 2006 by Ren Ng. Lytro started out developing light-field cameras, which capture the intensity of light in a scene, and also the direction that the light rays are traveling in space. This contrasts with a conventional camera, which records only light intensity. In 2016, Lytro had shifted focus and was working on a very-high-end VR video capture camera with companion custom compute server. This camera system, in theory, would allow the viewer to walk through The BizNest, experiencing the story in realtime and real space, much like game-engine VR only with photoreal moving images. It sounded amazing and perfect, until learning that the camera required to film was the size of a small room and that the amount of data captured in filming was so great that they could only film one actor at a time, and not including the background. From a production standpoint this seemed challenging—it would surely make it a longer and more complicated production process. Also, as so much of acting is reacting, it would steal a little bit of that theatre magic from the show.

That same month, Weston also pitched a version of the show to AltSpace VR in Redwood City, CA. AltSpace was, and still is, a social VR platform; it has since been acquired by Microsoft. Because AltSpace was a digitally built world, any version of *The BizNest* produced with them would use avatars instead of 3D scans of actors and participants. Actors could be filmed individually or in groups, most likely not all at the same time, presenting a similar disadvantage as Lytro's process, though not quite as extreme. The setting of the co-working space could either be CGI or filmed, but the action would be filmed on green screen or equivalent and placed in the space. Assembling the show this way would allow it to be "volumetric," which refers to a space that audience members could move through, and would also allow adjustments to be made to an episode even after the show has been assembled. In this way, it would be a little bit of a hybrid between live-action and animation. While this version definitely had a different feel than a live-action sitcom, it also provided true VR functionality, which was exciting. The biggest obstacle was that AltSpace was a small start-up and didn't have the requisite personnel to facilitate such a project. The two parties agreed to keep the idea on the back burner and work together on more easily executable projects in the meantime. That was the genesis of the first VR series that Weston produced, *I Feel You: The Empath Experience*, a groundbreaking social VR experience in which an Empath would read the feelings of strangers from around the world, live, based solely on the sound of their voice.[2]

The BizNest's early pitches had elements of social VR and integrated social media, a testament to the ambitious vision of the project and how it was always intended to make use of the unique possibilities presented by XR. The executive producer had a solid concept of what was possible in XR and was on the hunt to figure out "what was possible in XR now." As the aforementioned anecdotes make clear, even what was possible was not necessarily doable. This presented a question of Shakespearean import: to be or not to be. Was it best to wait until the project could be made in a way that fully executed the vision, with all the bells and whistles of VR, or was it better to exist? Ultimately, the team behind *The BizNest* decided that, given the state of the industry, it needed to exist, if only to ensure that the industry got to a place where that full vision could be executed. Even a simplified version of *The BizNest,* that didn't provide a volumetric or interactive experience, did provide the world with something that didn't yet exist. It had something new to say about storytelling and comedy in an immersive space; it would move the industry forward.

The other two companies that Weston pitched the show to were companies with whom the project would be realized as a 360 experience. Fittingly, the first of them was Experience 360, the second was Two-Bit Circus. The former is a 360 production company, while the latter is a location-based entertainment company that was, at the time, exploring how they fit into the VR landscape. By early 2017, both companies had sought to option *The BizNest* and for the following reasons: They hadn't met any other comedy writers who understood VR and immersive storytelling. The concept made a lot of sense for the medium in that the story could not be told the same way in any other media. And the viewer had a clear reason to be in the story, with their integrated first-person role as a member of the co-working space.

Both companies could potentially have made for good partners. When it came to immersive content production, all parties involved were making it up as they went along. There was talk of attaching digital production companies with no 360 experience but industry clout, and of adding *The BizNest* to a slate and then seeking funding for all the projects together as a sort of "investment package." Various factors were considered in deciding how to proceed. There are plenty of drawbacks to doing something that's never been done before. And it can be comforting to have partners—to feel like one isn't in it alone. On the other hand, there are also advantages to doing something that has never been done before. These are two of the biggest: No one knows better than you; you have a chance to be the first. Bringing on additional outside producers and/or waiting for funding would've eliminated these two big first-mover advantages. Another thing that pioneers have working in their favor is that folks involved in such endeavors often have a scrappy start-up mentality and are willing and able to get by with a lean team. *The BizNest* certainly had that and, so, the team behind *The BizNest* weighed their options and, instead, decided to form their own production company, Exelauno. Rather than concerning itself with courting producers and financiers, it would focus on finding what would show up on screen: a beautiful location and talented cast. But before the show could get to that, it had to develop a story that a location and talent would help bring to life.

Writing

With its roots in television comedy, *The BizNest* builds off the multi-camera sitcom structure. What is that structure? Well, anyone who's ever watched TV has likely noticed that there is often more than one story going on at once. After all, in *Friends*, Ross would make a play for Rachel, and Monica would need Phoebe's dating advice, and Joey would ask Chandler to help him prepare for an audition — all in the same episode. In a Hollywood television writers' room, each of these stories is designated by a different letter. In any episode, there might be an "A Story," a "B Story" and a "C Story."

The "A Story" is the main story, generally driven by the central character. In shows that have a character's name in the title, that character is generally the central character, i.e. *Seinfeld*, *Frasier*, Lucy in *I Love Lucy*. Then, there is usually a slightly smaller story going on at the same time—this is the "B Story." Early on in *Will & Grace*, there was always a story that had some weight to it and involved the two title characters, Will and Grace, and at the same time there was a smaller, often frivolous story, between Karen and Jack, the supporting characters. This Karen and Jack story was the "B Story." Sometimes the A and B stories affect one another, sometimes they don't. And, in some sitcoms, there might also be a "C Runner"—a light story, played more for comedy than character relationships—or a full "C Story" and potentially even a "D Story," which is more common in one-hour shows than half-hour shows.

Early in the development process, Weston, the writer of *The BizNest,* who had her roots in television comedy, having worked on shows like *Will & Grace* and Disney's *Wizards of Waverly Place,* realized that she was now painting on a larger canvas. A 360 experience gave her more physical space to fill in every episode: 360 degrees instead of the 60 to 90 degrees used by TV, depending on the size of the screen and its distance from the viewer. That means there could (and in her mind, should) be four to six times as much happening at any given time. Having C, D, E and even F stories seemed like a good way to keep meaningful action happening in every section of the space.

If *The BizNest* were done as a TV series, these would be the A, B and C stories of the pilot episode:

A Story:

When life-hacker Tim forgets his wallet and solicits money for lunch to avoid biking home, science writer Kate decides she'll stop at nothing to prevent Tim from being a lazy mooch.

B Story:

With Uri, her brother and business partner, breathing down her neck for missing an important meeting, Rebecca keeps her eye on the prize and proves to him that she can still get the job done, even if her process is a bit unconventional.

C Runner:

Under pressure from her publisher to hand in a draft by week's end, Donna comes to The BizNest in search of a quiet place to work, finds anything but, and somehow still gets exactly what she needs.

To create an expanded story world for VR, the writer included additional stories as follows:

D Story:

When your co-worker Sadie informs you that you need to figure out the tax stuff for your LLC today, you're at a loss for what to do until Wendell the CPA makes you an offer you can't refuse.

E Story:

Sadie's confused about why she's feeling off her game and hungrier than usual until an unexpected "visitor" provides an explanation... and a wardrobe disaster that requires immediate attention.

F Story:

When Rebecca misses her meeting with Claude, and Uri adds insult to injury, Claude bails on their ill-organized fashion label only to realize that, in the end, it's the work that matters to him the most.

G Runner:

With everyone in The BizNest wondering what his job is, Mike continues to evade the question while dropping highly intriguing and inconclusive clues.

H Runner:

Anna, the interior designer, prepares for, executes, and cleans up after a big client meeting.

It's worth speaking a bit about these "additional stories" and how they function. It is also worth noting that in a simul-story show such as this, all storylines are in motion simultaneously, with different storylines taking focus at different moments and the viewer concurrently having the option to look in whichever direction they desire.

The D Story is "your story" as the viewer in your assigned role as a member of this co-working space. It is something that XR allows for in a way that television never would. And not only does XR allow for it, in a way, it asks for it. The writer of *The BizNest* reports that a common question asked by VR production companies is "Why VR?" meaning why is the storyteller choosing to tell this story in VR; what makes VR the best medium for this particular story. She prefers the question, "Why is the viewer there?" If not carefully executed, a narrative VR experience can feel like a party where you don't know anyone. What is the viewer meant to do or, more importantly, feel?

This feeds directly into the idea of writing for the "camera character." *The BizNest* chose to make the viewer a character and, as the process of bringing the show to life progressed, realized the power of eye contact and engagement. This is a version of the power of YouTube discussed by Michael Wesch in *An Anthropological Introduction to YouTube* (Wesch, 2008), "Like people have this really profound deep connection with other humans through YouTube that maybe they couldn't experience in everyday life because they're not allowed to stare, because they're not allowed to just experience this person as a human being." It's interesting that Wesch finds this connection he's talking about so powerful that he uses both of the synonymous words "profound" and "deep" to describe it. Think then about how much more profound and deep a similar connection in VR has the power to be, given the immersive nature of the medium; people tend to register in-headset experiences as actual personal experiences (Segovia and Bailenson, 2019). This power and desire for connection is part of why the writer/director of *The BizNest* expanded the "camera character's" story. *The BizNest* now combines the connectivity of YouTuber content, in which the viewer feels a personal connection with the Influencer (often due to the Influencer directly addressing camera), with the structured narrative and character development of TV to get the viewer closer than ever to characters they love.

The E story is a great example of the benefits of the rehearsal process. It started as two separate bits: a co-worker of the camera character, and a moment where a woman comes out of the bathroom stall to get a tampon in the middle of Kate's rant. The second was a standalone moment and the first was a thin through-line that came from the realization that it would be satisfying for the viewer to have someone they connect with that could ground them in that world. As it happened, Amy Bury was cast as Sadie (the bathroom girl) around the same time the camera's co-worker was being woven into the story. Bury had been cast due to her excellent facial expressions and the writer/director quickly realized that having her interact with the viewer would be a real boon. Combining those two characters also gave a little more meat to the storyline; it helped give Bury a purpose or objective in every scene, which in turn leant even more of a sense of reality to the show.

The F Story and G and H Runners also serve to add to the reality of the show. If the F Story were a TV story, the character Claude would be present only in the moments where he serves the Uri/Rebecca storyline, leaving The BizNest after Rebecca's a no-show, returning to order the outfits, and departing after signing the order. In the 360VR show, there are no cuts or cutaways to other storylines; if someone is in the space, the viewer will see them. The conference room scene between Claude and Uri in the first segment—a continuous take that is more than a scene but less than an episode—could have taken place in an office off-camera; for example, in segment 1, Uri and Claude could've been in an office near the hallway where segment 2 takes place and Uri could've just popped into the bullpen for his lines. But really, that option would have just robbed additional action from the space. The writer/director felt strongly that having that action, which was driven by a clear-cut story and relationship, would really add to the atmosphere of the show. It also leant the ability to have moments like the one in segment 2 when Claude says, "Not now Tim, we're on our way to the bathroom" and then later, "That's why you asked me into the bathroom?!" These moments added comedy and also the vibrancy of a real space where one sees snippets of other peoples' daily lives as they pass through one's own. The latter is exactly what the G and H Runners also add. In G, Mike is just going about his day, business as usual, and, by doing so, arousing the suspicions of his co-workers. Landon Kirksey, the talented actor and improviser who portrays Mike, admits that he does indeed know what Mike's job is and that that informs the minutiae of his actions in any given moment, but he won't reveal it so that the mystery stays alive for Season Two. Anna's H Runner is an even more extreme version of the same. Her story has almost no dialog, but if one watches her throughout the show, one notices that there is a through line. Her actions connect in a meaningful, motivated way; they're not just busywork invented by an extra to pass the time. This intention is really key to lending a verisimilitude to *The BizNest*.

Having so many stories raises the question of what the script ultimately looked like—see sample (Figure 1). In the end, the script was about 100 pages, which is two to four times longer than a traditional multi-camera script. It didn't include all of every character's action; what was required for the story, story continuity or comedy was written down, what was largely for atmosphere and motivated by the story was entrusted to the actors and often made note of by the stage manager, associate producer Rachel Shanblatt. As a result of its length, the 360VR script ended up functioning much more as a reference book than as a readable story document. When watching the show, the viewer has the choice to look where they want and they can only see one thing—maybe two, if the two actions are in the same field of view—in any given moment. The script, however, has to contain everything story-relevant happening in every field of view at any given moment. As such, it's dense. It did, however, prove to be an indispensable reference so that everyone on set wasn't required to keep all that information in their heads.

GETTING THE SHOW ON ITS FEET

While much about getting *The BizNest* up and running was novel, there were processes and techniques from television that served as a valuable model, able to be modified to serve the needs of this new medium. This section will discuss casting (what special traits or skills *The BizNest* looked for in its actors); rehearsals and production (how *The BizNest* made accommodations for 360 while innovating a do-able schedule at a fraction of a "VR budget"); directing (where the challenges and opportunities lay in playing to an audience "inside" the show); and acting (how, in 360, it can be simultaneously both more and less intimate than other media).

Casting

Since *The BizNest* is a comedy, when casting, comedic sensibility and timing was key. What else was important? From the beginning, the director of *The BizNest* was interested in casting actors with a strong improv background. While the show was scripted, unlike multi-cam where an actor would rarely be on camera without having lines or participating in the main action, in *The BizNest*, the actors would often be on camera when not part of the main action. In life, one's story doesn't stop when one isn't being looked at, so neither should an actor's story in *The BizNest*. Skilled improv comedians could not only fill those moments with engaging action, but would also enjoy the opportunity to do so. Additionally, the plan for filming was to do long, continuous takes with no edits, which required not only reliability from the performers but also adaptability.

There's a great moment about a minute and nineteen seconds into the show that really showcases the cast's improv skills. A framed photo that had been propped up on the desk unexpectedly falls over; one actor acknowledges it with an improvised "uh-oh," the other stands it back up again, and the scene keeps going without missing a beat. It feels real—which was core to the desired experience of *The BizNest*. Thanks to the actors' skill sets, the photo frame accidentally falling makes the show even better; that would not have been the case if they ignored the accident or allowed it to throw off their performances. Another really important quality that the team behind *The BizNest* considered was an actor's general likability. Because, watching the show, the viewer would actually feel like they were hanging out with these characters, it was even more important than in television that the viewer like the performers. After the casting call went out, auditions were held live in Los Angeles and those who made it to callbacks

Figure 1. A sample script page from The BizNest segment 5, "Calling All Phones." Italics are used to indicate simultaneous action
Source: Exelauno, 2019

```
The BizNest: Season 1                                  37.
"Donna's First Day"- PRODUCTION DRAFT              (Seg. 5)

                    NELLIE

         That's what I would tell them.   That,

         and "shower."

As KATE'S PHONE RINGS, Wendell enters from the back.
Answering her phone, Kate reluctantly leaves Tim alone in
Nellie's company and, as she walks to your right, draws your
eyeline toward Sadie.

                    SADIE
              (to you)
         You've got something in your teeth.

Sadie makes faces over the following like, "Nope, you haven't
gotten it yet," she uses her teeth to show you where to go
fishing, she indicates to you that you should move one tooth
over, etc.

As you work to find this stuck piece of food in your teeth
and Sadie guides you, Wendell makes eye contact with Tim -
they have an understanding - and Tim engages Nellie in a way
that turns her back to Wendell, so he can enter and solicit
Mike.

As Nellie's rice cooks, she and Tim continue to chat. They
stay in the kitchen for the duration of this segment and the
next.

With Nellie enamored of Tim, Mike and Wendell converse:

                    WENDELL

         Hey Mike, you know the tax code is

         changing, could affect what you do.  In

         ways.

                    MIKE

         Oh yeah, how so?

                    WENDELL

         Ways. Hey, listen I'm giving a short

         presentation later if you're

         interested. You have a CPA that you

         use... or are?
```

were taped so that Sabrina Hyman, a casting director experienced in VR who has since been nominated for an Emmy for her amazing work in television, could weigh in from New York. With Hyman's input, the director then made final decisions as to who would play which role. The reader can see the final cast and crew in Table 1.

Rehearsals and Production

As the intention of *The BizNest* has always been to reinvent the multi-camera sitcom for immersive media, it may be instructive to first review the production process for television comedy so that it is easier to see the similarities and differences between TV and 360VR. Multi-camera sitcoms—unlike single-camera TV shows and movies—film in front of a live studio audience. As a result, rehearsal is key; the actors are effectively putting on a play on tape night. Tape night is the culmination of a week's work by the cast and crew. If a show has a Monday-through-Friday schedule—meaning the show tapes its episodes on Friday—the actors get the script on Monday morning. The writers, actors, directors and executives all gather for what is called a table read. There, the actors sit around a table and read the script aloud for the first time. After hearing that read, the writers and executives discuss the script: what's working, what's not; and the writers go off and do a rewrite. When the actors come in on Tuesday morning, there's a new draft of the script and they get to work rehearsing it. In the afternoon, the cast will do a run through for the writers and the studio and then, based on that, the writers will do another rewrite. On Wednesday morning, the actors will again get a new script, rehearse it, and then do another run through for the writers and the network. On Thursday, there is yet again a new script, which the actors rehearse. And after rehearsal, the director will let the writers know if anything isn't working. Then, on Friday, the cast performs the show in front of the cameras… and a live studio audience.

The BizNest benefited from many of the conventions of the multi-camera production process. *The BizNest*'s rehearsal process was helpful for discovering areas where a little rewrite could help. Since using the immersive medium for comedy is also relatively new, it was a great opportunity to make discoveries and then still have time to incorporate them into the show. And, while *The BizNest* didn't have a live studio audience or an audience that would be laughing along, it did have a co-working space full of extras. These extras were audience members in a way; they were reacting to the action "on stage." Like multi-cam, *The BizNest* rehearsed multiple segments at a time and then filmed several on the same day. For the most part, scenes filmed in the same section of the set were filmed on the same shoot day. This helped with continuity of extras, not to mention continuity of set and props. While the show filmed in a real co-working space, the furniture arrangement for the show was not the same as what it was on an average day in the location.

Knowing going in that every segment of *The BizNest* would be filmed in one continuous take that didn't allow for cuts or edits, developing a functional rehearsal process was key. And while it was great to have everyone in the same place at the same time for the duration when filming, for rehearsals, it wasn't feasible from a budgetary standpoint or sensible from a time-management standpoint to have all actors on set at all times. Accordingly, the director broke each segment down by storyline and then had all the actors in that storyline come to rehearsal on a given night. Actors in other storylines would rehearse on other nights. Then after each storyline group had their acting and blocking down, all the storyline groups would come together so that the director could integrate the action and figure out the timing.

Table 1. The BizNest final cast and crew

The BizNest Credits		
Main Role(s)	**Name**	**Department / Attribution**
Writer, Director, Producer Costumer Designer, Prop Master Rebecca Co-Editor	Eve Weston	Executive Producer/ Creator Crew Cast / Series Regular Post-Production
Associate Producer Prouction Coordinator, Stage Manager and Camera	Rachel Shanblatt	Associate Producer Crew
Assistant Director Wardrobe Stylist, Prop Assistant Anna	Anna Dufault Miller	Assistant Director Crew Actor / Guest Stare
Claude Co-Editor	Lloyd Ahlquist	Cast / Series Regular Post-Production
Donna	Ellie Araiza	Cast / Series Regular
Kate	Gillian Bellinger	Cast / Series Regular
Sadie	Amy Bury	Cast / Series Regular
Uri	Tommy Dickie	Cast / Series Regular
Nellie	Becky Flaum	Cast / Series Regular
JR	Joey Greer	Cast / Series Regular
Mike	Landon Kirksey	Cast / Series Regular
Tim	Chad Reinhart	Cast / Series Regular
Wendell	Atul Singh	Cast / Series Regular
Pupuseria Co-Owner	Ravi "Andrew" Gahi	Actor / Guest Stara
Cori	Cori Snelson	Actor / Guest Star
Benny "Bathroom Boy"	Benny Spiewak	Actor / Guest Star
Nadeya "Book Girl"	Nadeya Ward	Actor / Guest Star
Casting Consultant	Sabrina Hyman	Casting
Production Assistant	Jeffrey Blatt	Crew
Swing	Elaine Chu	Crew
Sound Mixer	Igor Kogan	Crew and Post-Production
Production Assistant	Isabelle von Lockner	Crew
Craft Services	Susan Weston	Crew
Music courtesy of	Joseph Miller and ALIBI Music Library	Music
Location Managers	Peter & Dan Pastewka Lilly Nguyen	Location
Filmed at	Phase Two co-working space in Culver City, CA	Location

The BizNest uses spatial audio, which favors having a clear recording of each actor's lines. Because the show was being filmed in 360, boom mics were not an option as they would have been visible in the recorded footage. Accordingly, the series used a combination of lavaliere mics on the actors and a few well-placed ambisonic microphones on set. Considering the number of lav mics needed, it made the most sense to rehearse multiple segments and then film them in one day. This method was used twice, with five segments shooting on each of two days. However, because one of those days included a reshoot, there was one leftover segment, segment 6, that provided an opportunity to experiment with a different rehearsal approach. segment 6, "The Water Runs Through It," was filmed in the gender-neutral restroom and required fewer actors than some of the other segments. It had fewer storylines crossing and needed fewer microphones. For this segment, the director gathered the actors the morning of the shoot, blocked the scene, rehearsed the scene for a couple of hours, and then filmed it. While this straight-through approach wouldn't work for all segments, it worked quite well for segment 6.

A Note on Notation from Stage Manager Rachel Shanblatt

With the 360 view, multiple storylines, and simultaneous action possible in immersive media, traditional storyboarding of shots and notating actor blocking is difficult. Because the camera functions as the viewer, the camera uses only a single shot in each segment--moving the shot would be quite disorienting! Rather than move the camera, the director gave the actors strategic blocking that played well to the camera; in short, the director moved the actors around the camera, instead of moving the camera around the actors.

Accordingly, rather than tracking shots by storyboarding, the stage manager tracked movement and blocking, initially in a theatre format, notated in reference to actors' lines in the script. However, because of the aforementioned script density, using lines in the script to follow blocking proved difficult. The theatre method of blocking notation also doesn't account for the plethora of action in a 360 shot-—it is difficult to notate the movement of every character in the shot, especially the many who don't necessarily speak.

Over time, a more collaborative approach developed. Large maps of the space were printed and used to keep track of camera placement and each character's movement in each segment. The camera was placed on the map, and each character's path and various positions around the camera were marked. These maps and blocking notes were maintained by the stage manager for the principal characters in each segment. Background action that was more improv-style and not as essential to advancing the storyline was largely entrusted to each actor to recall. In a traditional context, trusting actors to remember their blocking would never work. It worked in this medium for two reasons: Exact placement of secondary action or tertiary gags was not vital; the actors had strong backgrounds in improv.

The director and stage manager also filmed parts of rehearsal in 2D and posted the clips to YouTube to allow actors to review their placement and movement in segments---especially where notation and mapping became cumbersome and saturated with the principal characters' action and all of the background action taking place around the set.

The concluding point is that whereas, in film, storyboarding is used to keep track of shots, this doesn't work well in the 360 medium because essentially the camera can't be used for different shots within the same segment: rather, the director needs to give actors strategic movement and blocking that places them in desirable locations around the camera's chosen position.

Directing

Directing for 360 includes all the usual responsibilities of directing: deciding what the camera captures, getting performance from actors, and dramatic and comedic blocking. It also has some unique requirements. Placing the viewer within the show, directing the viewer's attention, planting moments of audience discovery, and pacing the action appropriately were all unique concerns demanded by the immersive medium and taken into account by the director of *The BizNest*.

It was inherent in the script that the camera would "be a member" of The BizNest co-working space. Still, that left some options as far as camera placement. Camera placement in this case involved both where the camera would be during the scene and also how the set was designed—and/or which room was chosen for the scene—as that often limited or opened up possibilities.

In segments 1 and 3, the goal was to have the viewer feel as if they were sitting at their very own desk within the co-working space. Accordingly, the camera was placed on a monopod on a wheeled desk chair so that the camera was approximately eye-level of an average person. Weston, who provided consistency of vision by directing her script, put a lot of thought into the set design and where in that set the camera was placed—aiming to keep the camera closest to the most interesting and most story-relevant parts of the space.

For example, viewers will notice there's a sitting area in front of and to the right of Kate, the red-headed science journalist, in segments 1 and 3 that's near the entrance to The BizNest (Figure 2). Interestingly, in our location--- the Phase Two co-working space,[3] which is a hub for the virtual reality industry in Los Angeles---there is also an entrance on the other side. But the director found the right side with the sitting area to be more visually pleasing and also to offer more story opportunities. Similarly, the assignment of desks to characters was carefully thought out, considering who would be where when. Uri wasn't spending much time at his desk and was spending time going through Rebecca's desk, so it made sense to have his desk farther away and hers closer, even though she's not around for the first few segments. J.R. had very little scripted action at his desk, but is a talented and engaging improviser; it was appealing to have him visible at close range if the viewer were to look opposite the main action. Kate is part of the A Story, so, it was ideal to have her front and center, helping the audience get on board with the plot from the get-go. The overall philosophy was to try and have most main action take place within about three to five feet of camera. Moments in *The BizNest* that take place farther away tend to be less story-essential and, if they are story-essential, are played larger.

A common question about directing VR content is "how do you get the viewer to look where you want?" *The BizNest* postulates that you don't. Viewer autonomy doesn't have to be a problem; it can be an opportunity. Skillful direction can guide the viewer to follow the primary action and give them engaging secondary action, tertiary action, and so on to discover for themselves. *The BizNest* utilizes a novel "choose your own attention" approach in which the viewer decides where to look and because of the clarity of the dialog, still follows the story.[4] An example of this can be seen in segment 1, where, early on, the viewer is likely watching Kate and J.R. Then, if the viewer were to follow Donna, with her backpack and purple fleece, they would still hear all of Kate and J.R.'s story-relevant dialog. Then, they would be in a position to see Uri cross out of the conference room. Their eye would likely follow him because he draws focus with a combination of action and dialog. If the viewer does follow him, they'll have the opportunity to see the logjam at the phone booth and then, can choose to stay on him or look around—with the dialog again keeping them in the loop story-wise wherever their eyes happen to be.

Figure 2. An equirectangular still image from segment 1 of The BizNest, "Pupusas & Coffee," showing the Phase Two co-working space and the blocking of the characters relative to camera. Actors closest to camera, left-to-right, include Joey Greer as J.R., Tommy Dickie as Uri, Landon Kirksey as Mike, Becky Flaum as Nellie, Gillian Bellinger as Kate and Chad Reinhart as Tim
Source: Exelauno, 2019

If they didn't follow Uri, they would likely have followed Tim, who, just a moment after Uri, crosses in the same direction.

And again, if the viewer chooses not to follow Tim, they still hear all relevant dialogue, and are redirected to Tim when he stands up on the coffee table and commands attention with "Attention, BizNest!" Knowing that Tim would be speaking for a bit, Weston intentionally crafts other moments of interest for the viewer to take in during this time: Donna feeling like she's in the spotlight and backing away, Claude coming to the glass doors to see what all the hubbub is about, J.R. tossing a basketball in the air, Uri's exchange with Nellie; this last instance may get the viewer to look to the side of the room opposite Tim and notice that Uri's searching for something. If they stay on Uri long enough, the viewer will discover that he's looking for the key to Rebecca's drawers, then going in and digging around, ultimately discovering a strip of condoms. Such moments are not story-crucial, but are story-relevant. The moment with Uri and Rebecca's drawer is a part of Uri's storyline in which Rebecca has missed their meeting and he's now looking for the pants to show the fashion buyer. If the viewer doesn't catch this moment, they won't fall behind, but if they do catch it, they get an extra story moment and laugh that still doesn't compete with or compromise the A Story. It is one of several times that the director uses skillful choreography and visual humor to tell an additional story in a given moment without having competing dialog.

This leads to another element worth mentioning: audience discovery. Audience discovery is something that a 360 experience can offer that a 2D show really can't. And it is valuable. The opportunity to discover something engages the viewer in this world and, when they do discover something, they feel that much more immersed. This chapter will note several things that provide increased audience immersion without requiring interactivity; this is one of them. Another reason that audience discovery is valuable is for its comedic potential. As Dan O'Shannon writes in his masterful treatise on comedy, *What Are You Laughing At? A Comprehensive Guide to the Comedic Event*, "…surprise is a powerful element in comedy—when we are startled, we go through the same rapid high-alert/cool-down process [as when

Figure 3. An equirectangular still image from The BizNest segment 8, "How to 'Do Your Taxes'," in which CPA Wendell, played by Atul Singh, is completely oblivious to what's happening in—and coming out of—the booth behind him
Source: Exelauno, 2019

we detect safe incongruity—the threat of danger followed by the realization that it is harmless]. It's not uncommon for people to have scrapes with death and then, finding themselves unharmed, to start laughing" (O'Shannon, 2012). TV shows and movies do often surprise audiences; 360 and VR provides more opportunities to surprise audiences thanks to the added opportunity for discovery.

An Anecdote from Director Eve Weston

"I remember the moment during rehearsals for *The BizNest* that I discovered the laugh of discovery. We were rehearsing one of the segments—I won't say which one, so I don't spoil it for viewers—and I was standing in a hallway outside of an office. During the scene, I just started looking around in different directions, to see what the camera would see. At one point, I found myself looking through a window and an actor was looking back at me. I laughed out loud; I hadn't expected anyone to be there. It was the laughter of genuine surprise. I realized that in television, a laugh like this was unlikely—we know that everything on screen has been put there intentionally and the whole scene is within our field of view from the get go. I loved this moment. Sadly, our location frosted the windows between that rehearsal and our shoot date, so we couldn't use that exact moment in the show. It did, however, influence the show and prompt us to look for other such moments; there's a great one in the bathroom scene, thanks to Benny Spiewak."

In addition to prompting the "laughter of surprise," audience discovery can also elicit "laughter of knowledge." This is when something is funny merely because somebody knows something that someone else does not. This is part of why segment 8, "How to 'Do Your Taxes'" is so funny, with the magazine flying out of the back booth, the audience sees something happening that Wendell, the CPA giving the tax presentation, is unaware of (Figure 3). There are two additional good examples in segment 7, "What It's Like to Be an Olympian." One of them is a spoiler, the other comes about 32 seconds in when the viewer can see what looks like Kate and J.R. making out in the phone booth, but Wendell, who's right

Figure 4. An equirectangular still image from The BizNest segment 7, "What It's Like to Be an Olympian," in which Wendell the CPA is unaware of what's going on just around the corner in phone booth 171
Source: Exelauno, 2019

on the other side of the viewer, can't (Figure 4). *The BizNest* provides the opportunity for the viewer to discover something that the characters don't know or haven't yet realized.

Another element that *The BizNest* paid attention to was pacing. There are two big differences between traditional multi-cam sitcom pacing and the pacing of *The BizNest*. One is a result of there being many fewer cuts, the other is a result of there being a much broader field of view. The cuts that multi-cam sit-coms rely on allow for focusing attention, for example by cutting to a close-up here or there. They allow for selecting the best take of any given moment. And finally, they also allow for manufactured comedic timing. *The BizNest* on the other hand had to rely on actor performance for timing in all instances, unable to make up for any lags later, in post-production. Segment 6 provides an excellent example of the effectiveness of well-rehearsed comedic timing—without cuts—in an immersive setting. This scene, which takes place in the gender-neutral restroom, is a bit of a farce, with Kate getting continuously blocked and rerouted by other characters coming in and out of bathroom stalls. The director had this vision from the beginning, and it was only through rehearsal and precise execution of timing that it worked. For the rehearsals, the director actually stood where the camera was and watched the scene. There were many run-throughs where the acting was good, but it just wasn't funny; once the actors nailed the pacing, the scene automatically elicited a laugh. The director informed the cast "that was it," then stepped out, turned the camera on and started filming takes, asking the cast each time whether they nailed it and trusting them to know when they matched that successful performance. Thankfully, they did.

The other big difference when it comes to pacing has to do with field of view. It's a different thing watching something directly in one's field of vision than watching something unfolding all around oneself. It takes more time to digest action happening in 360. At the beginning of the first segment of *The BizNest*, the viewer will notice that there's a little bit of downtime and it starts off slowly, to give the viewer the chance to take in and adjust to this virtual world. Such a moment is neither necessary nor productive in a television show. And while slower pacing in 360 helps allow the audience to keep up, it also lends the show a greater sense of reality. *The BizNest* has a nice balance of keeping action slow enough that it feels real and yet placing additional action in just the right locations so that the world feels full. There's a great moment in segment 2 where Donna is considering the membership options of The BizNest; she takes more time than a sitcom character in mulling over her options, enough that one could believe she was really reading and thinking over her choices. While she is, Claude says to Uri, "That's why you asked me into the bathroom?!," and Uri replies, "You should try them on—they're slimming and they won't leak!" The juxtaposition of Donna's reading and Uri and Claude's exchange feels real, even though the odds are slim that, in the real world, Claude would deliver that line squarely in the doorframe within the camera's field of vision and at the exact moment that he's not competing with anyone else's dialog. That is the beauty of skillful directing in immersive environments.

Acting

The immersive medium forces the actor to think in a 360 way, even beyond "in the round," as the audience can see everything all the time. Acting for 360 is its own form. An anecdote from auditions proves helpful when discussing acting for 360. The director had an actress in mind for a specific role, whom she'd seen perform many times. She was confident the actress could play the role, and yet, in the audition, the actress wasn't nailing it. The actress was, however, able to take direction and give several versions of the material in a cold reading. She gave a TV take, she gave a commercial take, she gave a multi-camera sitcom take, she even gave a theatre take. None of these were quite right. The director gave her the note "more grounded, real" and she did it again. It still wasn't a hundred percent, but it was much closer and, considering the actress hadn't seen the material until moments before, it was enough to show that she would get there. The director cast her and, sure enough, she did get there. All this to say that acting in 360 is it's own beast. Even experienced actors who have trained for various media and situations are encountering something new when they step onto a 360 set.

To address this situation, the director ran one-on-one camera tests with each actor. She would film them at several distances from the camera: far, medium, close and uncomfortably close, noting which take was at what distance. She would also give the actor the option of "wild card distances," having them pick a distance from camera they were curious about, in addition to the ones she encouraged, just to see what it felt like from the other side. Then, after rehearsal, the director would stitch the files,[5] upload them to YouTube and send them to the actor—to whom she'd given 360 viewing glasses—so they could experience how the viewer might experience the scene. That way, it would start to make sense for them. Distances that the actor might have initially thought were too close merely felt intimate. Distances that were closer still may have been too much for certain situations, but appropriate for others in which the goal was to make the viewer feel uncomfortable or crowded. Distances that were farther away, the actors now realized, required a larger performance, otherwise their acting just wouldn't read. Working with the actors in this way, the director discovered what she now calls the Three Foot Rule: When an actor is within in three feet of camera, they need to perform in a style similar to shooting for television and outside of that space, a style more indicative of theater.

As mentioned previously, there are multiple ways of achieving increased audience immersion without requiring interactivity. Audience discovery is one way that was already discussed. Another is by utilizing the power of eye contact. When a character on TV or in a movie looks at the viewer, it sort of seems like they're looking at the viewer; but they could be looking at the person on the couch next to that viewer. In 360 and VR, there's no doubt. When a cast-member looks at the viewer, the viewer feels it. In *The BizNest*, there are some moments that call for the actor to look at the camera, for example, when, in the first segment, Tim asks the viewer for money with, "How 'bout you?" There are other moments where looking the viewer in the eye allows the actor to convey a message to the viewer without interrupting the other storylines, for example, also in the first segment, when the manager points to the viewer and mouths "My office, five minutes." Both of these moments are tied pretty closely to the plot; they help drive it forward. Realizing the power of eye contact, the director of *The BizNest* also asked each of the actors to find one moment in every segment where they could make eye contact with the viewer via the camera. Doing this achieved three things. First, it facilitated a connection between the viewer and each and every character. Second, it helped to provide interesting, engaging, personal moments happening in all directions throughout the show. And third, in certain instances, it gave the viewer a sense of how the other characters felt about each other by how they reacted to other characters' actions and behaviors. It is largely as a result of the new techniques *The BizNest* employed that it bears rewatching; after several viewings, the viewer continues to discover new things. And, importantly, the viewer still enjoys spending time with these characters.

Thoughts from an Immersive Actress: Ellie Araiza (Donna in The BizNest, Philly in Marvel's Legion)

"I've performed on stage many times as a singer and actress, both alone and with a full cast. I've worked in TV, commercials and films in close ups and long shots for over 15 years. Nothing can compare to the audience being able to see you with a 360 view. There is no fourth wall, there is no frame. You cannot run, and you cannot hide! Any moment you could get caught out of character, so you have no choice but to stay in it. On top of it, when the 360 degree camera is also a person you interact with, you know that this is truly an immersive experience unlike no other, and that person is now a part of the story. They get to decide what part of the story to focus on and every detail matters. Every moment, movement and interaction colors the story you are trying to tell at every angle. It requires a lot of coordination with your fellow performers so that the timing of your dialogue and blocking can run in sync. It's like a dance, a play, and an orchestrated mechanical circus all at the same time. As a performer, it's challenging and fun, but most of all, incredibly exciting. As an actor, I thoroughly enjoyed my own immersion in the world's first 360VR sitcom. I'm very excited for people to drop into the world of *The BizNest!*"

GETTING THE SHOW OUT THE DOOR

As pioneers not only on the creative side of VR content but also on the business side, the team behind *The BizNest* realized that part of its goal was to create a sustainable business model so that they and their peers could continue to create quality, innovative content. There were various steps they took before, during and after production to help cultivate a sustainable industry.

The first step *The BizNest* took was in valuing the ability to work with professional-level talent. *The BizNest* was a union production, working both with Screen Actors Guild-American Federation of Television and Radio Actors (SAG-AFTRA)[6] and the Writers' Guild of America (WGA).[7] An important takeaway from the show's work is that whatever level production one is doing and whatever size budget that production has, there is a way to work with the unions. It requires a bit of planning and paperwork, and the unions have rules in place to make sure it is not cost-prohibitive for small, independent productions.

Next, *The BizNest* recognized that the method of monetization that has been most successful for television has been advertising. While at the time *The BizNest* was going into production, and still at the time of publication, there are not enough eyeballs in VR to lure advertisers, *The BizNest* has been planning ahead since the beginning. With the multifarious possibilities, and much potential marketing power, it seemed a shame to think of advertising in only two-dimensions. Banner ads also seemed a waste of the medium; a harsh reminder that virtual reality isn't real after all. Commercials—especially in 360—are an unnecessary occurrence and much more jarring in an immersive medium. *The BizNest* aimed to pave a path to a better future of advertising in immersive content. Specifically, the show, in its finished form, exemplifies a new approach to story-organic immersive marketing. It showcases product placement at three different levels: having the product placed in the scene, having the product used or referenced in the scene, and having the product woven into the story. Encountering a product in *The BizNest* isn't like seeing a commercial; it's like noticing a product at your friend's house when you're visiting.

This feeling of presence is why Bryan Icenhower, President of WME IMG's experiential agency says, "What takes traditional advertising weeks, months or years to do, [experiential marketing] can do in a moment." Examples of where the viewer has the opportunity to notice the product placed in the scene include the Eric Miller *City Lights* music CD on the viewer's desk in segments 1 and 3 as well as the nutrition bar alongside it. There's also a moment in segment 5 when Cori, the blonde, puts Donna's published book *The Phenomenal Future of Marjorie Dean* on the kitchen island. If the viewer liked Cori's character, the blonde in the black overalls, they might be curious what she was reading and, if purchasable, purchase it. That's a great segue to the next example of immersive marketing possibilities: having the product used or referenced in the scene. This is the case in segment 6 with *While You Were Pooping*, the book by "Anonymous Pooper" that Nadeya is reading to the viewer and absolutely convinced that Mike wrote. This book is actually available on Amazon should the viewer find themselves intrigued and wanting to read more. And finally, *The BizNest* also shows how a product or brand can be woven into the story. The best example of this is the fictional crowdfunding website, Jumpstarter.Com, that Kate is pitching an article to *Wired* magazine about. Jumpstarter.Com is mentioned in segments 1, 3, 4, 5, 6 and 10 and the website is actually shown in segment 4. Jumpstarter.Com could just as easily have been a real crowdfunding website looking to get some publicity.

It is worth noting that *Wired* magazine also gets a shout-out, showing yet another way that advertising can be effective in 360 without being disruptive. As was already mentioned, every experience a viewer has in *The BizNest* is a memory: not a memory of watching something, a memory of being somewhere and experiencing it. Additionally, because the *Wired* magazine mention is in a joke, it has an incredibly high chance of being remembered and recounted by viewers. This is backed up by science: Goel and Dolan's neuroscience research (2001) reveals that humor systematically activates the brain's dopamine reward system, and cognitive studies show that dopamine is important for both goal-oriented motivation and long-term memory. In addition, a 2010 study by Banas and others (Banas et al., 2010) indicates that correctly-used humor can improve retention in students from kindergarten through college. And, anecdotally, the director has found that the "*Wired* magazine moment" is something that viewers often reference as memorable and funny (talk about good word-of-mouth advertising!). That moment also made it into the trailer, a potentially big bonus for any advertiser. Mentions of Amazon and Anthropologie are similarly illustrative, as is repeated reference to the pupusas from the pupuseria across the street. These examples, shown using sample products and services, pave a path to eliminating traditional ads without eliminating advertisers.

But, for advertisers to buy in, there needs to be distribution. And *The BizNest* is well positioned to help pave a path. Many of the professional-quality pieces of 360 and VR content are made for or commissioned by a 360 or VR platform. This presents a quandary for independent content creators like the journalists Weston spoke to as a presenter at the 2018 National Science Writers' Conference in Washington DC. They were interested in starting to film and report in 360 but asked, "If we make it, what do we do with it?" Sadly, at the time there was no good answer. Putting it up on YouTube for free was an option, but not a reliable way for journalists to make a living or an impact. To ensure that immersive content creators down the road will be able to do both requires an additional effort from those independently producing content or producing platform-agnostic content. The team behind *The BizNest* is working hard to explore and carve out distribution options that will help create a sustainable ecosystem for immersive narrative content.

Why Comedy

While *The BizNest* does indeed have a lot to offer emerging immersive artists and forward-thinking marketers and advertisers, it also has a lot to offer its audience. "Humor serves a number of 'serious' social, cognitive, and emotional functions," notes Rod A. Martin in the preface to his authoritative text *The Psychology of Humor: An Integrative Approach*, "Surprisingly, however, despite its obvious importance in human behavior, humor and related topics like laughter, irony, and mirth are hardly ever mentioned in psychology texts and other scholarly books" (Martin, 2006, p. xv). Psychology texts are not the only place where comedy is sometimes underacknowledged. From 1927 to 2001, only 18% of Oscar nominees for Best Picture—and 14% of winners—have been comedies (Filmsite, 2019).

While comedy may be less likely to be regarded as serious art or science, its impacts are hardly laughable. Mirth, the distinctive emotion elicited by the perception of humor, causes subjective feelings of pleasure, amusement, and cheerfulness. This emotion is also accompanied by a range of biochemical changes in the brain, autonomic nervous system, and endocrine system, affecting neurotransmitters, hormones, opioids, neuropeptides and more (Panksepp, 1993). This neurochemical cocktail then goes on to have an effect on various parts of the body, including the cardiovascular, musculoskeletal, digestive, and immune systems (Fry, 1994). Moreover, when people are experiencing positive emotions (including comedy-induced mirth), as compared to neutral or negative emotions, they show improvements in a variety of social behaviors and cognitive abilities (Isen, 2003). As Martin summarizes, "They demonstrate greater cognitive flexibility, enabling them to engage in more creative problem solving; more efficient organization and integration of memory; more effective thinking, planning, and judgment; and higher levels of social responsibility and prosocial behaviors such as helpfulness and generosity" (Martin, 2006, p. 15) (see also Lyubomirsky, King, and Diener, 2005). And inducing mirth, for example by making someone laugh, also helps to reduce the physiological arousal caused by negative emotions (Fredrickson and Levenson, 1998). All this to say, comedy is good for people.

The question is then: how does experiencing comedy in VR compare to experiencing comedy in other media? A 2016 study used neuroscience technology to compare user response to the same content in three distinct mediums: VR, 360-degree video on a flat surface and 2D. Notably, VR experiences received a 17% higher emotional reaction than flat 360-degree video, and a 27% higher reaction than 2D video. This data suggests that if viewing TV comedy has a positive impact, viewing comedy in VR has nearly 30% greater positive impact. Without even considering the converse—what this means for content that might generate negative emotions, like fear (e.g. horror content or first-person shooter games)— it is clear that it would not be an overstatement to say that comedy in VR has the potential to make peoples' lives better. After all, positive emotions such as mirth are evolved adaptations that contribute to both mental and physical health. (Fredrickson and Branigan, 2005; Fredrickson et al., 2000). It's certainly worth considering when deciding what to create or what to consume in VR.

What's Next

The future is bright for the style of content *The BizNest* introduces. One Oculus executive cited all the unique things about *The BizNest* that challenge the status quo and set a precedent for effective narrative storytelling, while another spoke to the series' potential for building audience in VR, "I'm actually really impressed. I can't imagine a world in which this doesn't take off."[8] As Wesch put it, "what we're seeking then through technologies often is a form of connection without constraint, some way of connecting very deeply without feeling the deep responsibilities of that deep connection." It's no surprise, then, the model presented by *The BizNest* has great appeal. On a recent Southwest airlines flight, a passenger watching a free screening of *The BizNest* said, "It's really great. I'm not even a fan of TV sitcoms. I've never seen content like this before." The screening of the first multi-cam sitcom may have elicited a similar response; and it defined how we consumed comedy on television for decades. *The BizNest* is a similarly innovative approach to filmed comedy, providing a distinctive, replicable format that has the power to shape the future of entertainment as we know it. And somehow, this is still just the beginning.

As of the writing of this chapter, social viewing of 360 videos is a relatively new and very exciting development. It means that viewers can watch *The BizNest*, and discuss *The BizNest*, with their friends INSIDE *The BizNest*. Not only can viewers comment and laugh together as they would when watching TV together on the couch, but on platforms that support avatars, viewers can also communicate non-verbally, despite being in different geographic locations; when deciding which area of the 360 space to focus on, one viewer might notice that her friend is looking behind herself and also choose to check out what's happening in that space. Additionally, hand controllers allow for rudimentary pointing and gesturing. These nonverbal abilities will only grow as technology advances; hand-tracking is coming soon and photoreal 3D-models-as-avatars, complete with real-time facial expressions, are on their way. Social VR takes "viewing parties" to a whole new level; now the viewers are hanging out and engaging with each other and the characters, all in real-time. Additionally, thanks to technological advances, viewers will be able to bring pieces of the real world into the fictional world with them, and bring pieces of the fictional world into the real world with them. These are exciting eventualities in a world where fan culture, engagement, and social media are huge. The farther down the road to the future we go, the more we're going to see a blurring between the lines of entertainment, work and socializing. *The BizNest* provides an innovative structure through which we begin to explore blurring those lines and that will help lead us to the Golden Age of VR Storytelling.

REFERENCES

Adams, P. (2016). Report: VR delivers big on engagement, emotional response. *Marketing Dive*. Retrieved from https://www.marketingdive.com/news/report-vr-delivers-big-on-engagement-emotional-response/430113/

Bailenson, J. (2018). *Experience on demand: what virtual reality is, how it works, and what it can do*. New York, NY: W. W. Norton & Company.

Banas, J. A., Dunbar, N., Rodriguez, D., & Liu, S. (2010). A review of humor in educational settings: Four decades of research. *Communication Education*, (60): 115–144.

Cardinal, D. (2015). *Lytro's Immerge aims to make virtual reality video more realistic*. Retrieved from https://www.extremetech.com/extreme/217536-lytros-immerge-aims-to-make-virtual-reality-video-more-realistic

Filmsite. (2019). Academy Awards Best Picture: Genre Biases. *AMC Filmsite*. Retrieved from https://www.filmsite.org/bestpics2.html

Fredrickson, B. L., & Branigan, C. (2005). Positive emotions broaden the scope of attention and thought-action repertoires. *Cognition and Emotion*, *19*(3), 313–332. doi:10.1080/02699930441000238 PMID:21852891

Fredrickson, B. L., & Levenson, R. W. (1998). Positive emotions speed recovery from the cardiovascular sequelae of negative emotions. *Cognition and Emotion*, *12*(2), 191–220. doi:10.1080/026999398379718 PMID:21852890

Fredrickson, B. L., Mancuso, R. A., Branigan, C., & Tugade, M. M. (2000). The undoing effect of positive emotions. *Motivation and Emotion*, *24*(4), 237–258. doi:10.1023/A:1010796329158 PMID:21731120

Fried, I. (2011). Meet the stealthy start-up that aims to sharpen focus of entire camera industry. *All Things D*. Retrieved from http://allthingsd.com/20110621/meet-the-stealthy-start-up-that-aims-to-sharpen-focus-of-entire-camera-industry/

Fry, W. F. (1994). The biology of humor. *Humor: International Journal of Humor Research*, *7*(2), 111–126. doi:10.1515/humr.1994.7.2.111

Goel, V., & Dolan, R. J. (2001). The functional anatomy of humor: Segregating cognitive and affective components. *Nature Neuroscience*, *4*(4), 237–238. doi:10.1038/85076 PMID:11224538

IMDB. (2019). *Eve Weston*. Retrieved from https://www.imdb.com/name/nm2542598/?ref_=fn_al_nm_1

Isen, A. M. (1993). Positive affect and decision making. In M. Lewis & J. M. Haviland (Eds.), *Handbook of emotions* (pp. 261–277). New York: Guilford.

LaValle, S. (2016, January 24). Goals and VR definitions [Video file]. *Retrieved from*, *14*, 40m.

Lyubomirsky, S., King, L., & Diener, E. (2005). The benefits of frequent positive affect: Does happiness lead to success? *Psychological Bulletin*, *131*(6), 803–855. doi:10.1037/0033-2909.131.6.803 PMID:16351326

Martin, R. A. (2006). *The Psychology of Humor: An Integrative Approach*. Cambridge, MA: Academic Press.

O'Shannon, D. (2012). *What are you laughing at? A comprehensive guide to the comedic event*. Continuum International Publishing Group.

Panksepp, J. (1993). Neurochemical control of moods and emotions: Amino acids to neuropeptides. In M. Lewis & J. M. Haviland (Eds.), *Handbook of emotions* (pp. 87–107). New York: Guilford.

Sandler, E. (2007). *The tv writer's workbook: a creative approach to television scripts*. New York, NY: Bantam Dell.

Segovia, K. Y., & Bailenson, J. (2019). Memory versus media: creating false memories with virtual reality. *Brain World*. Retrieved from https://brainworldmagazine.com/memory-versus-media-creating-false-memory-virtual-reality

Troche, J., & Weston, E. (forthcoming). Virtual Reality Storytelling: Pedagogy and Applications. In *Proceedings of the Ancient Egypt – New Technology Conference*. Leiden, The Netherlands: Brill.

Wesch, M. (2008, July 26). *An Anthroplogical Introduction to YouTube* [Video file]. YouTube.

KEY TERMS AND DEFINITIONS

"A" Story: The main story in a show: film or narrative experience, generally driven by the central character.

Choose Your Own Attention: A style of immersive storytelling in which the viewer decides where to look and because of the clarity of the dialog, still follows the story.

Laughter of Knowledge: When an audience laughs because they know something that a character does not.

Laughter of Surprise: When an audience laughs on account of having encountered something unexpected.

Multi-Camera: A show filmed with multiple cameras rolling at the same time and capturing different angles and shots.

Path-Mapping: The process of noting the camera's position and each character's path and positions for a given scene or segment on a representation of the set or location.

Runner: A light story, played more for comedy than character relationships.

Simul-Story: A show or immersive experience in which multiple narrative storylines are progressing simultaneously within the concurrently existing space of the experience.

Story-Organic Immersive Marketing: A style of marking that takes advantage of the consumer's presence in a narrative experience of some kind and utilizes product placement at one of the following three levels: having the product placed in the scene, having the product used or referenced in the scene, and having the product woven into the story.

Three Foot Rule: When an actor is within three feet of camera, they need to perform in a style similar to shooting for television and outside of that space, a style more indicative of theater.

ENDNOTES

[1]   A trailer for *The BizNest* can be found at https://exelauno.co/portfolio/360-trailer-for-the-biznest/. For up-to-date information on where to view the show itself, see https://exelauno.co and JoinThe-BizNest.Com

[2]   A trailer for the series *I Feel You: The Empath Experience* can be found at https://exelauno.co/ portfolio/i-feel-you/

[3]   For more information on Phase Two and their role in the XR community, see https://phasetwospace. com/

[4]   The phrase "choose your own attention" originates from a discussion about *The BizNest* that Weston and Ahlquist had during post-production.

[5]   Stitching is the process of combining two or more images filmed with different lenses into one image of a 360 space. To stitch footage, a filmmaker or editor would use software of some kind. After Effects, Mistika and Action Director are all examples of stitching software.

[6]   The SAG-AFTRA website has information about how new media productions can work with SAG: https://www.sagaftra.org/production-center/contract/805/getting-started

[7]   The WGA website on how companies can work with the WGA: https://www.wga.org/employers/ signatories/become-a-signatory

[8]   Author's discussion with Samuel Jordan, Facebook production engineer, on April 12, 2019.

Chapter 11

Virtual eXperience as a Mass Market Phenomenon:
Spatial Computing and the World Building Challenge

Brett Leonard
Studio Lightship, USA

ABSTRACT

The focus of this chapter is twofold: How do we create immersive work that incorporates the best of our traditional media knowledge into this new realm? and How do we take new forms of immersive media to mass market? This chapter also covers the process of creating an innovative immersive new wave, independent cinema that incorporates a feature-length film done in multiple media formats with immersion at the core. Activating our own creative imaginations and unleashing participants and empowering them with this technology is the only positive route ahead into the future of immersive media.

INTRODUCTION

The current era of immersive media was ushered in with the astronomic sales of a crowd-funded Virtual Reality (VR) headset called the Oculus Rift. It didn't matter that mostly gamers were behind this sales push, because the next step was the attention and investment placed in this fledgling VR gear by Mark Zuckerberg of Facebook, who infused the nascent company with over two billion dollars. That action influenced other investors to start seeing where they could put their funding; surely Facebook knew something important.

Virtual reality has gone through several waves of development, from the earliest research in the 1960s, through the first wave of hope and hype in the late 1980s and early 1990s, to now, this third wave.

DOI: 10.4018/978-1-7998-2433-6.ch011

Now, five years after the launch of Oculus Rift, many of the promised riches have not materialized. Even Facebook is still waiting for their bet to pay off big time (Hoium, 2018). Other early investors have become disillusioned, and many early VR companies have been closing doors for lack of further cash (Rubin, 2017), (Jenkins, 2019).

But there are some players starting to take baby steps, as exemplified by Amazon's recent announcement about their Amazon Prime Portal (Dotson, 2019). With Portal, the company has opened all their traditional work (2D films and television shows) in their Amazon Prime Library for personal viewing in a VR device. To be clear, these are not native immersive works, they are traditional media simply viewed with the screen strapped to your face. However, Amazon is also including ten 360-degree videos in this launch, which starts to open the door to mainstream immersive content. Netflix, YouTube and others are also offering similar services. So a few companies are cautiously opening that door, although in a much more measured way than how the initial frenzy began.

Currently, true immersive media is largely "playing to its own room." Practitioners in this new wave have thus far failed to reach out and embrace what it means to actually create Virtual eXperiences (VX) that both appeal to and meet some need for the average person/participant/audience.

We are at a crux in the development of immersive media. There is currently a bit of a backlash from segments like early investors, who may have come too soon to the game and are now a bit disappointed things are not further along. Much of that early funding centered on gear such as headsets and cameras. What was lacking was the content, and funding for that content, but content requires the new medium to start defining itself.

We are finding ourselves at a transitional point where we have to leverage off of the best we have learned from previous media—find what DNA from earlier media fits naturally in the new immersive realm—and then investigate and test what needs to be invented. Finding the natural affordances of a new medium takes time and experimentation. Film itself went through many stages to get to the mature state we now enjoy. From adding camera techniques to including sound, film vocabulary has evolved through dedicated trials and errors. Immersive media will take a similar trajectory.

Many creators who came into the space came in from different disciplines. Many people coming from cinema didn't really understand the unique qualities of immersive media. The emergence of 360 video started as a transitional step; it was something cinema people could wrap their heads around. So a wall arose between cinema and immersion, which started to codify and calcify itself. For traditional cinema creators, 360 video became *the* mechanism of immersive media. Unfortunately, seeing this as the solution to immersive media/VR didn't really serve to advance anything about a new form of media and storytelling. It, in essence, stifled more critical advances.

The approach I took as a traditional film person who has a unique connection to VR was more open. It was an approach to embrace traditional cinematic techniques *and* immersion within the same work, to the best of the current abilities of both aspects.

This chapter details the story of my work, *Hollywood Rooftop*, a transitional hybrid cinematic immersive piece that keeps the best of cinematic techniques while exploring the new possibilities on true immersion in media. Within this chapter I share the creative process of this work—one that brings old and new aspects together in unique, novel ways. I include the discoveries along the way that required inventing techniques to link the best possibilities inherent in each media form, sharing the lessons learned from planning, to staging, to shooting, to post production and distribution.

VIRTUAL REALITY: STORYTELLING VS. WORLD BUILDING

The films I made early in my career, during the second wave of VR (from the mid-1980s through the 1990s) were about societal issues we might face with this new medium. *Lawnmower Man* (1992) and *Virtuosity* (1995) were cautionary tales about Virtual eXperience, about virtual characters, about the merging of human reality with the virtual. As part of the ethical framework I developed in my storytelling during that time, I recently published my five laws of VR[1], which were a bit of a tongue-in-cheek homage to Isaac Asimov's three laws of robotics (Asimov, 1950). My five laws of VR are:

1. Take it seriously!
   Don't underestimate the potential power of Virtual Reality to greatly affect actual reality.

2. Empathy not alienation
   VR must be designed to connect humans with more empathy and intimacy, not alienate them from each other to a greater degree than already exists.

3. VR is a new paradigm
   The rules governing VR must be organic to the medium itself, not simply modified from earlier paradigms of reality.

4. VR must be the ultimate 'safe space'
   Virtual reality needs to be a safe space to express ideas, even those that are considered 'dangerous'. It is THE medium to express and experience the far reaches of human imagination!

5. The stakes are high!
   VR must be the medium to awaken the inter-connected consciousness and freedom of the emerging Global Human. If not, it could be the ultimate medium of Global Control.

As the director of a film about VR that became a mass-market phenomenon, I was a little spoiled, you might say, and this gave me a different perspective. I wanted to stimulate the discussion about what it would take to make VR *itself* a mass-market phenomenon. I've believed from the very beginning that it needed to be a hybrid approach—that we couldn't abandon cinematic language and many of the elements of traditional storytelling—that we needed to incorporate the best of these within some of the new and fresh aspects of immersive and interactive storytelling. This hybrid approach is fascinating, and a bridge that combines the best of both mediums.

After *Lawnmower Man*, I was suddenly on every panel about interactive storytelling in VR, even though I'd made a passive experience—a movie about VR! So that was an irony for me. But it became fascinating for me to look at the true antecedents of interactive storytelling—where did it come from? I started looking further and further back in time, all the way back to forms of ancient tribal ritual. It was in the middle of a tribal ritual in Australia, with the Aboriginal people there, that I experienced this most amazing multimedia experience with no technology at all. This made me understand the structure of tribal ritual and the way in which the group mind or the hive mind was guided through a process of a meta-narrative that encompassed multiple clans, multiple tribal understandings, but an overall unifying cosmology. That, to me, was at the core of what Virtual eXperience could be about—the ancient native core of creating an interactive alternate *storyworld.*

Because of this I started working on a theory called *Narrative Magnets,* a technique to maintain storytelling, or *storyworlding*, in the context of an interactive experience that has true agency, that is not passive. Obviously, the gaming world has been on this track: a gamer has to have agency to make choices in the game. In some ways, game designers understand this concept a lot better than traditional narrative storytellers. But there is a blind spot with game design as well.

There is an undiscovered country between game design, or *game logic,* and linear narrative that I believe this true interactive narrative story experience can take place in—what I started calling a *StoryWorld* about 25 years ago. Since then many people have picked up that term and some were very significant collaborators. For example, Alex McDowell, who was my production designer on *Lawnmower Man,* went on to be the production designer on *Minority Report* (2002), and many other big films—he was also building StoryWorlds and came to many of the same conclusions even though we hadn't worked together for over 20 years. Alex is an amazing visionary in his own right, and has also run the World Building Lab at the University of Southern California.

We share so many of the same ideas: How can a creator incorporate agency in interactive storytelling, using (for now) a hybrid process that still embraces the traditional aspects of storytelling, of cinematic language that people are already inculcated in?

What I saw happening in the first seven years of this third phase of VR was a Chinese wall being put up between traditional narrative cinematic storytelling, or cinema, writ large, and immersive, agency-driven experience or Virtual eXperience (VX). It seemed the two could never meet. People that were proponents of 360 video would say, "You have to let go of the frame, you have to let go of everything you've learned as a filmmaker." I didn't want to let go of everything I've learned as filmmaker, because I dedicated my whole life to learn that language—cinema is one of my religions! I also saw that, even if you didn't use the frame, emotional engagement, use of atmosphere, all these things that you learn as a cinematic storyteller were very applicable in immersive storytelling.

ENTER THE IMMERSIVE NEW WAVE

Cinema has had many disruptive moments. John Cassavetes was an American actor who started using 16 millimeter cameras and his acting money to make his incredibly groundbreaking independent films that moved cinema (along with other significant talents in France, Japan, etc.) into a whole new direction in the 1960s. He was a significant part of igniting the independent American film spirit, an American New Wave commiserate with the French New Wave of that era. Cassavetes didn't care about perfection. He was using short ends—film rolls leftover from another production—because they were cheaper, and much of the time his shots were in and out of focus, with an erratic handheld aesthetic of close-ups keying on the fresh spontaneous, and often improvised performances of his actors. These methods became part of his unique style. His films were successful in part because they were new; they heralded a new spirit in filmmaking that was in contrast to what the major studios were producing. They were raw and true with a messy humanistic focus.

We need to bring that spirit into the creation of immersive experience, and immersive cinema. Without that spirit of raw creation, you're bogged down by "Well, if we can't do it perfectly on a technical level, then we shouldn't do it." Or "If we don't have the money, it won't be perfect." When I was starting

Hollywood Rooftop, producer Mark Rickard and I met with some technical partners that wanted to be a part of it, and they noted that there were things we couldn't do because we did not have the budget to do it "properly" in their opinion. My approach was not to focus on the money, but on what I *could do* on a micro budget. How could I do a film that will exist in two mediums? That will be eminently watchable and extremely interesting because of what's happening on screen and what's going on with the characters.

In *Hollywood Rooftop,* there's a lot of dialogue to listen to, and this is something not typically done in virtual reality content for a number of reasons. Some of those previously mentioned technical partners dropped out because they believed that what we wanted to accomplish was impossible without a huge budget. But it was more that their priorities were in a different place, about making that perfect shot, and that's not what this movie is about. This work is about getting the energy of an ensemble group of young actors to express a fairly radical socio-political statement about Hollywood. Mona Lisa Moru's uncompromising script focuses on young people coming into the maw, the meat grinder of Hollywood and meeting on a rooftop overlooking an iconic Hollywood landscape to share their experiences with each other. That's the primary focus: what it's like to be a millennial trying to make it in Hollywood right now in this era, which is very daunting, especially in this time of massive transition.

And our challenge then, is to use immersion to put *you* the audience *into* the mise en scène. You are on that rooftop with them. How do we accomplish this? With this new realm of immersive cinematic experimentation! The whole point of this production was to make an indie film with that New Wave spirit, just like Cassavettes did, or John Luc Godard going off the streets of France with his hand held camera, but using these new immersive technologies.

One of the most extreme indie experiments ever done was *Dogme 95* (1995) by Lars von Trier and Thomas Vinterberg in Europe. They literally said: you have to shoot with the lowest level camera you can, and sound has to be secondary, and it has to be as authentic as possible, and the technology of filmmaking cannot get in the way at all. This was the philosophy that these filmmakers signed on to at that time, and Lars von Trier was the *pater familias* of that whole movement. There were some good things and some bad things made within this movement. *Breaking the Waves* (1996) is amazing film, for example. There was so much improvisation going on, including not letting the camera and the sound get in the way of the acting. In addition to extreme indie filmmaking such as *Dogme 95,* there were many other independent filmmakers not trying to make a highly polished Hollywood product. Those super polished Hollywood releases do work for many things and huge audiences, but there are other people making films for just the pure energy and intensity. *Easy Rider* (1969) was done in this vein at the beginning of the American independent film movement, and it was incredibly rough compared to slick Hollywood product of the time, and it completely changed the entire nature of the American box office. New filmmakers such as Scorsese and Coppola, along with a new breed of actors, like De Niro, Pacino, and Nicholson, created innovative new films throughout the 1970s: Many films of this era were made in a crazy climate where nearly anything was permissible: innovation and experimentation were both the method and the goal. This new young generation of filmmakers changed the studio system and created the New Hollywood. *The Godfather* (1972), was a true studio film, but made by independent filmmakers within the studio system. It's the nature of independent filmmaking to allow the instincts of the filmmaker, the instincts of the cast to take primacy, and because this was allowed for that decade, it changed the studio approach for a while. That phase ended when the likes of Lucas and Spielberg created the summer blockbuster, starting with *Jaws* (1975)—Then the commercial approach started to return to being more and more polished, and now everything coming out of the studio system is super polished again. But here we are at another potentially disruptive moment.

We need to encourage an Immersive New Wave—just like there was a French New Wave, a Japanese New Wave, an American New Wave—we need an Immersive New Wave that embraces new *artistic* aspects of storytelling as opposed to focusing exclusively on the *technical* and on perfection at this early stage of this emerging medium.

CREATING A TRUE TRANSITIONAL IMMERSIVE FILM: A HYBRID APPROACH

I didn't embrace 360 video or other forms being used for many, many years while I was exploring all this, because I didn't see it as compelling enough. Then I partnered with Mona Lisa Moru, who wrote a screenplay called *Hollywood Rooftop,* which all takes place on a rooftop in Hollywood, about young actors—mostly millennial age—who are trying to make it in this crazy business. They have just graduated from Stella Adler theatre school,[2] and they talk about their loves, their lives, their disasters, how they're trying to break into the industry. Mona Lisa's screenplay was really edgy, a very strong indictment of modern Hollywood and what it meant to be a young person in it. It was set in this kind of fantasy environment of a rooftop overlooking Hollywood Boulevard. I saw how it could be an immersive work. It has a diverse cast, different ethnicities, a gender fluid character played by an actor who was gender fluid at the time of shooting. So it had these great compelling components. The original idea was to just shoot it with a 360 rig on a rooftop, but I wanted to push it further. So I asked. "Why not shoot it in traditional cinema and 360 simultaneously?"

Why? I realized I had great tools in my cinema toolbox that just weren't part of 360 vocabulary.

Am I going to walk an actor closer to the camera every time I need something that really conveys a strong emotion? You couldn't stage it that way in 360. But I knew exactly how to do it with traditional cinema; why throw that language away?

Everyone thought I was nuts. In the end, we'd shoot the first half of each day with a 360 VR video camera. And the second half we would switch to traditional HD cinema cameras, shooting it like a traditional indie feature. The key elements that required thought to make something truly immersive, that took the best of cinema and immersive VR, required revisiting many aspects of production, including getting funding, establishing performance techniques, creating the set, developing novel production practices, and inventing an entirely new post production approach and pipeline.

I call this new approach *Cinema VX.* We are only at the beginning, and the discoveries we have made thus far, in a true indie spirit, will hopefully help point the way to more native and robust forms of immersive media in the future.

An Immersive New Wave Approach: A Cinema VX Project

Just as in an effects driven superhero film, not every shot needs to be a money shot. The nature of cinema, even when you're shooting normally, is that not every shot has to be perfect, even if the end product of today's films seem super polished. Cinema at its core has never been about perfection. To oversimplify, it is about using a string of shots that kinesthetically work in the audience's mind, then BAM, along comes the shot that punctuates it, the money shot. That is the true sleight of hand of cinema. We believe it is all polished because certain key shots are; the rest support the overall experience of the story.

We need to bring that same sleight of hand to immersive experience, in part because it is necessary to make production time and cost effective enough to pull off. This approach allows for a creative friction that is not bogged down by wanting to make everything perfect. And yet, this perfection is what many of the technology-based companies in VR have focused on. Perfection is not what keeps people inside an immersive environment.

The raison d'etre of *Hollywood Rooftop* was to embrace making a full immersive feature film that also included cinematic language, with a total indie spirit. It wasn't meant to be perfect. For example, the stitching of the 360 video from the multiple camera rig isn't going to be absolutely perfect, as that should not be what people are focused on. The direction of the participants/audience attention should be on what is important: the story, the characters, the relationships, the meaning, and not on what is strictly technical or trivial.

This is challenging in immersive cinema, as we have not yet found all the solutions for the technical issues, nor developed a solid vocabulary for immersive storytelling.

Take finding the right 360 camera, for instance. The reason I picked the Google Jump camera, which is the YI Halo camera, was in part, because it had 16 lenses all around (and one looking up for our dome sky) so it creates an excellent stereoscopic effect, but more importantly, you could get very close to that camera and the stereoscopic immersion held up. Because I had a character driven piece, I needed actors to get close and this camera facilitated that.

Another reason for choosing this camera was that the Jump camera, when you bought it at the time we did, came with automatic stitching in the cloud from Google (which unfortunately they have just discontinued because they are moving away from 360 video). I was lucky to get an entire feature film captured, with 50 hours of 360 auto-stitching because I used the YI Halo camera. So that was absolutely a key decision—if we had had to stitch by brute force, we'd still be stitching, and we would never have done it under the micro-budget we had for the shoot.

There are other stitching software options coming along that are pretty much automated, but at the time we did this, a year ago, it would have been nearly impossible to stitch the amount of footage we shot for a full feature story.

A Feature-Length Immersive Experiment

Hollywood Rooftop is a feature-length film in 360 *and* in 2D, because we shot in those two distinct mediums. After we got all the 360 coverage, and the 2D shots, they are merged together for the *Cinema VX experience.* This utilizes the cinematic frame, multiple frames as a matter of fact, referencing experiments that filmmakers like Brian DePalma were doing in the 70s with split screen storytelling. 360 editor Steve Yoon and I used some of these techniques on steroids *in* an immersive environment, placing these multiplexed frames in the 360 stereoscopic space, so you are watching the story in immersive VR, and suddenly frames come up in your view, giving you close ups, allowing you to focus on moments of intimacy between the characters. Then that goes away, and you're back in the immersion environment, following the characters in that 360 mode. People who have viewed our initial finished scenes have remarked that they are fully engaged in the story and following it in a way unique in their viewing of 360 VR—They've said they haven't experienced this in a lot of other 360 video immersion, simply because the immersion is everywhere and they don't know where to look. For a dialogue-driven, ensemble character focused film, knowing when to focus on specific characters is critical. When something important is happening between the characters we direct your attention. You can also still look around the 360 environment at all times to see the reactions of the other characters, etc. Because you do have other places to look, you can watch scenes multiple times, and it will not be the same experience—It can be fresh with each multiple viewing.

We are also creating a traditional 2D "flatie" version of the story that will be a companion piece to the immersive version. The 2D will also reference and utilize some of the 360 footage (in flatie form) just as the 360 version utilizes the 2D footage. So we will utilize both mediums, with the idea that the two versions will be very different from each other stylistically, and yet are essentially the same story.

From a process standpoint we of course needed funding to start production. We received this from CEEK VR, a company headed by an amazing woman, Mary Spio, who is building a distribution platform for innovative VR content. CEEK, under Mary's leadership, has created successful 360 music immersion projects, first with Mega Death, and also with Lady Gaga and Katy Perry, as CEEK has a very strong relationship with Universal Music. CEEK had the courage to support the creation of a very experimental film done in two mediums, on a micro-budget. They embraced our indie immersive New Wave spirit, enabling such a transitional piece of work—This indie approach allows experimentation and finding compromises that can make new ideas work. Like choosing the right camera. The choice of the Yi Halo Google jump camera with its automatic stitching was very critical, so CEEK bought us that camera, enabling us to just shoot and get the stitched 360 VR scenes automatically, in the cloud. We shot 50 hours of 360, 100 hours of 2D, on a production schedule of just 18 days. It was a wild experimental experience for all of us involved!

Pre-Production and Creating the Set

In pre-production we focused on creating the environment, a set suitable for 360 immersive drama. In creating such a set for a work that is feature-length, you have to make something that the actors can live and work in, lay on and walk over. So, we built this rooftop at the Creative Technology Center stage in the Brewery Arts District in downtown Los Angeles. We had a high enough ceiling to place a projection dome into the stage, and we worked with Full Dome[3], who provided that "dome sky" for our set (Figure 1). We realized we had to build the whole set inside a stage in order to get the dialogue captured correctly, because this film is very dialogue driven—120 pages of dialogue! That, in itself, is unique for VR. The actors were all outfitted with lav mics for the 360 capture, with some hidden mics in the set, and we boomed it when we went in with the 2D cameras.

The stylized rooftop set was built in full 360 degrees under the tilted dome, on which sky elements were projection mapped. The set was built around the projectors, so you couldn't easily see them. The open end of the set, where you looked out on the Hollywood landscape was another projection environment: front projection by three projectors mounted above the dome. We had eight projections going simultaneously, which all had to be synced. And the projections changed during the scenes, the sky would react to the emotion, the landscape would react to the scenes, sometimes in a stylized way, sometimes in a more naturalistic manner. All the projections were plates we shot in HD. I call the way in which this set worked a "Hollywood of the mind;" it wasn't direct film shots of Hollywood but rather the way we imagine it; the emotional impact the iconic landscape of Hollywood has on us.

The cinematographer was pioneer Edward Button, who has worked on many high-profile immersive works, and was the artist in residence at Technicolor in New York City. His challenge was both lighting the set for 360, and then having to also come in and light it for 2D. The larger scenes were full 360,

Figure 1. Hollywood Rooftop dome set-up

with characters moving around the entire set, such as for the big party scenes on the rooftop. Some of the shots were staged for just 220 degrees, primarily because a lot of the drama happened in that space. I insisted that we only had one light to "paint" out of the equation at the back of the 360 set—that was the one light that gave us our key light of sun and moon.

Eddy Vajarakitipongse was our projection guru, and he artistically put together the powerful image landscapes, and was able to change the sky, have clouds go by, helicopters flying past, all as interactive elements that were projected in real time as backdrop while we were shooting the 360 and capturing the drama—it was a true real-time interactive immersive set!

This was a very ambitious piece, especially on a micro-budget, but I want to do something that really embraced all of these different techniques: There had to be enough to look at in the 360 environment so that it would be good for multiple viewings in a VR headset.

So much had to come together for this immersive experiment. The cast did a fantastic job, and really dedicated themselves to this very crazy performance experience. Mark Rickard did a herculean job as producer, putting together the deals for the dome and projections, and all the other elements that had to be there. And luckily, we had almost no technical glitches for the entire shoot, which is good because we couldn't afford any glitches on our budget and timeframe—One problem, like projectors going down etc., would have killed us, because we had only 18 days to shoot this feature-length piece in both mediums.

Performance and Shooting

Luckily, we had a great cast of young actors who recently graduated from the Stella Adler theatrical school, who were willing to do a month of rehearsals before shooting. This enabled us to get all the 360 staging worked out ahead of time. If we had had to stage it on each day of shooting, we could not have finished in anywhere near 18 days. So for multiple days a week we had rehearsals, and eventually we rehearsed in the 360 stage, marking out where everything was, and this was how we got the staging down pat. Because the actors were theatrically trained, they inherently understood staging in a 360 environment. Most of them had never acted in a feature film before. A cast of experienced film actors would have been much harder to work with I feel. As my background is also in theater, I had an innate sensibility of what kind of actors we needed and what they could do. The most interesting thing about working with the actors for this piece was what happened when we went to the second half of the day shooting with traditional cinema cameras—we had only rehearsed the 360 staging thoroughly, so when we switched to traditional cinema techniques, that's when confusion cropped up—the actors were used to thinking of the entire space immersively, so when we went in for something like a close up, it was mind blowing to them! Of course, they got used to that, but it was challenging to shift from one approach to the other in the same day, every day. It was also challenging for me as a director as well from a performance standpoint—switching to 2D was the first time most of these actors had to think within the context of a frame. It was as if we were doing a play in the first half of the day, a play for this 360 camera that is basically a spectator in the middle of the action, and then in the second part of the day a film crew walks in, focused on close-ups in a Cassavetes hand-held style, as well as tripod-based stable shots for integrating into the immersive version, oriented to cinematic language—a true process experiment for us all!

Inventing a Post-Production Process

The processes that we worked out for our 360 VR post-production are very technically advanced, such as looking at the geometry of how to put these multiplexed cinematic frames into an immersive stereoscopic space, which is now our proprietary process for *CinemaVX*. We have developed a number of these proprietary processes at my company Studio Lightship, which I co-founded with social media content pioneer Josh Shore, as part of new ways to do immersive cinema and a *World Building Process* we plan to license to content creators in the future.

At the end of shooting, we've got 100 hours of 2D cinema and 50 hours of immersive VR video in the can: We have an unbelievable amount of data! After making triplicate copies of all that data, we partnered with Artists & Algorithms, a company owned and run by effects and 3D innovator Tom Polson, and engaged 360 editor Steve Yoon, and together we literally had to re-invent the post-production process, because not only do we have over/under 8K stereoscopic 360 VR, we have all the 2D cinematic footage that we needed to blend in many complex multiple layers on the timeline. Without the brilliance of collaborators like Tom and Steve, we never would have been able to figure this out!

This blending is not as simple as combining imagery in a flat space; this had to blend in a 360 3D stereoscopic space—Everything has to inhabit that immersive environment. We want to create an ultimate cinema experience, where cinematic language is expressing itself inside its own fully immersive mise en scène, which the audience experiences as a 360 VR environment.

Figure 2. Cutouts technique used in Hollywood Rooftop

Another technique we developed we call *cutouts*, which is a way to have multiple layers of focus for the audience, even while the audience is in a pure 360 environment without other cinematic elements. One example of this is in a scene we've completed where these cutouts follow separate dancers who are moving around the camera in 360 stereoscopic space. The cutouts allow you to follow individual dancers, and then at one point those cutouts fade away, and you are back in the full 360 environment. This is one technique to use a framing device in a unique a way while maintaining full immersion.

These cutouts (Figure 2), are essentially like a moving matte, dark and translucent in parts, and fully clear in other parts; framing things in the stereoscopic 3D space. We use them to acclimate the viewer to the 3D immersive space, and then let them go into the fully 360 space as the cutouts fade away. You are then inside the drama, watching the characters talk to each other as they move around in the 360 environment—the effect is that you are a passive character on the rooftop hanging out and observing the other characters.

Once the drama begins in 360, we had to figure a way of bringing the frames of our 2D cinematic coverage into the immersive environment in a way that guides the viewer through the story and allows them to emotionally engage in a very deep, intimate way with the characters, as cinematic language allows with the use of close ups—this hybrid approach allows things that you usually don't get in pure 360 VR immersion. We came up with different ways of *matrixing*, or *multiplexing* the 2D image elements, such as creating complex split screen environments *within* the 360 stereoscopic space of the rooftop (Figures 3 and 4). Sometimes you might see a strip of film coming across your view, showing the main frame, then moving to the next shot as in a timeline of a series of images—this technique expresses cinematic time as the images move in the strip of film— the future coming to you—the present in the main position—and the past receding as the images move along the embedded film strip in the 360 space.

In this way, in one short scene segment, we infuse something like 20 minutes of actual footage, creating a deep cinematic environment to explore in multiple viewings. We multiplex the footage in this way because we had all this coverage, all of these matching elements in both mediums, so why not experiment with new techniques? I am inspired by filmmakers like Brian De Palma, who have really experimented with visual language in the service of story, by combined all sorts of multiplexed images

Figure 3. The matrixing or multiplexing technique used in Hollywood Rooftop

Figure 4. Another view of the matrixing or multiplexing technique used in Hollywood Rooftop

and split screens in bravura stylized sequences. So Steve, Tom, and I experimented with these ideas, and figured out how to technically combine up to 24 layers of 2D cinematic coverage in our 8K 360 VR rooftop environment, which makes for a very rich visual and emotional experience.

This immersive visual environment had to be complemented by a truly immersive soundtrack. My music and sound collaborator on many of my films, Gregg Leonard, a pioneer in immersive sound in his own right (and who also happens to be my brother) heads up the team creating that 360 audio landscape for *Hollywood Rooftop*. It begins with Gregg's composition of a brilliant music score, just like for any feature film, and continues with creating an immersive sound design with the help of 360 audio mixer Eric Hemion. The goal is to place the viewer in the immersive audio world of the rooftop, with all its stylization, while delivering the dialogue-driven story in a seamless manner that references the traditional cinema-going experience that everyone is familiar with—we want everyone to feel like they are inside a movie, not some alien experience, and the immersive soundtrack as a whole, music included, is a huge part of delivering that in technically transparent way that also carries the participant into the emotional streams of the story and characters. I believe music and sound design create 80 percent of the emotional impact of any film—there are plenty of great films that don't have especially good cinematography, but there are no great films (of the modern sound era) that don't have a terrific music score and/or sound design. There has been a lack of focus on sound for VR in general, and that is something that has to change if the immersive medium is ever to gain mass-market adoption.

Frag Film

Now, a full feature-length immersive film can't really be watched in a VR headset in a comfortable way today; at least that's the common knowledge. Now this may change as the technology of VR delivery changes, but for now we are making what I call a *Frag Film*—A Frag Film is viewed in 10 minute fragments that fit together into a full feature—it's not a series: a series is in episodes that continue, that can be connected, or be consumed independently. A Frag Film is still a feature film, period—It just happens to be delivered in terms of the immersive experience with VR in *Frags*. I coined the term *Frag Film* many years ago, and actually won the *2010 Digital 25 Award* for this concept: doing feature-length films in fragments for the Internet. Why? Attention spans are getting shorter, and there's a whole new way of experiencing content on smartphones, so the Frag Film idea just seemed right for the Internet era of content, and now there are new content platforms based on this concept, like Quibi. I ended up making several Frag Films over the last decade, including on for Disney.

The 360 VR version of *Hollywood Rooftop* will comprise 10 to 12 Frags that make up the full feature film, and that's how the audience will be able to experience it on the CEEK VR platform.

Lessons Learned: Measuring Success of Immersion in This Form

These experiments in techniques that make sense for the audience in immersive media are new. Time will tell if we achieved our goals of combining the best of traditional methods with new immersive possibilities. We think we have created something both meaningful for the audience and true to the story—and to the World Building. Such experimentation is the first stage of a getting to a true *World Building Process,* taking multiple hybrid elements, multiplexed elements, and coming up with a multimedia expression that is built around immersion as a critical native principal.

How will we measure success? If people come back to re-experience the story, seeing it from different perspectives; if they feel it is new and fresh on repeated interactions, then we can feel like we found some new ideas that might stick. But true immersive media is still developing and needs a great deal more work to find what will engage future audience/participants who will no doubt be more and more demanding. It needs to be based on World Building, a more holistic approach to the creation of immersive media.

WORLD BUILDING AS THE FOUNDATION OF IMMERSIVE MEDIA

The development of a World Building process thus far has been fragmented, because the money has gone to individual technologies, hardware, software, and widgets. We need to look at it from a 30,000 foot level and ask what is an overall process that encompasses all aspects of both the technical and creative, and puts them into an economical and time efficient process that can actually be pragmatically used for building world assets around an IP. There also has to be a new transmedia ecosystem for servicing all of these new tools and techniques emerging in this era of immersive content. Most people don't look at the overall process because it is a hard thing to get perspective on—right now there are many unknowns.

We must start preparing for what is being called spatial computing. Spatial computing really is the underlying phenomenon—a mega-trend that encompasses all virtual experiences (all the virtual "Rs" like VR, AR, MR and XR). Spatial computing is the next phase of how we understand our computing mechanisms—not as separate devices, but as an integral part of everything we know. It is how humans and computers will relate and interface from here on out. That is the 3,000 foot immersive spatial computing tsunami coming right at us, and it will change everything. Companies like VERSES, which is headed up by my friend and longtime collaborator Dan Mapes, are forging the foundational infrastructure of the new spatial web, which is what all spatial computing and Virtual eXperience will sit upon—they are building the surfboard that will let us ride and survive that tsunami—which is going to inundate us sooner than you think!

Computers, virtual and physical, will mesh into one reality. This is a natural progression—a continuum—from where computing began, to its natural, most efficient way for humans to interact with that computer and the data that it represents, where the interface is one with the natural human environment. That's what we've done with every other technology—the technology becomes invisible, and it becomes part of our world. So there is a rigor and processes and expertise required for the craft of these Virtual eXperiences, these things that sit on top of spatial computing. These VX components (and how they are crafted) constitute the ways in which humans will interact with spatial computing—it's going to be this invisible infrastructural thing, and you need to have VX crafted properly in order to do anything with it.

The tenants of entertainment are incredibly important in all aspects of VX for spatial computing, even the most utilitarian, because when you're talking about spatial computing, you're talking about immersive experience, and you're talking about something that's more intimate than just tapping on or watching a flat screen—it is intimately a part of you. This becomes a second or third or fourth or fifth skin, as part of our identity, what we think of as being human, and what we consider reality. Children that grow up in this spatial computing universe are not going to think of themselves as separate from those other "skins" of reality. We barely think of ourselves as separate from our automobiles now, or our cell phones. Technology becomes part of us in a way that's seamless in a very short amount of time.

Think of the anxiety people have over losing their smartphone. It is one of the most stressful things that happens today for human beings, because we are so addicted to that device being an extension of ourselves: we are intertwined with it as a part of our person. The intertwining with spatial computing will be so much more than what we now have with a little flat screen that we get to touch and scroll on. Can we even imagine what's it going to be like when everything around you is touchable, and react-able, and interface-able?

Ethically, the stakes are very high. The type of things happening at such a rapid rate of change currently with social media (such as the nature of representative democracy and changes in fundamental societal structures) will happen at an even much greater level and pace when true spatial computing becomes ubiquitous. Maybe these interim steps have been showing us where the foibles are, where the dangers are located. But when spatial computing is fully integrated as part of being human, we may hopefully come back to a humanist oriented imperative around how we interface with these extensions of ourselves. By keeping human imagination at the core and allowing human imagination to run free (which is literally the last line of *Lawnmower Man*), this technology can be a hugely positive thing. We have a responsibility to design these things with that purpose in mind as creators of the technology, creators of the content, creators of the interface—The user interface is literally going to become the user interface for being human on this planet!

That is why it is critical to look at the process of creation, writ large, because it's so easy for us to lose control. To support mass adoption, immersive media has to be more time efficient and more cost effective than anything else in media creation history, or it won't happen. If it's just more widgets, and more complexity, and more things you have to wear without it creating efficiency, the market forces will not allow it to take hold.

And beyond efficiency, there is meaning. What does it do for our lives?

In this vein I am working on my follow-up to *Lawnmower Man,* which is about a world in which spatial computing is imbedded everything. It's ubiquitous in this nearly invisible way. What does that mean for the nature of being human? This is the Transhuman question. My belief is that as storytellers, it is imperative right now that we tell positive stories and positive visions about this future. Yes, there has to be cautionary tales, but just showing a dystopian vision is not what we need at this transitional moment in human history. We've had tremendous amounts of dystopian vision that have been brilliantly executed over the decades. I can't do better than that. Trying to make a better dystopian vision is flogging a dead horse. But making a *utopian* vision of how the future of immersivity can express greater human intimacy, greater human connection, and activate the genius of the hive mind and the better angels of our nature, that is the imperative for storytellers right now!

This all goes back to the challenge of World Building—the *meaning* needs to be one of the animating factors for all of us from the very beginning. Better human meaning and understanding wasn't one of the main factors for the titans who came up with today's social media, and we are now living the results of that. We are seeing those creators having to deal with the reality of their creations, which have turned out to pose incredible challenges for humans. Social media is currently based on making money, not on providing meaning for humans. The new immersive world order must do better—that's the true center of an Immersive New Wave!

Going hand in hand with who builds it, is who controls it? When spatial computing reaches mass adoption, what structures will it be under? Current corporate global society is not about empowering the hive mind—its goal is more in *controlling* the hive mind so people make good consumers. The data sovereignty movement, to enable personal control of your data, is one of the most important things happening right now[4].

We can't build this new world order on top of today's social media structures; there are no protections. It's like the Vatican controlling everything in the Middle Ages. Today's system has to be broken down to give sovereignty and power back to the individual, and to an empowered hive mind. Enabling the genius of the human hive mind, not its primal reptilian-brainstem theater, is the next stage of us activating our evolution.

This is why the process of World Building is a challenge: integrating all these multi-disciplines, including an ethical framework, including an understanding of sociology, including understanding human psychology, including the idea of sovereignty, and how you empower people as opposed to disempowering them—all this has to be parts of the table that's set for us to truly address this challenge. It's not just a technical challenge. It's not just a creative challenge. It's a challenge of human nature.

THE NATIVE ELEMENTS OF TRUE IMMERSIVE VIRTUAL EXPERIENCE (VX)

As we approach worldbuilding for the future, we are already starting to see some main tenants of what will define true Virtual eXperiences. The Holy Grail for me is developing what is native to this medium, which goes far beyond what we are doing with *Hollywood Rooftop*. That was creating a hybrid transition towards a full immersive experience (though I'd love to eventually make some of the Frags fully interactive, using the rich cinematic resources we have captured).

One key tenant is that immersive media will natively be real time. It will not be pre-rendered and unable to be changed after creation. Creation will be an ongoing process facilitated by every person inside the media. For example, I have this concept of the emotion glass. You're in the middle of a drama and you bring out the emotion glass, and it stops the drama for a moment. Then you are able to zoom in on a deeper level of the drama between this character and that character, utilizing the cinematic elements. This takes cinematic language and makes it an interactive user experience within the larger story. This idea puts you into the drama in a different way, with *emotional agency*.

How we create worldbuilding assets will also undergo a radical transformation. We will use rapid scanning and procedural techniques to bring forth the environment and its elements in real time. In this way anyone could alter the world during the experience. Your actions and the actions of others in that StoryWorld with you are *writing through actions* what the world is, moment by moment, and creating the consequences of the world in real time. Procedural world generation is not only important, but absolutely critical to native immersive media. If you're not creating something that is real time and eventually procedural, you're not native to what immersive experience is truly about.

Take your avatar representation. You will be seeing others as they are seeing you. You will be able to interact with them in this new dimension with real time generated avatar representations in the immersive space. People will need to be generated the way they actually appear and move, with their own textures in real time. Since you are typically viewing an immersive experience in first person, this is key, but most VR platforms don't give you a personalized avatar if they provide one at all. In the future, your avatar will be generated on the fly; in first person mode you will be able to look down to see your own body. In other modes you might be watching yourself in third person—from behind or overhead. There's going to be ways of toggling your viewpoint in real time.

Because these worlds of the future will be shared as part of the all-encompassing nature of spatial computing, we can also use community techniques, connecting people in real time and leveraging that, to create a really expansive experience.

Real time experimentation is astonishing right now because it forces you to think in a different way. It forces you to think in concepts that work in the here and now, and that lead to procedural environmental changes based upon the interaction of the people in that environment. The worldbuilding challenge must incorporate things that are native to an interactive experience. Creators have to think in real time to solve the problems and—this is critical—not compromise that native real time process.

I also believe this experimentation to drive the discoveries of immersive media must be project driven. You've got to actually produce something and be on fire about it creatively. The team, whatever their level of expertise is, whatever their specific focus is, each team member has to be on fire about being able to execute something from their expertise set that is going to be different and new, and not worry about making it perfect. Perfection is the enemy of the good sometimes, and of the pragmatic.

Eventually real time asset generation will be of high enough quality to create real worldbuilding assets that can service both immersive real time and top quality feature films. At that level of quality, immersive experiences will constitute the whole world, all the elements. The worldbuilding challenge is to find that sweet spot of process tools to create, something that can serve one aspect and automatically be ready for the other. When this spot is reached, immersive media will take off as a market because it is cost effective enough to do it that way, and being cost effective will be the thing that convinces the gatekeepers.

The current status quo in digital is all about super photorealistic imagery as something that can be rendered, and *not* how *alive it is*. Super realism is a heavy outlay in time and money for getting stuff done. Its path is somewhat parallel, and somewhat opposed to the path of real time processing.

Each mode has its place. Real time gains a liveliness and responsiveness that high rendering may miss; and vice versa. The real time solution may not be a perfect photorealistic depiction, but it may feel more responsive and alive. For the time being the photo real will try to keep the real time in a corner. But we need to, in some ways, wipe the slate clean and embrace real time as a great process right off the bat. Such new approaches can bring things like visualization in early at the ideation and writing stage, rather than much further down the line as they tend to be now.

The first successful immersive world property will be immersive from the get go. A feature film of that IP will come out of the immersion, not the other way around.

Wizards—the people who have always been on the creative edge, developing or refining the latest and greatest to keep the technology advancing and entertaining us in new ways—are beginning to turn their focus forward from the way it has "always been done," and embracing new concepts and ideas, especially the newer generations. Where is the new generation? Solidly in real time, solidly in these new technologies. That's what they have been raised in, with games and interaction, not passive forms of media. Democratized tools, not super expensive software locked behind limited licenses. This is the new talent pool, the new wizards. Immersion is firmly in their sights.

All this change is starting to erode the foundation of the current systems—the current ways things are done in the visual effects and digital innovation business. This change is going to affect not just entertainment, but everything. Because if you're not ready for spatial computing writ large, which is all real time, everything all the time, you're going to miss the boat. That wave is coming, and we are in the moment of transition and disruption that happens just before it actually hits.

TOWARDS A MASS MARKET FOR IMMERSIVE MEDIA

Film box office revenues are going down every year, and that indicates a sea change. With companies like Netflix and Amazon disrupting on all levels of the entertainment business, everyone's experiencing downward price pressure. Technology must address keeping innovation and quality at a high level, while being more cost effective. And we have to embrace that in our industry. In order for immersion to truly become a mass market phenomenon it must start on the inside professional level first, then the market gets created because there's enough content that's compelling enough to actually attract a mass market. So, most importantly, we've got to create content that is so compelling, that it starts to bring about a mass market adoption.

A true Virtual eXperience is a form of spatial computing, and worldbuilding, in particular, is the way creating such experiences must be approached. If you start with native VX techniques, then every experience is unique, and people don't feel like they know exactly what's going to happen; they can return and have a different experience.

True spatial immersion is by definition, real time. Real time must be part of the worldbuilding process because it puts creation directly in the hands of each individual in the hive mind, not some distant entity making all the decisions and sending it down to be dealt with and consumed. That real time component needs to extend as creative empowerment into the experiences themselves. All individuals experiencing these real time forms in this way, all become empowered creators.

Take the idea of brands, which are part of the fabric of our society. The best of these must empower consumers to become collaborators in the creation of the brand. They must figure out what consumers really are attracted to, and then creatively push that forward in a positive way with virtual elements, World Building elements that fit into the spatial computing structure. That's what a brand needs to do if it doesn't want to be left in the dust. *(Editors' note: See Linda Ricci's chapter in this book for a deeper look at brands and how immersive media is affecting them.)*

There's a whole generation coming up, especially Gen Z, that absolutely demands the agency that is native to immersive media. Their demand: "Don't tell me what to do," is not just a trend, it is existential. If brands, entertainment, media don't do this, they simply won't be part of the New Immersive World Order with consumers who are no longer okay with being passively fed something someone else decided they want. Gen Z is demanding agency and demanding more and more immersion, because they're growing up with media devices that essentially immerse them in media all the time.

A concept often brought up as the essence of real time experiences is that of *Presence*—that feeling that your *self i*s totally living in a space that may not be part of the physical reality, but feels as if it is. Your senses and actions have an effect in such a space, and your embodied self receives feedback and responses that have believability similar to what can be experienced in our everyday reality.

Mass market adoption also requires more attention to long term, as opposed to short term, gain. Trying to get a quick return may be the biggest obstacle to getting immersive spatial out there quickly. It may lengthen the adoption cycle by years, if not decades.

There needs to be a slow, true, concerted effort to create mass market adoption. We have to be market creators, not market followers. This is critical. Understanding that the mega-trend of spatial computing is emerging from and fueled by huge changes in computing and data, as well as the wants and desires human imagination, requires us to embrace that challenge in everything we do. This leads me to describe my next, natively immersive project.

TECHNOLOGY AND PHILOSOPHY OF THE MACGYVER-WORLD PROJECT

Lee David Zlottof, the brilliant guy who created the TV series and character *MacGyver* in 1985, has teamed up with Studio Lightship to create *The MacGyverWorld* project, a new work that will incorporate the full scope of immersive techniques as we understand and can implement them today. The technology is still under development, but rapidly advancing. The experience is a real time virtual escape room for four simultaneous players in its first iteration.

MacGyverWorld is slated to be offered at family entertainment centers, amusement parks and beyond, sometime in 2020, at many sites all around the world. Now, MacGyver is literally a verb in many dictionaries; it represents the idea of having ingenuity with common objects, using just your wits and your skill, and your expertise and your smarts, to solve problems. An interesting note is that MacGyver never used a gun—violence is never the solution—which fits an ethos building in society at this moment in time. We have these intractable human-caused problems that seem impossible, but maybe there are commonplace solutions that we're just missing because they're so close to us. So we're going to try to embed this kind of problem solving into *MacGyverWorld*. This also fits into current concepts like DIY, and Maker Spaces, and even life-hacking.

Each person in the experience will appear as a voxel-based avatar with their own textures, using a technology created by Swiss company IMVERSE—Your avatar is captured on the fly, in real time. Why voxels[5]? There are two basic methods to model objects and people in virtual space. One is a surface or mesh approach, which makes lovely representations, but with the overhead of a large amount of computer processing. It is not really efficient and therefore does not run in anything like real time. Voxels, on the other hand are succinct, mathematical representations of small atomic shapes that can be combined and moved quickly with much less computational burden.

Therefore, unlike other systems where each player is assigned or chooses some sort of default avatar, in *MacGyverWorld* the avatar is constructed on the unique aspects of the individual being scanned in real time. With most avatar representations, a surface model is utilized, which, while it can look exceptionally photorealistic, cannot reflect real time changes. Voxel-based modeling and rendering is, at its core, much faster and can be updated in real time, making it native to true VX.

Imagine if Mom, Dad, and the kids are working collaboratively in the experience, not simply as the same avatars that anyone gets, but as themselves. The dynamics are much more personal, and the experience perhaps more memorable. Not only are you in VR, but you look down and you are yourself, and the people you are in the story with, they are people you know and recognize. This is a game changer, literally, for VR and immersive experiences in general—VX. This is the way VX should be. We have accepted the alternative, which is either having a fictionalized character that is not you, or a fully captured "holographic" type form, which *is* you, but pre-captured and therefore "on rails" and limited to only the actions performed during the capture session. *MacGyverWorld* will be a multi-player real time Virtual eXperience, and seeing others in their true personas is something we believe will make the entire situation more personal and meaningful.

CONCLUSION

There is a major transition that's happening in the overall digital imaging world, which is moving from workstation based programs that are very artist intensive and time intensive to real time processes. This changes the nature of the creative process, changes the nature of action in ways we are only just beginning to fathom. Our entertainment properties, our worlds and universes that are inhabited by the characters we know and love are changing in fundamental ways. With real time components in play from the start, which are more efficient and mutable, the entire game—the creative process—is redefined in a major way.

We have to remember to capture people's imaginations and allow them to exercise this unique human power that we have. We have started to forget about this in our hundred years of passive media. Activating our own creative imaginations and unleashing participants and empowering them with this technology is the only positive route ahead into the future of immersive media. This technology can start to reflect the better angels of our nature, if we have the willpower and vision to guide it in that direction. And even AI factors into this, because the management of these StoryWorlds can't be done at a human level, it has to be done at a faster level than human processing. So, AI will be part of it, and real time, and our own personas, and our imagination and creativity—all embedded in the creation of Worlds for this immersive spatial computing paradigm that's coming sooner than most realize.

ACKNOWLEDGMENT

All images used in the chapter are courtesy of the author.

REFERENCES

Asimov, I. (1950). Runaround. In I, Robot (The Isaac Asimov Collection ed.). New York: Doubleday.

Constantine, J. (2014). Facebook's $2Billion Acquisition of Oculus Closes, Now Official. *Techcrunch.com*. Retrieved from https://techcrunch.com/2014/07/21/facebooks-acquisition-of-oculus-closes-now-official/

Dotson, K. (2019). Amazon Prime releases streaming VR shows and movies for Oculus headsets. In *SiliconAngle: The Voice of Enterprise and Emerging Tech*. Retrieved from https://siliconangle.com/2019/07/25/amazon-prime-releases-streaming-vr-shows-movies-oculus-headsets/

Hoium, T. (2018). Why Facebook's Oculus Acquisition Hasn't Paid Off... Yet Facebook has a lot of work to do growing its virtual reality business. *The Motely Fool*. Retrieved from https://www.fool.com/investing/2018/08/31/why-facebooks-oculus-acquisition-hasnt-paid-off-ye.aspx

Jenkins, A. (2019). The Fall and Rise of VR: The Struggle to Make Virtual Reality Get Real. *Fortune*. Retrieved from https://fortune.com/longform/virtual-reality-struggle-hope-vr/

Rubin, P. (2017). VR's First Major Casuality Was One of Its Smartest Startups. *Wired Magazine*. Retrieved from https://www.wired.com/story/altspace-vr-closes/

ADDITIONAL READING

Ochanji, S. (2019) MacGyver-Themed VR Escape Room Coming Soon, Complete With 3D Holograms. *VR Times*. Retrieved from https://virtualrealitytimes.com/2019/07/28/macgyver-themed-vr-escape-room-coming-soon-complete-with-3d-holograms/

KEY TERMS AND DEFINITIONS

Escape Room: An adventure-type game typically played with others in a physical location and including missions and puzzles to be solved.

Flatie: A colloquial term for part of an immersive video presented in a 2D, or flat, format.

Frag Film: A feature-length film that can be viewed in smaller segments that fit together into a full feature.

Mesh: Another term for a computer graphic or digital surface model.

Procedural: This term refers to using mathematical formulas or rule generation techniques to form digital models, as opposed to tediously building the points that make up a model's form by hand.

Real Time: Refers relating to a system in which data is processed within the shortest amount of time, such as milliseconds, so that it is perceived as immediately responsive.

Surface Model: A computer graphic or digital representation that is defined by a collection of points (usually a very large number) that together form the surfaces of an object or person.

Voxel: The basic unit—a "volume element"— in a solid geometry-based computer model of an object. Voxels can be combined in endless ways to form a specific representation. Because each voxel, such as an elementary cube, can be stored in the computer as a small mathematical formula rather than a huge database of points as for a surface model, it requires far less computational power in actual use.

ENDNOTES

[1] https://www.techradar.com/in/news/world-of-tech/these-are-the-5-laws-of-virtual-reality-according-to-the-director-of-the-lawnmower-man-1317795

[2] The Stella Adler Theater School is known for training actors is a specific methodology that is suited for expressive theatrical acting. It includes connecting to an actors own emotional experiences. In 1988, she published *The Technique of Acting* with a foreword by Marlon Brando.

[3] The set-up of the dome stage can be seen at https://www.youtube.com/watch?v=46EzCJKeroY

[4] See, for example, this article by Samantha Matthews, an important voice in the area. https://medium.com/global-citizen-foundation/5-easy-steps-to-secure-your-data-in-2019-f975164f8d45

[5] A voxel is the short name for a volume element. Just as in 2D imagery the simplest unit of imagery is a pixel, a voxel, which can be thought of as a tiny cube, is the elemental unit of a 3D form.

Chapter 12
Cinematic Virtual Reality:
Inside the Story

Brian Seth Hurst

StoryTech Immersive, USA

ABSTRACT

This chapter presents a case study of the groundbreaking PBS digital studies cinematic VR film My Brother's Keeper. It covers all aspects of cinematic VR from conception and writing for the medium to ensuring the technology serves the story, filming, and postproduction. The piece set a bar for innovation in cinematic VR as the first production to combine 360- and 180-degree stereoscopic image capture to forward story and character interaction, the first to use true slow-motion 120 frames-per-second in VR and the first to establish intimacy with camera movement and close-ups, among other innovations. Six key videos are discussed, illustrating and demonstrating the principles of filmmaking innovation articulated in the chapter, as well as insights from behind the scenes interviews with the directors, producers, cast, and technologists talk about the making of the piece.

INTRODUCTION

For centuries, regardless of the medium, it has been the deepest desire of storytellers to immerse their audience into the storyworlds that they create; to have the characters come alive in front of and all around them; to make the story as real as possible. Virtual reality filmmaking holds the promise to realize the storyteller's dream to put the audience *inside the story*. This chapter will cover the current and evolving state of what is referred to as *cinematic VR*, defined as immersive story-driven narrative films in 360 or 180-degree mono and/or stereoscopic formats. From technology to technique it will document both the leveraging of best practices over 100 years of cinematic production history into the new medium of virtual passive and interactive reality, and the establishment of a new language of filmmaking. The chapter, told from a first person perspective, presents the cinematic VR film *My Brother's Keeper* from PBS Digital Studios as a case study to familiarize readers with the evolving storytelling medium of cinematic virtual reality from concept to screen. It focuses on six key innovations developed for this film, along with links to the videos that illustrate them.

DOI: 10.4018/978-1-7998-2433-6.ch012

BACKGROUND

I am a storyteller. And I know now, it has always been that way. The imaginary worlds that children create and inhabit may be child's play for others but for me, it was training. I had one of those mothers who proudly saved everything I wrote growing up. Not long ago, in digging through the "archives" after her death I found a short story written on construction paper called *The Lonely Petunia*. It was the story of a beautiful sole petunia growing up in a rose garden. Setting aside the probable autobiographical aspects of the second grader who wrote it, the story world created was rich, and colorful, the characters well defined, the cannons of gardening duly observed and an ending that was well, tragic and yet poignantly impactful. As the writer, I wanted people to "immerse" themselves in the story I was telling; perhaps more importantly I wanted them to feel what it was like to be that petunia.

Hindsight being what it is I can see how the training progressed over the decades. It seems to me that it is never the "what" of storytelling that changes. All those prime elements of the fine art of story remain essential: great characters, a rich world in which they come to life, a story that absolutely must be told, and of course the opportunity for the audience to imagine themselves as part of that story and storyworld. It is the "how" of storytelling, thanks to technology, that changes. From the printing press, to the motion picture, from television to the internet, from 2D to 3D, advances in technology continue forward giving creators more and more tools to author story-driven experiences for the audience.

Mastering new technologies of storytelling will forever present both the challenge and the excitement of innovation as well as numerous cautionary tales of making sure that technology serves the story rather than the other way around. While experience is said to be the best teacher, sometimes you must set aside what you know and approach the "new" with both wonder and deliberateness at the same time. Recently, while working with a very accomplished and award-winning director of what we now have come to call "traditional" media, I put it this way. "I truly respect all that you know and all that you have done in this industry. Now, here, can you, if only for a moment, forget what you know and what you have done before and the way you have done it? And, can you resist, again just for a moment, comparing the technology or the process to anything that has come before? With an open mind you will 'get' this. And once you do, you'll be able to bring back everything you know—all of your experience. You'll experiment and bring your wealth of knowledge to the platform. You'll see what works and what doesn't. The more open you are to the technology the more open the technology will be for you." I didn't tell him about the potential for motion sickness. That would come later. And there, experience *would* be the best teacher.

I had first seen "Virtual Reality" at the University of British Colombia in 1997. It was heavy, bulky and anything but portable. I actually don't even remember what I saw because I think my imagination of what it could be took off. But it made impression enough that I remember thinking "Someday, I am going to be doing this." Then, in December 2014, the Samsung Gear VR Innovator Edition arrived. I put it on and watched "Introduction to Virtual Reality" produced by Felix & Paul Studios (2016). I cried. I remember thinking: "This is what I have been waiting for my entire life. And I know exactly what I want to do with this." It has always been my deepest desire to immerse the audience in the storyworlds I create; to have the characters and the story world come alive in front of and all around them and to make the story as real as possible. Perhaps that is every storyteller's desire. I know that we want to move people. Whether I had realized that consciously before or not didn't matter because I knew I had the answer then and there. I felt like immersive storytelling was in my DNA.

The reason I was able to dispense that bit of wisdom to the traditional director was because I had learned that myself. I would have to forget everything I knew, not about the "what" of storytelling but about the "how." I'd have to experiment. I'd have to resist making rules that would limit the possibilities while working to establish best practices and I would have to ascend a very steep learning mountain on a road that albeit was less traveled, but was in the over-hype danger zone. And finally, I'd had to bring everything I knew about storytelling in any and every medium back to the table.

The Category is Immersive Entertainment

In 2015, I decided to follow gut instinct and take the leap into Virtual Reality filmmaking. I didn't know how I was going to do it; I just knew I didn't have a choice. I also knew—having lived through interactive television, Internet originals, and "transmedia"—that I would need to be prepared for the "long game." As a new form of storytelling, and the dating and subsequent marriage of storytelling and VR tech, I knew it was going to take years to develop. But it has and will continue to do so with on-going contributions and innovations from artists, directors, writers, postproduction and sound professionals, actors and yes—technology companies.

Back in 2015, I thought that the term "VR" might actually be limiting. So while other companies sprang up with "VR" as part of their names, my background as a brand strategist led me to look at something that would allow for future and even unpredictable discovery. Essentially, it was going to be the rise of a new category of entertainment, not to mention enterprise applications. And so StoryTech® Immersive was born. The motivation behind the name StoryTech® was to emphasize that the story comes first and that technology needs to serve and enable the story rather than detract from it, and the word "immersive" to help define that new and larger category. This category began, in 2015, as primarily focused on 360 degree Virtual Reality but has now expanded and is referred to as XR encompassing Augmented Reality (information/content superimposed or layered over the real world in real time) and Mixed Reality, which even at this moment has several explanations which seem to combine AR and VR. An industry finding its footing is prone to want to name and define things, and make rules as quickly as possible. Regardless, this evolution of tech presents opportunities for storytellers: new and wonderful ways to tell stories. Yet, the category of Immersive Entertainment is so much more. It includes location-based virtual reality entertainment, which is redefining theme park experiences, immersive domes, Augmented Reality, Live 360 broadcasts and more.

To my mind the art and science of immersive storytelling first started in the theater, but the "language" of modern immersion was first spoken by 3D and 4D Dark Ride companies who using projection, movement and haptic technology transported theme park visitors to other worlds such as and *Captain Eo* (Disney, 1986) and *Star War's Star Tours* (Disney, 1987) up to *Harry Potter and the Forbidden Journey* (Universal Creative, 2016) and *Godzilla: King of the Monsters* (Universal Creative, 2019). As a matter of fact, as I entered the world of immersive production, my first stop was to visit themed entertainment company Super 78 Studios to learn how they did what they did. Their wealth of experience would provide a solid foundation.

An Evolving Industry: Context for Immersive Storytelling

Virtual Reality presented opportunities for documentary, animation, games and various forms of interactivity; but by early 2016 I had decided that producing, writing and eventually directing cinematic narrative in virtual reality would be where I would put my attention. As I had back in 1997 when I first got involved in what was called "convergence," I once again became the autodidact learning everything that I could about how stories could be told. In all honesty it was a singular mission bordering on obsession. I was a prepared as I could be, revved up and ready but the reality of virtual reality as an industry was a different story. The business of VR was in the hyper-drive reminiscent of other industries driven by tech, a train was leaving the station and no one wanted to miss it. This train was a bullet train fueled by hype and technology investments.

Early on there were plenty of experiments in VR being filmed and released. There were some diamonds in the rough, but for the most part what consumers saw was long on wow and short on story. Image capture was improvised with GoPro action cameras in self-built rigs. Post production tools and workflow were being invented on the fly. It was, and still is if you're innovating, a hacker's world. The Samsung GearVR progressed to a consumer edition accommodating different models of Galaxy phones that would maneuver into place in the headsets. No matter what conference or film festival you attended it was the headset and the platform of choice for creators. Phones overheated and batteries drained and resolution was not great, but the industry was off and running and investments poured into technology companies making cameras (Jaunt, Ozo, Lytro) and headsets.

In 2014 Facebook bought Oculus for what actually turned out to be $3 billion based on Mark Zuckerberg's belief that VR would be the next computing platform. This may turn out to be correct but it is more likely to be Mixed Reality combining aspects of VR and AR into spatial computing that will succeed. Enamored by the technology, convinced of a bright future and gaining a quick foothold in an industry that held the promise of billions of dollars, storytellers and would-be storytellers jumped in and seemed to forget the general tenets of good storytelling. Money flowed into tech but to a much lesser extent into content. So basically you had a platform in search of much needed content. While some of the technology companies funded content (Samsung and HTC) others started award-winning studios (Oculus Story Studio 2015-2017, Google Spotlight Stories 2013-1019). And standing out above that seemed to be thousands of independent production companies. North America had Felix & Paul and Within (formerly VRSE). Canada, France and other countries actually had and still have government programs and tax incentives to fund immersive content. As 2018 came around most inside the industry felt a "trough of disillusionment" had been entered. Independent production companies folded, and camera companies disappeared or pivoted (Ozo, Jaunt). As sobering as it was, it had to happen and technology marched on with new head-mounted displays that were more comfortable, more versatile with better processing power and higher resolution.

Some things however were painfully clear: there was a lack of truly great content with high production values and great story for commercial distribution, solid business models were still in development and there was a bottleneck and a lot of friction when it came to consumers understanding and getting into VR. The industry had cooled and it was now time for some sanity. The "wow" can only go so far. It was time to evolve and the true artistry of VR filmmaking as rare as it had been now had to become the standard. The time for truly great immersive storytelling had arrived.

My Brother's Keeper: A Case Study

I have been fortunate enough to have had the opportunity to produce a cinematic virtual reality film with American public broadcaster PBS and PBS Digital Studios. This work would not only focus on story but also would help define an industry. This project was promoted to the world as follows.

My Brother's Keeper is a Civil War inspired narrative that pushes the boundaries of immersive storytelling while remaining anchored in historical fact. It is the story of two estranged brothers who, fighting on opposing sides, unknowingly reunite one last time on the battlefield at Antietam. As we walk into battle with Ethan, 19 and Jackson, 16, we also take a journey through their brief lives to understand what has led them to this one life-altering moment that is surrounded by carnage and the brutality of war (Figure 1).

The project, produced for PBS Digital Studios by StoryTech® Immersive and Perception Squared in collaboration with the Technicolor Experience Center, uses the latest technologies and techniques for creating narrative Virtual Reality (Cinematic VR). The purpose of the project is to give audiences a better understanding of the Civil War in a story-driven experience that places them not only at but *in* the Battle of Antietam. The short VR film is available in head-mounted displays such as the HTC Vive but also as 360 video on the web and mobile. *My Brother's Keeper* is a companion piece to the PBS primetime Civil War drama *Mercy Street*.

Thanks to the imagination and skill of its directors, the incredible support from PBS and an amazing crew, *My Brother's Keeper* is considered to have set a new bar for cinematic VR. Released in 2017 it still stands up today for its moving story and its groundbreaking use of technology. It continues to make its way around the world carried on multiple VR distribution platforms and has even been on exhibition at the Shanghai Modern Art Museum and the United Nations Office in Geneva. Shot on location in Virginia with over 150 Civil War reenactors, the production broke new ground in a number of ways that have contributed to the artistic and technical knowledge base of the industry. I'm grateful to have the opportunity through this chapter to share some of these innovations. Six of these techniques, which will be catalogued in this case study, have now become part of the immersive filmmaker's toolbox. It is my hope that not only will they show what is possible in virtual reality but also that creators will be inspired to hack, invent, reach new heights and set new bars for cinematic VR.

In April of 2016, Don R. Wilcox, Vice President of Multiplatform Marketing and Content at PBS contacted me about PBS Digital Studio's desire to do something in VR that would be related to *Mercy Street*, the network's Civil War prime time drama. Previously Don had asked me to speak at the organization's annual TechCon conference on the subject of VR. From that session Don had a glimpse of what was possible and was now asking for ideas.

Years ago, as a young writer I had a wonderful agent who secured new clients by trolling university film schools and film festivals. That stuck in my head and so, I did the same trolling at VR festivals that were popping up. It was at Kaleidoscope's 2016 Los Angeles Festival that I saw not just the future but also my future. I was rushed that night as I had a plane to catch and zipped through to see as much as I could. The local filmmakers section was my last stop. I found myself inside a headset watching a film called *Real* from director Connor Hair. I only saw two minutes of the almost 13-minute piece before I had to leave but right away I knew in my gut that I was going to work with this director. As it turns out, Connor was one half of a brilliant directing duo, the other being Alex Meader. Connor and Alex were "traditional" film directors but also gamers and hackers who I knew truly "got" storytelling in VR. After a quick call about the opportunity Connor and Alex were in.

Figure 1. My Brother's Keeper one-sheet poster

Don, along with Natalie Benson, then Director of Social Media Strategy & Digital Communications at PBS asked that we present them with three story ideas for a virtual reality film that would be a companion piece for the series and *My Brother's Keeper* was born. One of the themes in *Mercy Street* focused on a pair of brothers fighting on opposite sides during the Civil War. Connor, Alex and I fleshed out the story and then they wrote a first draft of the script. One of the first questions I always ask myself as a producer is "Why does this story have to be told in VR?" Connor and Alex understood the medium and the opportunity. We had the "what" of the story and I was certain that the "how "of the story was in their very capable and innovative hands. They wanted to place the viewer on the battlefield. They wanted to allow the audience to experience the relationship between the brothers on a much deeper level. They did not want to glorify war but rather show the deep effects of it on family. The intention: the end of *My Brother's Keeper* not only would you have experienced the Battle of Antietam, you would be moved to mourn the loss of the brother's relationship and (spoiler alert) their lives. *My Brother's Keeper* premiered with HTC at "VR on the Mountain" at Sundance 2017 and as I watched people come out of the headset with tears in their eyes, I knew that we had indeed moved the audience as we so had wanted to do.

DEVELOPMENT

Getting the Greenlight

Once the choice of story had been made, and as part of development, we wanted to be able to give the executives at PBS an idea of how the story would play out and the experience the viewer would have. We began with an "experiential script" which I refer to as a combination of prose, theater and film. Rather than the stage directions you find in a traditional script, first person descriptions of what the viewer would be seeing and experiencing inside the head-mounted displays were included along with the dialog. I believe that unlike in traditional film and much like in theater, the power rests with the writer and the success of any cinematic VR piece is a function of close collaboration between the writer and the director. In our case, the writers and directors were one in the same.

Once the first draft of the script was completed, Connor and Alex chose to create both a visual and emotional reference in a 2D cinematic "mood piece." Dialog in *My Brother's Keeper* consisted of the inner dialog via voice over that each brother was having as they reminisced about their lives and marched into battle. And so, key sections of the script were married to selected scenes using voice-over and pieces from existing films. It was in essence a cinematic approximation of tone, feel and pacing. Key considerations for me as producer were to ensure that the production values and innovation of *My Brother's Keeper* met the standards of the network, that the piece was historically accurate down to the buttons on a confederate uniform, and that the look, tone and feel matched the story world that the producers of *Mercy Street* had created. It had to present a believable story world in which our viewers would be transported to another time, another place and be situated between two brothers marching to their fate. The combination of the experiential script and the mood piece let the PBS executives know that those considerations were handled. We received the greenlight.

Building the Team

I am fond of saying a great producer gives the directors and creative team everything they need and then gets out of the way. Connor and Alex had a plan for doing things that had never been done before (and some that still have not be done again) in virtual reality. As with any production, every decision made has a cost attached to it and the desire of so many experienced professionals to help kept the numbers in line. We were incredibly fortunate that from the very beginning there were people that truly believed in what we were doing and honestly made my job a joy as things fell into place. Many partners, including Radiant Images, Jaunt, and the Technicolor Experience Center, not only gave their expertise to the project but provided services in-kind or at great rates. Connor and Alex, given their knowledge, demeanor and certainty of what they wanted, their solutionist hacker skills and mentality, and their previous experience and success in traditional film garnered instant respect and willing collaboration no matter where we went.

Innovations included the first true slo-motion sequences shot in stereoscopic virtual reality, the combining of 360 degrees and 180-degree imagery in a single film and its use to drive the story forward, camera movement, and close-ups. These are described in more detail below.

As previously introduced, this chapter focuses on six innovations, which I personally believe moved the technical and creative needle for the industry. To enhance and illustrate these innovations rather than showing you the film in what is called "equirectangular" fashion where the sphere is flattened out and the picture distorted, I am providing links to segments that were recorded inside the headset. While not in 360 stereoscopic, these segments will give you an idea of the experience of the viewer. Given the innovation, especially if it worked the way we thought it would, I also wanted to make sure that we had a record of how we made *My Brother's Keeper* to document the innovations. You can find *My Brother's Keeper: Behind the Scenes* here.[1] I am honored on behalf of the directors, PBS Digital Studios, Don R. Wilcox and Natalie Benson and our entire team to say that *My Brother's Keeper* is a part of coursework in an increasing number of colleges and universities teaching immersive filmmaking. Here then are the six examples.

The Cornfield

"Clear the Sphere!" shouted our First Assistant Director Tony Sanchez. After telling 150 reenactors to "never break character" because of the nature of 360 filming, the man who had never done a VR production before had just coined a new phrase that signaled just how innovative this production would be.

Camera selection is crucial to any VR production. Different cameras have different capture capabilities in terms of sensors, frame rates, stitching, and syncing. In the "early" days of VR (c. 2013-14!), pioneers were using GoPro action cameras to build 360 monoscopic and stereoscopic rigs with anywhere from six to 24 cameras. Everything, and I mean everything was done manually, from clapping your hands to have a sync mark from all the cameras to creating a system to catalog SD cards and the shots on them. Sound capture both in camera and externally mic'd had its challenges. And—stitching was anything but automatic. You crossed your fingers and hoped that any single camera would not go down or overheat. Those early days laid the foundation for the automation that we now have from on-board stitching to plugins and postproduction tools. Today camera companies are using the collective knowledge gained over the last five years as well as talking to storytellers in the field to develop better and better solutions. New technologies such as volumetric scanning by which multiple cameras shooting from the outside in produce 3D filmed imagery and light-field technology which captures imagery more closely approximat-

Figure 2. The "Johnny 4" camera rig used in My Brother's Keeper

ing the way the human eye sees hold great promise for storytellers. Having mentioned this, it should be noted that those on the cutting edge of VR filmmaking are still hacking rigs.

Knowing what you want to do and then matching the camera to it may require extensive testing. Thanks to Michael Mansouri's belief in the project and his crew at Radiant Images we had the opportunity and time to test cameras so that the directors could get what was in their heads in and on to the spherical screen. You can be well versed in camera technology but sometimes; the available VR cameras and rigs just don't do what you need them to do. And so, you hack, you take what's available and build a rig. The camera used in the opening scene was fictionally named the "Johnny 4" (Figure 2) a hat tip to the robot Johnny 5 from the 1986 movie *Short Circuit*. The camera, which did seem to have its own robotic personality, was purpose built by Connor and Alex, using four Go Pro action cameras, Entaniya 220 degree lenses and Back-Bone modifications. It allowed the directors to get within less than five feet of the subject without distortion or stich errors, which prior to this had been limiting factors. In a headset, in stereoscopic 3D it enables a more intimate relationship between the viewer and the main characters as well as placing them on the battlefield at Antietam with the regiment. In the beginning of the film just prior to this segment viewers are given some time as the story begins to acclimate to VR, to the environment and the story. First on a field, next at creek then another field they are in solitude. The scene is peaceful with the sounds of nature surrounding them. The serenity belies what is about to happen. This is war after all.

In this segment, the opening scene, Ethan, the older brother and Union soldier emerges from the tall stalks of the cornfield. To his and our right and left are his fellow soldiers. Ethan pauses as the other soldiers move warily forward. We hear his thoughts and the opening line of the film, "There's a kind of feeling that comes over you when you know this could be the last day of your life." The video can be seen here.[2]

The Creek

We wanted to give the viewer the experience of being in battle, and Connor and Alex had dreamed of slow motion battle sequences. This was one of those instances where imagination drives innovation. At the time of preproduction, no camera was ready to shoot at the 120 frames per second necessary for true slow motion. We did know however that the capability was on Jaunt's product roadmap, but we were told it wouldn't be ready in time for our shoot. All that changed with a phone call to Art Van Hoff, Jaunt's CTO. We had known each other from a few conferences. When we spoke on a Monday I told him both PBS's and the directors' vision for *My Brother's Keeper*. By Friday he affirmed that they would be able to unlock the 120 fps capability for us and would send camera tech, Cael Liakos-Gilbert, to the set to assist. Radiant, Cael and the directors worked to make sure the Jaunt was ready to go. This now meant that come postproduction time we would be integrating not only 60 and 120 fps footage but also footage from two different cameras, sometimes in the same scene, a production and post-production challenge!

If you have ever had the experience of working with true and professional reenactors then you know they will hold your feet to the fire in the name of accuracy and authenticity. I consider them a gift in this respect. There is only one place in the entire piece were authenticity had to be sacrificed in the name of budget, and in the nicest possible way, I defy you to find it. In this battle scene that takes place in the riverbed of what is standing in for Antietam Creek, reenactors as the Federal soldiers and the Rebels are in carefully calculated, precise and choreographed close quarters combat. Rehearsals were at quarter and then half speed as far as action but when it came time to shoot it was full on at full speed and yes, guns a blazing. Such authenticity paid off. In this clip the directors' vision of the emotional power and impact of slow motion is realized. It also represents the transfer of language and ideas from traditional film into virtual reality, and can be seen here.[3]

The Whipping

As we began postproduction at the end of 2016 a friend drew my attention to an article written by an academic on the ten rules of VR (since removed from the Internet). As I read each one of them I became just a bit incensed. Here was someone in authority in what I considered to still be the early stages of the industry listing rules that to my mind would stifle creative innovation. Taking a breath, I reread each one carefully only to realize that Connor and Alex had basically blasted through most of them. Two of those rules were "no voice-over" and "no camera movement." I feel that any rule that limits your ability to tell a story in the way you imagine it could be told is a rule that is begging to be broken. If I have one rule, it is to keep breaking rules. We had cast great actors in Alexander Neher and Jacob Kyle Young and their skill at speaking from the depth of their character's souls created an emotional undertone that was undeniable. The love the brothers feel for one another is palpable and only magnified by the presence that VR engenders. So…one rule broken. As far as camera movement, it was and is a delicate subject in VR. A viewer can so easily be made sick by not only quick cuts but also camera movements that are too fast or unsteady.

The "Johnny 4," light in its weight, was a versatile rig. It could be placed in a riverbed for the close up of a struggling soldier crawling through rock filled shallow water or mounted on a camBLOCK for steady and precise camera movement. Here, as the camera slowly moves through the young brothers' bedroom, we see them kneeling on a bench looking out the window as their father whips a slave. The slow movement of the camera from the back of the room to the window in the scene gives the viewer enough time to survey the boy's childhood bedroom which through the art direction of Mark Davis gives you important insight into their lives through the objects in the room. But the viewer is drawn by the sound in front of them: the cracking of a whip and its subsequent thwack on the slave's back. As the camera moves towards the window where the boys sit, we see over their shoulders. They flinch with each crack and as the camera moves closer the scene out the window and the father's brutal treatment of the slave comes into clear view. We then see Ethan the older brother ushering his little brother Jackson from the room in order to spare him the pain of watching. Prior to *My Brother's Keeper* camera movement had not been done in this manner.[4]

The Battlefield

Bokeh is a film convention whereby a deliberate use of shallow focus technique blurs aspects of an image while applying sharp focus to a specific area. One of the challenges in VR is in the direction of viewer's attention. In this scene the directors have brought the convention into Virtual Reality filmmaking. *My Brother's Keeper* opens in 360 degree stereoscopic. Yet as the brothers move closer and closer towards battle and each other a shift is made from 360 to 180 degree stereoscopic. Some viewers have said that they were so focused on the story and the brothers that they didn't even notice the shift. At the time, VR purists insisted that VR was only a 360 medium and therefore the whole sphere must be used. Yet what Connor and Alex chose to do in combining the two was to take the audience deeper into the brother's relationship and quite simply to unavoidably feel what they feel.

In this scene Ethan and Jackson are in the throws of battle and in a stunning moment of recognition after years of separation, they see each other. In this moment they are removed from the battle and their love for each other takes over. The viewer placed between them bears witness. A rifle shot snaps both the brothers and the viewer back to reality.

During the Civil War the smoke coming from canon, musket and rifle fire would be thick as it rose up from the battlefield obscuring the soldiers' view. This fog of war provided the perfect opportunity for the directors to focus the attention of the viewer not just on the faces of the brothers as they recognize each other across the field but on the look in their eyes. Using the technique of Bokeh, each brother is framed at the center of a 180 shot. To the right and to the left is the blur of the smoky clouds of battle. It is at this point in the story that sound becomes even more crucial. Designed by Scott Gershin of Technicolor Sound, the sounds of the battle surround and consume the viewer, which only adds to the tension. Camera movement is literally front and center in this scene moving closer to each brother; filling the frame as they and by our presence, we close in with them on the inevitable. Connor and Alex, knowing where the viewer would be looking in this 180 frame were able to cut back and forth between the brothers in editing. These kinds of cuts had also not been done prior to *My Brother's Keeper*.

A couple of notes here. Connor and Alex were consumed by prep work. The experiments they worked on prior to the shooting paid off and allowed for smooth on-location production. While there were some experiments on set these were carefully calculated and all of them, some with adjustments, worked. You learn a lot during experimentation. When you watch this segment and the younger brother Jackson raises his rifle pointing just over your shoulder it is a particularly effective moment. There is a reason that rifle is pointed over your shoulder and not directly at you. In the experimentation Connor and Alex discovered that pointing the gun directly at the viewer caused motion sickness. Connor had to lie down for 45 minutes to recover. Back on his feet again they learned it would not happen if the rifle were pointed over the viewer's shoulder. It's the little things, right? Another note here, Connor and Alex worked diligently to direct the viewer's attention inside the sphere. Two months after *My Brother's Keeper* was released, a new heat mapping analytical tool became available. Samsung VR supported the technology being developed and asked if PBS and we wanted it applied to *My Brother's Keeper*. The results were a huge affirmation. More than 98% of the viewers were looking exactly where the directors wanted them to throughout the entire film. And one final note relative to this scene, within six months after our release, YouTube enabled the uploading and viewing of 180 degree VR.[5]

Death

This scene presents perhaps the most emotional moment of the film. After having both been shot, the brothers fall to the ground. The war that will soon end for them continues to rage on. As the life drains slowly out of each of them Ethan, the older brother speaks of the sorrow of war and the regret he feels having realized he abandoned his brother when he was needed the most. Again shot in 180 using Bokeh the camera cuts back and forth between each brother. Yet, here Connor and Alex took another risk. They placed the "Johnny 4" in 180-degree configuration rig on its side at ground level. You are now on the same visual plane as each brother. You have the point of view that they have of each other and you are looking directly into their eyes.[6]

You have perhaps noticed—or it would actually be better if you didn't—the fine acting in *My Brother's Keeper*. You'll recall earlier how I spoke of virtual reality filmmaking being in my DNA. Well as you probably suspect by now it is also Connor and Alex's DNA even more so. It was up to them with PBS approvals to cast actors that not only could gain a rapid understanding of acting in this new medium but for whom it was also second nature. I was happy to have the directors do the casting because first, they knew what they wanted, second they could communicate and rapidly train the actors for VR and finally, I wasn't certain that a traditional film or television casting director would understand the medium. I have watched bad acting detract from more than a few cinematic VR films.

Ghosts on the Battlefield

In this final scene of the film, we return to the two young brothers side-by-side looking through the smoke onto the battlefield strewn with the dead. Jackson's voice is heard. He speculates, "Maybe someday, we can make sense of it all."[7]

IT TOOK MORE THAN A VILLAGE

The segments I selected for this case study have hopefully inspired ideas and possibilities in pushing the boundaries of virtual reality storytelling as a cinematic art. I am sincerely encouraged these days by the work that is coming out in VR live action, animation and documentary. And it is work that is available on commercial platforms for growing audiences to see. They are also increasingly available at location based entertainment venues and VR arcades. I hope these innovations are solid foundational blocks upon which to build. For those that want to produce write or direct Cinematic VR I tell them to spend as much time in a headset as possible and to take the opportunity to look for both the great and the not so great. To look and see how you might do things differently. Most Friday mornings you can find me inside a headset doing that very thing.

Like traditional film and television there are elements that support great storytelling and that are integral to the production level of the film and its ability to resonate with viewers. Over 100 years of filmmaking has resulted in best practices and workflows that are standard and continue to improve. VR is not there yet, and therefore is, for now, a bit more labor intensive, but it sure is rewarding. While technology is advancing quickly and enabling a measure of automation, the skill sets and expertise are not widely available. Perhaps it is because the business models aren't solid yet or that standards have not settled in, or that production and postproduction technology is constantly changing for the better. But we are getting there.

As the credits roll by on the screen on any production, I am usually reminded that each person named has something special to do—one piece, one element that adds to the whole. When the job is done well… well, no one notices. I am happy to say that was the case with *My Brother's Keeper.*

As we now know, different VR cameras—even if you build your own rig—will have both capabilities and issues. It is vital that none of these issues take the viewer out of the story. It is important to identify as many of these issues before you even shoot. To that end, there are a many forums online where directors and postproduction professionals are sharing their experiences and their fixes. But to add to the old adage "experience is the best teacher," whenever you have to chance to play, play. The camera is like a musical instrument: the more you know your instrument the more you can do with it. Fortunately there are ever increasing numbers of directors and directors of photography that truly play a camera to visual symphonic results. But capturing image is only half the battle.

Connor and Alex's innovation would carry right on through to postproduction. In this respect we were fortunate to have been the first project at the Technicolor Experience Center (TEC), a facility wholly dedicated to immersive filmmaking, under the leadership of Marcie Jastrow. Marcie's mission and dedication to deliver the highest quality images whatever it took ensured the development of innovative processes in post that indeed raised the bar. This made certain that everything on screen would support the story and nothing would distract or detract. This required a close collaboration between the directors and the TEC's postproduction professionals. In addition to the Edit Decision List, Connor and Alex, who are also accomplished editors, made a VR editing video tutorial for the rig that they had built to assist the staff at the TEC. They and editor Brian Zwiener, also coming from traditional film, worked to deliver perfection, or as close to perfection as you could get given the limitations of time and technology.

Marcie Jastrow also brought Scott Gershin and the team at Technicolor Sound to the project. Scott's experience in both film and video games was perfect for what we needed, not to mention a deep rich sound library. As I stated earlier, spatial sound design in virtual reality storytelling is crucial. Scott combined the ambient sound captured on location with assets from the library, the recorded narration and the hauntingly beautiful score by Davey Thomas Tucker. Also his first VR project. When we walked into the studio and sat down to hear the first cut joined to picture Scott said, "You know, I had to develop a whole new workflow for you guys." Not surprising.

Sitting in the studio surrounded at the center of an array of speakers and eyes closed, I heard the final version. Surrounded by the sounds of battle, moved by the beautiful score and feeling the emotion of the brothers as they spoke, I cried. The story in sound alone was stunning. In headset picture and sound combined into the film and experience that we had all imagined.

CONCLUSION

I am happy to have had the opportunity to share some of the innovations in VR filmmaking that were a part of PBS Digital Studio's *My Brother's Keeper* with you in this chapter. The film is available on the leading VR platforms and watching it in stereoscopic 3D you'll be able to see how these firsts discussed here impact your experience of the story. There were several members of our team who came from traditional film, who were ready and willing to learn VR. The one thing everyone understood was that first and foremost it was about the story and everything that was done was done in support of that story.

There are immersive filmmakers who continue to inspire me. Like the pioneers of other storytelling technologies before them, they rise to face the challenge of the unknown. They take risks, they make mistakes, and they define, refine and redefine. The most successful in my opinion are those who are about the story rather than about the hype or even the glory. I have seen work where I come out of the headset dumbfounded. And, I have done location based-entertainment story-driven experiences where when finished I wanted to turn right around and do it again. In those instances whether it was with familiar intellectual property and franchises or original work, the storytellers welcomed me into the worlds they had created with precision, skill, attention to detail, and amazing storytelling and I was so thrilled to be there that the technology much to their credit became invisible.

You can probably tell that I am bullish on VR. I am because I trust the storytellers and as I watch the means by which the stories are produced, told and experienced get better and better, I have complete faith that as far as a business there is money to be made. And, where there is money to be made the friction points for consumers and the business models get worked out. What I do know is that no platform can survive without great content and a great experience. At the risk of being cliché (a relatively new cliché at that) we have the ability, in the hands of great producers, writers, directors, actors, sound designers and postproduction professionals, to transport audiences into our imaginations: into what we have seen in our heads, and we have the ability to move them viscerally as never before. How we do that has to be done not only with great story but also with the utmost care, concern and integrity for this medium to thrive.

Once upon a time as an 8-year-old I had a dream of being a lonely petunia in a rose garden, and I mean a real dream, the kind you have when you are asleep. I took that dream and wrote a story. But the limitation was that people could never experience that story as I had in my dream—a 360-degree world of color, sound and feeling. Now, they can.

ACKNOWLEDGMENT

There is nothing as satisfying as when you are given the time, the belief and the space in which to innovate. This is my wish for anyone in immersive production. I'll be forever grateful to Don R. Wilcox at PBS for giving us just that. His trust and faith in the team set the foundation for what was possible. We also had the freedom to choose our partners in innovation from Radiant Images, to Jaunt to the Technicolor Experience Center. I'm convinced that when the good of the project is placed above all else—a challenge to be sure, then magic happens. The blessings extended to the experience of filming in the state of Virginia, to the excellent crew. Of the crew, which numbered more than 50, only four had done VR before. Kudos goes to Connor and Alex who were able to onboard them all so quickly. Historical Producer, Guy Gane and the reenactors, also who had not done VR before, brought authenticity to every aspect of production. All of the actors who with coaching from the directors were able to quickly adapt to the 360-degree nature of VR. And finally, to Andrew Hancock who was able to document beautifully in behind the scenes content what we did for the sake of posterity.

REFERENCES

Universal Creative. (2016). *Harry Potter and the Forbidden Journey motion simulator ride*. Author.

Universal Creative. (2019). *Godzilla: King of the Monsters 3D theme park film*. Author.

Félix and Paul Studios. (2016). Introduction to Virtual Reality. 360 degree video for the Oculus Rift platform. Montreal, Canada: Author.

Walt Disney Imagineering with Industrial Light and Magic. (1986). *Captain Eo, 3D theme park film*. Author.

Walt Disney Imagineering with Industrial Light and Magic. (1987). *Star War's Star Tours motion simulator ride*. Author.

KEY TERMS AND DEFINITIONS

CamBLOCK: CamBLOCK is a brand that has a product line of "portable motion control systems for cinematographers" (www.camblock.com).

Dark Ride: An attraction at a theme park that audiences experience in an immersive, dark space, such as a roller coaster racing through a space-themed environment.

ENDNOTES

[1]   https://www.youtube.com/watch?v=7Z_fVCA_D0E

[2]   https://youtu.be/fcO_xTYbITk

[3]   https://youtu.be/EtkcAAucuXw

[4]   https://youtu.be/w2zNRdhY4M4

[5]   https://youtu.be/vToRvWiSVs4

[6]   https://youtu.be/BAVVSME7xNA

[7]   https://youtu.be/-U4SQlAAY0E

Chapter 13
Immersive Storytelling:
Leveraging the Benefits and Avoiding the Pitfalls of Immersive Media in Domes

Michael Daut

Independent Researcher, USA

ABSTRACT

This chapter compares and contrasts the development of traditional cinema and fulldome cinema, describing the way their origins shaped not only their current success and potential as unique cinematic mediums, but also how their cinematic languages developed. There is a vastly different approach to storytelling that filmmakers must understand when creating shows for immersive digital dome theaters versus the approach they would take to tell stories in a traditional film. This chapter identifies key differences between cinema and fulldome and provides a primer for immersive storytelling on the dome from understanding the technology to understanding how most effectively to use the strengths of fulldome while avoiding its weaknesses. Ultimately, this discussion is designed to help creative artists become more effective immersive filmmakers for the fulldome canvas.

INTRODUCTION

Modern society is experiencing an explosion of immersive media in a nearly overwhelming number of forms: Virtual Reality (VR) that requires a headset that feeds 360° imagery in the user's eyes and pours immersive audio into their ears; Augmented Reality (AR) that creates visual and auditory overlays on top of reality using a smart phone or a semi-transparent pair of glasses; Mixed Reality (MR), that uses a combination of VR and AR to create new and unexpected experiences through a headset that can change from fully transparent to fully opaque based on the content creator's design. Then there are hybrid forms of immersive media that blend theatrical stagecraft with a VR system that allows free roaming through physical spaces with walls people can see virtually and touch in reality, props they can use, and other tactile sensations that powerfully blur the lines between virtual and reality. These are just some examples of immersive media that involve some sort of device that the audience must either use

DOI: 10.4018/978-1-7998-2433-6.ch013

Figure 1. Inside a digital fulldome theater with immersive visuals
Source: ©2019 Greg Downing, Hyperacuity.com. Used with permission.

or wear, and more times than not, these "vehicles to immersion" create a sense of isolation, not a shared community experience.

On a more basic level there is 3D stereo technology that exists in cinema, VR, home theater, video games, lenticular stereo printing, giant screen theaters, and even giant 3D dome theaters to add visual depth to the experiences. In a completely different type of experience, interactive media platforms like Twitch add to the viewer's sense of agency and therefore immersion.

These "new media" experiences have brought with them new ways of telling stories and a new type of cinematic and aesthetic language that creatives and consumers alike are still trying to understand and unravel. New media storytellers are experimenting with new ways of immersive expression and developing and inventing a new lexicon of techniques and understanding how to speak this immersive visual language. It is an exciting time as creatives are blazing a trail through this largely undiscovered country. Exploring the art of immersive storytelling opens a deep well that branches in nearly infinite directions that would overwhelm this chapter and spill over into a series of books.

This chapter focuses on a specific type of immersive medium: digital fulldome theaters (Figure 1). From their origins as planetarium spaces to their continuing growth into VR Theaters of the future, this exciting medium has developed its own cinematic language that is part traditional cinema, part live theater, and a lot of something magical that when leveraged effectively can transport audiences as a small community into shared virtual experiences. Technological advancements and system features still impact digital domes as much as the format's differences from traditional cinema. How has cinematic language developed in traditional cinema, and how has it formed in digital immersive domes? How can these languages be the same? How must they be different? Are immersive digital fulldome theaters effective spaces for storytelling, or are these spaces best used for documentary-style programs and purely educational experiences? These questions are only the jumping-off points for this fascinating exploration.

The Development of Cinematic Language

Modern cinema was born with the invention of the motion picture camera, and as often happens, many pieces of this technology were being developed simultaneously and independently by a number of inventors across the world. It is therefore difficult to pinpoint exactly who invented the motion picture camera, although most historians attribute this honor to American innovator, Thomas Edison, who incidentally would have willingly accepted this attribution. The truth of the matter is more complicated, of course, with Edison's Kinetograph, motion picture camera, built upon the work of early pioneers, Francis Ronalds, Wordsworth Donisthorpe, Louis Le Prince, William Friese-Greene, and William Kennedy Laurie Dickson. Even the exact year the world-changing camera came into being is up for debate. For further background on the story behind the creation of the motion picture camera, explore the many resources listed in the Additional Reading section at the end of this chapter.

Regardless of its specific origins or authorship, in 1891 or 1892, the motion picture camera ushered in the age of cinema. Cinema exhibition started with Edison's Kinetoscope (Figure 2): a mechanical device in which one person at a time would look through an eyepiece or "peephole" at the top to view the images printed sequentially on a strip of film. Sprocket holes along the film's edges allowed the film to be pulled through the device across an illuminated image plate below the peephole. A high-speed shutter hid the transition between frames, completing the illusion of movement. Later the Lumière brothers would transform the Kinetoscope into the Cinématographe, the first motion picture projector, allowing an entire audience to view the film at once (Library of Congress, n. d.).

It took over two decades for filmmakers to truly understand and exploit its visual language. D.W. Griffith was one of the early masters of visual cinematic storytelling, using the close-up and careful editing to build the experience shot by shot. Legendary pioneering filmmakers such as Buster Keaton, Charlie Chaplin, Cecil B. De Mille, and others further contributed their legerdemain to advance the art.

In step with (or more accurately, many steps behind) developing creative and aesthetic techniques, the technology itself advanced, sometimes at a snail's pace; other times blindingly fast, creating an interdependency that exists to this day. Filmmakers developed their stories within the confines of the technology while pushing diligently against technology's limits. At the same time, the inventors both responded to the creative needs and leveraged new, even groundbreaking developments to reinvent the process of motion picture image capture and exhibition (and all the steps in between) over and over again with nearly relentless fervor. In the same way, filmmakers would leverage these new innovations to further elevate visual storytelling and define new ways to create movies in the ever-changing technological landscape.

This interdependent growth cycle between art and technology is not unique to cinema. The same patterns can be seen in computer technology, science, engineering, music, even accounting and finance. Technology creates opportunity; users drive technology; technology advances creating new opportunities; users find new applications and drive technology further; technology advances again, and the cycle goes on indefinitely. The cycle itself is not as crucial to this discussion as is the interdependence of art and technology. They cannot be separated, and they enable one another. Just as oil paints as a medium

Figure 2: A person watching a movie with Edison's Kinetoscope
Source: Public domain image from Wikimedia Commons

Figure 3. The interior of Edison's Kinetoscope showing the film path
Source: Public domain image from Wikimedia Commons

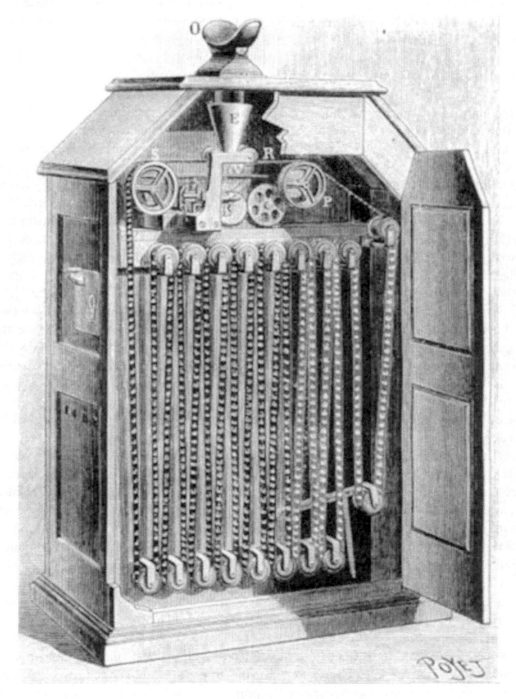

influence and affect the outcome of the art on the canvas, so the technology of cinema affects those who paint with its cinematic language. The creation of the art must leverage the available tools and the strengths and limitations of the medium to harness its full potential. This required deep understanding and experience on the part of the artist.

The Development of Immersive Digital Dome Systems

Just as motion pictures, immersive dome systems began with analog technology. In 1923 the Zeiss Corporation in Jena, Germany developed a revolutionary optical mechanical projection device, a metal sphere studded with lenses and a cylindrical appendage that extended underneath, affectionately called, *The Wonder of Jena*, that could realistically reproduce the starry night sky. This device required a new physical structure and projection surface that approximated the apparent shape of the sky overhead. A large hemispherical dome, 360° around by 180° high became the obvious choice (Lambert, 2012).

The world's first planetarium opened at the Deutsche's Museum in Munich, Germany in 1925 with the first Carl Zeiss optical mechanical star projector. The projector used light inside of a mechanism that could project points of light that replicated the starry sky as seen from Earth, enabling them to move across the sky as night transitioned to day and back again into night. It could even adjust its orientation to show the accurate night sky from any location on Earth. This optical mechanical projector also featured planet projectors that through precise mathematical calculations could mirror the forward and retrograde movement of planets through the night sky. This technology caught worldwide attention, inspiring a generation of astronomers and science educators. The first planetarium in the US, the Adler Planetarium in Chicago, opened its planetarium in 1930, with other, now legendary planetariums, like the American Museum of Natural History in New York, and Griffith Observatory in Los Angeles opening shortly thereafter (Marche, 2005).

It goes without saying that Carl Zeiss and other companies that followed, designed and built domes with the express purpose of showing audiences the wonders of the night sky. These theaters provided astronomy education spaces where people could learn about and identify constellations, planets, and seasonal changes in the sky. The original theater and seating design that supported this purpose consisted of a hemispherical dome screen hung directly above the audience with its base completely parallel to the ground (with no tilt forward or backward in any direction). The audience sat in concentric rows with their backs to the outside walls, each guest facing into the center of the theater where the optical mechanical projector resided. This orientation allowed guests to view the night sky in all directions simultaneously while highlighting the magnificent star projector as the centerpiece to the experience (Figure 4).

The modern planetarium was born (incidentally, only about 40 years after the birth of the motion picture camera). This new medium that was purpose-built for teaching astronomy would embark on its own wild ride and hard-fought path to be a legitimate cinematic and immersive medium in its own right, and the battle has only begun.

Even with the star projector's exquisite ability to recreate the stars and planets of the night sky, the instrument could only depict stellar observation from the surface of earth. The audience could never take off into space and fly through the stars. Because star projectors were large mechanical devices, they could only move the night sky at relatively slow speeds to simulate Earth's rotation and the eventual sunrise.

In the early 1970's, Ivan Dryer created *Laserium*, a visual music experience for planetarium domes. Ivan and his team created a custom laser projector that could be preprogrammed and choreographed to a musical soundtrack and performed live across the dome's interior in front of an audience. *Laserium*

Figure 4. Inside a concentric planetarium with a non-tilted 180° dome and star projector
Source: Public domain image from Wikimedia Commons

stepped into history at the Griffith Observatory in Los Angeles on November 19, 1973. For the first time pure entertainment shows entered planetarium domes, and the impact of *Laserium* continues to inspire producers and inspire new creative uses for the dome's hemispherical canvas (Ehrman, 2002).

Then in the early 1980's something revolutionary (and at the time somewhat primitive by today's standards) happened. Evans & Sutherland (E&S) a company based in Salt Lake City, Utah largely known for their pioneering work in computer graphics, introduced a *digital* star projector called Digistar, and the planetarium changed forever, but certainly not overnight. In fact, the planetarium is still in the process of changing to this day. Digistar introduced two significant groundbreaking capabilities: 1) the ability to lift off of Earth and fly through the stars (and view them from essentially any point in the known universe and at any point in history); 2) the ability to create vector graphics allowing the display of any sort of wireframe computer graphics imaginable. These digital tools expanded the types of experiences that were possible inside planetarium domes.

Because of *Laserium* and Digistar's paradigm shifts, the dome theater started to become more than just a planetarium, but its metamorphosis would be slow: very, very slow.

The 1990's introduced yet another giant leap forward: fulldome video (Figure 5). The concept was straightforward and ingenious. Take a number of video projectors—initially six—install them in a circular arrangement at the bottom edge of the dome screen and project imagery from these projectors across the dome to create one fulldome video display. These projected images would overlap each other, creating regions where the images could be blended together. Precise, painstaking alignment of the blended im-

Figure 5. Inside a digital fulldome theater
Source: Adam Kozak distributed under a CC-BY 2.0 license

ages would create the illusion of a single fulldome video. A cluster of PCs or a real-time computer image generator (essentially a powerful custom computer built for flight simulation) processed a sequence of circular fisheye images into the system, sliced into tiles that would synchronize and feed each individual projector, allowing video to display across the fulldome canvas.

Once fulldome video existed, dome productions could tell more immersive and sophisticated visual stories, but the fact that domes were nearly exclusively found in planetariums, most fulldome content stayed within the astronomy genre. This is a critical reason that it has been (and continues to be) difficult for fulldome films to break free from their astronomical origins and become more mainstream. Theater design shifted from domes that were parallel to the ground with omnidirectional seating to domes that tilted forward in front of the audience with unidirectional seating that faced the front of the dome tilted down anywhere from 10° to 30°. This has produced a daunting inconsistency in theater layout, dome tilts, projector resolution, placement, quality, and seating configurations, which presents significant challenges for producers who hope that their content will look equally good in all venues.

Today's advancements have dramatically improved image quality in the theaters. Auto-alignment and auto-blending technologies have allowed even more projectors to be tiled together across the screen and look visually seamless, as if projected from a single source. The most advanced domes use laser video projection and enough 4K projectors to create a fulldome canvas that is over 8192 x 8192 pixels (over 64,000,000 pixels). At the time of writing, the most compelling new technology to be introduced is a self-illuminating dome constructed of LED tiles, eliminating the need for video projection.

Fulldome's planetarium origins and the fact that almost its entire network of existing theaters exists within planetariums and science centers have largely prevented content to break free from a science education focus to general entertainment. Planetariums' general lack of marketing budget and lack of budget in general often prevents them from being able to afford higher quality shows. The low revenue stream from theaters that license fulldome shows has kept production budgets low, maybe 1% or less of the typical budget spent on a Hollywood film.

Still, the powerful immersive nature of the medium is propelling it forward into new types of content and into new and unexpected venues including themed entertainment, pop up experiences, concerts, theatrical performances, and touring shows.

As mentioned in the introduction VR, AR, MR and most other immersive technologies require some sort of apparatus and some degree of individualized isolation for the experiences to work. Not so in fulldome. This exciting medium has the true potential to deliver on the promise of VR while remaining a communal, shared experience. Fulldome is essentially the platform for the VR Theater of today and the future. Fulldome also has the potential to attract audiences in a way that traditional cinema is struggling to maintain.

Because of its uniqueness and its ability to exceed the power of VR, it's important to understand the distinguishing characteristics of fulldome, its potential, and its cinematic language. The rest of this chapter is designed as a primer, of sorts for the medium and a guide to harnessing its abilities to create a powerful new form of storytelling.

UNIQUENESS OF THE FULLDOME CANVAS

The fulldome medium itself stands at the intersection of theater and cinema, yet it is neither both nor one or the other. It is its own blended experience that can be leveraged to produce a powerful sense of presence within an immersive theater. Also, whereas VR is an individual, isolating immersive experience, akin to Edison's Kinetoscope, fulldome is a shared audience experience more like the Lumière brothers' Cinématographe motion picture projector.

Looking at vs. Being Inside

Unlike traditional cinema, where the audience is looking *at* a screen, digital fulldome places the audience *inside* of the screen. Cinema uses a framed window in front of the audience to slowly invite them into the experience through emotional connection and the willing suspension of disbelief. Fulldome cinema surrounds the audience in such a way that they start inside the experience, even before the audience's engagement can draw them in. This instant or "forced immersion" can be difficult to overcome, especially if the audience feels overwhelmed and pushes back from this intrusion. It's the cinematic version of coming on too strong romantically. It can be uncomfortable and off-putting. More subtle techniques at the start of a fulldome film/immersive experience should be employed to create an emotional connection or conversely, a fascinating spectacle could be created that entices the audience to want to see more. A live presenter to warm up the audience or even participate in the dome show can function as the audience surrogate in the immersive presentation and bridge this gap even further. Once the audience engages in the experience, the feeling of deep immersion and sensation of simulated reality can be extraordinarily impactful.

Sense of Presence

The visuals that surround the audience create a strong sense of presence, simulating the sensation that the audience actually exists in the place depicted around them on the dome. This is a powerful illusion that is analogous to subjective camera in traditional cinema, where the audience is seeing through the camera as if they are participating in the scene. This effect is more powerful in immersive fulldome, since there is no perceived or implied camera. The virtual world simply surrounds the audience and transports them into the scene's setting, much like the legendary Holodeck from *Star Trek: The Next Generation* (1987). Cinematically there are two major types of scenes in fulldome: subjective scenes and objective scenes.

Subjective scenes (designed to make the audience feel as if the experience is happening to them personally) inherently play in real time, since that is the only way humans can move through time and space. Most transitions should not be used in these sequences, since there are no transitions or gaps in time or space when moving from one place to another in reality. When scene changes are necessary within subjective sequences, dips to black, or a time/space travel device, like a visual time warp, launch to light speed, or some similar visual effect, can preserve the audience's sense of being a participant in the scene.

In the early days of digital fulldome, essentially all scenes were subjective scenes. Producers were concerned about breaking the audience's sense of presence in time and space. This greatly limited the types of storytelling that could be done and eliminated the possibility for editing and adjustments to the show's pacing.

Experiments with editing, specifically cutting, revealed that if properly integrated into a sequence, cuts could produce objective scenes in which the audience felt they were in the experience, but not directly inside the scene. Looking at the main action from a physical and emotional distance, rather that always feeling like they were directly inside of the action. Objective scenes allow the audience members to become close bystanders rather than feeling like the actions in the scene are happening directly to them.

Alternating between subjective and objective scenes allows emotional ebbs and flows in the structure of a show, so that producers can employ subjective techniques to "grab" or "fully immerse" the audience and objective techniques to offer the audience a safe distance from the impact of the scenes.

Finding this balance is one of the most important keys to immersive storytelling on the dome. Misunderstanding and misusing these techniques are the quickest way to break the audience's willing suspension of disbelief and pull them out of the experience.

A Different Kind of Frame

Ben Shedd called fulldome a "frameless medium," which it is to a large degree; however, the audience is almost always looking up to some degree, even in a severely tilted (30° forward tilt) dome. The audience can also see below the edge of the dome and see the edges of the dome to either side of them when facing forward in a unidirectional dome (or even in a non-titled dome with omnidirectional seating). In most fulldome theaters, the audience is aware of at least the lower edge of the frame.

Domes also have the inherent challenge of needing lots and lots of image resolution, since the dome surrounds the audience on all sides, and half of the pixels are behind the audience. This causes the individual pixels themselves to be closer to the audience and larger than they would be if they were all out in front of them. Imagine an HDTV folded over the heads of each audience member. The pixels would appear too large and too close. For optimum resolution, more and smaller pixels are necessary. VR has a similar resolution problem, since even a "retina display" that is too close to the viewer appears

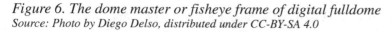

Figure 6. The dome master or fisheye frame of digital fulldome
Source: Photo by Diego Delso, distributed under CC-BY-SA 4.0

to have large pixels and low resolution. This is why many modern fulldome theaters and shows have at least 6K x 6K resolution or even 8K x 8K resolution. The standard master frame for digital fulldome is a circular equidistant azimuthal fisheye with a 1:1 (or square) aspect ratio. The circular fisheye frame is called a dome original or dome master (Figure 6). Dome master hemispherical sequences are typically produced at 4K x 4K (4096 x 4096 resolution) up to 8K x 8K (8192 x 8192 resolution) for each frame. Fully spherical scenes can also be mastered in equirectangular format (the standard frame format for VR production) at 8192 x 4096 for 4K spherical content or 16384 x 8192 for 8K spherical content.

Furthermore, standard 24 fps cinema frame rate looks "steppy" and appears to judder in the dome. Higher frame rate (HFR) capability smooths out the experience, especially for digital astronomy presentations. For pre-rendered shows, the standard fulldome frame rate is 30 fps, and for real time graphics, the standard frame rate is 60 fps. Higher frame rates up to 120 fps and higher are also possible

3D stereo fulldome is also possible, requiring additional technology in the theater to play back 3D and a complete dome original frame sequence of left eye frames and right eye frames at a rate of 60 fps per eye.

This resolution and HFR requirement can be a significant burden for producers especially when combined with fulldome 3D. 8K x 8K frames are four times the resolution of 4K x 4K frames, which are also four times the resolution of 2K x 2K (essentially HD) frames. This means that 8K frames take four times longer to render and are four times larger than 4K x 4K frames. HFR shows that play back at 60 frames per second require twice as many frames as a standard 30 fps show. Adding 3D doubles the number of frames that must be produced, since 3D requires a complete set of frames for the right eye and for the left eye. The math on this is staggering: each 8K x 8K file (uncompressed) would be approximately 192 MB. For 60 fps 3D, this would require 120 8K frames per second. At 192 MB per frame, this translates to 23 GB per second. The average length of a fulldome show is 22 minutes; therefore, a 22-minute 8K 3D 60 fps per eye show would require 79,200 frames per eye at a total data size of 15 TB per eye (uncompressed) or a total of 158,400 frames and 30 TB for such a show. This assumes no image compositing, or one layer per frame, which is not realistic given standard "layered" production workflows. Producing layered elements for each frame would make the production process even more daunting.

With this said, the results of 8K fulldome production can be truly astonishing, surpassing any other conventional form of media in terms of resolution, immersion, and raw impact. GPU based rendering technology has made 8K production more possible, but it is far from practical or cost effective at this time.

STORYTELLING TOOLS

Traditional cinema has a well-established collection of visual storytelling tools. These include the following:

- Editing
- Composition
- Camera Movement
- Actor Blocking
- Color
- Light
- Camera Angles
- Lenses
- Special Effects
- Many, many others

Over 100 years, filmmakers have refined the uses of these techniques within the constraints of the medium.

Two key attributes define the essential capabilities of cinema: the frame itself and editing. In traditional cinema, the frame itself is one of the most powerful tools filmmakers use to direct the audience's attention and guide them through the story. The frame inherently restricts the audience's view and perspective and only presents what the director wants the audience to see at any given time. Combined with skillful editing, the visual story ebbs and flows according to the director's vision, focusing the audience exactly where they want it shot by shot, and scene by scene throughout the film. In traditional film, the frame confines, restricts, and contains the imagery within each shot. The art of editing transitions these pictures rhythmically and structurally, using shots as building blocks of the visual story. Editing combines shots with varying fields of view (wide shots to close ups), and the frame itself helps define the type of shot within it, since the subject in a close up fills more of the frame than the subjects in a wide shot.

Also, in traditional cinema, the audience is looking at the film voyeuristically. Through empathy and emotional resonance, the audience may feel very connected to the experience, but they never feel that they are actually inside the film, since it clearly exists out in front of them. Surround sound and more advanced dimensional sound systems like Dolby Atmos, Fraunhofer, Iosono, Barco Auro, IMAX 12.0, and others envelop the audience with sound to help create a stronger sense of immersion.

With all of its storytelling power, however, traditional cinema cannot place the audience inside a scene.

FULLDOME FILMMAKING CHALLENGES

Fulldome filmmaking is inherently immersive, as previously described. The audience starts out inside the experience and remains immersed throughout the film. This effect can be very powerful, but there are many challenges to storytelling that this sense of presence and the medium itself creates.

Here are just some of the challenges to storytelling in domes:

Size of Actor(s) on Screen

Because the dome evokes such a strong sense of presence inside a place, there is a natural expectation that objects should look the way they would appear in real life, especially when employing subjective camera techniques that anchor the audience in the scene as if they are actually there. Humans depicted on screen need to look scaled properly against their environments on screen, which is also true of traditional cinema, but in subjective scenes, the actors on screen should also feel properly sized relative to the theater screen and the audience. If a human on the dome appears too large aesthetically, they appear giant, and if they appear to be too small aesthetically, they seem to miniaturize. This seems particularly problematic, since dome sizes vary dramatically from venue to venue. In practice, however, if the human character feels right on the dome, any dome, the scale of the actor will work regardless of the dome size, since the angle of light emanating from the object on the dome will be the same whether the dome is very large or relatively small. Larger domes expand out equally in all directions, so everything scales up equally, appearing the same relative size. The converse is true of smaller domes. An interesting phenomenon, but it works consistently because of the applied physics of light and the equal curvature of the dome despite its size.

The team that produced the fulldome show for New York's Madame Tussaud's Wax Museum in 2000, did extensive compositing tests to determine the specific placement and scale of the on-screen actor who played the hansom cab driver who guided the audience through the history of New York City. It was key to the effectiveness of the attraction that the cab driver appeared to be the proper size relative to the immersive space.

Editing

Cuts can work, but not in a traditional sense. Scenes built through inductive editing (lots of close ups) don't usually work. The dome canvas creates too large and too wide of a view to achieve the same "restricted" view that closer shots provide in cinema when they are contained by the frame. There is no

Psycho "shower scene" that exists in the fulldome medium any more than such a scene could exist on a live theater stage, at least not using traditional cinematic editing techniques.

Directors must creatively employ other techniques like camera movement, blocking and choreography in front of the camera, fades to black, and other methods borrowed from the world of theater to keep the audience oriented and anchored inside the virtual space as much as possible.

Fast Cuts Don't Have Same Sizzle

There is a lot to see on the dome canvas that spreads across the audience's field of vision. Fast cutting from one shot to another doesn't give the audience adequate time to see what is in a given shot, since it is replaced quickly by another shot. According to *Wired* Magazine (https://www.wired.com/2014/09/cinema-is-evolving/) modern Hollywood films have an average shot length of 2.5 seconds. This type of cutting is way too fast for fulldome. Also, consider the similarity to a theatrical experience that the dome provides. Audiences can't get up and rapidly shift from one seat to another every 2.5 seconds in the theater. That would be absolutely exhausting and ridiculous. Even with objective scenes on the dome, longer shots work much more effectively on the dome than shots that are less than 3 seconds in duration.

With that said, a good rule of thumb is the less complex the shot, the shorter it can be on the dome (within reason). The more complex the shot, the longer it needs to be for the audience to perceive it properly.

In traditional cinema, fast editing can add to the intensity and create a percussive rhythm to a scene; not so in fulldome. This type of editing is absolutely disorienting to the audience unless used sparingly for effect.

Short Shots are Hard to Read

Think of the dome as a portal to put the audience inside a shot that physically surrounds them. There is a complete and large hemispherical canvas of information for the audience to absorb and comprehend. Shots that are too short don't give the audience time to orient themselves in the space of the film. If the goal is disorientation, then this technique can be extremely effective, but if disorientation is not the intent, it is best to give the audience time to be absorbed into the scene.

Speed of Movement

Motion must be slowed down to feel correct and natural on the dome, compared to cinema and television, since a dome has more real estate to cover. Think of the fulldome canvas like being on the front row in a movie theater with a giant screen. Super-fast movements can be overwhelming. On a computer monitor, for example, if an object moves from one edge of a 27" screen to the other edge in 2 seconds, that movement may feel somewhat slow (a speed of 13.5" per second), but on a 60' wide dome that same 2 second movement would move at a speed of 30' per second: dramatically faster perceptually. This is not to say that fast movement isn't possible on the dome. It is. It's just vital to understand the acceleration effect the medium provides and to compensate for this accordingly.

The Fulldome Canvas

The canvas itself is circular and distorted as if by a fisheye lens. As stated previously, this circular frame is often called the dome original or dome master. The center of the circle represents the top, or zenith, of a dome hemisphere with 0° tilt, or the spot directly above the audience. For tilted domes, this spot moves forward by the exact number of degrees the dome is tilted forward. For example, a dome tilted forward 30° will have the zenith point tilted 30° forward of the actual point that is directly above the audience's heads. The bottom of the circle represents the front of the dome, the top of the circle represents the back of the dome, the left side of the circle is audience left, and the right side is audience right.

One of the challenges of the production workflow when creating dome originals is that they are always visually distorted. Pixels compress near the zenith of the image and they stretch dramatically near the edges of the circular frame. Only when these images are projected inside the dome do they properly undistort by mapping to the three-dimensional geometry of the hemisphere itself.

It is imperative to screen material on the dome to determine and evaluate proper scale, placement, sense of motion, shot duration, etc. since these phenomena are virtually indistinguishable when watching playback of a fisheye preview on a computer monitor.

More experienced fulldome creators can get a good sense of how a scene is playing from a fisheye preview, but even seasoned professionals can miss important details if they don't view their work on a dome.

Live Action Photography

Interestingly, the advent of Virtual Reality has contributed to the development of innovative new camera technology that allows filmmakers to capture real world imagery in 180° and 360°. In fact, there are significant parallels in processes between VR production and fulldome production. VR often requires a completely spherical image, but fulldome only requires half of that, a 180° hemisphere. Spherical VR cameras used for fulldome production offer filmmakers the flexibility to adjust the tilt and orientation of the spherical imagery for optimum placement on a non-tilted and a severely tilted dome without having to reshoot content for display on multiple types of dome configurations. The appropriately formatted hemispherical dome originals can be extracted from spherical equirectangular frames.

There are modern cameras that have up to 4K vertical resolution, and for a majority of domes these offer enough resolution for the live-action imagery to look reasonably good on a 4K x 4K digital dome. The problem is that for the images to look as crisp and as realistic as possible, they really need to be produced at a higher resolution than 4K to allow pixel sub-sampling to optimize each pixel on the dome. Furthermore, 180° fisheye lenses cut off the horizon if they are pointed straight up during a shoot. Fisheye lenses with fields of view over 200° are needed to see below the lens and photograph the horizon below the camera.

A single 8K camera can be mounted on a Nodal Ninja, which is a camera mount that has built in nodal points around a shared center point, allowing a scene to be photographed multiple times from a fixed position. The camera points in a different direction for each take as the camera angle shifts from nodal point to nodal point until capturing all angles of a hemisphere or complete sphere. This technique can produce phenomenally high-resolution master frames: 16K x 8K spherical, but without computer-controlled tripods or dollys, all shots captured this way must be stationary with no camera movement at all. This technique provides ultimate resolution at the cost of camera movement.

Multi-camera rigs tend to integrate short focal length lenses in order for each camera to see the widest possible field of view. This reduces the total number of cameras needed for the rig and creates fewer recordings that will have to be stitched together to create the hemispherical or spherical imagery.

Spherical cameras come in all shapes and sizes, from the GoPro Max with two fisheye cameras mounted back-to-back, to larger rigs containing multiple RED, ARRI, or other professional cameras in a spherical array, and everything in between including the Insta360 Pro camera, which is essentially a point-and-shoot spherical camera with multiple lenses and cameras imbedded around a sphere. Companies such as Radiant Images in Los Angeles specialize in these types of camera systems, offering a varied assortment of choices for purchase or rental.

Stitching software to combine images from each camera into a unified spherical image is often rather primitive and requires considerable physical tweaking and painstaking adjustments to optimize and master an image that looks seamless. Additionally, the physical layout of the cameras in the spherical rigs creates dead zones in the spaces between cameras in the rig especially if a subject comes too close to the camera rig. Choreography in front of a spherical camera must be carefully orchestrated to keep actors and key objects far enough from the rig to prevent them from splitting apart visually across the seams between the cameras in the array.

Lens selection is also extremely limited for fulldome live action photography. Traditional cinematographers rely on a variety of lenses to produce visual aesthetic effects to structure the depth of field (how much of the background is in focus) and field of view (how much the audience can see inside the frame). In fulldome photography, the audience generally sees everything, since the imagery inherently surrounds them, and generally everything is in focus deep into the frame.

Of course, filmmakers may also choose to shoot live action elements in front of a green screen with traditional video cameras, and then composite these assets into hemispherical CG environments using fulldome production tools produced by Evans & Sutherland, Sky-Skan, Multimeios, and others.

Filmmakers must consider and navigate the complexities of the fulldome technical workflow in order to deliver shows on time and on budget.

For single camera production, there is one type of lens: the fisheye (Figure 7) that captures a single view that is 180° to 250° wide. Fisheye lenses are the least flattering lenses for people since their extreme optics will severely distort objects that come too close to the lens, creating an unflattering effect known as foreshortening (Figure 8). The part of an object that is close to the camera appears extremely large while parts of the object further away appear unnaturally small. This is especially disastrous with human faces, since noses and chins can become enormous relative to the rest of the face when a person is too close to the lens.

Fisheye lenses also have infinite depth of field, so everything is always in focus, removing one of the classic cinematic techniques that shallow depth of field allows: blurry backgrounds. Soft focus in the background and sharp focus on the subject draws the audience's attention to the subject that is in sharp focus and away from the soft-focus background. This technique facilitates moments in which the director wants to amplify the emphasis on the subject and minimize distractions. Live action lenses for digital fulldome can't do this, so directors must employ other techniques to direct the audience's focus and attention.

Current digital transforms developed to stretch and warp 4:3 aspect ratio produced by 15/70 IMAX film enable flat screen imagery to cover 80% of the dome (as IMAX Dome systems have done since the 1970s). Live action footage can be shot with any lens in 4:3 aspect ratio and then warped to the dome. This technique leaves a 20% gap of black in the back of the dome that needs to be filled in with CGI or

Figure 7. An 8mm focal length fisheye lens.
Source: Photo by Jud McCranie distributed under CC-BY-SA 4.0

just feathered to black. This workaround allows cinematographers access to essentially any lens, letting them break free from constantly having to choose a fisheye or wide-angle lens.

A dome is a very challenging environment for projection. Because light falls on every part of the dome, the light from the back of the dome bounces back toward the front, scattering light into the dark areas of the scene, thereby reducing the contrast. This phenomenon called *cross-reflection* has a similar effect to what happens in a movie theater when the house lights come on during the credits roll at the end of the film. Blacks on the screen turn gray, and the contrast ratio of the image drops dramatically. LED domes are self-illuminating, solving the cross-reflection problem, producing bright images with phenomenal contrast. Currently LED domes are quite expensive, but as with all new technology, its price will drop and become more affordable over time.

There is also only one perfect seat in the dome, and that is right in the middle, right under the zenith. This is the only place where all the images perfectly unwrap from their distorted dome original to look straight and undistorted on the dome. Anywhere else in the dome, vertical lines will curve. It's simply a physics problem. Domes are compound curves, and they are curved everywhere. Domes warp everything, so directors need to be careful of straight lines. They won't stay straight. This isn't always a problem, but it is something to consider when designing an experience for an audience.

Figure 8. Foreshortening effect caused by being too close to a fisheye lens
Source: Dr. Denny Vrandečić, distributed under CC-BY-SA 4.0

KEY VISUAL STORYTELLING TOOLS FOR DIGITAL FULLDOME

The following list of tools work extremely well to help craft visual stories in the fulldome medium. By using these techniques separately and together, directors can tell amazing stories despite the aforementioned limitations of the fulldome medium.

Composition

The arrangement of items across the fulldome canvas is one of most powerful resources in the director's toolkit. There is an expansive world to paint both in terms of the imagery that surrounds the audience, but also what exists overhead. The fulldome canvas is surprisingly supple and can easily take the shape of the environment placed around it. Low ceilings and close walls can simulate a confined space; conversely tall trees stretching high above the audience can create the strong sensation of an expansive space.

Many of the other tools below, except for the last two, work within the composition of the scene to create show's visual aesthetic. More than virtually any other medium, fulldome does not have an obvious point of focus or place to look; therefore, it is imperative to skillfully and constantly guide the audience's attention and visual focus throughout a show. The techniques below are some of the time-tested methods that can do just that.

Camera Movement

Moving the perspective of the entire scene, crafting dynamic and changing compositions by moving the camera, provides visual interest to scenes, allowing them to develop over time and stay on screen longer without the need for cuts. The more the scene can change within the shot and the camera's choreography, the more the audience will stay anchored within the location or place of the scene.

Camera movement must be handled skillfully, since the audience often feels that they are actually moving with the camera through the scene. It is quite a powerful kinetic connection that immersion creates in the audience.

Just like any technique this can be underused and overused. Some notable fulldome films are comprised of one continuous shot over their 20 to 25-minute running time. This can be quite effective, but also has the unexpected complication of forcing the camera path over time into dead moments that have to be enhanced to liven them up (much like long stretches of open highway on an endless road trip) or to restricting your view to what can logically fit along that unbroken camera path. Intentionally leading with a technique or gimmick can diminish the overall creative possibilities and highlight the technique at the expense of the impact of the overall experience. Everything in moderation, unless there is a compelling creative reason to lean heavily into one technique or another. It's a delicate artistic balance that the director must constantly evaluate.

Actor Blocking

Just as in a stage play, blocking helps define the scene's action and the actors' characters. Whereas a pure theatrical experience is limited by the confines of the available performance areas inside the theater, in a fulldome show, actors can appear and move anywhere within the immersive canvas. This needs careful balance as well, but in a dynamic shot, even if the camera is stationary, actors moving toward and away from the camera or moving through the scene can help guide the audience's attention within a frame that has no clear director or point of focus. As humans, we like to look at other humans, and our eyes follow them throughout a scene. This is a powerful way to guide the audience's gaze inside the frame, which is more crucial than ever considering the inability to use traditional cinematic editing to restrict the audience's view.

Movement Within Frame

The human eye also follows movement. Objects that move against others that are stationary grab attention. Something that moves causes humans to want to know *what* is moving, *where* it is going, and what it may be up to. This could relate to simple survival skills or basic curiosity. Either way, object movement inside the frame is a highly effective way to guide the audience's attention through the expansive fulldome canvas.

Visual Balance of Frame

Humans seem to have a desire for order and organization. Even a picture that is slightly off of perfect level screams out to be adjusted. Visual balance in a fulldome frame is no exception. Similar objects or those that have a symmetrical layout on screen are easily ignored, but anything that stands out because of its size (smaller or larger than other objects) or because of its visual isolation within the frame draws focus. This orchestration of visual balance is not nearly as powerful as movement or a human in the frame, but the choreography of visual elements and the balance of their visual symmetry and asymmetry can cause viewers to look at the objects that stand out. This is pure visual composition and the creation of an area of interest inside the fulldome frame and is most analogous to composition principles in conventional cinema.

Color

In a similar way, color asymmetry can cause the audience to focus on colors that look different or draw attention. For example, a green object will pull focus in a scene that is largely blue. Humans are very aware of differences, and unique colors in a scene will stand out. Also, warm colors (reds, yellows, oranges) command attention and push to the foreground while cool colors (blues and purples) recede and move to the background. Greens are neutral and can serve either purpose. White and black can switch roles based on the surrounding colors. In other words, either black or white can be dominant or recessive based on the context of the scene. With that said, white tends to grab our attention more than black if all other factors are neutral.

Light

Human eyes are basically light receptors. Light activates sight. Light on objects in a scene makes people look at them. It's the same reason people follow the beam of light from a flashlight in the dark, even if it isn't illuminating anything interesting. Light directs the viewer's attention very powerfully. Once again this is a time-honored tool from the beginning of cinematography and theater. Lighting is a very useful too that can guide the audience attention throughout a show.

Visual Simplicity vs. Complexity

As much as humans like to think they are very complex and sophisticated, they default to what is simple and easy to understand. The human eye may be fascinated by complex imagery but will always try to simplify it or find the least complex place to look. This is why tunnels work so well on the dome. The audience looks right down the center of the tunnel to see where it is leading. The choreography and interplay of simple and complex visual structure can effectively show the audience exactly where to look in a scene. This can be everything from a tunnel to an alleyway blocked by tall buildings on both sides, to the tracks on a rollercoaster.

Vectors

Vectors are imaginary lines that point in certain directions within a frame. These cause the audience to look in the direction the vector is pointing or moving. Vectors on the dome can be caused by graphical composition where a line or curve forms from the spatial arrangement or simple patterns among a complex scene as described above. These are known as graphic vectors, which tend to be subtle. Other vectors that point in a certain direction, like an arrow, a street sign, or a finger pointing at something are called index vectors. These are a bit more powerful than graphic vectors. Finally, there are motion vectors where an object is moving in a direction, and the audience watches with interest where it is going. Motion vectors have the most weight and ability to direct the audience's eyes through the scene.

An Actor's Eye Line

This is a specific type of vector generated by an actor looking in a particular direction on the screen. Wherever the actor looks, the audience is compelled to look as well. Part of this likely springs from innate curiosity; part may result from the fact that looking at something is a less obvious form of pointing. For this vector to work most effectively, the actor should look at something in the scene. This way the audience can follow the actor's gaze to a landing point within the frame.

There is little offscreen space in fulldome, since the frame is so vast, but it is possible to use clever editing to connect the actor's eye line from inside one shot into an object in the next shot.

Editing and Scene Transitions

As previously discussed, editing is possible and often necessary in digital fulldome. Editing allows directors to shift between subjective and objective scenes and to change the audience vantage point within an objective scene. Editing can also transition between subjective sequences to string larger sections of a film together.

There is no shortage of authoritative reference material for cinematic editing techniques, and there is neither space nor need to delve into these in this chapter. Suffice it to say that most time-honored principles of traditional editing still apply to digital fulldome, even if the frame or the immersive medium itself does not respond the same way as a cinematic frame that sits out in front of the audience. Experimentation and careful shot/sequence planning is essential to discover what can work the most effectively in a given project.

When used most effectively, cuts can become largely invisible and feel completely organic to the visual story. This places pacing and scene sequencing back in the hands of the director even in the fulldome medium.

Sound Design

Audio cues are extremely effective in grabbing the audience's attention, especially in moments where the director wants the audience to look up, to the sides of the screen or behind them toward the back of the dome. Even though fulldome is an immersive medium with 360° imagery, when an audience is seated, they typically look forward unless there are reasons for them to look elsewhere. Sound cues are an organic and elegant way to help direct the audience's attention to different parts of the dome. This technique must be used gently, because it is uncomfortable for the audience to require them to move their bodies around to physically look behind them, especially when they are in a seated position. Better to use sound in the back of the dome to bring in something that quickly moves to the sides of the dome or across the zenith, such as a spaceship entering from behind and moving overhead. In this example the audience will only have to look up as the ship is passing above them.

The tools highlighted above can help directors navigate and craft the visual story for maximum impact, while avoiding the pitfalls of immersive media.

EXAMPLES AND ADVANTAGES OF EFFECTIVE FULLDOME STORYTELLING

The immersive fulldome canvas is not inherently better than traditional flat screen cinema, but as explored in this chapter, it is inherently different. In addition to the variety of specific aesthetic effects immersive content provides, fulldome creates a unique connection with the audience. They feel like they are inside the story, sometimes in first person point of view (POV) and other times in third person POV, but in both cases they are watching from inside the story as opposed to watching as a voyeur in traditional cinema where the audience is outside the experience looking in through the frame.

There are a host of films produced specifically for the fulldome medium that have leveraged these principles effectively within certain scenes and in some cases throughout the films.

- **Microcosm: The Adventure Within:** (Daut, 2002). The first science fiction and non-astronomical fulldome film ever created (written, produced, and directed by the author) was also the first time that a fulldome film moved from entirely a first person POV and made extensive use of cinematic editing to propel the story and change audience perspective in the immersive space. What started as a grand experiment actually helped define and clarify modern fulldome cinematic techniques.

The conceit of the film placed the audience inside a human-crewed submersible that could shrink down to microscopic size for injection into the bloodstream of a dying patient. After an introduction that set up the scenario, the audience finds themselves inside the submarine's cockpit looking out the front window with controls and hardware of the submarine's interior surrounding them. The show established this as the first person POV for the entire show. Rather than anchoring the entire experience inside the sub, the perspective cuts to a view outside the sub, watching the scene from within the scene from a third person POV. This change in perspective within a scene enabled editing to allow the viewer to move easily from one POV to the other; in fact, from the third person POV, cuts from shot to shot were easier to achieve because of the aesthetic distance created by the third person POV. This continuous sense of presence in the scene creates a dynamic effect that could not be possible in a traditional cinematic experience.

- **Stars of the Pharaohs:** (Murtagh & Daut, 2004). This film broke ground with its stunning rec- reations of temples and tombs of ancient Egypt including the temple of Denderah (built in 3D as a photorealistic representation of how it exists today in its partially ruined state) and the temple of Luxor (built in 3D as a depiction of how it may have looked 3,000 years ago). By establishing a first person POV, the audience was allowed to travel inside these amazing locations in such a way that they felt transported not only to Egypt, but also back in time on a walk-through of these astonishing destinations. Traditional cinema does not allow this sensation of transportation inside virtual worlds.
- **Dawn of the Space Age:** (Sip, 2007). Telling the story of mankind's efforts to take the first steps into space, the competition between the USA and the Soviet Union, the moon landing, and human- ity's future in space, this show uses the third person POV throughout the entire film. This is a per- fectly appropriate technique for this particular narrative, since the filmmaker invites the audience to become a bystander inside defining moments of the space race, but not to take the first-person perspective of those pioneers who changed mankind's destiny in the universe. The audience was never allowed to become the historic space pioneers, but only to be with these pioneers to expe- rience these seminal moments with them as never before. This third person perspective allowed

freedom of editing from one shot and one scene to another, since the audience never perceived that they were the people in the story, but only very close observers.

- **Dream to Fly:** (Heavens of Copernicus & Majda, 2013). Just before the midpoint of this film, the filmmakers place the audience inside a conventional theater facing a curtained proscenium that towers in front of them. This motif riffs on the theatrical nature of fulldome immersion, previously discussed in this chapter, and then pulls set pieces off the stage and moves them around the audience space, everything from sketches on parchment paper and aerodynamic equations to prototype planes that fly around the interior of the theater. This sense of theatrical immersion does not directly translate into flat screen cinema experience, and is therefore unique and completely fitting for use in the fulldome medium.
- **Expedition Reef:** (California Academy of Sciences & Wyatt, 2018). The film begins with a scene inside an aquarium facing a large floor-to-ceiling glass tank containing a coral reef environment. The audience is in the building looking at the aquarium, an interesting play on "looking at" versus "being in" a scene. As the camera moves toward the glass on tank, the interior of the aquarium melts away and blends into the coral reef, placing the audience in the middle of the open ocean on a journey of exploration into the biodiversity of the coral reef. This is a powerful immersive storytelling technique that would not be possible in traditional cinema.

The show continues with long-duration shots featuring complex camera moves sweeping through the reef, pausing to introduce new creatures and story points to the audience, anchoring them in a first-person POV with a highly choreographed camera paths that efficiently move from one story point to the next with very infrequent cuts and scene transitions. The opening shot lasts nearly five minutes, starting underwater, breeching the surface, hovering over the shoreline, then flying out into space to look at the Earth holistically. This type of sweeping, complex shot would not have the same sense of presence in traditional cinema and would likely need more edits to preserve the pacing for the flat screen experience.

HOW TO TELL STORIES ON THE DOME

Show, Don't Tell

The fulldome canvas is huge. If a picture is worth a thousand words, then a fulldome picture is worth ten thousand words. Directors should strongly consider designing the visual story first, almost as if crafting a silent film. They should ask what story the visuals are telling and how many words are actually needed to complement the scenes. It is not necessary to use words to state what is obvious in the visual story.

Action, camera movement, blocking, light, color, composition, and the other visual storytelling techniques described should build each shot and sequence to guide the audience through each beat of the story.

Design Objective and Subjective Scenes

Choosing whether to design an objective or subjective scene or sequence is most directly analogous to the throttle or gas pedal for immersive storytelling. Subjective scenes, where the audience feels like they scene is happening to them, are the most potent and impactful. Objective scenes where the audience feels like they are close to an event as just an observer or bystander have slightly less impact and offer directors more opportunities to cut.

Subjective scenes, for example place the audience inside a car in the driver's seat (maximum emotional and kinetic impact), whereas objective scenes place the audience outside the car to witness what another driver is doing (one step removed from personal participation, but still strong involvement). Subjective scenes anchor themselves in real time, since they mimic real experiences. Temporal flow must remain natural and uninterrupted. Objective scenes can jump between places and time can be left out when an edit takes place.

Structuring a balance between objective and subjective scenes effectively can allow directors to most powerfully guide the audience through a visual story while balancing the thematic arc and emotional impact.

Choreograph Longer Shots with Higher Degrees of Complexity

Think of the medium as immersive theater with an audience that can move around the theater to a limited degree. In digital fulldome, when the perspective moves, the audience moves. Rather than rely on editing to structure and build a sequence, the dome more natively wants to present shots that are highly choreographed from camera movement, to blocking, to art direction, to the arrangement of items in the frame, to the dynamic, unfolding interest generated by a longer shot that is constantly changing and developing as the audience moves through the scene.

The more complex the scene, the more it holds the audience's interest, and the longer it can be sustained without a cut. This is an extraordinarily important technique to learn and implement.

Edit with the Medium and Audience in Mind

Don't rely on editing to build scenes the way it can in traditional cinema

Don't rely on close ups, master shot, medium shot, over the shoulder shots, since the dome is largely frameless, and these shot descriptions can't apply in the same way. There is no direct correlation to this type of shooting or sequence editing. The scenes are either objective with limited editing or subjective with little or no editing except for transitions from one scene to another. Craft shots that are visually interesting and transform into different looks as the camera moves and as subjects move within the fulldome frame.

Leverage the Dome's Ability to Transform Itself

The canvas itself is very big. Make it smaller when needed or let it be giant. The shape of the dome mimics the sky or infinite space. Its geometry does not make itself obvious to the audience; instead, it seems to transform its shape and size to perfectly match and reproduce any environment projected onto its surface. That makes the dome somewhat magical, when it can use these "superpowers" to mold itself into a tiny passageway through an underground cavern or a giant cathedral with 60' vaulted ceilings. Both are entirely possible as is everything in between. The aesthetic feeling of each space can also help shape and convey the story.

Most Important

Don't tell fulldome stories: tell stories. Don't let the medium itself force story choices that don't best serve the story's intent. This means that the story may require live actors inside the dome theater that interact with moments on the dome. This may mean that set pieces, props, a preshow, or seamless branching between story segments may be required. Let the story shape the experience NOT the medium. Definitely consider all the medium's uniqueness qualities, but don't be confined by the restrictions of the medium itself.

Examples

A number of feature films have begun experimenting with longer, highly choreographed shots that illustrate sensibilities that work perfectly for fulldome production.

Here are just a few:

- **Gravity:** Directed by Alfonso Cuarón - 2013

The film opens with a single shot that runs for 13 minutes and 7 seconds with no cuts. This shot is exquisitely choreographed with camera movements, actor blocking, staging of the spacecraft in the scene. This groundbreaking shot is extremely dynamic and provides masterful pacing and remarkable storytelling (Cuáron & Heyman, 2013).

- **Creed:** Directed by Ryan Coogler - 2015

The first boxing match in the film is shot with a moving camera and no cuts at all. Once again, the shot never loses energy and does not suffer from a lack of fast edits. The scene constantly changes (Winkler, et al., 2015).

- **Black Panther:** Directed by Ryan Coogler - 2018

The director employs a long uninterrupted shot in the middle of the film where a battle breaks out at a casino where unsavory activities are taking place. Another excellent example of camera and actor choreography in a sustained, dynamic shot (Fiege & Coogler, 2018).

- **Birdman:** Directed by Alejandro G. Iñárritu - 2014

Much of this film's entire running time is one single shot with no observable edits (but of course the film was not shot in one take. Clever edits are hidden as the camera moves across a neutral background. More inspiration for choreography on the dome (Iñárritu et al., 2014).

Tricks and Tips

- Don't lead with the technology
- Don't move too quickly
- Don't rush your shots. Give the audience time to experience the scene. Base shot duration on complexity of the scene
- Don't forget to move the camera
- Don't forget the audience moves with you. Guide them through the experience like an expert docent at a museum or historical site

CONCLUSION

Cinema and dome cinema grew up in very different ways. Their technology and their origins have led to their current maturity and the depth of content that is possible in each medium. Similar tools exist in both mediums, but their use is very different. Education, not entertainment, was the origin of digital fulldome; whereas, cinema could educate, entertain, and explore any genre from its inception. Storytelling and entertainment experiences are not only possible, but game-changing in digital fulldome, and effective storytelling techniques and best practices exist and are continuing to expand.

The fulldome medium has the potential to attract large audiences and to deliver a mind-blowing VR shared theater experience for audiences of all ages and even eclipse the storytelling capabilities of Hollywood films, potentially kicking off a revolution in fulldome filmmaking and even the establishment of a dome theater network across the world. The future of fulldome is yet to be written, but its potential is absolutely unlimited.

REFERENCES

California Academy of Sciences. (Producer), & Wyatt, R. (Director). (2018). Expedition Reef [Fulldome Film]. United States: California Academy of Sciences.

Cuarón, A., & Heyman, D. (Producers), & Cuarón, A. (Director). (2013). *Gravity* [Motion Picture]. United Kingdom, United States: Warner Bros. Pictures.

Ehrman, M. (2002). The Last Laser Show Laserium, once playing at an observatory near you, has gone the way of the pet rock. Mark Ehrman tracks the history—and future? —of the light fantastic. *CNN Money*. Retrieved from https://money.cnn.com/magazines/fortune/fortune_archive/2002/02/18/318144/index.htm

Feige, K. (Producer), & Coogler, R. (Director). (2018). *Black Panther* [Motion Picture]. United States. Marvel Studios.

Heavens of Copernicus Productions (Producer), Majda, P. (Director). (2013). *Dream to Fly* [Fulldome Film]. Poland: Heavens of Copernicus Productions.

Iñárritu, A. G., Lesher, J., Milchan, A., & Skotchdopole, J. W. (Producers), Iñárritu, A. G., (Director). (2014). *Birdman* [Motion Picture]. United States. Fox Searchlight Pictures.

Lambert, N., & Phillips, M. (2012). Introduction: Fulldome. *Digital Creativity*, *23*(1), 1–4. doi:10.108 0/14626268.2012.666980

Library of Congress. (n.d.). *Early Motion Picture Productions*. Retrieved from https://www.loc.gov/collections/edison-company-motion-pictures-and-sound-recordings/articles-and-essays/history-of-edison-motion-pictures/early-motion-picture-productions/

Marche, J. (2005). *Theaters of Time and Space: American Planetaria, 1930-1970*. New Brunswick, NJ: Rutgers University Press.

Michael, D. *(Producer), & Michael, D. (Director). (2002). Microcosm: The Adventure Within* [Fulldome Film]. United States: Evans & Sutherland.

Murtagh, T., & Daut, M. (Producers & Directors). (2004). Stars of the Pharaohs [Fulldome Film]. United States: Evans & Sutherland.

Sip, R. (Producer & Director). (2007). *Dawn of the Space Age* [Fulldome Film]. Netherlands: Mirage3D.

Winkler, I., Chartoff, B., Winkler, C., Winkler, D., King-Templeton, K., & Stallone, S. (Producers), & Coogler, R. (Director). (2015). *Creed*. [Motion Picture]. United States: Warner Bros. Pictures.

Chapter 14
POV in XR:
How We Experience, Discuss, and Create the Virtual World

Eve Weston

ⓘ https://orcid.org/0000-0002-8841-5491

Exelauno, USA

ABSTRACT

This chapter will introduce and explain the applications of a taxonomy for discussing point of view (POV) in XR. The simple designations of first, second, and third person that are used to categorize books, movies, and video games don't cover all the options and combinations available in immersive media. Accordingly, XR requires a new taxonomy that will allow for clear communication about content and experiences. This chapter will do three things: (1) present the four main POV tiers: narrative, visual, effectual, and experiential; (2) address less common tiers and how they might be incorporated and acknowledged in future XR experiences; and (3) show the taxonomy in action by using it to describe contemporary XR content.

INTRODUCTION

Literary point of view and its complications have been analyzed in detail by French literary theorist Gerard Genette (1983), and Dutch cultural theorist Mieke Bal (1997), each of whom has contributed significantly to the study and discussion of narrative. In film studies, many of their terms were taken up and expanded to include the complexity of image and sound. With virtual reality, new complexities, opportunities, and fields present themselves. The world of storytelling has expanded. With the development of immersive media---collectively known as extended reality (XR)---comes a need to extend the vocabulary we use to define and discuss point of view concepts. The simple designations of first, second, and third person used to categorize books, movies, and video games don't cover all the options and combinations available in XR. Accordingly, the immersive medium of virtual reality requires a new

DOI: 10.4018/978-1-7998-2433-6.ch014

taxonomy for discussing point-of-view. Having a taxonomy that specifically addresses what is possible in virtual reality will facilitate better and clearer discussion, analysis, and communication about this medium.

This chapter first reviews the existing terms for Point of View (POV) from traditional media. Next, it explores how these terms do and don't apply to virtual reality. Then, to help facilitate clearer communication about the options available in XR, this chapter presents and explains applications of the taxonomy as used within virtual reality. This proposed taxonomy, represented in Figure 1, is a marriage of old and new ideas and includes four POV tiers: 1) narrative, 2) visual, 3) effectual and 4) experiential. The shared vocabulary that this taxonomy provides is both descriptive and prescriptive, serving as a way to describe existing work and also as a menu of options for what's possible.

NARRATIVE POV

POV is most commonly thought of in terms of narrative point-of-view: first, second or third person, which is the point of view from which the story is being told. Before examining how narrative point-of-view intersects with the other tiers in virtual reality, it serves to have a brief review of narrative point of view.

In a first-person narrative, the narrator is telling you his or her own story. *Moby Dick*'s famous opening line, "Call me Ishmael," is a classic example. First person narrative POV is also exemplified by Ernest Cline's *Ready Player One* (2012).

<u>My</u> *mom once told* <u>me</u> *that* <u>my</u> *dad had given* <u>me</u> *an alliterative name, Wade Watts, because he thought it sounded like the secret identity of a superhero.*

The words "my" and "me" in the passage above, along with the word "I" in general are excellent first-person indicators. From them, we can determine that Wade, the narrator, is telling us his own story, in the first person.

Second person narrative POV can be found in the Choose Your Own Adventure books. As exemplified by the following passage from R.A. Montgomery's *The Trail of Lost Time* (2011), the narrator is telling not his or her, but your, experience.

<u>You</u> *stare at the envelope with* <u>your</u> *name written in faded ink. The lawyer handed it to* <u>you</u> *an hour ago after he read* <u>your</u> *grandfather's will.*

And examples of third-person narrative POV are plentiful in books, from Jane Austen's *Pride and Prejudice* to Michael Crichton's *Jurassic Park*. Third person POV can be limited in scope or omniscient, knowing only one characters' thoughts, everyone's thoughts, or somewhere in between. An example follows below from J.K. Rowling's *Harry Potter & the Deathly Hallows* (2007).

<u>Harry's</u> *mind wandered a long way from the marquee, back to afternoons spent alone with Ginny in lonely parts of the school grounds.*

The key is that a third person narrator is neither telling his or her own thoughts or experiences, nor yours, and, rather, is recounting another, third person's thoughts.

Figure 1. Tiers of immersive POV
Source: Exelauno, 2019

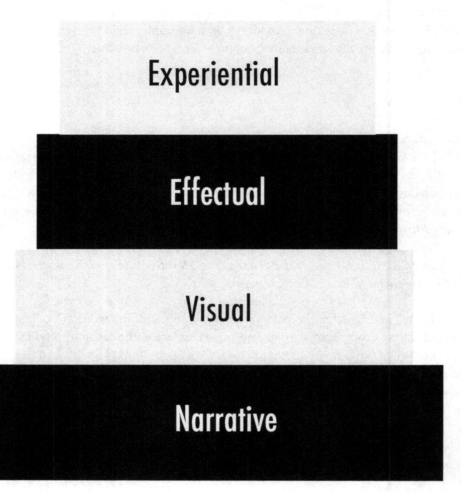

This recap of narrative POV will be useful after the next section, when looking at how narrative and visual POV work together in immersive experiences.

VISUAL POV

In addition to narrative point-of-view, in film and other visual media such as television and video games, there is also visual point-of-view, the POV from which the story is being *seen*. Visual point-of-view can be similarly broken down into the three categories of person: Third Person Objective, First Person, and Second Person, which are next discussed in this order.

Third Person Objective point-of-view is the most common visual point-of-view utilized in film. Movies that use this POV include *Casablanca, Indiana Jones*, *Star Wars, Wonder Woman*, and most others. When a movie uses third person objective POV, it means that the moviegoer is not a character in the film, no matter how good their Captain America costume or how many lines of *Endgame*'s dialog they're reciting from that second-row aisle seat.

First person visual point-of-view means that the viewer is a character in the film, namely the protagonist in the visual experience. First person POV is incredibly common in video games. Most people are familiar with the concept of "first person shooter" where the player is the one holding the gun and shooting it at the enemies within the game. Even in a 2D world, this engages the player as a character in the story. In film, however, first-person visual point-of-view is rare, though it has been done. The 1947 American film noir *Lady in the Lake* is an adaptation of the 1943 Raymond Chandler first person murder mystery novel by the same name. First-time director Robert Montgomery's ambition was to create a cinematic version of Chandler's Philip Marlowe novels, known for their first-person narrative style. As a result, the entire film is shot from the viewpoint of the central character, with the exception of a couple of moments when the central character addresses the audience directly. Because of this POV, the film was promoted by MGM with the claim that it was the first of its kind. Another example of first person visual POV is when a wedding videographer entreats a guest to, "Say something to the happy couple!" The videographer anticipates that the couple will be watching the video and the intention is for the couple to feel like they're experiencing their wedding day all over again. As a side note, the happy couple watching that wedding video moment was the closest thing to first person visual POV plus first person narrative POV… until virtual reality.

So, if in third person visual point-of-view the viewer *isn't* in the story and in first person visual point-of-view the viewer *is* in the story, what is second person visual point-of-view? It splits the difference: the viewer is straddling the worlds. "You," the viewer, have one foot in the story and one foot outside of it; second person point-of-view acknowledges the medium. In books, second person acknowledges there's a reader: you. In film, it acknowledges there's a viewer: you. Sometimes this is done fantastically, by the character breaking the fourth wall and talking to the audience, sometimes it's done logically with the conceit of a documentary film crew: as is the case in the television show *The Office* and even in the video game *Mario 64,* where the player sees action from the POV of Latiku, a monster and cameraman, while still controlling Mario.

To recap, with third person visual POV, the viewer is outside the story, in first person visual POV, the viewer is inside the story, and with second personal visual POV, the viewer is very aware it is a story.

NARRATIVE AND VISUAL POV TOGETHER IN VIRTUAL REALITY

So, how do narrative and visual point-of-view work in virtual reality? In virtual reality the viewer *becomes* the camera or the player. Figure 2 is representative of that, showing the image from each of two

Figure 2. A modified, unstitched 360 production image from the set of the world's first immersive sitcom, The BizNest, showing Associate Producer and Stage Manager Rachel Shanblatt, right, hard at work
Source: Exelauno, 2019

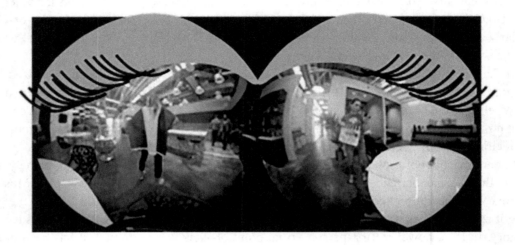

180 lenses, fashioned as eyes. As a result of the viewer "being" the camera, it is easy to think that POV in VR is as simple as saying that virtual reality is always first person. In the purely visual sense, it is. The virtual reality participant is always having a first person visual experience of the 360 degree space around them in which they are immersed. However, POV is not simply about the viewer's relationship to the space; it is also about the viewer's relationship to the story. Since, at this point in the VR industry most experiences do provide a first person visual perspective (1PPV) on the story, this section will begin with a focus on first person visual perspective and then address some other (at the time of this writing) less common options.

1PPV is employed in VR experiences as diverse as *Beat Saber*, *Notes on Blindness*, *The BizNest* and *The Dinner Party,* all of which will be examined more closely later in this chapter.

One might think that by defining a VR work as 1PPV, most of the heavy lifting regarding POV is done. However, there is more to be resolved. Certainly, the viewer is seeing a story from the first-person perspective, but whose story is it? And, is the viewer (you) learning the narrative from that person or someone else? In other words, what is the narrative point of view? In visual media, there is more than one way to convey narrative. To illustrate the difference between narrative and visual point of view and the importance of being able to distinguish between them, it will be instructive to examine VR experiences with voiceover narration.

Take for example the above-mentioned immersive virtual reality project *Notes on Blindness*. This VR project premiered at Sundance in 2016, complementing the story world of its eponymous, coordinate feature film (Puschmann, 2016). It is based on author John Hull's sensory and psychological experience of blindness.[1] The voiceover narration that provides the backbone for the *Notes on Blindness* VR experience is Hull's actual audio diary; he is narrating, in the first person, his experience of going blind. He is describing what he is seeing in real time. This gives the experience a first person narrative POV. At the same time, in the VR experience, the viewer is seeing the filmmakers' approximation of what John Hull would have been seeing, recreated with real-time 3D animations. This gives the experience a first-person visual point of view. And, because the visuals match the narration—the viewer is witnessing firsthand what is being described in the first person—the viewer can conclude that the viewer is meant to be John Hull. Such an experience, in which there is first person narrative and first person visuals that "match," is an example of embodied first-person narrative (e1N).

Another immersive experience worth looking at is *52 Places to Go: Iceland*, a 360° travel experience produced by the New York Times.[2] In *52 Places to Go: Iceland*, the viewer is traveling with Jada Yuan, a 52 Places Traveler, and Lucas Peterson, Frugal Traveler. The main narration for the 360 piece is Jada's first-person narration. This gives the experience a first person narrative POV, much like *Notes on Blindness*. However, in contrast to *Notes on Blindness*, in *52 Places to Go: Iceland* the viewer sees the narrator Jada, and not her visual point of view. Because the viewer is seeing Jada, the viewer can conclude that the viewer is not meant to be Jada. While both *52 Places to Go: Iceland* and *Notes on Blindness* have first-person narrative plus first-person visuals, they clearly provide different types of experiences; in one, you are the "main character," in another, you are not. *52 Places to Go: Iceland*, an immersive experience in which the first person narrative and first-person visuals do not match, is a disembodied first-person narrative (d1N).

It is an important point to note that an embodied experience will immerse the viewer in the narrative and a disembodied experience will detach the audience from the moment at hand. An embodied experience will encourage empathy and a disembodied experience will shut down the participant's emotional response and ignite their intellectual response, prompting them to think and question. An embodied experience helps the viewer believe they are living the virtual experience. By contrast, a disembodied experience is Brechtian in its nature. The theatrical practice of Bertolt Brecht—German theatre practitioner, playwright, and poet—embodied his belief that a play should not cause the spectator to identify emotionally with the characters or action but should instead provoke rational self-reflection and a critical view of the action on the stage (Squiers, 2015). He wanted his audiences to adopt a critical perspective and employed techniques that reminded the spectator that the play was a representation of reality and not reality itself, a philosophy that is certainly relevant to VR. This discussion should serve as a reminder that there is no right or wrong way to construct an immersive experience, but rather, there are ways to succeed or fail at achieving one's ultimate objective. Creators should be mindful not only of what decisions they make, but also of why they make them.

As mentioned previously, experiences providing first person visual perspective (1PPV) on the story are quite prevalent. However, there are other options, and it is worth taking a moment to acknowledge some of these and how they might be created. Narrative POV is about the viewer's narrative relationship to the story. And visual POV is about the viewer's visual relationship to the story. As such, it is possible to give the viewer a third-person visual perspective on the story while still having them see the 360 space "first-hand" in VR. As has already been alluded, if the viewer is the protagonist in the VR experience and is controlling their avatar with their real body, the viewer is engaged in a first person narrative experience. If the viewer has first person perspective (1PPV), they would experience an embodied first person narrative; in the virtual world, they might see their hands and arms in front of them, but they could not see their back or the top of their head, etc. However, if there were a virtual camera mounted behind their avatar or body, as in Figure 3, they could then see their back or the top of their head. The viewer could, in such an instance, control their body in the virtual world while at the same time viewing it as an outside observer. These two different experiences are exactly what were created by a team of European researchers. Geoffrey Gorisse, Olivier Christmann, Etienne Armand Amato, and Simon Richir set out to compare the impact and potentialities enabled by first person perspective (1PPV) versus third person perspective (3PPV) in immersive virtual environments. However, virtual environments are not the

Figure 3. This camera mounted in the viewer's backpack with the visual feed going directly into his headset allows the viewer to have a third-person visual perspective on his own real-world first-person experience
Source: Mei.pi. Real World Third Person Perspective VR / AR Experiment, 2014

only place that this sort of out-of-body experience is possible. The following still images from a video by the team at Mepi.pl shows how it's possible to use XR to give someone a third person perspective in the real world (Gorisse, 2017).

Thanks to the VR headset being worn by the gentleman in the photo on the left, which is receiving a visual feed from the cameras mounted from his backpack, he is able to view himself in the real world from a third-person visual perspective (3PPV). Accordingly, it is possible to give the viewer a third-person visual perspective on the story while still having them see the 360 space "first-hand" in VR. While it was not necessarily intuitive that this might be done in 360, third person visual POV was clearly a possibility for game-engine built VR games and has indeed been adopted by VR games. Even so, *Lucky's Tale* and *Edge of Nowhere* made waves by opting for third person over first person POV. When *Lucky's Tale* was released by Playful Corp back at Electronic Entertainment Expo (E3) in Los Angeles in 2014 it was a heated topic of discussion on account of its then-uncommon third person POV. The game tells the story of a young fox, Lucky, who sets out to save his friend Pig, when Pig gets taken by a purple tentacle beast with large eyes and an appetite for pork. The player can lean in to see the fox they control, or they sit back to take in the whole level at a distance—in "god mode"—but at no time does the player take Lucky's POV. In *Edge of Nowhere,* Victor Howard is searching for his fiancé, Ava Thorne, who is part of a lost expedition in Antarctica. However, the player controls Victor while seeing Victor, not seeing as Victor. The idea of third person POV VR games has proven to have some staying power. More recently the industry has welcomed *Chronos,* an atmospheric hero's quest Role Playing Game, or RPG, among others.

As for what a second person visual perspective (2PPV) might be in VR, there is still much room for exploration. Since visual POV is about the viewer's visual relationship to the story, one way to achieve second person visual perspective in a fully immersive virtual world is to have the viewer take the visual perspective of a character in the game or story, but not the character they are controlling. To use *Mario 64* as an example, if the level with Latiku the cameraman was turned into a VR game, the player would be seeing the story world as Latiku, from his visual point of view, while controlling Mario.

Table 1. A breakdown of the different types of effectual POV and their determining factors

Effectual POV	Detectable in scene?	Has agency?
Non-Entity	No	No
Entity	Yes	No
Participant	Yes	Yes

The narrative and visual points-of-view discussed thus far describe the viewer's narrative and visual relationship to an immersive story. But are those the only types of relationships that a viewer can have with an immersive story? In *Notes on Blindness*, the viewer is a character, John Hull. But that's not the case in *52 Places to Go: Iceland*. What are the options for how the viewer can "be" in the space? That's the next topic of discussion.

EFFECTUAL POINT OF VIEW

The Effectual POV describes the effect the viewer's presence itself has on the scene. In the simplest terms, can the person experiencing an immersive work impact it? If so, to what extent? There are three effectual points of view: non-entity, entity and participant. This section gives a description of each, followed by examples.

As a non-entity, the viewer is an invisible observer. The viewer is present in the scene, but no one and nothing in the scene can tell. The viewer has no impact on the scene and it's as if the viewer is not even there. One example of this is Baobab Studios' *Crow: The Legend,* which takes place in a world where, when Winter comes for the very first time, much-admired Crow is cajoled by his friends into flying to the Heavens to bring back Spring. In this story, the viewer is not Crow. Rather, the viewer is sometimes standing on the ground, sometimes floating in the air, but never looked at. The viewer is not a character; moreover, the viewer is not acknowledged, addressed or given any indication that they exist. Another example of non-entity effectual POV is Felix & Paul's *Traveling While Black,* a 360 video exploring the complicated legacy of the Jim Crow-era travel guide for African-Americans, The Green Book (Freedom du Lac, 2010). Multiple times during this piece, the viewer is seated in a restaurant booth with people, but none of these people ever talks to the viewer or looks at the viewer.

By contrast, with an entity effectual POV, the viewer is acknowledged and interacted with but has no agency. Characters in the story or scene are aware of the viewer's presence—they see the viewer and they may interact with the viewer. In this way, the viewer has an impact on the scene even though they can't actively make choices that affect it. One example of entity POV is Exelauno's *Human/Art/ Object*, in which the viewer gets to experience what it is like to be a work of art in an art gallery. This experience, fimed at bG Gallery in Los Angeles, has been shown at numerous galleries and art shows in the US and, at time of publication, is available free on Exelauno's website www.exelauno.co. In this 360 experience, the viewer, tagged with a gallery label (shown in Figure 4, top), is examined by gallery visitors and clearly feels present in the space as something—in this case a work of art. The viewer-as-art is impacting the scene in the sense that his or her presence influences the behavior of the other people in the scene. Another example of entity is Felix and Paul's *Miyubi*. The viewer in *Miyubi* is cast as a robot that can engage with people. The conceit of the piece is that Miyubi was given as a birthday gift in 1982 to a young boy, Dennis. Early in the piece, the viewer sees the birthday boy looking at him or her. And when Dennis requests that Miyubi say his name, Miyubi does. But the viewer doesn't control if or when he or she speaks or what he or she says as Miyubi; that's all pre-programmed. The viewer doesn't have agency but does have a place within the story world.

The next and highest level of effectual POV is participant. As a participant, the viewer has agency. He or she feels like—and is—somebody or something that can do things. The viewer is no longer just a viewer: he or she can do things that are perceived by or affect the scene. A great example of this is the popular VR game *Beat Saber*, a rhythm game in which the player slashes the beats of adrenaline-pumping music, visually represented as boxes that fly toward the player. The player can use their saber to hit the boxes and, when he or she does, the box goes away, the player's score goes up and, ultimately, the player can win or lose. Other examples include VR games where the player is moving themselves around, opening a door or employing a tool (i.e. paintbrush, weapon, laser pointer). *Tilt Brush*, Google's 3D-painting experience, is another good example of participant effectual POV. The viewer-as-participant isn't affecting a narrative or game but is affecting the space around them and how it is going forward.

Some interactive VR experiences fall under participant, depending on what the interactivity allows the viewer to affect. If the interactivity affects the scene or story, it would be participant. Hulu's *Door No. 1*, a live-action multiple choice comedy adventure, is an example of an interactive experience with participant effectual POV. In it, the viewer is "Alex", attending his ten-year high school reunion. At various junctures, the viewer gets to choose whether to follow one high-school classmate or another. By contrast, when an XR experience's interactivity allows the viewer to affect things beyond the scene or story, such as the way the viewer experiences the scene, it falls under a different POV tier, which will be explored in the next section.

It is the impact the viewer has on the scene (as summarized in Table 1) that determines an experience's effectual POV, not the mechanism by which they impact the scene. To elaborate on this concept a bit, in addition to the aforementioned tools, as the XR industry advances there will be an increasing number of ways that the viewer-as-participant can have agency. There are currently VR games that respond to the player's heart rate. In *Bring to Light*, a horror title from Red Meat Games, the player's level of fear affects the virtual world. On the more calming side of the spectrum, StoryUP Studios' *Healium* offers data-driven virtual escapes powered by the user's brain and proven to decrease stress and anxiety. Thanks to an electrical-activity-sensing headband and smart watch, the participant can use their brain's positive vibes to hatch butterflies from a chrysalis and their heart rate to illuminate the planets. Hopefully these examples help to illustrate that it is not the way that the player impacts the scene (e.g. using buttons, triggers, brainwaves, heart rate, etc.) but simply the fact that the viewer/player/user is able to impact the story and/or scene that makes an immersive experience participant effectual POV. Because of this, the taxonomy for XR will still hold as the industry evolves and as additional means of influencing XR experiences come to market.

Figure 4. Top: The gallery label associated with the viewer in Human/Art/Object. Bottom: Still image from Human/Art/Object of a woman examining the viewer as a work of art
Source: Exelauno, 2019

Table 2. A breakdown of the different types of experiential POV and their determining factors.

Experiential POV	Control Over Degrees of Freedom (DOF)
Robot	Has no control over at least 1 DOF
Mortal	Has control over 1-6 DOF
Deity	Has control over more than 6 DOF

EXPERIENTIAL POINT OF VIEW

Experiential POV describes the impact that the viewer has on how they experience the scene or story. There are three types of experiential POV: robot, mortal and deity. This section gives a description of each, followed by examples.

As robot, the viewer's experience is programmed. The viewer can't control it. Included in this designation is any experience where the viewer experiences the sensation of moving but is not actually walking or in or on a vehicle. One example of this experiential POV is Breaking Fourth's *BroBots,* a four-part series available on SamsungVR in which two British robots, Otis and Roberto, arrive in New York and join the NYPD. Another is Secret Location's *The Great C,* in which the viewer follows Clare, a young woman who finds her life upended when her fiancé is summoned for this year's pilgrimage to the all-powerful supercomputer, The Great C. Of the latter, Mike of Virtual Reality Oasis says, "The camera movement itself may be a bit intense for some as you have no control over it" (Virtual Reality Oasis, 2018); that is robot experiential POV, case in point. In both the aforementioned titles, the viewer has an experience much like that of riding on the crane of a crane-shot from traditional cinema: their effectual POV is non-entity and they move through the space seeing the action from the vantage point desired by the director. Many "cinematic" VR experiences fall into the category of robot experiential POV, however, one should be wary of jumping to such conclusions as "cinematic," much like "interactive," can be more broadly descriptive and is not a taxonomic term. Robot experiential POV also includes experiences that exercise control over the viewer's field of view at any given moment in the narrative or experience. A much-talked about concern when it comes to VR filmmaking is that the director doesn't have control over what the viewer is looking at in any given moment. To combat this, Sean Liu, Stanford PhD student and recipient of the Brown Institute for Media Innovation's Magic Grant, is creating *NeverEnding 360.* Her team built a 360-degree video editor that allows authors to specify "visual triggers" which deploy when an important event is approaching in the video and the viewer is looking elsewhere (The Brown Institute for Media Innovation, 2018). *NeverEnding 360* will allow the creator of a project to freeze the VR experience so that it won't continue until the viewer looks where the director wants them to be looking.[3] Any experience that employs *NeverEnding 360* will then have robot experiential POV. To recap, Robot covers any experience with forced perspective or movement. Some Positron chair VR experiences will likely also fall under this experiential POV.[4] As discussed above with regard to effectual POV, an experience's experiential POV is determined by what impact the viewer has on how they experience the scene, not the mechanism by which they are able or unable to control their experience.

With mortal experiential POV, the viewer can control their experience much as they would in real life. An example of an experience with mortal experiential POV is the 2019 Auggie Award Finalist and the world's first 360VR immersive sitcom, *The BizNest* (also described in a dedicated chapter in this book.). Imagine if instead of watching the TV show *The Office* from the couch in their apartment, a viewer could

Figure 5. Sadie, the viewer's co-worker in Exelauno's immersive sitcom, The BizNest, tells the viewer that they have food in their teeth
Source: Exelauno, 2019

watch it from the desk next to Jim, a fellow employee. That's the experience of *The BizNest*, a workplace comedy that takes place in a co-working space where the viewer is one of the members. The viewer sits at their desk or stands in the hallway, and the other characters in the show engage with them: giving them a sidelong glance, reminding them of an assignment, telling them they have food in their teeth, as pictured in Figure 5. In the mortal experiential POV, the viewer has control over all of the experience's provided Degrees of Freedom (DOF), which may include anywhere from 1-6 DOF.

For those readers who may not be familiar with Degrees of Freedom, each degree is an independently variable factor affecting any of the directions in which independent motion can occur in three-dimensional space. The first three degrees include rotational movement: rolling (head pivots side-to-side), pitching (head tilts along a vertical axis), and yawing (head swivels along a horizontal axis). The next three degrees include rotational and translational movement: elevating (moving up or down), strafing (moving left or right), and surging (moving forwards or backwards). In robot experiential POV, the experience itself may provide some degrees of freedom—the aforementioned examples allow rolling, pitching and yawing—but at least one of them is being controlled by the experience. In mortal experiential POV, the viewer/player has control over all degrees of freedom in the 1-6 DOF range available within the immersive experience. And, as Table 2 summarizes, in deity experiential POV, the viewer/player has control of degrees of freedom beyond the 1-6 DOF range.

With this knowledge, one can see how a whole range of XR experiences might fall under the mortal experiential POV. To give an example from the world of Augmented Reality, the game *Pokémon Go* (one of the most used and most profitable apps of 2016) uses mortal experiential POV. In it, the player uses their smartphone to reveal the game world overlaid on the real world and then has to locate, capture, battle, and train virtual creatures, called Pokémon. Because the player is navigating through the real

Figure 6. A menu of immersive POV options
Source: Exelauno, 2019

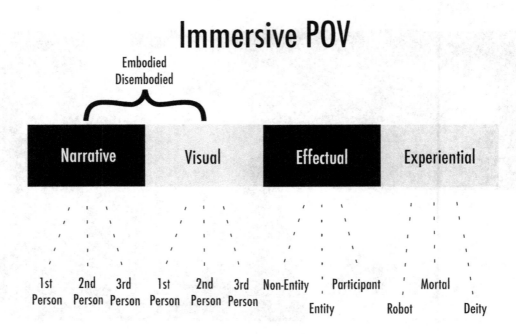

Figure 6. A menu of immersive POV options
Source: Exelauno, 2019

world as they navigate the virtual world, they logically have the ability to exercise control over 6 degrees of freedom. Alejandro González Iñárritu's location-based art experience, *Carne y Arena*, also gives the viewer mortal experiential POV, placing them among a group of immigrants who are led by a coyote across the Mexican border into the U.S. until they are stopped by the border patrol.

The viewer having control over any more than six degrees of freedom makes the immersive experience a deity experiential POV. Since the six degrees of freedom cover all the possible independent motions in three-dimensional space, to get more than six degrees of freedom, one needs to be able to move in or through more dimensions. For example, the fourth dimension is time. So, if a VR experience allows the viewer to travel through time, then it is giving the viewer more than six degrees of freedom. Superstring Theory posits that the universe exists in ten dimensions (Williams, 2014). This leaves many future possibilities for what might fall under deity experiential POV. To focus on what might be most relevant, without getting too deep into Superstring Theory, a simple way to think about it is that, as deity, the viewer can experience the world as various people or things, teleport or time travel. It is helpful to provide a few examples of deity experiential POV. *U Turn,* a 360 narrative about what happens when a young female coder joins a male-dominated floundering startup, provides an excellent example of how the viewer can experience the world as various people or things. This award-winning piece, produced by Nathalie Mathe, gives the viewer a choice: in any given moment, simply by turning their head, the viewer can experience the story as a dedicated female coder or as a male tech entrepreneur. This choice won't affect the narrative path or outcome of the story—that's predetermined; it only affects how the viewer experiences the story. Jessica Kantor's *The Dinner Party* provides a useful example of teleportation as a means of providing experiential options. Hers is a gaze-based experience. This means that where the viewer is looking determines the vantage point from which they'll experience the next scene.

For example, if the viewer is focused on the hostess of the dinner party, they might be near her in the kitchen for the next scene. If they're focused on her ex-boyfriend, they might be situated near him, in the foyer, for the next scene. Either way, wherever the viewer is situated, the story of that next scene plays out the same. And finally, Flyover Zone Productions' *Rome Reborn* series, particularly *Rome Reborn: The Roman Forum* is a great example of how a viewer can have the experiential option of time travel. In the VR experience, which offers a guided tour of the Roman Forum, the viewer can toggle back and forth between the Roman Forum in ruins, as it is today, and the Roman Forum in its prime, as it was in Ancient Rome.

THE FOUR (OR MORE?) POV TIERS

This proposed taxonomy summarized in Figure 6 is a successful marriage of old and new concepts and terms. While there will be an initial learning curve, ultimately, it will greatly simplify and streamline conversations about existing and forthcoming 360 and/or VR content.

This taxonomy should allow for description of any possible XR experience. It also raises some questions. The first two tiers—narrative and visual—as used in relationship to VR seem to correlate to two of the five senses: hearing and sight. That is not entirely accurate. While examples of narrative that utilized voiceover were particularly helpful for showing the contrast between narrative and visual point of view, and while dialog is also a way in which people aurally consume narrative, auditory narrative is by no means the only method to achieve this VR POV. Narrative can be expressed in many other ways, such as by written text, or by physical action, and the list goes on. That leaves visual POV as the only purely sensory POV tier. However, it begs an important question: if there is a POV specifically for what one experiences visually, shouldn't there be a POV specific to each of the five senses? Yes, there should be.

The reason those were not laid out earlier is because use of them is incredibly uncommon and, in some cases, still technically impossible. But this doesn't mean that innovative storytelling using all five senses in a wide variety of ways won't happen in the future. The question, really, is not if, but why. For the right story, the various sensory POVs could prove to be valuable storytelling tools. And the era of XR storytelling has just begun; people are about to be able to tell stories that they could never tell before.

The other potential sensory POVs would include olfactory POV, tactile POV, gustatory POV and auditory POV. Olfactory POV is possible thanks to the innovations being done by folks like Jacquelyn Ford Morie and Simon Niedenthal, who have created scent devices that can pair with VR. First-person olfactory POV would involve a faithful scent map of the virtual scene so that the viewer would experience any smells present in the scene from the appropriate distance and at the appropriate strength. Third-person olfactory POV would be if the viewer smelled something completely unrelated to the scene at hand, like smelling the pungent bird guano of the seaside while inside a kitchen in the mountains where a chef is baking banana bread. And second person olfactory POV would be if the viewer smelled what another character in the scene were smelling; for example, in a scene that takes place in a bedroom, the viewer is looking through the closet—which may have the scent of mothballs—but the viewer doesn't smell mothballs and instead smells the rose that his or her companion in the scene is smelling, from where they're sitting next to the planter in the window box. This pattern of first, second and third person experience can be applied to all of the sensory POVs. In this way, the taxonomy presented here covers a wide range of possible XR experiences, experiences that transcend even what is possible in the real world.

USING THE TAXONOMY TO DESCRIBE 360 AND VR EXPERIENCES

It is certainly instructive to have all four or more POV tiers defined and explained. But how does one use them in practice to describe immersive experiences? This section will put theory into practice, applying the taxonomy for XR to specific pieces of immersive content.

The following abbreviations will allow for concise denotation:

Abbreviations
1PP = 1st person perspective*
2PP = 2nd person perspective
3PP = 3rd person perspective
e = embodied
d = disembodied
1N = 1st person narrative
2N = 2nd person narrative
3N = 3rd person narrative
N = Non-Entity
E = Entity
P = Participant
R = Robot
M = Mortal
D = Deity
If multiple sensory POVs are being used, it will be helpful to follow PP with the first letter of the relevant sensation: V (visual), O (olfactory), T (tactile), G (gustatory), A (auditory)

Examples

U Turn: *U Turn*, as discussed, is a live-action VR series set at a floundering tech startup. The first person visuals are complemented by first person narrative. This narrative is provided not by narration but by characters in the scene. The viewer's character does speak and because the first person narrative matches the first-person visuals, it is clear that *U Turn* is an embodied 1st person narrative. The viewer's character—either the female coder or the male tech entrepreneur—is acknowledged and interacted with, but has no agency, so the effectual POV is entity. However, the viewer does have agency when it comes to how they experience the scene, either as the female coder or the male tech entrepreneur. This is more than any human could do in real life; it is deity experiential POV.

e+1N+E+D = embodied 1st person narrative entity deity

The BizNest: *The BizNest* is a comedy that takes place in a co-working space where you are one of the members, so like *U Turn*, *The BizNest* is also embodied first person narrative entity. However, where *U Turn* allows the viewer to affect how they experience the scene, as a male or female, *The BizNest* aims to ground the viewer more completely in reality, using one scene to fill all 360 degrees and having the viewer's ability to affect how they experience the scene be in keeping with a person's ability to affect how they experience any given moment in life.

e+1N+E+M = embodied 1st person narrative entity mortal

Henry: *Henry* is an Emmy award-winning VR experience by Oculus Story Studio. It's the animated tale of a lonely Hedgehog celebrating his birthday and wishing for more. In this experience, there is voiceover narration, but it is not first person, it's third person. As such, it doesn't match the first person visuals, so the experience is disembodied third person narrative. As the viewer looks around in this experience, it becomes clear that they are not a character of any sort; they are not acknowledged or a part of the story, and they do not affect the scene in any way. The viewer is a non-entity. And, as far as how the viewer can affect their experience of the scene… well, their experience is not programmed—the viewer has the freedom to use one to six degrees of freedom—but they don't have the ability to teleport, travel through time or see the story unfold from the perspective of another character. The viewer's experiential POV is mortal.

d+3N+NE+M = disembodied 3rd person narrative non-entity mortal

Beat Saber: In *Beat Saber*, while there is no voiceover narration or dialog, there is a narrative: the player's progression in the game. How the player fares in the game is connected to their actions; the player's score matches up with what they are seeing and doing. Accordingly, the game experience is embodied first person narrative. Because the player can affect the scene and has agency, their effectual POV is participant. And because they can affect their experience of the scene using only 1-6 Degrees of Freedom, their experiential POV is mortal.

e+1N+P+M = embodied 1st person narrative participant mortal

The Dinner Party: In this 360 dramatic comedy short about a young woman throwing a dinner party to raise funds for her new company, the viewer is not a character. As such, *The Dinner Party* presents a third person narrative that the viewer witnesses first-hand—1PP visual, the default option—offering a third person disembodied narrative experience. Not only is the viewer not a character, their presence is never acknowledged, and they are unable to be seen by the characters in the story, so the effectual point of view is non-entity. However, the viewer does have some control over how they experience the story. Thanks to gaze-based technology built with game-engine based VR creator tools, where the viewer looks determines what vantage point they will view the next scene from. As a result, the viewer's effectual POV is deity.

d+3N+N+D = disembodied 3rd person narrative non-entity deity

Pokémon Go: In this popular AR experience, the viewer/player has a first person visual perspective and is experiencing the story world first-hand. They also have agency; the player can throw Poke Balls, catch Pokémon, battle other Trainers and more. In keeping with the fact that, as this game is actually Augmented Reality, or AR, it is played with the visuals overlaid on the physical world, the player cannot affect how they experience the game; they have a mortal experiential POV.

e+1N+P+M = embodied 1st person narrative participant mortal

Chronos: Gunfire Games' VR action roleplaying game has the player exist outside of the character he or she is controlling. As a result, it is a disembodied third person narrative experience. Because the player has agency, it is participant effectual POV. One interesting twist that *Chronos* has is that every time the player dies, they come back a year older. This aging actually shows up on the player's character as graying hairs and a wrinkling face. Because the player seemingly defies the rules of the real world by coming back from death and suddenly being and looking a year older when less than a year has passed, it is tempting to wonder if the experiential POV is deity. However, it is worth remembering that experiential POV is determined by the degree to which the player can control how they experience the scene. The player isn't controlling their aging. They are forcibly moved forward in time and they cannot move backward in time. Because the player has no agency as to how they experience time, the experiential POV is not deity. Rather, because they can affect their experience of the scene, but only using 1-6 degrees of freedom, the experiential POV is mortal.

d+3N+P+M = disembodied 3rd person narrative participant mortal

The Blu (Dreamscape Immersive): *The Blu* is one of the three social, location-based "adventures" with which Dreamscape, a VR experience company, launched. In *The Blu*, the viewer is one of several divers that plunges into the depths of the ocean on a mission to help reunite a family of whales. Wearing a virtual diver's suit and an actual haptic backpack, the viewer has an AquaScooter at his or her disposal to maneuver through the depths of the sea. Because the viewer is a character in the space and what they see is—and matches—their story, it is an embodied first person narrative experience. As hinted at by the mention that you have an AquaScooter, the viewer's character has agency. Another example of the viewer's agency that won't end up being a story spoiler is that if the viewer chooses to poke at any of the sea anemones in the underwater scene, the anemones will react to that touch and close up. The viewer does not, however, have the ability to affect their own experience of the story or scene by more than 6 degrees of freedom.

e+1N+P+M = embodied 1st person narrative participant mortal

Door No. 1: In Hulu's interactive comedy, the viewer is "Alex," who has returned to his high school for a reunion. As such, the 1st person narrative experience matches the visuals, making this an embodied first person narrative. The viewer is a character and, on top of that, has the agency to decide which of two paths he wants to take at various moments throughout the experience, making the viewer a participant. These decisions affect the story, but not the way the viewer experiences the story; the viewer experiences the story as a human would, in keeping with the laws of physics. As such, the experiential POV is mortal.

e+1N+P+M = embodied 1st person narrative participant mortal

Healium: Butterflies: Using a brain-wave-sensing headband, StoryUP Studios' VR experience and AR app encourages the viewer to think happy thoughts and rewards them by hatching virtual butterflies when the viewer successfully recalls a time when they felt love, joy or appreciation. The viewer is having a first-hand experience of the butterflies hatching and their visual experience matches the narrative of their brain-wave activity. The viewer's brain waves have an impact on the narrative of the scene—butterflies hatching or not hatching—so the viewer has agency. And the viewer can only affect how they experience the scene using 1-3 degrees of freedom, so the experiential POV is mortal.

e+1N+P+M = embodied 1st person narrative participant mortal

CONCLUSION

This taxonomy of immersive POV and story experience doesn't change what can be possible in VR. There's nothing that people can talk about by using this taxonomy that they couldn't talk about without it. However, using it provides several advantages. Without the taxonomy, it might take up to ten minutes or more to describe the functionality and POV of a VR experience; with this taxonomy, as seen in the above examples, that description shrinks down to five words and takes less than one minute. The advantages of this are multiple: it saves time, it gets everyone on the same page, and it promotes clarity of vision and of comprehension, making it easier for developers to move forward and for buyers to make decisions. It also gives VR creators a clear framework in which to think about what's possible in VR, as it provides a menu of options, a visible toolkit. Having these tools visible enables a creator to better make informed decisions, choosing a certain POV for the desired effect that it has on the viewer or player, rather than because it's the option that came to mind first or one of the few options that occurred to them. The common language provided by this taxonomy also facilitates critical literature and community, increasing transparency of ideas and the ability to communicate widely about the medium.

VR doesn't just allow us to look at the world in a new way, it allows us to look at the world in many new ways. And, in order to explore, discuss, recount, critique, develop and promote virtual reality successfully, we need to be able to communicate clearly about the various points of view that virtual reality gives us. This taxonomy facilitates that collective conversation.

REFERENCES

Bal, M. (1997). *Narratology: Introduction to the Theory of Narrative*. Toronto, Canada: University of Toronto Press.

Brown Institute for Media Innovation. (2018). *NeverEnding 360*. Retrieved from https://brown.columbia.edu/portfolio/neverending-360/

Cline, E. (2012). *Ready Player One: A Novel*. New York: Broadway Books.

Freedom du Lac, J. (2010). Guidebook that aided black travelers during segregation reveals vastly different D.C. *Washington Post*. Retrieved from http://www.washingtonpost.com/wp-dyn/content/article/2010/09/11/AR2010091105358.html

Genette, G. (1983). *Narrative Discourse: An Essay in Method*. Ithaca, NY: Cornell University Press.

Gorisse, G., Christmann, O., Amato, E., & Richir, S. (2017). First-and third-person perspectives in immersive virtual environments: Presence and performance analysis of embodied users. *Frontiers in Robotics and AI, 4*(33).

Guarino, B. (2016). Edge of Nowhere, Lucky's Tale, and the case for third person VR. *Inverse*. Retrieved from https://www.inverse.com/article/9996-edge-of-nowhere-lucky-s-tale-and-the-case-for-third-person-vr

Hayden, S. (2016). 'Sequenced' creates truly reactive storytelling in VR. *Road to VR*. Retrieved from https://www.roadtovr.com/vr-animated-series-sequenced-creates-truly-reactive-storytelling-vr/

Joyce, K. (2017). Review: Lucky's Tale: Playful Corp.'s Lucky's Tale defines what it means to be a platform videogame in VR. *VR Focus*. Retrieved from https://www.vrfocus.com/2016/03/review-luckys-tale/

mei.pi [Username]. (2014, June 25). *Real World Third Person Perspective VR/AR Experiment* [Video file]. Retrieved from https://www.youtube.com/watch?v=RgBeRP4dUGo

Miller, L. (2018). Hulu tests whether VR can be funny with new interactive 360 experience 'Door No. 1.' *IndieWire*. Retrieved from https://www.indiewire.com/2018/05/hulu-door-no-1-interactive-video-nora-kirkpatrick-1201968459/

Montgomery, R. A. (2011). *The Trail of Lost Time*. Chooseco, LLC.

Puschmann, M. (2016). Notes on Blindness, a virtual reality journey into the world of blindness. *The Drum*. Retrieved from https://www.thedrum.com/news/2016/10/21/notes-blindness-virtual-reality-journey-the-world-blindness

Rowling, J. K. (2007). *Harry Potter and the Deathly Hallows*. Bloomsbury.

Squiers, A. (2015). A Critical Response to Heidi M. Silcox's 'What's Wrong with Alienation?'. *Philosophy and Literature, 39*(1), 243–247. doi:10.1353/phl.2015.0016

Sundance Institute. (2016). Notes on Blindness. *Sundance Institute Projects*. Retrieved from https://www.sundance.org/projects/notes-on-blindness

Tarrant, J., Viczko, J., & Cope, C. (2018). Virtual reality for anxiety reduction demonstrated by quantitative EEG: A pilot study. *Frontiers in Psychology, 9*(1280). PMID:30087642

Turner, N. K. (2017). Virtual Reality + Digitizing Scent with Simon Niedenthal and Jacki Morie. *Art and Cake*. Retrieved from https://artandcakela.com/2017/07/18/virtual-reality-digitizing-scent-with-simon-niedenthal-and-jacki-morie/

Virtual Reality Oasis [Username]. (2018, October 11). *The Great C: The first 5 minutes of this cinematic virtual reality movie* [Video File]. Retrieved from https://youtu.be/lwL9FpnSlrk

Williams, M. (2014). A Universe of 10 Dimensions. *Universe Today*. Retrieved from https://phys.org/news/2014-12-universe-dimensions.html

ENDNOTES

[1]   As of the date of publication of this book, according to the film's website, http://www.noteson-blindness.co.uk, the *Notes on Blindness* VR experience is available for free on Samsung Gear.

[2]   As of the date of publication of this book, *52 Places to Go: Iceland* is available for free on the TimesVideo website and also on the NYTimes 360 app.

[3]   Author's discussion with Sean Liu on May 17, 2019.

[4]   Positron is a company that makes chairs designed specifically for fully immersive cinematic VR that move in tandem with the VR content.

Chapter 15

Location–Based Entertainment:
How Immersive Technology Can Make Us More Human

Leila Amirsadeghi
MESH, USA

ABSTRACT

This chapter goes on a journey through time, highlighting key milestones, present-day realities, and future possibilities in the unbounded world of location-based entertainment (LBE). It explores the constant human desire for connection and play and looks at the role immersive entertainment has played in getting us out of the house, thus encouraging social interaction and mental stimulation in the most unconventional of ways. The chapter explores the impact that this growing industry will have on the (traditional) entertainment, retail, hospitality, art and education spheres, and touches on the history and background of venues and players (old and new), demonstrating diversity, creativity, and inimitability in execution. By taking a look at the power of immersive storytelling, the authors touch on the future of location-based entertainment and its ability to inspire ideas, conversation, and community.

INTRODUCTION

Over the last 10-15 years, we have witnessed a growing addiction to our screens, from social media to video games. Technology has become a divider between people and the real world, resulting in a more disconnected and dysfunctional social discourse.

Human beings are by nature a social species, and connectivity is our core human need, vital to every aspect of our development. In his book, *Social: Why Our Brains Are Wired to Connect*, scientist Matthew Lieberman (2013) reaffirms that "our need to connect is as fundamental as our need for food and water."

With exponential growth in what has now been coined 'the experience economy,' we are seeing a move away from isolation, towards socially connected experiences. Over 70% of Americans believe that attending a live event or experience makes them feel more connected to other people, to their community and the world at large.

DOI: 10.4018/978-1-7998-2433-6.ch015

A study commissioned by Eventbrite, released in 2017, states 78% of Americans choose to spend their money on experiences versus stuff, preferring to accumulate memories over material things (Eventbrite, 2017). This fact is validated by the 70% increase in the US that consumers spent on live experiences over the last 30 plus years, an increase that will likely keep growing as we seek out more interactive, participatory experiences.

We want to be participants in our lived experiences, events and entertainment mediums. We want to be able to engage en masse, connect with a purpose and share the moment for inspiration, awareness—and more times than we'd care to admit—for pure vanity.

Living in a digital world, we crave real world connections to create memories over material experiences, a perspective shared across generations, and led by millennials. Our bar is set ever higher as we expect to have purpose-driven entertainment made available to us, especially at a time of intensified political debate across the globe, and an increasingly deteriorating environmental climate.

80% of Americans believe it's essential for people to come together in-person to promote positive change, and 84% believe that all sorts of events (not just political), can inspire positive change. (Eventbrite, 2017, p. 3)

These statistics continue to grow with the increasing popularity of location-based, immersive and experiential entertainment. The LBE market witnessed crazy growth between 2017 and 2019, with a significant number of LBEs coming to market in the US and abroad. We are seeing variety and quality through the evolution of existing, and the introduction of new, business models and experience types—many of which have been built around the notion of connection, community and play.

With the current political and socially charged climate in most democracies in America and Europe, our physical and social environment is left to deteriorate at a faster pace than has been witnessed in the last half-century. Growing divisions amongst the world's publics calls for new means of mediation of viewpoints, and transmission of new and better ideas. We need to look to immersive entertainment as a means to an end on several fronts: to platform ideas and dialogue and to catalyze and inspire change. Immersive entertainment gives us tools and platforms of opportunity to create experiences that evoke empathy, compassion and love in the most visceral of ways—by reconnecting with ourselves, with each other and with Mother Earth.

We are seeing new paradigms developing in entertainment, ones that are more immersive, interactive, collaborative, purpose-driven, influential and socially adaptive by design, connecting our lives at the intersections of storytelling, and human connection.

WHAT IS LOCATION-BASED ENTERTAINMENT (LBE)?

Location-Based Entertainment (LBE) is any form of entertainment that is experienced at a particular location that's not one's home. Also referred to as immersive entertainment, experiential entertainment or digital out-of-home entertainment, LBEs are diverse and can include family entertainment centers, multisensory digital experiences, theme parks and immersive art installations.

LBE was born from the traditional out-of-home entertainment (OOHE or OHE) industry, a label given to experiences housed at theme or amusement parks, as well as regional venues from cultural institutions to family entertainment centers.

LBE is most commonly used to describe companies and events that offer a wide variety of out-of-home immersive or interactive experiences. Whether describing the cinematic Virtual Reality (VR) experience *Carne y Arena,* by Alejandro G. Iñárritu, a multi-person, themed VR experience at *The VOID*, the interactive art park *Meow Wolf*, or the Instagram museum, *the Museum of Ice Cream*, LBE has become a catch-all for all types of immersive entertainment experiences, pop-up or permanent, small and large.

As a way to get people out of their living-rooms and into a social setting with friends, family and strangers, location-based entertainment venues deliver opportunities for connection, engaged play, personal creativity and a sense of community. Immersive entertainment is no longer about experiencing content in an alternative form, but rather becoming the content, living the story and interacting in ways that inspire and transform.

A Brief History

Out-of-Home/Location-Based Entertainment is not an invention of the 21st century, it dates back thousands of years. Early examples include the theaters of ancient Greece, and the Coliseum in Rome (Harrison, 1951).

Fast forward a thousand years to the launch of the Bartholomew Fair in 1133, considered to be an early precursor of the modern fairs: a place one could go to hear live music, see performers and puppet shows. It's remarkable that such destinations remained part of the scene for over 700 years (Cavendish, 2005).

The next wave in OOHE/LBE came with the advent of 'Pleasure Gardens' in cities across Europe, laying the groundwork for modern-day amusement parks, which feature theatrical performances, acrobatic shows, singing, food stalls, games and more. The most notable of these is Bakken. Launched in 1583 in Denmark, it is the world's oldest operating amusement park with over 150 attractions, still in operation today.[1]

In the world of cinema, the first Kinetoscope Parlor opened in 1894, allowing audiences to pay to watch different films on an array of kinetoscopes on site (Library of Congress, n. d.). Its wild popularity was what led to the birth of the modern movie theater just two years later.

About the same time, the world's first modern amusement parks opened, with Sea Lion Park, Coney Island, NY in 1895, and Blackpool Pleasure Beach, Blackpool, England, in 1896. The world's first theme park, Santa Claus Land, opened its gates in 1946 and Disneyland launched in 1955, in Southern California. Amusement parks are a melting pot of live entertainment, rides, games and more, while a theme park is a kind of amusement venue that has a core theme or group of themes, Disneyland, for example. Walt Disney Resorts and Universal Studios have since become the world's largest theme park operators, with Walt Disney World and Universal Studios Orlando, leading the way (Botterill, 1997; Davis, 1996).

From the amusement industry emerged the Family Entertainment Centers (FEC)—mini-amusement parks, often indoors either inside a theme park or at a stand-alone location. FECs target teenagers and families with young kids and can include a variety of entertainment-based attractions and activities, including traditional arcade games, dining, virtual reality, escape rooms, bowling alleys, miniature golf, movie theaters and laser tag (White Hutchison, n. d.).

According to Allied Market Research, the global family entertainment centers market was valued at $18.91 billion in 2017 and is projected to reach $40.81 billion by 2025, registering a CAGR of 10.2% during the forecast period (Rake, 2019).

Fast forward 50 years to the 2010s, when we see a rise in popularity for Escape Rooms with permanent, independent locations emerging outside of the family entertainment centers such as the world's first, SCRAP, launched in 2007 in Japan (Corkill, 2009). And the largest, Diefenbunker, located in Canada. There are over 10,000 escape rooms worldwide in operation today, with almost 25% located within the United States (CBC, 2016).

Referred to as the modern-day laser-tag, Location-Based Virtual Reality (LBVR) was born a few years later and made popular in 2016 with the launch of the VOID. This LBE segment has seen the fastest growth to date, with LBVR estimated to represent more than 10% of the total VR industry market size (Mordor, 2019). Other players dominating the global LBVR market today include Dreamscape Immersive, Zero Latency, Sandbox VR, Hologate, Spaces and VRStudios. Some LBVRs are designed to integrate seamlessly within an existing entertainment property like an amusement park or FEC, while others operate as stand-alone businesses inside of a retail or resort space.

LBVR went mainstream in 2018 with Dave & Buster's, who in partnership with VRStudios launched a number of IP-based experiences including *Jurassic World Expedition* and *Men In Black* in over 100 locations across the United States (Takahashi, 2018). 2016 also saw growth across other areas of location-based entertainment, with the successful launch of two very different immersive art experiences, Meow Wolf (Staugaitis, 2018) and the Museum of Ice Cream (Luckel, 2016), influential in cementing the experience and attention economies.

Combined with the success of LBVR, exponential improvements in immersive technology hardware, the sheer volume of pop-ups entering the market, and an increase in investment made into immersive entertainment companies, we have seen the global birth of a new generation in entertainment, one that has changed the face of the OOHE/LBE market, and which continues to grow exponentially today.

According to the 2019 Immersive Design Industry Annual Report, "2018 saw more than 700 new or updated immersive experiences in North America alone" (Immersive Design Industry, 2019, p. 14). An industry with a potential to surpass the motion-picture and video games markets with its rapid rate of growth and success within the next decades.

A New Generation of LBE is Born

As noted early in this chapter, connection with others is, and will continue to be, a priority for us as humans. New technology developed over the last 15 years has augmented the quantity, quality, frequency and level of engagement we can now have with others.

Social media and our addiction to online living, has empowered us to connect more often, widely and deeply through all digital devices we have at our disposal, from home or on the go. Immersive media has given us the ability to step inside other worlds and connect with story and character in new ways. Immersive technology creates a bridge between the real world and the digital world and expands our sense of reality to enable more meaningful connectivity and impactful experiences, shared and memorialized through social media. Location-based entertainment venues are the place for such experiences to exist.

To quote co-founder and CTO of Zero Latency, Scott Vandonkelaar: "We are finally abstracting the technology from the experience, so that you can truly focus on consuming the content with every one of your senses without the medium getting in the way. The more we can continue to push the technology out of the way while enhancing the seamlessness of human interaction, the more powerful immersive media will get" (personal email, Dec 12, 2019).

In the blink of an eye, the immersive, location-based entertainment industry has exploded, taking the attractions industry and consumer market by storm with experiences that run the gamut from escape games and virtual reality, to projection-mapped wonderlands, and interactive art exhibits. The popularity of entertainment that engulfs, engages and embodies audiences into storyworlds is on the rise. The people have spoken (with their pocketbooks), and they want more immersion, as evidenced by the steady decline in number of tickets sold in cinemas across the United States between 2007-2019: from 1,420,036,680 to 1,217,885,661—a drop of more than 15% (Nash, 2019).

The growth of both the 'experience and attention economies' is demonstrative of our dissatisfaction with passive media consumption (like cinema), which in turn is responsible for the booming immersive, location-based entertainment industry. Spearheaded by millennials, and swiftly followed by boomers, 75% of these social strata now choose to buy an experience, rather than a consumer product. They want more immersion, interactivity and ultimately, community—and they want to be able to share their adventures across social media, for the entire world to see.

The global Immersive Media market, estimated at $18.4B in 2018, is projected to grow to $179B by 2022, with the US leading the way with over 30% market share (NASSCOM, 2019, p. 4). In 2018, the immersive entertainment market was valued at 10% of the total value of the theme park industry that same year. At this pace, it could outgrow the motion picture business in the not too distant future.

The global location-based entertainment market reached over $1B at the end of 2018 and is projected to reach over $12B by 2023 according to a Greenlight Insights report published in 2018. With investment and spending on immersive entertainment & LBE exceeding people's expectations in 2019, this number could be much higher than originally estimated (Giardina, 2018).

Such positive growth is a combination of consumers increasing desire for experiences over things and rapid innovations made in immersive tech. At the current rate that new experiences are entering the marketplace, LBE will be seen as one of the fastest growing industries of all time—an industry that caters to ALL age groups and audience types, inspiring family and group-based outings, shared experiences and deeper bonding.

With nascent immersive technologies such as AR/VR/MR/XR becoming more ubiquitous, with costs decreasing and hardware improving and the promise of 5G and edge computing, with the evolution of wearables, and with companies like Apple, Qualcomm and Samsung introducing their version of smart glasses launching XR into the everyday consumer market, the location-based entertainment industry will continue to see colossal gains over the coming years.

An Experience Is an Irreplaceable Memory

A great LBE can

- Be a powerful storytelling platform, delivering emotive, visceral experiences that can create a lasting impression
- Introduce audiences to the magic of reality, bringing them one step closer to the beauty and joy the world has to offer
- Bring people closer together to create new connections with absolute strangers or tighter moments with friends, through collaborative, quest-based experiences, with or without the use of a head mounted display
- Open up our minds and imaginations

- Surprise and delight
- Incite play and bring out the inner child
- Inspire community and trigger action
- Be socially aware and shareable across class and division

From themed-attractions to XR technologies like AR/VR, projections, 360 video and everything in-between, we now have the ability to immerse audiences, young and old, together, in ever-changing story worlds rooted in fantasy, reality or a mix of the two.

Disney's latest attraction and addition to the *Star Wars* franchise, *Rise of the Resistance*, opened in December 2019. It puts visitors in the middle of a clash between the Resistance and the First Order. A mixed reality attraction, the ride integrates multiple systems with physical sets, screen-based media, audio-animatronics and projection-mapping, to submerge guests inside the movie and an element of the *Star Wars* universe. Hailed as the next generation in theme park rides, it sets a new bar in location-based entertainment with its size, scale and flawless integration of ride systems. Described as transportive, surprising and delightful, it cleverly brings together a number of complicated components to deliver experience in way never-before-done, surpassing Disney's own bar in innovation (Farkas, 2019a).

The accelerated rise of immersive, location-based entertainment is unprecedented. Even the once passive out-of-home entertainment experiences are reaping the benefits of the immersive revolution and its evolution. Where once artist, content and audience were separated, immersive places the experiencer squarely at the center of the tale, changing the relationship between audience and content/actor/artist/musician. Not only game-changing, it is influential in transforming many entertainment mediums in the process, including cinema, theater, museums, concerts, sporting events and stage shows, while introducing new models in art, education and retail, LBE benefits go far beyond mere entertainment.

The *War of the Worlds* immersive experience in London combines seated and free-roam VR with live actors, richly detailed physical sets, and various projection technologies (Willmott, 2019). Disney is building a cruise-ship that never physically leaves the dock, in the form of a *Star Wars* themed starship hotel where all the windows have been replaced with digital screens and live actors invite guests along on adventures (Farkas, 2019b).

Any kind of storytelling requires a certain level of suspension of belief. When immersive techniques are employed well, belief and disbelief melt away faster and more comprehensively than any other form of storytelling has achieved. The feeling of presence, which is unique to immersive entertainment, enables participants to truly feel a part of the story instead of a passive observer. This also allows for immediate empathy to be imparted on participants, as there is a feeling that whatever is happening, it is happening to them.

You cannot simply look away, as you're there in the thick of things.

The LBE revolution is a global phenomenon, with hundreds of installations, locations and pop-ups opening regularly across Asia, Europe, the Middle East, and the United States. This indeed is a space to watch. Let's look next at the many types of LBE available today.

THE LBE UNIVERSE

The LBE universe is big, broad and growing. Immersive, location-based entertainment has seen steady growth over the last 30 years, it is in the last 10 years that we have witnessed the explosion of this category. Today's LBE has become its own vertical, within which are multiple genres and experience types. These categories will continue to see steady growth as the technology advances and investment increases. A few examples within each category are provided, each representing a unique model within the genres. The company or attraction website is included in each example for access to direct information.

360 Video/Domes

Fulldome refers to immersive dome-based (360) video projection environments. A technology that has been around since the 1990s, fulldomes have become more popular in recent years, made so by location-based entertainment-use cases, from planetariums that deliver story-based educational experiences to immersive art shows integrating multiple technologies for mixed reality adventures.

Domes allow for immediate otherworldly immersion without the need for a headset of any kind. The very nature of enveloping the audience inside a spherical space filled with content delivers a powerful visceral experience. A dome is the perfect venue to create a suspension of disbelief when mixing realities that blend physical props, 360 video and XR technology to deliver a mobile interconnected, interactive experience that people can walk around in, engaging with the story, and with each other. Notable dome examples include:

- *MSG Sphere,* Las Vegas, NV. (www.msgsphere.com)

A new development by the Madison Square Garden Entertainment company, a 350-foot round dome, completely covered in and out with customizable LED panels and screens, 17,500 seats, and a 170,000 square foot display inside, is claimed to be the largest and highest resolution capable of 25M pixels. The outside canvas can become anything from a glowing globe to a soccer ball to celebrate the World Cup for example, displaying an experience of its own to the high-rise hotels and landing planes as they make their final approach into Las Vegas.

With the power of 360 video, the immersion of a dome and the resolution of the Sphere, the next generation of life-changing and transformational experiences is upon us. "The lines between the different types of immersive location-based entertainment are blurring and will continue to cross-pollinate in the future until they are difficult to tell apart any longer." states Aaron Pulkka, Senior Director of Interactive Design for MGM Sphere (Personal conversation & email, 1/4/2020).

- *Wisdome,* Los Angeles, CA. (www.wisdome.la)

Wisdome LA, self-described as a five-dome immersive art park in the heart of downtown Los Angeles, offers inimitable immersive art experiences where guests can see the art and interact with it. Using immersive technologies including AR, VR and 3D, visitors can take a cultural journey through mystical dimensions.

Since opening, visionary artist Android Jones' show *Samskara*, has been an anchor and popular experience at the park (Barrett, 2019). An award-winning 360 project show, interactive VR and augmented reality art installations, combines ancient Vedic wisdom with visionary art to deliver an almost ceremonial experience exploring self, and the cosmos. *Wisdome* plays host to a series of parties, concerts and art experiences that leverage the power 360 video to engage and immerse audiences.

Escape Rooms

Escape rooms are the fastest growing segment within immersive entertainment, with an industry valuation of $513.7M. A highly profitable business, the US escape room market saw a hockey stick level spike in the number of escape rooms, from 22 in 2014 to 2,300 in 2019 (Mallenbaum, 2018). An escape room or escape game, inspired by the 'escape-the-room' style video game in which a group of people work together to solve puzzles, find clues and (literally) escape the room. Immersive technologies have evolved the escape room from a physical to a digital experience, and in many cases, blending the two for a hybrid experience.

- *Dragonborn The Innkeeper's Son*. Vitoria, Spain. (www.dragonbornvitoria.es)

A 90-minute experience for two to five players, *DragonBorn Vitoria Escape Room* is a novel live escape experience developed by Mad Mansion.

Story: In *DragonBorn* you will be put in the shoes of a group of adventurers who will have to try to discover the mysteries surrounding a strange inn located on a remote mountain in a fantastic world inhabited by magical beings. The enigmatic innkeeper has promised a great reward to anyone who finds his lost son, who disappeared one stormy night, but it will not be as easy as it seems since you are not the first to try.

- *Ghosthunter Brandon Darkmoor*. Berlin, Germany. (www.the-room-berlin.com)

A 75-minute experience for two to four players, *Ghosthunter Brandon Darkmoor* is a traditional escape room laden with puzzles and clues for audiences from 18 and up.

Story: An internship with the famous ghost hunter Brandon Darkmoor—that was your plan. You didn't expect to be sent off to a case on your first day though. In the past, the building of "THE ROOM" was part of the Carl Bonhof clinic. This asylum experienced a horrible fire in 1987. Everybody survived—except for one person—the former opera singer Anna Morana, who haunts the basement ever since.

- *The Man from Beyond*. Houston, TX. (strangebirdimmersive.com)

A 90-minute experience for four to eight players, The Man from Beyond is an original story combining immersive theater and an escape room.

Story: Madame Daphne cordially invites you to a private séance to contact the spirit of Harry Houdini. But all is not what it seems, and when the ghost appears, things take a dramatic turn. Unravel mysteries a century in the making, and you could find yourselves doing more than escaping a room.

Family Entertainment Centers

A family entertainment center, fun center, indoor amusement park, indoor theme park and other names that it is nowadays referred to as, is a mini-amusement park usually indoors, targeted to teenagers and families with small children, promoting an all day long experience that includes shows, games, food and in some cases, alcoholic libations available for the parents!

These FECs can be standalone or part of a larger amusement/theme park. Smaller than traditional amusement parks, FECs can most commonly be found in regional areas spread across smaller cities and suburbs made for locals, not tourists.

- *Dave & Busters*, Dallas, TX. (www.daveandbusters.com)

Dave & Buster's is a restaurant and entertainment, also referred to as a "barcade" business, hosting a sports bar, restaurant and video arcade, including the VR attractions of today. Dave & Buster's mission includes offering fun, amazing food and drink, and ensuring they carry the latest and greatest in games and experiences.

- *Joypolis*, Tokyo, Japan. (https://tokyo-joypolis.com/language/english/)

Joypolis is a chain of indoor amusement parks operated by Sega in Japan and China, featuring arcade games, attractions, and amusement rides based on Sega IP. Joypolis locations are large scale entertainment properties with retail, food and beverage and arcades throughout.

Its main attractions are Sega's medium and large-scale amusement rides and attractions, such as bumper cars, indoor roller coasters, and virtual reality simulators, which the company began designing and building in the late 1980s.

Immersive/Interactive Art

A new generation of art exhibits using digital technologies to immerse audiences into the art and mind of the artist is taking the art and entertainment world by storm.

- *ZeroSpace*, New York, New York. (www.zerospace.co)

ZeroSpace is a 25,000 sq. ft. immersive art playground showcasing a collection of large-scale installations a set of digital artists from around the world. In addition, *ZeroSpace* is an immersive theater show placing the audience at the center of a digital multiverse, with meta story and narrative, a choose your own adventure style exploration in an extended reality world of art.

Immersive Bazaar

A new sub-category, a first with the upcoming launch of Area15, the entertainment complex or immersive bazaar combines eating, shopping and play in a highly designed and curated space that takes you into another dimension— think Amusement Park or Family Entertainment Center meets Mall. The

Immersive Bazaar invites audiences to spend all day lost inside unique and interactive art, culinary and fashion experiences.

- *Area15*, Las Vegas, NV. (www.area15.com)

Area15, an entertainment offering that blends immersive and interactive art, retail, food and beverage and live music over 120,000 square feet is opening late in Las Vegas in the latter part of 2020. Self-described as Art, Entertainment and Retail redefined into an 'Immersive Bazaar,' Area15 is a canvas for artists to show their work.

The mall of the future, filled with a variety of immersive entertainment properties and activations, from Escape Rooms to LBVR and everything in between, including an axe throwing station, Meow Wolf and a zip line, Area15 has something for everyone.

"The blurring boundaries between commerce and experience is the future. Despite all the digital world has to offer, consumers still crave physical connection and real human interaction, and they are increasingly gravitating toward new artful forms of entertainment that provide immersive experiences, authentic connections, and real emotions. I believe the new retail landscape is the intersection of commerce and experiential entertainment designed with engaging narratives in "bricks and mortar" settings that will truly resonate with today's sophisticated consumer." – Winston Fisher, CEO of AREA15 and partner at Fisher Brothers (Personal email, 1/9/2020)

Immersive Dining

Immersive dining is considered to be the modern-day dining theater. These experiences can combine many elements physical, projections, lights, actors, interactive storytelling, XR technologies, smell, touch and of course, food, resulting in multisensory gastronomic experiences that evoke emotions and memories that go well beyond the food.

- *Beetlehouse*, New York, NY & Los Angeles. (www.beetlehousela.com)

Described as a "Halloween party with a Burtonesque feel, curated by Alfred Hitchcock, with a 90s goth band on stage and everyone is wearing weird costumes," *Beetlehouse* is a pop-up restaurant with locations in New York City and Los Angeles.The experience in New York is more intimate with up to 45 guests, whereas Los Angeles is a much larger production, a la Hollywood, catering for 500 people.

- *Cow by Bear*, San Diego, CA. (https:cowbybear.com)

Cow by Bear is a very different kind of dinner party experience, located across different, secret locations in San Diego. Taking place on weekends, the experiences bring together 14 diners around a delicious meal cooked by a bear, an Alaskan brown bear.

With a backstory around Chef Bear and his pop-up dining events, the Food by Bear dinner series was born in May 2019, highlighting chapters from a cookbook with the same name, immersive guests inside the stories while serving dishes from the book, the chapters or individual experience themes run for two months before switching up.

- *F.E.A.S.T.,* San Francisco, CA. (www.electricplayhouse.com)

An acronym for Fine dining, Entertainment, Art, Story and Technology, *F.E.A.S.T.* is an immersive and interactive dining experience, launched in San Francisco in 2019, *F.E.A.S.T.* is a collaboration between Electric Playhouse and Onedome.

Combining three to five courses with 32 guests, immersive video, interactive projections and sound, *F.E.A.S.T.* is a great example of a social dining experience with its series of thematic narratives integrating food and art, operated as pop-up and permanent installations across the United States (Barmann, 2019).

- *Le Petit Chef*, Dubai, UAE. (www.dinnertimestory.com)

Le Petit Chef has made waves with a variety of 3D projection-mapping story experiences, integrated into a two-hour dining experience. At the bleeding edge of interactive storytelling, Le Petit Chef is a culinary storytelling experience delivered through immersive content, flavors, ingredients, tastes and sounds over six courses, this delightful experience explores the places visited by Marco Polo on his travels through the Silk Road.

Immersive Theater

A type of intimate, personal entertainment characterized by interaction between performers and audience members has become increasingly popular in recent years. The first time the world of theater placed the audience at the center of the story, effectively enveloping them in the tale was in 1981 with Tamara by John Krizanc, a play about the painter Tamara de Lempicka (Isenberg, 1989).

Immersive theater allows spectators to follow the story or character of their choice, not always being able to experience the whole play, and certainly not at once. A choose your own adventure guided by actors, the medium eliminates the separation between actor and audience, and places the audience at the center of the story, a player rather than observer.

- *Accomplice*, New York, NY. (www.accomplicetheshow.com)

Tom and Betsy Salamon's unique adventure—part interactive theater, part scavenger hunt, part walking tour—draws participants into an amusing web of puzzles and intrigue. You can choose between the three-hour New York tour, which takes participants through various neighborhoods of lower Manhattan, or the two-hour Village tour, which travels through quirky Greenwich Village. Groups of as many as 11 people are booked in every half hour.

- *Punchdrunk: Sleep No More*, New York, NY. (www.mckittrickhotel.com)

Sleep No More, the longest running immersive theater production in the world, based out of the McKittrick Hotel in New York City, is loosely modeled after the noir genres, Shakespeare's Macbeth and Hitchcock films with references to the 1697 Paisley witch trials. Punchdrunk's *Sleep No More* continues to be the longest continuously running immersive theater production in the United States with earnings of over $4.9M to date (Immersive Industry Design, 2019, p.15).

Immersive Theme Parks

In recent years, we have seen the theme park industry evolve their approach to rides and attractions, focusing their attention on more interactive experiences that go beyond immersive audiences into the story universe, treating them as an active participant and part of the story.

Through Disney's *Star Wars Galaxy's Edge*, we've witnessed the increasing complexity of environments, details, story, interactivity and technology integration, all designed to support the theme and narrative. A fully immersive experience that surrounds guests with the sights, smells, sounds and characters of the Star Wars Universe.

A new kind of theme park emerged in 2018 with Evermore, no rides, no attractions, instead a storybook world with highly designed physical environments, interactive storytelling with live actors and immersive tactics.

The same popularity and growth patterns are being seen in the area of haunted attractions, with over 300% growth between 2013 and 2017, when it was valued at over $1B. Traditional walk-through or ride-through haunted experiences have expanded to include live actors, immersive technologies and interactive content (Immersive Industry Design, 2019, p.14).

The American Haunts website (https://www.americahaunts.com) states the following facts on the industry:

We estimate there are over 1,200 haunted attractions charging admission fees to their events. We additionally estimated that there are over 300 amusement facilities producing some sort of Halloween or Haunted House event such as an amusement park or family fun center. Lastly there are over 3,000 charity attractions that open for one day on Halloween or one or two weekends in October produced by a local charity group.

- *Castle of Chaos*, Midvale, UT. (www.castleofchaos.com)

Castle of Chaos 20-year old experience, offers overnight extreme haunts that tests the mental and physical stamina of participants across its multilevel, twisting adventure experience.

- *Evermore*, Pleasant Grove, UT. (www.evermore.com)

Evermore Park is an amusement park set against the backdrop of Evermore Village, themed on older European cities, visitors can interact with characters, chase down adventures and seek out quests and become a part of the storyworld.

- *Knotts Scary Farm*, Buena Park, CA. (www.knotts.com)

Knott's Scary Farm or Knott's Halloween Haunt is a seasonal Halloween event at Knott's Berry Farm in Buena Park, California, filled with haunt-themed rides and attractions and said to be the first, largest and longest-running Halloween event to be held at a theme park.

- *Star Wars: Galaxy's Edge*, Anaheim, CA. (www.disneyland.com)

Star Wars: Galaxy's Edge is a 14-acre themed area inspired by the Star Wars franchise at Disneyland and Disneyworld locations. Opened in 2019, with a series of theme attractions launching, it is considered Disney's most ambitious project yet.

Instagram Museums

Since the successful launch of the Museum of Ice Cream in 2016, a large number of pop-up and permanent Instagram-friendly installations have come to market, the largest portion of which have been in the US.

Though many of these experiences are deemed vacuous, their success is undeniable. A success driven by millennials and their influence on the rise of the experience economy and the selfie generation, needing to document and share their experiences. People want to take photos of themselves in front of "artistic or art" environments, though their definition is subjective in this case.

The minds behind such pop-ups and businesses have taken advantage of this new consumer behavior to launch a new sub-segment, the Instagram Museum, taking the LBE market by storm. And why wouldn't they take advantage, since its opening in 2016, the Museum of Ice Cream has earned over $30M in revenues and closed a Series A of $40M with a valuation of $200M in August 2019 (Roof, 2019).

Some pop-ups brand themselves as museums, and others shy away from the term, but they're all exhibits of sorts that are also mostly a series of backdrops for Instagram.

Though many have been launched around the subject of food, we are seeing more culturally-driven activations like Sneakertopia, a large-scale immersive experience placing audiences inside the world sneakers, the history and the influences from pop-culture, fashion and entertainment, to the celebrities within. Instagram Museums as a concept could be leveraged by brands to bring immersive audiences into their worlds, products and branding, and are a great way to drive affinity and engagement.

- *Candytopia*, Miami, FL. (www.candytopia.com)

This pop-up interactive art installation celebrates the vibrant colors and flavors of our favorite sugary delights across over a dozen environments, from flying unicorn pigs to a marshmallow tsunami.

- *Museum of Ice Cream*, San Francisco, CA. (www.museumoficecream.com)

Described in *NY Ma*gazine as, "a sprawling warren of interactive, vaguely hallucinatory confection-themed exhibits: brightly colored rooms with flattering lighting that contain, among other things, a rock-candy cave, a unicorn, and a swimming pool of rainbow sprinkles, now Instagram-influencer-infamous."

- *Sneakertopia*, Los Angeles, CA. (www.sneakertopia.com)

A celebration of one of the most unique cultural phenomenons of this generation. *Sneakertopia* brings guests along the journey of what started as an article of clothing and turned into a global culture. Through immersive art installations, the audience is encouraged to step into the world of sneakers and all of its connected cultures—sports, music, film, art, design, fashion. Ultimately, guests are empowered to put their own footprint on each scene. This is a sneaker utopia.

Like stepping into the history of sneaker culture, this fully enveloping storyboard mural brings you through the deep, multi-faceted journey—from the first Converse All Stars in 1917 to the debut of the first Jordans in 1984 to the prevalence of limited-edition retailers and resellers of today. Once inside the mural, you will notice a sketch of a 1980s retro TV set light up with an intro video that visually narrates the transition of sneaker to culture.

Location-Based Augmented Reality (LBAR)

The most nascent of LBEs as head mounted display (HMD) technology has not been readily available or cost-effective, and mobile-AR not yet immersive enough for location-based experiences, this segment has been lagging behind the others.

However, with continuous improvements to the technology and more penetration into the consumer market, we will see a significant rise in LBAR experiences. Microsoft, first-to-market with its HoloLens in 2016, and released its latest version, the HoloLens 2, at the end of 2019. With improved field-of-view, anchoring and tracking capabilities, the HoloLens 2 is the leading market technologically when it comes to AR goggles.

Another player dominant market player is Magic Leap, who first released their HMD in late 2018, and who's focus has been on the development of content and experiences for their platform, coined the *magicverse*, which they hope to make accessible by any device, not just their own, in years to come.

Magic Leap and AT&T launched a *Game of Thrones* experience ahead of the premiere of the show's final season at select AT&T stores, *The Dead Must Die: A Magic Leap Encounter*, though not ground-breaking as far as LBAR goes, did demonstrate how immersive brand marketing and experiential activations can become the driver for consumer adoption. It also enabled a large number of the consumer market to try out HMD AR for the first time.

There are currently very few types of LBAR experiences across the US and Asia, but the ones that do exist, demonstrate a breadth of event type and use of technology.

- *HADO*, Tokyo, Japan. (www.meleap.com)

HADO is the combination of motion sensor, smartphone, AR (Augmented Reality) tech, and sports that creates a whole new experience coined Techno Sports by its creators. A high-impact experience, HADO gets users hearts racing and blood pumping bringing out the competitive edge of players.

HADO players run freely within real-world arena battles, wearing wireless head mounted displays and wrist motion sensors, using only gestures to unleash super powered projectiles on opponents.

- *The Chainsmokers AR Concert*, San Francisco, CA. (www.thechainsmokers.com)

A progressive and game-changing approach to mobile-AR at a live concert, where artist and audience, and audience and audience were connected at different times during the show. With the ability to view, create and collaborate on AR content, this event signals a pivotal moment in live experience engagement with the advent of 5G and the possibilities it brings into the LBE space (Reichard, 2019).

Location-Based Virtual Reality

Out of all the sub-categories, LBVR is by far the most expansive, has its own sub-genres and can be loosely organized as Gaming, Art, Education, Film and Music, examples of which can be found below. According to Kevin Vitale, CEO of VRStudios, it seemed clear that the LBE market could be a driver in the adoption of VR technology for two important reasons:

1. Investment in technologies, products and content to make experiences that can scale. Meaning the same content must be able to run in volume to be financially successful, and LBE has the available market to do so.
2. It can begin to monetize immediately with available and loyal LBE customers willing to pay for amazing experiences. (Personal Communication & email, December 12, 2019)

The popularity of LBVR is undeniable; and it was backed-up by some incredible events in 2019:

*   Sandbox VR received upwards of $80M in funding by the end of 2019
*   Zero Latency exceeded one million plays in August 2019
*   Hologate hits 5M players, worldwide
*   The VOID has teamed up with mall operator Unibail-Rodamco-Westfield (URW) to open 25 new outposts in the U.S. and Europe by 2022

Some of the world's leading LBVR companies include Dreamscape, Exit Reality, Hologate, Nomadic, Omni by Virtuix, SandboxVR, Spaces, The VOID, VRStudios and Zero Latency. We will next look at some of these.

Carne y Arena (Flesh & Sand), Multiple locations. (https://carneyarenadc.com/)

Oscar-winning (Special Achievement Academy Award) *Carne y Arena*, Spanish for Flesh and Sand, is a 2017 American short virtual reality project written and directed by filmmaker, Alejandro Iñárritu, which premiered at the Cannes Film Festival that year (Tapley, 2017).

Created in collaboration with ILMxLAB, Legendary Entertainment and the Fondazione Prada in Italy, the installation toured globally hosted at prestigious cultural institutions including the Prada Foundation in Milan, LACMA (Los Angeles County Museum of Art) and the Smithsonian in Washington D.C.

Revered for its innovative tactics and politically-charged story, this incredibly emotional journey, immerses the participant at the US/Mexico border along with several others (real immigrants attempting to cross the border) captured on film. Beyond being immersed in the environment, the viewer connects viscerally to the characters and story through sensory tactics such as wind, to mimic a helicopter above, or touch, having had to remove shoes and socks before stepping into the experience, the viewer finds themselves walking on the same ground as their fellow immigrants.

*   *Chained: A Victorian Nightmare* (www.becomechained.com)

A hair-raising VR adaptation of Charles Dickens's *A Christmas Carol,* the audience is dropped into the center of the story and presented with an avant-garde representation of interactive storytelling. Between the haunting nature of the story, 360-degree immersion through VR, integrated physical props, sensory tactics (like smell and heat), cinematic animation and live actors. Chained: A Victorian Nightmare takes you on a journey of deep self-reflection, compelling you to confront your past, present and future.

As noted in a recent article in *No Proscenium, the Self-Styled Guide to Everything Immersive,* "Unlike most other VR experiences, immersive VR theater allows audience members to interact inside of VR in real time with *both performers and physical objects* to create a sense of deep immersion and presence" (Yu, 2019).

If the combination of Immersive + VR + Real People + Haptics in a live experience can be so incredibly powerful to affect and impact its audience this much, imagine its applications beyond entertainment. Such visceral, emotionally-charged and visually stimulating methodologies can be used in areas beyond entertainment such as mental health, where a condition such as PTSD can be more quickly, effectively and scalably treated.

- *Dreamscape Immersive*, Los Angeles, CA. (www.dreamscapeimmersive.com)

Currently featuring four adventures, including "DreamWorks Dragon Flight Academy", a collaboration with the movie studio and the first popular entertainment IP-driven title.

Founded by entertainment industry veterans with deep roots in the movie business, Dreamscape Immersive venues began rolling out in December 2018.

- *Hologate*, Munich, Germany. (www.hologate.com)

Hologate creates multi-user immersive media platforms for location-based entertainment that easily integrate with venues like family entertainment centers, laser tag bowling or cinemas. Hologate has over 300 locations in 30 countries and has served over five million customers.

Following the success of Hologate Arena, the company has launched Hologate Blitz—a motion simulator platform designed for flying, racing and even underwater VR experiences.

- *Miro Shot,* Paris, France *(*www.miroshot.com)

With a global collective of multidisciplinary creatives, Miro Shot is paving the way for accessibility and innovation in live performance with immersive technology. CONTENT, the live immersive concert by Miro Shot, presents an experience like never before in a showcase of the latest technology.

In these shows, the audience enters a room filled with projection mapping, digital art, VR headsets, and a stage. With VR headsets on, the audience is immersed in an audiovisual journey as the band plays live, the music augmented with haptics, custom scents, and dreamscape visuals to blend the concept of being physically present in the non-physical world of VR.

The band first tested this notion in 2017 in underground performances in cinemas and warehouses across Europe, and at the Institute of Contemporary Art in Amsterdam where attendees would look at their hands to see if they were real or not.

- *VRStudios*. Seattle, WA. (www.vrstudios.com)

"In terms of using immersive technology (in my case, VR) to make us "more human," the first step might be to define what it means to be more/or less human. From my point of view, one of the most important characteristics is interactivity and social engagement with other humans, not just digital media and LED screens." Kevin Vitale, CEO (Personal Email, Dec 12, 2019).

VRstudios is a leading provider of commercial-VR systems, technology and integrated VR attractions, built expressly for the LBE enterprise. With a broad portfolio of original VR attractions, custom-branded attractions and high-profile IP assets, VRStudios platforms are installed in over 100+ locations in the United States.

VRstudios creates virtual reality experiences delivered as a complete commercial solution that is serious business and new revenue for location-based entertainment operators. VRstudios offers premium wireless attractions that are modular and flexible, integrating its own innovative Attraction Management Platform (AMP) technology and portfolio of exceptional quality content titles with the best compute and VR hardware from market-leading manufacturers.

- *Zero Latency*. Melbourne, Australia. (www.zerolatencyvr.com)

The first-to-market with free-roam, multiplayer, VR entertainment, Zero Latency was founded by Tim Ruse, Scott Vandonkelaar and Kyel Smith. Zero Latency opened the world's first VR entertainment venue, in Melbourne, Australia in August 2015. Today, Zero Latency has over 40 locations worldwide.

"There is a simple key to creating great immersive entertainment experiences and while it isn't complex in theory it takes practice to get right because it affects everything. To make an amazing and memorable experience, your players need to feel like they are the best or even better version of themselves. We don't enter an immersive experience to replicate the real world, we want to exceed it," says Scott Vandonkelaar, Co-founder & CTO (personal email, December 12, 2019).

Mixed Reality Experiences

Mixed Reality Experiences are ones that combine the physical and virtual elements of an experience in novel ways that enhance the sense of presence in an alternate space.

- *The Unreal Garden*. San Francisco, CA. (www.enklu.com)

Though also an example of a location-based augmented reality experience, The Unreal Garden can best be described as a 'mixed reality' experience as it integrates the digital and real worlds in ways that enable a greater suspension of disbelief. A collaboration between Enklu and Onedome and built on the Enklu platform, *The Unreal Garden* launched in San Francisco in October 2018, and is the first-to-market large-scale multiplayer augmented reality experience using numerous technologies to deliver a fully immersive, interactive social experience with collaboration and connection at the core.

Blending physical forestscapes, spatial sound, interactive projections, haptics and immersive augmented reality using the Microsoft HoloLens, *The Unreal Garden* invites 40 plus guests into a world filled with magical flora and fauna. By bridging the physical and virtual in a social environment where players can see all the layers of reality on top of one another, as well as see and interact with other guests, you can deliver a highly impactful visceral experience.

A 6,000 square foot pop-up of *The Unreal Garden* was brought to this year's E3 (Electronic Entertainment Expo), a video game conference held in Los Angeles annually, hosted by the Electronic Software Association (ESA), with over 6,000 attendees experiencing the installation over the three-day conference (Enklu 2019).

VR Arcades

Virtual reality arcade (VRcade) is exactly that, a location filled with single and multiplayer virtual reality games. China had an estimated 3,000 such sites in 2016 and the market was forecast to grow 13-fold by 2021, to $782M (Lan, 2019).

- *Headrock VR*, Sentosa, Simgapore. (www.headrockvr.sg)

Using state-of-the-art virtual reality technology, leading South Korean production company Mediafront launched an interactive digital theme park at Resorts World.

- *CTRL V*. Waterloo (Ontario), CA. (www.ctrlv.ca)

Ctrl V is North America's first virtual reality arcade, with over 15 locations, Ctrl V has a goal to bring VR to the masses. Ctrl V was among the very first operational VR arcade business in North America, with a couple of other US companies opening VR arcades shortly after.

SHOWCASE

Let's take a trip to visit an eclectic mix of venues with diverse offerings of experiences and activities. From household names to new-to-market, we explore the magic world of modern immersive, location-based entertainment along with some personal author's notes.

- *THE VOID*, Lindon, UT. (www.thevoid.com)

Launching in 2016 with the term, *hyper reality,* to describe a new generation of immersive VR, one that plays to the senses, the VOID has opened 16 locations in four countries, with another 14 countries in the works across the U.S. and Europe. The VOID is well known for its high-profile IP-based franchises their experiences are themed on. The VOID combines cutting-edge VR technology, sound, immersive 3D visuals, physical environments and multisensory effects to place players inside the story universe, as an active participant in the experience.

The VOID debuted with a *Ghostbusters*-themed experience at Madame Tussaud's in New York City in 2016, quickly launching multiple locations and experiences worldwide with *Secrets of the Empire.* Through its partnership with ILMxLAB, The VOID and Disney have collaborated iconic-IP themed experiences, including *Star Wars, Marvel Cinematic Universe* and *Wreck-It-Ralph.*

"Location based entertainment has been a passion of mine since I was very young. Ultimately, I wanted to transport people beyond the veil of a grey world and into a world of color, magic, and wonder. I would argue that this sort of transcendent (if transitory) teleportation of guests is the final goal of every LBE venue," states Curtis Hickman, Co-founder & CCO (personal email, January 4, 2020).

Author's Note: I grew up with the *Star Wars* franchise, with my first cinematic experience in 1980 with *Empire Strikes Back*, I immersed myself in the *Star Wars* universe with toys, books and films. I would later find myself one step closer to the world in my agency life, building marketing campaigns and experiences for both film and video games, collaborating with the studios for theatrical and home entertainment. You can imagine my mind blown when first experiencing the VOID, *Secrets of the Empire*, now at the heart of the story and able to participate inside of a world that has played a significant role throughout my life. It also happened to be my first experience in immersive VR, and the moment that I fell in love with the bridging of the virtual and the real.

- *Meow Wolf,* Santa Fe, NM. (www.meowwolf.com)

Meow Wolf is an arts collective and entertainment group based in Santa Fe, New Mexico, and has earned over $24M from more than 1.5 million visitors since opening the *House of Eternal Return* in 2016 (Immersive Design Industry, 2019, p. 14). *The House of Eternal* is a multi-layer (physical) immersive art installation with over 100 artists contributing designs, to create a labyrinth of spaces and rooms that deliver a different experience to the voyeur as it does to the gamer looking for the deeper narrative and story thread, uncover an alternate-reality game of sorts. The LBE also hosts an event space, a cafe/bar and children's learning and art center.

Partially funded by George R.R. Martin (who now serves as its "chief world builder"), the art collective Meow Wolf's installation environment/fun house in Santa Fe, complete with secret passages and a labyrinthine back story, has quickly exploded into something that has slipped out of the category of art and into a whole other new thing. In the brief years since the debut of the *House of Eternal Return*, the "Meow Wolf Model" has quickly spread, with the group opening massive, multi-million-dollar environments in other cities (Davis, 2020).

Since launching *Kaleidoscape*, a dark ride, at Elitch Gardens in Denver (also the location of a permanent venue opening in 2021), Meow Wolf has plans to open other locations in Las Vegas, Nevada, at Area15, Washington D.C. and Phoenix, which will also have a Meow Wolf-themed hotel.

Author's Note: Having visited the *House of Eternal Return* a few times, I was pleasantly surprised to discover something new each time. The attention to detail is extraordinary, the depth of story and connectivity between every piece, remarkable. There is nothing quite like it and very hard to describe, though if I had to hazard a try, I would say: mash-up Lewis Carroll's vision with *Alice in Wonderland*, Roald Dahl's imagination with *Willy Wonka*, the multidimensional story in Erin Morgernstern's *The Night Circus*, peppered with psychedelic nuances you'd expect from Timothy Leary, and otherworldly creations that might exist in a Tim Burton film. A sort of Burning Man in a 20,000 square foot building, my advice would be to go and experience it for yourself, nothing substitutes for the experience, and if you go, be sure to visit a couple of times, going deeper each time.

"We create an opportunity for people to be explorers, and to be scientists," he said. "When you come inside of a Meow Wolf exhibition, you're finding clues, you're discovering rooms, you're venturing into unknown spaces. That excites a part of humans that we have long forgot about. At the heart of it, we're all scientists." Vince Kadlubek, co-founder & CEO (Sutton, 2018).

Author's Note: Having visited the *House of Eternal Return* a few times, I was pleasantly surprised to discover something new each time. The attention to detail is extraordinary, the depth of story and connectivity between every piece, remarkable. There is nothing quite like it and very hard to describe, though if I had to hazard a try, I would say: mash-up Lewis Carroll's vision with *Alice in Wonderland*, Roald Dahl's imagination with *Willy Wonka*, the multidimensional story in Erin Morgernstern's *The Night Circus*, peppered with psychedelic nuances you'd expect from Timothy Leary, and otherworldly creations that might exist in a Tim Burton film. A sort of Burning Man in a 20,000+ square foot building, my advice would be to go and experience it for yourself, nothing substitutes for the experience, and if you go, be sure to visit a couple of times, going deeper each time.

- *Two Bit Circus*, Los Angeles. (www.twobitcircus.com)

Two Bit Circus is a new concept—blending amusement park, carnival and arcade in the most unique of ways. Self-described as a "micro-amusement park," *Two Bit Circus* is admission-free with a pay-to-play attraction model using a reloadable Playing Card.

With a vision to bring play to the world and help people "find their fun," Two Bit Circus is beautifully designed space in the heart of the arts district in Downtown Los Angeles with plans to expand nationally and internationally with multiple locations due to open in coming years. 38,000 square feet bringing together VR, Escape Rooms, an interactive social club, a modern-take on the carnival midway, an immersive arcade of digital goodness and, a bar and restaurant, the park offers hours of fun that keeps people coming back.

Brent Bushnell, Two Bit's CEO says "I'm excited for LBE to get more personalized, immersive, and persistent. The most magical moments in immersive theater are when the production responds to you personally be it one on one time with an actor, a special event, or content customized to you. As technology gets better, conversational agents, AI and robotics will help to provide these personalizations for a fraction of today's costs" (Personal Email Jan 2, 2020).

Author's Note: Two Bit Circus has reimagined fun in ways that keep you on premise for hours! Going to Two Bit is like being a kid again, you get to be silly, play all day long and end it with a nice cocktail before heading home, so much fun! Their unique take on the escape room, which they call story rooms, blend the traditional with digital to immerse you into fun, themed environments. An awesome night out with friends or a great space to host an event, it has become a favorite go-to of mine in LA.

- *teamLab*, Tokyo, Japan. (www.teamlab.art/en)

teamLab is an art collective and interdisciplinary group of ultra-technologists whose collaborative practice seeks to navigate the confluence of art, science, technology, design and the natural world. Various specialists such as artists, programmers, engineers, CG animators, mathematicians and architects form teamLab.

Isolde Brielmaier, curator, International Center for Photography, and professor at Tisch's Department of Photography, Imaging and Emerging Media at New York University, describes the group thusly: "team Lab crew works at the intersections of art and technology. Their work, which we have seen all over the world (I saw their massive Tokyo installation in July) in the past year or two is pushing the limits of machine learning as in integral part of experiential work. They are bold, forward-thinking, and orienting us toward the future" (Artnews, 2019).

With hugely successful pop-up exhibitions in major cities like London, Shanghai, Seoul, and Tokyo, teamLab opened their flagship location called *Borderless* at the Mori Building Digital Art Museum in Tokyo in June 2018. Fifty art installations computer-generated in real time over 100,000 square feet, *Borderless* is an incredibly gorgeous and fully-immersive location-based art experience.

"Visitors can explore five virtual exhibitions generated by 520 computers and 470 projectors. With digital flora and kaleidoscopic light patterns that spill from one room to another, the main exhibit, Borderless, evokes an undelineated, pre-cartography natural world. Museum-goers are invited to scatter butterflies with a glance of the hand or bend waterfalls around their bodies" (Travelogues, 2018).

Author's Note: My first experience with teamLab was in London in 2017 with an exhibition they held at the Pace Gallery called *Transcending Boundaries.* I could not believe what I was seeing and experiencing—a vision I have had for years, to use digital technologies to immerse audiences into art—was realized. So beautifully designed, so eloquently executed, teamLab has brought art into the mainstream and opened up art—considered to be the most powerful medium in history—to the masses. I cannot wait to visit *Borderless* in Tokyo as see it at scale.

- *Cages*, Los Angeles, CA. (cagesdtla.com)

Cages blends immersive and traditional style theater into a three-hour journey and adventure. A rock opera from *Woolf and the Wondershow* that pushes the limits immersive storytelling to new heights, bringing technology and animation to the stage in a way never-before-done.

Though the show itself does not immerse the audience into the content, the experience does immerse you into their world through a beautifully designed facade, art and actors, all to be enjoyed pre-show and during the intermission.

Using projection technology in unique ways, delivering story with old school cinema-esque animations that nod to German expressionism, to tell a beautiful love story with layers of inspirational and uplifting messaging.

Described as a new medium of storytelling, CAGES has the ability to touch upon all of the senses as it transports audiences through a carefully curated journey that alters your perception of reality with groundbreaking technology, an all-consuming sphere of sound, and state of the art visuals.

CAGES transports attendees into the dystopian world of Anhedonia—where emotions are forbidden, and everyone's hearts are locked in cages. When Woolf meets his muse, Madeline, he struggles to find the words that describe what he is suddenly feeling. With music as the universal language, Woolf sets out on a surreal journey to master his emotions in order to write a symphony powerful enough to make the world feel and set their hearts free.

Ian McEvily, CAGES Co-Founder says "For us, the immersive elements are really worldbuilding that all point to a larger narrative. We aim to not force interactiveness, instead focus on piquing the interest of the consumer to explore on their own terms. We believe this is an important factor in allowing the consumer to experience something new in a way that feels comfortable and makes them want to return. The theatrical and musical components of the experience is what truly excites us as it's an industry that is ripe for disruption and lends itself well to more of the immersive world building that we're playing with. A well-made cocktail certainly doesn't hurt" (personal email Jan 2, 2020).

Author's Note: CAGES is magnificent and a must-see! Let's hope it stays around for a long time, ideally touring the world so many more people can experience it. An incredible mix of story mediums and technologies, CAGES has you at the edge of your seat from start to finish, hoping it actually won't ever end! With pre and post show theatrics through art and actors, the whole experience was refreshingly original and absolutely mind-blowing.

- *Electric Playhouse*, Albuquerque, NM. (https://electricplayhouse.com/)

Have you ever wanted to enter a digital fun house filled with games, dining and interactive experiences that are designed for a group? *Electric Playhouse*, a recent addition to the location-based entertainment scene in Albuquerque, New Mexico, which soft opened in December 2019, offers exactly this. A digital wonderland, *Electric Playhouse* (EP), with their new 30,000+ square foot campus, has something for everyone.

Veterans of immersive entertainment formerly known as *Storylab Interactive*, with numerous installations and pop-ups under their belt, the creators at *Electric Playhouse* know how to design social experiences that deliver hours of fun using responsive projection mapping technology to deliver experiences that appeal to all age groups, resulting in new connections and shared memories.

Reporting in a personal email to the author, John-Mark Collins, co-founder and CEO of EP describes this venue as:

'How Immersive Technology Can Make Us More Human' is essentially why we build what we build. Shared experiences (more importantly, physical shared experiences) are the gateway to long standing positive memories with other people. Think of dining out, sports, walking through an incredible location (real or virtual), building something in a group—these things all have a component of the physical that provide an array of data and stimulation to the senses that make them more powerful than something strictly digital or in a known setting (like your home). It is the inputs, sights, sounds, smells and textures that really drive memory and connection. The opposite of this is the lack of all of those things in a text message (well, outside of the annoying ding or buzz). (personal email Jan 4, 2020)

Author's Note: I have had the pleasure of working with the EP team for a couple of years now, building interactive installations and immersive dining activations together, so I know first-hand how creative and fun their experiences are. A team of engineers, designers and visionaries, Electric Playhouse has manifested a vision that can easily scale across cities, be their own space or fit into other LBEs easily and deliver unique experiences that are fun for the whole family.

IMPACT: THE LBE EFFECT

Let's now take a look at the positive impact location-based entertainment is having on other verticals.

The Human Side

Immersive media in entertainment is a powerful force, and immersive experiences have the ability to impact, influence and transform audiences in longer lasting ways. The medium can be used to develop an audience's understanding of environmental, political or social issues, resulting in empathy, compassion and action.

Reading a book, watching a movie or playing a game does not present the same capabilities as immersive entertainment does, not only connecting us with issues that matter but affecting us in ways that cannot be ignored.

We have an opportunity to bring audiences closer to the beauty that exists on earth, to connect them emotionally to fauna on the path to extinction, flora that can speak to the damage and destruction, and narrative that helps us understand the ramifications of our actions or inaction.

Beyond empathy, compassion and love, we can teach behavior such as mindfulness or presence. Let's take the HoloLens AR headset for example, which has an accelerometer that can track movement and speed, relevant as follows:

We are inside of a magical mixed reality forest filled with a variety of vibrant looking creatures including a pride of very colorful peacocks that draws the attention of an audience member. In their excitement and joy, they rush over to take a closer look but their pace/speed scares away the birds. In that moment of disappointment as the audience member stands in contemplation wondering what happened, there is a moment of presence and in that moment, the pride step back out.

What if one out of ten individuals makes a connection that their behavior is what drove and brought back these birds? This is one of many ways, the simplest of ways to leverage immersive tech to create emotional that can create lasting change—a kind of immersive neuro linguistic programming (NLP), so to speak.

Beyond the individual influence, much of today's immersive entertainment is group-based or collaborative in nature, requiring audiences to connect with others in space from friends to strangers, to explore, navigate and solve in experience. Though LBVR currently has limitations in throughput, other LBE experiences such as LBAR, interactive art and immersive theater cater to large groups.

Let's also look at the impact that immersive experiences can have on the world of nonprofits and their fundraising efforts. The very visceral nature of the experience can evoke feelings that lead to action - bring a VR installation to a Fundraising Gala and watch how quickly donors open their wallets!

At a time when our planet's health is rapidly declining, killings through terrorism or war are increasing, and the very nature of democracy is being challenged, immersive media presents us the opportunity to inspire *being* human.

A beautiful example of how this medium can leave an imprint, is the Ocean of Air installation at the Saatchi Gallery in London. A multi-sensory immersive installation illuminating the fundamental connection between animal and plant. The experience takes place in Sequoia National Park, home to the Giant Sequoia trees. Standing at over 30-storeys high, they are the largest living organisms to ever to be sustained by the planet. Using a unique combination of technologies from untethered virtual reality, heart rate monitors and breath sensors to body tracking, visitors will be completely immersed in a world beyond human perception. Existing in the liminal space between art, science and technology, this is a rare and exciting opportunity to not only learn about the symbiotic systems of nature, but also to experience it firsthand (Daniel, 2019).

Art

Advancements in immersive technologies are inspiring new horizons, offering audiences intriguing ways of viewing, interpreting and experiencing art.

- Audiences can be completely immersed inside of an artwork (Projections, VR & AR)
- Greater information about the artwork and artist can be explored
- Artworks can be interacted unlike traditional museums where one cannot touch the works (AV/VR/MR)
- Audiences can become part of the artwork (AR)
- Audiences become the artist

These technologies are revolutionizing artworks across all mediums. From Jeff Koons to Björk to Android Jones staging VR installations everywhere from the Royal Academy of Arts in London, to the Smithsonian in Washington DC, and artists like Yayoi Kusama and teamLab enveloping audiences inside of art, we are seeing an *art renaissance* emerge. Whether incorporating facial-recognition technology or movement and behavioral responsiveness, immersive installations deliver a personalized gallery experience to attendees.

Atelier des Lumieres is one such example, their latest digital exhibition in Paris immerses visitors in the paintings of Vincent van Gogh. Projected on all the surfaces of the Atelier, this new visual and musical production retraces the intense life of the artist, who, during the last ten years of his life, painted more than 2,000 pictures which are now in collections around the world (Stenson, 2019).

In 2020, Christie's will sell the first mixed-reality work ever, Marina Abramović's *The Life*, a 19-minute augmented reality piece featuring a 3D digital rendering of the performance artist wandering around London's Serpentine Gallery, using volumetric capture and Magic Leap headsets (Shaw, 2019). Abramovic's installation allows viewers to explore the artist's movements as if she was in the room.

The adoption of emotion-responsive technology in exhibitions, galleries and institutions and art being the change agent that it has always been, immersive technology may usher in the next renaissance. Digital technology has allowed art to liberate itself from the physical and transcend boundaries.

Education

The visceral nature of immersive technologies is such that any knowledge or information learned via experience has the ability to remain with us forever. Location-based experiences can amplify the learning experience by placing us inside the worlds, invoking empathy, compassion, love, and other human emotions that trigger transformation and memory.

Field trips are seen as the most effective learning experiences, and with immersive, location-based experiences, this is taken one step further by offering trips to locations that would have been impossible without the new technology. Location-based education allows for greater accessibility, engagement, interactivity, involvement and team work.

Félix Lajeunesse, Co-Founder of Felix & Paul Studios, who recently created an immersive experience visit to the ISS explains this power:

In the coming years, immersive technology will allow these locations to become gateways to other worlds. For instance, you can certainly learn about the International Space Station in a museum but being transported to low-Earth orbit using VR and meeting the astronauts who work there in a highly realistic way is a completely different experience. One that is more entertaining, that cultivates deeper understanding, and that results in a far more emotional and memorable experience for audiences. (As quoted in Porges, 2019)

National Geographic's commitment to education through entertainment comes to life in many forms from their park to a large-scale immersive experience in New York, taking guests on a journey under the ocean in ways that impart knowledge and compassion. Combining immersive technologies, video and audio, *National Geographic Encounter: Ocean Odyssey* (Nat Geo, 2017) is an extraordinary underwater experience that brings visitors in touch with the ocean world. It is a fantastic example of how LBE can work for education.

Another great immersive educational experience worth noting is the National Geographic Ultimate Explorer Center in Shenyang, China. It boasts 15 different experiences—from simulator rides to hands-on dinosaur digs. Lead Creative Director on the project, Michelangelo Capraro, shares his goals for the project:

We set out on the project with the intent to create an immersive setting where we combined the National Geographic brand values of conservation and staying true to science, a place where learning was done through play, and parents could be part of the adventure. Our goal was to create a place where kids can feel like real explorers, and teach them through taking them on wild, hands-on adventures, encouraging them to be responsible stewards of our planet and all its inhabitants—and inspiring them to become actual explorers themselves! (Personal email Jan. 7, 2020)

Retail and Real Estate

The last few years have witnessed a dramatic pivot when it comes to brick and mortar retail, with almost 10,000 stores closing in 2019 alone (Doctor RJ, 2019). Blamed on the increasing popularity and ease of online shopping, consumers are no longer flocking to malls as often as they used to and are certainly no longer looking at these properties as 'hang out' destinations—the days of the mall rat are long gone! Not only do retailers need to solve for new traffic, they also need to solve for time spent on site.

We are seeing an evolution in the space, coined "retailtainment," malls, big box retailers, real estate developers and hoteliers are increasingly looking to implement lifestyle, food and beverage (F&B), and entertainment choices for a new generation of shoppers. Location-based experiences are traffic drivers, drawing in new audiences and increasing dwell time within a mall.

Kim Schaeffer, President of Parks at *Two Bit Circus*, recently wrote in an article in *VentureBeat* in which she says: "Numerous businesses have already shown success by grouping a variety of experiences in one area, adding entertainment value and accommodating a much broader audience—which makes for a more compelling, inclusive business model, and heightens the user experience" (Schaefer, 2019).

Companies like Area15 are seen to be revolutionizing the space by introduction. A first-of-its-kind experiential and interactive entertainment, retail, dining and nightlife complex, Area15 is scheduled to open in Las Vegas towards the latter part of 2020, launching with Meow Wolf as its anchor tenant and a series of modern-day experiential, retail and culinary experiences.

"Area15 is a radical re-imagining of retail," said Winston Fisher, a principal of Fisher Brothers. "It will be a 21st century immersive bazaar and an entirely new concept in retail and entertainment. We're excited to debut this groundbreaking concept off the Las Vegas Strip, attracting tourists and locals alike, and we are thrilled to have Meow Wolf join as the premier anchor tenant." (as quoted in Area15, 2018).

THE FUTURE

Location-based entertainment will become the driver for more community-driven human interaction. The movies originally were a motivator for more engagement within the community—a place to go and socialize alongside the entertainment. Today, that is no longer the case—most of humanity can now access media on demand, without going anywhere. Media needs to change shape—in some ways, physically. Building something that can only be experienced in a specific location and with other people is the quintessential driver of location-based entertainment. We will see more immersive stories because it's about the story, not just the tech. Immersion is about storytelling and the crafting of the actual narrative. The tech can be high or low, people in costume or VR or projection domes, but LBE is transforming because we are putting people into stories, into roles and places they only wish they could go to.

Today, we are competing with the screen. Kids and families can immerse themselves in movies and games right now at home, so to get them to experience that deeper immersion, we need to take them out of that confined space, and create a physical experience for them with the sights, sounds, smells, and movement you would expect in the adventure you are crafting. This, combined with the social nature of being in an out-of-home environment, will ensure growth in this segment.

We will see more meaningful experiences and less violent shooters and zombie killers. Though these will not go away, they will no longer become a main driver for our LBE day out.

We will see a democratization of content as digital immersive technologies open the door to *all creators,* known or unknown, connecting them directly into an experience and distributed across multiple locations in a scalable, fast and cost-effective manner.

We will see new ways for artists to monetize their work, offering digital artworks that can now live across devices and the virtual space. And we will leverage blockchain technologies for digital rights management (DRM) controls such that digital art can be on display and sold across multiple channels.

We will see a new generation seek out 'art experiences,' opening the once niche and exclusive art world up to the masses.

We will see the entree of even more LBEs, traditional and non-traditional as technology improves, latency decreases and bandwidth increases, and things like edge computing become ubiquitous.

We will see the democratization of Free Roam VR as hardware becomes more prevalent, costs decrease and 5G technology rolls out. These trends can effectively empower locations to become an LBE— imagine the Macy's store with their own experience in their shoe department.

We will continue to see a separation between the technology and the experience, and a willingness to partner across the spectrum versus owning the entire ecosystem.

The future is immersive: the lines between the different types of immersive location-based entertainment are blurring and will continue to cross-pollinate in the future until they lose their boundaries and become difficult to tell apart any longer.

CONCLUSION

Never has there been a medium so powerful that it that it can inspire and transform—all in the spirit of play and fun—and for that reason, the immersive location-based entertainment industry will likely surpass the motion picture and video game industries in the coming years.

LBE is the portal to play and along the way, you may learn a thing or two. Like sugar-coated vegetables, LBEs use entertainment as the way in and the experience as the inspiration. Whatever the underlying mechanics, whether they be educational, artistic, cinematic, playful, heady or hearty, the one constant is that one is guaranteed a good time!

As our world gets smaller and we become more connected to another through our digital world, our desire to connect and engage in the physical realm increases exponentially. Everyone is looking for a way in or out of reality and would prefer that whatever it is they step into has some meaning behind it. Purpose-driven experiences, the next wave of the location-based entertainment industry and, at a time we need it the most.

With the current global climate, we are all seeking an escape, and to marry these two worlds, we are able to witness the magic of reality in a communal setting is not strictly bound to the seclusion of goggles and headsets.

The future of LBE will continue to see a rise in multi-generational, personalized and shared immersive experiences that are designed for social media. We will continue to see the bar grow, artistically and commercially, push the boundaries of what's possible, blur the lines between realities, while finding new ways that connect and resonate with people at the deepest of levels.

As the LBE market grows, so does the opportunity for operators to ensure that they are delivering meaningful moments that go beyond a great memory.

While olfactory and haptic technologies are advancing rapidly, they are nowhere near the 'Netflix' of changing the way people dine, play sports and engage—physically. Location-based entertainment will help to keep us human in the next decades, as automation and access drive us farther away from the need to connect face-to-face.

REFERENCES

Area15. (2018). *AREA15, A First-of-Its-Kind Experiential and Interactive Entertainment, Retail, Dining and Nightlife Complex, Opening in Las Vegas Mid-2019*. Area15 Press Release. Retrieved from https://www.prnewswire.com/news-releases/area15-a-first-of-its-kind-experiential-and-interactive-entertainment-retail-dining-and-nightlife-complex-opening-in-las-vegas-mid-2019-300584326.html

Artnet News. (2019). What Was the Most Influential Work of the Decade? We Surveyed Dozens of Art-World Experts to Find Out. *Artnet News*. Retrieved from https://news.artnet.com/art-world/what-was-the-most-influential-work-of-the-decade-we-surveyed-dozens-of-art-world-experts-to-find-out-1736172

Barmann, J. (2019). Former Bisou Chef Now Cooking for Instagram Centric Mid-Market Pop-Up Called F.E.A.S.T. *SFIST*. Retrieved from https://sfist.com/2019/03/21/former-bisou-chef-now-cooking-for-instagram-centric-mid-market-pop-up-called-f-e-a-s-t/

Barrett, S. (2019). BWW Review: SAMSKARA at Wisdome: Immersive Art Park Dazzles Audiences with Digital Artwork by Android Jones. *Broadway World*. Retrieved from https://www.broadwayworld.com/los-angeles/article/BWW-Review-SAMSKARA-at-Wisdome-Immersive-Art-Park-Dazzles-Audiences-With-Digital-Artwork-by-Android-Jones-20190502

Botterill, J. (1997). *The Fairest of the Fairs: a History of Fairs, Amusement Parks, and Theme Parks* (Doctoral dissertation Theses). School of Communication, Simon Fraser University.

Cavendish, R. (2005). London's Last Bartholomew Fair: September 3rd, 1855. *History Today*, *55*(9), 52.

CBC News. (2016). Diefenbunker Museum escape room promises interactive Cold War history lesson. *CBC News*. Retrieved from https://www.cbc.ca/news/canada/ottawa/diefenbunker-escape-room-cold-war-1.3445576

Corkill, E. (2009). Real Escape Game brings its creator's wonderment to life. *The Japan Times*. Retrieved from https://www.japantimes.co.jp/life/2009/12/20/general/real-escape-game-brings-its-creators-wonderment-to-life/

Daniel, E. (2019). We Live in an Ocean of Air: How VR art is capturing the hearts and minds of audiences. *The Verdict Podcast*. Retrieved from https://www.verdict.co.uk/vr-art/

Davis, B. (2016). Is This Art Space Backed by 'Game of Thrones' Author George R. R. Martin a Force of Good or Evil? *Artnet News*. Retrieved from https://news.artnet.com/art-world/george-r-r-martin-backed-art-collective-556880

Davis, S. G. (1996). The theme park: Global industry and cultural form. *Media Culture & Society*, *18*(3), 399–422. doi:10.1177/016344396018003003

Doctor, R. J. (2019). The slow death of the American mall and the social imperfections it exhibited. *Daily Kos*. Retrieved from https://www.dailykos.com/stories/2019/11/27/1901730/-The-slow-death-of-the-American-mall-and-the-social-imperfections-it-exhibited

Enklu. (2019). Success for The Unreal Garden at E3. *Enklu in the News*. Retrieved from https://www.enklu.com/

Eventbrite. (2017). *The Experience Movement: Research Report: How Millennials are Bridging Cultural & Political Divides Offline*. Retrieved from https://www.eventbrite.com/l/millennialsreport-2017/

Farkas, J. (2019a). Inside the innovative Disney ride that's key to its *Star Wars* strategy. *CNN Business*. Retrieved from https://www.cnn.com/2019/12/03/tech/star-wars-rise-of-the-resistance-ride

Farkas, J. (2019b). Disney's Star Wars hotel is a cruise ship in space. *CNN Travel*. Retrieved from https://www.cnn.com/travel/article/disney-star-wars-epcot-d23

Giardina, C. (2018). NAB: Location-Based Entertainment Could Be $12 Billion Industry in Five Years. *Hollywood Reporter*. Retrieved from https://www.hollywoodreporter.com/behind-screen/nab-location-based-entertainment-could-be-12-billion-industry-five-years-1100772

Harrison, J. E. (1951). *Ancient Art and Ritual*. New York: Greenwood Press.

Immersive Design Industry. (2019). Interactive, Intimate, Experiential: The Impact of Immersive Design. *2019 Immersive Design Industry Annual Report*. Retrieved from https://immersivedesignsummit.com/2019industryreport.pdf

Isenberg, B. (1989). Secrets of the Play that Refuses to Close. *Los Angeles Times*. Retrieved from https://www.latimes.com/archives/la-xpm-1989-02-12-ca-3037-story.html

Lan, L. (2019). China's virtual reality arcades aim for real-world success. *The Jakarta Post*. Retrieved from https://www.thejakartapost.com/life/2019/04/07/chinas-virtual-reality-arcades-aim-for-real-world-success.html

Library of Congress. (n.d.). *Early Motion Picture Productions*. Retrieved from https://www.loc.gov/collections/edison-company-motion-pictures-and-sound-recordings/articles-and-essays/history-of-edison-motion-pictures/early-motion-picture-productions/

Lieberman, M. (2013). *Social: Why Our Brains Are Wired to Connect*. New York: Crown Publisher.

Luckel, M. (2016). Yes, There's a Museum of Ice Cream. And It's Everything You'd Imagine. *Vogue Daily*. Retrieved from https://www.vogue.com/article/museum-of-ice-cream-august-2016-nyc

Mallenbaum, C. (2018). Why Escape Rooms Have a Lock on the U.S. *USA Today*. Retrieved from https://www.usatoday.com/story/life/people/2018/04/25/escape-rooms-trend-us/468181002/

McConnon, A. (2018). Breaking into the boom in escape rooms: what entrepreneurs need to know. *The New York Times*. Retrieved from https://www.nytimes.com/2018/04/11/business/escape-room-small-business.html?

Mordor Intelligence. (2019). Location-Based Virtual Reality (VR) Market: Growth, Trends, and Forecast (2020-2025). *Mordor Intelligence*. Retrieved from https://www.mordorintelligence.com/industry-reports/location-based-virtual-reality-vr-market

Nash Information Services. (2019) Domestic Movie Theatrical Market Summary 1995 to 2019. The Numbers: Where Data and Business Meet. *Nash Information Services*. Retrieved from https://www.the-numbers.com/market/

NASSCOM. (2019). *Growth of Immersive Media: A Reality Check*. Retrieved from https://www.nasscom.in/knowledge-center/publications/growth-immersive-media-reality-check

Nat. Geo. (2017). *National Geographic Press release*. Retrieved from https://www.nationalgeographicpartners.com/press/2017/09/national-geographic-encounter-ocean-odyssey-opens/

Porges, S. (2019). The Future of VR? Site-Specific Art Installations. *Forbes*. Retrieved from https://www.forbes.com/sites/sethporges/2019/11/04/the-future-of-vr-site-specific-art-installations

Rake, R. (2019). Family Entertainment Centers Market Overview. *Allied Market Research*. Retrieved from https://www.alliedmarketresearch.com/family-entertainment-centers-market

Reichard, K. (2019). Closer Chainsmokers 5G Experience on Tap at Chase Center. *Arena Digest*. Retrieved from https://arenadigest.com/2019/11/27/closer-chainsmokers-5g-experience-on-tap-at-chase-center/

Roof, K. (2019). Museum of Ice Cream Valued at $200 Million. *The Wall Street Journal*. Retrieved from https://www.wsj.com/articles/museum-of-ice-cream-valued-at-200-million-11565782201

Shaefer, K. (2019). Malls Have a Future: Location-Based Entertainment. *VentureBeat*. Retrieved from https://venturebeat.com/2019/09/25/malls-have-a-future-location-based-entertainment/

Shaw, A. (2019). Marina Abramovic's *The Life* to become first mixed reality work ever auctioned. *The Art Newspaper*. Retrieved from https://www.theartnewspaper.com/news/marina-abramovic-s-the-life-to-become-first-mixed-reality-work-ever-auctioned

Staugaitis, L. (2018). Meow Wolf Explains their Origin Story in a Feature-Length Documentary. *Colossal*. Retrieved from https://www.thisiscolossal.com/2018/11/meow-wolf-documentary/

Stenson, B. (2019). Immersive Van Gogh show opens in Paris – in pictures. *The Guardian*. Retrieved from https://www.theguardian.com/travel/gallery/2019/mar/04/immersive-vincent-van-gogh-show-opens-paris-digital-art

Sutton, R. (2018). *Investing in Creativity*. Retrieved from https://www.arts.gov/NEARTS/2018v3-pushing-boundaries-look-visionary-approaches-arts/investing-creativity

Takahasi, D. (2018). VRstudios launches Jurassic World VR attraction at Dave & Buster's restaurants. *Venture Beat*. Retrieved from https://venturebeat.com/2018/06/06/vrstudios-launches-jurassic-world-vr-attraction-at-dave-busters-restaurants/

Tapely, K. (2017). Oscars: Alejandro G. Inarritu's Virtual Reality Installation 'Carne y Arena' to Receive Special Award. *Variety*. Retrieved from https://variety.com/2017/film/awards/oscars-alejandro-g-inarritus-virtual-reality-installation-carne-y-arena-to-receive-special-award-1202601265/

Travelogues. (2018). Borderless: Tokyo's New Digital Art Museum is a Creative Paradigm Shift. *Travelogues*. Retrieved from https://www.remotelands.com/travelogues/tokyos-new-digital-art-museum-is-simply-stunning/

White Hutchinson. (n.d.). What is a Family Entertainment Center? *White Hutchinson Leisure and Learning Group*. Retrieved from https://www.whitehutchinson.com/leisure/familyctr.shtml

Willmott, P. (2019). Review: The War of the Worlds Immersive Experience at 56 Leadenhall Street. *London Box Office*. Retrieved from https://www.londonboxoffice.co.uk/news/post/review-war-of-the-worlds-immersive-experience

Yu, K. (2019). How Immersive Virtual Reality Theatre Pushes the Limits of Storytelling. *No Proscenium*. Retrieved from https://noproscenium.com/how-immersive-virtual-reality-theatre-pushes-the-limits-of-storytelling-8265b198bfc7

ENDNOTE

[1]   See the park's website for more information. http://www.denmark.net/denmark-guide/attractions-denmark/dyrehavsbakken/]

Chapter 16
Immersion Domes:
Next–Generation Arts and Entertainment Venues

Edward Lantz
Vortex Immersion Media, USA

ABSTRACT

Large-scale immersion domes are specialized embodiments of spatial augmented reality allowing large groups to be immersed in real-time animated or cinematic virtual worlds with strong sense-of-presence. Also called fulldome theaters, these spaces currently serve as giant screen cinemas, planetariums, themed entertainment attractions, and immersive classrooms. This chapter presents case studies for emerging applications of digital domes, reviews dome theater design basics, and suggests that these venues are on track to become mainstream arts and entertainment centers delivering global impact at scale. Standard venue designs will be necessary to realize the full potential of an immersive media arts and entertainment distribution network. This chapter provides rationale for standardization of immersion domes for multi-use events spaces, immersive cinemas, and live performing arts theaters.

INTRODUCTION

Spatial augmented reality (SAR) maps pixels onto physical objects to produce visually immersive or digitally augmented experiences. SAR embodiments include architectural projection mapping and digital domes (fulldome theaters) which are general-purpose immersive visualization environments capable of accommodating large groups without the need for VR headsets, glasses or goggles. Digital domes can incorporate a variety of extended reality (XR) modalities including the incorporation of live performers with interactive tracking, stage and prop projection mapping, and real-time display of cyber worlds and metaverse environments.

Because of their large capacity, high throughput and ease of use (no wearables or controllers), digital domes have the potential to become a mass medium for XR similar to cinemas. Domes and other SAR environments cannot replace VR—they are a medium in their own right. They are advanced storytell-

DOI: 10.4018/978-1-7998-2433-6.ch016

ing environments capable of touring audiences through virtual worlds, scientific datasets cinematic environments and more. Walk-through and stand-up SAR environments can also be highly interactive.

Digital dome venues do have a number of limitations when compared to VR. For instance, dome theaters accommodating large audiences are typically limited to a hemispheric field of view—half the visual field of VR—because large standing or seated audiences block a large portion of the audience's visual field-of-view. And with large audiences the sense of personal agency is muted, with the experience being more akin to a tour bus ride or a large window into virtual worlds.

The tour bus analogy accurately describes contemporary immersion dome experiences in planetariums, giant screen cinemas and IMAX® Domes. It would be tempting to classify dome theaters as passive group immersive cinema displays, or group immersive portals into cyberspace. However, our recent work involves the merging of live performers into real-time rendered environments, allowing performers to command and interact with the immersive world. This moves digital domes more firmly into the realm of mixed reality.

The integration of stadium seating for optimal immersion, a projection-mapped stage and foreground props utilizing SAR techniques, in combination with 360 scenes projected on the dome create a unique format that we call CineTheater™. In addition, multipurpose dome venues without seating can serve as community hubs for connecting, creative placemaking, black box theaters, and special event venues. It is suggested that both designs will find utility and should be pursued in the development of next-generation, location-based arts and entertainment venues.

BACKGROUND

Immersion domes typically map 360 visuals onto spherical, hemispheric, or ovoid screens to deliver visual experiences similar to VR headsets but without the need for glasses or goggles (Lantz, 1997). It's like putting a giant VR headset on a large group of people. The resulting wide field-of-view imagery can trigger brain states not usually accessible via film or other digital media such as sense-of-motion (vection), presence, scale, awe, and have been shown to communicate concepts better, create a greater interest in learning, and are more effective than a movie screen or television at conveying certain scientific concepts (Lantz, 2011).

Digital domes can provide a greater instantaneous visual field-of-view than consumer VR headsets, nearly encompassing the viewer's entire peripheral vision. Peripheral vision is associated with vection, spatial learning, and navigation skills (Yamamoto & Philbeck, 2013). Because the audience is free to use head motion to observe immersive scenes without the need for head tracking, higher frame rates are not strictly required. Anecdotal experience with audiences indicates that VR experiences presented in digital domes are preferred by many who otherwise feel confined, experience vertigo, or have other difficulties with VR headsets.

The first digital domes were pioneered for military vehicle simulation and training, but it is the planetariums that first embraced video projection in domes for public exhibitions. At last count over 1,665 digital domes—mostly planetariums, science centers, giant screen theaters and portable domes—are documented worldwide, with nearly half in the U.S. (Petersen, 2019a). And over 335 titles have been produced for this market ranging from astronomy and space science, earth science, and more (Petersen 2019b).

While narrative storytelling has long been a mainstay of planetarium programming, with the advent of laser graphics in the 1970s and now 360 "fulldome" video graphics and VR content creation, arts and entertainment programming has increasingly found a home in planetarium programming (Lantz, 2009; Lantz, 2018).

DIGITAL DOME DESIGN

Digital dome theaters include portable (inflatable) planetariums, smaller classroom planetariums in universities and school districts, public or private institutional digital domes largely in museums and science centers, giant screen film theaters which have converted to digital including, most recently, IMAX® Domes. In addition, a number of theme park rides employ domes and other wide FOV screens (Fraser, 2018).

While there are now 1,665 digital domes in the world, there are only a small number of pioneering arts and entertainment dome theaters that have emerged in the past decade. It is a now a good time to establish industry standards for the coming generation of arts and entertainment domes.

There are existing industry standards that can apply to arts and entertainment domes (Lantz, Wyatt, Bruno, & Neafus 2004). *The Dome Master Specification*, first drafted in 2004 at the Fulldome Standards Summit in Valencia, Spain, has allowed the free exchange of cinematic digital dome programming between digital planetariums, and continues to be updated by the trade association IMERSA: Immersive Media, Entertainment, Research, Science, Arts (2014) which was founded in 2008 to foster the fulldome video format. This format was subsequently incorporated into the *Digital Immersive Giant Screen Specifications*, developed by the Giant Screen Cinema Association for the conversion of 70mm film theaters to giant screen digital cinema (DIGSS, 2018).

If immersion domes are to become a recognized mainstream entertainment format at scale—allowing mass distribution of immersive experiences—basic design principles must be adopted, and specific design features must be chosen and adhered to by the industry. This section focuses on some of the more critical design parameters and principles that must come into play when designing next generation immersive venues.

In general, immersive theaters typically utilize one or more video projectors to cover the entire surface of a dome screen. LED domes are also emerging but are currently limited to specialized applications such as theme parks by their high cost. Therefore, the focus of this chapter is on projection domes, with an eye towards future emissive screens such as LED. Audio systems are more flexible and do not dictate theater design to the same degree as display systems so they will not be covered in as much detail.

Venue Design

Permanent Dome Venues

Most permanent dome theaters utilize one or more video projectors to cover the entire surface of a perforated aluminum dome screen. Perforated aluminum screens are nearly seamless when panels are precisely butt-seamed and are also nearly transparent to sound. This allows sound absorbing material to be placed behind the dome to mitigate unwanted reflections. It also allows speakers to be mounted behind the screen as well as fire sprinklers.

Figure 1. Cutaway of geodesic dome with hanging vinyl cover and internal negative-pressure screen
Source: ©2019 Pacific Domes, Inc. Used with permission.

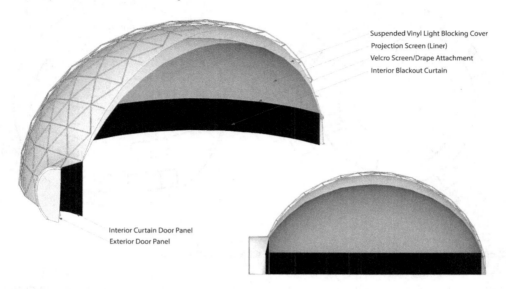

Suspended Vinyl Light Blocking Cover
Projection Screen (Liner)
Velcro Screen/Drape Attachment
Interior Blackout Curtain

Interior Curtain Door Panel
Exterior Door Panel

Mobile Dome Venues

Building digital planetariums and giant screen theaters is an expensive affair. Less expensive prefabricated mobile dome theaters are a popular alternative and can be found at festivals, sporting events, conventions, and more. The most common mobile domes utilize a geodesic frame with vinyl cover and negative pressure internal fabric projection screen supported via a suction fan (Figure 1). With a UV resistant heavy vinyl cover, HVAC and an interior deck or slab, these structures can also be used as semi-permanent theaters up to 37 meters in diameter with a lifetime of 20 years or more. Air-supported domes are also popular for larger venues of 60 meters or more. These structures require positive air pressure requiring revolving doors or airlocks to maintain interior air pressure.

Dome audience viewing and interaction modalities include seated, standing and walkthrough.

Dome imagery can be unidirectional or omnidirectional. Each configuration has its own unique properties.

Audience Arrangements

There are two primary viewing configurations in immersion domes—unidirectional, where all audience members face the same direction—and omnidirectional or concentric, where audience members all face the center of the theater like sitting or standing around a campfire (Figure 2). Standing configurations often use handrails to guide visitors since the strong sense of vection can cause a standing audience to lose balance if exclusively focused on a dome presentation.

For concentric seating (a) the dome screen equator or "springline" is almost always level to the ground—typically raised just above the audience's heads. Unidirectional seating (b) allows the dome to be tilted in the front to provide foreground. Stadium seating takes full advantage of the dome tilt to further improve viewer sight lines. More on this shortly.

Figure 2. Dome seating/standing configurations

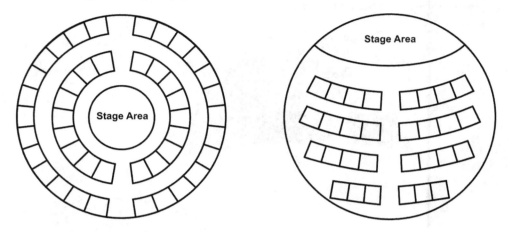

Unidirectional viewing is especially advantageous for storytelling because:

- The entire audience is looking in the same direction towards a "sweet spot" on the dome
- Single point of focus facilitates character-based storytelling, informational text
- Audience can be flown through or over terrain with everyone flying in same direction
- Audience attention can easily be captured and directed to the left or right
- Provides the most consistent and controlled audience experience
- Stage lighting is simplified – elevated lights can be placed behind the audience

Concentric viewing presents a number of challenges especially when delivering a cinematic experience, but there are some interesting possibilities as well:

- In concentric seating the audience could be looking in any direction
- The zenith (top) of the dome screen is the only common area of focus
- Flying audience up towards sky or falling are powerful omnidirectional experiences
- Image orientation on the zenith depends on seat location
  - Nearly half of the audience will see zenith image upside down
  - Especially problematic with text, faces and other objects dependent on orientation
- Text and characters on dome generally need to be repeated around dome for all to see
  - Limits use of full dome images (which are the most powerful)
- When flying audiences over landscapes, half of the audience will be flying backwards
- Stadium seating is not possible without raising the entire dome image which reduces the dome image field-of-view for the audience.
- Easily accommodates random standing audience such as cocktail party or networking
- Omnidirectional seating generally results in greater audience capacity

Figure 3. Standard ergonomic field-of-vision for a) seated and reclined and b) standing

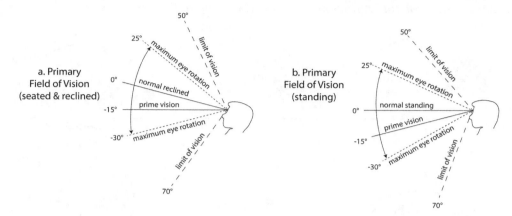

Theater Seating

Theater seats are a key component in sit-down environments. As will be seen, it is important to assure that the seat tilt provides audiences with an optimal view of the dome screen. In general, seat backs should tilt back further the closer they are to the front of the screen. Removable seats are desirable in multipurpose domes. A number of multisensory "4D" special effects can also be built into theater seats including vibroacoustic "bass shakers," personal sound environments, seat cushion pokers and air bladders that inflate and deflate in sequence, mist, buzzers, neck and leg ticklers and motion seats.

Sight Lines and Dome Tilt

In dome theater design we assess the degree of audience immersion by measuring the image field-of-view (FOV). The FOV is defined by the horizontal and vertical angles over which the dome image extends in a typical viewers eye when seated or standing naturally. FOV is a function of where the person is seated or standing in the dome. We use standard ergonomic field-of-view angles for both (a) seated (leaning back) and (b) standing configurations (Figure 3).

We can assess the degree of visual immersion by projecting these "sight lines" from a typical viewer's eye and measuring the vertical and horizontal angle covered by the dome image. Since the horizontal FOV is almost always at least 180 degrees, the vertical FOV is typically the limiting factor in creating a powerful sense of immersion. Ideally, the entire surface area of every viewer's retinas would be completely mapped with pixels.

The (4a) standing configuration (Figure 4) provides the narrowest vertical FOV in natural standing head position. Viewers must look up to maximize their sense of immersion. Slightly reclining seats (4b) provide viewers with an improved FOV. Note that the front seats would ideally be reclined at a greater angle to maximize immersion. Tilting the dome as shown in (4c) improves immersion, especially for viewers towards the front of the theater. Increasing dome tilt and adding stadium seating as shown in (4d) maximizes vertical FOV and is an optimal design for immersive theater where it is desired to deliver a collective audience experience. Optimal immersion is also attained when floating or reclining in a level dome as shown in (4e), or when rows are vertically stacked in a 90-degree tilted dome as shown in (4f).

Figure 4. Unidirectional dome designs including a) standing, b) seated, c) seated with dome tilt, d) stadium seating with dome tilt, e) floating or reclined viewing and f) vertical seating

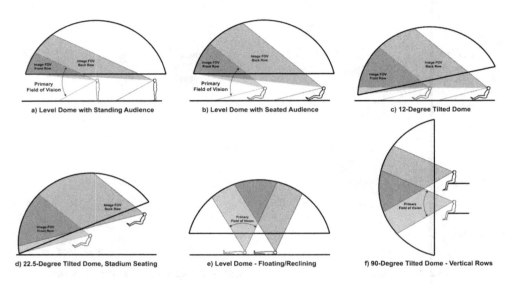

Figure 5. Variations in dome tilt and formation of a virtual "gravity horizon"

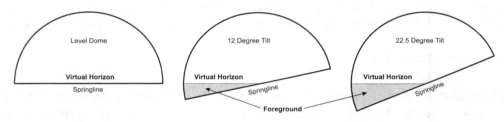

Floating and vertical designs provide greater isolation from other audience members which is not desirable in a shared theater environment but is ideal for special applications such as digital wellness environment (floating design), flying theater or theme park dark ride (vertical design).

Note that tilting the dome towards the front of the theater allows the projection of foreground under the average viewer's virtual "gravity horizon" line (Figure 5). In a level dome the spring line is the same as the horizon line. As the dome is tilted, foreground imagery under the horizon is revealed. In practice this virtual horizon can actually be placed anywhere to achieve a desired aesthetic and does not need to follow the audience's gravity horizon, although the experience is the least disorienting when the two coincide. Since most of the audience is seated behind dome center, the "design eyepoint" can be lifted into the center of the seating deck, thereby lifting the horizon higher up onto the dome.

Figure 6. Variations in dome vertical elevation or aperture angle

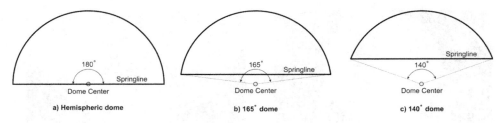

Figure 7. Sightline criteria for placement of springline and stage

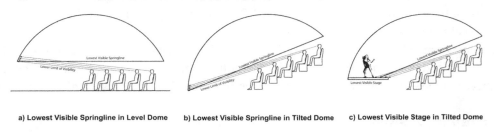

Dome Elevation Angle

Another variable in screen design is the vertical elevation of the dome with respect to dome center (sometimes called "sweep" or "aperture angle"). Most planetarium domes are perfect hemispheres (180-degree vertical elevation) for legacy reasons. There are, however, advantages to constructing domes that are less than (6a) a hemisphere (Figure 6). Hypohemispheric dome screens have less surface area and thus tend to cost less, are easier to project onto using multiple projectors, and result in improved contrast as we shall see. The 165-degree dome (6b) was originally chosen by IMAX Corp. since it dropped the spherical center closer to the audience's eye plane which minimizes geometric distortion as viewers move off-axis.

Springline Height

Finally, we look at image field-of-view and placement of audiences within immersive spaces and placement of the springline. It is certainly possible to completely surround a viewer with complete sphere with no springline at all. Full-sphere theaters have been built for research such as the AlloSphere (Kuchera-Morin, et al., 2014), and have found applications in exhibitions and museums (Maceda, 2015; GOTO, 2016; Proctor, 2017).

However, the presence of a fully populated audience—whether seated or standing—limits a typical viewer's unobstructed field of view to approximately a hemisphere. That is because, in a densely populated space, there are audience members sitting or standing in front of, behind, and to the sides of us which obscures our field of view. So, while we could extend the dome screen to the floor level or below, sightlines to these pixels—which are costly—are blocked for most audience members and do not appreciably add to the audience experience. Note that this primarily applies to performing arts theaters, concert venues and other densely populated venues.

Figure 8. Fisheye projection options for single projector with 1.9:1 aspect ratio

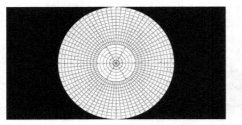 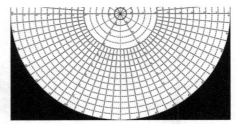

a) Full-frame fisheye - limited to vertical pixel resolution over 180 degrees   b) Truncated fisheye - utilizes full horizontal resolution over 180 degrees but truncates image

(Figure 7) shows the lowest sight lines for a seated audience terminate slightly above the heads of the audience (7a)—often referred to as the "eye plane." This suggests placement of the springline no lower than what is visible for a majority of the audience.

A tilted dome demands a tilted eye-plane which is satisfied by stadium seating as shown in (7b). And when a stage is placed in the theater, if it is desirable for the audience to see the surface of the stage, then the front surface of the stage should not be much lower than the lowest visible springline as shown in (7c).

Display System Design

Most dome theaters utilize one or more projectors illuminating a perforated aluminum or fabric dome screen. The projection system must seamlessly map a 1:1 aspect ratio Dome Master frame over the entire surface of the dome. Various projection display configurations are outlined below.

Single Projector Systems

Single-projector systems utilize ultra-wide angle "fisheye" lenses to illuminate all or most of the dome screen. While high-brightness single-projector systems have been introduced for large domes including IMAX® Dome, the limited resolution and brightness of a single projector can be an issue. Most high-resolution projectors have a 1.6:1, 1.78 or 1.9:1 aspect ratio which does not match the 1:1 fisheye fulldome format. This either requires vertically truncating the projection in the back of the theater or limiting the full fisheye frame to the vertical resolution (Figure 8).

In general, most single-projector systems are found in smaller domes up to 10-12m in diameter and require 4k or 8k pixel resolution projectors for best results (Figure 9). The projector is ideally placed in the center of the dome (9a) but may be placed towards the front or rear of the dome with appropriate digital remapping and intensity gradient compensation. Single projector systems are simpler to setup and align and are therefore much better suited to portable dome applications. Dual fisheye configurations are also possible that use a second projector to fill in the truncated area as shown in (9b). A single edge-blend between two projectors is accomplished using geometric warping and soft-edge masking. Navitar (2019) publishes an excellent tutorial on single and dual projector dome systems.

Figure 9. Single, dual & six-projector edge-blended projector layout

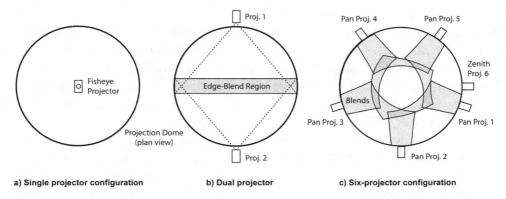

a) Single projector configuration   b) Dual projector   c) Six-projector configuration

Multi-Projector Edge-Blended Systems

Larger systems typically require multiple projectors to allow scaling of brightness and resolution. The majority of larger domes use multiple video projectors—up to two dozen or more in large-scale domes or specialized simulator applications. The projectors must sufficiently overlap to allow geometric alignment and soft-edge-blending to create a single seamless image covering the entire surface of the dome screen. Auto-alignment systems use one or more cameras in conjunction with structured light grids to compute u/v warping and blending maps to create a single seamless image from multiple overlapped projectors. Projectors are typically mounted around the periphery of the dome, projecting across the dome diameter (9c).

Note that the projector black level in blend regions is additive which introduces a distracting hard-edged fixed pattern in the black level which effectively reduces the sequential (on/off) system contrast. There are two solutions to restore black level uniformity. The first is to simply raise the black level outside of the blend regions—a simple solution for auto-edge-blend systems. This reduces black-level contrast to a lesser—but uniform—value across the frame. This approach works particularly well with projectors that have high sequential contrast (ideally without the use of dynamic contrast). But most large-venue projectors are limited to 2000:1 to 5000:1 sequential contrast a best, resulting in discernable loss of contrast.

The second solution applies a physical optical mask somewhere in the optical train (outside of the projection lens in some systems) to create physical blends that function at all light levels. This is not an ideal solution however it can work very effectively. Emerging HDR (high-dynamic range) projectors promise to alleviate the need for masks or black-level boosting altogether.

Projectors and Lenses

There are numerous choices for video projectors and lenses. The most popular choices of projection technology are single-chip or three-chip DLP (Texas Instrument's Digital Light Processor), LCOS (liquid crystal on silicon) or organic LCD (liquid crystal display) spatial light modulators (SLMs), with DLP technology clearly leading in high-end projectors. Projectors with up to 4k horizontal pixels have been manufactured with some 8k projectors entering the market. Lower cost versions use "wobulators" to optically displace pixels by a fraction of a pixel into several positions per frame—each position a fraction of a pixel—to attain higher virtual frame rates.

Projector lenses are rated according to throw ratio. The throw ratio specifies the ratio between image width and throw distance. A 1.5:1 throw ratio, for instance, will produce an image one unit wide when the projector is placed 1.5 units of distance from the screen. Ultra-short throw lenses are now available with throw ratios of 0.3:1 or less. Precautions must be taken, however, to assure that the lens will properly focus across the curvature of the dome. It is rare that projector manufacturers publish this data—empirical testing is a must.

Sequential contrast is another parameter that must now be tested empirically. In recent years manufacturers have universally abandoned the ANSI intra-frame (checkerboard) contrast specification in favor of dynamic contrast specification. Dynamic contrast uses variable iris to throttle down projector brightness in low light scenes, achieving dynamic contrast ratios of 20,000:1 or more. Dynamic contrast cannot be used on multi-projector systems unless the dynamic parameters of all projectors are synchronized. And, because of the very wide field of view, dome imagery does not lend itself to dynamic contrast over the entire display. Most projectors allow dynamic contrast to be disabled, and some allow detailed control over parameters or synchronization of multiple projectors. Without dynamic contrast activated some projectors are left with sequential contrast of 500:1 or worse, so empirical evaluation of contrast is recommended.

Stereoscopic 3D

Stereoscopic 3D is also possible in digital domes; however, it is difficult to fabricate large polarization-preserving projection screens with sufficient precision. Instead, active sequential LCD shutter glasses or optical wavelength multiplex imaging technology such as INFITEC® (used by Dolby and others) is typically required for eye separation. There are also geometric compromises in 3D stereo imagery in domes with a large off-axis viewing volume that make it more difficult for audiences to fuse stereo images from obtuse viewing angles.

Graphics Server

A basic multiprojector digital dome system is shown in (Figure 10). One or more central media servers takes dome master frames, breaks them into sub-frames with proper warping and feeds the sub-frames to multiple video projectors. Image source can either be realtime 3D rendered visuals or pre-rendered video streaming from SSD drives in high-speed RAID configuration. An outboard digital audio processor takes synchronized audio stems or multiple audio tracks in virtually any surround or 3D audio format and remaps them into the theater's speaker array. A separate audio channel is provided for vibroacoustic transducers on the chairs, seating deck or floor.

The system includes an auto-alignment camera or array of cameras to capture projected structured light allowing the display to be geometrically aligned and automatically edge-blended using one of several commercial algorithms. Another array of cameras allows tracking of performers on the stage. The server plays video clips and 3D interactive scenes according to a cue list or timeline.

Multiple auxiliary video inputs fed by a video switcher allowing external video sources to access the display. The server accepts any planar or 360 format (rectangular, equirectangular 360, equipolar dome masters, cubic etc.) and remaps it into dome coordinates with low latency using 2D or 3D map-

Figure 10. Basic multiprojector display system for live-performance dome theater

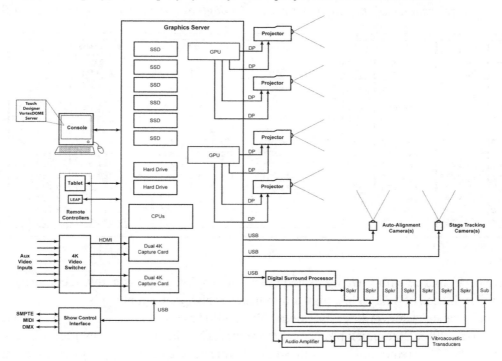

ping. External inputs may be layered or mixed with internal realtime 3D or pre-rendered 360 video. In this manner the dome server becomes a dedicated remapping server allowing multiple outboard image generators including stage mapping computer, audience interactive computer, digital lighting server, GPU supercomputer, multiple VJ servers, live immersive camera feeds and other third-party sources to be seamlessly orchestrated to deliver powerful audience experiences.

A show control interface allows coordination with lighting, motion control rigging, stage props, musical instruments, audio mixers, sensors and other peripheral devices through SMPTE timecode, MIDI, DMX and related control interfaces.

Image Brightness

With their large surface areas, digital dome projection screens are hungry for light. In cinema systems image "brightness" or luminance is often measured in US units of foot-Lamberts (fL). The corresponding SI units for luminance are candela/m^2 and are often referred to as nits (1.0 fL = 3.426 candela/m^2). The SMPTE standard ST 431-1:2006 for digital cinema requires screen luminance of 14 fL or 48 nits for full white (SMPTE, 2006). Projection domes, whether film or digital, rarely achieve these brightness levels. The Giant Screen Cinema Association's DIGSS 2.0 requirements for giant screen theaters requires at least 3 fL for full white with an aspirational goal of 6 fL (DIGSS, 2018). Table 1 lists required projector luminous flux (in lumens) to achieve various luminance values (in both fL and nits) for a range of dome diameters.

Table 1. Projector luminous flux (in lumens) versus screen luminance (fL) for various dome diameters. Assumes screen reflectance of 0.2, dome elevation 165 degrees and projector overlap factor 0.8

Dome Diameter (m)	Surface Area (sq. m)	Projector Lumens Required to Produce *n* foot-Lamberts							
		n = 2 fL (6.9 nits)	4 fL (14 nits)	6 fL (21 nits)	8 fL (27 nits)	10 fL (34 nits)	12 fL (41 nits)	14 fL (48 nits)	16 fL (55 nits)
2.5	9.8	1,200	2,300	3,500	4,600	5,800	6,900	8,100	9,200
5.0	39	4,600	9,200	13,800	18,400	23,000	27,600	32,200	36,800
7.5	88	10,400	20,700	31,000	41,400	51,700	62,000	72,400	82,700
10.0	157	18,400	36,800	55,200	73,500	91,900	110,300	128,600	147,000
15.0	353	41,400	82,700	124,000	165,400	206,700	248,000	289,300	330,700
20.0	628	73,500	147,000	220,500	293,900	367,400	440,900	514,300	587,800
25.0	982	114,800	229,600	344,400	459,200	574,000	688,800	803,600	918,400
30.0	1414	165,400	330,700	496,000	661,300	826,600	991,900	1,157,200	1,322,500
40.0	2513	293,900	587,800	881,700	1,175,500	1,469,400	1,763,300	2,057,100	2,351,000
50.0	3927	459,200	918,400	1,377,600	1,836,700	2,295,900	2,755,100	3,214,200	3,673,400
60.0	5655	661,300	1,322,500	1,983,700	2,644,900	3,306,100	3,967,300	4,628,500	5,289,700
70.0	7697	900,000	1,800,000	2,700,000	3,599,900	4,499,900	5,399,900	6,299,900	7,199,800
80.0	10053	1,175,500	2,351,000	3,526,500	4,701,900	5,877,400	7,052,900	8,228,400	9,403,800

For live performance with stage lights and other ambient lighting it is highly recommended to have a minimum luminance of 4 fL. While higher luminance is always desirable, it is often not economically feasible. For instance, achieving 4 fL in a relatively small 15m dome (seating capacity 120) can be accomplished using three 30k lumen projectors. However, achieving the same light level in a 60m dome (seating capacity 2500) requires 44 ea. of those same projectors. Even using the brightest commercially available projector (75,000 lumens) still requires 18 ea. projectors. It is easy to see the temptation to economize by a) reducing the number of projectors and decreasing image luminance, b) reducing the number of projectors and using a higher screen reflectance to maintain the same image luminance (which sacrifices contrast as we shall see) or c) reducing the vertical elevation (aperture angle) of the screen thereby allowing a reduction in the number of projectors without sacrificing either luminance or contrast (although there may be loss in vertical resolution depending on projection geometry).

Note that projectors can be double-stacked and aligned using internal warping, thereby halving the required number of unique server channels. Double-stacking is common in the industry and most projectionists can quickly manually align projector stacks.

Image Resolution

Image resolution is another critical measure when designing dome displays (or any display, for that matter). Note that, since the introduction of digital projection, display application engineers now typically express resolution in resolvable pixels (pixel resolution) rather than the optical engineering definition of resolution which is based on resolvable line-pairs. Resolution in digital domes is expressed in pixels per degree or—quite often—in the number of pixels per 180 degrees. This is because the standard image map for domes—known as the Dome Master—is an equidistant polar (fisheye) frame with vertical and horizontal axes both representing 180 degrees (from springline to springline). The same 180-degree dome master frame is mapped to the entire dome, regardless of dome elevation (aperture) or dome tilt.

Digital domes have an interesting property. If one stands at dome center, domes with the same number of pixels will appear to have the same pixel resolution regardless of scale. Resolution is measured by pixels per degree, a factor that remains constant with dome diameter. Of course, the pixel size itself

Figure 11. Eye-limited resolution as a driver for pixel resolution at various viewing locations expressed as a fraction of dome radius (scales with dome size), with resultant pixel width for various diameters

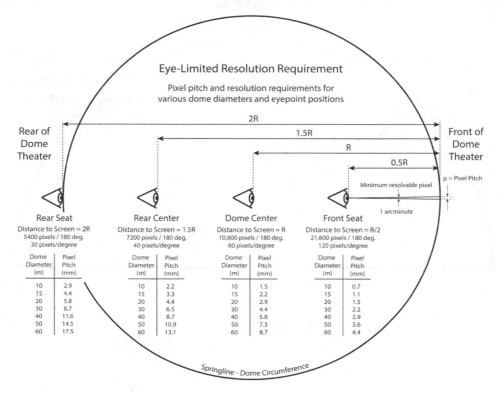

does scale with dome diameter, since the number of pixels around the circumference remains fixed as the circumference increases. If we design theaters with seating or standing areas measured in fractions of dome radius, then our pixel resolution design criteria will also scale with dome diameter.

The acuity of the human eye with 20/20 vision is approximately one arcminute. Dome resolutions resulting from requirement of eye-limited resolution at four different viewing locations (Figure 11). These viewing locations (front seat, dome center, rear center and rear seat) are expressed in units of dome radius, therefore the resolution requirements are scale-invariant with respect to dome diameter.

Large-scale digital planetariums and giant screen domes typically employ an industry standard of 4k x 4k dome master resolution with a small number of 8k x 8k systems deployed. As shown, a resolution of 5.4k is required to match the resolution of the human eye from the rear-most seat. An 8k dome display falls below eye-limited resolution just behind dome center. And if eye-limited resolution is desired at the front row—assumed to be 0.5 radii in front of dome center—a 22k dome master is required.

This raises the question of the need for eye-limited resolution. Projection systems have evolved to have very high pixel fill factors—up to 92% - which minimizes the "screen door" effect when viewing the projected image at closer distance than the eye-limited resolution limit. From experience, the eye is very tolerant to a factor of two (or more) drop in pixel resolution below eye-limited resolution. So an 8k dome master will likely be sufficient into the foreseeable future. Such is not the case with LED displays which have a very low fill factor, allowing the eye to easily discern individual pixels when under the

Figure 12. Crossbounce of incident light ray with luminance (L) onto screen with reflectance (r)

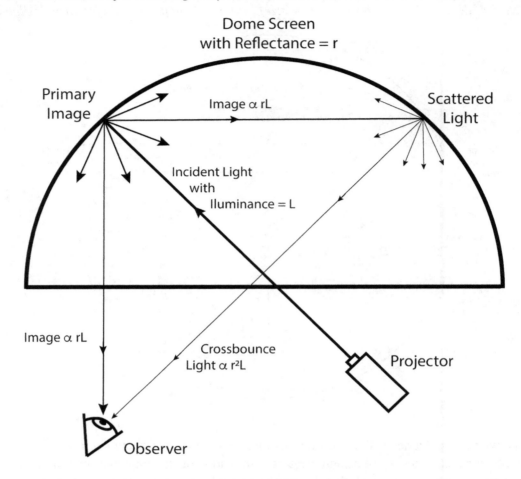

eye-limited resolution threshold. So, even in the case where 8k content is being projected on an LED screen, the pixel resolution will want to be near eye-limited resolution to prevent screen-door artifacts.

Crossbounce Contrast

An often-overlooked factor in dome theater design is the effect of scattered light or "crossbounce" (also called inter-reflection)—that is, light from projected images that scatters back onto the dome instead of into the eyes of the audience causing loss of contrast. This is one of the most common, difficult to solve and often most misunderstood limitations of projection dome image quality. Unlike standard cinema screens that are substantially flat, dome screens are concave, allowing them to reflect not only projected light which forms the primary image, but light from the primary image that scatters back onto the dome itself. The effect is a reduction of image contrast due to an increase in ambient light that limits the blackest black that can be obtained.

Interestingly, crossbounce contrast is highly dependent upon the nature of the projected dome imagery. Bright images such as white clouds – as one might expect when looking up at a daytime sky—can substantially raise the black level over the entire dome screen. Should such an image also contain dark

Table 2. Checkerboard contrast vs dome gain and vertical dome elevation

Dome Gain	Vertical Dome Elevation (Aperture Angle), Degrees										
	130	135	140	145	150	155	160	165	170	175	180
10%	34.6	32.4	30.4	28.6	27.0	25.5	24.2	23.0	21.9	20.9	20.0
20%	17.3	16.2	15.2	14.3	13.5	12.8	12.1	11.5	11.0	10.5	10.0
30%	11.5	10.8	10.1	9.5	9.0	8.5	8.1	7.7	7.3	7.0	6.7
40%	8.7	8.1	7.6	7.2	6.7	6.4	6.1	5.8	5.5	5.2	5.0
50%	6.9	6.5	6.1	5.7	5.4	5.1	4.8	4.6	4.4	4.2	4.0
60%	5.8	5.4	5.1	4.8	4.5	4.3	4.0	3.8	3.7	3.5	3.3
70%	4.9	4.6	4.3	4.1	3.9	3.6	3.5	3.3	3.1	3.0	2.9
80%	4.3	4.0	3.8	3.6	3.4	3.2	3.0	2.9	2.7	2.6	2.5

areas, such as looking into the mouth of a cave or dark shadows under trees or rocks, these dark areas of the image will appear quite washed out. On the other hand, sparse imagery against black—such as a starry night sky—produces very little scattered light. In this case contrast is likely limited by the projector's sequential contrast (on/off black level) or ANSI contrast (typically limited by scatter in lens and optics) and not contrast loss due to crossbounce.

In (Figure 12) we illustrate crossbounce by tracing a single ray of light with illuminance L. This ray strikes a grey Lambertian screen (which scatters equally in all directions) with reflectance r. The resulting image illuminance seen by an observer is therefore proportional to r. Crossbounce light is attenuated a second time relative to the primary reflected image. Therefore, the intensity of a crossbounce ray varies proportional to r^2 as r is varied. The overall crossbounce contrast ratio (r / r^2) varies approximately as 1/r. So as the reflectance is lowered, crossbounce contrast, which is inversely proportional, increases.

This simple model neglects image shape and intensity variation and more complex specular properties of dome screens. The real-world factors contributing to crossbounce on arbitrary images are complex and can be solved through numeric modeling (Hazleton, 2016).

In practice a standard method for measuring the crossbounce contrast ratio is to project a black and white checkerboard over the entire dome surface and measure the ratio of luminance between the white squares and the black squares (Lantz, 2004).

Checkerboard contrast can be derived using integrating sphere theory (Ganter, 2012) and is given by:

$$C = 2 (1 + A/2) / A$$

Where A is the amplification factor given by

$$A = 1 / (1 - r/2 * (1-\cos(Ø/2))) - 1$$

Where r is the dome screen reflectance (also called gain) and Ø is the vertical dome elevation.

Checkerboard contrast as a function of dome gain and vertical elevation is shown in Table 2. Many traditional planetariums utilize hemispheric screens (elevation of 180 degrees) with a gain of 0.65 which works well for star projection where the imagery is mostly black with pinpoint stars and planets. However, this results in a checkerboard contrast of less than 4:1 which is concerning for cinematic content creators as it severely limits image quality for brighter content. In comparison, digital cinema systems are generally expected to maintain checkerboard contrast of 100:1 or more.

Lowering screen gain and decreasing elevation angle can drastically improve the crossbounce contrast ratio. Halving the screen reflectance approximately doubles checkerboard contrast. IMAX® Dome screens designed for cinema have typical reflectance of 0.28 or less. The Vulcan Holodome, a spherical theater designed by Vortex Immersion Media, Inc., used a screen with reflectance of 0.13. This dark grey screen decreased image brightness nearly by a factor of eight requiring much brighter projectors to compensate for the optical loss. Unfortunately, many existing digital domes were originally constructed for star projection with a screen reflectance exceeding 0.6 which is entirely unsuitable for cinematic content.

Even the best projection dome screens would be hard pressed to achieve 100:1 checkerboard contrast. A dome with elevation angel of 155 degrees would need to have a reflectance of 0.025 to achieve 100:1 contrast which would attenuate projected light by a factor of 40. Clearly, if digital domes are to achieve their full potential to faithfully reproduce real or simulated imagery, another solution must ultimately be found.

Another method for increasing crossbounce contrast is to increase screen gain. Basically, a high-gain screen concentrates reflected light into the specular direction rather than scattering light equally in all directions. If the projector is a single-lens design placed near dome center, a high-gain dome screen will concentrate reflected light back down towards the projector—and thus, concentrate reflected light into the audience seating area. High gain dome screens have been manufactured for IMAX® Ridefilm and specialty simulator systems. However, while this approach works for smaller single-projector systems it does not scale up to multi-projector edge-blended systems in theaters since image brightness of overlapped projectors in blend regions varies according to viewer position within the theater. Simulator systems have a single viewer with a small "viewing volume" and therefore can compensate for viewer position. Larger dome theaters require multiple projectors to scale up brightness and resolution.

Novel approaches to compensating for crossbounce have been summarized by Rößner, Christensen, and Ganter (2016) and include real-time computational "reverse radiometry" (Bimber, Grundhofer, Zeidler, Danch & Kapakos, 2006), dome screens with microstructures to provide selective gain (Bublitz, D. 2011), camera based approaches (Habe 2007) or photochromic screens that can selectively subtract light (Takeda, 2016). These approaches have not been applied to large-scale digital domes as they are either highly computationally intensive, expensive to manufacture or not suitable for large-scale dome theaters.

The ultimate digital dome display will likely require a departure away from projected display technology altogether.

LED Display Systems

The use of discrete LED panels has the potential advantage of greatly reducing cross-dome scatter, opening the door to high-dynamic range (HDR) dome theaters (Kleiman, 2019; Campos, 2019; Brennesholtz, 2019). LED's are also brighter, easily exceeding the 55 nits requirement for digital cinema resulting in better perceived color saturation. Recent innovations in LED domes include perforated panels for sound transmissivity and custom fabricated panels for spatial pixel uniformity over the spherical surface.

The primary barrier to entry for LED domes is cost, which is bound to come down as LED technology advances. LED screens and other emissive surfaces (OLED, printed polymers) are likely the future of this format. Dome theaters should be designed to be future-proof and accommodate potential upgrade to emissive screens.

As shown in Figure 10, a 60m diameter 22k pixel dome requires 4.4mm pixel pitch to be eye-limited resolution—well within the capabilities of current discrete LED panel design.

Stage Projection Mapping

Projection mapping is a powerful tool to transform any spatial environment where ambient light levels can be controlled. Textures can be projected onto walls, floors, furniture, and more. In the case of a live stage performance, large digital sets can be computer cut or 3D printed to exactly resemble objects projected within the immersive dome scene.

The "holy grail" of live performance immersive design is where a vast spatial scene on the dome comes seamlessly into the room and onto an LED or projection-mapped stage. The effect is working when the eye cannot tell where the dome ends and the stage begins. This effectively opens a portal bridging the virtual cyber world and the real physical world (Zhang, Shen, Zhang, Zhu & Ma, 2019).

These two worlds become seamlessly stitched together when, for instance, a sun (projected onto the dome) arcs across the sky and the shadows of stage props (projected onto the stage) shift position, tracking the sun. A performer then lifts a glowing orb and the light rays illuminate 3D objects in the cyber world (projected onto the dome), seemingly emanating from the orb which is being tracked across the stage. The performer then walks on a treadmill while the 3D projected imagery on the dome scrolls past.

Another powerful effect is the tracking of performers and use of video projectors as stage lights. By placing light onto the performers only we can avoid spillage of ambient stage lighting onto projected scenes. We can also project textures onto moving performers.

Audio Systems

There are numerous surround sound configurations utilized in dome theaters, from 5.1 surround, 7.1 and 11.1 to custom 23.2 systems and beyond (Gaston, 2008). Three-dimensional audio processing is also coming into vogue. Standard commercial systems may conform to THX, be modeled after open source formats such as ambisonics or proprietary formats such as Dolby Atmos, Auro 3D and DTS. It is highly desirable to place audio in spatial configurations to match immersive visuals. More sophisticated wavefield synthesis techniques such as IOSONO and Auro 3D Max offer holographic sound reproduction allowing virtual audio sources to appear anywhere within the dome space.

The primary goal of a modern digital dome audio system should be the ability to accept nearly any set of audio stems with directional information or any set of surround channels and re-map the audio to the venue's speaker configuration. Vibroacoustic transducers on the floor or chairs can also transmit low frequency vibration through the sense of touch. This is best provided by a separately mixed channel rather than deriving it from the sub bass channel.

Figure 13. Multipurpose event dome configurations. © 2019 Vortex Immersion Media, Inc. Used with permission

DIGITAL DOME APPLICATIONS

Theater Types

Two primary theater types are recommended for standardization as arts and entertainment venues: Multipurpose domes and CineTheater™ domes.

Multipurpose Domes

The first and most popular design for mobile domes is a simple non-tilted dome with level floor and removable seats. This architecture is a multipurpose design that serves as a digitally themed ballroom or event center and is suitable for banquets, dance parties, concerts and simple theatrical productions (Figure 13). Provisions must be made for storage of chairs, tables bars and other equipment that may be swapped in and out according to event type.

CineTheater™

The optimal design for shared theatrical productions is the CineTheater™ with tilted springline, stadium seating deck and projection mapped (or LED) stage (Figure 14). Such a theater can maximize the illusion of a seamless merging of real and virtual worlds.

There are substantial challenges to the seamless integration of video backdrops and set pieces in dome theaters since there is no theatrical proscenium to hide lights or drop scrims, set backdrops, props and rigging. These effects must instead be raised from underneath the stage or dropped from overhead through moving ports in the dome screen. A number of innovations in theatrical staging are now being developed and standardized allowing productions to be easily distributed to a network of CineTheaters™.

Figure 14. Mobile Vortex CineTheater™ design. © 2019 Vortex Immersion Media, Inc. Used with permission

Immersive Experiences

Digital domes are general purpose immersive environment that are extremely flexible and can be used in a variety of ways to deliver sit-down, stand-up and walk-through experiences.

360 Cinema Experiences

Domes are best known for delivering amazing 360 cinematic journeys, from IMAX films to thrill rides and visual music entertainment. Like VR, 360 cinemas can evoke deep empathy and create breathtaking spectacles.

Live CineTheater™ Performances

Live performers can step into and interact with projected immersive environments which can serve as digital sets. CineTheaters™ have features that support live performances including projection mapped stage and props, video-based lighting, talent facilities, and more.

Broadway, Cirque and large-scale theatrical stage shows rely on extensive physical sets, props, and expensive stages to create massive spectacles for attendees. As discussed by Passy (2013), mounting a Broadway show typically costs $5 million to $25 million. At the high end, for the Cirque du Soleil show *KA* they built a custom $135 million theater with a moving stage. The show itself has 72 performers and cost $30 million to produce (Fink, 2004).

CineTheaters™ require a one-time investment in AV equipment which—similar to cinema— utilize live-action cinematography or visual effects to create the illusion of nearly any scene imaginable. But instead of viewing the scene within a rectangular frame on a wall, the digital dome wraps the environment around audiences to evoke a strong sense-of-presence. Live characters can enter the virtual environment and command it, effectively commanding the nervous systems of the audience.

While visual effects can be expensive, once produced, a CineTheater™ show can be rapidly and inexpensively mounted from a hard drive along with a handful of simple projection-mapped set pieces and minimal rigging. The cast is reduced because some of the performers can be rendered into pixels instead of being physically present for each performance.

The CineTheater™ brings cirque-scale spectacle into regional dome performing arts theaters with relatively inexpensive show mounting costs.

Ambient Visuals

A wide variety of events can be enhanced using 360 environmental backdrops. Cocktail parties, banquets, and gatherings of all kinds can benefit from abstract immersive scenes such as starry night sky, beaches, palaces, cityscapes, popular art and more. Scenes can be static or slowly changing with looping visuals (i.e. moving clouds, trees blowing in wind, birds soaring overhead). This is sometimes referred to as "digital wallpaper."

Interactive Experiences

The dome can serve as a group immersive portal into virtual worlds including interactive games, esports, and metaverse-based events. Walk-through immersive environments can be created that include projection mapping gesture-based textures onto real-world sets and objects.

Virtual World Experiences

Massively multi-user online virtual environments and games (MMO's) such as *Second Life*, *Fortnite* and *World of Warcraft* have attracted millions of users. Virtual world participants don avatar personalities and navigate through 3D shopping malls, nightclubs, games, and other user-generated virtual worlds. Avatars can work, eat, sleep, meet one another, make love, get married, raise children, purchase real estate, attend game shows, change gender, and act out fantasies. Users of MMO's build personalities, skills and attributes over time, just as in the real world.

Virtual worlds including user generated environments created in MMO's can ported into physical worlds as walk-through SAR environments using 3D-printed objects from the virtual world.

Lectures and Presentations

Slide-show presentations cannot compete with the power of immersive intelligent spaces. Panelists and presenters can teleport audiences into virtually any place on Earth or beyond, including rare ecosystems, astronomical datasets, microscopic domains, or virtual worlds. Executive presentations can command vast amount of information and visual simulations. Self-help speakers can add dramatizations and experiential elements.

Theatrical Experiences

Performers or dancers can create live interactive art on the dome and audiences can interact with dome content with user interfaces such as mobile phones, wands, game controllers, motion-captured gestures, or speech. The resulting "digital Cirque" performances can simulate massive theatrical spectacles that would otherwise be costly to fabricate. Virtual characters and sets can transcend reality as they are not bound by physical limitation. AI-driven "synthespians" can access personal data to personalize the audience experience for those who opt in.

Figure 15. Streaming options for live immersive media experiences
Source: © 2019 Vortex Immersion Media, Inc. Used with permission

Live Concerts and Dance Music Events

Video jockeys (VJ's) can take over the dome and perform to live music, bringing stand-up concerts and dance music events to an entirely new level. Advanced dome re-mapping servers support real-time frame capture and re-mapping allowing VJ's to directly drive the dome using their own VJ server and content. Advanced AI image generation allows real-time style transfer and other artistic effects. The powerful nature of 360 visuals elevates the VJ to equal status with the DJ. Gesture-driven "dome jockey" interfaces go further to allow a single performer to command both musical and visual performance from a single console.

Domecasting and 360 Multicasting

Global audiences can be engaged in live events (Figure 15) through 360 multicasting (15a) and dome-casting (15b). In these scenarios a 360 camera captures a scene, either within an immersion dome – such as a concert performance—or other live event and streams the event into other domes or headsets. In domecasting, the remote domes can enhance the experience with the addition of a local moderator or "shoutcaster" and additional video streams and information channels which can be displayed around the dome to augment the 360 "God's eye" view.

CASE STUDIES

To illustrate trends and state-of-the art in the industry here are a handful of real-world case studies across several application areas from pioneering companies making strides in this field.

Figure 16. Nokia Lab tri-dome featuring real-time 3D graphics, live music stage with VJ and live
Source: © 2019 Vortex Immersion Media, Inc. Used with permission

Experiential Marketing

Big brands want to dazzle audiences with memorable experiences and are willing to pay handsomely for it. Experiential marketing continues to be an on-ramp for newcomers in immersive media and an important proving ground for new tech coming out of the labs. These case studies demonstrate the power of immersive media to deliver unique and compelling brand experiences.

Nokia Lab Dome

The Nokia Lab immersion dome and digital projections were created by VIM for the 2012 SXSW festival in association with High Beam Events and featured a tri-dome translucent air-supported design with three 12m diameter dome sections. Air-supported structures require revolving doors or air-locks for ingress and egress that maintain the required positive inflation pressure. This project used an unusual projection architecture with a dome server built upon an interactive engine by Derivative called TouchDesigner which provided real-time 3D animation capability. Experiences included a variety of immersive environments created in cooperation with Pixomondo (water, igloo blocks, rotating brand elements, and a "*Tron*-like" world), slowly rotating real-time 3D models of Nokia's new phone and real-time simulated northern lights that users could interact with using a touch table. Live moderated Twitter feeds were also projected onto the dome and a VJ performed visuals in real-time with live band. The VJ visuals initially filled the entire dome but induced vertigo in some attendees, so the art was scaled down and projected onto the screen of the 3D phone model which was positioned to appear floating above the band.

Twitter Feeds

This and other translucent dome projects identified the need to both reduce ambient light inside and outside the structure and increase projector brightness (Figure 16). In (16a), the luminous bar washed out projections from the interior, while (16b) shows how exterior street lights (along with automobile headlights) interfered with the experience inside the dome. Text on the dome also had to be constantly rotated so it appeared correctly to viewers both inside and outside the dome.

Figure 17. Xbox Dome at Super Bowl XLVIII in New Orleans
Source: © 2019 Vortex Immersion Media, Inc. Used with permission

Super Bowl

The NFL Super Bowl Host Committee commissioned an 18m inflatable "Stratosphere" dome structure in 2012 to serve the nearly one million visitors anticipated at the Super Bowl Village, a temporary entertainment zone in downtown Indianapolis. Microsoft's Xbox came in and sponsored the dome. 3D animated visuals were projected onto the dome interior and exterior.

A second Xbox dome venue was commissioned for Super Bowl 2013 (Figure 17). The interior included a Kinect interaction station allowing visitors to throw simulated Mardi Gras beads, levitate a playing field with running football players or spin Xbox brand elements around on the dome. The 15 m opaque vinyl covered negative pressure dome was seamlessly projection-mapped on both the exterior and interior. The exterior featured rotating brand elements and provided visibility from many points along the Mississippi river. Snorkel doors reduced the amount of ambient sunlight entering the dome as audiences entered allowing a more controlled ambient light environment. Lighting on interior signage

Figure 18. EMC World 2013 exterior and interior dome
Source: © 2019 Vortex Immersion Media, Inc. Used with permission

was also delivered using projection mapping to reduce interior ambient light. A smaller 7m dome was attached to the main structure which housed a photo booth experience as visitors exited the venue. Approximately 10,000 visitors passed through the dome over several days.

4D Storytelling

Storytelling journeys use immersive media to amplify the experience.

EMC World Domes

EMC[2] commissioned an 11-meter tilted tradeshow dome and a series of 5-minute "thrill rides" into the world of electronic information (Figure 18).

In 2012 VIM worked with EMC brand managers to craft a story to fly audiences through a "dataverse" showing how private and public clouds could be trusted to serve corporations. In 2013 the same team created a *Tron*-like world that we navigated in a "dataship" while that illustrated tools for IT security and governance. Both pieces included animation with live-action elements and visual effects produced with support from Pixomondo, an Academy award-winning visual effects house that won three Emmys for their dragon animations on HBO's *Game of Thrones* (2011-2019) and an Oscar for its work on Martin Scorsese's *Hugo* (2011).

Constantine Dome

NBC Universal commissioned the creation of an original experience for the launch of *Constantine* (2014), a TV series based on the DC Comics character and 2005 film starring Keanu Reeves. The 3.5 minute animated themed experience was produced in six weeks and included a flythrough of a creepy sanatorium and collision with a ghost train while combating demons. Synchronized 4D effects included wind and strobes. The show was screened 1,200 times over five days.

Figure 19. Stella Sensorium in Toronto, Canada
Source: © 2019 Vortex Immersion Media, Inc. Used with permission

Immersive Dining

The Stella Artois' Sensorium immersive pop-up dining experience in Toronto, Canada featured a sense of taste, sight, smell, sound and touch throughout a five-course meal by celebrated chef Richie Farina. Show in in Figure 20, the event sold out an entire month of servings at $125/plate prior to opening.

Arts and Entertainment

A number of immersive arts and entertainment projects have been pioneered in digital planetariums over the years (Lantz, 2009). However, only a small number of dedicated arts and entertainment immersion dome venues exist at this time.

Vortex Dome LA

The Vortex Dome, established in 2010 at Los Angeles Center Studios in downtown Los Angeles has served as a public showcase and testbed for immersive mixed-media productions including; 360 ballet, live painting, musicals, EDM experiences, concerts, solo performances, 360 cinema and more (Lantz, 2018). The 15m dome accommodates up to 130 seated or 240 standing and continues to serve as an immersive media development, R&D lab, and showcase studio.

Productions at the Vortex Dome include; *Migrations* (2011) with visual artist Audri Phillips and composer Winter Lazerus, *Blue Apple* ballet with visuals by Audri Phillips and choreographer Stefan Wenta, *BollyDoll* by artist and singer Amrita Sen and composer Anthony Marinelli, *Deep, Deeper Deepest* with visuals by Audri Phillips and space music artist Steve Roach, *Refractor Piano* performed by Peter Manning Robinson with visuals by Hana Kim and Klaus Hoch (multicast in 360 VR), a performance by the band Braves with visuals by Brianna Amore, and *Ceremony* and *Mesmerica* visual music performances with musician, James Hood.

Other productions explored in the Vortex Dome including traditional film screenings, performance art, EDM events, poetry readings, experimental art, sound and light meditations, workshops, panels, symposia, immersive film festivals, immersive dining experiences, a *Teletubbies* premiere party for Nickelodean and more. Next-generation interactive performances are now in production including Audri Phillip's *Robot Prayers*.

Video shoots in The Votex Dome include an MTV pilot for a global multicast dance party, two *60 Minutes* episodes, a scene from the TV series *Castle*, an independent sci-fi film, music videos, documentary interviews with legendary jazz musician Wayne Shorter, with rapper Chuck-D from Public Enemy, and most recently a futuristic set for Jay Z's music video called *Family Fued* with Beyoncé. Events are regularly live-streamed in 360 video for viewing in VR headsets.

SAT

Montreal's SAT (Société des arts technologiques) in CANADA features the Satosphère, an 18 m projection dome with unique multipurpose design dedicated to artistic creation and visualization events (Husband & Barsalo, 2005). The theater opened in October 2011 and has hosted numerous fine arts performances. SAT is one of the world's first permanent dedicated arts and entertainment dome theaters. The successful business model includes an innovation lab, restaurant and bar making it a frequented local destination in addition to a successful immersive theater.

Wisdome

And in late 2018 the Wisdome Immersive Art Park opened in Los Angeles' Arts District featuring two mobile projection domes and three exhibition domes. The venue is open daily featuring the works of visionary artist Android Jones and holds special events such as tribute bands, sound healing, screenings and more.

IAIA Digital Dome

The Digital Dome at IAIA (Institute for American Indian Art) is dedicated to exploring "new applications for creative expression, scientific and technical exploration, and the merging of art and technology." It features a 7m suspended dome that can rotate from a level dome to 90-degree tilt, a 15.1 surround sound system and up to 55 removable seats. The dome has featured numerous art installations and screenings.

Pharos

Pharos was a temporary mobile dome show featuring Childish Gambino (aka Donald Glover) located in the Joshua Tree desert. Gambino performed five shows over three days in a 49m inflatable dome theater with a 2500-person capacity. The Microsoft-backed production team led by animators Mikael Gustafsson and Alejandro Crow spent two weeks in The Vortex Dome in downtown LA preparing the show which was VJ'd live from dual Unity servers outputting 4k x 4k and re-mapped onto a 12-projector display at 60 fps. *Billboard* raved that "...the dome was truly the highlight of the night," and Hip-Hop DX called it "... the most innovative live show this decade." The second Pharos dome in New Zealand featured five Unreal servers feeding a single re-mapping server, with one rendering the sides of a hemicube.

The largest dome VIM has delivered was a 60m inflatable structure at the Los Angeles Coliseum produced by The Production Club for a well-known game designer. Over 3,000 people enjoyed the world's most immersive EDM party with performances by Skrillex, Diplo and DJ Snake.

Mesmerica 360

Mesmerica is an extremely successful cross-platform production including a live performance with James Hood (still running at the Vortex Dome LA), a fulldome film for distribution (currently playing in over 23 planetariums and IMAX® Laser Domes) and a companion VR experience. Directed by Michael Saul, it features James Hood's cheerful music set to world-class fulldome art. The show is expressly designed to activate positive brain states and a sense of wellbeing. Contributors include Jonathan A.N. Fisher, PhD., an Assistant Professor and the Director of the Neurosensory Engineering Lab in the Department of Physiology at New York Medical College who provided brain visualizations from Neurodome® and Mark Subbarao, PhD from the Adler Planetarium in Chicago who provided a galactic zoom and brain sequence renders. Other artists include Brianna Amore, Ken Scott, John Banks and Tatiana Plakhova.

Other Case Studies

Paul Allen's Holodome

In late 2015, a Request for Proposals (RFP) from Paul Allen's Vulcan was released seeking proposals for a "Holodeck." The resulting system used four each 4k laser projectors aimed into a semi-spherical screen driven by full-sphere equirectangular movies from TouchDesigner playback and remapping server and two separate Unity servers. Vulcan introduced the Holodome into the MoPop museum in Seattle in early 2019 [3].

Universal Sphere

The Universal Sphere opened in April 2019 in the lobby of Philadelphia's new Comcast Technology Center. The 34' diameter dome theater features a free 7-minute film called *The Power of I* about the origin and power of ideas produced by Steven Spielberg in cooperation with DreamWorks Animation, Universal Parks and Resorts and Comcast Labs.

The theater, two years in the making, was designed by Foster + Partners, a London-based architectural firm led by architect Norman Foster. It is ADA-compliant with wheelchair access and closed captioning devices. The development team rented the Fels Planetarium at The Franklin Institute Science Museum as part of their show development.

Comcast CEO Brian Roberts explained "The first 50 years for our company were about finance and entrepreneurship. If we're going to thrive for the next 50 years, it's going to be about innovation, media, and technology" (Stephens, 2019).

THE FUTURE

Immersion domes have been called the "next big thing" for live immersive performances [Csathy 2018]. Two companies have announced major brick-and-mortar developments that promise to kick off a rapidly expanding ecosystem of immersion dome theaters.

Figure 20. Vortex DomePlex conceptual rendering
Source: © 2019 Vortex Immersion Media, Inc. Used with permission

Vortex DomePlex

Vortex Immersion Media has announced a new project in development called the Vortex DomePlex (Roettgers, 2019) (Figure 20). This immersive arts and entertainment complex includes a 2500 seat performing arts CineTheater™, two 1,000-capacity Vortex Dome events domes and smaller dome spaces for retail, experiential lounges and VR arcades. The facility is designed as a major exhibition venue for stand-up, sit-down and walk-through immersive experiences.

The CineTheater™ features an advanced projection-mapped elevator stage, video-tracked theatrical lighting and 3D sound including infrasound and vibroacoustic chairs. The theater will be fitted with a multicamera 360 video capture and streaming system for domecasting and VR multicasting. An MMO metaverse version of the venue will encourage remote pre- and post-event engagement and community building around a wide range of entertainment themes.

One of the Vortex Domes will serve as an after-party venue allowing story extension. It will be equipped with photonic go-go booths, elevator stages for DJ's (dome jockey), full audience tracking and multi-VJ performance consoles. The open architecture design will allow artists to perform from their own servers which can be installed on site. Another Vortex Dome will serve as flex space to expand storytelling worlds into walk-through immersive experiences, host travelling exhibits and more.

Vortex's business model is designed to be flexible, accommodating an ever-evolving technical, artistic and consumer market. The company seeks to present family programming in the daytime, "digital cirque" entertainment residencies in the evening and interactive electronic entertainment for late night.

MSG Sphere

Madison Square Garden Entertainment has announced the MSG SPHERE, a 17,500 seat LED-based digital dome to be constructed in Las Vegas and London. The project – currently estimated at $1.7b, features a 152m LED-mapped spherical exterior and an interior LED dome screen. The project is currently under construction in Las Vegas.

FUTURE RESEARCH

Immersion domes suggest a wide range of academic and commercial research opportunities spanning neuroscience and cognitive science, computer graphics and interactive techniques.

Cognitive research is needed to better understand the effect of immersive media on consciousness and it's use in storytelling and delivering impact. It is possible that unique brain states such as the pilomotor reflex and the release of pleasurable brain chemicals such a dopamine, serotonin, oxytocin and endorphins could be optimized in highly immersive and interactive experiences (Salimpoor, Benovoy, Larcher, Dagher & Zatorre, 2011; Manninen, et al. 2017). And how can audience biometrics combined with AI be used to optimize these responses?

The economics of dome theaters allows the installation of GPU supercomputers for real-time raytracing and deep learning algorithms. What new experiences can be offered with such computing power? If we can specifically identify audience members and—through their opting in—can access their "big data" social media assets, how can AI use these assets to enhance the audience experience? And how can AI be used to assist the interpretation of music through immersive visuals, or vice versa?

Rendering, animation and computing algorithms are often biased towards planar imagery and cartesian coordinates. What shortcuts might be possible when serving graphics exclusively for spherical environments?

The dome is effectively a portal into cyberspace. XR technologies can bring cyberspace into the real space of the theater as well. Stage performances within immersive environments are greatly enhanced by tracking both props and performers and altering the immersive environment in response to their movements. Lighting and textures can be mapped onto moving performers, providing avatar-like capabilities to transform. Performers can be volumetrically scanned and placed into MMO metaverses and role-playing games.

And what AR/VR/XR/360 interfaces and devices and applications can be developed for in-dome or at-home audience participation? Can a billion people attend a single immersion dome event?

CONCLUSION

Arts and entertainment in digital immersion domes have been steadily growing, first appearing in domes intended for astronomy and space science and giant screen documentary films. Market growth is evidenced by the success of *Mesmerica*, the Vortex Dome, SAT, IAIA's Digital Dome and the more recent success of the Wisdome Art Park plus the success of *Pharos* which received praise from *Billboard* and Childish Gambino's many fans. Recent announcements of MSG Sphere and the Vortex DomePlex indicate that arts and entertainment domes are on a growth trajectory.

If digital arts and entertainment dome networks are to be established there will need to be standards in dome designs. Two general venue designs have been suggested for standardization efforts; the Multi-purpose Dome and the CineTheater™. A number of relevant design factors were reviewed to support such an effort. It is hoped that industry-wide cooperation will lead to a robust distribution network, allowing artists and producers to benefit from digital distribution of powerful immersive experiences.

It is also hoped that the power of this next-generation immersive format is used mindfully for positive societal impact. Digital domes are part of an immersive media ecosystem that will have profound and far-reaching impact on humanity.

ACKNOWLEDGMENT

All images © 2019 Visual Bandwidth, Inc. unless otherwise denoted.

REFERENCES

Bimber, O., Grundhofer, A., Zeidler, T., Danch, D., & Kapakos, P. (2006). Compensating Indirect Scattering for Immersive and Semi-Immersive Projection Displays. *IEEE Virtual Reality Conference (VR 2006)*. 10.1109/VR.2006.34

Brennesholtz, M. (2019). NAB's 2019 Display Awards: DesignLED Technology. *Display Daily*. Retrieved from https://www.displaydaily.com/article/display-daily/nab-s-2019-display-awards

Bublitz, D. (2011). *Projektionsfl¨ache zur Frontprojektion*. Patent Disclosure Document DE 10 2011 008471 A1.

Campos, G. (2019). Kraftwerk Living Technologies launches LED dome solution. *AV Magazine*. Retrieved from https://www.avinteractive.com/news/products/kraftwerk-living-technologies-launches-led-dome-solution-04-04-2019/

Csathy, P. (2018). Fearless Media 2.0: An insider's guide & call to action for today's media 2.0 world & where it's going. *CREATV Media, Ch.*, *3*(Part III), 269–271.

DIGSS. (2018). *Digital Immersive Giant Screen Specifications 2.0 (DIGSS)*. Giant Screen Cinema Association. Retrieved from https://www.giantscreencinema.com/Member-Center/DIGSS

Fink, J. (2004). Cirque du Soleil spares no cost with 'KA.' *Las Vegas Sun*. Retrieved from https://lasvegassun.com/news/2004/sep/16/cirque-du-soleil-spares-no-cost-with-ka/

Fraser, P. (2018, Feb.). Giant-Screen Biz Meets Themed Entertainment...and They Get Along Just Fine! *LF Examiner*.

Ganter, C. (2012). Projectors and Dome Effective Contrast. *IPS 2012 Conference Proceedings*. Retrieved from http://media.definititheaters.com/node/43

Gaston, L., Dougall, P., & Thompson, E. D. (2008). Methods for Sharing Stereo and Multichannel Recordings among Planetariums. *Proceedings of the AES 124th Convention*.

GOTO, Inc. (2016). *Second full-sphere projection system installed at Fukushima Prefectural Government Environmental Creation Center*. Retrieved from http://www.goto.co.jp/english/news/20160908/

Habe, H., Saeki, N., & Matsuyama, T. (2007). Inter-reflection compensation for immersive projection display. *Proceedings of the IEEE International Workshop on Projector-Camera Systems (ProCams)*.

Hazleton, A. (2016). *CrossBounce Simulation*. GitHub, Inc. Retrieved from https://github.com/zicher3d-org/domemaster-stereo-shader/wiki/CrossBounce-Simulation

Husband, J., & Barsalo, R. (2005). *The SAT Urban Hub. Vision, issues and opportunities and future directions*. SAT Metalab White Paper. Retrieved from https://bibbase.org/network/publication/husband-barsalo-thesaturbanhubvisionissuesandopportunitiesandfuturedirection-2005

IMERSA. (2014). *IMERSA/AFDI Dome Standards Group, Dome Master Standards*. Retrieved from https://www.imersa.org/standards

Kleiman, J. (2019). Evans & Sutherland launches DomeX LED display for fulldome planetariums and giant screen theaters. *InPark Magazine*. Retrieved from http://www.inparkmagazine.com/about/

Kuchera-Morin, J., Wright, M., Wakefield, G., Roberts, C., Adderton, D., Sajadi, B., ... Majumder, A. (2014). Immersive full-surround multi-user system design. *Computers & Graphics*, *40*, 10–21. doi:10.1016/j.cag.2013.12.004

Lantz, E. (1997). Future Directions in Visual Display Systems. Guest Editor. *Computer Graphics*, *31*(2), 38–45. doi:10.1145/271283.271301

Lantz, E. (2004). Fulldome Display Specifications: A Proposal. IPS 2004 Fulldome Standards Summit, Valencia, Spain.

Lantz, E. (2009, June). The Planetarium: A Transitional Animal. *Planetarian*, *38*(2), 6–12.

Lantz, E. (2011, July). Planetarium of the Future. *Curator*, *54*(3), 293–312. doi:10.1111/j.2151-6952.2011.00093.x

Lantz, E. (2018). From space to the stars: Ten years of arts and entertainment at The Vortex Dome-Los Angeles. *Planetarian*, *47*(2), 22–28.

Lantz, E., Wyatt, R., Bruno, M., & Neafus, D. (2004). *Proceedings of the IPS 2004 Fulldome Standards Summit, Valencia, Spain, 7 July 2004*. Retrieved from http://extranet.spitzinc.com/reference/IPS2004/default.aspx

Maceda, C. (2015). Take a tour of Dubai in 3.5 minutes: 'The Sphere'-a first of its kind in the Middle East-offers virtual tour to visitors. *Gulf News*. Retrieved from https://gulfnews.com/travel/destinations/take-a-tour-of-dubai-in-35-minutes-1.1469766

Manninen, S., Tuominen, L, Dunbar, R., Karjalainen, T., Hirvonen, J., Arponen, E., ... Nummenmaa, L. (2017). Social Laughter Triggers Endogenous Opioid Release in Humans. *The Journal of Neuroscience*.

Navitar. (2019). HemiStar™ Application Notes. *Navitar*. Retrieved from https://navitar.com/products/download-document/2359/

Passy, C. (2013, June 10). How to invest in a Broadway show. *Market Watch*.

Petersen, M. (2019). *Fulldome Theater Compendium*. Lochness Productions. Retrieved from http://lochnessproductions.com/lfco/lfco.html

Proctor, D. (2017). Inside South Korea's first spherical projection theatre. *AV Technology Europ*. Retrieved from https://www.installation-international.com/technology/inside-south-koreas-first-spherical-projection-theatre

Roettgers, J. (2019). Vortex Plans to Open 2,500-Seat Dome Multiplex for Headset-Free VR Experiences. *Variety*. February 12, 2019. Retrieved from https://variety.com/2019/digital/news/vortex-domeplex-arizona-headse-free-vr-1203136609/

Rößner, M., Christensen, L., & Ganter, C. (2016). Characterising Fulldome Planetarium Projection Systems: The Limitations Imposed by Physics, and Suggestions on How to Mitigate, In IPS 2016 Proceedings. Retrieved from https://www.semanticscholar.org/paper/Characterising-Fulldome-Planetarium-Projection-%3A-by-R%C3%B6%C3%9Fner-Christensen/eddb673f09666d9468e04c9cd0d1ab5dfc93e9fb

Salimpoor, V. N., Benovoy, M., Larcher, K., Dagher, A., & Zatorre, R. (2011). Anatomically distinct dopamine release during anticipation and experience of peak emotion to music. *Nature Neuroscience*, *14*(2), 257–262. Retrieved from https://www.academia.edu/5008150/Anatomically_distinct_dopamine_release_during_anticipation_and_experience_of_peak_emotion_to_music. doi:10.1038/nn.2726 PMID:21217764

SMPTE. (2006). SMPTE Standard-D-Cinema Quality—Screen Luminance Level, Chromaticity and Uniformity. In ST 431-1:2006. 18 April 2006. pp.1-5. Retrieved from http://ieeexplore.ieee.org/stamp/stamp.jsp?tp=&arnumber=7292124&isnumber=7292123

Stephens, R. (2019). You'll Be Surprised by Steven Spielberg's Latest Project. *Fortune*, July 27, 2019. Retrieved from https://fortune.com/2019/07/27/steven-spielberg-universal-sphere-comcast/

Takeda, S., Iwai, D., & Sato, K. (2016). Inter-reflection Compensation of Immersive Projection Display by Spatio-Temporal Screen Reflectance Modulation. *IEEE Transactions on Visualization and Computer Graphics*, *22*(4), 1424–1431. doi:10.1109/TVCG.2016.2518136 PMID:26780805

Yamamoto, N., & Philbeck, J. W. (2013). Peripheral vision benefits spatial learning by guiding eye movements. *Mem Cogn 41*: pp. 109-121. Retrieved from https://link.springer.com/content/pdf/10.3758%2Fs13421-012-0240-2.pdf

Zhang, Y., Shen, Y., Zhang, W., Zhu, Z., & Ma, P. (2019). Interactive spatial augmented reality system for Chinese opera. In Proceedings of SIGGRAPH 2019. Article 14. pp. 1-2. Retrieved from https://dl.acm.org/citation.cfm?id=3338566

Section 3

Immersive Media and the Human Experience: Wider Implications From Entertainment to Beyond

Chapter 17
The Promises and Challenges of Immersive Education

Jacquelyn F. Morie
https://orcid.org/0000-0002-4934-4715
All These Worlds, LLC, USA

ABSTRACT

This chapter covers immersive media as an educational tool, from its origins as a simulation training device for military applications to more recent examples of how it is being used in education and training today. Educational immersive media provides firsthand experiential learning opportunities. Educational theorists have supported the use of experiential learning as an effective approach even before the current development of digital applications, and these ideas are mentioned briefly. A continuum of immersion is discussed to include several approaches from low cost to high-end simulation. The chapter provides several examples of the ways today's immersive education is being utilized. Benefits as well as challenges and issues of this approach are outlined. A call for future research concludes the chapter.

INTRODUCTION

"Education is our passport to the future, for tomorrow belongs to the people who prepare for it today."
  -Malcolm X

In the beginning—millennia ago—learning was a done by one of two methods: self-exploration in the physical world, or by being guided by someone who knew something you didn't and wanted to share this information. Learning was embodied and immersive, relying on the direct experience of our human being within the world and with others around us. In the intervening millennia that brought us to today, we developed ways to encapsulate knowledge and wisdom, going beyond the embodied mechanisms, abstracting information to something "out there"—something external—that could be accessed indirectly. We invented writing, and books, and were able to encapsulate knowledge as a separate thing unto its own.

More recently we have devised electronic methods to capture, analyze and make knowledge and data accessible to the connected. And through our technological tools we can now bring people together in ways once unimaginable. However, these tools tend to circumvent the original immersive nature of

DOI: 10.4018/978-1-7998-2433-6.ch017

learning and understanding in many ways. They oblige us to read, look and be alone in our quest for knowledge—interacting with a screen or book in an abstracted way.

Moving forward, we are now in an age when the very tools that connect us are becoming themselves immersive. This situation provides a unique opportunity to be able to revisit the forms of learning that supported our species in its formative years. Immersive technologies, such as the ones described in this book, are on the cusp of impacting the very way we consume and share our ever-widening forms of knowledge and understanding. In the very near future, education is poised to undergo transformation for how it is created, delivered and absorbed. Imagine a class where students across the globe can gather together without having to leave their home base and where they learn by being immersed within the lesson itself. In immersive learning scenarios, learners of all ages have the key learning objects, functions and people in the same virtual space, and experience them as embodied, spatial constructs. This is much more aligned with how humanity learned in its genesis years.

Education experts have explored the benefits of "Experiential Learning" for decades. John Dewey's early theories introduced the idea of experiential education as opposed to learning pre-digested material or rote facts, and claimed that the quality of that experience was critical, and that in part was due to the way individuals can create meaning from their interactions with the content of the experience (Dewey, 1938).

In the 1980s Seymour Papert took this idea even further by discussing how a learner can become the very thing about which they are learning.

The gear can be used to illustrate many powerful 'advanced' mathematical ideas, such as groups or relative motion. But it does more than this. As well as connecting with the formal knowledge of mathematics, it also connects with the "body knowledge," the sensorimotor schemata of a child. You can be the gear, you can understand how it turns by projecting yourself into its place and turning with it. It is this double relationship—both abstract and sensory—that gives the gear the power to carry powerful mathematics into the mind. (Papert, 1980, p. 2).

Virtual reality and immersive scenarios can facilitate a learner becoming that gear. One of the most engaging, informative and memorable virtual experiences I have encountered was being a particle in a particle accelerator (though extremely slowed down to meet my mere human perceptual constraints). "I" (my point of view) was whizzed through the accelerator and I came away with a new understanding of the twists and turns of the journey. This was on a Department of Energy (DOE) island in the virtual world Second Life (Bojanova and Pang, 2011, p. 223), itself a hotbed of instructional experimentation from about 2006 through roughly 2014.[1] It was this first-person viewpoint transporting me into the mode of *being* that particle that enabled a deeper understanding of the concepts involved.

According to Christian Itin, Experiential Learning consists of: "1) action that creates an experience, 2) reflection on the action and experience, 3) abstractions drawn from the reflection, and 4) application of the abstraction to a new experience or action" (Itin, 1999; p. 91).

Beyond the mental imagining that Papert envisioned, Virtual Reality can actually provide us a cognitively real, embodied mode of becoming the object of a lesson. From gears to particles, to foraging as a dinosaur in some Jurassic landscape, VR can engage our sensory mechanisms in visceral ways that impresses our mind into believing the experience is on a par with that which we experience in our physical reality.

Not only is Virtual Reality able to present realities—past, present and future—and the lessons we can glean from those, but also topics that are theoretical—such as mathematics or music—which can be presented and perceived in tangible ways. VR experiences can allow learners to interact with these constructs, learning more by direct manipulation, which brings into play a kinesthetic learning process known as embodied cognition that suits our physical nature. Immersive multi-sensory, embodied inter-actions have been shown to support stronger neural pathways in our brains beyond what simply reading about abstract concepts might do (Fisher & Coello, 2016). Immersive methods of distributing knowledge also can allow for failure in safe ways. Just as for the past several decades, aircraft pilots have trained in simulators that allow mistakes to be non-fatal (and less expensive than crashing a multi-million-dollar plane), many more types of training and learning can also benefit from more intensive lessons learned by safe failures.

And VR can even take us into realms of pure imagination. Early VR pioneer Jaron Lanier often opined about using VR to become creatures like lobsters that require a different body configuration to expand our modes of thinking (Lanier, 2010). Different types of navigation allow people to experience flying, changes in scale from macro to micro, time that goes super-fast or slow, and physics that challenge our understanding of our normal waking life, like trying the gravity on Mars. This ability to present different realties allows for participants to gain new understandings and points of view.

The promise of immersive education, of course, has challenges. The gear required to provide im-mersion into a spatial, embodied learning environment is only just emerging from companies, and there are no standards as yet. Head-mounted displays are bulky and one size does not fit all. Tracking, an essential core technology that supports embodiment and immersion, has made great strides in the past few years, especially with inside-out solutions, but still needs refinement. Input devices are still at the game controller stage and could be much more intuitive and closer to our normal ways of interfacing with the world. User interface design demands new techniques for immersion, but still has no agreed-upon best practices that designers can access. And incorporating additional senses such as haptics (touch) and smell, is still on a distant horizon for consumer use. We will certainly see improvements in all these areas, as buyers decide which devices best suit them and vote with their dollars. Other challenges include utilizing techniques to avoid the nausea that plagues a certain percentage of users, bringing costs down, and maintaining and upgrading rapidly developing technologies.

None of this should stop us. In fact, these emerging promises and challenges should spark ever more concerted efforts to bring the immersive educational future to everyone. This chapter will outline several efforts underway to deploy education topics in an immersive setting. Some are collaborative; some are not. Some do better with delivering a high level of embodied interaction. Some are unique one-off solu-tions. A very few are part of studies to see what works effectively and what doesn't in this new means of delivering education. We certainly need more formal studies, but we can learn from each and every experience being created. Each one tells us something—about what connects, what inspires, what is remembered. Some day we will look back at these efforts and see in them the seeds of the immersive transformation of education and learning that is our birthright and our future. First, however, we will explore some of the history of immersive learning.

BACKGROUND

Virtual Reality Origins (as Immersive Media)

To the current public, VR as the exemplar of immersive technology appears to have emerged fully blown with the announcement of Facebook buying a small company called Oculus that was experimenting with a low-cost headset for gamers to jump inside their 3D games (Harris, 2019). Arguably, this was less of a start and more a culmination of sorts, as VR in some form had been around since the mid 1960s as a research vector for the US military (Aitoro, 2016) and in its first commercials forays that happened (and eventually stalled) from the mid-1980s to about 2000 (Kawalsky, 1993). This second burst of VR activity saw a number of notable pioneers who worked diligently in the "second wave" of VR, but in the end, the technology was simply not cost effective enough for consumer prime time. And yet, alongside VR endeavors in entertainment, games, and health purposes during those years, some education applications were also developed.

The VR pioneers of the second wave were very aware of how immersive VR could be used for learning. Early VR expert Meredith Bricken stated in her 1991 article:

Virtual Reality as a Learning Environment

Using a head-mounted audio-visual display, 6-D position sensors, and tactile interface devices, we can inhabit computer-generated environments. We can see, hear and touch virtual objects. We can create, modify and manipulate them in much the same way we do physical objects, but without those pesky real-world limitations. VR is not only virtual: we can meet real people in virtual worlds, we can tele-exist in real places all over the world and beyond, and we can superimpose virtual displays onto the physical world (Bricken, 1991).

Training Simulation and VR

Even from the earliest days, virtual reality was considered an aid to training. Its history can be traced back several decades to pre-digital times. In 1929 Edwin Link created a training simulator called the "Blue Box" (Figure 1) for pilots to learn to fly when visuals were compromised, such as at night or in bad weather, a process now known as instrument flying. As such, his simulator had no display to speak of, but it did have pneumatic motion platform so the trainees felt some of the physical sensations of the flying experience (Courtney, 2017).

Ultimately this device was to find use as an entertainment device, much like mechanical horses and other coin operated "kiddie rides." Link himself patented the device for entertainment use in 1930.[2]

Years later the United States military, still interested in simulator training, paid for the earliest research into both Augmented and Virtual Realities with the ultimate goal of making better simulation devices. Connected Abrams tank simulator systems, collectively called SIMNET, allowed a crew to operate the various components of the tank such as driving, observation and handling ordinance. Visual were not worn but were digital displays that replicated the type of windows the tank would have. However, their primarily educational advantage was on how to communicate via the radio comms made necessary by the noisy environment (Miller, 2015).

Figure 1. Aircrew training during the 1940s with a link trainer
Source: The National Archives

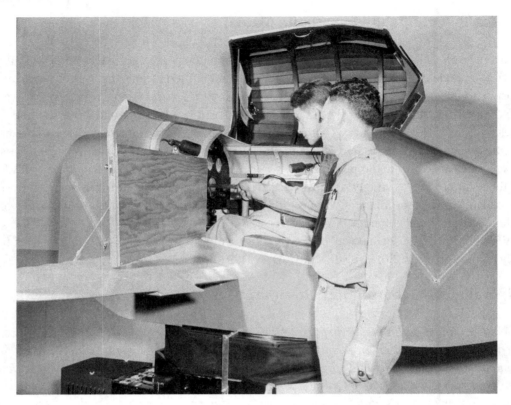

The Advanced Research Projects Administration (ARPA, later known as DARPA) funded the building of early immersive headsets that could project a computer display in front of a person's eyes. The 1960s version, created by Ivan Sutherland, a researcher, and Bob Sproull, then head of ARPA, consisted of two cathode ray tubes affixed to the sides of a user's head that projected a stereo wireframe display to a virtual space that appeared to be in front of the wearer's eyes. This computer-generated scene was actually overlaid onto the view of the room in which the person was standing and therefore was more like Augmented Reality rather than fully immersive VR that shuts out the physical world.

This system, which included mechanical parts to keep track of where the user was looking, was so heavy that it required a counterweight to keep the user's head from being too impacted. As such, it became known as "The Sword of Damocles" after the old Greek tale about a courtier who was jealous of a king until forced to sit under a heavy sword suspended by a single hair to illustrate how those is power are also always in danger. [Roman philosopher Cicero in his 45 B.C. book *Tusculan Disputations*.]

Sutherland's original definition of what has become to be known as a Head-mounted display (HMD) is this, from his 1968 paper in the Fall Joint Computer Conference, 1968: "The fundamental idea behind the three-dimensional display is to present the user with a perspective image which changes as he moves" (Sutherland, 1968). The fact that a user's actions can affect the presentation of images in a logical, spatial and embodied way is a key tenant of VR.

Sutherland had broader futuristic visions for such devices and how they would be used. In 1965 he published a short paper called *The Ultimate Display*. In this he envisioned:

The ultimate display would, of course, be a room within which the computer can control the existence of matter. A chair displayed in such a room would be good enough to sit in. Handcuffs displayed in such a room would be confining, and a bullet displayed in such a room would be fatal. With appropriate programming such a display could literally be the Wonderland into which Alice walked (Sutherland, 1965).

As the goal for this research was better training devices, Sutherland continued to work in this area, both in creating the fledgling field of computer graphics and the hardware to run and display these digital images. By 1968 he had partnered with David C. Evans to form a company called Evans and Sutherland, which commercialize computerized immersive training. During the 1970s, 1980s, and into the 1990s, it was one of the most popular flight simulators in use by the US military. These systems had the best real time graphics and audio coupled with a six degree of freedom motion platform to realistically convey believable motion of an aircraft to a participant or trainee.

A CONTINUUM OF IMMERSION

With this background firmly placed in the reader's mind, the boundaries of immersive education as discussed in this chapter can be presented. Immersion is one of the key tenants of Virtual Reality systems, as is physical tracking of a person's body. Immersion is typically achieved via a visual system that shuts out the surrounding physical world from a user's perceptions, replacing it instead with the object of the immersive experience. This method allows a participant to focus fully on the immersive, actively generated space with fewer distractions from external world inputs.

Secondly, physical tracking allows the immersive system to include participant actions such as head orientation, body position, gaze direction, gestures and navigation (and sometimes facial expressions) as input into the system in real time, with those actions directly affecting the Virtual Reality environment itself. This aspect brings an embodied sensibility to the resulting experience as the visuals, audio and other sensory presentations are computed directly from changes resulting from a participant's actions; the resulting space of the VR environment changes with whatever the participant does. These techniques support what is known as embodiment in the virtual space.

Embodiment is a powerful construct that affects us much like physical reality because our brains are evolutionarily wired to believe the inputs of our sensory mechanisms, even when those have been "hijacked" or replaced by other forms.

Now there are many other types of digital or computational media placed around the periphery of this definition that are also valuable approaches to more engaging educational roads. These include Augmented Reality, where the physical world is still in view, collaborative spaces where one learner has control and agency and others are passive observers, and 360 video-based experiences where a user's only activity is the turning of their head, though these will be covered only briefly in this chapter.

In fact, immersivity can be considered a continuum, from a passive viewing of a two-dimensional screen (which can often engage and feel cognitively immersive) to more active viewing of a 360 "surround" video (most likely not stereo), to stereo viewing in passive mode of an experience where one participant is the active "driver," to AR that overlays the physical world and, if done well, can integrate the virtual and the physical in a tightly coupled way. Closely related to full immersion is the fulldome venue, first utilized as a means for scientific education about the nighttime skies. At the extreme end of the continuum is fully immersive virtual reality, where a person's body, eye gaze and head orientation are tracked in real time, allowing for full interaction with elements of the VR environment. This final mode of full embodiment is the ultimate realization of interaction and immersion. Add to that multiple senses, and the experience comes as close to simulating a physical world experience as our technology currently allows.

IMMERSION IN EDUCATION AND TRAINING: SOME RECENT EXAMPLES

It is critical to remember that immersion forms of education are not a pedagogical approach in and of themselves, but rather modules that support curricular objectives and goals. Immersive educational modules need to be matched to the intent of the lesson as well as the subject matter. They should provide an enhancement to traditional learning methods that immersion best fulfills.

For example, it makes sense to use immersion if the lesson has an interactive or kinesthetic component such as learning how to handle hazardous equipment, or how to perform a specific surgery. These lessons are difficult to teach via basic book learning or other symbolic methods. Being within the environment—what Meredith Bricken describes as the 'inclusive interface' (Bricken, 1994) is a much more intuitive human situation.

You don't see text much in nature, so you cannot rely on it necessarily in critical learning situations. …. As instructors, if we imagine how we place the learner in the middle of a natural, unfolding story, in which their behavior determines the next outcome, we create a learning environment in 3D (Wankel & Heinrich, 2011. p. xiv).

The field of immersive education is growing, and more and more offerings are being added as developers realize that educational experiences can provide new and powerful ways of understanding for learners. Some notable examples are provided here to show the scope of what may be coming in the future. This is not meant to be a comprehensive listing, merely ideas of what can be done. The larger questions of how such examples might be deployed and what the assumed benefits could be will be addressed in the section outlining issues.

Example 1: Domes as an Educational Vehicle

Starting in the 1920s, projections of the night sky onto hemispherical domes heralded the start of the modern planetarium as a venue for scientific education about our nighttime skies. The Zeiss optical company came up with the concept of projecting patterns of light via a multi-lens projector onto the inner surface of such a dome measuring 16 meters (Zeiss, n.d.). The first such facility was installed in Munich, Germany and was called the *Sternentheater*, or star theatre (Firebrace, 2017; Kukula, 2017).

These planetariums surged in popularity during the Sputnik era, when attention to space became a critical aspect of new space exploration efforts, primarily by Russia and the United States of America. (In fact, Russia for many years boasted the largest planetarium at 37 meters wide.). Multitudes of school children visited planetariums in the 1950s and 60s to better understand the skies, stars and planets above them (Nadworny & Anderson, 2017).

By the 1980s the projections systems for planetariums were transitioning from optical to a digital format, with Evans and Sutherland, a simulation training company in Salt Lake City, Utah launching their Digistar systems that were installed in many global educational and entertainment venues (Faidit, 2009).

These were the predecessors to what we now call fulldome venues. Today we are seeing an explosion of dome installations, many for entertainment but often now with an educational component. These range from pop-up installations and festivals to more permanent structures that are open to use for multiple purposes.

At least one company—Spitz[3]—today offers an easy to use educational planetarium system called SciDome specifically designed for teachers. It includes the project system and a full curriculum covering topics from astronomy, to weather patterns and the composition of earth's core, to basic physics concepts where variables can be changed interactively in real time.

While not fully immersive as VR (participants have no body, face or gaze tracking so these systems fall in the 360/180 degree video category where your only agency is to turn your head to change your view as if you are inside a spherical screen) they still provide a large feeling of immersion with imagery filling your full field of view. This and the interactivity provided make them a great use case for future immersive learning.

Example 2: Google Expeditions

Perhaps one of the best-known recent deployments of a type of VR technology in the classroom is Google's Expedition (GE) Project, wherein Google provided a selection of classrooms with their low-cost cardboard viewers into which a smartphone could be placed running the Google Expeditions app. This app allows students to take virtual field trips to hundreds of locations that have been captured with a 360-degree camera. The teacher leads the students through the field trip via the guide mode on a tablet, and students, using the cardboard viewer, follow along in 'student' mode.

The Open University recently conducted a large-scale study of the affordances and efficacy of this low cost VR approach (Minocha et al., 2017). Participants in the study included not only the students (grades 4-11), but also educators, curriculum experts and fieldworkers. The study aimed to answer the following questions: 1) how effective were the GE VR simulations in representing the concepts and processes, 2) can such virtual field trips support physical fieldwork, and 3) can these modules support inquiry-based learning.

Even though the GE setup did not permit direct manipulation of any objects within the 360 recording, it still provided a unique and authentic viewpoint to a world that students would otherwise be unable to experience. Other aspects particular to standard field trips were also woven into the GE experience (e.g. preparing for data collection, understanding the purpose of the trip, assessing the impact of the trip after the fact). In this way the virtual field trips proved to be quite effective. In using the GE resources in conjunction with an actual physical visit to a location, an added benefit was perceived in that additional or hard-to-see details could be showcased and emphasized. And finally, the study concluded that inquiry-based learning was supported by the geography and science modules provided and tested.

In addition to these findings, the thrill of discovery from a class of excited students underscores the ability of such technology to capture the attention of today's youth (Brown & Green, 2016).

Example 3: NASA Astronaut Candidate Training

NASA has been a prime user of VR for Training, and in fact accelerated the development of the gear necessary to support their training efforts. The NASA Ames Research Center developed a full 120° FOV HMD (monochrome) in 1984 followed by a Virtual Environment Interface Workstation (VIEW) with stereo visuals, a full spatialized auditory system powered by a DSP Board called the Convolvotron (Crystal River Engineering), head and hand tracking via a Polhemus magnetic tracker, and gesture input that used a prototype glove (Kalawsky, p. 27). Scott Fisher led the VIEW Project, which pushed the development of the technology under NASA's sponsorship far more than hopeful commercial prototypes of those early days.

NASA's interest was specific: astronauts' teleoperation of equipment such as robotic arms that would be attached to the space station. These would have to be operated remotely, but in a way that gave the user a feeling of actually being in proximity to the objects being manipulated. Not only would the system provide functionality on the station at some point, they could be used to practice the actions needed to successfully maneuver the equipment. This became a critical training component when the Hubble Telescope, launched in 1993, required repair that could only be done remotely.

To support training needs for these very complex operations, NASA has taken the immersive training of astronauts to ever more sophisticated levels. At the VR Training Center at the Johnson Space Center, advances are researched and implemented by a team led by Dr. Evelyn Morales. There are four main areas of focus: training for EVA walks, rehearsing how to get back to the ship if separated using a backpack rocket, telerobotic activities, and practicing in low levels of gravity, this latter use facilitated by a pool which more closely resembles zero gravity (Carson, 2015). In addition, networked VR training situations also help hone communication skills.

Example 4: On the Job Training

On the job training is widely considered the best way to train in industry, but it is a time and cost consuming method that can tie up both people (as trainers) and facilities. This is an area where immersive systems are proving invaluable and are starting to be extensively deployed. Immersive learning promotes what Chris Dede calls effective transfer by simulating the real world effectively.

Transfer is defined as the application of knowledge learned in one situation to another situation and is demonstrated if instruction on a learning task leads to improved performance on a transfer task, ideally a skilled performance in a realworld setting (Dede, 2009. p. 67).

A new employee can take the immersive training module not only for initial learning, but also for refresher and certification classes. Walmart uses VR to prepare its employees to deal with the conditions they will encounter in Black Friday sales days (Thompson, 2019). Several energy companies are testing out immersive scenarios for operating complex and dangerous equipment, some of which have embedded assessment tools as part of the learning experience (Joshi, 2019). Especially in this latter category, the ability to gain experience with dangerous equipment in a safe manner is invaluable.

Figure 2. An immersive science lesson with Michael Faraday and James Clerk Maxwell
Source: Image courtesy of ScienceVR and Jackie Chia-Hsun Lee

Example 5: Social Training

In addition to on the job training, many companies are investing in using VR for more socially-oriented skills. These include training for diversity, inclusion and harassment mitigation, interviewing skills for professionals such as HR personnel and doctors, cultural training with language and social skills, and safe role playing for various types of social encounters. The benefits are that the VR experience can be done multiple times, with the learners gaining valuable knowledge from each encounter (Gillies, 2018). This leaves them better prepared to deal with a variety of circumstances, without worrying about the effect a naïve decision may have on another human being.

Example 6: Learning Science from the Scientists in VR

Imagine learning scientific principles from the people who invented or discovered them: magnetism from Michael Faraday, the theory of electromagnetic radiation from James Clerk Maxwell, and the secrets of radioactive elements from Marie Skłodowska Curie (Figure 2). This is the approach of Jackie Chia-Hsun Lee's company ScienceVR, which has a created number of these engaging, interactive experiences. From Archimedes' "Eureka" moment to Volta's development of batteries, science gets personable and real, and therefore quite memorable!

Example 7: Learning Complex Concepts in VR

Dede et al. (1997) were among the first to see the potential in virtual reality for a new form of interaction with the material to be understood. This team explored the very nature of learning as it was supported by specific affordances of VR. In the mid-1990s they built three ScienceSpace worlds to "enable unique, extraordinary educational experiences that help learners challenge their intuitions and construct new understandings of science" (p. 2). This work included evaluations of the VR environments from a "learner-centric strategy." Their description of one of their Scienceworlds, NewtonWorld, is particularly intriguing:

In NewtonWorld, users experience laws of motion from multiple points of view. In this world with neither gravity nor friction, balls hover above the ground. Users can become a ball; see, hear, and feel its collisions; and experience the ensuing motion (Dede, 1997. p. 3).

But what of complex and or abstract concepts? Can immersion provide an advantageous edge for these sometimes difficult to grasp topics? Many can be aligned with the 3D, agency-oriented features of VR.

For example—one can learn the Pythagorean Theorem via direct algebraic formula, but often a better and more complete understanding is achieved through geometric derivations or what is called rearrangement. Being able to take the geometry into visuals that can be manipulated in three dimensions can lead to an "a hah" moment for some learners.

Indeed, this was observed during one of the class sessions in a 2018 ten-week curriculum for Building VR Experiences of which the author was a part. Students were struggling with the concepts of adding vectors and understanding their impact on objects in VR.[4] By allowing students to actually manipulate those vectors while inside VR with controllers and an immersive HMD led to revelations for many students that allowed them to more fully comprehend the core ideas.

Scott Greenwald, who is pioneering the use of VR within MIT's curriculum, recently completed a study comparing complex concepts as presented via VR and traditional means (Greenwald et al., 2018). He states: "VR was perceived by learners to have advantages. We did find significant quantitative differences in learners' completion times. We share findings, based on the quantitative and qualitative feedback received, about what makes VR environments beneficial for learning about complex spatial topics, and propose corresponding design guidelines."

ADDITIONAL VR LEARNING APPROACHES

Learning to Create VR Experiences: Robert Eagle Staff Middle School

Creating a virtual reality experience involves a number of disciplines working in concert, such as computer science, computer graphics, design, user interfaces, physics, modeling, code writing, and iterative assessment. Using VR production as a multidisciplinary learning process can teach not only these skills but also collaboration, communication and more.

A recent example of this was the efforts of Tom Furness and several Virtual World Society (VWS) members to teach 28 middle schoolers at Robert Eagle Staff Middle School in Seattle how to create their own VR experiences (Figure 3).

The worlds the students created illustrated several STEM concepts such as gravity and light. With equipment provided by HTC Vive, each student worked with mentors from the VWS to learn how to setup and use the VR systems, critically analyze the concepts they wanted to create, and form teams to tackle the production process. Having a project that came from their own ideas empowered these students to create exciting experiences.

Figure 3. Students at the Robert Eagle Staff Middle School creating their own VR experiences
Source: Image courtesy of the Virtual World Society

This class was successful because of the dedication of the VWS volunteers, who had the technical expertise. Most teachers would need this type of support to enable such a class, but the rewards would be invaluable.

Using VR as a Creation Tool

Simple to learn and use VR apps that do not require programming have just started to arrive. Many of these fall into a creative arts categories such as dimensional painting and sculpting or animation. Examples include Google's TiltBrush, Oculus Medium, Quill, AnimVR and more. These programs allow someone to learn a relatively simple interface quickly and create in full 3D while being immersed in the creation space.

A number of college levels course are being designed around these programs, including one the author teaches at Otis College of Art and Design in Los Angeles. Not only are the students being very original with their artistic output, they are learning a great deal by being immersed in this creation space (Figure 4). Many of the students have stated that they never fully understood 3D modeling and animation programs they were using in their Digital Media classes until they were able to be inside the 3D space. One student used the VR programs to build and measure a sword he was taking from a 2D sketch to a physically built object to ensure that his hand would fit into the hilt properly. Such creation is, as one said, designing from "a more spatially informed point of view." Another described it as "a limitless me-

Figure 4. Students creating with VR art programs at Otis College of Art and Design
Source: Photo by the author

dium" and many remarked on it being an integral part of the future of art, and that VR art could be the "barely explored immersive three-dimensional experience medium that the art world has been missing."

BENEFITS OF VR FOR LEARNING

These examples begin to illustrate some of the many positive ways in which immersive, experiential learning can supercharge the educational process. Studies have been done in which VR has been shown to improve a wide range of cognitive aspects as diverse as *response times* (Sankaranarayananet al., 2018), *procedural knowledge retention* (Zhang, 2019; Babu, et al., 2018), *second language vocabulary learning* (Legault, et al., 2019; Cho et al., 2018), *attitudes and empathy* (Formosa, et al., 2018), *manual skill acquisition* (Pulijala, et al., 2018), and *spatial understanding of complex objects*, (Parkhomenko et al., 2018; Stepan, et al., 2017). Some of these show significant improvements in short and long-term retention of information after an active immersive learning session.

Chris Dede notes:

Studies have shown that immersion in a digital environment can enhance education in at least three ways: by allowing multiple perspectives, situated learning, and transfer (Dede, 2009. p. 66).

The presentation of multiple perspectives VR can provide reinforces the understanding of the lessons to be learned. And by accurately simulating the physical world, learners can transfer the skills used from the virtual to the actual world. This more direct transfer of skills allows for the application of that knowledge to other similar situations.

Other benefits include:

- Motivation

The novelty and wow factor in immersive experiences can provide enhanced motivation and willingness to explore.

- Focused attention

Immersive experiences separate us from the ordinary world, whether through a head-mounted display or being in a separate dome space. This situation leads to fewer distractions and more concentration on the material being presented.

- Exploration in a natural way

The three-dimension and tracking affordances of VR allow us to navigate, look around and even pick up objects in an intuitive manner. Its spatialized audio means that we understand where a sound is coming from and can turn, or look up or down, to find that source. The benefit of this immersion is that it mimics many of the ways we interact naturally with the world.

- Safe exploration of dangerous environments or situations

Many experiences are inherently dangerous in the physical world. And yet people may need training to interact with such spaces. A spatial virtual environment allows safe exploration of dangerous machines or distant places, while still providing many of the benefits of being in the actual place.

- Kinesthetic learning "hands-on" experiential

Because we are moving (and being tracked) in the virtual space, we use many of the same physical actions there that we use in the physical world. Even if the controllers and navigation devices are not mapped congruently, they still tend to activate the same motor areas in our brains and thus give us the feeling that we are acting with our body kinesthetically.

- Ability to transcend physical reality

The only limitation of what can be presented in an immersive lesson is one's imagination. From micro to macroscopic, from ancient history to predications of the future, from this planet to the stars—all forms of experiences can be presented.

- Opportunities for shared or social experiences

VR is rapidly advancing to allow for shared experiences whereby participants can log into a common VR space from anywhere in the world. Learners can access the best teachers anywhere, as well as their peers in other countries. This presents many new opportunities for learning, and most especially for cultural understanding.

- New forms of creative expression

Recent VR offerings allow participants to actually create *within* an immersive environment, as illustrated in the VR art class example described earlier in this chapter. This is a new method of creation fundamentally different from traditional forms of artistic expression. As such, VR can be utilized in diverse forms of creative expression, including dance, music, theater, plastic and fine arts and narrative storytelling. It may open up a new age of innovation and imagination in these areas.

- Opportunities for tailored learning

VR learning environments are flexible and can be tailored to individuals both in the physical aspects as well as to address varied cognitive learning styles. Especially with the inclusion of rapidly evolving artificial intelligence (AI) technologies, unique and customized variations of a lesson can be presented that matches the learner's particular needs.

ADVANCED CONSIDERATIONS

Two modalities that are just starting to be implemented within immersive learning environments are the use of personal avatars and the briefly mentioned inclusion of AI techniques to customize the educational module. These are powerful aspects that deserve a much fuller consideration, as they may stimulate news concepts in how we use these technologies for all forms of instruction. Two questions that these techniques raise are discussed next.

Does the Use of an Avatar Enhance the Learning Potential of Virtual Experiences?

The idea that avatars could become the ultimate somatic learning objects came to Jaron Lanier during the-early mapping of his body onto a that of a lobster avatar mentioned in the beginning of this chapter. He noted is was not difficult to map a very differently formed creation into something our human body could control, which he states is based on the concept of homuncular flexibility, or the ability of parts of our motor cortex to be repurposed rather rapidly when needed. Channeling Papert's becoming gear idea, Lanier states:

My favorite experiment so far involved turning elementary-school kids into the things they were studying. Some were turned into molecules, dancing and squirming to dock with other molecules. In this case the molecule serves the role of the piano, and instead of harmony puzzles, you are learning chemistry.

Somatic cognition offers an overwhelming emotional appeal for education, because it leverages vanity. You become the thing you are studying. Your sensory motor loop is modified to incorporate the logic of a science, and you develop body intuition about that logic (Lanier, 2010).

By the mid-2000s virtual worlds that people entered via an avatar (a personal digital representation) were gaining popularity.[5] KZero, a research firm that tracked their usage from age groups starting as early as five years old through mature adults, showed that in 2014 there were almost 100 million registered user avatars (though not unique) from age 25 up, 250 million in the 15-25 age range, almost a billion in the 10-15 segment, and approximately 400 million in the youngest range from 5 to 10 years old (Mitham, 2014). These are astonishing numbers! The important idea here is that the young generations that six years ago were using avatars in online flat screen virtual worlds are well-primed to jump into fully immersive spaces with avatars. What has been overlooked are the benefits that understanding avatar use can have for VR education. Online avatars were often designed or customized by their users, often involving an emotional attachment to these surrogates. While today's VR worlds often provide avatars for participants, they have a long way to go before they are customizable in the way the online avatars were. However, having an avatar that means something to its owner may enhance the educational experience in constructive ways. More research is needed to fully understand the educational potential for avatar engagement.

How Can AI Fit into Making the Educational Experience Better?

The move from instructor-led education to the more self-directed approach that VR provides presents some additional challenges. How does the student navigate the experience to maximum effectiveness?

Best practices need to be developed and evaluated as to their effectiveness, both in steering the student through the experience as well as in assessing learning outcomes and material retention. This is where AI technologies can play a role. From AI assistants who can recognize when a student is stuck and offer just-in-time help, to fully developed systems that ascertain a student's optimal learning approach and deliver that in VR in real time, the potential enhancements are unbounded.

ISSUES, CONTROVERSIES, PROBLEMS

Because immersive technology is evolving at a rapid rate, it is not surprising that there are several challenges associated with using it for education and training. Of course, any new technology will raise concerns that need to be addressed. A short list of these include:

1. Initial cost
2. Upkeep and staying up on the rapid technology advancements
3. Space for trackers and other equipment
4. Security for equipment and users
5. Hygiene for shared systems
6. Simulator sickness (simsickness)
7. Training the educators
8. Age controversies

9.   Uncomfortable or ill-fitting gear
10. Bullying in shared environments
11. Incomplete understanding of long-term effects
12. Lack of definitive studies

The initial cost as well as funds targeted at upkeep is a given, even with VR systems being the most affordable they have ever been. The ongoing advances in the gear alone demands a change out approximately every three years. An organization's IT department also has to keep up with the frequent software and computer updates (Steam, the VR portal for many applications, seems to require an update every time it is launched!), and often a dedicated employee is needed to know about keeping things both secure and updated. Space for the VR gear and security issues will also be considerations for the foreseeable future. There is overhead in the setup and tear down if there is not a dedicated space for the equipment. This is especially true in the classroom, which tends to be scheduled by different kinds of classes sharing the same space.

Classroom use currently seems to be an afterthought to the main VR companies. Educational institutions expect such support as site licenses for software so all students can access what they need. Currently this is not possible with VR content, so often each student must purchase their own copy of something like TiltBrush or Medium. And the constant software and firmware upgrades require administrator access, which is not often provided to students.

For shared systems, there are other issues that are small but might make the difference between people disliking the VR training and not—such as promoting hygiene (e.g. wearing masks or cleaning an HMD between users). There is also the issue of simsickness, which can cause some people to become nauseous when using VR. This is often caused by badly designed content, or by tracking and display issues such as low frame rates on older equipment, but some people are simply prone to it no matter how good the VR program.

Educators might ask: "Where does this VR module really fit in my curriculum?" and there may well be a mismatch between the available created experiences and what actually needs to be taught to students. There is also the need to train the trainers, who may be initially unfamiliar with VR systems.

A current controversy revolves around the best age to allow young people into immersive media. Most of the VR hardware manufactures state their product is for ages 12 or 13 and up. Many say that young children should not use their products at all (probably to limit liability and out of an abundance of caution). Supposed negative ramifications include physical concerns like kids developing near sightedness over time (Hill, 2016), as well as psychological ones due to children not being able to discern whether something is actually virtual or real. Segovia and Bailenson (2009) suggest that children may be unable to remember whether an experience initiated from a real world or virtual world space, due to the richness of the immersive media. This could result in the introduction of what are sometimes called "false memories."

As well, there are problems related to the form factors of the equipment itself, which is not adaptable to the range of potential users. Very young or small people have difficulty using the current HMDs, as do those with certain types of hair or head-worn religious garb. Even displays that allow for adjustable interpupilary distance may not cover the full extent of what some people need. Users with glasses are also left out, though some manufacturers are starting to address this with better spacing or additional lenses.

In social VR platforms there is the threat of bullying or other unwanted interactions. These challenges have garnered the attention of the software companies and there are several solutions that help a bit in this area, but certainly more can be done beyond safety bubbles, making one's avatar invisible, and better reporting methods.

Unfortunately, many of the educational examples provided in this chapter are prototypes, and few have been deployed to any scale within modern educational systems. And very little has been done to study them widely. It's somewhat a chicken and egg problem. Do we study the effectiveness in a small population and then deploy more broadly, or deploy broadly, then gather data on the effectiveness? Immersive education won't replace existing teaching methodologies any time soon, but may be used as supplemental modules within existing curricula. We really don't yet know the best ways to incorporate technology-based immersive modules in a classroom. For the foreseeable future, we will be most likely be gathering anecdotal and small study data to determine these best practices. This leads into a call for more research to underscore the beneficial uses of VR as an experiential educational tool.

FUTURE RESEARCH DIRECTIONS: A CALL FOR MORE RESEARCH

In a recent Venture Beat article by Amir Bozorgzadeh (2019), he states: "AR and VR have delivered on the promise to supercharge the enterprise's education and training industry." However, that article differentiates the successes that are primarily happening in enterprise training, as contrasted to public education, which the author characterizes as "a bureaucratic jungle of red tape."

While we may be beginning to understand what works for industry training, we are still far from knowing what the best instructional design approaches for immersive learning are. School-aged children span a wide range of ages and learning styles. A recent report from The Joan Ganz Cooney Center at Sesame Workshop outlines a possible research agenda to address the needs of young children using immersive media (Sobel, 2019). Such testing is needed to see how different learners adjust to and get the most out of a VR immersive experience. Currently we are at the early testbed phases of using VR for education. Meredith Bricken again, wisely states:

By making VR tools and environments available to educators, we may discover more about the very process of learning. By participating in the development of VR, educators can guide the growth of the technology, and perhaps influence the course of educational change. As we test and refine this unique learning environment together, we might even hope that VR really will help us to teach more effectively, and that we will see more often that bright light of understanding in our students' eyes. (Bricken, 1991)

This is how we should look at VR for learning—as a radical change and improvement for how we deliver and consume information in a learning context. Its promise is to change education for the better—back to how we originally learned in the beginnings of time—by direct exploration of our world (which now can be virtual or real), and by knowledge being shared with others who are in that environment with us. In addition, the use of AI and avatars within immersive education is barely starting and there is an abundance of understanding we need to research to effectively incorporate these technologies into immersive learning. For every dollar spent on developing new experiences, investment in the research to see what we can learn must be considered as equally important.

CONCLUSION

J.R. Pierce, the chairman of the President's Science Advisory Committee (PSAC) wrote a report in 1963 that included this quote: "After two decades of unprecedented development, the computer is approaching its infancy" (in Sproull, 2006). We are now approaching the "infancy" of VR within educational contexts, and this inception is both remarkable and exciting as we contemplate the impacts it may have going forward!

There are many benefits we already know immersive education provides, and more we will learn over time. We already know this approach:

VR will add a layer of detail and realism to a student's experience of the curriculum, but it should not be seen as an end in and of itself. It seems to work best as a complementary tool to previously taught information, or as a fun and engaging introduction to a topic. (Black p. 57)

What we continue to discover while VR and its kin carry on their meteoric rise may change the very fabric of learning. VR is showing promise at changing the way we actually think (Bailenson et al., 2008). And in many ways, this is a paradigm shift. I often note, "We have underestimated the plasticity of the brain, and VR is a way to unlock it." With such unlocking comes marvelous new opportunities for learning.

REFERENCES

Aitoro, J. (2016). 30 Years: Virtual Reality—Training Transformation. *Defense News*. Retrieved from https://www.defensenews.com/30th-annivesary/2016/10/25/30-years-virtual-reality-training-transformation/

Babu, S. K., Krishna, S., Unnikrishnan, R., & Bhavani, R. R. (2018). Virtual reality learning environments for vocational education: A comparison study with conventional instructional media on knowledge retention. In *2018 IEEE 18th International Conference on Advanced Learning Technologies (ICALT)* (pp. 385-389). IEEE. 10.1109/ICALT.2018.00094

Bailenson, J., Yee, N., Blascovitch, J., Beall, A. C., Lundblad, M., & Jin, M. (2008). The Use of Immersive Virtual Reality in the Learning Sciences: Digital Transformations of Teachers, Students, and Social Context. *Journal of the Learning Sciences*, *17*(1), 102–141. doi:10.1080/10508400701793141

Black, E. R. (2017). *Learning then and there: An exploration of virtual reality in K-12 history education* (doctoral dissertation). Accessed on August 23, 2019 at https://repositories.lib.utexas.edu/handle/2152/63616

Blascovich, J., & Bailenson, J. (2005). Immersive virtual environments and education simulations. In P. Cohen & T. Rehberger (Eds.), *Virtual decisions: digital simulations for teaching reasoning in the social sciences and humanities*. Mahwah, NJ: Lawrence Earlbaum Associates, Inc.

Bojanova, I., & Pang, L. (2011). Enhancing Graduate Courses through Educational Virtual Tours. In C. Wankel & R. Hinrichs (Eds.), *Transforming Virtual World Learning* (pp. 215–240). Bingley, UK: Emerald Group Publishing Limited. doi:10.1108/S2044-9968(2011)0000004013

Bozorgzadeh, A. (2019). The future of immersive education will be live, social, and personalized. *Venture Beat*. Retrieved from https://venturebeat.com/2019/07/26/the-future-of-immersive-education-will-be-live-social-and-personalized/

Bricken, M. (1991). Virtual reality learning environments: Potentials and challenges. *Computer Graphics*, *25*(3), 178–184. doi:10.1145/126640.126657

Bricken, M. (1994). *Virtual Worlds: No Interface to Design. Technical Report R-90-2. Human Interface Technology Laboratory (HITL)*. Seattle, WA: Washington Technology Center University of Washington. Retrieved from http://papers.cumincad.org/data/works/att/5dff.content.pdf

Brown, A., & Green, T. (2016). Virtual reality: Low-cost tools and resources for the classroom. *Tech-Trends*, *60*(5), 517–519. doi:10.100711528-016-0102-z

Carson, E. (2015). How NASA uses virtual reality to train astronauts. *TechRepublic*. Retrieved from https://www.yahoo.com/news/nasa-uses-virtual-reality-train-151645861.html

Cho, Y., Biocca, F., & Biocca, H. (2018). *How Spatial Presence in Virtual Reality Affects Memory Retention and Motivation on Second Language Learning*. Syracuse University.

Courtney, C. (2017). Edwin Albert Link: Inventor of the First Flight Simulator. *Disciples of Flight*. Retrieved August 24, 2019 from: https://disciplesofflight.com/edwin-albert-link-flight-simulator/

De Freitas, S., Rebolledo-Mendez, G., Liarokapis, F., Magoulas, G., & Poulovassilis, A. (2010). Learning as immersive experiences: Using the four-dimensional framework for designing and evaluating immersive learning experiences in a virtual world. *British Journal of Educational Technology*, *41*(1), 69–85. doi:10.1111/j.1467-8535.2009.01024.x

Dede, C. (2009). Immersive interfaces for engagement and learning. *Science*, *323*(5910), 66–69. doi:10.1126cience.1167311 PMID:19119219

Dede, C., Salzman, M., Loftin, R. B., & Ash, K. (1997). *Using virtual reality technology to convey abstract scientific concepts. Learning the Sciences of the 21st Century: Research, Design, and Implementing Advanced Technology Learning Environments*. Hillsdale, NJ: Lawrence Erlbaum.

Faidit, J. M. (2009). Planetariums in the world. *Proceedings of the International Astronomical Union*, *5*(S260), E9. doi:10.1017/S1743921311003292

Firebrace, W. (2017). *Star Theatre: The Story of the Planetarium*. London: Reaktion Books.

Fischer, M. H., & Coello, Y. (Eds.). (2016). *Foundations of embodied cognition: Conceptual and interactive embodiment*. Routledge/Taylor & Francis Group.

Formosa, N. J., Morrison, B. W., Hill, G., & Stone, D. (2018). Testing the efficacy of a virtual reality-based simulation in enhancing users' knowledge, attitudes, and empathy relating to psychosis. *Australian Journal of Psychology*, *70*(1), 57–65. doi:10.1111/ajpy.12167

Gillies, M. (2018). Purposeful Practice for Learning Social Skills in VR. *Medium*. Retrieved from https://medium.com/virtual-reality-virtual-people/purposeful-practice-for-learning-social-skills-in-vr-362657cbfc88

Google Patents. (2017). *Combination training device for student aviators and entertainment apparatus.* Retrieved from https://patents.google.com/patent/US1825462

Greenwald, S. W., Corning, W., Funk, M., & Maes, P. (2018). Comparing Learning in Virtual Reality with Learning on a 2D Screen Using Electrostatics Activities. *J. UCS, 24*(2), 220–245.

Harris, B. J. (2019). *The History of the Future: How a Bunch of Misfits, Makers, and Mavericks Cracked the Code of Virtual Reality.* New York: HarperCollins Publishers.

Hill, S. (2016). Is VR too dangerous for kids? We asked the experts. *Digital Trends.* Retrieved from https://www.digitaltrends.com/virtual-reality/is-vr-safe-for-kids-we-asked-the-experts/

Hodgson, P., Lee, V. W. Y., Chan, J. C. S., Fong, A., Tang, C. S. Y., Chan, L., & Wong, C. (2019). Immersive Virtual Reality (IVR) in Higher Education: Development and Implementation. In Augmented Reality and Virtual Reality: The Power of AR and VR for Business. New York: Springer International Publishing.

Itin, C. M. (1999). Reasserting the philosophy of experiential education as a vehicle for change in the 21st century. *Journal of Experiential Education, 22*(2), 91–98. doi:10.1177/105382599902200206

Joshi, N. (2019). AR and VR in the Utility Sector. *Forbes.* Retrieved from https://www.forbes.com/sites/cognitiveworld/2019/09/29/ar-and-vr-in-the-utility-sector

Kalawsky, R. S. (1993). *The Science of Virtual Reality and Virtual Environments: A Technical, Scientific and Engineering Reference on Virtual Environments.* Wokingham, UK: Addison-Wesley.

Kukula, M. (2017). Planetariums and the rise of spectacular science. *Nature Magazine.* Retrieved from https://www.nature.com/articles/d41586-017-08441-9

Lampton, D. R., Knerr, B. W., Goldberg, S. L., Bliss, J. P., Moshell, J. M., & Blau, B. S. (1994). The Virtual Environment Performance Assessment Battery (VEPAB): Development and Evaluation. *Presence (Cambridge, Mass.), 3*(2), 145–157. doi:10.1162/pres.1994.3.2.145

Lanier, J. (2010). On the Threshold of the Avatar Era. *Wall Street Journal.* Retrieved from: https://www.wsj.com/articles/SB10001424052702303738504575568410584865010

Legault, J., Zhao, J., Chi, Y. A., Chen, W., Klippel, A., & Li, P. (2019). Immersive Virtual Reality as an Effective Tool for Second Language Vocabulary Learning. *Languages, 4*(1), 13. doi:10.3390/languages4010013

Miller, D. C. (2015). *SIMNET and Beyond: A History of the Development of Distributed Simulation.* Interservice/Industry Training, Simulation, and Education (IITSEC) Fellows Paper. Retrieved from https://www.iitsec.org/-/media/sites/iitsec/link-attachments/iitsec-fellows/2015_fellowpaper_miller.ashx

Minocha, S., Tudor, A., & Tilling, S. (2017). Affordances of Mobile Virtual Reality and their Role in Learning and Teaching. *Proceedings of the 31st British Human Computer Interaction Conference.* 10.14236/ewic/HCI2017.44

Mitham, N. (2014). Virtual Worlds: Industry and User Data: Universe Chart for Q2 2014. *KZERO, Worldswide.* Retrieved from https://www.slideshare.net/nicmitham/kzero-universe-q2-2014

Nadworny, E., & Anderson, M. (2017). Relics of The Space Race, School Planetariums Are an Endangered Species. *NPREd: How Learning Happens.* Retrieved from https://www.npr.org/sections/ed/2017/01/03/504715174/relics-of-the-space-race-school-planetariums-are-an-endangered-species

Papert, S. (1980). *Mindstorms: Children, Computers, and Powerful Ideas.* New York: Basic Books.

Parkhomenko, E., O'Leary, M., Safiullah, S., Walia, S., Owyong, M., Lin, C., ... Clayman, R. (2018). Pilot Assessment of Immersive Virtual Reality Renal Models as an Educational and Preoperative Planning Tool for Percutaneous Nephrolithotomy. *Journal of Endourology, 33*(4), 283–288. doi:10.1089/end.2018.0626 PMID:30460860

Pulijala, Y., Ma, M., Pears, M., Peebles, D., & Ayoub, A. (2018). Effectiveness of Immersive Virtual Reality in Surgical Training: A Randomized Control Trial. *International Journal of Oral and Maxillofacial Surgery, 76*(5), 1065–1072. doi:10.1016/j.joms.2017.10.002 PMID:29104028

Recalled by Robert Sproull. (2006). *In DARPA Case No. 13-01968.000048 Interview: December 7, 2006.* Retrieved August 23, 2019 from https://www.esd.whs.mil/Portals/54/Documents/FOID/Reading%20Room/DARPA/15-F-0751_DARPA_Director_Robert_Sproull.pdf

Salzman, M. C., Dede, C., Loftin, R. B., & Chen, J. (1999). A model for understanding how virtual reality aids complex conceptual learning. *Presence (Cambridge, Mass.), 8*(3), 293–316. doi:10.1162/105474699566242

Sankaranarayanan, G., Wooley, L., Hogg, D., Dorozhkin, D., Olasky, J., Chauhan, S., ... Jones, D. B. (2018). Immersive virtual reality-based training improves response in a simulated operating room fire scenario. *Surgical Endoscopy, 32*(8), 3439–3449. doi:10.100700464-018-6063-x PMID:29372313

Segovia, K. Y., & Bailenson, J. N. (2009). Virtually true: Children's acquisition of false memories in virtual reality. *Media Psychology, 12*(4), 371–393. doi:10.1080/15213260903287267

Sobel, K. (2019). *Immersive media and child development: Synthesis of a cross-sectoral meeting on virtual, augmented, and mixed reality and young children.* New York: The Joan Ganz Cooney Center at Sesame Workshop.

Stepan, K., Zeiger, J., Hanchuk, S., Del Signore, A., Shrivastava, R., Govindaraj, S., & Iloreta, A. (2017). Immersive virtual reality as a teaching tool for neuroanatomy. *International Forum of Allergy & Rhinology, 7*(10), 1006–1013. doi:10.1002/alr.21986 PMID:28719062

Sutherland, I. E. (1965). The Ultimate Display. *Proceedings of IFIP, 65*(2), 506–508.

Thompson, S. (2019). VR for Corporate Training: Examples of VR already Being Used. *Virtual Speech.* Retrieved from https://virtualspeech.com/blog/how-is-vr-changing-corporate-training

Thorpe, J. A. (2010). Trends in Modeling, Simulation & Gaming: Personal Observations About the Last Thirty Years and Speculation About the Next Ten. *Interservice/Industry Training, Simulation, and Education Conference (I/ITSEC).*

Wankle, C., & Hinrichs, R. (2011). Introduction. In C. Wankle & R. Hinrichs (Eds.), *Transforming Virtual World Learning.* Bingley, UK: Emerald Group Publishing Limited.

Zeiss (n.d.). *History of ZEISS Planetariums: How it all began.* Retrieved from https://www.zeiss.com/corporate/int/about-zeiss/history/technological-milestones/planetariums.html

Zhang, J. (2019). *Immersive Virtual Reality Training to Enhance Procedural Knowledge Retention* (Doctoral dissertation). Purdue University.

ADDITIONAL REFERENCES

Brewer, D. N., Wilson, T. D., Eagleson, R., & De Ribaupierre, S. (2012). Evaluation of neuroanatomical training using a 3d visual reality model. MMVR 2012 Proceedings, 85-91.

Huang, H. M., & Liaw, S. S. (2018). An analysis of learners' intentions toward virtual reality learning based on constructivist and technology acceptance approaches. *International Review of Research in Open and Distributed Learning*, *19*(1). doi:10.19173/irrodl.v19i1.2503

Merchant, Z., Goetz, E. T., Cifuentes, L., Keeney-Kennicutt, W., & Davis, T. J. (2014). Effectiveness of virtual reality-based instruction on students' learning outcomes in K-12 and higher education: A meta-analysis. *Computers & Education*, *70*, 29–40. doi:10.1016/j.compedu.2013.07.033

ENDNOTES

[1] In other words, up until the third wave of VR started to gather steam. For more information see Wankel and Heinrich's edited volume: *Transforming Virtual World Learning* (2011).

[2] https://patents.google.com/patent/US1825462 "Combination training device for student aviators and entertainment apparatus." *Google Patents*. Retrieved 24 September 2017.

[3] https://www.spitzinc.com/planetarium/educate/

[4] A Euclidean vector is a mathematical construct comprising a geometric object that has magnitude and direction. Vector algebra allows for vectors to be added or subtracted to other vectors within the rules of Vector Algebra. Because it is Euclidean, the direction of a vector can point anywhere in 3 dimensional space.

[5] Virtual worlds can be considered a predecessor to today's fully immersive VR environments. The KZERO numbers come from the more easily accessed online virtual worlds, used typically with a mouse and a flat screen, including multiplayer games such as Everquest, as well as offerings like Linden Lab's Second Life (for adults) and Disney's Club Penguin for young children.

Chapter 18
Spatial Immersion and Human Interaction:
Comparing Cross–Generational Experiences of Pokémon GO Play

Shaojung Sharon Wang

Institute of Marketing Communication, National Sun Yat-sen University, Taiwan

ABSTRACT

This study investigated how Pokémon GO play may integrate players' gaming experiences and physical environments to facilitate spatial-human immersions in psychologically meaningful ways. Two age groups that represent generational players were further compared. A survey of 1031 players found that co-presence was positively associated with game enjoyment and game involvement, and nostalgia was positively associated with game enjoyment. The mediation effect of nostalgia on game involvement through game enjoyment was significant and game involvement completely mediated the relationship between game enjoyment and place attachment. In the 35 years and older age group, the direct effect of nostalgia on game involvement and the indirect effect of nostalgia on game involvement through game enjoyment were both significant. Theoretical implications on linking spatial relationships and the process of movement in the immersive AR environment and connecting the media experiences from one's formative youth period to the world of technological advances are elaborated.

INTRODUCTION

Pokémon GO is a popular mobile game that applies augmented reality (AR) and geolocation technologies to integrate the physical universe into its virtual world. The game uses a global positioning system (GPS) to situate virtual creatures called "Pokémon" overlaid on top of the players' physical surroundings. The player takes on the role of a trainer in order to capture Pokémon. Using GPS while moving around in the real world, players are notified via their smartphones when Pokémon are nearby. The design of the game not only immerses players into actual geographical places but transforms real-world places into

DOI: 10.4018/978-1-7998-2433-6.ch018

"PokéStops" and "Gyms," the specially marked virtual spots located throughout the physical world at landmarks and local businesses.

Although location-based AR games entered the market in 2003 in Japan, this game genre did not draw worldwide attention until the release of *Pokémon GO*. In fact, GPS, AR, and mobile games had all been on the market for several years. The success of *Pokémon GO* may not be due only to the integration of technological advances but rather may have been constructed by its appeal to the fans who grew up collecting the cards and building "Pokedexes" on *Game Boys* during their childhoods in the 1990s. Today's millennials who once dreamed of catching Pokémon in real life now account for the majority of the *Pokémon GO* players (Cummings, 2016). Keogh (2017), particularly, attributes this phenomenon to the importance of nostalgia. Nostalgia, as the specific form of passion derived from past moments of significance in one's life course, is one component in the generational experience that is relative to media (Bolin, 2016). While nostalgia may explain the motivation for the millennials to play *Pokémon GO*, the relationship between the remembrances of media content connected to one's earlier life phases and the enjoyment of the media experience in one's present time through the accessibility of technologies has remained largely unanswered.

From a technical perspective, recent developments in the contemporary media environment have enabled and made possible mapping spatial distribution and how different spatial patterns relate to one another. While social media interfaces have increasingly been employed for individuals to facilitate interpersonal communication goals, current geolocation technologies and the characteristics of AR games allow the connection between players, spaces, and *locations*, facilitating a sense of physical coexistence between people. Co-presence—the sense of being there together with others (Harms & Biocca, 2004)—allows for an increased awareness of the everyday lives and activities of distant others through the mediated interactions that present themselves within the ubiquitous media environment, enabling deeper emotional aspects of relationships to be developed. Thus co-presence that includes one's movement may serve as a function of spatial configuration that connects the physical and virtual spaces with the social occupation of space. However, social and personal variables can also mediate a perception of crowdedness (Stokols, Rall, Pinner, & Schopler, 1973) by reflecting one's spatial needs. This suggests that an investigation of an environment in order to integrate one's surroundings may develop spatial–human interaction in psychologically meaningful ways.

Given that spatiality and sociality can provide individuals with contexts in which they can understand media (Berland, 2009), the interpretation of *Pokémon GO* may become inseparable from spatial-human interactions. Klimmt, Hartmann, and Frey (2007) have suggested that the enjoyment of players' causal effects on the gaming context can motivate them to interact with the environment. *Pokémon GO* play that is mediated by geolocation and AR technologies may not only simply be considered as a media experience, but a necessary condition defined by spatial relationships and the process of movement. However, while technologies affect and mediate one's perception of the environment, nostalgia, a longing for the past (Batcho, 2013), seems to play a contradictory position by connecting the media experiences from one's formative youth period to the world of technological advances. Therefore, this study sets out to explore the generation-based socialization that may contribute to the enjoyment of *Pokémon GO* play and how the gaming experiences in a fictional world may elicit players' affections toward their real-world surroundings. Two age groups are compared in this chapter to understand how generations and technologies are intertwined in the process of media enjoyment and spatial–human relationships.

BACKGROUND AND THEORETICAL FRAMEWORKS

Environmental Psychology's Place And Crowding Aspects

Environmental psychology focuses on the reciprocal relationships and the transactions between humans and their physical settings. Places that integrate natural and social aspects of the environment are more than geographic surroundings with distinct physical boundaries and textual features; in fact, places are movable, changeable, dynamic contexts of social interactions and human memories (Williams & Vaske, 2003). The positive emotional bonds between the selves and their surroundings or the meanings that one attributes to such places constitutes what is considered to be place attachment (Williams et al., 1992). Place attachment emphasizes the importance of a physical location in the self-definition of an individual, as well as on the community members' sense of group identity (Brown & Perkins, 1992). As place attachment highlights both the personal effects—as well as social components—of specific locations, it can explain the emotional affiliation between individuals and their meaningful surroundings.

Williams et al. (1992) have distinctively identified two components of place attachment: place identity and place dependence. The former is the extent to which one emotionally connects to a place in relation to what the setting stands for and it provides the opportunity for one to both express and affirm one's identity, whereas the latter highlights the level of satisfaction that the place creates in relation to one's functional or cognitive needs. Scannell and Gifford (2010) proposed the person–process–place framework to theorize place attachment as a link between an individual or a group and a physical place that can be manifested through affective, cognitive, and behavioral psychological processes; the attachment to places with specific social or physical characteristics can thus provide a sense of belongingness and enhance self-identity.

Further, one's interpretations of the geographic settings are also central to the investigation of perceived crowding in the field of environmental psychology. However, crowding is an adverse condition encountered in the environment due to the physical density of a setting, which results in potential inconveniencies such as the restriction of movement and the obstruction of privacy as perceived by an individual (Stokols, Rall, Pinner, & Schopler, 1973). To understand human behaviors, two types of density are further identified: spatial density and social density. While spatial density and the number of encounters are objectively descriptive terms, perceived crowding as a subjective evaluation of density levels and the frequency of encounters in a specific location generally emphasizes the negative psychological reaction of crowding and a negative assessment of a given area (Shelby, Vaske, & Donnelly, 1996).

When individuals perceive an environment as crowded, they tend to compare the conditions they have experienced using norms as standards to evaluate the situations, activities, or environments as acceptable or not (Vaske & Donnelly, 2002). Given that crowding can have a direct social impact on interactions in outdoor recreational activities, the effect of crowding has been largely examined in recreational management studies to explore how it may affect tourists' satisfaction. In these studies, perceived crowding is often used to explain a high frequency of encounters with other visitors or a high density in tourist spots to imply a negative personal evaluation of touristic experiences (Zehrer & Raich, 2016). *Pokémon GO* requires players to find and capture rare virtual creatures or hatch eggs in real-world places in order to level up. A recent study has found that the game has the potential to increase physical activities and decrease sedentary behaviors (Mateo, 2017), allowing for an opportunity to investigate the crowding effect on *Pokémon GO* play context.

MEDIA ENTERTAINMENT'S CO-PRESENCE AND NOSTALGIA ASPECTS

The Concept of Co-Presence

Co-presence consists of particular properties that are relevant to ubiquitous media technology. Slater, Sadagic, Usoh, and Schroeder (2000) define it as the feeling of being and acting together with another individual in either a virtual space or a remote physical environment, and thus consider co-presence as a social or physiological reaction to an embodied entity. However, other researchers view co-presence as a sharing of the same space with another person or both parties' mutual awareness of each other's accessibility and availability. For example, Harms and Biocca (2004) define co-presence as an individual's sense of the other's presence, while Blascovich et al. (2002) emphasize the extent to which one regards an embodied agent as a real human being. Campos-Castillo and Hitlin (2013) conceptualize co-presence as a continuous, intra-individual variable and emphasize the mutual feeling of entrainment that is facilitated between actors.

The advance of media technology has extended human's reach across space and time, allowing researchers to particularly examine co-presence in the context of social interactions with remote users in a virtual environment. For example, IJsselsteijn et al. (2001) stress the sense of physically being that is embodied in a virtual space together with the mediated actors. Lee (2004) focuses on the mental simulation of other humans or nonhuman intelligences and views co-presence as an experience of an artificial social entity perceived through an avatar or an artificial intelligence agent via technology. Schroeder et al. (2001) use co-presence to depict one's engagement in being and acting together with the other in a shared, computer-mediated environment. Researchers further distinguish the mediated environment from telepresence (such as videophones or video-conferences) to simulated virtual presences such as avatars inhabiting a virtual game world (Schroeder et al., 2001; Zhao, 2003).

Although the definition of co-presence may vary depending on the phenomena and the environment being studied, two elements may be highlighted: psychological involvement and behavioral engagement. According to Biocca, Harms, and Burgoon (2003), the former is the degree to which an individual is aware of the other agent and can empathically respond to the thoughts and intentions of the other. It measures how much the other person can also correctly comprehend an individual's emotional states. The latter is the extent to which an individual considers that his/her actions are influenced by the other agent and can feel the other's reactions to his/her actions. To reconcile both sociological and psychological aspects of co-presence, Zhao (2003) proposes two dimensions of co-presence—a mode of being with others and a sense of being with others—to depict the phenomena in both a mediated and physical setting. Zhao's (2003) taxonomy generally dichotomizes co-presence into physical proximity and electronic proximity; the former emphasizes human co-location in which interpersonal interactions occur, while the latter stresses one's subjective experience of being with others. As such, human interaction can occur in a mode of co-presence in which both actors are within physical proximity and in situations involving digitally-participating actors, in that an agent is in electronic proximity to the actor. In light of this concept, location-based media technology approximates physical closeness whereas the actual existence and tangible proximity of the other person can be grasped. *Pokémon GO* play involves encountering other players in the physical world and, at the same time, collaborating with other players by trading and battling with each other in the virtual world, which facilitates the co-presence modes of being with others and a sense of being with others, as Zhao (2003) proposes.

The Role of Nostalgia

While co-presence is often linked to the advance of media technology, the relationship between media and nostalgia is, to a certain extent, intertwined. The concept of nostalgia, once regarded as a medical diagnosis in the 17th century, has been substantially changed over the past three centuries, from the psychiatric disorder to psychodynamic approaches to the discipline of psychology itself. Nostalgia has been associated with psychological disorders for much of the 20th century as the term has long been an equivalent of homesickness, at least up until late 20th century. Davis (1979) specifically distinguishes nostalgia from homesickness as college students tend to associate the words *warm*, *old times*, *childhood*, and *yearning* more often with the former than the with the latter. Schindler and Holbrook (2003) defined nostalgia as one's preference toward people, places, or things that were more popular, trendy, or widely circulated when one was younger or even before one's birth. Thus, nostalgia depicts a bittersweet yearning for past times and spaces (Batcho, 2013), pleasant memories of the "good old days." In comparison, homesickness is a longing for one's place of origin while experiencing an absence from it (Van Tilburg, Vingerhouts, & van Heck, 1996).

Media has long been regarded as a means of eliciting nostalgic emotions through the visual, appearance-based, audio, and narrative portrayal of the past, as well as through technological objects of nostalgia that recall one's own past (Niemeyer & Wentz, 2014). The intimate and passionate relation that has developed toward media content and technologies such as the musical genres and stars, comics, and reproduction technologies—such as vinyl records and cassette tapes—that were popular during one's formative youth period is an important reflection of the collective memories of generational experience that are activated by nostalgic sentiments to past media use and consumption (Bolin, 2016). As such, nostalgia has long been linked to the media as it provides the opportunity to reflect on mediation, media, and related technologies, and vice versa (Boym, 2008).

In the 1990s, the original *Pokémon* anime reflected on the creator's childhood experiences of exploring rice fields and rivers to collect insects, and the first *Pokémon* game played on the *Game Boy* further drew on these nostalgic components in order to amplify young children's imaginations (Keogh, 2017). The mobile version of the game, *Pokémon GO*, taps into the emotions and storytelling elements of one's childhood experiences in the 1990s, allowing players to once again indulge in their early obsession, given that the embodied nostalgic elements may enable players to experience their own nostalgic feelings for the video game in a similar manner (Lange, 2011). Therefore, the *Pokémon GO* study explores how nostalgia may evoke a player's emotions toward the game and further compares how nostalgia may take effect across two different generations.

THE *POKÉMON GO* STUDY: HYPOTHESES DEVELOPMENT AND THE RESEARCH MODEL

The *Pokémon GO* study investigates elements of game enjoyment and involvement and how they may affect players' immersive gaming experience in the AR environment. Two generational groups are further compared to understand spatial-human interactions in psychologically meaningful ways.

Game Enjoyment And Involvement

Enjoyment, an attitude with affective, cognitive, and behavioral antecedents and consequences (Nabi & Krcmar, 2004), is the extent to which performing an activity is perceived to be fun and enjoyable in its own right, quite apart from any performance consequences. As such, enjoyment is considered to be the pleasant experience one has when exposed to media (Tamborini & Bowman, 2010) in the context of using media to pursue entertainment. Video games provide players with various entertainment gratifications and possess ideal characteristics through which we can explain those media experiences that can be labeled as media entertainment.

Involvement is defined as the degree of psychological connections (Funk, Ridinger, & Moorman, 2004) and perceptions of personal relevance (Kyle & Chick, 2002) that one attains during an activity or while inhabiting a location, as well as the extent to which one is committed to an object, activity, place, or experience (Gross & Brown, 2008). According to Lee and Faber (2007), involvement with the game is "a motivational state to exert cognitive effort at playing a game" (p. 77). Game involvement is generally accepted as the extent that the personal self-relevance of a player has with the game, which can be concretely demonstrated by a player's high investment of time, effort, and expense in terms of playing the game (Brown & Cairns, 2004).

Factors Impacting Game Enjoyment

Perceived crowding as a negative psychological reaction to the physical density in an environment is often described in negative terms, such as one feeling confined, constrained, or restricted (Stokols et al., 1973). Past research has constantly found negative affective and behavioral outcomes of perceived crowding in retail (Eroglu, Machleit, & Barr, 2005), café/restaurant, (Yildirim & Akalin-Baskaya, 2007), and recreational (Zehrer & Raich, 2016) settings. *Pokémon GO* play involves catching Pokémon in specific places that include both indoor and outdoor environments. The game has turned many physical locations into tourist spots and prompts players to enjoy the experience of interacting with others in the real world. However, being stuck in a crowd of Pokémon hunters might intrude on the players' own sense of personal space, causing anxious and uncomfortable emotions that could ultimately impede the enjoyment of the game. The following hypothesis is thus proposed:

H1: There will be a negative relationship between perceived crowding and game enjoyment.

Co-presence with remote individuals can be achieved through being consciously aware that the social interactions are mediated within the virtual world. In the video game world, co-presence emphasizes the sense of being and acting together with other players (Takatalo, Häkkinen, Kaistinen, & Nyman, 2010). Gajadhar, De Kort, and Ijsselsteijn (2008) empirically investigated the interplay between game enjoyment and social context and found that a co-located co-player significantly affects the enjoyment, challenge, and perceived competence of the game. Hartmann, Klimmt and Vorderer (2010) also claim that much of the contemporary development of media technology—such as high-definition (HD) and surround-sound systems—tends to pursue an increase in the sense of presence as a path to enjoyment. *Pokémon GO* encourages players to play outside rather than staying at home. Players of the game often encounter other players while chasing rare Pokémon or form a team together to collaborate with previously unacquainted players at the nearby PokéStop. In addition, the game has hosted numerous real-world activities. For example, there were 31 events, 12 Community Days, and four special raiding days in 2018, and a total of 10 activities in 2017 (Tassi, 2019). During *Pokémon GO* play, being with other players in the virtual world while they may also physically co-locate in the real world may promote a high level of engagement and increased interactions among players. Therefore, it is likely that a sense of co-presence is able to be generated through the social interactions and collaborations with other players during *Pokémon GO* play in order to elicit game enjoyment. Thus, this study posits that:

H2: There will be a positive relationship between co-presence and game enjoyment.

Nostalgia, as a social emotion, has a restorative function on one's past memories, on stimulating social bonds (Sedikides & Wildschut, 2016), and promoting psychological growth via engagement in novel activities (Baldwin & Landau, 2014). These elements act against negative effects (Barrett et al., 2010), boredom (Van Tilburg, Igou, & Sedikides, 2013), loneliness, and social exclusion (Sedikides & Wildschut, 2016). Research on consumer psychology has demonstrated that music, motion pictures, and automobiles that were popular during one's youth can influence lifelong preferences (Schindler & Holbrook, 2003). Media-induced nostalgia, the bittersweet and fundamentally social emotion elicited by remembering or re-experiencing media content and technologies from the past, may contribute to hedonic and non-hedonic entertainment experiences and affect one's psychological and subjective well-being (Wulf, Rieger, & Schmitt, 2018). Research on *Pokémon GO* play revealed that the game can trigger the nostalgic feelings, which in turn contribute toward resiliency, a particularly important factor in terms of well-being (Bonus, Peebles, Mares, & Sarmiento, 2018). For those who played *Pokémon* on their *Game Boy* during their childhood in the 1990s, *Pokémon GO* allows them to once again indulge in their old obsession. It is therefore plausible to assume that players who are more prone to experiencing nostalgia may enjoy the game more. Thus, this study posits:

H3: There will be a positive relationship between nostalgia and game enjoyment.

Factors Concerning Game Involvement

According to Calleja's (2007) model, spatial immersion sets players within a wider game environment than is visible on the screen and that may be embodied in the form of mental influence from other players or aspects that are related to the exploration and exploitation of the game space for the sake of completing strategic goals. Researchers have suggested that when players perceive a sense of spatial presence, they are then embodied within the game, and this might be more likely to trigger their involvement in the game (Takatalo et al., 2010). *Pokémon GO* encourages players to interact and engage with fellow players in both the virtual and real worlds. The feelings of co-presence with other players may further foster their sense of game involvement. Thus, this study posits:

H4: There will be a positive relationship between co-presence and game involvement.

Nostalgia, the fondness for the tangible or intangible feelings of possession or activities that are linked to one's past experiences (Schindler & Holbrook, 2003), can contribute toward personal identity based on a shared heritage and memories that coincide with that of one's group members (Brown & Humphreys, 2002). Collective nostalgia is found to promote one's involvement in in-group collective actions (Cheung, Sedikides, Wildschut, Tausch, & Ayanian, 2017). Within marketing research, nostalgia connects consumers to the brand, the brand community, and the in-group consumers (Koetz & Tankersley, 2016). In addition, nostalgia that causes personal connections to evolve with the foci of one's attention can also elicit higher levels of ad involvement (Muehling & Pascal, 2012). *Pokémon GO* revitalizes the *Pokémon* game that was popularized in the 1990s in order to tap into the players' nostalgic feelings (Keogh, 2017). Therefore, it is likely that those who are ranked higher in terms of their nostalgic feelings may form in-group shared identities with other players in order to generate higher involvement in the game world. Thus, the following hypothesis is proposed:

H5: There will be a positive relationship between nostalgia and game involvement.

Furthermore, as is mentioned above, nostalgia can foster hedonic experiences, one major component of making video games enjoyable (Wulf et al., 2018), and nostalgic feelings that can motivate consumers to engage in online communities (Koetz & Tankersley, 2016). Players with nostalgic feelings and those who hold affection toward *Pokémon* may be unconsciously motivated to search for, collect, and evolve particular Pokémon creatures, as opposed to those who do not have a nostalgic connection and who may be less motivated to do so (Loveday & Burgess, 2017). As affective involvement emphasizes the effect of positive emotions through gaming experiences (Calleja, 2007), it is likely that *Pokémon GO* players who experience a higher degree of nostalgia may become more involved in the game due to their positive gaming experiences. Thus, the following hypothesis is proposed:

H6: The relationship between the levels of nostalgia and game involvement will be mediated by the levels of game enjoyment.

Place Attachment And The Mediation Effect

We here recall that place attachment refers to an individual's positive emotional bonds with a place and how they attribute meanings or feelings of excitement to that place (Williams et al., 1992). Past study has suggested that one's involvement in outdoor leisure activities can foster affection for, and feeling of connection with, the places in which these activities take place (Gross & Brown, 2008). In the education-based gaming environment, game enjoyment can encourage learning activities (Pivec, 2007). *Pokémon GO* players explore real-world places, obtaining information about these places, and the game also converts various locations into recreational areas, facilitating positive attitudes toward these places (Oleksy & Wnuk, 2017). Therefore, it is likely that players are motivated to immerse themselves in the game if they have pleasant gaming experiences and the positive emotion toward the game can further trigger their affections for the places they have visited through gaming. Thus, this study posits:

H7: The relationship between the levels of game enjoyment and place attachment will be mediated by the levels of game involvement.

Figure 1 illustrates the proposed model, including the hypothesized paths.

Figure 1. Research model

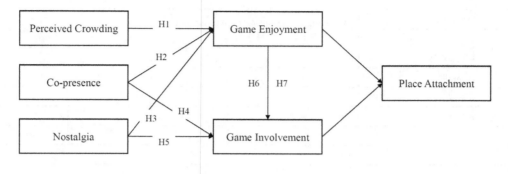

Age Differences and Pokémon GO Play

Pokémon was the game that was enjoyed by many children on their *Game Boys* in the 1990s. Researchers have suggested that those who enjoyed the game in their childhood may perceive a higher state of flow due to their greater level of autotelic control, clearer goals for play, as well as prior knowledge of, and familiarity with, the game (Loveday & Burgess, 2017). While feelings of fun, achievement, and nostalgia are significantly correlated to *Pokémon GO* play and nostalgia also motivates those who are playing the game (Loveday & Burgess, 2017; Yang & Liu, 2017), it is likely that players who enjoyed the earlier versions of the *Pokémon* game in their childhood may develop different perceptions and feelings toward *Pokémon GO* play than those who did not. Therefore, this study investigates the following research question:

RQ: In what way do players who enjoyed Pokémon in the 1990s possibly differ from those who did not in terms of their perceptions, feelings, and experiences of Pokémon GO play?

STUDY METHODOLOGY

Sampling Procedure and Participants

Pokémon GO launched in Taiwan on August 6, 2016 and Taiwan has remained in the top five countries that spend the most on the game worldwide (SensorTower, 2018). Although initially the millennials may have been the first who adopted *Pokémon GO*, more and more middle-aged and older people also started to play the game (KYODO NEWS, 2017). As the game can be enjoyed by players of all ages, a stratified sampling method was employed, which divided Taiwanese *Pokémon GO* players by age. However, due to the difficulty involved in verifying parental consent online, this study excluded players aged under 18 years old. The targeted sample was partitioned into five non-overlapping strata. The estimated proportion of each strata was calculated based on Media Palette (2016) and InsightXplorer's (2016) big data analysis, which delineated the age distribution of *Pokémon GO* players in Taiwan (Table 1).

To recruit survey participants, announcements were posted on some of Taiwan's popular game discussion boards and *Pokémon GO* fan groups on *Facebook*. Participants were instructed to click through one of the five survey links that corresponded to their age group. To ensure the composition of the

Table 1. Sample distribution

Strata		Estimated distribution of population per age group	Distribution of sample per age group
	Age		
	below 24	28.8%	27.8%
	25-34	36.7%	38.0%
	35-44	19.4%	17.9%
	45-54	9.6%	9.8%
	over 55	5.5%	6.4%
Total		100%	100%

participants matched the sampling frame, each survey link was automatically closed after reaching the number of estimated responses. Thirty gift certificates were provided. A live lottery draw using a computer program was hosted on *Facebook* and each participant had an equal opportunity of being picked to win any one of the certificates.

The survey was filled in online for three days. After excluding 141 respondents who were either non-*Pokémon GO* players, gave duplicate responses, or completed the survey in a much shorter time, 1,031 respondents remained for analysis. Table 2 shows the sample demographics.

Measures

Co-presence, as previously established, is the sense of being together with co-located fellow *Pokémon GO* players. Four items were developed based on Biocca et al.'s (2003) study. Sample items include "I feel the emergence of *Pokémon GO* players during the course of playing the game" and "While playing *Pokémon GO*, I have a sense of being part of the group."

Perceived crowding, as mentioned previously, measures the *Pokémon GO* players' evaluations of the restriction of movement and the frequency of encounters experienced during gameplay. Based on Shelby, Vaske, and Donnelly's (1996) study, four items were developed—for example, "While playing *Pokémon GO*, I feel my movement would be restricted in the crowd" and "While playing *Pokémon GO*, I seldom encountered other players (reverse coded)."

Nostalgia, as discussed earlier, measures the players' connection with, and affection for, *Pokémon* based on their childhood memories and experiences. Based on Schindler and Holbrook's (2003) definition, five items were developed. ample items include "*Pokémon GO* reminds me of my good old times in my childhood" and "I had enjoyed playing *Pokémon* video games in my childhood."

Game enjoyment, also as previously established, is the pleasant feelings that *Pokémon GO* players perceive while playing. Five items were adapted from Shafer and Carbonara's (2015) and Skalski, Tamborini, Shelton, Buncher, and Lindmark's (2011) scales with wording changes to reflect the context of the current study. Sample items include "While playing *Pokémon GO*, I feel very cheerful" and "Playing *Pokémon GO* is pleasurable."

Game involvement, as previously surmised, measures the extent to which *Pokémon GO* players feel cognitively and emotionally immersed while playing. Five items were developed based on Kyle and Chick's (2002) and Takatalo et al.'s (2010) studies, all of which required changes to the wording.

Table 2. Sample demographics

Variables			N=1031	
			N (%)	
Gender			Male	Female
			547 (53.1%)	484 (46.9%)
Age/Gender	<24		164(15.9%)	123(11.9%)
	25-34		188(18.2%)	204(19.8%)
	35-44		98(9.5%)	87(8.4%)
	45-54		60(5.8%)	41(4.0%)
	55 and above		37(3.6%)	29(2.8%)
Education	High school and below		43(4.2%)	58(5.6%)
	College		330(32.0%)	307(29.8%)
	Graduate school and above		174(16.9%)	119(11.5%)
Monthly income (USD)	Less than 300		189(18.3%)	169(16.4%)
	300-less than 1300		150(14.5%)	209(20.3%)
	1300-less than 2600		170(16.5%)	94(9.1%)
	More than 2600		38(3.7%)	12(1.2%)
Pokémon GO play experience	Less than 3 months		113(11.0%)	120(11.6%)
	3-less than 6 months		80(7.8%)	54(5.2%)
	More than 6 months		354(34.3%)	310(30.1%)
Pokémon GO play/day	Less than 30 min.		188(18.2%)	168(16.3%)
	30-less than 1h		153(14.8%)	122(11.8%)
	1h-less than 2h		114(11.1%)	76(7.4%)
	2h-less than 3h		51(4.9%)	62(6.0%)
	3h and more		23(4.0%)	41(5.4%)
Average spent on Pokémon GO (USD)	0		385(37.3%)	335(32.5%)
	Less than 10		46(4.5%)	27(2.6%)
	10-less than 35		52(5.0%)	56(5.4%)
	35- less than 70		32(3.1%)	24(2.3%)
	70 and above		32(3.1%)	42(4.1%)

Sample items include "Playing *Pokémon GO* is part of my daily life" and "I would feel sad if there was no *Pokémon GO* to play."

Finally, place attachment, also as mentioned above, measures the affective bond between *Pokémon GO* players and the specific places that appeared in the game world. Items were developed based on Williams and Vaske's (2003) study. Sample items include "I enjoy visiting some Pokéstops and Gyms more than visiting any other places" and "The places that I often visit while playing *Pokémon GO* are meaningful to me."

Table 3. Descriptive statistics and correlation for the measured variables

	M	SD	α	AVE	CR	Factor loading	1	2	3	4	5	6
1.Perceived Crowding	3.88	1.24	0.88	0.65	0.88	0.63-0.96	**0.81**					
2.Co-presence	5.16	1.18	0.86	0.61	0.86	0.67-0.83	-0.08	**0.78**				
3.Nostalgia	4.58	1.78	0.92	0.75	0.92	0.80-0.91	0.05	0.12	**0.87**			
4.Game Enjoyment	5.39	1.07	0.94	0.80	0.94	0.83-0.93	-0.07	0.62	0.27	**0.89**		
5.Game Involvement	4.86	1.21	0.87	0.63	0.87	0.77-0.82	-0.11	0.64	0.16	0.79	**0.79**	
6.Place Attachment	4.41	1.26	0.92	0.70	0.92	0.68-0.93	-0.04	0.50	0.06	0.45	0.57	**0.84**

Results

A structural equation modeling analysis coupled with maximum likelihood estimations using AMOS 22 was conducted. All of the endogenous variables in the model were found to have acceptable skewness (absolute values = −.65–.04) and kurtosis (absolute values = −.80–.75) values (Kline, 2015). The Mardia's coefficient was 260.96, which demonstrates a multivariate normality distribution (Mardia, 1970). There was no negative error variance and every error variance was significant. The absolute value of each factor loading was below one. Thus, no offending estimate affected the loading of the items (Bagozzi & Yi, 1988).

The reliability and convergent validity were examined (Table 3). The values of Cronbach's α and the composite reliability (CR) for all the constructs surpassed .80, indicating the internal consistency of all measures (Hair, Black, Babin, Anderson, & Tatham, 2006). Factor loadings for all of the items were above .60, and all of the average variance extracted (AVEs) were above .60, which demonstrated convergent validity (Fornell & Larcker, 1981). All of the squared roots of the AVEs were greater than the off-diagonal correlations and discriminant validity was conformed (Fornell & Larcker, 1981).

Hypotheses Testing

A confirmatory factor analysis was conducted and the $\chi 2$ statistic ($\chi 2$/df = 5.56, $p < .001$) of the measurement model was acceptable due to a larger sample size (> 250) and the greater indicator variables (≥ 30) (Klin, 2015). Following current conventions (Hair et al., 2006), the fit statistics demonstrated that the measurement model was a good fit (CFI = .929; TLI = .921; RMESA = .066 with a 90% CI [.063, .070]). An empirical structural equation model was then developed (χ^2/df = 5.61, $p < .001$). The fit indices also exhibited an acceptable fit with the data (CFI = .906; TLI = .899; RMESA = .067 with a 90% CI [.064, .070]).

To test the research hypotheses and the hypothesized model, a path analysis was employed. As shown in Figure 2, the paths from co-presence to game enjoyment ($\beta = .59$, $p < .001$) and game involvement ($\beta = .27$, $p < .001$) were significant. H2 and H4 were supported. The path from nostalgia to game enjoyment was also significant ($\beta = .20$, $p < .001$), supporting H3. However, the paths from perceived crowding to game enjoyment and from nostalgia to game involvement were not significant and H1 and H5 were rejected.

Figure 2. Results of the path analysis (full sample)

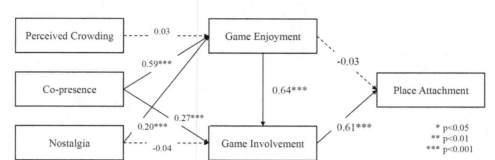

To test the mediation effects, bootstrapping analyses were performed with 5000 samples and a bias-corrected 95% CI. As shown in Table 4, although the direct effect from nostalgia to game involvement ($\beta = -.04$, $p = .13$) was not significant, the indirect effect ($\beta = .13$, $p < .001$) was significant, suggesting that the relationship between nostalgia and game involvement was mediated by game enjoyment. Thus, H6 was supported. In addition, the direct effect of game enjoyment on place attachment ($\beta = -.03$, $p = .062$) was not significant. However, the indirect effect of game enjoyment on place attachment through game involvement existed ($\beta = .39$, $p < .001$) and H7 was supported.

Research Question

To answer the research question, this study further split the sample into two age groups: one group included those were under 35 years old, and the other group was compiled of those who were 35 years and older and who may have enjoyed the *Pokémon* game during their childhood in the 1990s (Fahey, 2018). Two structural models—the model for those who were below 35 years of age and the model for those who aged 35 and above—were then created. The $\chi 2$ statistic and fit statistics of the age < 35 model (χ^2/df = 3.99, $p < .001$; CFI = .94; TLI = .93; RMESA = .066 with a 90% CI [.062, .071]) and the age $\geq$ 35 model (χ^2/df = 2.92, $p< .001$; CFI = .93; TLI = .92; RMESA = .074 with a 90% CI [.068, .080]) both demonstrated an acceptable fit to the data, based on current conventions (Hair et al., 2006; Klin, 2015).

A path analysis on this age data was then conducted. The significance of each path in the age < 35 model (Figure 3) did not differ compared to the model that consisted of a full sample (Figure 2). In the age $\geq$ 35 model (Figure 4), the significance of each path generally remained the same as the model that consisted of a full sample (Figure 2); however, the path from nostalgia to game involvement was significant ($\beta = .13$, $p < .01$) in this age group.

This study then moved on to bootstrapping analyses to examine the mediation effects. In the age < 35 model, the indirect effect ($\beta = .25$, $p = .002$) of nostalgia on game involvement through game enjoyment and the indirect effect ($\beta = .37$, $p = .001$) of game enjoyment on place attachment through game involvement were both significant (Table 4). In the age $\geq$ 35 model, the direct effect ($\beta = .06$, $p = .008$) and the indirect effect ($\beta = .13$, p = .003) were both significant, suggesting that the relationship between nostalgia and game involvement was partially mediated by game enjoyment. The direct effect of game enjoyment on place attachment was not significant ($\beta = -.08$, $p = .54$), but the indirect effect ($\beta = .37$, $p = .002$) of game enjoyment on place attachment through game involvement was significant (Table 4).

Figure 3. Results of the path analysis (age under 35 group)

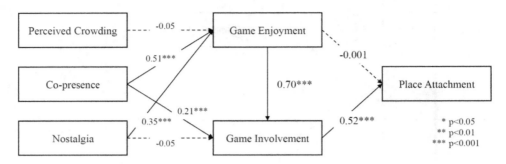

Figure 4. Results of the path analysis (age 35 and above group)

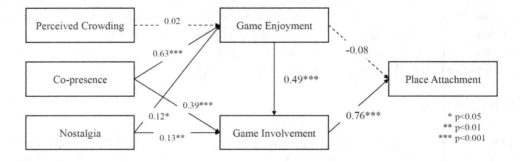

DISCUSSION

This study investigated how *Pokémon GO* play may integrate players' gaming experiences and physical environments in order to facilitate spatial–human interactions in psychologically meaningful ways: Two age groups that represent generational players were further compared. As predicted, co-presence was positively associated with game enjoyment and game involvement, and nostalgia was positively associated with game enjoyment. The mediation effects of nostalgia on game involvement through game enjoyment was significant. Game involvement mediated the relationship between game enjoyment and place attachment.

Although perceived crowding is considered to be one's negative evaluation of usage levels, settings, or the number of encounters with others (Shelby et al., 1996), the negative relationship of perceived crowding with game enjoyment was not salient, despite the result indicating the negative correlation between these two variables ($\beta = -.002$, $p = .21$). It may be understood that crowding is a multifaceted and subjective variable and its effect may depend on situational and social variables (Stokols et al., 1973), reducing the significant relationship between crowding and enjoyment. This antecedent variable of crowding and its effect on game enjoyment may therefore vary depending on players' expectations of the number of other players present in the setting who could possibly interfere with their goals of play. In addition, although the direct relationship of nostalgia with game involvement was not supported, the mediation effect of nostalgia on game involvement through game enjoyment was significant. The findings

Table 4. Mediation analysis

Full sample					
				Bias-corrected 95% CI	
Nostalgia → Game Enjoyment → Game involvement	**Path coefficient**	**Standardized error**	**p-value**	**Lower**	**Upper**
Total Effect	0.09	0.03	0.004	0.03	0.14
Indirect Effect	0.13	0.02	0.001	0.09	0.17
Direct Effect	-0.04	0.03	0.13	-0.10	0.01
Game Enjoyment→ Game involvement→ Place Attachment	Path coefficient	Standardized error	p-value	Lower	Upper
Total Effect	0.36	0.04	0.001	0.29	0.43
Indirect Effect	0.39	0.05	0.001	0.29	0.49
Direct Effect	-0.03	0.06	0.62	-0.16	0.09
< 35 years old group					
Nostalgia → Game Enjoyment → Game involvement	Path coefficient	Standardized error	p-value	Lower	Upper
Total Effect	0.20	0.04	0.002	0.11	0.28
Indirect Effect	0.25	0.03	0.002	0.18	0.32
Direct Effect	-0.05	0.04	0.16	-0.12	0.02
Game Enjoyment→ Game involvement→ Place Attachment	Path coefficient	Standardized error	p-value	Lower	Upper
Total Effect	0.37	0.04	0.002	0.28	0.45
Indirect Effect	0.37	0.07	0.001	0.25	0.53
Direct Effect	-0.001	0.09	0.95	-0.19	0.15
≥ 35 years old group					
Nostalgia → Game Enjoyment → Game involvement	Path coefficient	Standardized error	p-value	Lower	Upper
Total Effect	0.19	0.05	0.001	0.09	0.29
Indirect Effect	0.06	0.03	0.008	0.02	0.12
Direct Effect	0.13	0.05	0.003	0.04	0.22
Game Enjoyment→ Game involvement→ Place Attachment	Path coefficient	Standardized error	p-value	Lower	Upper
Total Effect	0.29	0.08	0.003	0.13	0.44
Indirect Effect	0.37	0.10	0.002	0.22	0.62
Direct Effect	-0.08	0.12	0.54	-0.32	0.14

here showed that players who have higher ratings for nostalgia may not form in-group identities and, in turn, may not promote their involvement in the game unless they find the game to be more enjoyable.

To further understand how *Pokémon GO* play may be a cross-generational phenomenon due to the long history of the *Pokémon* game, this study split the sample into two age groups. For the under 35 age group, the results were not much different from the full sample model. Interestingly, the relationship between nostalgia and game enjoyment is also significant in the under 35 age group, and it may be that because the history of the *Pokémon* media franchise has spanned over two decades since the first game was released in the 1990s, many young generations may also have watched *Pokémon* cartoons in their childhood. However, the relationship between nostalgia and game involvement was only significant in the 35 years and older age group. The direct effect of nostalgia on game involvement and the indirect effect of nostalgia on game involvement through game enjoyment were both significant in this group. The findings here suggest that there may be two distinct groups of players; those who fondly recalled *Pokémon* in their childhoods may involve themselves with the game more than others who did not.

The theoretical implications of this study are trifold. Firstly, the individuals' lives are comprised of continual changes in multiple intermittently existing and non-existing models. Amid this process of change, people, objects, thoughts, ideas, and influences can cross multiple geographical distances via travel (i.e., movement in a physical space) and various communication technologies (Büscher & Urry, 2009). *Pokémon GO* utilizes AR technology to connect gameplay with the real-world environment, turning gameplay into an outdoor leisure activity. From an environmental psychology perspective that concerns providing a systematic account of the relationship between the individual and the environment (Russell & Ward, 1982), this study set out to understand how players may develop emotional bonds to the places they visit through gaming and how the evaluation of crowding during gameplay may interfere with their behaviors and perceptions and sense of immersion. Furthermore, from the media entertainment perspective, being present within the environment of video games is directly related to game enjoyment (Tamborini & Bowman, 2010) as games that create a sense of spatial presence, allowing players to feel that they physically immerse within their gaming locations, result in the facilitation of enjoyable experiences (Skalski et al., 2011). Therefore, this study integrates the concepts of environmental psychology and media entertainment to demonstrate that location-based AR games may enable the affectional interactivity of players and their surroundings, facilitated by their positive gaming experiences.

Secondly, technology as a variable can have profound implications on co-presence and human interaction, two important factors of immersion, in a virtual environment due to the development of mediated systems and media interfaces. In particular, from a media-orientated perspective, researchers have long been interested in exploring the features of media that can facilitate one's ability to interact with another person and how one can perceive another mind in the virtual environment (Nowak, 2001). Furthermore, media has long been a means of bringing back memories as well as becoming objects of memory (Niemeyer & Wentz, 2014). Nostalgia is one's fondness for tangible or intangible possessions and activities that have been learned vicariously from the past through the media (Fairley, 2003). While technology strives toward the future, it also continually revises how we recall the past. Therefore, this study explores how co-presence, the manifestation of technology, and nostalgia—the historical context imbuing technology—may influence *Pokémon GO* players' game enjoyment and involvement from the media entertainment perspective. The results demonstrated that co-presence and nostalgia are positively associated with game enjoyment. Co-presence is also positively related to game involvement. The findings of this study suggest that the advance of AR game technology that blends players' physical embodiment across the virtual and real worlds may facilitate the goal of achieving satisfactory connections with one another. Although nostalgia refers to the past, it is, in fact, forward-looking in the sense that it connects and assimilates individuals' pasts with their presents—and even their futures (Sedikides & Wildschut, 2016). The fusion of nostalgia and technology may therefore have a measurable implication for media entrainment that can drive innovation to move forward.

Finally, *Pokémon GO* may evoke reflective longing for bygone days due to the popularity of *Pokémon* games, movies, and trading cards during the 1990s. One major component in the generational experience that is related to media entertainment is the passionate disposition that has developed toward media personnel, content, and technology from one's earlier life phase. Considering that one's passionate relationship may be activated through past media experiences, this study compared two generational players and the results demonstrated that the relationship between nostalgia and game involvement was only salient for players older than 35 years of age who had more childhood memories of *Pokémon*-related media experiences. The findings from this study may echo the idea that one's tendency to engage in nostalgic feelings varies over the course of one's lifetime and nostalgia proneness may peak as one moves into middle age (Holak & Havlena, 1992). As game involvement emphasizes the player's self-relevance with the game (Brown & Cairns, 2004), *Pokémon GO* may particularly lend itself to the presentations, expressions, and sensations of the older players. It further argues that technological advances may affect and mediate one's perception of the world—the world of new technology that views the experience and perception of time as perhaps depending on one's lifelong experiences of and immersion into new forms of media.

LIMITATIONS AND FUTURE DIRECTIONS

This study compared two age groups of *Pokémon GO* players; however, the stratified sample was recruited based on the industry's big data estimation of the age distribution of *Pokémon GO* players, resulting in participants younger than 35 outnumbering the older participants. While the proportion of the younger *Pokémon GO* players dropped, the proportion of players aged over 40 rose when it concerned playing the game to stay healthy and physically active (KYOTO NEWS, 2017; Low, 2017). Future studies may particularly focus on the older generation to explore how the game may encourage them to perform outdoor activities and exercises and how such collaborative gameplay may help them to cope with loneliness or other emotional and physical stresses that go along with aging. In addition, as the game's developer continues to host real-world Community Day events to encourage players to meet fellow Pokémon trainers at their local parks and experience what it means to be a part of the game community, an online-to-offline (O2O) location-based AR game mode has emerged. How the game may encourage community engagement, pro-environmental activity, or even O2O commerce may also be of interest to future researchers.

Finally, *Pokémon GO*'s creators have released a new immersive augmented-reality game, *Harry Potter: Wizards Unite*, based on popular book-to-movie franchise. Likewise, the Harry Potter game share some gameplay elements and features as *Pokémon GO*. For example, players take on the roles of the wizards and the game map will reveal traces of magic, highlighting the location of magical Foundables. This game also encourages players to physically move around to explore the real-world surroundings to encounter certain Foundables, creatures, or iconic characters and to interact with other players at real locations. Given that AR games are built on the ideas of exploration, exercise, and social activities, co-presence addresses the connections of physical and virtual spaces with the social interaction can thus explain the immersive experience of these games. In addition, Harry Potter is a series originally based on British nostalgia and the franchise continues to expand since the release of the first book 21 years ago. How the AR game may immerse players in the wizard world by stimulating their longing to the past or by emotionally reacting the passing of time may also be interested to explore.

ACKNOWLEDGMENT

This research was supported by the Ministry of Science and Technology, Taiwan.

REFERENCES

Bagozzi, R. P., & Yi, Y. (1988). On the evaluation of structural equation models. *Journal of the Academy of Marketing Science*, *16*(1), 74–94. doi:10.1007/BF02723327

Baldwin, M., & Landau, M. J. (2014). Exploring nostalgia's influence on psychological growth. *Self and Identity*, *13*(2), 162–177. doi:10.1080/15298868.2013.772320

Barrett, F. S., Grimm, K. J., Robins, R. W., Wildschut, T., Sedikides, C., & Janata, P. (2010). Music-evoked nostalgia: Affect, memory, and personality. *Emotion (Washington, D.C.)*, *10*(3), 390–403. doi:10.1037/a0019006 PMID:20515227

Batcho, K. I. (2013). Nostalgia: The bittersweet history of a psychological concept. *History of Psychology*, *16*(3), 165–176. doi:10.1037/a0032427 PMID:23646885

Biocca, F., Harms, C., & Burgoon, J. K. (2003). Toward a more robust theory and measure of social presence: Review and suggested criteria. *Presence (Cambridge, Mass.)*, *12*(5), 456–480. doi:10.1162/105474603322761270

Bolin, G. (2016). Passion and nostalgia in generational media experiences. *European Journal of Cultural Studies*, *19*(3), 250–264. doi:10.1177/1367549415609327

Bonus, J. A., Peebles, A., Mares, M.-L., & Sarmiento, I. G. (2018). Look on the bright side (of media effects): Pokémon Go as a catalyst for positive life experiences. *Media Psychology*, *21*(2), 263–287. doi:10.1080/15213269.2017.1305280

Boym, S. (2008). *The future of nostalgia*. New York: Basic Books.

Brown, A. D., & Humphreys, M. (2002). Nostalgia and the narrativization of identity: A Turkish case study. *British Journal of Management*, *13*(2), 141–159. doi:10.1111/1467-8551.00228

Büscher, M., & Urry, J. (2009). Mobile methods and the empirical. *European Journal of Social Theory*, *12*(1), 99–116. doi:10.1177/1368431008099642

Calleja, G. (2007). Digital game involvement: A conceptual model. *Games and Culture*, *2*(3), 236–260. doi:10.1177/1555412007306206

Campos-Castillo, C., & Hitlin, S. (2013). Copresence: Revisiting a building block for social interaction theories. *Sociological Theory*, *31*(2), 168–192. doi:10.1177/0735275113489811

Cheung, W.-Y., Sedikides, C., Wildschut, T., Tausch, N., & Ayanian, A. H. (2017). Collective nostalgia is associated with stronger outgroup-directed anger and participation in ingroup-favoring collective action. *Journal of Social and Political Psychology*, *5*(2), 301–319. doi:10.5964/jspp.v5i2.697

Cummings, C. (2016, July 24). Infographic: Pokemon Go Could Be What Farmville Never Was—Successful: Here's how brands can catch 'em all. *ADWEEK*. Retrieved from http://www.adweek.com/digital/infographic-pokemon-go-could-be-what-farmville-never-was-successful-172626/

Davis, F. (1979). *Yearning for yesterday: A sociology of nostalgia.* New York: Free Press.

Eroglu, S. A., Machleit, K., & Barr, T. F. (2005). Perceived retail crowding and shopping satisfaction: The role of shopping values. *Journal of Business Research*, *58*(8), 1146–1153. doi:10.1016/j.jbusres.2004.01.005

Fahey, R. (2018, November 16). *Pokémon's strategy is cross-generational: By balancing nostalgia for parents with appeal to children.* Retrieved from https://www.gamesindustry.biz/articles/2018-11-16-pokemons-strategy-is-cross-generational

Fairley, S. (2003). In search of relived social experience: Group-based nostalgia sport tourism. *Journal of Sport Management*, *17*(3), 284–304. doi:10.1123/jsm.17.3.284

Fornell, C., & Larcker, D. F. (1981). *Structural equation models with unobservable variables and measurement error: Algebra and statistics.* Los Angeles, CA: SAGE Publications Sage CA.

Funk, D. C., Ridinger, L. L., & Moorman, A. M. (2004). Exploring origins of involvement: Understanding the relationship between consumer motives and involvement with professional sport teams. *Leisure Sciences*, *26*(1), 35–61. doi:10.1080/01490400490272440

Gajadhar, B. J., De Kort, Y. A., & Ijsselsteijn, W. A. (2008). *Shared fun is doubled fun: player enjoyment as a function of social setting. In Fun and games* (pp. 106–111). Berlin: Springer-Verlag.

Gross, M. J., & Brown, G. (2008). An empirical structural model of tourists and places: Progressing involvement and place attachment into tourism. *Tourism Management*, *29*(6), 1141–1151. doi:10.1016/j.tourman.2008.02.009

Hair, J. F., Black, W. C., Babin, B. J., Anderson, R. E., & Tatham, R. L. (2006). *Multivariate data analysis.* Upper Saddle River, NJ: Pearson Prentice Hall.

Harms, C., & Biocca, F. (2004). Internal Consistency and Reliability of the Networked Minds Measure of Social Presence. In M. Alcaniz & B. Rey (Eds.), *Seventh Annual International Workshop: Presence 2004.* Valencia: Universidad Politecnica de Valencia.

Holak, S. L., & Havlena, W. J. (1992). *Nostalgia: An exploratory study of themes and emotions in the nostalgic experience.* ACR North American Advances.

Keogh, B. (2017). Pokémon Go, the novelty of nostalgia, and the ubiquity of the smartphone. *Mobile Media & Communication*, *5*(1), 38–41. doi:10.1177/2050157916678025

Kline, R. B. (2015). *Principles and practice of structural equation modeling.* Guilford publications.

Koetz, C., & Tankersley, J. D. (2016). Nostalgia in online brand communities. *The Journal of Business Strategy*, *37*(3), 22–29. doi:10.1108/JBS-03-2015-0025

Kyle, G., & Chick, G. (2002). The social nature of leisure involvement. *Journal of Leisure Research*, *34*(4), 426–448. doi:10.1080/00222216.2002.11949980

Kyodo News. (2017, July 15). One year after release, Pokemon Go is fitness tool for older people. *Kyodo News*. Retrieved from https://english.kyodonews.net/

Lange, P. G. (2011). Video-mediated nostalgia and the aesthetics of technical competencies. *Visual Communication, 10*(1), 25–44. doi:10.1177/1470357210389533

Lee, M., & Faber, R. J. (2007). Effects of product placement in on-line games on brand memory: A perspective of the limited-capacity model of attention. *Journal of Advertising, 36*(4), 75–90. doi:10.2753/JOA0091-3367360406

Loveday, P., & Burgess, J. (2017). Flow and Pokémon GO: The Contribution of Game Level, Playing Alone, and Nostalgia to the Flow State. *E-Journal of Social & Behavioural Research in Business, 8*(2), 16–28.

Low, A. (2017, July 10). These seniors are kicking ass in Pokemon Go: And staying healthy while doing so. *CNET*. Retrieved from https://www.cnet.com/

Mardia, K. V. (1970). Measures of multivariate skewness and kurtosis with applications. *Biometrika, 57*(3), 519–530. doi:10.1093/biomet/57.3.519

Mateo, D. J. (2017). Pokémon GO May Increase Physical Activity and Decrease Sedentary Behaviors Regular physical. *American Journal of Public Health, 107*(1), 37–38. doi:10.2105/AJPH.2016.303532 PMID:27854536

Muehling, D. D., & Pascal, V. J. (2012). An involvement explanation for nostalgia advertising effects. *Journal of Promotion Management, 18*(1), 100–118. doi:10.1080/10496491.2012.646222

Nabi, R. L., & Krcmar, M. (2004). Conceptualizing media enjoyment as attitude: Implications for mass media effects research. *Communication Theory, 14*(4), 288–310. doi:10.1111/j.1468-2885.2004.tb00316.x

Nelson, R. (2018). *Pokémon GO revenue hits $1.8 billion on its two year launch anniversary*. Retrieved from https://sensortower.com/blog/pokemon-go-revenue-year-two

Niemeyer, K., & Wentz, D. (2014). Nostalgia is not what it used to be: Serial nostalgia and nostalgic television series. In K. Niemeyer (Ed.), *Media and Nostalgia: Yearning for the Past, the Present and the Future* (pp. 129–138). London: Palgrave McMillan. doi:10.1057/9781137375889_10

Nowak, K. (2001). *Defining and differentiating copresence, social presence and presence as transportation*. Paper presented at the Presence 2001 Conference, Philadelphia, PA.

Oleksy, T., & Wnuk, A. (2017). Catch them all and increase your place attachment! The role of location-based augmented reality games in changing people-place relations. *Computers in Human Behavior, 76*, 3–8. doi:10.1016/j.chb.2017.06.008

Pivec, M. (2007). Play and learn: Potentials of game-based learning. *British Journal of Educational Technology, 38*(3), 387–393. doi:10.1111/j.1467-8535.2007.00722.x

Russell, J. A., & Ward, L. M. (1982). Environmental psychology. *Annual Review of Psychology, 33*(1), 651–689. doi:10.1146/annurev.ps.33.020182.003251

Scannell, L., & Gifford, R. (2010). Defining place attachment: A tripartite organizing framework. *Journal of Environmental Psychology*, *30*(1), 1–10. doi:10.1016/j.jenvp.2009.09.006

Schindler, R. M., & Holbrook, M. B. (2003). Nostalgia for early experience as a determinant of consumer preferences. *Psychology and Marketing*, *20*(4), 275–302. doi:10.1002/mar.10074

Schroeder, R., Steed, A., Axelsson, A.-S., Heldal, I., Abelin, Å., Widestrom, J., ... Slater, M. (2001). Collaborating in networked immersive spaces: As good as being there together? *Computers & Graphics*, *25*(5), 781–788. doi:10.1016/S0097-8493(01)00120-0

Sedikides, C., & Wildschut, T. (2016). Past forward: Nostalgia as a motivational force. *Trends in Cognitive Sciences*, *20*(5), 319–321. doi:10.1016/j.tics.2016.01.008 PMID:26905661

Shafer, D. M., & Carbonara, C. P. (2015). Examining enjoyment of casual videogames. *Games for Health Journal*, *4*(6), 452–459. doi:10.1089/g4h.2015.0012 PMID:26509941

Shelby, B., Vaske, J. J., & Donnelly, M. P. (1996). Norms, standards, and natural resources. *Leisure Sciences*, *18*(2), 103–123. doi:10.1080/01490409609513276

Skalski, P., Tamborini, R., Shelton, A., Buncher, M., & Lindmark, P. (2011). Mapping the road to fun: Natural video game controllers, presence, and game enjoyment. *New Media & Society*, *13*(2), 224–242. doi:10.1177/1461444810370949

Slater, M., Sadagic, A., Usoh, M., & Schroeder, R. (2000). Small-group behavior in a virtual and real environment: A comparative study. *Presence (Cambridge, Mass.)*, *9*(1), 37–51. doi:10.1162/105474600566600

Stokols, D., Rall, M., Pinner, B., & Schopler, J. (1973). Physical, social, and personal determinants of the perception of crowding. *Environment and Behavior*, *5*(1), 87–115. doi:10.1177/001391657300500106

Takatalo, J., Häkkinen, J., Kaistinen, J., & Nyman, G. (2010). Presence, involvement, and flow in digital games. In R. Bernhaupt (Ed.), *Evaluating User Experience in Games. Human-Computer Interaction Series* (pp. 23–46). London, UK: Springer. doi:10.1007/978-1-84882-963-3_3

Tamborini, R., & Bowman, N. D. (2010). Presence in video games. In C. Campanella Bracken & P. D. Skalski (Eds.), Immersed in media: Telepresence in everyday life (pp. 87–109). Academic Press.

Tassi, P. (2019). How on earth did 'Pokémon GO' make almost $800 million in 2018? *Forbes*. Retrieved from https://www.forbes.com/

Van Tilburg, W. A., Igou, E. R., & Sedikides, C. (2013). In search of meaningfulness: Nostalgia as an antidote to boredom. *Emotion (Washington, D.C.)*, *13*(3), 450–461. doi:10.1037/a0030442 PMID:23163710

Williams, D. R., & Vaske, J. J. (2003). The measurement of place attachment: Validity and generalizability of a psychometric approach. *Forest Science*, *49*(6), 830–840.

Wulf, T., Rieger, D., & Schmitt, J. B. (2018). Blissed by the past: Theorizing media-induced nostalgia as an audience response factor for entertainment and well-being. *Poetics*, *69*, 70–80. doi:10.1016/j.poetic.2018.04.001

Yang, C., & Liu, D. (2017). Motives matter: Motives for playing Pokémon Go and implications for well-being. *Cyberpsychology, Behavior, and Social Networking, 20*(1), 52–57. doi:10.1089/cyber.2016.0562 PMID:28080150

Yildirim, K., & Akalin-Baskaya, A. (2007). Perceived crowding in a café/restaurant with different seating densities. *Building and Environment, 42*(9), 3410–3417. doi:10.1016/j.buildenv.2006.08.014

Zehrer, A., & Raich, F. (2016). The impact of perceived crowding on customer satisfaction. *Journal of Hospitality and Tourism Management, 29*, 88–98. doi:10.1016/j.jhtm.2016.06.007

Zhao, S. (2003). Toward a taxonomy of copresence. *Presence (Cambridge, Mass.), 12*(5), 445–455. doi:10.1162/105474603322761261

Chapter 19
Immersive Media and Branding:
How Being a Brand Will Change and Expand in the Age of True Immersion

Linda Ricci

ⓘ https://orcid.org/0000-0002-0985-6660

Decahedralist Consulting, USA

ABSTRACT

This chapter explores the impact immersive technologies—augmented reality and virtual reality—will have on consumer branding and business in the near- and longer-term future. Weaving multiple use cases and examples throughout, the author discusses the next phase of experiential marketing: how immersive branding will develop as spatial computing becomes more mainstream, and how brands can start thinking about how they can leverage the technology. The author examines the rise of virtual influencers, how they will affect social media marketing—and how artificial intelligence will ultimately enable true one-to-one interaction with customers through virtual avatars. Finally, the author discusses risks, rules, and recommendations for how to successfully proceed as a brand curious about how to best harness the technologies.

INTRODUCTION

It's an old story.

There are new technologies on the scene—immersive media, experiential marketing—and brands are watching, struggling to figure out what it will mean for them. How they should be involved? What opportunities do they bring? What are the risks? Some will hang back, waiting; some will dive right in, wanting to be first. Many brand efforts won't even be noticed, but others that embrace these new frontiers will achieve successes, winning customers and establishing deeper relationships with the ones they have.

Virtual Reality, Augmented Reality and Mixed Reality (VR/AR/MR)—or the more inclusive term, XR—form the latest tools in the brand arsenal. They are part of emerging **spatial computing** revolu-

DOI: 10.4018/978-1-7998-2433-6.ch019

tion, fueled by immense computing power, unbridled connection speed, and increasingly sophisticated artificial intelligence, combining to create a new generation of immersive technology.

Although it is very early in the mass adoption of these immersive technologies, now is the time for brands to strategize, plan and/or experiment in the spatial computing worlds. Brands that take this leap will be ahead of the curve when these media develop more mainstream methods in the marketing and communications domains. Brands that position themselves to harness immersive technologies are positioning themselves for the next big disruption. This isn't the future ... this is now.

BACKGROUND

The evolution of what the word "brand" means has morphed over time. Originally it was a promise: a shortcut for choice in a marketplace. In a sea of sameness, being a brand allowed a product or service to stand out, be recognized, and say something about itself that would encourage purchase or even status.

Brands have come a long way from being logos and signage; with each incremental addition of media, brands have adapted. Where once it was important for brands to simply have a name that was memorable or a recognizable logo, they evolved to encompass sound and voice for radio and memorable (though short) stories for television. But in all these cases the method was to broadcast a message in the hopes it would resonate and build rapport with customers.

The arrival of digital technologies and the mass penetration of the Internet around 25 years ago—and subsequently, the connectivity brought by mobile networks—has changed the relationship between consumers and brands. Some brands such as Apple or Nike have inspired tribal fandom bordering on cult status. Brand has become a relationship between a consumer and a product, one that has evolved to thrive on dialogue and listening (on the company's part). Technology now lets consumers become content creators and sharers, taking brands from out of the driver's seat to serving as copilots and collaborators. Peer groups have become stronger influencers on brand choices than any paid-for media or planned brand positioning. Customers have become content creators who are partners, allies and advocates, versus target audiences.

The meteoric growth and influence of social media has created social platforms that are an incredible opportunity for brands to engage with their audiences and gather insightful data on who they are, what they do, and identify what they want and deliver it in a personal way. The rise of influencers and social networks as a key element of a brand's marketing strategy has changed the relationship between brands and consumers. The power of influencers cannot be overstated. "Influencers" is a nebulous term that can include paid influencers, and social networks themselves, such as online groups, peers, friends, and reviews.

WHAT IS IMMERSIVE BRANDING

There is no definitive definition of the term *Immersive Branding*. Generally speaking, it is used in reference to a brand experience that's translated into a variety of mediums, working together to create a metaphorical 360° experience of the brand thus creating a holistic brand experience.

With the arrival of VR/AR/MR on the scene, that definition takes on new dimensions as literally, a person can be completely surrounded by the brand. For purposes of this chapter, "immersive" refers to branding on an experiential level where the user is experiencing "brand" via an enhanced or upgraded combination of sense-stimuli, data and technology. Just as humans can be "embodied" in VR, brand can be "embodied" through sight, sound, experience, and eventually touch.

The bedrock that next-generation, immersive branding practices are founded upon includes harnessing lessons from digital best practices and extending them into this new medium. For the first time there can actually be an embodied experience: one where the individual is part of and interacts with both the medium and the participant/consumer, connecting and interacting with brands in far more personal, intimate and interactive ways than ever before. These technologies will, properly applied, revolutionize marketing efforts and drive quick conversions. Both offer an unprecedented way for brands to create a 1:1 relationship with consumers. A quote from Graeme Cox, CEO of Emteq sums it up:

The next evolution will move from devices in our hands to devices on our faces. These devices will need to collect data on the emotional responses of consumers to experiences, so brands can make informed decisions on how to connect with consumers. (as cited by Roland, 2018)

VR/AR/MR are all still in their commercial infancy; few companies use AR regularly, and even fewer consumers have VR headsets. As these technologies continue to develop there will be multiple opportunities for brands to integrate immersive technologies into their marketing initiatives. And while many important uses for these emerging technologies are applications in Business-to-Business (B2B) sectors (healthcare, education, manufacturing, training, industrial design, architecture), the focus of this chapter is around how the Business-to-Consumer (B2C) brands of today can transform what they are doing into the brand experience of the future.

AR and VR naturally have different methods and techniques for brands to engage with consumers and create an immersive brand experience. The opportunities for each will be addressed separately.

IMMERSIVE BRANDING AND AUGMENTED/MIXED REALITY

Augmented Reality/Mixed Reality takes the tangible, real time/real world experience and overlays new information on it to create an enhanced, expanded and more interactive reality. It augments the consumer's existing visual and audible experience with information that engages the senses, adding to and hopefully improving the experience. AR/MR is an opportunity for brands to engage in and be a part of the daily experience of the user. It has the potential to act as a co-pilot throughout someone's day, enhancing what is being experienced in real time. It can build an empathy bridge that comes through co-experiencing something together; it's an opportunity for brands to become an experience, rather than just a sometimes conversation or relationship.

Currently, viewing AR/MR experiences is primarily accomplished via a smartphone or tablet screen (a few in-store installations exist) held up in front of a physical scene. This is a limiting factor for brands to get involved. Getting people to use your brand's AR app is a huge leap for most businesses, although retailers like Amazon are blazing a trail in the mainstream with their furniture placement app. Convenience is and will continue to be the main driving force behind adoption, not the technology itself.

Figure 1. The Patrón Experience

AR isn't just visual; our world can also be augmented by sound as well. Capsure is a San Francisco-based AR startup that was launched when the founder's wife found a recording of her mother's voice after her death; it aggregates sounds, pictures and other private, emotional memories into an enhanced and interactive family album (Mark Wayman, personal communication, 2018).

Fun and Utility: Drivers Of AR/MR Adoption

Fun comes from the novelty and serendipity that can be the happy result of a well-designed experience AR: the joy of discovery, the "connect the dots" moments where the individual has data, information and context overplayed on their reality in interesting ways.

It can be a phenomenally fun way to add interest to everyday life with games, such as the 2016's surprise hit *Pokémon Go*, which was also an early model for AR as a social platform. Playing this game was a surprisingly social experience, with players running into each other and striking up conversations, exchanging tips, giving directions, and generally having a tremendous time meeting people during a digital treasure hunt. Brands have a huge opportunity to weave this type of fun into a consumer's day and increase engagement when they do. Surprise and delight are powerful motivators to return to the experience, and to share with friends, and enabling those moments with augmented reality is an excellent way for a brand to engage repeat customers.

Patrón Tequila uses AR to tell their story in a unique and engaging way (Figure 1). A brand with a deep history, storytelling is their method of choice to convey their brand's authenticity. Information and education tell a story about tequila and conveys what is special about Patrón's version. This brand also helps prospective customers by explaining the different tasting notes of the various tequilas they offer. It is an entertaining and memorable way for their brand to take their positioning (quality, authenticity, luxury) and use experiential marketing to enhance that story.

Figure 2. Jack Daniel's Augmented Reality App
Source: © 2019, Jack Daniel Distillery. Used with permission

Jack Daniel's whiskey also uses AR to tell the story of its origins (Figure 2). By scanning their label, the customer can watch an engaging animation showing the first Jack Daniel's distillery, and listen to a description of the process of making their product. The decision to integrate non- traditional media such as AR into their marketing mix came from wanting to signal to both potential and existing customers that the brand values tradition but also innovation. Additionally, AR presents an opportunity to tell a story way beyond the confines of the physical space offered (in this case the real estate is a bottle label), but there is no physical limit to what can be presented through the smartphone screen.

Utility is the other important aspect that drives engagement with AR. With an unmatched ability to deepen everyday experiences by overlaying images and information: 2D and 3D, visual as well as aural. Some of the most powerful AR use cases include social media-driven campaigns, virtual in-store displays, and mobile apps with AR capabilities to try products from the comfort of home. According to Harris Interactive Digital Consumer Survey for Accenture, four out of the top six reasons consumers are looking forward to using AR are utilitarian in nature. The fifth is to help with instructions and user manuals, the sixth is gaming (Sovie et al. 2018). The first four reasons for AR use are:

1. **To Shop for Household Items and Furniture**: Examples of companies already successfully helping customers shop for household items and furniture include Home Depot, Amazon, and Ikea. According to IBISWorld, 15% of the $70 billion US furniture market has moved online (Sonsev, 2017), and while reviews can be helpful for things such as quality and feel, they can't help buyers visualize what a sofa will actually look like in their home. Plus returning large items can be difficult and expensive.

So using AR to visualize how a large item will look in someone's home has proved valuable. Enter augmented reality "try before you buy" AR apps. They work with the consumer's phone camera to virtually place items in their homes so consumers can "see" how it looks before buying, increasing customer satisfaction since there's a much smaller window for disappointment if the couch doesn't look quite the way a customer thought it would.

Similarly, Sherwin-Williams' "ColorSnap® Visualizer" AR app (www.sherwin-williams.com/homeowners/color/try-on-colors), lets people "paint" their walls in the full spectrum of paint colors they offer to help visualize the finished look before picking up a paint brush, and helps them color match their paint to anything the app can be pointed at.

2. **To Visualize how Clothes Might fit**: While not clothing, beauty is also a natural category for AR; L'Oréal, Estée Lauder, Sally Hansen, Mac Cosmetics and an increasing number of other makeup brands have introduced phone-based AR apps and in-store mirrors to help customers visualize products in use and to learn new skills or techniques.

Facebook is working with L'Oréal to introduce AI driven chatbots that use facial mapping to demonstrate L'Oréal cosmetics in Facebook's Messenger app (Williams, 2017); all in an attempt to bring innovation to cosmetics for (as L'Oréal puts it) "the selfie generation" (PYMNTS, 2019).

Warby Parker has developed an AR virtual try on app that allows shoppers to try on any of their frames, to check for fit and style. Their brand has stood for simplicity and ease since they launched in 2010. There's no need to foster ongoing engagement since people don't typically buy more than one or two pairs of glasses a year; but the high cost of returns and even higher risk of customer dissatisfaction that comes from being a predominantly Internet-based accessory brand is greatly reduced if you can help customers decide on the right frames before ordering. And if you can increase customer delight, they are more likely to share and recommend that experience with a friend, and return when they do need another pair of glasses.

3. **To Learn More About a Place They are Visiting**: AR is revolutionizing the travel industry in so many ways. The simplest (but useful) example includes Google translate, which uses AR to translate street signs in real time (Whitney, 2017).

Museums are using AR to further educate (and entertain) visitors about their exhibits; The National Museum of Natural History's Skin and Bones app adds animations, x-ray vision and sound to their displays, allowing visitors to peer into the inner lives of animals exhibited (Smithsonian, 2015).

And travelers have a myriad of AR apps to help them navigate foreign terrain, be it nature parks or cities. From needing to find the best pastry shop to learning more about the history of the street you're on (and having a virtual concierge guide you on a discovery journey), AR is being used to enrich travel (Joseph, 2019).

4. **To Learn new Skills or Techniques**: Sephora's Visual Artist AR app is an intuitive and consumer friendly way to try on the makeup they carry, and learn how to apply, with an e-commerce module to buy directly from the app (Burkard, 2018). With an already huge database of customers subscribed to their loyalty program, they are ensuring that customers keep coming back to the app for new tutorials, to play with each season's new makeup, and brings the "fun" of trying on

makeup—something they revolutionized with their retail stores—to people's homes. It's a clean and easy way for shoppers to engage with their Sephora brand (Liu, 2018).

The brand benefit to all of these is, of course, brand engagement. It puts the customers in the story's driver seat, while helping them create viral content (e.g. pictures) that they can easily share on social media for feedback, following, and opinions. There's a huge social component; sharing your results, asking your real or virtual tribes for input. This is a winning formula for supercharging a brand.

Social Networks and Augmented Reality

It's been roughly 15 years since the first social networks launched (Terrell, 2016). They have tapped into a primal human need to connect and communicate, resulting in a meteoric growth in adoption and use.

As of Q2 2019, Facebook had roughly 2.41 billion monthly active users (people who those which have logged in during the last 30 days) (Clement, 2019a). During the last reported quarter, the company stated that 2.7 billion people were using at least one of the company's core products (Facebook, WhatsApp, Instagram, or Messenger) each month (Clement, 2019a). Twitter reports 330 million monthly active users (Clement, 2019b). These numbers are staggering and reflect a major opportunity for augmented reality to have a place in the social lives of customers and brands.

Snapchat is one of the players creating the foundation for an AR social network (Dachis, 2016). While it may seem like a silly children's toy, with augmented reality filters that add cat's ears or rainbow eyeglasses over your face, the future is compelling. Without much commotion they have created a social network that uses AR as the glue that connects. How is this social? And how do brands monetize this?

Brand engagement is the answer. Snapchat has 300 million global monthly active users (190 daily users) who create a staggering 3 billion snaps and watch more than 10 billion videos a day. 75% of Snapchat users are under 34 years old, with 30% of US millennials using Snapchat regularly (Salman, 2019).

Snapchat filters are a brilliant way to encourage consumers to engage with your brand, as Gatorade discovered when they launched a branded filter for the Super Bowl. With only a branded "G" on a cooler that splashed on screen for a split second—the Snapchat filter allowed users to dunk a virtual Gatorade cooler over people's video selfies. This resulted in driving 160 million impressions, more than the 115 million who actually tuned in to the game (Garett, 2016).

The social element comes in when your Snapchat enhanced video is shared, creating a viral campaign. It's subtle, but users generally end up sharing their AR creation—creating a fun micro brand moment that gains momentum and spreads brand awareness.

Brands often have a strong visual identity or a mascot—people can embody these via filters in AR. Snapchat has done a great job with this and as we move towards webAR, we'll start to see more brands develop this outside the Snap ecosystem. (Harding, personal communication, 2019)

In order to engage with and educate a younger, more diverse audience, museums and other physical locations are using Snapchat to offer contextually relevant AR to their real world experiences. They see it as adding a layer of authentic storytelling over what they offer.

The Los Angeles County Museum of Art, among others, has gained notoriety for their pithy Snapchat accounts. Museums report loving Snapchat and customer AR filters because it encourages visitors share their collection, and the excitement of being there; it's actually a form of direct marketing (Museum

Hack, 2016). By adding Snapchat custom filters, museums are encouraging the use of social media to tell their story.

Although pundits and dystopian futurists like to paint the future of AR and brand being about billboards and brands interfering with visual clutter everywhere someone looks, the best way to engage with customers will more likely be by making people's lives easier, more fun and more connected. Using technology like AR to enable sharing and creation around with your brand as the (subtle) fuel will be a much more effective way to create a relationship with a consumer that by placing a virtual ad over what they see.

Augmented Reality: The Near Future

As discussed above, the current most popular way to experience AR is by holding up a phone or tablet. However, in the near future, we will be able to experience AR in multiple ways. It could be via a HUD (heads-up display, like in a fighter jet) built into your car dashboard, projecting navigation and other car data directly onto the window, or a data-enabled rear-view mirror that signals your car's distance from another. It could be a mirror in the home, showing you the time and weather along with recommendations for accessories based on the outfit you are wearing. A personal device (smartphone? Something else?) may trigger experiences by proximity, serving personalized experiences that only that person can see using eyeglasses or contact lenses.

This smartphone/device will be a personal concierge and guardian, adding AR over our surroundings in sync with stored personal preferences and information. It will use a collection of behavioral and location-based data to mold an individual's surroundings to their personal, preferred profile. For brands, greater capacity to interact with products will lead to more data points that brands can use to adapt to consumer needs. Consumers will have the power to customize the brand experience and alter the consumer's environment in real time according to their desires (Corbett-Drummond et al., 2017).

IMMERSIVE BRANDING: VIRTUAL REALITY

Virtual Reality allows for the complete immersion of an individual into a computer-generated environment. It replaces the user's physical field of view with something specially created and allows for embodied exploration, experience, emotion and connection. The participant becomes a fully captive and interactive audience. Because of this, VR can elicit very powerful emotions, from an adrenaline rush, to empathy, to wonder.

Completely controlling the narrative is one of the attractions to using VR as part of a brand strategy. The experiences you build can be immensely impactful and memorable, as nothing is more personal than being transported to an alternate reality, as it is something you experience with full visual immersion. In an instant it's happening to you: you're somewhere completely different. It's also possible as a brand to be featured in another virtual world: you can stream Red Bull television content while virtually sitting in the Oculus Lounge.

VR technology has many applications. Four of the major categories of VR opportunities for brands in the B2C space include 1) branded entertainment, 2) sales tool, 3) journalism and 4) social good. (Education, training and healthcare are other major areas for VR, but primarily fall under the B2B umbrella and are not discussed in this chapter).

1. **Branded Entertainment**: It is natural for entertainment companies to expand their entertainment into VR, either as a preview or an accompaniment to their traditional content. From *Star Wars Battlefront Rogue One: X-Wing VR Mission* where you virtually fly an X-Wing and shoot down Tie Fighters, to playing virtual Holochess as seen in *Star Wars: Episode IV—A New Hope*, Disney is using VR to create anticipation for their movies with experiences that mimic and complement scenes in their movies.

Gaming is a major component of Virtual Reality and a natural use for complete immersion. But it is not realistic for most brands to create, distribute and drive traffic to a Virtual Reality game, nor is it something that aligns with their brand to do so. So what does a brand do to become involved with VR, when they don't own an entertainment franchise to leverage, and aren't a gaming company?

VR is also a natural channel for any product or services that has a visual, experiential aspect to it. Fashion, for example, is perfect for VR, as fans of fashion and apparel brands can be rabid. Experiencing an upfront seat at Gucci's fashion week show sitting next to your favorite celebrity or model would be a dream for most, and highly entertaining with a high social/viral component.

Here's a scenario: you log onto Kim Kardashian's live stream. You're standing next to her, mobbed by paparazzi and blinded by the flashes; you clutch your Birkin bag, call out to Giselle and slip through the crowds to take your front row seats. Anna Wintour waves, a quick peek shows you're surrounded by celebrities ("Hi Leonardo!") as the exclusive 4k 360° VR stream of New York Fashion Week 2019 starts.

And then everything freezes. "*Want to see more? $39.99 will get you an all access spot. Kim's waiting!*"

- **VR streaming** like this offers brands and advertisers access to a highly targeted and willfully engaged audience. Livestream and *New York Magazine* surveys found that 45% of live video audiences would pay for live, exclusive, on-demand video from an influencer (Mallet, n.d.). Imagine how many would be thrilled to "attend" that event in 3D with VR; the impact on brand recognition and loyalty of each element of that event (the watch, the outfits, the accessories) would be incredible.
- **Choose your own experiences** are another creative tactic for immersive VR events. Combining VR, branching narrative, and vcommerce, they creatively created a whole new category of immersive experiences. Accenture and Specular Theory (Figure 3) combined storytelling and VR with interactive "choose your own" choices and actual shopping shop in 2018's "Behind the Style." This interactive VR story of a fashion shoot seamlessly blended fashion, tech and vcommerce (commerce in the virtual space) in a way that was highly engaging, fun and natural (Accenture, 2017).

Other retail and apparel brands could use a similar creative approach to entice viewers into immersive interaction in a thoroughly impactful and memorable way. This is a fresh, creative, memorable, and relevant way to stand out from the crowd when consumers are increasingly not responsive to traditional marketing tactics.

Why not partner with synergistic events or brands to bring viewers into a new world of experience? Why wouldn't Swarovski sponsor an "experience a Venetian masquerade ball" experience, complete with your own sparkly costume? You could choose your Swarovski-encrusted ball gown, and your earrings - which happen to be for sale? Why not gamify it and create a treasure hunt? Brands can, and should, be creative with this new frontier.

Figure 3. Behind The Style
Source: © 2017, Accenture and Specular Theory. Used with permission

2.   **Sales Tool**: Brands with longer and more involved sales cycles are also using VR to differentiate and become involved earlier in the brand decision process.

Luxury brand Cadillac faced a challenge: increasingly consumers are not engaging with an actual Cadillac dealership—or a person there—until the decision to buy one had already been made. We have entered what Robert Spierenburg, CEO of All Things Media calls the "age of Amazon," (Robert Spierenburg, personal communication, 2019) where the transparency and ease of online shopping has changed the very nature of how people shop and what they expect. Home-based research online, comparison shopping, soliciting opinions and reading reviews had taken over visits to the dealership and asking questions; Cadillac had lost the opportunity to influence the consumer at any stage of the purchase funnel. This was weakening any potential brand relationship and was commoditizing the car shopping experience.

Cadillac's solution was to create a VR experience where a potential customer who was "just shopping" could do so, without the hassle and perceived pressure of having to talk to a live Cadillac sales person. There they could use options to create their perfect Cadillac in VR, with or without a Cadillac's representative (i.e. their avatar) there to answer their questions. If prompted and approved, a representative from a local Cadillac dealership would appear as their avatar. Thus, the brand representative would be there much nearer to the beginning of the sales process, instead of at the end when the customer only wants to discuss price. It is an opportunity to establish virtually, earlier in the sales cycle, and carry that relationship into the real world (Robert Spierenburg, personal communication, 2019).

In addition, the metrics collected can be parsed to better anticipate future conversations and then used to train salespeople and ultimately, artificial intelligence customer service agents.

•   **Virtual Staging with VR**: VR technology is being used by developers to help customers visualize how a prospective residence might look with different types of interior décor (Steele, 2019). Shoppers can use a VR headset during an in-person property tour to see true-to-life visualizations (with inventory from participating retailers). This opportunity to envision a prospective home converts to sales; 77% of buyers' agents reported staging a home made it easier for a buyer to visualize

Figure 4. Natuzzi Augmented Store
Source: © 2019, Natuzzi S.p.A. Used with permission

the property as a future home (The National Association of Realtors, 2017). In this way Virtual Reality improves the flexibility, ease and cost of staging.

- **Virtual Showroom**: As of January 2019, Macy's has added VR based in-store furniture shopping experiences in 90 of its stores (O'Shea, (2018), where customers can design their homes with furniture pieces and decor elements from Macy's inventory. This is a huge sales tool for Macy's, not only increasing sales but reducing buyer's remorse. Macy's can feature many more items virtually that can be dropped shipped than they could ever carry on the store showroom floor, so their product offering is multiplied without any overhead cost. Macy's reports in the stores with VR installations furniture sales increase by more than 60% compared to non-VR sales, with returns down to less than 2% (Shayon, 2016).

Virtual showrooms are being used by luxury brands as well. At NYCxDesign 2019 (Chouinard, 2019) Italian luxury furniture maker Natuzzi launched a preview of its future mixed reality showroom using VR, AR and holographs (Figure 3). There were multiple benefits for both the brand and potential consumers, "This gives us an incredible opportunity to showcase our collection without boundaries; to lower the stock and inventory at our stores; minimize the space and architectural investments required to set up a location; and dramatically increase our sales per square foot," says Pasquale Junior Natuzzi, creative director and stylist (Chouinard, 2019). Customers enjoyed immersing themselves in a 3D representation of what the brand stood for and could decide whether the brand's vision appealed to their aesthetic sense; and they had a memorable experience that was fun.

3. **Journalism**: According to Adobe's "The Future of Experience" report, VR is best used to "foster empathy and create meaningful experiences that have the potential to power social good" (Adobe, 2018). To build stronger connections, brands, artists, and organizations—including advocacy groups and marketers—are exploring the medium for a variety of uses, from showcasing their corporate social impact work to creating virtual, mission-driven art installations, and raising awareness of the ramifications of negative behavior on others.

In 2015, *The New York Times* in partnership with Google, distributed 1.3 million Google VR Cardboard headsets to subscribers and made the bold move to establish themselves as the pioneers of VR journalism. The ability of VR to communicate the realities of a situation is unparalleled; a visual story holds far more ability to communicate than a typed word and picture, and a completely immersive one even more so. You can be standing with their reporters in the middle of Fallujah as bombs are falling, or as with the story that launched with the Google Cardboard distribution—give viewers a taste of what it's like to be a child refugee in Ukraine, Syria, South Sudan. It provided a powerful and moving experience, and offered a glimpse of the VR and journalism could do best: tell a story, and create empathy, moving the journalism needle higher.

4. **Social Good:** The shoe brand TOMS has used VR to tell the powerful story of their charity work: they match every pair of shoes purchased with a new pair for a child in need, located in some of the poorest location in the world. The VR experiences that *TOMS Giving Trip* brings the viewer along on one of their trips, showing how TOMS employees and partners fit kids for shoes and highlight the work they are doing to improve education and health programs (Nafarrete 2015). For a brand whose core brand identity revolves around giving, VR provides an intimate glimpse into the work they do. TOMS stores each include an in-store VR headset so shoppers can see the good their purchases are doing. It is an excellent example of how VR can further the best kind of social good marketing.

In addition, VR can be a shared experience in social VR applications. Enabling multiple people to co-experience VR is currently in very early stages, but early indications of how much it will grow is already there. Experiencing sharing with others in the virtual space will turbo charge the adoption of VR, which can currently be a solitary pursuit.

In this area it is now possible to watch streaming television or movies with another person's avatar on a shared "couch" with Oculus Cinema, and one can attend VR events in AltspaceVR, interacting with body motions through the Microsoft Kinect and sharing the experience with millions of other people across the globe.

Alejandro Mainetto, EY partner and digital transformation leader points out that "Interacting in Social VR will be conceptually similar to interacting in the real world, except that we will be interacting with avatars: digital beings, digital representations of humans in the virtual space" (Alejandro Mainetto, personal communication, 2019).

People have gathered in virtual worlds since the late-1990s (Ah-young, 2013). The digital platform *Second Life*—a 3D virtual world with only a computer screen for an interface—boasted 1.1 million active users at its peak in 2007 (Axon, 2017). But the recent VR concert in *Fortnite* featuring DJ Marshmello broke a new record, with roughly 10 million people concurrently attending in the game's "showtime" mode (Tassi, 2019). Although only 10 minutes long it gave us a glimpse of what the future of VR events will be like: people using avatars to enjoy a shared interaction in a geographically irrelevant space, enjoying a mass scale event together.

The potential benefits of holding a VR event for brands are many: the cost per event is much lower than holding a physical event; there's no venue to book, no security to hire, no stage to decorate. It also avoids the logistics or risks associated with holding a large-scale event, as there's no possibility of injury, with all associated potential lawsuits. Attendance isn't limited to those who can geographically make it, or by how large the stadium is. You can monitor and track participation and engagement to better understand what your audience is enjoying (Robert Spierenburg, personal communication, 2019). And the enthusiasm is real; you've created something that will ensure brand engagement with your target audience, and they get to enjoy something without having to leave the safety and comfort of their own living rooms.

Brands can and will continue to play a key role in facilitating virtual tribes, as they have done in the traditional sense, creating communities around love of a product. Such brands will need to foster the creation, curation and management of these communities.

A big win for everyone.

VIRTUAL BEINGS AS INFLUENCERS AND BRAND AMBASSADORS

The newest trend is the development of virtual influencers on Instagram and other digital platforms, which are computer-generated virtual humans that "synthesize the most attractive traits of real influencers and even manufacture interpersonal drama to promote very real brands" (Kulp, 2019).

What is a *virtual being*? A virtual being is a created character. You (ideally) know they aren't real. They offer varying levels of interaction, and they can definitely influence real life brand decisions.

The term virtual being encompasses everything from a simple chatbot on a website to Google's Alexa, digitally created influencers like the Instagram phenomenon Lil Miquela who "interacts" through social media posts, up to artificially intelligent agents like Mica (an avatar chatbot from Magic Leap) and ultimately, Lucy, who is an interactive virtual being that incorporates Natural Language Processing into interactions, allowing for personalized conversations in real-time.

These last two examples are very cutting edge, and artificial intelligence technology is not quite yet able to interact at the level of a real human. That will change as the technology improves, and when that happens the line between real and fake influencers will blur.

Although not yet perfect human duplicates, virtual beings already influence people's purchasing decisions. Dubbed as the world's first digital supermodel, Shudu has modeled for the likes of Balmain and Fenty Beauty. Created by British photographer Cameron-James Wilson in 2017, she has also been featured in editorials in *Vogue* Australia and *Cosmopolitan* magazine (Barker, 2019).

Lil Michaela has become a huge Instagram celebrity and influencer with a 1.6 million-strong following in less than three years: everything from her bangs, freckles, heritage (Brazilian and Spanish) and beautiful friends has been a cause célèbre since then. Her followers closely follow her every move (and fashion choice), while her fakeness is celebrated. She updates Instagram daily with photos of herself wearing real products from prestigious fashion brands such as Chanel, Proenza Schouler and Vans (Morency, 2018). 80,000 fans on Spotify stream her songs every month (Hsu, 2017). She also recently crossed out of the digital realm and caused quite a stir by kissing Bella Hadid in a Calvin Klein ad.

The technology to convincingly make her—and her success—has intensified the discussion by brands around how necessary it is to hire expensive celebrities, models, or even "regular" social media influencers, when you can take consumer insights specific to your market, brand, and product, and turn them into supercharged brand ambassadors from scratch.

Another benefit: virtual influencers are less regulated than their human counterparts and can work 24/7. They won't get hired away and they won't go on strike. They won't age either, or gain weight (unless you want them too); they won't appear in tabloid scandals (unless it's on brand to do so), throw tantrums or demand more money (although their creators might). Alexis Ohanian, Co-founder of Reddit said it best: "Brands like working with avatars—they don't have to do 100 takes (as cited by Hsu, 2017)." He also believes, "Social media, to date, has largely been the domain of real humans being fake. But avatars are a future of storytelling."

This is no flash-in-the-pan trend. Lipps LA is a modeling agency recently expanded their traditional services to become a "digitally focused celebrity, influencer and model agency (SparkCGI, 2019)." Their first "sign on" is Daisy Page, a 100% computer generated model. She is seen as the first in a rapidly expanding market for custom characters, who will literally personify brands and/or be the influencers that brands will enthusiastically adopt data and insight driven computer-generated models, as a pipeline to Millennials and GenZ audiences.

Designing your own branded digitally created influencer versus partnering with one that already exists (like Lil Miquela) is actually just the next step in personifying a brand with a character. Tony the Tiger has been selling cereal for decades; The Colonel has been the face of KFC since 1952. The difference is that now not only are the brand characters more real, but the opportunity to actually engage is becoming reality. Using consumer insights and data it's possible to design a fleshed out brand driven, personality rich persona in conjunction with an appearance that synergizes with a brand's values.

In conversation with the Author, Samantha Wolfe, Managing Partner of PitchFWD and Author of *Marketing New Realities* describes the challenge for brands: "Embodiment is making something concrete and perceptible (as it will be when consumers interact with it in VR) (Samantha Wolfe, personal communication, 2019). How can you "embody" a brand and what does that look like to the consumer? "Being considerate is a great first step and making sure that anything you do is in context of your brand" (Samantha Wolfe, personal communication, 2019).

Brands have the opportunity to create fully fleshed out and interactive 3D versions of brand personas, developing a truly interactive interaction with their brand—and the opportunity to nearly literally "flesh out" what they stand for when interacting with consumers.

Robert Spierenburg, CEO of All Things Media made the point in conversation that although true artificial intelligence is still a few years away, the general public has embraced voice interaction and digital home assistants with Siri, Alexa, and others (Robert Spierenburg, personal communication, 2019). Enhancing virtual avatars with artificial intelligence will develop artificial avatars even further and in the not so distant future consumers will be able to talk to your brand in the form of an embodied avatar that is responsive and conversational, taking immersiveness and interaction to a new level.

Spark CGi's lead artist and designer, and the creator of Daisy—Phillip Jay, believes this is a new and exciting opportunity for both fashion and brand marketing. He says, "We're moving into a new era where Artificial Intelligence and CGI characters will coexist with humans in many traditional roles including acting, modeling, presenting and influencing" (SparkCGI, 2019).

And give brands, ironically, the ability to once again control the well-informed data-driven story.

PERSONALIZATION AND PRIVACY

As consumers increasingly demand the power to experience brands in their own, personalized way through a myriad of channels, the need for data collection, processing, storage and use becomes monumental. Delivering a personalized micro-targeted experience or interaction—such as a retail chatbot that remembers your past conversations and favorite color, or a store that knows who you are and remembers you don't mind getting a coupon from them on your phone when you come within three blocks of their store (but only once!)—requires ever increasing amounts of data.

This is something that many consumers have become more and more comfortable with. Google maps knows your entire location history; Stitcher recommends podcasts based on your tastes; Spotify tailors your music feed to your listening history; and Alexa has made listening ubiquitous. Consumers happily trade personal data for the convenience of having things work the way they want them to: it has just become a way of life. "We are growing accustomed to being known and to expect companies to personalize to us as individuals—same will be the case in VR space—there is no going back to mass targeting (Alejandro Mainetto, personal communication, 2019)."

But the sheer amount of data that can and will be collected with immersive technology/spatial computing is staggering: geo-location, physical movements, eye tracking, positional data, brand and retailers you interact with, speech, and proximity sensor data, to name a few. VR headsets map your living space; they know how tall you are. VR doesn't just enable hearing what users say, but how they how they talk, what they do, who they interact with, and more. In VR is it possible to surveil every single interaction a user makes, store it forever and use that data for any purpose.

The benefit to this data collection for brands is that they can create experiences and marketing campaigns that are incredibly relevant to the customer. To quote Alejandro Mainetto, Partner & Digital Transformation Leader, EY:

Personalization will be exactly what it means in the current world. Your digital being or avatar will be in constant communication and alignment with the VR/AR/MR platform which will know what you like, what you don't—who are your friends, essentially just like how Facebook works today but it will be the VR/AR/MR version of it. Trust will have to be built in the same way it did in the early days of the internet. As with e-commerce, as the masses will flock and adopt these environments others will flock there as well trusting it will safe. (Alejandro Mainetto, personal communication, 2019)

The challenge though is that the experience is already "closer to home" than just logging onto a 2D screen; interactions and experience can feel *too* personal.

Providing the right amount of personalization means gathering data on customers. How to use that data without annoying customers is the key. Brands will need to walk a very fine line between using that data to provide a personalized experience, without crossing the line: consumers don't want to be reminded of how much companies know about them. Particularly, brands need to be sensitive to "invading" personal space, a line that can easily and inadvertently be crossed.

That will require brands keep the customers first and foremost when designing immersive experiences, keeping their needs at the north star rather than the company's desire for more data. Smart brands will be able to walk the fine line between being an invited guest and an unwelcome intruder.

As people move to virtual meetings and social interactions, the need for secure use of your personal avatars will become increasingly more important. Blockchain may be one of many solutions that can mitigate risks of losing digital identity. This makes it vital to create rules and standards that prevent it from being abused. (Alan Smithson, personal communication, 2019)

RISKS, RECOMMENDATIONS AND CONCLUSION

Along with the opportunities for engagement, influence and commerce, immersive technologies have the significant, non-trivial risks inherent in any new medium. What follows is a list of seven risks that should be top of mind for any brand intending to engage in AR or VR development. This is by no means an exhaustive list but should be considered a strong starting point.

1. Poor strategy, weak execution and lack of relevance are common and preventable problems facing brands every day in print, radio, out of home advertising (billboards, bus posters, subway posters, etc), TV and digital. The same challenges face brands as they contemplate building VR/AR/MR experiences. Because they are so experiential, VR/AR/MR works require more focus on the strategy and relevance to the consumer. Based on consumers' experiences with gaming, science fiction and television entertainment, the gap between expectations and the actual experience might be quite large. *Your* execution will also be constantly measured against other experiences available, including those put out by industry behemoths such as Disney. Any effort needs to exchange significant value to that user immediately and keep it going in order to keep their attention and engagement.

2. The second risk brands face is being smart about how they commit to and invest in VR/AR/MR efforts. Whether building their own virtual worlds or AR apps, engaging on others' platforms, or sponsoring experiences, brands need to focus as much on the diversity of experiences as their quality, particularly as they navigate this new space. Finding their target audiences and reaching them in meaningful ways means making lots of small and medium sized investments of time and budget. Launching an app and not updating it, releasing a virtual product and not supporting it, opening a new platform on a virtual world and not having a calendar of events and content that users can engage are all avoidable. Brands need to keep this in mind as they plan and build.

3. Earlier in this chapter we talked about brands and trust, which leads to a third risk, reputation and brand safety. Brands are valuable and cultivated reputation engines. They stand for things and mean something to customers beyond packaging and specific product attributes. In immersive branding brands are entering spaces that they don't wholly own. Even if you launch a branded virtual space, you are sharing it with the consumers experiencing it. Brands in these new media are, in a number of cases, co-creating with the consumers who engage. As we have seen in social media and in the 2000s with *Second Life* there are individuals who will troll, bully, and vandalize a space or experience (Daily Mail, 2007). As the host, sponsor or maker of the experience, brands need to consider and implement "codes of conduct" for the spaces they are building/funding as well as mitigation strategies (moderation, report-block signaling, force-fields, etc.) for keeping participants safe and appropriate responses and action for these types of issues.

4. The fourth risk within Immersive Branding concerns consumer privacy and control. As two forms of embodied media, AR and VR may have a set of different expectations than the mobile or desktop internet. One of the features of these technologies is the sense of agency, of control that they

bring to the consumer and their interactions. AR and VR aren't passive media: the user is an active participant, even if the only interaction is to change their point of view. As AR is an overlay to the real world, users will want to understand how AR experiences they interact with are reporting back and to whom. In VR, especially Social VR where you aren't alone in the experience but "hanging out" with other consumers or chatbots, the consumer's privacy and control are intertwined. *Who* can see a consumer's avatar is as important as what that avatar looks like. Will a VR user have the ability to set rules on who can approach them? Will they have a "force field" preventing other users from approaching them if they aren't from the same tribe or clan? Brands need to be extra careful in why, how and where in their AR and VR experiences the value of the brand is in friction with the privacy and agency of the consumer.

5. Where brands decide to build, sponsor or engage users in different AR or VR experiences, consumer data will be collected, and this is our fifth risk. Data collection for advertising and marketing purposes is happening every day online with targeted/display advertising and even in the offline world with events and out of home advertising. User expectations are mixed in regard to their privacy and data. Some give personal data away willingly in exchange for a free product or service. Others use ad blockers and VPNs to prevent third parties from snooping on them and their web surfing, etc. What is critical is the awareness of the consumer that data is being collected, how the data is collected, how it is processed and used, where it is stored and if it is shared or sold to another party. Brands should consider data minimization policies whenever they are directly or indirectly collecting data on consumers engaging their experiences. In addition, adhering to public regulations on personal data such as GDPR (a legal framework that sets guidelines for the collection and processing of personal information from individuals who live in the European Union (Frankenfield, 2019) can go a long way in building trust with consumers.

6. Our sixth risk, specific to AR but may also apply to some VR experiences, is a concept called "Virtual Air Rights" a term coined by the writer, John C. Havens (Havens 2011). In theory, augmented reality can replace objects, surfaces and people within a consumer's point of view. As a consumer walks down the street, mailboxes transform to look like steam punk mail engines, Pokémon peek out from behind corners and directional arrows fed from our map application appear in the air at an intersection indicating where we should turn. If AR can add to my point of view or alter things in my point of view, what is stopping it from becoming an augmented reality ad blocker, removing billboards and OOH ads in my field of view? Worse, what if instead of removing ads from my POV, my AR provider allowed brands to pay to replace ads in my field of view? Brands need to consider the best way to handle these concerns.

7. Platform dependence is the final risk enumerated in this chapter. Brands make investments of time, attention and budget on platforms like TV networks, social networks, live events, etc. all the time. It is unrealistic that every brand will have its own virtual world (although with WebVR this is a distinct possibility). As brands engage consumers on multiple platforms, they are growing their own audience *and* bringing new users to the platforms. Brands should work to make sure they aren't becoming too dependent on any one platform, be open to as many opportunities and possible and push for interoperability of identity and experience for consumers.

RULES OF BRAND ENGAGEMENT

Rules of brand engagement in the immersive space are the same ones that would apply to any digital campaign, and they are that much more important to be sensitive to since the experiences in the medium are so close in people's personal space.

1. Listen carefully to what consumers are talking about, saying to you, and saying to each other—brands do not want to facilitate bullying, trolling or abuse. They need, especially if they are building or renting their own VR/AR/MR products, to police their experiences. Silence is not acceptable

2. Be deliberate in analyzing the takeaways and, if possible, test what you are hearing with market research. Know what your brand stands for and use that as guard rails for developing immersive experiences.

3. Add Augmented or Virtual reality to your brand's portfolio of marketing tactics but start slowly and test small. Don't jump in with a big splash and expect huge results immediately. Add incremental efforts where possible, and always within the boundaries of your brand values and position. Evaluate, analyze, learn, fine tune from every effort, and apply those takeaways into your next effort.

4. Wait to be invited in; don't interrupt! Since AR and VR are such personal experiences, interrupting user's experiences with in-their-faces advertising—or even worse, interstitials—would be a hugely disruptive; something no brand wants to do (especially to vocal users who will complain on social media and social VR). Instead strive to facilitate, enhance, and integrate. Don't be the enthusiastic puppy bounding in, be the aloof cat.

5. Provide only as much interaction as you customer desires: don't force interaction or content on them unless they ask for it. Help customers create experience and interactions that facilitate what they desire.

6. Enable connections to their virtual tribes, the ones that share their passion for your brand (or an activity/product that synergizes with your brand). Use a values-based approach to connect experiences and people; foster brand appropriate emotion and connection, not brand messaging and positioning.

7. Give customers a platform to yell from: it's stronger to enable other people's content creation than it is to get them to listen to your message. Your message will be better accepted if there is a relationship

8. Don't focus on ROI. Immersive technology enables brand awareness and engagement: it does not yet lend itself to rigorous ROI analysis. Treat it as you would any brand engagement exercise: as something valuable for the longer term, and part of a marketing ecosystem, with a portfolio of marketing tactics that work together to achieve a goal. It's a marathon, not a sprint.

9. Technology is a new frontier, and just like all frontiers it is full of opportunities and potential pitfalls for brands. If you want to get involved, keep in mind the following:

10. Integrate any efforts in AR or VR into your portfolio of marketing activities. Nothing successful happens in a vacuum, and every customer touch point is inextricably linked together. Keep the experience consistent with who you are, and what you stand for.

11. What stories are you trying to tell? Bring experiences to life. Think of what you're designing in terms of an experience, not an application.

12. Technology is only a tool: it can evoke strong emotions and build solid customer bridges, but it should not be used to do something just because it's there. If it makes sense for what your brand stands for, what you're trying to achieve—and if it will resonate with your customers—then test the waters.

13. Fight the urge to try and control how people interact with your brand, instead make then co-creators, travelers on your brand journey whose contributions you celebrate and value.

14. Although sense of touch is still severely limited and the field of haptics is still in its infancy, it will become an integral part of the VR experience as the technology progresses. From gloves to full body suits, to exoskeletons and brain computer interfaces—the future will definitely include simulated weight, force and touch—and there are a plethora of companies working on delivering that more complete experience. Despite the current limitation of not being able to feel and touch, though, VR still delivers surprisingly experiential moments in a fully immersive—and often highly emotional—way. Use this strength of the medium to create empathy and an emotional bonding experience with consumers.

15. And lastly, don't just try something because it's creative, or cool. Like any other technology, AR, VR and MR will be best used when a well-defined business case is laid out. Nothing can substitute for having a rock-solid brand strategy to build on. Don't forget what you want to achieve and design an approach that will help move toward that goal.

CONCLUSION

We are on the precipice of a new dimension. Human imagination has brought us storytelling through books, films, theater, but have always been limited by what our eyes could physically see—or what our minds could imagine. This is an exciting frontier for brands. For the first time in history, there is an opportunity to not just interact with customers, but to actually embody the values and personality of your brand, bringing new meaning to the concept of "experiential branding."

Get involved. Because as in the early days of the internet, the brands that experimented and learned early on were at the forefront when it became mainstream; you don't want to miss this train.

ACKNOWLEDGMENT

The author would like to extend a sincere thank you to Cortney Harding of Friends with Holograms, Alejandro Mainetto of EY, Alan Smithson of XR Ignite Community Hub & Hyper-Accelerator, Robert Spierenburg of All Things Media, LLC and Samantha Wolfe of PitchFWD for being so generous with their time, insights, and intellectual contributions.

REFERENCES

Accenture. (2017). *Accenture and Specular Theory Create Interactive Vcommerce Experience "Behind the Style."* Retrieved from https://newsroom.accenture.com/news/accenture-and-specular-theory-create-interactive-vcommerce-experience-behind-the-style.htm

Adobe Communications Team. (2018). *Using VR as a Force for Social Good*. Retrieved from https://theblog.adobe.com/using-vr-force-social-good

Ah-young, C. (2013). Can holograms replace real K-pop stars? *The Korea Times*. Retrieved from http://koreatimes.co.kr/www/news/culture/2013/07/135_139321.html

Aslam, S. (2019). Snapchat by the Numbers: Stats, Demographics & Fun Facts. *Omnicore*. Retrieved from www.omnicoreagency.com/snapchat-statistics

Axon, S. (2017). Returning to Second Life. *Ars Technica*. Retrieved from https://arstechnica.com/gaming/2017/10/returning-to-second-life

Barker, S. (2019). What is the Future of CGI Influencers in the Marketing World? *Shane Barker Blog*. Retrieved from https://shanebarker.com/blog/cgi-influencers

Blair, K., & Hoy, C. (2006). Paying attention to adult learning online: The pedagogy and politics of community. *Computers and Composition*, *23*(1), 32–48. doi:10.1016/j.compcom.2005.12.006

Burkard, K. (2018, July 13). *The Top 10 Best Customer Experiences (and What You Can Learn From Them)*. Retrieved from https://blog.smile.io/top-10-best-customer-experiences

Chouinard, H. (2019). Is virtual reality the end of the physical showroom? *Business of Home*. Retrieved from www.businessofhome.com/articles/is-virtual-reality-the-end-of-the-physical-showroom

Clement, J. (2019a). Number of monthly active Facebook users worldwide as of 2nd quarter 2019 (in millions). *Statistica*. Retrieved from www.statista.com/statistics/264810/number-of-monthly-active-facebook-users-worldwide

Clement, J. (2019b). Number of monthly active Twitter users worldwide from 1st quarter 2010 to 1st quarter 2019 (in millions). *Statistica*. Retrieved from www.statista.com/statistics/282087/number-of-monthly-active-twitter-users

Corbett-Drummond, T., Carole, N. R., & Strum, B. (2017). The Future of Immersive Branding and Retail According to the AT&T Foundry. *AT&T Foundry*. Retrieved from https://foundry.att.com/media/The-Future-of-Immersive-Branding-and-Retail.pdf

Dachis, A. (2016). How Snapchat Quietly Became the First Social AR Platform. *Next Reality*. Retrieved from https://mobile-ar.reality.news/news/snapchat-quietly-became-first-social-ar-platform-0171923

Daily Mail. (2007). Warning over cyber-bullying in Second Life. *The Daily Mail*. Retrieved from www.dailymail.co.uk/sciencetech/article-458743/Warning-cyber-bullying-Second-Life.html

Frank, P. (2016). An Art Museum in Los Angeles Is Killing the Snapchat Game. *Huffpost*. Retrieved from https://www.huffpost.com/entry/you-need-to-start-following-lacma-on-snapchat_n_55b136afe4b08f57d5d3fdf7

Frankenfield, J. (2019). What is the General Data Protection Regulation (GDPR)? *Investopedia*. Retrieved from www.investopedia.com/terms/g/general-data-protection-regulation-gdpr.asp

Gotter, A. (2017). What Your Brand Can Learn from Warby Parker's Massive Success. *Pixlee*. Retrieved from www.pixlee.com/blog/what-your-brand-can-learn-from-warby-parkers-massive-success

Havens, J. (2011). Who Owns the Advertising Space in an Augmented Reality World? *Mashable*. Retrieved from www.mashable.com/2011/06/06/virtual-air-rights-augmented-reality

Hsu, T. (2017). These Influencers Aren't Flesh and Blood, Yet Millions Follow Them. *New York Times*. Retrieved from www.nytimes.com/2019/06/17/business/media/miquela-virtual-influencer.html

Joseph, T. (2019). How Is Augmented Reality Reshaping Travel and Tourism? *Fingent*. Retrieved from www.fingent.com/blog/how-is-augmented-reality-reshaping-travel-and-tourism

Kulp, P. (2019). A Small But Growing Startup Scene Is Exploring Uses for Digital Human Avatars. *Adweek*. Retrieved from www.adweek.com/digital/a-small-but-growing-startup-scene-is-exploring-uses-for-digital-human-avatars

Liu, Y., & Berger, P. D. (2018). The Sephora Mobile-App and Its Relationship to Customer Loyalty. *Business and Management Horizons, 6*(1). Retrieved from: www.macrothink.org/journal/index.php/bmh/article/view/13005/10285

Mallet, C. (2018). Is Kylie Jenner going to save VR? *VR Influencer Marketing*. Retrieved from www.somewhereelse.co/vr-influencer-marketing

Morency, C. (2018). Meet Fashion's First Computer-Generated Influencer. *Business of Fashion*. Retrieved from http://www.businessoffashion.com/articles/intelligence/meeting-fashions-first-computer-generated-influencer-lil-miquela-sousa

Museum Hack. (2016). Snapchat Filters for Museums: Our Paid Results at AAM 2016. *Museum Hack*. Retrieved from www.museumhack.com/snapchat-filters

Nafarrete, J. (2015). Tom's Brings Virtual Reality Giving Trips to Retail Customers. *VR Scout*. Retrieved from https://vrscout.com/news/toms-virtual-reality-giving-trips

O'Shea, D. (2018). Macy's expanding VR furniture shopping to 90 stores by January. *Retail Dive*. Retrieved from www.retaildive.com/news/macys-expanding-vr-furniture-shopping-to-90-stores-by-january/539873

PYMNTS. (2019). *L'Oréal To Partner with Amazon On Makeup Tech*. Retrieved from www.pymnts.com/news/retail/2019/loreal-amazon-makeup-augmented-reality-tech

Roland, C. (2018). The Future of Immersive Branding and Retail. *AT&T Shape*. Retrieved from https://shape.att.com/blog/future-of-immersive-branding-and-retail

Shayon, S. (2018). Macy's Rolls Out VR to Sell More Furniture in Less Space. *Brand Channel*. Retrieved from www.brandchannel.com/2018/10/19/macys-vr-furniture

Sloane, G. (2016). Gatorade's Super Bowl Snapchat filter got 160 million impressions. *Digiday.com*. Retrieved from https://digiday.com/marketing/inside-gatorades-digital-ad-playbook-snapchat-facebook

Sonsev, V. (2017). How Augmented Reality Is Giving Furniture A Boost in Sales. *Forbes*. Retrieved from www.forbes.com/sites/veronikasonsev/2017/12/20/how-ar-is-giving-furniture-a-boost-in-sales/#7e2cd2d21d3a

Sovie, D. R. G., Murdoch, R., McMahon, L., & Schoelwer, M. (2018). Time to Navigate the Super MyWay. *Accenture 2018 Digital Consumer Survey Findings*. Retrieved www.accenture.com/us-en/_acnmedia/PDF-69/Accenture-2018-Digital-Consumer-Survey-Findings.pdf

Spark, C. G. I. (2019). World First: Virtual Female Model Signs to Top US Agency. *Cision PR Newswire*. Retrieved from www.prnewswire.com/news-releases/world-first-virtual-female-model-signs-to-top-us-agency-300871973.html

Steele, J. (2019). Multifamily Marketers Using Virtual Staging to Make Real Impact. *Forbes*. Retrieved from www.forbes.com/sites/jeffsteele/2019/06/28/multifamily-marketers-using-virtual-staging-to-make-real-impact/

Tassi, P. (2019). 'Fortnite' Had 10 Million Concurrent Players in The Marshmello Concert Event. *Forbes*. Retrieved from www.forbes.com/sites/insertcoin/2019/02/03/fortnite-had-10-million-concurrent-players-in-the-marshmello-concert-event/

Terrell, K. (2016). *The History of Social Media: Social Networking Evolution!* Retrieved from https://historycooperative.org/the-history-of-social-media

The National Association of Realtors Research Department. (2017). *2017 Profile of Home Staging*. Retrieved from www.nar.realtor/sites/default/files/migration_files/reports/2017/2017-profile-of-home-staging-07-06-2017.pdf

Whitney, L. (2017). How to Use Google's Translate App. *PC Magazine*. Retrieved from www.pcmag.com/news/352206/how-to-use-googles-translate-app

Williams, R. (2017). Estée Lauder's AR chatbot offers advice on lipstick colors. *MobileMarketer*. Retrieved from http://www.mobilemarketer.com/news/estee-lauders-ar-chatbot-offers-advice-on-lipstick-colors/447096

KEY TERMS AND DEFINITIONS

Immersive Branding: Is the next evolution in branding: the newest addition to traditional customer touch points, retail experiences, and mobile phones. AR/VR/MR—ultimately fueled by artificial intelligence and virtual beings with "brand personality"—is turning branding into and actual verb, giving consumers the opportunity to directly engage brands, and redefine the brand experience.

Spatial Computing: Is the blend of technologies that use the space around humans as a medium, blurring the lines between physical and digital worlds. Either digital augmentation is superimposed over the physical world, or a virtual one that completely immerses the viewer in an alternate version of one is possible. These technologies "see" the physical world, map to it, understand and interpret it, and/or create alternate realities for us to experience.

Virtual Beings: Are representations of humans that live in digital spaces but cross over into the physical world through interaction on social media, advertising, and others. Unlike computer generated or animated characters, Virtual Beings are so detailed as to appear indistinguishable from humans. Advances in artificial intelligence are fueling the development of "smart" virtual beings, providing the opportunity to interact and co-experience in a highly naturalistic way.

Virtual Influencers: Are virtual beings being used to engage audiences on behalf of brands and companies and movements. Much like human celebrities have historically been contracted to champion various efforts, they are being used in social media, advertising and PR campaigns to be effective salespeople, brand endorsers, and spokespeople.

Chapter 20
Immersive Media, Scientific Visualization, and Global Umwelt

Julieta Cristina Aguilera
https://orcid.org/0000-0002-3620-7535
Independent Researcher, USA

ABSTRACT

This chapter deals with the global implications of immersive media: First, it considers how the concept of the umwelt can be used to address the extension of sensory motor capabilities of the human body. Next, it discusses what the implications are when the concept of the human umwelt is applied to scientific visualization in astronomy, which scales space and time to present data. Then, these scientific visualizations are discussed in the context of planetarium domes and what it means to collectively experience an immersive environment based on large scale data. As a case study, the final section articulates what this entails for the understanding of the effects of collective human interactions with our planetary environment at this stage of climate change.

INTRODUCTION

Can immersive media bring forth a new global understanding of the interconnectedness of humans and other life forms that stem from and inhabit our planetary environment? In architecture and design studies there is a dominant focus on immediate space (architects) as well as on symbolic space (designers). This focus affords the development of a practice that observes spatial abstractions as well as the interactions that happen within spaces. Add to this mix Virtual Reality (VR), immersive environments and other synthetic experiences that accommodate human senses and actions, and space becomes a deeper construct that supports and informs the human umwelt. That is, the planetary environment experienced through the sensorimotor structure of the body that has evolved there (Von Uexküll, 1934/1957) across economies of scale and meaning (Lakoff & Johnson,1980; Johnson, 1987).

DOI: 10.4018/978-1-7998-2433-6.ch020

I began exploring these thoughts during a class on Body Culture at the School of Architecture of the Universidad Católica de Valparaíso (Pendleton-Jullian, 1996) that was geared towards reflections about the body in space. Ideas that years later emerged from this inception include my work Unfolding Space (Aguilera, 2006) that investigated the three dimensional shadow of a four dimensional grid in VR, with interactions that cover both abstract spatialities and abstract temporalities in the form of tangible and digital mapped spaces. Next, I used these ideas for scientific visualization during my work at the Adler Planetarium's Space Visualization Laboratory (Aguilera et al. 2008) in order to look at seemingly impossible spaces while considering the different interaction modalities of immersion inside the museum and its dome (Aguilera, 2014). Projects such as historical astronomy illustrations envisioning the 3D structure of our Milky Way galaxy helped to refine those visions in virtual spaces and brought forward concepts about how point of view is resized in relation to the larger scales of the planet, the galaxy and the Universe. Finally, teaching a class at the University of Hawai'i at Hilo that focused on collaboration across VR, printmaking and ceramics (Aguilera et al., 2017) inspired the three faculty members involved to consider perception, three dimensional space, and scale across disparate media. The experience of developing the class helped further refine my emerging ideas about the senses in space by having students work with hand modeling, scanning, digital alterations, 3D prints in different sizes, capturing 360 spaces via photography, and moving through space in VR, while also adding animated particle effects that required considering time as texture (Varela, Thompson & Rosch, 1991). The notion of the body as a device came from observing how perception changes when transferring models across the different media utilized in the class, so the models could be experienced as objects and environments when moved from one media to another.

Informed by these experiences and diverse settings regarding space and time, in this chapter I will explore what the human umwelt has to do with immersive environments, that is, spaces that accommodate human senses and actions (Aguilera, 2013). Then I will connect virtual environments with experiences informed by large scale sensor and detector data in scientific visualizations, such as that of vast spaces examined in astronomy (Aguilera, 2015). Along this arc, I will offer some insights on what happens when the senses break down at very large scales, and how these large scales can be coupled to the human body that inhabits its home planet within these vast realms (Aguilera, 2019a). Finally, I will discuss how the awareness of this scaling of space and time can tailor seemingly unfathomable realities to the human temporal and spatial experience which is dependent on a subjective point of view (Damasio & Damasio, 1996). The awareness of how scaling subjectivity works (Aguilera, 2019b) becomes, then, a necessary kind of literacy that can afford understanding the effects of real and direct collective actions and their effects on planet Earth.

IMMERSION AND UMWELT

Even though the concept of space may seem obvious (we humans live in our home planet Earth, spatially interacting with the environment in order to sustain ourselves, as do other life forms), the awareness of reality at different scales is not necessarily the same for all people. In fact, reality itself is a cognitive construct when navigating space in three dimensions and over time. Our reality is the virtual model in our minds (Noë, 2004) that we create when we notice the effects of our present actions within the larger, past and future inhabited world. These are spatial and temporal models of the mind, not too different from those that astrophysicists build to understand and share the knowledge about the Universe that humankind is immersed in at grander scales (Aguilera, 2019).

At human scale, the bodily senses are used to create these models or structures of inhabited space. But each of our senses has different spatial and temporal ranges and utilizes different amounts of sensory and motor resources in the brain (Iacoboni et al., 1999). In this context, it can be said that the proportions of resources allocated to the senses and to actions in the human body point to its umwelt. Mental models contain not just sensory input but cross modal connections between what is sensed (Giard & Peronnet, 1999). If the body is considered as an immersive device, these cross modal connections shape a structure that is already in place to condition how other models that amplify and extend the understanding of reality are created. The sensors that humankind has put together to look at the Universe allow seeing beyond what human eyes can perceive, to hear beyond what human ears can hear, feel forces that are beyond what human muscles can gauge, and assess physical and atmospheric conditions that exist beyond the body. Such sensor data can only be experienced by bringing the data into the actual embodied perceptual capabilities and umwelt of human existence in the planetary environments humans have evolved in (Aguilera, 2019a), where the experiences that ground human ideas have accumulated.

Whereas the word immersion is used in media to explain installations or devices that fill the visual field of a person, the strict definition is that of mental involvement. When considering dynamic physicality, on the other hand, immersion in the natural world can be described as a kind of inhabiting interdependence between being and environment. Likewise, when Jakob Von Uexküll defined umwelt (Von Uexküll, 1934/1957), he was looking at the bodies of different species of animals in terms of their sensory motor connections within the inhabited environment, articulating a bio-semiotic approach to describing the body as a model of interaction in the world. Models and simulations that present aspects of the world not directly accessible to the human umwelt bring to focus today, not the electronic or immersive media per se, but the person that enacts (Petitmengin, 2017) the models and the simulations as the media itself. In this regard, the body can, by extension, be considered as the holder of its umwelt when experiencing abstract data in immersive media, which, when transposed to the mediated experiences, may reconfigure how the body connects to these virtual spaces in contrast to real inhabited space. Furthermore, reality exists beyond what the human body can perceive within its surroundings, and it is through the extending of sensory capabilities via devices that present data gathered by different kinds of detectors, in order to immerse the body in the data, that humankind can finally come back to its senses. In other words, extending the senses affords the opportunity to understand how a body is present in the Universe—the ultimate subjectivity—at any temporal or spatial scale via bridging the knowledge of accumulated direct experience. By considering this, it is the immediate experience of time and space that is the starting point to connect to those extended senses, tailoring what cannot be reached to what can.

SCIENTIFIC VISUALIZATION DATA AND THE IMMERSIVE EXPERIENCE

… as far as possible from the earth, sits a human being. He has so transformed his eyes, with the aid of gigantic optical instruments, that they have become fit to penetrate the universe up to its most distant stars. In his Umwelt, suns and planets circle in festive procession. Fleet-footed light takes millions of years to travel through his Umwelt space (Von Uexküll, 1957 (1934), p. 76).

Von Uexküll also had a notion of sensory extensions when he described the astronomer as the human with the farthest sensory reach. Yet in direct experience, the spatial reaches of the different human senses in relation to planetary space are not equal but have a distinctive kind of spatial fingerprint (Aguilera, 2015). Astronomical spans of time and space reveal the spatial sensory boundaries of the planetary human experience today, for example when light changes color according to the direction of stellar motion (cosmological redshift) which cannot be detected with un-augmented senses, or the inability to perceive the high speed at which the Milky Way galaxy is moving because of how small human scale is relative to the cosmos at a galactic scale. The spatial and temporal breaking down of the senses at larger scales reveals some of those boundaries or ranges. Also, the Universe known to humans until relatively recently can only be directly seen from Earth and it has been constrained in terms of spatial human-designed navigation (considering the location of the two Voyager spacecraft) to roughly a little further than the boundary of the solar system. Modern instruments have improved visual resolution and in turn allowed perceptual expansion far beyond our human sensory limitations through innovative detectors and telescopes that reach out into deep space. Today astrophysicists can also reconstruct the dynamics of stars and galaxies from the physical laws that explain what is detected by these devices that extend the human experience, further affording the exploration of the data gathered by telescopes and detectors over time. In the same manner, their reconstructions are data scaled back to the confines of human experience. As previously mentioned, the proportions of sensory motor resources in the body reveal the attentional connections to the environment (Maunsell & Treue, 2006). It is the reach of the senses and motor capabilities of the human body that, in turn, point to the kind of environmental models afforded by the human mind (Aguilera, 2019) in its planetary evolution and upbringing. In this context, humankind observes the Universe with the affordances of the planetary spatio-temporal vocabulary of the direct experience exerted there.

Immersive scientific visualization involving space and time for data exploration is particularly relevant in astronomy because of the immense ranges and spatial complexity at which celestial bodies exist (McCormick et al., 1987). In that regard, the act of mapping spatial and temporal data to human scale is becoming a research branch of astrophysics in its own right, invaluable to explore dynamics, matter and causal relationships that cannot be directly translated to a form that is perceptible to humans. Scaling space and time in immersive scientific visualization brings together the extended senses of data, physical actions and externalized simulation in the form of media (Aguilera, 2019a). Conversely, immersive, sensory rich and interactive models of phenomena at cosmic scales position the embodied mind in space to explore data in the form of scientific visualizations (Aguilera, 2019a). In this way, immersive media bring large spatial and temporal scales to the size and the pace of human experience and the human species' umwelt (Von Uexküll, 1934/1957). Whether a temporal and spatial scale is geographical, planetary, solar or galactic, immersive media has the capability of resizing it to the literal proximity and perceptual velocity range of the human body, for the body to be able to explore the given temporal and spatial scales as a scientific visualization. Therefore, understanding how immersive scientific visualization mediates the human experience of space and time implies a new kind of literacy that encompasses both body aesthetics and scientific knowledge.

Virtual Reality and Scientific Visualization can also help reveal and support a deeper understanding of large scale global human interaction with the planet (Aguilera, 2019). The multisensory understanding of the world (Zuidhoek et al., 2004), both direct and mediated—as experienced through Virtual Reality and other immersive media—is part of a new form of literacy that is now also required in order to personally, collectively, and at various scales reflect and act on the consequences of human activity on the planet.

Immersive media, in this manner, has shifted the paradigm of esthetic endeavors from the object to the environment, presenting not what is in front of the individual or the collective, but where the person or group of people are in relation to the environment. Immersive media then changes the paradigm of the outsider view to the view from within as individual and as collective.

Another important aspect of being in a body in relation to immersive media is that a single point of view in other kinds of media like drawings, paintings or film, where what the viewer sees is the unique point of view of the artist (Alberti, 1966 (1436); Panofsky, 1927/1991), may have inferred that there is such a thing as a unique idea of a view at all scales. Immersive media in turn affords the articulation of the interaction of different viewpoints and various scales in a common space. Furthermore, in immersive scientific visualization, changing spatial and temporal scales affords perceiving changes that humans would not otherwise notice. Conversely, those models connect to the ranges of human sensory-motor capabilities: smallest, largest, slowest and fastest sensations and actions, including what can be recalled and what can be predicted, as well as assumptions of the amount of space and degree of motion existing between a viewer and what is being focused on in the environment. Immersive scientific visualization thus affords accessing other temporal and spatial scales, and modeling them in the body-mind continuum. Dominant cues of distance such as stereoscopy, motion parallax and differential size are used in immersive scientific visualization to present not just actual aspects of reality, but relationships that escape average human perception (as in the 3D spatial relationships and motion of stars and galaxies in relation to each other). This creates interaction affordances to unreachable objects by bringing them into the human dimension, for example by presenting planets and galaxies at a scale where one can spin them, navigate around them, or affect their motion.

It should be noted that the amount of change in space and time perceived through detectors reveals that aspects of phenomena which appear constant at human scale are not so at cosmic ones. When remote objects in the Universe are observed, the behavior of common phenomena such as light is not constant as when experienced at human scale. In using sensors to detect phenomena that exist beyond human perception, the electromagnetic radiation that lies above or below the average human visual range is used to sense various non visual qualities of the Universe, such as motion or chemical composition. This is to say that part of understanding phenomena through data captured by sensors or detectors that reach outside human perception is to be able to understand how extending the senses affects the appearance of objects and matter themselves, by creating novel mappings that make sense and do scale to our perception of them in time and space.

For example, sensing radiation in the multi-wavelength spectrum through specific telescopes[1] implies a mapping activity to the human umwelt because said radiation in the wavelengths of infrared, x-ray, and gamma ray are moved, scaled and modulated into the area of the spectrum that is visible to the human eye, increasing contrast when patterns are detected just so they can be better observed. It is also in this manner that infrared sensors reveal heat, giving visual appearance to thermo-perception regarding cosmic phenomena. X-ray in turn penetrates dust matter that obscures human vision, very much as our flesh prevents us from seeing our bones. Light waves that compress or stretch afford knowing the direction in which stars are moving and inform the creation of dynamic simulations of the distribution and overall flow of stars in the galaxy. Type 1b Supernova explosions which can be measured in constant candle units assist in ascertaining the amount of space that exists between Earth and the galaxy where the supernova occurred, allowing for the measuring of the space that separates the Milky Way from said galaxy, which in turn can be used to create 3D models for the distribution of galaxies. The LIGO gravitational data, for example, was famously presented as a sound pitching upwards. In these many ways, sensor data is utilized not only to make space phenomena visible or audible but also dynamic and interactive, so it can be accessible to the human senses for patterns and intensity to be considered within the experiential capabilities of the human umwelt.

SCALING SPACE AND TIME FOR IMMERSION

When looking at the environment that surrounds the human body, only changes that are either sufficiently slow or fast to be perceived by the human senses and human memory are apparent enough to deserve attention. However, data collection over time reveals a more detailed picture of temporal patterns and cycles to focus on, which can afford a deeper understanding of how those patterns affect inhabited space. Because a human experience is attached to its immediate environment and the present within perceptual range, there is an expectation—same as with light as previously discussed—that what is static or constant at human scale, will continue to be so at larger ones, but again, this is not the case. The continents, the solar system and the galaxy where humankind exists, which all seem static to the present moment for a human, are moving at vastly different speeds. They move immensely slow in the case of continents, and immensely fast in the case of galaxies, where continents appear static relative to human temporal perception (human motion being too fast), and static for galaxies relative to human spatial perception (human scale being too small, while also contained in the planet's atmosphere, to notice the speed of the galaxy). In this regard, perhaps it is the vastness of deep space that provides the best example of spatial and temporal relativity. Creating scientific visualizations in immersive media that represent spatial and temporal scales brings up the importance of defining a viewer's point of view, that is, the constructive process of the sense of being there, in space and time, in relation to the perceptually present surroundings.

The occasional experience of large scale planetary phenomena has given different societies, living in various geographies, a glimpse of the planet's dynamic cycles and how cumulative effects work, as in storms, volcanic eruptions, earthquakes, floods, droughts and forest fires. Not only can the ground change faster than one is used to in daily routines, but air velocity, temperature and humidity in various combinations can become inhospitable. In that sense, considering the larger environment shows that humankind has requirements that encompass more than those of the immediate location where a person is, where phenomena are experienced from an understanding of how the human body relates to them in terms of dependency. A higher proportion of modern living detaches a significant percentage of the human population—over half of which now live in the mediated spaces of an urban setting—from having the immediate need of being at ease within the environment, and instead increases attention to constructed and mediated architectural and digital environments that emphasize individual presence, where the surrounding space is held in perceptually reachable and sometimes isolated interactive situations. One important aspect of noticing how a person relates to constructed scales that are built on the planet and around the body is the ability to access these mediated environments and still be grounded in the body, because the ability to inhabit and embody what one experiences still relies on the understanding of how the body inhabits planetary space (Aguilera, 2019). On the other hand, noticing the accumulative effects of small parts of massive planetary phenomena like dust particles in a tornado, the number of insects feeding on plantings and so on, grants an opportunity to, in turn, consider the effects of the human population and the consequences of its constructions as a whole. At the same time, scientific visualizations in immersive spaces have the ability to recreate and rearrange the actual planetary environments that exist, past and future, and can resize time and space around the human body to access not only aspects of the vast Universe as it has come to be at grand scales, but aspects of collective human impact in the planetary environment over time that cannot be directly and perceptually assessed by an individual alone.

Astrophysicists and artists creating scientific visualizations have come up with models of the evolving Universe based on what can be observed from the point of view of the Earth (Bond et al., 1996) where the farther away a star or galaxy appears, the farther back in time it is: humankind can only see as far as its light has had time to travel towards Earth. In such an immense range (just like an ant and a bridge cannot be captured visually in the same picture when observed at the same distance) there are different qualities of the Cosmic Web formed by the galaxies that have been detected, which cannot be observed in one constant spatial and temporal measuring unit. Images from distant outer space objects detected by advanced telescopes as well as scientific visualizations based on detector data show how large systems work, even when separated by immense spatial vastness. The choices that go into coupling astronomical data to the human umwelt for designing the visualizations when it is not possible to just scale everything by the same amount, must structurally correspond to the relationships established in the data. At the same time, the choices must aesthetically be mapped to the sensorimotor structure of the human body and its perceptual and dynamic connections to the planetary environment. But astronomical data being numeric, visual, or some other kind of detector based product, may not show change per se, or afford the perception and appreciation of complex patterns when there are subtle differences involved. To that end, change and patterns first need to be found and then amplified via sufficient contrast. This is informally referred to as "massaging the data". The aesthetic balancing of contrasting aspects of the data has to then be coupled to physical presence and, when suitable, physical motion. Do the waves of galactic mergers evoke the physical experience of paddling through water or of long blades of waving grass? If one could feel those forces at human scale, what could they reveal about the interactions of dust and gases taking place at the galactic scale? What can different speeds reveal about the merger? It soon becomes clear in the process that creating a scientific visualization is not a linear job that is performed by a scientist in step one and an artist in step two and then finished, but a recursive operation. As such, scientific and esthetic knowledge must be shared and expanded in collaboration of expertises and concerns so data can be coupled to the human experience and thus, take advantage of human cognitive capabilities. Therefore, extending the body when it is not possible to just scale everything by the same amount implies the integration of data and aesthetics as a kind of embodied understanding.

COLLECTIVE IMMERSION IN PLANETARIUM DOMES

Although architectural sensory-social constructions do exist (Pallasmaa, 2012), the situation of planetariums in relation to immersive experiences and VR is an interesting and distinctive one in terms of collective dynamic simulation for the purpose of accessing space at various spatial and temporal scales. This because of the structure of shared subjectivity in the form of an immersive representation in a physically social space, where an experiencer is arguably not alone. The room to be accompanied by a crowd inside a dynamic representation is a very different environment from static architectural constructions, if architecture is to be considered in its aspect of a kind of immersive representation.

Dynamic representations can make temporal changes apparent, which is something that architectural constructions utilize but may not bring to the conscious level. Even as light traverses buildings during the day cycle, the speed of Earth turning while orbiting the sun is not obviously noticeable from moment to moment. Understanding the day cycle has always been common in daily routines where activity and rest demand said states from each person, but understanding the seasons and being able to travel guided by the stars as well as planetary phenomena was traditionally the role of the astronomer/navigator in many ancient communities, that person being the one who understood larger spatiotemporal scales (Aguilera, 2019a). For some time now, that understanding of longer spans of time over the motion of larger bodies has become part of common knowledge regularly utilized when communicating and traveling across the globe. Applying larger spatial and temporal scales has become a practical endeavor in many aspects of modern life, while moving through immersive experiences in a planetarium dome affords a shared reconstruction of change over scales, which provides a much deeper understanding of time and space itself.

One of the key aspects of VR in relation to spatial change is tracking, especially that of the head, which determines what is in front of the individual exploring the immersive world or scientific visualization. The tracking capability that connects the visual field to the orientation of the head and position of the body in space brings up a level of agency that activates the body to read space in three dimensions through visual cues. One of those cues is motion parallax which compares past and present views in order to mentally calculate the relative expanse between observer and observed, where the observer is moving in relation to a nearby tree or something much larger like a mountain. In those cases rapid change would indicate closeness and slow change, remoteness. Without stereoscopic vision, which is the dominant cue to represent proximity and interaction that engages touch (as in handling of objects (McNeill, 1992)), it is this motion parallax and also differential size that come into play to bring agency to immersion in planetarium domes. In other words, not all degrees of agency in relation to actual scale involve the senses in the same manner. It is important to also note that whereas a head-mounted display (HMD) may update the visual field based on head movement, people in a planetarium dome can turn their heads at will to look at what is displayed on different parts of the dome surface. Moreover, digital planetariums can fly in any direction and showcase stars and galaxies from the point of view of other stars, other galaxies and at various scales while viewers retain the ability to look around when doing so. Navigating this kind of space is physically comparable to various physically assisted modes of displacement and transportation that many have access to around the world such as elevators, walking conveyor belts, electric escalators, cars, trains and airplanes. But it is the focus on the resizing of space, where scale can be stretched or compressed within scientific visualizations around a group of people, is what distinguishes domes from other representations of collective experience. This capability is not unheard of since the CAVE system (Cruz-Neira et al., 1993) was developed in the 1990s, which could accommodate a dozen or so people besides the person "driving" the immersive experience while moving through virtual space. However, a CAVE experience is typically not focused on the scaling of space and time, as is the astronomical content of planetarium domes. On the other hand there have been stereoscopy capable domes, but since the cue of stereoscopy merely scales the person to the approximate size of planets and galaxies just like other kinds of VR experiences, that is not a unique aspect of domes either. However, being in a planetarium dome experiencing spatial and temporal relationships while space and time stretch and compress to accommodate the attention of a group of people beyond what one can focus on is different than being with a dozen people exploring a place. In a planetarium dome, a kind of collective agency is directly accessible because in a sense, the group may represent humanity in the larger cosmic context.

Sharing the experience of vast or minuscule phenomena, where one is not alone but in a social context has implications (Van Bavel, 2014), not the least of which is the context of a shared representation (Turner & Whitehead, 2008). Unlike a mental simulation or a real experience, the shared point in space of dome navigation externalizes the representation of a context where people can focus on an almost fully immersive field of view compared to what would be possible in flat or wider angle cinema screens. These situations afford a kind of participatory attentional navigation that can help corroborate aspects of what a person looking in a different direction from another person may have missed, more so in a live show where there is an actual person maneuvering the direction centered in the front area of the dome. This is the same reason telescopes and detectors work in arrays and are scattered around the world, looking at the sky in the northern and southern hemispheres while the planet rotates, capturing a full picture of the surrounding sky. Even though something similar could be said when different people focus on different aspects of a photo, for example, there is a spatial shared referent that derives from the actual location of the participants in the space of the dome relative to each other. The point in space is therefore shared, but the points of view are oriented in different directions just like when looking through different windows or when being driven in a car, train, bus, or other mass means of transportation at the direct experience of human scale, where travelers retain gaze agency within the boundaries of the windows or the direction of the vehicle. Whereas moving towards an object, for example a planet, may be the choreographed focus of the experience in a planetarium dome, the appearance of moons or satellites nearby may be noticed by viewers at different times, pacing the awareness of the different celestial objects across the crowd until everybody in the presence of the representation is on the same attentional page. This spreading level of attention functions while retaining a degree of agency in the ability to look around the immersive environment as opposed to having visual boundaries like those of screen displays or a picture window. The immersive and collective dynamic representation/visualization of space and time stretching or compressing with the variable attentional focus of viewers is the unique experiential structure of a planetarium dome, capable of simultaneous individual agency and, to an extent, social collective agency.

IMMERSION AND CLIMATE CHANGE DATA

The notion of immersion in virtual and dynamic representations experienced in a collective setting affords access to data about the larger environments inhabited by humankind, whether it is a city, a continent, the planet or the galaxy where the planet exists in the Universe. At all these scales there is codependence and forces at work that reveal the dynamics of the system and the cumulative effects where events at one scale build up to sometimes affect other scales. The technological visualization ability to work with patterns among distant cosmic bodies is basically the same used to detect patterns at the microscopic scale and at the planetary one. Most significantly, visualizing planetary scale patterns on the Earth based on data—more and more utilized in weather forecasting channels and sites via a kind of presenter augmented reality over scientific visualizations—and informed by scientific visualization literacy encompassing measurement, number of entities and viewing location, allows access to connecting individual and collective actions or intentions of actions to global consequences. This is why data of collective human presence and influence is important and why being able to apply agency over those collective intentions or actions, in a manner that is akin to what is practiced in immersive media, is paramount at this stage of social awareness for the human species.

Regarding collective actions, there is no debate that climate change is a global phenomenon which is the result of cumulative matter in space derived from pollution-inducing human activity over time. Climate change threatens the habitat of interdependent life forms which have co-evolved adapting to a common and relatively stable environment. Even in human-made urban environments, functions like breathing and eating directly rely on the planet and do not manifest the self-contained environment of an astronaut. This critical situation urgently requires civilization to become scientific visualization literate. In this literacy, scientific visualization can be presented in immersive media so as to encompass simulations that provide a degree of agency via a dynamic and interactive point of view. This dynamic point of view provides an understanding for the located aspect of being in the planetary environment together with other human agents, not as an outside isolated viewer, but within the pacing and the scaling of interdependent individual, collective and global points of view informed by the data being presented.

Whereas older, passive media may have unconsciously promoted the pervasive assumption that the media experience carries the same circumstantial view for everybody, the importance of interaction in tracked immersive media (Krueger, 1977)—where camera motion is dependent on the actual position and motion of the head of the viewer—cannot be overstated (Ginsburg, 1999). Considering that a view depends on one's motion and location in space affords the understanding that others in the space have a different view and therefore a somewhat different experience. This understanding of how spatial interaction is articulated, in turn, gives a particular access to the scientific process. In such access, theories and methods are tested through simulations to collectively assess common phenomena found under different circumstances in the world of humans. Furthermore, understanding the uniqueness of awareness in the individual has the potential to bring aesthetic (Freedberg & Gallese, 2007) spatiotemporal empathy. Such a kind of aesthetic empathy could in turn have the potential to better support human populations without assumptions that may be merely projecting the context of one population over another. Such empathy can further aid in understanding the worlds of the many life forms with which humankind has co-evolved and with which human life exists in interdependence.

In sum, the shift from single point of view in passive media to active point of view in immersive media implies a key element of survival in the environment directly connected to the human mind. This shift is not only bringing back the notion of dynamic space and singular placement, but the scaling of agency to larger dynamic systems that exist beyond the scale of a person, and the reach and uniqueness of systems in larger spatial scales that join the points of view of all humanity in the single planetary environment of Earth. The knowledge achievable by understanding the scaling and mapping process, which is afforded by immersive media for scientific visualizations, is a necessary step forward towards the global understanding of climate change and other larger than human scale concerns on planet Earth, because it is the very way in which perception is resized to better understand planetary phenomena coupled to the human experience.

CONCLUSION

Humankind makes sense of a model of the Universe that is scaled to the human umwelt. The kinds of data that are being collected today may go beyond direct experience, whether it be citywide, geographical, planetary or cosmic, and are being tailored to human spatial and temporal attention for navigation and dexterity, affording agency over phenomena at a global scale. The immediate experience of time and space is the starting point to connect to the extended senses of data collection, tailoring what cannot be reached to what can. Astronomical data is utilized not only to make cosmic space phenomena perceptible but also dynamic and interactive, so unreachable patterns and intensities can be accessible to the human senses. Scientific visualization literacy is the understanding of the parsing and mapping process that can bring aspects of reality that are beyond direct experience to human perception by giving shape and timing to simulations in immersive media.

The case of climate change poses a challenge to immersive media as it requires a new kind of literacy that understands how our bodies are connected to the immediate environment via direct and cumulative experience. In this way, experience can then be extended, and have the extrasensory data mapped and paced to comprehend phenomena larger than that available via direct experience. This literacy also includes the ability to have an understanding of the larger spatiotemporal realms that in the past were the exclusive knowledge of the astronomer. Scientific visualizations in immersive spaces have the ability to simulate the actual specific data from planetary environments that exist, past and future, and can resize time and space around the human body to access not only aspects of the vast Universe as it has come to be, but aspects of collective human impact in the planetary environment over time that cannot be directly or perceptually assessed in media by an individual alone. In this regard, understanding the effects of collective actions on the planet is nothing less than aligning collective behavior with larger scales, informed by the coupling of sensors and effectors that present the data to different degrees, in order to manage the global impact of humanity on the planet through conscious individual and collective behavior aligned to the data.

In summary, we inhabit a Universe scaled to the human umwelt through media and scientific visualization, and scientific visualization literacy is the understanding of the parsing and mapping process when building shared models of reality. Understanding how the human umwelt exists on Earth and how dynamic simulations in immersive media work by giving a place to the body in virtual spaces, shifts the focus of attention from different media to the body in space where the body itself becomes the media with which to decode the experience. In other words: for immersion, the body is the media. Finally, the common experience of climate change requires us to be thus literate in order to understand the pacing and the scaling of each of the individual points of view within larger human communities, as to be able to adjust individual, collective, and global behavior accordingly.

ACKNOWLEDGMENT

The Congregation of Holy Cross, Notre Dame, IN
Electronic Visualization Laboratory, University of Illinois at Chicago, IL
Adler Planetarium, Chicago, IL
Mind and Life Institute, VA
Academy of Creative Media, University of Hawai'i, HI
This research received no specific grant from any funding agency in the public, commercial, or not-for-profit sectors.

REFERENCES

Aguilera, J. (2013). The perceptual world of a virtual Umwelt. *Technoetic Arts: a Journal of Speculative Research*, *11*(3), 193–198. doi:10.1386/tear.11.3.193_1

Aguilera, J. (2015). Senses in space: Mapping the Universe to the human body. In *International Conference on Universal Access in Human-Computer Interaction* (pp. 177-185). Springer. 10.1007/978-3-319-20681-3_16

Aguilera, J. (2019a). *Mindfulness and Embodiment in the Design of a Synthetic Experience* (Doctoral dissertation). University of Plymouth.

Aguilera, J. (2019b, July). Point of View When Designing Around Behavior. In *International Conference on Human-Computer Interaction*, (pp. 3-13). Springer. 10.1007/978-3-030-23570-3_1

Aguilera, J., Goebel, J., & Mann, M. (2017). 3D across media: ceramics, print and VR. *ACM SIGGRAPH 2017 Educator's Forum*, 1.

Aguilera, J., Roberts, D., SubbaRao, M., Minerva, C., Nichols, M., Salgado, J.F., & Kooima, R. (2008). The SVL, a Working Laboratory Inside a Museum. *Proceedings of IPS 2008, 19th Biennial Conference of the International Planetarium Society*.

Aguilera, J., Tsoupikova, D., Sandin, D., Plepys, D., & Kauffman, L. (2006). Unfolding Space (Unpublished Doctoral dissertation). Electronic Visualization Laboratory, University of Illinois at Chicago.

Aguilera, J. C. (2014). Museum as spacecraft: a building in virtual space. In *The Engineering Reality of Virtual Reality 2014, 9012* (p. 90120D). International Society for Optics and Photonics.

Alberti, L. B. (1966). On Painting, Book II (J. R. Spencer, Trans.). Yale University Press.

Bond, J. R., Kofman, L., & Pogosyan, D. (1996). How filaments of galaxies are woven into the cosmic web. *Nature*, *380*(6575), 603–606. doi:10.1038/380603a0

Cruz-Neira, C., Sandin, D. J., & DeFanti, T. A. (1993, September). Surround-screen projection-based virtual reality: the design and implementation of the CAVE. In *Proceedings of the 20th annual conference on computer graphics and interactive techniques* (pp. 135-142). ACM. 10.1145/166117.166134

Damasio, A. R., & Damasio, H. (1996). Making images and creating subjectivity. The mindbrain continuum. *Sensory Processes*, 19–27.

Freedberg, D., & Gallese, V. (2007). Motion, emotion and empathy in esthetic experience. *Trends in Cognitive Sciences*, *11*(5), 197–203. doi:10.1016/j.tics.2007.02.003 PMID:17347026

Giard, M. H., & Peronnet, F. (1999). Auditory-visual integration during multimodal object recognition in humans: A behavioral and electrophysiological study. *Journal of Cognitive Neuroscience*, *11*(5), 473–490. doi:10.1162/089892999563544 PMID:10511637

Ginsburg, C. (1999). Body-Image, Movement and Consciousness. In J. Shear & F. J. Varela (Eds.), *The view from within: First-person approaches to the study of consciousness*. Imprint Academic.

Iacoboni, M., Woods, R. P., Brass, M., Bekkering, H., Mazziotta, J. C., & Rizzolatti, G. (1999). Cortical mechanisms of human imitation. *Science*, *286*(5449), 2526–2528. doi:10.1126cience.286.5449.2526 PMID:10617472

Johnson, M. (1987). *The Body in the Mind*. Chicago, IL: University of Chicago Press. doi:10.7208/chicago/9780226177847.001.0001

Krueger, M. W. (1977, June). Responsive environments. In *Proceedings of the June 13-16, 1977, national computer conference* (pp. 423-433). ACM. 10.1145/1499402.1499476

Lakoff, G., & Johnson, M. (1980). *Metaphors we live by*. Chicago: University of Chicago Press.

Maunsell, J. H., & Treue, S. (2006). Feature-based attention in visual cortex. *Trends in Neurosciences*, *29*(6), 317–322. doi:10.1016/j.tins.2006.04.001 PMID:16697058

McCormick, B. H., Defanti, T. A., & Brown, M. D. (1987). *Visualization in scientific computing: Report of the NSF Advisory Panel on Graphics*. Image Processing and Workstations.

McNeill, D. (1992). *Hand and mind: What gestures reveal about thought*. Chicago, IL: University of Chicago Press.

Noë, A. (2004). *Action in perception*. Boston, MA: MIT Press.

Pallasmaa, J. (2012). *The eyes of the skin: architecture and the senses*. Hoboken, NJ: John Wiley & Sons.

Panofsky, E., Wood, C. S., & Wood, C. (1991). Perspective as symbolic form. New York: Zone Books.

Pendleton-Jullian, A. M. (1996). *The road that is not a road and the open city, Ritoque, Chile*. Boston, MA: MIT Press.

Petitmengin, C. (2017). Enaction as a Lived Experience. *Constructivist Foundations*, *12*(2).

Turner, R., & Whitehead, C. (2008). How collective representations can change the structure of the brain. *Journal of Consciousness Studies*, *15*(10-1), 43-57.

Van Bavel, J. J., Hackel, L. M., & Xiao, Y. J. (2014). The group mind: The pervasive influence of social identity on cognition. In *New frontiers in social neuroscience* (pp. 41–56). Cham: Springer. doi:10.1007/978-3-319-02904-7_4

Varela, F. J., Thompson, E., & Rosch, E. (1991). *The embodied mind: Cognitive science and human experience*. Boston, MA: MIT Press. doi:10.7551/mitpress/6730.001.0001

Von Uexküll, J. (1957). A stroll through the worlds of animals and men. In C. Schiller (Ed.), *Instinctive behavior: The development of a modern concept*. Madison, CT: International Universities Press, Inc.

Zuidhoek, S., Visser, A., Bredero, M. E., & Postma, A. (2004). Multisensory integration mechanisms in haptic space perception. *Experimental Brain Research*, *157*(2), 265–268. doi:10.100700221-004-1938-6 PMID:15197527

ADDITIONAL READING

Ilardo, M. A., Moltke, I., Korneliussen, T. S., Cheng, J., Stern, A. J., Racimo, F., ... van den Munckhof, I. C. (2018). Physiological and Genetic Adaptations to Diving in Sea Nomads. *Cell, 173*(3), 569–580. doi:10.1016/j.cell.2018.03.054 PMID:29677510

McConville, D. (2014). On the Evolution of the Heavenly Spheres: An Enactive Approach to Cosmography. (Doctoral dissertation, University of Plymouth). Retrieved from https://pearl.plymouth.ac.uk/handle/10026.1/3530

Miller, S. (2010). Delhi: Adventures. In *A Megacity*. India: Penguin Books India.

Price, C. A., Lee, H. S., Subbarao, M., Kasal, E., & Aguilera, J. (2015). Comparing Short and Long Term Learning Effects Between Stereoscopic and Two-Dimensional Film at a Planetarium. *Science Education, 99*(6), 1118–1142. doi:10.1002ce.21185

Stoker, C. R. (1993). Telepresence in the human exploration of Mars: Field studies in analog environments. NASA. Retrieved from https://ntrs.nasa.gov/archive/nasa/casi.ntrs.nasa.gov/19940022857.pdf

ENDNOTE

[1]   Many other kinds of detectors exist such as that at the Laser Interferometer Gravitational-Wave Observatory, or LIGO, that can capture gravitational forces.

Chapter 21

Virtual Reality as a Tool for Mental Health and Conscious Living and Death:
Immersive Contemplative Approaches to Existential Anxieties

Dorote Weyers-Lucci

Institute of Transpersonal Psychology, Sofia University, USA

ABSTRACT

In this chapter, the authors look at the possibilities of impact of VR in the mental health and wellness area through the lens of contemplative practices and immersive experiences. The area of existential anxieties is often stigmatized or difficult to address directly. Death is the most transformative journey possible but may not be viewed this way. Immersive experiences designed to encourage and allow for non-dual experiences can support this transition. They are difficult to design since non-dual experiences by their very nature are both deeply personal and yet totally impersonal at the same time. Yet, the authors examine how existential anxieties are the perfect framework for a non-dual experience. The wellness app StarflightVR serves as an explorative tool. We mention a past study in this area, which revealed that it is possible to mitigate depression by addressing anxiety on a daily basis through this immersive contemplative VR experience. The authors build on this study with existential fear mitigation examined through an online workshop experience and StarflightVR.

INTRODUCTION

In this chapter, we first focus on Virtual Reality (VR), and its positive impacts on mental health. It has been shown to have therapeutic benefits, offering a bridge between transpersonal psychology and the latest technology (Carvalho, Freire, & Nardi, 2010; Chirico et al., 2016; Cukor, Spitalnick, Difede, Rizzo, & Rothbaum, 2009; Diers et al., 2015; Freeman et al., 2014; Glantz, Rizzo, & Graap, 2003). VR has been

DOI: 10.4018/978-1-7998-2433-6.ch021

shown to improve quality of life (Anderson, Rothbaum, & Hodges, 2001), reduce post-traumatic stress disorder (PTSD) (Cukor et al., 2015), and to be effective as a tool in psychotherapy (Rizzo, 2010). The use of VR to work with anxiety disorders is ideal because of its immersive quality. Immersion can be defined by the ability to get into a different point of view. It has also been defined as taking on another story: "A Zen-like state where your hands just seem to know what to do, and your mind just seems to carry on with the story" (Brown & Cairns, 2004).

Immersion is especially promising if mixed with testing physiological mechanisms of the anxiety response as well. Physiological measures such as heart rate, brain waves changes, respiration rate, and skin conductance in response to a virtual environment can be easily and objectively measured. This in turn contributes to an objective assessment of anxiety and depression (Wilhelm & Roth, 2001).

VR may well prove to be a major mental health tool in the future. Immersive virtual environment technology has already been used in therapy for phobias (Côté & Bouchard, 2008; Wiederhold et al., 2002), stress (Bouchard, Baus, Bernier, & McCreary, 2010, Riva et al., 2006; Villani, Preziosa, & Riva, 2006), anxiety (Harris, Kemmerling, & North, 2002; Repetto & Riva, 2011), exercising (Bryanton et al., 2006), and memory problems (Brooks & Rose, 2003; Klinger, Chemin, Lebreton, & Marié, 2006). Additionally, the effects of VR on anxiety symptoms has been examined. In their study, Gorini et al. (2010) concluded that VR for relaxation represents a promising approach in the treatment of general anxiety disorder (GAD). This is because VR enhances the quality of the relaxation experience through the elicitation of the sense of presence generated within the immersive experiences. Slater et al. (1994) define presence as a psychological sense of being in a virtual environment. This sense of presence is that which supports the quality of the relaxation. These types of studies underline the fact that clinical cases such as GAD can also benefit from the VR treatments.

Over the past few decades, VR has been used successfully in a myriad of psychotherapeutic applications. For example, VR has a long history of use for the treatment of PTSD within exposure therapy (Cukor et al., 2015) which reintroduces the patient to the traumatizing event. VR-based therapies allow the clinician to present compelling and controllable scenarios which can be immediately stopped or de-escalated if patients become too anxious during treatment (Kwon, et al., 2009).

VR is also useful for habit training within behavioral therapy. Iribarren, Prolo, Neagos, and Chiappelli (2005) listed the following evidenced-based psychotherapeutic methods for treatment of PTSD: Cognitive-behavioral psychotherapies (i.e., systematic desensitization, relaxation training, biofeedback, cognitive processing therapy, stress inoculation training, assertiveness training, exposure therapy, combined stress inoculation training and exposure therapy, combined exposure therapy and relaxation training, and cognitive therapy), psychological debriefing, pharmacotherapy, and eye movement desensitization reprocessing therapy (EMDR). According to Iribarren et al., evidence-based practice (EBP) is a clinical approach requiring that decisions about health care be based on the best available, current, valid, and relevant evidence. These practices are a conglomeration of the best available resources in clinical treatment (Dawes et al., 2005).

Conversely, VR is also useful in the mental health arena due to its ability to generate a relaxing experience that stimulates the senses while it integrates with the polyvagal system (Porges, 1995, 2009). Porges is vastly cited in this field for his polyvagal theory. The polyvagal theory proposes that the evolution of the mammalian autonomic nervous system provides the neurophysiological substrates for adaptive behavioral strategies. It further proposes that physiological state limits the range of behavior and psychological experience. This vagal integration therefore, can help to provide a deep sense of relaxation and give patients the ability to build vagal muscle. This in turn facilitates autonomous stress regulation. VR is also key in delivering Mindfulness practice. By focusing a person's attention through the immersive qualities of VR, the sense of being there is more easily achieved (Navarro-Haro et al., 2017; Rice & Schroeder, 2017).

Another compelling aspect of VR is that one's visual system's ability to interpret the surrounding environment is duped into accepting the provided visual stimuli as real. This leads to repercussions in the body, and therefore in one's psychophysiology as well. The viewer reacts as if this is happening here and now. This psychophysiological connection is important for the mental health field because it is the basis for permanent behavior change. Antonio Damasio (1996), scientist, researcher, and expert in neuroscience, proposed the somatic marker hypothesis which describes the capacity of the ventral medial prefrontal cortex and the amygdala to monitor the body's past and hypothetical responses through somatic markers. These markers are located in the brainstem and the VS/nucleus accumbens (reward center) for the involuntary system and the higher cortex for the voluntary system. Both systems are a part of the upward and downward loops within the body to and from the brain. According to Damasio (2010), "the brain's protoself structures are not merely about the body. They are literally and inextricably attached to the body. They are resonant loops that connect back to the brain and then back to the body. A body brain bond." (pp. 470-473). If these loops are broken, such as with PTSD or chronic anxiety, then the person will not be able to integrate the exterior information properly. However, equally important, if these bonds are reconnected permanent behavior change becomes possible. In other words, exposure therapy is effective because the VR environment exposes the whole person to an event, which they can then process and integrate psychophysiologically.

If continuously exposed to in small doses, VR can help to shift one's whole countenance, approach to life, and provide a platform for transformation in their lives (Weyers-Lucci, 2016). VR has been used for healing in other ways as well. VR in combination with EEG technology has been shown to heal certain neural imbalances such as stroke, aging, and autism. Studies that employed brain-computer interface (BCI) technologies and VR included using this interface for rehabilitating stroke (Lechner et al., 2014), the motor-imagery BCI for stroke rehabilitation (I Badia et al., 2013) and paraplegic patients (Donati et al., 2016), and the use of BCI for training normal aging subjects (de Tommaso et al., 2016) as well as those subjects with autism disorder (Amaral et al., 2017) and attention deficit hyperactivity disorder (Rohani & Puthusserypady, 2015). Additionally, VR has shown a capacity to reengage and/or build multiple cortical functions (Baumann et al., 2003; Carrieri et al., 2016; Lin et al., 2008; Schedlbauer et al., 2014) and showed a capacity to optimize the coding efficiency of the sensory cortex (Ansuini et al., 2006; Keller et al., 2012; Ravassard et al., 2013; Schindler & Bartels, 2013; Sofroniew et al., 2015).

Currently there is a need for more research focused on the therapeutic process within VR and not purely on its effectiveness. Maples-Keller, Bunnell, Kim, and Rothbaum (2017) proposed investigating factors such as emotion processing, psychophysiological markers during exposure, and the therapeutic alliance. Their view is that research testing hypothesized mediators and moderators of VR-based treatment will prove informative in the future. This ongoing research study will be focusing on this need.

Working with VR enables mental health practitioners and researchers to create the environment necessary for an immersive, whole body experience that could mimic the state of these feelings of knowing (FOK), a type of metacognition coined by Damasio in his neurocognitive approach of whole body sensing (2010). An example of whole body experience of the feelings of knowing could be a Gestalt or a felt sense (Oleary, 2013; Gendlin, 1992, 1994). This is another aspect that makes VR uniquely suited for working with existential fears.

STARFLIGHTVR AS A NEUROAESTHETIC/ NEUROPHENOMENOLOGICAL TRANSPERSONAL EXPERIENCE OF DEATH/LIFE

StarflightVR is a mobile VR experience set up to engage a whole body experience of a contemplative, non-dual state of death/life. It was designed using hypnotherapeutic principles focused on dehypnotization (Casey, 1987 and Elias, 2006) and neuroaesthetic principles of the integrative and meaning making power of art (Pelowski, et al., 2017). It is an immersive experience that is visually and auditory-based and is meant to give the illusion of letting go into the unknown, very much like it would be to let go into an entirely different state such as a nondual experience, or an experience resembling a near death experience (NDE) like a mindfulness-induced NDE (van Gordon et al., 2018). It is used in this study as one of the immersive experiences.

StarflightVR is also based on the "perceptual illusion of non-mediation" (Lombard and Ditton 1997), which proposes that the illusion becomes reality for the user. In this case, it is the disappearance of the body that actually reinforces the feeling of being fully present in the moment within oneself. Therefore, while experiencing letting go into this environment, flying and without a physical body it becomes possible to experience a state similar to a non-dual state, a meditative state, an egoless experience, or a near-death experience (NDE).

This hypnagogic-based design of a space also impacts emotions according to aesthetic perception, which has been shown to activate the bilateral insula which we attribute to the experience of emotion (Cupchik, 2016). In this case the emotions are soothed, and the ability to observe their fluctuations is supported.

Tracking the movement of the eyes is optional in the experience but could be used to track a participant's focus, whether open or closed focus (based on mindfulness meditation principles). This has a direct effect on brain integration. Deliberate eye movements in therapy have been demonstrated to induce a state of relaxation, or decreased psychophysiological arousal (Shapiro, 2014). One hypothesis is that this relaxation response is a reaction to changes in the environment, part of an orienting response that is elicited by the shifts of attention caused by the repeated bilateral stimulation, which links into processes similar to what occurs during R.E.M. sleep (Shapiro, 2014).

Within the StarflightVR experience there are five chapters or function: sleep, energize, guided meditation, story, and experiences. The sleep experience will be used for the current ongoing research study.

The sleep experience itself can be described as follows: The cadence and design of the star field and the accompanying audio track helps bring the user into a state of flow and calm. The background at first appears to be static and the user is encouraged to observe this with a non-critical mind. It evolves in both color and pattern first into a green and golden background, as if one is in the center of the galaxy, and then gradually, through a color progression, into a calming violet field.

These immersive visuals are able to provide a safe environment to experience a shift of state. The visual and auditory experience can become a whole body experience:

When we relax into our senses, and into our body sensations we are able to access the full picture of the situation at hand. From a neural perspective this means that we are using our lamina1 nerve information from the body and integrating that in various ways into the brain. (Siegel, 2012. p. 172)

Users can open their focus to the field and or choose to follow an object as it glides by. Alternatively, they can observe the quasars with their peripheral vision as those appear and become absorbed into black holes.

Virtual Reality allows for a 360° experience, and therefore allows full peripheral vision to help attenuate existential anxieties. The use of peripheral vision has been shown to be an excellent method for shifting from the awake, aware state into calmness and quiet (Lachenmayr, 2006).

StarflightVR's audio track is designed to resonate with a heartbeat at rest, giving hypnotic cues to settle the sympathetic nervous system (Elias, 2006). It helps shift the brain, and therefore the psychophysiology, into the alpha, alpha/theta state of deep, restful relaxation helping to encourage and enhances the sleep experience (Weyers-Lucci, 2016). This technique induces the breathing to automatically synchronize with the visual and audio flow.

The Greater Good Center in Berkeley completed a recent study on awe and its benefits to human health (Keltner, 2003). The practice of noticing moments of awe is in itself an amazing healing therapy for inflammation, and other stress-related diseases. The momentary experiences of awe stimulates wonder and curiosity (Keltner, 2003). In this case travelling through space in StarflightVR, gently rocked by the rhythm of the heartbeat at rest supports this sense of awe. Awe, in itself, also automatically invites the experience of the present moment. In this way it has the effect of binding social collectives, and enabling more collaborative actions.

From a transpersonal perspective the link existing between art and the artist are examples of transpersonal connection. Ultimately, this is the point of immersion. The painter of an artwork for example, and the viewer are engaged not only in the process of making sense of the existing reality, but they are also linking to an engagement and a transformational property. This is a form of absorption (the ability to be immersed in inner imagery) (Luhrmann, Nusbaum and Thisted 2010) and is important from a pedagogical as well as an artistic perspective. The relationship of the viewer to the painting is similar in some way to that of the relationship of the artist to the painting, however, the viewer becomes the observer in this case and the painter becomes the creator together they are then, as Steiner would qualify it, "the knowing doer" (Steiner, 1964). The knowing doer of Steiner, is also the psychologically mature individual who has attained "embodied consciousness" under Assagioli (1965), who is also the person who has become aware of his own depths and shadow formations as with Jung (1959). In other words, once internal imagery is expressed harmoniously and clearly as an outer form, the sense of presence in everyday life is reflected in a sense of flow.

From a neuroaesthetic perspective such an experience is a complex artistic process that crosses cognitive, kinesthetic and emotional functions, (Pelowski, et al, 2017) and sparks the activation of mirror neurons while the individual is "connecting" with art (Schott, 2015). The reaction or resonance that is established with a work of art or a specific relationship and connection reminds one of the *participatory spirituality* (Ferrer, 2017), approaches. In conjunction with the painting the viewer can possibly attain higher levels of self-awareness:

Most religious and spiritual endeavors, we should stress here, are aimed not so much at describing or explaining human nature and the world, but at engaging and transforming forming them in creative and participatory ways, and may therefore call for different validity standards than those emerging from the rationalistic study of the natural world. (Ferrer & Sherman, 2000. p.150-152)

Therefore, in this case, both the creator and the viewer engage not only in the process of making sense of the existing reality, but also linking to an engagement and a transformational property.

A symbol using abstract visuals supports a transcultural approach that is based in archetypal imagery (Jung and Franz, 1964). The abstract approach itself can be seen as a lack of cultural interpretation or methodology of presentation and reception of information. The cultural code, or subcontext, is left open and therefore interpretation becomes transculturally rooted:

The visions of the Jewish mystic are not entirely constituted by his or her subjective imagination, but actually reflect ontological realities that have the capacity of being seen within the imagination of the visionary. This is so because the imagination is...the organ that puts one in contact with spiritual realities that are perceptible to each individual according to the dominant images of one's religious and cultural affiliation. (Ferrer & Sherman, 2000. p.150-152)

This transcultural approach informs the way colors are used in StarflightVR. Distinct wisdom traditions and theories around color differ in their approach yet converge in interesting ways. For example, the colors of sleep within StarflightVR reflect a progression through the color system and are designed to be experienced in an immersive and symbolic manner. This approach to color therapy is grounded in transpersonal psychology. Distinct wisdom traditions and theories around color differ in their approach, yet converge in interesting ways. Rudolf Steiner, founder of Anthroposophy (a philosophical system, and a base for healing methodologies, and other systems such as pedagogy and agricultural systems), was less interested in providing a steep ladder for awakening methodologies, rather than to "awaken at a higher level," meaning a higher level of psychological maturity so that the humans become "stronger souls." (Steiner, 1995). His priority in his approach towards transpersonal phenomena and higher levels of consciousness was directed towards a training of the senses, and a targeted methodology and pedagogy to achieve embodiment, and psychological maturity. Therefore, his way of handling color is entirely different from for example the point of view of the Kabbalah (Lancaster, 2011) or Wilber's pyramid where color is a reflection of a state of consciousness and an energy (Wilber, 2006). Or as Sufi Junayd would say, "the water takes on the color of the cup," (Ferrer & Sherman, 2000, p.150-152). Therefore, wherever the person is, in terms of transpersonal development, they reflect that particular state as a color. The inner maturity reflects in the level of consciousness, which in turn reflects a color (Wilber, 2006). How the individuals interpret, live, and evolve within that color scheme is very personal. Yet Steiner also proposes that there is an aura color specific to every individual. This color is exuded as part of the personal color scheme within the four temperaments in Anthroposophy, and reflects the soul state of being (Steiner, 1995). Allowing for an immersion in color in StarflightVR then mimics this transformative potential. In the end, the intent is to unite, to bring together that which has been held as separate into one non-dual experience of life/death.

Ultimately, the intention of StarflightVR, from a neurophenomenological perspective, is to produce the same changes and transformation in the human brain that is triggered by mindfulness states (Davidson et al., 2003; Hölzel et al., 2011; Kilpatrick et al., 2011). These have important clinical implications, such as reducing automatic affective processing, altering one's relationship to pain and addiction, and leading to the cultivation of compassion (Farb, Anderson & Segal, 2012, pp. 6–7, Garland et al., 2018). For the purpose of mental health it is not necessary to experience death/life as in the Mahasi Sayadaw tradition of Vipassana for example, where there are the stages of insight, called "dukkha nanas," which can generate fear of death and terror (Koster & Oosterhoff, 2004). The proposition here is that of generating an experience which gives a taste of the non-dual state while gently supporting transformation and neurogenesis. Instead of working with mindfulness-induced NDEs, we are working here with VR-induced NDEs. StarflightVR's content was created to be gentle and avoid any possible negative side effects of VR exposure therapy.

FEAR OF DEATH AND IMMERSIVE EXPERIENCES

Immersive experiences are uniquely effective in inviting transformation because they work on a deep-rooted phenomenological level and may also integrate socially. Therefore, they can address both individuality and social transformation. Diana Eck, a professor of comparative religion at Harvard University, recognizes in her work that the diversity of cultures is a demographic fact and shares in *Death Makes Life Possible*, a research project and book by Dr. Marilyn Schlitz and Deepak Chopra which takes an immersive approach to coming to an understanding about death (Schlitz & Chopra, 2015):

Because pluralism allows us to celebrate the differences in an effort to find our own deeper truths and paths of meaning, engaging in the world's traditions approach to death and existential anxieties also engages the individual to become more fully human and reflect and examine their own lives and world-view (ibid., p. 93)

An immersive experience in which we engage with the conversation of death and its surrounding myths, archetypes, and psychology can be an incredibly powerful experience.

This integration of different sensing and perceptive methodologies mimics a case study on the same subject of an immersive six-week experience of the *Gestalt of Death* (Weyers-Lucci, 2018). The study was set up with a regular weekly online Zoom meeting rhythm with two participants and myself. Every online meeting included meditation, reflection, sharing, and support in the same order. Discussion points were based on *Death Makes Life Possible* (Schlitz, 2015), NDEs that both participants revisited and shared, as well as other inner and outer experiences related to existential anxieties or feelings of wellness and growth. Sensing, inner knowing, spiritual co-creation also known as *participatory spirituality*, (Ferrer, 2017), and deeper experiencing were a part of every meeting. Other elements included the journaling exercise. All participants continuously practiced focusing on the *Gestalt of Death* for those six weeks. This is the manner in which Anderson (1998a), for example, approached her methodology of intuitive observations: "Each cycle contains both intuitive and analytic activities that invite the researcher's psyche to roam freely within the boundaries set by the cycle. The researcher's psyche roams freely but not aimlessly" (p. 244).

In this example, the participants were also involved in the same activity. We used steps delineated by Claire Petitmengin-Peugeot (1999) to set up an environment for intuitive knowing, or focus. She described four "interior gestures" (p. 246) that pervaded her research: (a) the gesture of letting go, slowing down, and of interior self-collection; (b) the gesture of connection with a person, object, problem, or situation; (c) the gesture of listening with senses and awareness open and attentive; and (d) the intuition itself (in Anderson, 1998). We also discussed and shared diary entries and photography. At the end of the six weeks, both participants made a collage of their journey into death and rebirth. The organic inquiry brought out the need to discuss rebirth as an integral part of the *Gestalt of Death*, rather than a separate area. Ferrer (2017) stresses this type of experiencing when he speaks of *knowing by virtue of being*. This for him entails a rejection of the subject-object dilemma that is, according to him, part of the Cartesian worldview. In his view of "bringing forth" an experience, rather than a point of view that is divided between object and subject, it is rather something that happens in unison and is never divided. In this case, both the participants and the researcher became absorbed into the experience of death and rebirth as a continuum.

An immersive experience then, resembles a meditative training in which skills are learned that encourage the individual to change habit patterns and neurological/epigenetic expression and engage in life in a transformed manner. Stages of transformation such as those proposed by Wilber (2006) can be applied here. It is through a phenomenological pattern of insights that transformation can occur because it leads to self-knowledge and dehypnotization in a regular rhythmic fashion of perception and expression. Essentially this is based in a non-dual approach:

The action of meditation can be very simple. It is perceiving the process of becoming, with its wanting, desiring, pushing, and pulling. You can just be aware of all that because it is not Being. The more you are aware of this movement of becoming and allow yourself the possibility that it is not working regardless of what it is moving towards, the more you can observe and experience the gap directly. And if you don't follow any movement, attitude, or reaction to it, you may find yourself to be complet (p. 93, Almaas, 2000)

Or as Elena Avila, practitioner states (cited in Schlitz, 2015):

Healing is remembering who we are—re-remembering, not being dismembered, but remembering. We are already given to the power that rules our fate, and we cling to nothing so we have nothing to defend. We have no thoughts, so that we can see. We have no fear, so that we can re-member ourselves, detached and at ease. We will dart past the ego to be free. (pp. 173-174)

USING A GESTALT RESEARCH APPROACH WITH IMMERSIVE EXPERIENCES

Gestalt is a German term signifying a particular formation, patterning, shape, or even person that is perceived as holistic unit over its component parts. Every gestalt is unique, as is every person or situation. Listening to a gestalt is then feeling the particular flavor of the essence or uniqueness of a person, situation, or process. This essence could be seen as being a reflection of consciousness itself (Almaas, 1986). This unique sense, or gestalt, emerges in the immersive environments. The gestalt will manifest differently for every participant, yet certain types of data will reflect a group process accompanied by physiological data underlining state changes from an objective, biological, and existential perspective.

Gestalt therapy was founded by Fritz Perls (Encyclopedia Brittanica, 2012), who was born in Germany and was a student of Sigmund Freud. In gestalt therapy, the client learns to listen into one's own unique sense of what is true using the same skills as the integrative research skills listed above. It is concerned with developing a client's ability to connect with what is true, and in expressing this authentically to others in everyday life (Perls, 1951). In gestalt, therapy finding the "unique sense" of something is called "finding your unique contact boundary" (Oleary, 2013, p. 24). Gestalt is a relational therapy: congruence, authenticity, and honesty are some of the key terms describing the relational capacities that are fostered in this approach. In the same way, using gestalt principles in research aims toward the discovery of the *unique contact boundary* (Oleary, 2013) of the research matter and how it influences itself and its surroundings, as well as how it expresses itself in the world. Working with gestalt means enhanced awareness of sensation, perception, bodily feelings, emotion, and behavior in the present moment. It is, in effect, taking research skills and using them intentionally to bring out a specific "shape" of something, (in this study, for example, the gestalt is that of death). In gestalt, relationship is also emphasized along with contact between the self, the environment, and the other. It is about finding the connections between the points within the research and letting them emerge from the unconscious as well as from the subconscious and conscious. To do this, it is possible to work with two types of emergence that are related to the kinesthetic and proprioceptive skills and, in that way, to the gestalt of something. These are the lightning flash of recognition and the slower coming to of inspired knowing. The flash can be described in the following manner:

Brilliancy arrives at insight in one shot, at a glance, as if intuitively. It doesn't need to go through the various correlations. It is fast and breathtaking. However, it does not see the details of interactions and relationships between the various elements of the situation. We arrive at insight, but most of the time we don't know how we got there. There isn't as much perception, understanding, or knowledge in the process of arriving at the insight, which often makes it difficult to communicate it to others. However, since the Diamond Guidance has Brilliancy as an aspect, it can use the capacity for direct illumination by simply seeing the **gestalt** *without also seeing how the illumination came about. (Almaas, 2000, p. 412)*

The researcher can slow the process and delve into more somatic aspects, or make use of the *Felt Sense* approach (Gendlin, 1992), to inquire into the details of the experience of gestalt and the way the participants are *touching* this essence and the way they are being *touched* by it. This *sensing* quality also ties back to Damasio's *Feelings of Knowing* mentioned earlier (Damasio, 1999).

This gestalt approach to the research may also be useful to address the difficulties that can arise through encountering difficult emotions or feelings:

Some people can withdraw from reality by means of profound spontaneous trances, usually secondary to stress or psychological trauma, and create a fantasy experience by narrowly focusing their attention on imaginary structures or remembered traumatic events while blocking out external reality. (Castillo, 2003, pp. 13-14)

These trances, or unconscious and subconscious overlays, cut off the ability to inquire more deeply and effectively stop the ability to see things as they are.

This is the same phenomenon looked at earlier from the different perspectives of neuroscience, existentialism, and transpersonal psychology. Grounding through feeling the sensation of the body in the moment is helpful in seeing things more clearly, as in *focusing* (Gendlin, 1992). Playfulness, added onto kinesthetic and proprioceptive, is a welcome tool as well. Playing with a gestalt or a sense of an essence through the body could help with triggers and difficult emotions as they may emerge while dealing with topics like death.

From the perspective of neuroscience and neuroplasticity, applying gestalt therapy principles and combining them with immersive experiences and virtual reality exposure is an opportunity to create behavioral changes that could be permanent (Rizzo, 2017). The connection between gestalt and immersive experiences from this perspective lies at the heart of the visual and perceptive networks—those networks from without and those generated on their own from within, those attention-demanding tasks, and the stimulus-dependent tasks. The network associated with attention-demanding tasks is referred to as the task-related network, and the network associated with stimulus-independent thought during the resting state is referred to as the default mode network (DMN). The two networks are believed to be negatively correlated (Josipovic, 2016).

There are, however, challenges in observing and collecting data about the DMN because by definition, it is activated when the brain is not triggered by any outside factor. According to Lifshitz, Cusumano, and Raz (2013), it is challenging to manipulate the DMN in experiments since it activates spontaneously when there are no external task stimuli. Actually, the brain is capable of generating a whole independent universe of conscious experiences when it is disconnected from an outside environment; that is, the brain generates this universe without the task network activation (Nir & Tononi, 2010). How does the visual system then activate without external stimuli? It seems that sensory deprivation increases neuroplasticity, and that therefore the state of sensory deprivation within meditation is also an area of interest. Dehypnotization is essentially the act of self-remembrance. The common aspect to meditative practices from different traditions is the element of progressive dis-identification from thought (Walsh, 1979). Walsh (1979) posited that the normal state of being revolves around thoughts and cognitive constructs, which are layered to produce a hypnotized or trancelike state. From a transpersonal psychology perspective, meditation is a tool in the process of self-remembering (Walsh and Shapiro, 2006, Casey, 1987).

The visual system operates by distinct rules; it is an interoceptive system, driven by the subconscious with distinct patterning. A gestalt is a phenomenological shape incurred through internal perception and underlined by neurophysiological expression (Varela, 1995). The sum of a vision is not just the image produced in the eye when one is looking at something, but it is also influenced by the internal gestalt. When looking at an image, the visual networks only register a fraction of this same image. The rest is aggregated through information from the past and the networks of memory and past experience (the hippocampus comes into play here. This processing of information may be the root cause for continuous negative interpretation of the environment in depressive subjects. As shown by Dainer-Best, et al. (2018), sustained attention for negative stimuli in subjects suffering from depression symptoms shows how what is seen is sustained by the perception of the information provided by the visual sense. This sustained attention seems to alter what is perceived from person to person. This change in perception, of self and of the people and things in the world around one, is what changes behavior.

The visual sense is also social, since there are instances of similar brain activity when watching the same movies. The inter-subject correlation analysis used in the Hasson study (2010), for example, shows the impact or control that a given movie may have on the brains of spectators. The analysis measured similarity in brain activity amongst participants. One hypothesis is that certain visual stimuli are processed in the same manner, and that the integration of these particular signals are also similar between people. These universals would be the same universals as the signals of fear and fear of death, especially in crowds or larger audiences. The neurological connection between humans affects the field of vision as well it seems. This fine attunement is the basis for mirror neuron theories (Siegel, 2006) and attachment theory (Bowlby, 1982, 1988). It is also a possibility for transformation, as shared from the research of DMLP and *Living Deeply* (Schlitz, 2015, Vieten, Amorok and Schlitz, 2007). And like others who have reported having near-death experiences, renowned remote viewer, Joseph McMoneagle found a doorway into personal growth that leads away from a primary focus on self-enhancement and toward supportive and meaningful social behaviors. As research on the positive trajectories of terror management and worldview transformation suggest, the experiences guided him to reprioritize intrinsic over extrinsic goals and priorities. "It shifted his view from a small "me" to a larger interconnected "we."" (ibid., p. 54).

It seems that most visual signaling is interpreted from the subjectivity of the first-person perspective, and from the memories attached to that particular body mind, as well to the viewpoint coming from its subconscious structure. What is not known is where are these networks of activity and sensory information integrated?

According to Cavanna and Trimble (2006), some visuo-spatial imagery studies suggest the involvement in internally guided attention and manipulation of mental images, as well as the integration of mental imagery from the first-person perspective (i.e., introspective integration). These studies support the hypothesis that the precuneus (area of the brain involved in a variety of complex functions, which includes recollection and memory, integration of information (gestalt) relating to perception of the environment, cue reactivity, mental imagery strategies, episodic memory retrieval, and affective responses to pain) is the center point for this integrative activity, and for the visual network as well. Is it possible to postulate that the fear of death is likely to be seen in the brain as a lack of integration? If so, brain structures such as the precuneus would be smaller and structures such as the amygdala would be larger in subjects with chronic, unconscious existential anxiety and depression.

The sense of sight is also of primary importance in embodiment, in other words, the sense of being in a body. Sight seems to have an integrative function in self-perception of the body, coupled with the vestibular system. This system is divided into visual exteroception—the visual perception of the location and movement of the limbs (Crook, 1987)—and visual proprioception and kinesthesis. This combination makes gestalt a powerful tool to work with when researching existential fears and their brain and body maps.

EXISTENTIAL PERSPECTIVE ON THE FEAR OF DEATH

The existential psychotherapist and writer Yalom (1980) outlined what he considered to be the ultimate concerns of humankind: (a) death, (b) isolation, (c) meaninglessness, and (d) freedom. As a psychotherapist, Yalom was primarily interested in how these existential concerns inform the therapeutic process. He believed that psychological difficulties stem from an inability to reconcile with these existential concerns. Thus, his sessions included a thorough examination of the way every individual accommodates these concerns. Yalom believed that the liberation of suffering and sorrow would occur once the client has made peace with their circumstances.

According to psychodynamic theory, Yalom's view represents the specific tension of dual instincts of ego and libidinal instincts (Greenberg & Mitchel, 1983). The demands of the external and internal environments are the birthplace of the superego. This is the force that manages interpersonal demands and the need of the child for approval from their security-providing adults. Failure to find balance among these demands may freeze life-enhancing movement forward that resides in the libido. Character structure rests in part on the role of the superego. The superego manages the safekeeping of its owner. According to Greenberg (1983), "Growth is always compromised for the sake of security" (p. 107). Therefore freezing, whether it be muscles themselves or the lack of movement that comes from a suppressed libido, could easily lead to frozen expressions, frozen muscles, and frozen facial traits. In other words, frozenness itself becomes a "being" (Greenberg, 1983, p. 107), blocking movement forward as growth is compromised for security. Greenberg (1983) stated, "In Freud's revised view, meaning is determined by the ebbs and flows, and a complex interplay of life and death instincts" (pp. 552-553). In the end, Yalom (2009) provides a solution to the existential psychologists' dilemma:

A denial of death at any level is a denial of one's basic nature and begets an increasingly pervasive restriction of awareness and experience. The integration of the idea of death saves us; rather than sentence us to existences of terror or bleak pessimism, it acts as a catalyst to plunge us into more authentic life modes, and it enhances our pleasure in the living of life. (pp 89-91).

A denial of death causes stress, anxiety, and possibly depression in the individuals experiencing this *death denial*. The physiological effects of denial should become measurable because stress stimulates the sympathetic nervous system while inhibiting the vagus nerve (Porges, 1995; Sahar et al., 2001). Therefore, typical stress-related brain wave patterns and their relaxed counterparts could clearly demonstrate a stress state or a parasympathetic-based state. These can be analyzed to understand the effects of the fear of death, and of relaxation/natural flow. It seems possible to defreeze individuals by having them be immersed in a gestalt of death experience. This invites an examination of the possible effects of immersive experiences, including VR, as a psychotherapeutic tool for existential anxieties.

FEAR OF DEATH AND EXISTENTIAL ANXIETY AND DEPRESSION

As mentioned previously, fear of death/existential anxiety is considered to be a basis for anxiety and depression in existential psychotherapy (Yalom, 2009), cognitive based therapy (CBT) (Lazarus, 1997; Scherer, 2005), and terror management theory (Becker, 1973). At its core, the existential perspective proposes that dread is the basis of human emotional life. This theory stipulates that it is the fear of death that motivates our reality, and is the core of human experience, which results in existential anxiety. This anxiety in turn sets up a filter to create a specific experience of reality. However, the processes associated with the creation of filters are typically nonconscious.

Nonconscious fear processes themselves cannot not be approached in the same manner as conscious fear processes (LeDoux, 2014) and may require a different approach to managing uncontrolled fear states. Existential psychotherapy focuses specifically on the fear of death (Yalom, 2009). Fear of death is considered to be at the basis of unconscious, uncontrolled fear states (Beck & Weisshaar, 1995; Lewis, 2014; Ottens & Hanna, 1998). The distinction between conscious and unconscious is important because the predisposing factors for each may be different and therefore need to be addressed in a different manner (LeDoux, 2014). Fear conditioning is one form of Pavlovian conditioning that has received considerable attention (Fendt & Fanselow 1999, LeDoux, 2000) and has been studied extensively. Pavlovian fear conditioning posits that certain environmental stimuli predict certain aversive events. Pavlovian conditioning forms neural representations of the conditioning itself and, therefore, an alteration in the perception of the subjects who are conditioned (Maren & Holt, 2000).

One experiment that clearly shows this is the *Little Albert Experiment* (Watson, 1920). The researcher, Watson, presents Albert, a human infant, with a novel white rat. Albert responds with curiosity and reaches out to touch the animal. Watson then subsequently pairs appearances of the white rat with a loud and aversive noise. Watson again presents Little Albert with the white rat after the rat had been paired with the loud noise. Unlike his initial reaction of curiosity to the rat, Albert now responds to the rat with fear. He moves away from the rat and cries. The circuits associated with this conditioned response are not the same as those that respond to natural threats occurring in the environment (LeDoux, 2014). The unconditioned fear response is one that responds unconditionally, naturally, and automatically to fear triggers. An unconditioned fear response could, for example, be rats who are exposed to a predator odor (trimethylthiazoline), to elicit unconditioned freezing behavior.

Terror management theory associates an increase of self-esteem when confronted with death with a reduction of death anxiety (Becker, 1973). The existential approach proposes that it is the fear reaction to mortality that causes social reactivity and hatred towards unaccepted population groups. There seems to be a hierarchy of fear reactions, that goes from attachment patterns (Bowlby, 1988) to social worldview and acceptance into social groups. Acceptance into social groups then entails existential fear reactions based on perceived threats to the group worldview. According to Freud the individual literally rescinds their individuality and becomes a barbarian. A group Freud claims, is impulsive, changeable and irritable, and is led almost exclusively by the sub conscious (Freud, 2005).

The fear of death or existential anxieties is deemed to be a basis for general anxiety disorders and therefore depression, lack of self-esteem and other psychological and social pathologies (Becker, 1973; Yalom, 2009; Schlitz, 2015; Sapolsky, 2001).

Is it possible to attain a more objective, clearer view life through an immersive six-week experience of the gestalt of death? The elemental movement when faced with death is a reactive, instinctual race into safety. The fear of death is a deeply wired biological reaction to threat faced by an organism. As Solomon, Greenberg, and Pyszczynski (2015) mentioned in their analysis of the fear of death in *Worm at the Core*, "The fear of death is one of the primary driving forces of human action" (ibid., p. 119-120). This natural driving force, however, can flip into a chronic state. According to Sapolsky (2001), being stuck in the state of chronic anxiety can lead to other psychological and physical imbalances such as depression.

Psychological pathologies related to existential anxieties that could be addressed are to name a few: General Anxiety Disorder (GAD), Obsessive Compulsive Disorder (OCD), Seasonal Affective Disorder (SAD), Panic Disorder (PDA), Post Traumatic Stress Disorder (PTSD), Major Depressive Disorder (MDD), as well as other anxiety-related disorders. Developing a tool for patients or people with these disorders is of prime importance. The current figures for these existential anxiety-related disorders are alarming, nationally within the U.S., and on a world scale.

According to a global study by the World Health Organization (WHO; 2017), GAD affects 6.8 million adults, or 3.1% of the U.S. population, yet only 43.2% are receiving treatment. Women are twice as likely to be affected as men. GAD often co-occurs with major depression. PDA affects 6 million adults, or 2.7% of the U.S. population. Women are twice as likely to be affected as men. SAD affects 15 million adults, or 6.8% of the U.S. population. The leading cause of disability in the U.S. for ages 15 to 44.3, MDD affects more than 16.1 million American adults, or about 6.7%of the U.S. population age 18 and older, in a given year.

The figures worldwide are equally concerning. Depression is the leading cause of disability worldwide. Almost 75% of people with mental disorders remain untreated in developing countries with almost 1 million people taking their lives each year. In addition, according to the WHO (2017), one person in 13 globally suffers from anxiety. The WHO reports that anxiety disorders are the most common mental disorders worldwide with specific phobia, major depressive disorder, and social phobia being the most common anxiety disorders.

Virtual Reality (VR) and/or an immersive experience of the gestalt (phenomenological form/shape) of death may prove to be a unique, comforting, and supportive approach to treat these existentially based anxieties and provide a microcosmic, detailed, and scalable approach to a global problem. Even though mental health is crucial for all development (economic, educational, labor, etc.), the WHO notes that based on the WHO Global Health Expenditure database (2017), the global median of domestic general government health expenditure per capita in 2015 was US $141, thus making government mental health expenditure less than 2% of global median of government health expenditure.

Additionally, low-income countries are faced with a lack of resources that is apparent in the distribution of mental health tools nationally. However, responses vary significantly across income groups with 85% of high-income countries reporting that income support is provided compared to only 11% of low-income countries.

As clinical psychologist Dr. Daniel Freeman says, there is "something beautiful" (Freeman et al., 2016, p. 63) about how VR works. Findings show that patients report satisfaction with VR-based therapy and may find it more acceptable than traditional approaches.

Researching VR and other immersive techniques, such as an experience of the gestalt of death in a workshop, is friendly to the research participants and can eventually be successfully implemented as a future treatment modality. An early study on virtual reality exposure (VRE) for patients with post-traumatic stress disorder (PTSD) due to motor vehicle crashes demonstrated that patients reported very high satisfaction with VRE. In a sample of 150 patients with specific phobias, the refusal rate for VR exposure (3%) was lower than for in vivo exposure (27%), providing preliminary evidence that VR-based exposure may be more acceptable to patients.

One study in a PTSD sample found equivalent satisfaction between VRE and imaginal exposure, while another found increased satisfaction for VRE (Delarosa et al., 2012). In a sample of 352 post-9/11 US soldiers, the majority reported that they would be willing to use most of the technology-based approaches for mental health care included in the survey (e.g., VR; Wilson et al, 2008). Additionally, 19% of those who reported that they would not be willing to talk to a counselor in person reported being willing to use VR approaches to access mental health care, suggesting that VR may potentially address some barriers to treatment (Wilson et al., 2008).

A combination of different approaches, including technological, and non-technological, need to be examined as well. For example, a small-scale RCT ($n = 20$) study used VR in conjunction with biofeedback for patients to practice relaxation exercises during treatment (Kim et al., 2008). Patients were randomly assigned to VR with biofeedback, VR without biofeedback, or wait-list control condition. Although the study did not have enough power to examine between group differences, it provides preliminary support for the feasibility of using VR for patients with GAD. Thus far, this study has been the only one to examine the use of VR in treating GAD in this manner. In the same way, there needs to be additional research done on non-technologically based treatment immersive methodologies in the area of existential anxieties (Cukor et al., 2009).

The dearth of studies may be due to the difficulty associated with creating standardized VR scenarios that are able to capture the numerous, varying, individualized worries of patients with GAD. Given this complication, VR-based treatment programs could focus on some of the more common worries among patients with GAD (e.g., health anxiety, something happening to a loved one). Alternatively, or if a patient's worries are not readily addressable with such scenarios, VR- based treatment could serve as a visual guide for breathing exercises and for practicing relaxation or mindfulness-based approaches. Another interesting area is the study of the use of avatars in immersive experiences and how they shift our deepest perceptions of self (Bailenson, 2018; Bailenson & Kim, 2007).

CONCLUSION

The aim of the current study on the effects of immersive experiences on the fear of death is to understand the individual's personal gestalt of death, and then apply this understanding to the individual's fear of death/existential anxieties. The mental health imbalances associated with these existential anxieties will be addressed in this manner. The research encompasses the applicability of technology such as VR to help mitigate and/or measure symptoms of existential anxiety (depression and neuroses). The rhythm and structure of the study is based on the natural or organic process of insight (Clements, 2004), the cognitive loop process of transformation through perception/expression (Perceptual Shift Hypothesis) (Weyers-Lucci, 2018), or clear thinking as per the scientist, academic, and nondual teacher (Almaas,1986). This loop of insight enables access to a gradually increasing *objective* or clear view of internal and external processes. As Almaas described:

We mean seeing things, seeing internal or external things as they are, instead of subjectively. Subjective is the antithesis; it means according to our positions, feelings, filters, beliefs and attitudes. So objective perception means pure perception, free from all positions, bias, filters, conflicts, intentions etc. It is perceiving whatever it is without any obscuration or intermediacy, so we see it just the way it is in itself. (ibid., p. 5)

REFERENCES

Almaas, A. H. (1986). *The void: Inner spaciousness and ego structure.* Boulder, CO: Shambhala.

Almaas, A. H. (2000). *Diamond heart book three: Being and the meaning of life.* Boulder, CO: Shambhala.

Amaral, C. P., Simões, M. A., Mouga, S., Andrade, J., & Castelo-Branco, M. (2017). A novel brain computer interface for classification of social joint attention in autism and comparison of 3 experimental setups: A feasibility study. *Journal of Neuroscience Methods, 290,* 105–115. doi:10.1016/j.jneumeth.2017.07.029 PMID:28760486

Anderson, P. L., Rothbaum, B. O., & Hodges, L. (2000). Virtual reality: Using the virtual world to improve quality of life in the real world. *Bulletin of the Menninger Clinic, 65*(1), 78–91. doi:10.1521/bumc.65.1.78.18713 PMID:11280960

Anderson, R. (1998a). Intuitive inquiry: Exploring the mirroring discourse of disease. In F. Wertz, K. Charmaz, L. McMullen, R. Josselson, & R. Anderson (Eds.), *Five ways of doing qualitative analysis: Phenomenological psychology, grounded theory, discourse analysis, narrative research, and intuitive inquiry* (Kindle version). New York, NY: Guilford. Retrieved from www.amazon.com

Anderson, R. (1998b). Intuitive inquiry: A transpersonal approach. In W. Braud & R. Anderson (Eds.), *Transpersonal research methods for the social sciences: Honoring human experience* (pp. 69–94). Thousand Oaks, CA: Sage.

Ansuini, C., Pierno, A. C., Lusher, D., & Castiello, U. (2006). Virtual reality applications for the remapping of space in neglect patients. *Restorative Neurology and Neuroscience, 24,* 431–441. PMID:17119316

Assagioli, R. (1965). *Psychosynthesis: A Manual of Principles and Techniques*. New York: Hobbs, Dorman & Company.

i.   Badia, S. B., Morgade, A. G., Samaha, H., & Verschure, P. F. (2013). Using a hybrid brain computer interface and virtual reality system to monitor and promote cortical reorganization through motor activity and motor imagery training. *IEEE Transactions on Neural Systems and Rehabilitation Engineering*, *21*(2), 174–181. doi:10.1109/TNSRE.2012.2229295 PMID:23204287

Bailenson, J. N. (2018). *Experience on Demand: What Virtual Reality Is, How It Works, and What It Can Do*. New York: W.W. Norton.

Bailenson, J. N., & Yee, N. (2007). Virtual interpersonal touch and digital chameleons. *Journal of Nonverbal Behavior*, *31*(4), 225–242. doi:10.100710919-007-0034-6

Baumann, S., Neff, C., Fetzick, S., Stangl, G., Basler, L., Vereneck, R., & Schneider, W. (2003). A virtual reality system for neurobehavioral and functional MRI studies. *Cyberpsychology & Behavior*, *6*(3), 259–266. doi:10.1089/109493103322011542 PMID:12855081

Beck, A. T., & Weishaar, M. E. (1995). Cognitive therapy. In R. J. Corsini & D. Wedding (Eds.), *Current psychotherapies* (pp. 229–261). Itasca, IL: Peacock.

Becker, E. (1973). *The denial of death*. New York, NY: Free Press.

Bouchard, S., Baus, O., Bernier, F., & McCreary, D. R. (2010). Selection of key stressors to develop virtual environments for practicing stress management skills with military personnel prior to deployment. *Cyberpsychology, Behavior, and Social Networking*, *13*(1), 83–94. doi:10.1089/cyber.2009.0336 PMID:20528298

Bowlby, J. (1982). Attachment and loss: Retrospect and prospect. *The American Journal of Orthopsychiatry*, *52*(4), 664–678. doi:10.1111/j.1939-0025.1982.tb01456.x PMID:7148988

Bowlby, J. (1988). *A secure base: Parent-child attachment and healthy human development*. New York, NY: Basic Books.

Brooks, B., & Rose, F. (2003). The use of virtual reality in memory rehabilitation: Current findings and future directions. *NeuroRehabilitation*, *18*, 147–157. PMID:12867677

Brown, E., & Cairns, P. (2004). A grounded investigation of game immersion. *Proceedings of CHI 2004*, 1279–1300.

Bryanton, C., Bosse, J., Brien, M., McLean, J., McCormick, A., & Sveistrup, H. (2006). Feasibility, motivation, and selective motor control: Virtual reality compared to conventional home exercise in children with cerebral palsy. *Cyberpsychology & Behavior*, *9*(2), 123–128. doi:10.1089/cpb.2006.9.123 PMID:16640463

Carrieri, M., Petracca, A., Lancia, S., Basso Moro, S., Brigadoi, S., Spezialetti, M., & Quaresima, V. (2016). Prefrontal cortex activation upon a demanding virtual hand controlled task: A new frontier for neuroergonomics. *Frontiers in Human Neuroscience*, *10*, 53. doi:10.3389/fnhum.2016.00053 PMID:26909033

Carvalho, M., Freire, R. C., & Nardi, A. (2010). Virtual reality as a mechanism for exposure therapy. *World Journal of Biological Psychiatry, 11*(2_2), 220-230.

Casey, E. S. (1987). *Remembering: A phenomenological study.* Bloomington, IN: Indiana University Press.

Cavanna, A. E., & Trimble, M. R. (2006). The precuneus: A review of its functional anatomy and behavioural correlates. *Brain, 129*(Pt 3), 564–583. doi:10.1093/brain/awl004 PMID:16399806

Chirico, A., Lucidi, F., De Laurentiis, M., Milanese, C., Napoli, A., & Giordano, A. (2016). Virtual reality in health system: Beyond entertainment. A mini-review on the efficacy of VR during cancer treatment. *Journal of Cellular Physiology, 231*(2), 275–287. doi:10.1002/jcp.25117 PMID:26238976

Clements, J. (2004). Organic inquiry: Toward research in partnership with spirit. *Journal of Transpersonal Psychology, 36*, 26–49.

Côté, S., & Bouchard, S. (2008). Virtual reality exposure for phobias: A critical review. *Journal of Cyber Therapy and Rehabilitation, 1*(1), 75–91.

Cukor, J., Spitalnick, J. S., Difede, J., Rizzo, A. A., & Rothbaum, B. O. (2009). Emerging treatments for PTSD. *Clinical Psychology Review, 29*(8), 715–726. doi:10.1016/j.cpr.2009.09.001 PMID:19800725

Cupchik, G. (2016). The Aesthetics of Emotion: Up the Down Staircase of the Mind Body. *Empirical Studies of the Arts, 36*(1), 114–121.

Dainer-Best J., Lee H.Y., Shumake J., Yeager D. S. & Beevers C.G. (2018). Determining optimal parameters of the self-referent encoding task: A large-scale examination of self referent cognition and depression *Psychological Assessment*, Advanced Online Publication.

Damasio, A. (1999). *The feeling of what happens: Body and emotion in the making of consciousness.* Fort Worth, TX: Harcourt College.

Damasio, A. (2010). *Self comes to mind: Constructing the conscious brain* (Kindle version). Knopf Doubleday. Retrieved from www.Amazon.com

Damasio, A. R. (1996). The somatic marker hypothesis and the possible functions of the prefrontal cortex. *Philosophical Transactions of the Royal Society of London. Series B, Biological Sciences, 351*(1346), 1413–1420. doi:10.1098/rstb.1996.0125 PMID:8941953

Davidson, R., Kabat–Zinn, J., Schumacher, J., Rosenkranz, M., Muller, D., Santorelli, S. F., ... Sheridan, J. F. (2003). Alterations in Brain and Immune Function Produced by Mindfulness Meditation. *Psychosomatic Medicine, 65*(4), 564–570. doi:10.1097/01.PSY.0000077505.67574.E3 PMID:12883106

Davidson, R., & Lutz, A. (2008). Buddha's Brain: Neuroplasticity and Meditation. *IEEE Signal Processing Magazine, 25*(1), 176–174. doi:10.1109/MSP.2008.4431873 PMID:20871742

Dawes, M., Summerskill, W., Glasziou, P., Cartabellotta, A., Martin, J., Hopayian, K., & Osborne, J. (2005). Sicily statement on evidence-based practice. *BMC Medical Education, 5*(1), 1. doi:10.1186/1472-6920-5-1 PMID:15634359

De la Rosa, A., & Cárdernas-López, G. (2012). Posttraumatic stress disorder: Efficacy of a treatment program using virtual reality for victims of criminal violence in Mexican population. *Anuario de Psicología, 42*, 377–391.

de Tommaso, M., Ricci, K., Delussi, M., Montemurno, A., Vecchio, E., Brunetti, A., & Bevilacqua, V. (2016). Testing a novel method for improving way finding by means of a P3b virtual reality visual paradigm in normal aging. *SpringerPlus, 5*(1), 1297. doi:10.118640064-016-2978-7 PMID:27547671

Diers, M., Kamping, S., Kirsch, P., Rance, M., Bekrater-Bodmann, R., Foell, J., ... Flor, H. (2015). Illusion-related brain activations: A new virtual reality mirror box system for use during functional magnetic resonance imaging. *Brain Research, 1594*, 173–182. doi:10.1016/j.brainres.2014.11.001 PMID:25446453

Donati, A. R., Shokur, S., Morya, E., Campos, D. S., Moioli, R. C., Gitti, C. M., ... Nicolelis, M. A. (2016). Longterm training with a brain-machine interface-based gait protocol induces partial neurological recovery in paraplegic patients. *Scientific Reports, 6*(30383). PMID:27513629

Elias, J. (2006). *Finding true magic: Transpersonal hypnosis and hypnotherapy/NLP (Kindle version)*. Seattle, WA: Five Wisdom Press. Retrieved from www.Amazon.com

Encyclopaedia Britannica. (2012). *Gestalt therapy*. Retrieved from https://www.britannica.com/science/Gestalt-therapy

Farb, N., Anderson, A., & Segal, Z. (2012). The Mindful Brain and Emotion Regulation in Mood Disorders. *Canadian Journal of Psychiatry, 57*(2), 70–77. doi:10.1177/070674371205700203 PMID:22340146

Fendt, M., & Fanselow, M. S. (1999). The neuroanatomical and neurochemical basis of conditioned fear. *Neuroscience and Biobehavioral Reviews, 23*(5), 743–760. doi:10.1016/S0149-7634(99)00016-0 PMID:10392663

Ferrer, J.N., & Sherman. (2000). Transpersonal Knowledge: A Participatory Approach to Transpersonal Phenomena. In T. Hart, P. Nelson, & K. Puhakka (Eds.), *Transpersonal Knowing: Exploring the Farther Reaches of Consciousness*, (pp. 213-252). Albany, NY: State University of New York Press.

Ferrer, J. N. (2017). *Participation and the mystery: Transpersonal essays in psychology education, and religion (Kindle version)*. Albany, NY: State University Press. doi:10.1215/08879982-4252974

Freud, S. (2005). Massenpsychologie und Ich-Analyse. Die Zukunft einer Illusion [Group psychology and the analysis of the ego: The future of an illusion]. Frankfurt-on-Main, Germany: Fischer Verlag. (Original work published 1921)

Garland, E. L., & Howard, M. O. (2018). Mindfulness-based treatment of addiction: Current state of the field and envisioning the next wave of research. *Addiction Science & Clinical Practice, 13*(1), 14. doi:10.118613722-018-0115-3 PMID:29669599

Gendlin, E. T. (1992). The wider role of bodily sense in thought and language. In M. Sheets Johnstone (Ed.), *Giving the body its due* (pp. 192–207). Albany, NY: State University of New York Press.

Gendlin, E. T. (1994). *The primacy of perception: An ancient and modern mistake*. Unpublished manuscript.

Glantz, K., Rizzo, A., & Graap, K. (2003). Virtual reality for psychotherapy: Current reality and future possibilities. *Psychotherapy (Chicago, Ill.)*, *40*(1-2), 55–67. doi:10.1037/0033-3204.40.1-2.55

Gorini, A., Pallavicini, F., Algeri, D., Repetto, C., Gaggioli, A., & Riva, G. (2010).. . *Studies in Health Technology and Informatics*, *154*, 39–43. PMID:20543266

Greenberg, J., & Mitchell, S. (1983). *Object relations in psychoanalytic theory (Kindle version)*. Cambridge, MA: Harvard University Press. doi:10.2307/j.ctvjk2xv6

Harris, S. R., Kemmerling, R. L., & North, M. M. (2002). Brief virtual reality therapy for public speaking anxiety. *Cyberpsychology & Behavior*, *5*(6), 534–550. doi:10.1089/109493102321018187 PMID:12556117

Hasson, U., Landesman, O., Knappmeyer, B., Vallines, I., Rubin, N., & Heeger, D. (2008). Neurocinematics: The neuroscience of film. *Projections: Journal for Movies and Mind*, *2*(1), 1–26. doi:10.3167/proj.2008.020102

Hölzel, B., Carmody, J., Vangel, M., Congleton, C., Yerramsetti, S. M., Gard, T., & Lazar, S. W. (2011). Mindfulness Practice Leads to Increases in Regional Brain Gray Matter Density. *Psychiatry Research*, *191*(1), 36–43. doi:10.1016/j.pscychresns.2010.08.006 PMID:21071182

Jung, C. G. (1959). *The archetypes and the collective unconscious* (R. F. C. Hull, Trans.). Princeton, NJ: Princeton University Press.

Jung, C. G. (1965). *Memories, dreams, reflections*. New York, NY: Vintage Books.

Keller, G. B., Bonhoeffer, T., & Hübener, M. (2012). Sensorimotor mismatch signals in primary visual cortex of the behaving mouse. *Neuron*, *74*(5), 809–815. doi:10.1016/j.neuron.2012.03.040 PMID:22681686

Keltner, D., & Haidt, J. (2003). Approaching awe, a moral, spiritual, and aesthetic emotion. *Cognition and Emotion*, *17*(2), 297–314. doi:10.1080/02699930302297 PMID:29715721

Kim, K., Kim, C. H., Cha, K. R., Park, J., Han, K., Kim, Y. K., ... Kim, S. I. (2008). Anxiety provocation and measurement using virtual reality in patients with obsessive compulsive disorder. *Cyberpsychology & Behavior*, *11*(6), 637–641. doi:10.1089/cpb.2008.0003 PMID:18991527

Klinger, E., Chemin, I., Lebreton, S., & Marié, R. M. (2006). Virtual action planning in Parkinson's disease: A control study. *Cyberpsychology & Behavior*, *9*(3), 342–347. doi:10.1089/cpb.2006.9.342 PMID:16780402

Koster, F., & Oosterhoff, M. (2004). *Liberating Insight: Introduction to Buddhist Psychology and Insight Meditation*. Chiang Mai: Silkworm Books.

Kwon, J. H., Chalmers, A., Czanner, S., Czanner, G., & Powell, J. (2009). A study of visual perception: social anxiety and virtual realism. *Proceedings of the 25th Spring Conference on Computer Graphics*, 167-172. 10.1145/1980462.1980495

Lancaster, L. (2011). The cognitive neuroscience of consciousness, mysticism and psi. *International Journal of Transpersonal Studies*, *30*(1-2), 11–22. doi:10.24972/ijts.2011.30.1-2.11

Lazarus, A. A. (1997). *Brief but comprehensive psychotherapy: The multimodal way*. New York, NY: Springer.

Lechner, A., Ortner, R., & Guger, C. (2014). Feedback strategies for BCI based stroke rehabilitation: Evaluation of different approaches. In W. Jensen, O. K. Andersen, & M. Akay (Eds.), *2nd International Conference on NeuroRehabilitation (ICNR)*. 10.1007/978-3-319-08072-7_75

LeDoux, J. (2014). Coming to terms with fear. *Proceedings of the National Academy of Sciences of the United States of America*, *111*(8), 2871–2878. doi:10.1073/pnas.1400335111 PMID:24501122

Lewis, A. M. (2014). Terror Management Theory applied clinically: Implications for existential integrative psychotherapy. *Death Studies*, *38*(6), 412–417. doi:10.1080/07481187.2012.753557 PMID:24666148

Lifshitz, M., Cusumano, E. P., & Raz, A. (2013). Hypnosis as neurophenomenology. *Frontiers in Human Neuroscience*, *7*, 469. doi:10.3389/fnhum.2013.00469 PMID:23966930

Lin, C.-T., Lin, H.-Z., Chiu, T.-W., Chao, C.-F., Chen, Y.-C., & Liang, S.-F. (2008). Distraction related EEG dynamics in virtual reality driving simulation. In *IEEE International Symposium on Circuits and Systems,* (pp. 1088-1091). Seattle, WA: IEEE.

Maples-Keller, J., Bunnell, B., Kim, S. J., & Rothbaum, B. (2017). The use of virtual reality technology in the treatment of anxiety and other psychiatric disorders. *Harvard Review of Psychiatry*, *25*(3), 103–113. doi:10.1097/HRP.0000000000000138 PMID:28475502

Maren, S., & Holt, W. (2000). The hippocampus and contextual memory retrieval in Pavlovian conditioning. *Behavioural Brain Research*, *110*(1-2), 97–108. doi:10.1016/S0166-4328(99)00188-6 PMID:10802307

Navarro-Haro, M. V., López-del-Hoyo, Y., Campos, D., Linehan, M. M., Hoffman, H. G., García-Palacios, A., ... García-Campayo, J. (2017). Meditation experts try Virtual Reality Mindfulness: A pilot study evaluation of the feasibility and acceptability of Virtual Reality to facilitate mindfulness practice in people attending a Mindfulness conference. *PLoS One*, *12*(11), e0187777. doi:10.1371/journal.pone.0187777 PMID:29166665

Nir, Y., & Tononi, G. (2010). Dreaming and the brain: From phenomenology to neurophysiology. *Trends in Cognitive Sciences*, *14*(2), 88–100. doi:10.1016/j.tics.2009.12.001 PMID:20079677

O'Leary, E. (Ed.). (2013). *Gestalt therapy around the world*. Hoboken, NJ: John Wiley & Sons. doi:10.1002/9781118323410

Ottens, A. J., & Hanna, F. J. (1998). Cognitive and existential therapies: Toward an integration. *Psychotherapy (Chicago, Ill.)*, *35*(3), 312–324. doi:10.1037/h0087832

Pelowski, M., Markey, P. S., Forster, M., Gerger, G., & Leder, H. (2017). Move me, astonish me... delight my eyes and brain: The Vienna Integrated Model of top-down and bottom up processes in Art Perception (VIMAP) and corresponding affective, evaluative and neurophysiological correlates. *Physics of Life Reviews*, *21*, 80–125. doi:10.1016/j.plrev.2017.02.003 PMID:28347673

Perls, F., Hefferline, G., & Goodman, P. (1951). *Gestalt therapy*. New York.

Petitmengin-Peugeot, C. (1999). The intuitive experience. In F. Varela & J. Shear (Eds.), *The view from within* (pp. 43–77). Exeter, UK: Academic-Imprint.

Porges, J. (1995). Orienting in a defensive world: Mammalian modifications of our evolutionary heritage. A polyvagal theory. *Psychophysiology*, *32*(4), 301–318. doi:10.1111/j.1469-8986.1995.tb01213.x PMID:7652107

Porges S. W. (2009). The polyvagal theory: new insights into adaptive reactions of the autonomic nervous system. *Cleveland Clinic Journal of Medicine, 76*(Suppl 2), S86–S90.

Ravassard, P., Kees, A., Willers, B., Ho, D., Aharoni, D. A., Cushman, J., ... Mehta, M. R. (2013). Multisensory control of hippocampal spatiotemporal selectivity. *Science*, *340*(6138), 1342–1346. doi:10.1126cience.1232655 PMID:23641063

Repetto, C., & Riva, G. (2011). From virtual reality to interreality in the treatment of anxiety disorders. *Neuropsychiatry*, *1*(1), 31–43. doi:10.2217/npy.11.5

Rice, V. J., Houston, F. S., & Schroeder, P. J. (2017, September). The Relationship between Mindful Awareness and Cognitive Performance among US Military Service Members and Veterans. *Proceedings of the Human Factors and Ergonomics Society Annual Meeting*, *61*(1), 843–847. doi:10.1177/1541931213601684

Riva, G., Raspelli, S., Algeri, D., Pallavicini, F., Gorini, A., Wiederhold, B. K., & Gaggioli, A. (2006). Interreality in practice: Bridging virtual and real worlds in the treatment of posttraumatic stress disorders. *Cyberpsychology, Behavior, and Social Networking*, *13*(1), 55–65. doi:10.1089/cyber.2009.0320 PMID:20528294

Rizzo, A., Cukor, J., Gerardi, M., Alley, S., Reist, C., Roy, M., ... Difede, J. (2015). Virtual reality exposure for PTSD due to military combat and terrorist attacks. *Journal of Contemporary Psychotherapy*, *45*(4), 255–264. doi:10.100710879-015-9306-3

Rizzo, A., Difede, J., Rothbaum, B. O., Reger, G., Spitalnick, J., Cukor, J., & Mclay, R. (2010). Development and early evaluation of the virtual Iraq/Afghanistan exposure therapy system for combat-related PTSD. *Annals of the New York Academy of Sciences*, *1208*(1), 114–125. doi:10.1111/j.1749-6632.2010.05755.x PMID:20955333

Rohani, D. A., & Puthusserypady, S. (2015). BCI inside a virtual reality classroom: A potential training tool for attention. *EPJ Nonlinear Biomedical Physiology*, *3*(1), 12. doi:10.1140/epjnbp40366-015-0027-z

Sahar, T., Shalev, A. Y., & Porges, S. W. (2001). Vagal modulation of responses to mental challenge in posttraumatic stress disorder. *Biological Psychiatry*, *49*(7), 637–643. doi:10.1016/S0006-3223(00)01045-3 PMID:11297721

Sapolsky, R. M. (2001). Depression, antidepressants, and the shrinking hippocampus. *Proceedings of the National Academy of Sciences of the United States of America*, *98*(22), 12320–12322. doi:10.1073/pnas.231475998 PMID:11675480

Schedlbauer, A. M., Copara, M. S., Watrous, A. J., & Ekstrom, A. D. (2014). Multiple interacting brain areas underlie successful spatiotemporal memory retrieval in humans. *Scientific Reports*, *4*(1), 6431. doi:10.1038rep06431 PMID:25234342

Scherer, K. R. (2005). What are emotions? And how can they be measured? *Social Sciences Information. Information Sur les Sciences Sociales*, *44*(4), 695–729. doi:10.1177/0539018405058216

Schindler, A., & Bartels, A. (2013). Parietal cortex codes for egocentric space beyond the field of view. *Current Biology, 23*(2), 177–182. doi:10.1016/j.cub.2012.11.060 PMID:23260468

Schlitz, M. (2015). *Death makes life possible: Revolutionary insights on living, dying, and the continuation of consciousness.* Boulder, CO: Sounds True.

Schlitz, M., Vieten, C., & Amorok, T. (2007). *Living deeply: The art and science of transformation in everyday life.* Berkeley, CA: New Harbinger.

Schott, G. D. (2015). Neuroaesthetics: Exploring beauty and the brain. *Brain, 138*(8), 2451–2454. doi:10.1093/brain/awv163

Shapiro, F. (2014). The role of eye movement desensitization and reprocessing (EMDR) therapy in medicine: Addressing the psychological and physical symptoms stemming from adverse life experiences. *The Permanente Journal, 18*(1), 71–77. doi:10.7812/TPP/13-098 PMID:24626074

Siegel, D. J. (2006). An interpersonal neurobiology approach to psychotherapy. *Psychiatric Annals, 36,* 248–256.

Siegel, D. J. (2012). *The developing mind: How relationships and the brain interact to shape who we are* (2nd ed.). New York, NY: Guilford Press.

Slater, M., & Usoh, M. (1994). Representation systems, perceptual position, and presence in immersive virtual environments. *Presence (Cambridge, Mass.), 2*(3), 221–233. doi:10.1162/pres.1993.2.3.221

Smolenski, D. J., Pruitt, L. D., Vuletic, S., Luxton, D. D., & Gahm, G. (2017). Unobserved heterogeneity in response to treatment for depression through videoconference. *Psychiatric Rehabilitation Journal, 40*(3), 303–308; Advance online publication. doi:10.1037/prj0000273 PMID:28604014

Sofroniew, N. J., Vlasov, Y. A., Hires, S. A., Freeman, J., & Svoboda, K. (2015). Neural coding in barrel cortex during whisker-guided locomotion. *eLife, 4,* e12559. doi:10.7554/eLife.12559 PMID:26701910

Solomon, S., Greenberg, J., & Pyszczynski, T. (1991). A terror management theory of social behavior: The psychological functions of self-esteem and cultural worldviews. *Advances in Experimental Social Psychology, 24,* 93–159. doi:10.1016/S0065-2601(08)60328-7

Solomon, S., Greenberg, J., & Pyszczynski, T. (2015). *The worm at the core: On the role of death in life (Kindle version).* New York, NY: Random House. Retrieved from www.Amazon.com

Steiner, R. (1995). Intuitive Thinking as a Spiritual Path: A Philosophy of Freedom (M. Lipson, Trans.). Hudson, NY: Anthroposophic Press.

Van Gordon, W., Shonin, E., Dunn, T. J., Sheffield, D., Garcia-Campayo, J., & Griffiths, M. D. (2018). Meditation-Induced Near-Death Experiences: A 3-Year Longitudinal Study. *Mindfulness, 9*(6), 1794–1806. doi:10.100712671-018-0922-3 PMID:30524512

Varela, F. (1995). The emergent self. In J. Brockman (Ed.), *The third culture: Beyond the scientific revolution* (p. 209). New York, NY: Touchstone.

Vieten, C., Amorok, T., & Schlitz, M. M. (2006). I to we: The role of consciousness transformation in compassion and altruism. *Zygon, 41*(4), 915–932. doi:10.1111/j.1467-9744.2006.00788.x

Villani, D., Preziosa, A., & Riva, G. (2006). Coping with stress using Virtual Reality: A new perspective. *Annual Review of Cybertherapy and Telemedicine, 4*, 25–32.

Walsh, R. (1979). Meditation research: An introduction and review. *Journal of Transpersonal Psychology, 11*(2).

Walsh, R., & Shapiro, S. L. (2006). The meeting of meditative disciplines and western psychology: A mutually enriching dialogue. *The American Psychologist, 61*(3), 227–239. doi:10.1037/0003-066X.61.3.227 PMID:16594839

Watson, J. B., & Rayner, R. (1920). Conditioned emotional reactions. *Journal of Experimental Psychology, 3*(1), 1–14. doi:10.1037/h0069608

Weyers-Lucci, D. (2016). *The impact of an 8 week daily exposure to a VR experience for anxiety and depression.* Unpublished study. Palo Alto, CA: Institute of Transpersonal Psychology at Sofia U.

Wiederhold, B. K., Jang, D. P., Gevirtz, R. G., Kim, S. I., Kim, I. Y., & Wiederhold, M. D. (2002). The treatment of fear of flying: A controlled study of imaginal and virtual reality graded exposure therapy. *IEEE Transactions on Information Technology in Biomedicine, 6*(3), 218–223. doi:10.1109/TITB.2002.802378 PMID:12381038

Wilber, K. (2006). *Integral spirituality: A startling new role for religion in the modern and postmodern world.* Boston, MA: Shambhala.

Wilhelm, F. H., & Roth, W. T. (2001). The somatic symptom paradox in DSM-IV anxiety disorders: Suggestions for a clinical focus in psychophysiology. *Biological Psychology, 57*(1-3), 105–140. doi:10.1016/S0301-0511(01)00091-6 PMID:11454436

Wilson, J. A., Onorati, K., Mishkind, M., Reger, M. A., & Gahm, G. A. (2008). Soldier attitudes about technology-based approaches to mental health care. *Cyberpsychology & Behavior, 11*(6), 767–769. doi:10.1089/cpb.2008.0071 PMID:18991533

World Health Organization (WHO). (2017). *World mental health atlas.* Geneva, Switzerland: WHO.

Yalom, I. (1980). *Existential psychotherapy (Kindle version).* New York, NY: Basic Books. Retrieved from www.amazon.com

Yalom, I. (2009b). *Staring at the sun: Overcoming the terror of death (Kindle version).* San Francisco, CA: Jossey Bass. Retrieved from www.amazon.com

Yalom, I. D. (2009). *The gift of therapy: An open letter to a new generation of therapists and their patients.* New York, NY: Harper Perennial.

Chapter 22
Immersive Experience:
Convergence, Storyworlds, and the Power for Social Impact

Kate M. McCallum
ⓘ https://orcid.org/0000-0002-6152-8891
Bridge Arts Media, LLC, USA & Vortex Immersion Media, USA

ABSTRACT

This chapter examines the evolution of trends in the arts, storytelling, and immersive media, along with the emerging awareness, expansion, and deliberate application of social impact entertainment (SIE). The author discusses how the ideas and concepts of transmedia, convergence, and storyworld-building have now expanded beyond academic theory into more organic commercial and artistic applications. The focus is on how this approach relates to extending intellectual properties and stories into immersive media platforms and beyond. Additionally, the author presents several case studies and examples of emerging arts and media formats to support what we might expect to experience in the near future.

INTRODUCTION

Immersive Media (IM) has become an umbrella term for content that extends beyond the boundaries of the traditional rectilinear screen format. The related term Immersive Experience (IE) is also being applied to live encounters that immerse audiences and participants in a more interactive, visually embodied experience. This chapter provides a variety of examples of the "immersive" arts and technologies emerging in entertainment, arts, media, and cultural landscapes.

The chapter also examines the concept of storyworld-building, transmedia and convergence strategy, and on how immersive media and arts can be used to extend intellectual properties (IP), or create original IP, via these emerging platforms. It also reviews the use and potential use of immersive media for social impact.

DOI: 10.4018/978-1-7998-2433-6.ch022

Much like the birth of early traditional cinema, immersive arts and media offer a paradigm shift on how viewers consume visual and audio storytelling and experiences. And—just as there were content concerns in the days of early cinema that resulted in censoring, the birth of the Motion Picture Association of America (MPAA) ratings systems, and the National Association of Broadcasters (NAB) Television Code of Content, so too the power of these formats raises a new level of concern about their impact. As a response, the popularity and adaptive use of Social Impact Entertainment (SIE) is increasing in the entertainment industry, a critical step for the future of immersive media. Additionally, this chapter includes references to organizations supporting the education and application of SIE for content creators, as well as simple guidelines on how to incorporate SIE into the immersive space.

BACKGROUND

The author has spent the last 37 years as both an educator and a practitioner working in immersive media, as well as being involved with futurist organizations, professional trade organizations, new media companies, and emerging technologies. Her experience provides on-the-ground insights about trends in the media and arts space. As new media technologies emerge and are implemented by the creative and business communities, new languages and applications are borne out and discovered. This chapter explores how these emerging platforms can be utilized for social impact as well as entertainment and education.

THE EVOLUTION OF IMMERSIVE MEDIA

In the 19th Century humanity implemented two powerful inventions that changed the course of human evolution—the gas engine and electricity. In less than 130 years, this new "Promethean Fire" accelerated our experience of life on Earth and we now find ourselves catapulted into the start of a new evolutionary era. For those who study mythic aspects of astrology this era marks the romantic narrative notion of the end of the Piscean Age and the beginning of the Aquarian Age. We've gone from a period in humanity which was dominated by a devotional approach, and a hierarchy, power-based society, to a more unified network of individualized power with access to technologies and vast information once accessible to only a few. Over the last decades, we have come to realize the tremendous power of global media and imagery to advance our consciousness and understanding of the human condition, life on Earth, and our place in the universe.

On December 24, 1968, during the Apollo 8 mission, astronaut William Anders photographed Earth and a portion of the Moon's surface from lunar orbit (Figure 1). That photo—*Earthrise*—has become one of the most influential images of all time as it provided humanity with a truly unique perspective of our place in the universe, much like the invention of the telescope did circa 1608.

Figure 1. Earthrise
Source: NASA Image Credit: NASA, Apollo 8 Crew, Bill Anders; Processing and License: Jim Weigang

THE EVOLUTION OF MEDIA

As we moved into the 20th Century, electricity gave rise to technological inventions that expanded our ability to communicate and experience life from around the world, and from the universe, starting with media like radio and the phonograph, and moving into cinema, television, electronic musical instruments, video games, theme parks, and even mobile phones. As well, the invention of the personal computer and the World Wide Web afforded humanity an ever-widening array of entertainment and communication choices.

One hundred years ago, cinema was in its early stages and inventors and creators were moving distribution of these films from the Nickelodeon to vaudeville, to small movie theaters, then—on to the grand movie palaces. Filmmakers and studios were being cultivated and formed, and the public was becoming aware of the power of this new medium. The public was also concerned about the ever-growing liberal morality in Hollywood and by association, the movies themselves. Cities and states began creating localized censorship boards. These trends caused the heads of the movie studios to grow concerned about federal regulations becoming eminent, so in 1922 a group of the business leaders created the Motion Pictures Producers and Distributors Association as an industry trade and lobby organization, which eventually became the Motion Picture Association of America (MPAA) in 1945. (Encyclopedia Britannica, 2019) The association was headed by Will H. Hays, a Republican lawyer who had previously served as United

States Postmaster General. Hays worked in tandem with the motion picture industry to help alleviate any attempt to institute federal censorship over the movies.

The 21st Century has brought us even more advanced communication tools. On January 9, 2007, Steve Jobs and Apple announced the release of the first iPhone (Silver, 2018). Who could have imagined the impact of this device and the immersive experiences it has made possible? We now have the power to connect with billions of people around the world, research the most obscure knowledge, access directions, watch and read media, create media, make music, amuse ourselves with games, access millions of apps and so much more, and we can be anywhere at any time! So too, the advancements in Extended Reality (XR), Virtual Reality (VR), Augmented Reality (AR), Mixed Reality (MR), and the commercialization and liberation of fulldome projection spaces from science centers into the mainstream have all provided new and exciting immersive possibilities.

ISSUES AND CHALLENGES

Over these past two centuries, our world has seen tremendous advancements and changes: civil rights, environmental consciousness, women's rights, gay rights, global consciousness, and more. We have also been experiencing the rise of terrorism, greed, fundamentalism, racism, partisan politics, random violence, environmental concerns, homelessness, suicides and mental health issues.

Storytelling and media have accelerated our awareness of these issues, and in many cases have helped provide solutions to these challenges, whether through fictional entertainment or non-fictional documentaries and news. The media has been the message and we've advanced human consciousness through these tools, whether we've done this consciously or not.

BACKGROUND AS STORYTELLER

As an artist, storyteller and media maker fresh out of college and new to Hollywood, I aspired to become a creative producer, and had the great fortune to work in two major media studios (NBCUniversal Studios and Paramount Studios) from 1985 to 2005, in the areas of television and feature film development and production. During this period the industry experienced technological advances that caused major changes in many of its business aspects—from production to distribution. From cinema cameras to video cameras and the advent of digital media, from four major broadcasters (ABC, CBS, NBC and FOX) to a plethora of cable outlets (starting with WTCG–Turner Communications Group in 1976, HBO, Showtime, etc.) to the activation of YouTube, Facebook, and the web via streaming services such as Netflix, Amazon, Hulu and Disney+, the technological platforms through which stories can be created, distributed and shared has continued to expand to where we are today.

During this time in the studios, working with writers and storytellers on major primetime dramatic television series such as *Equalizer* (1985-89), *Miami Vice* (1984-1990), *Law and Order* (1990-2010), and on half-hour sitcoms like *Charles In Charge* (1984-1990) and *Together We Stand* (1986-1987), I also authored screenplays, TV series concept bibles, and later became a creative development executive. It was during this phase of my career that I truly learned the concept and the power of "intellectual property" (IP), the legal term for a story, or character or a storyworld created by the author or creator of original source material. The first movie that I sold as a producer became a TV movie for NBC. It was based on a true story found in the *Pasadena Star News*, a local newspaper, in article titled *Lessons in Love*. At the time (mid-90s), many movies for TV were based on true stories, and as an aspiring producer I'd been given valuable advice by a writer/producer mentor to option material, which is to pay for exclusive rights to produce a work for a specific period of time. From his perspective, this was the most powerful way for a neophyte producer to get a movie or TV project bought and produced. He was right. I optioned the story from the family, and my agent at International Creative Management (ICM) put me together with an independent production company that specialized in TV movies that she represented. They, in turn, optioned my story, and I was brought on as a producer. Together, we pitched the story to NBC, sold it right away, and two years later it aired on NBC as a TV movie called *What Kind of Mother Are You?* (1996) starring Mel Harris of *Thirtysomething* and Nicole Thom who played her daughter.

As I spent more time in the studios and became familiar with their development slate (and legal contracts), what I began to realize is that the majority of feature films, and much of television is made from other existing source materials—novels primarily, and as of late—comic books, which have become a most popular source IP (consider Marvel and DC Comics for example). Ideas can come from other IP such as toys (*Transformers*), dolls (*Bratz* and *America Girl* dolls), games (*League of Legends, Warcraft, Angry Birds*), operas and musicals (*Phantom of the Opera, Carmen*), plays (*Death of a Salesman, A Streetcar Named Desire, Driving Miss Daisy*), theme park rides (*Pirates of the Caribbean, Haunted Mansion*), children's books and art books (*Dark Crystal, Shrek, The Grinch*), magazine and newspaper articles, and of course, remakes of old films or TV shows.

My personal favorite development projects during this time included optioning all the covers that artist Norman Rockwell painted for the *Saturday Evening Post* and developing a TV series concept from these images with partner Alan Fine, and executive producer and writer, Carmen Culver (of the 1983 *Thorn Birds* TV miniseries fame). I felt that the wonderful characters in these images cried out for their stories to be shared. Though we didn't sell the series, the project got me my first agent. Another favorite venture was researching a concept to develop a series from the comics found in *Bazooka Bubblegum*. I loved these ideas as they spanned generations.

INTRODUCING TRANSMEDIA AND CONVERGENCE

In the late 1990s, I met and worked with entertainment professional Robert Gould, an illustrator/artist colleague who was brought in as a development executive at Sony to work on a development deal at the studio. Afterwards Gould left the studio to start a company called Imaginosis, which specialized in "transmedia" development and production. Realizing the power of IP, it was his strategy to work with artists to develop projects and concepts in more accessible mediums, primarily illustrated art books, that could be optioned for film or television projects yet still stand alone as viable assets when published, thus sustaining the artists creating them. He created *The World of Froud*, my first introduction to the idea of "storyworlds." Illustrator/Artist Brian Froud, and Wendy Froud (known for her work on *The Dark Crystal, Labyrinth, Good Fairies Bad Fairies*, and for modeling the Yoda character in *Star Wars*) were his top clients and he worked with them to develop books, dolls, music, wine labels, divination cards, and a website devoted to their brand—truly trans many media! During the time I was associated with Robert, he also launched the *Faeriewolds Festival* inspired by the art of the Frouds and then went on to launch *FaerieCon*, both very popular festivals in the realm of fantasy. Through this association, I understood even more about the power of IP to move across media platforms and experiential transoms.

The concept of transmedia started to become more refined as a narrative approach, especially in the academic domain. Professor Henry Jenkins sought to clarify the concept of transmedia storytelling in his book *Convergence Culture: Where Old and New Media Collide* (2008). The takeaway from his work and other theories about transmedia is that a creator extends a larger storyworld universe into enhanced aspects with multiple characters and/or plot lines that are unique to specific platforms, thus resulting in unique experiences for those audiences of those platforms. Thus, the core origin storyworld can be sustained and expanded to a greater degree and for an extended period of time. The evolution of the web accelerated the ability to "cross platforms" which resulted in advancements in the industry.

PGA Establishes the Transmedia Credit

This strategic approach and methodology became increasingly popular, and in April of 2010 the Producers Guild of America (PGA) made an official announcement that they had created a new "Transmedia Producer" credit to add to the Guild's Producers Code of Credits (PCOC).

The Guild's decision to expand the Code of Credits to recognize the Transmedia Producer underscores the changing media landscape and the critical role of the producer within new creative mediums," said PGA President Marshall Herskovitz." As technology evolves, it's no longer adequate to think of a project as simply a television show or a movie; we now understand that the audience will want to experience that content across several platforms—online, mobile, VOD, Blu-Ray, and now iPad—often with different or additional material. It's the producer who oversees the complex and creative process that allows that to happen. (PGA, 2010)

The Guild defines a "Transmedia Narrative" project or franchise as one that consists of three (or more) narrative storylines existing within the same fictional universe on any of the following platforms: Film, Television, Short Film, Broadband, Publishing, Comics, Animation, Mobile, Special Venues, DVD/Bluray/CD-ROM, Narrative Commercial and Marketing rollouts, and other technologies that may or may not currently exist. These narrative extensions are custom made and are NOT the same as repurposing material from one platform to be ported to another.

A Transmedia Producer credit is given to the person(s) responsible for a significant portion of a project's long-term planning, development, production, and/or maintenance of narrative continuity across multiple platforms, and creation of original storylines for new platforms. Transmedia producers also create and implement interactive endeavors to unite the audience of the property with the canonical narrative and this element should be considered as valid qualification for credit as long as they are related directly to the narrative presentation of a project.

The Concept of Transmedia in History

There is precedence for this type of approach that can also be found in history, such as Richard Wagner's concept of the *'Gesamtkunstwerk.'* Gesamtkunstwerk translates into 'a total work of art,' and the term was first introduced by the German writer and philosopher K.F.E. Trahndorff is an essay titled *Ästhetik oder Lehre von Weltanschauung und Kunst* in 1827 (Trahndorff, 1827).

In many of Wagner's theoretical writings, such as *Die Kunst und die Religion, (Art and Religion)* (1849), *Das Kunstwerk der Zukunft* (*The Artwork of the Future*, 1849) and *Oper und Drama* (1852), the concept of the '*Gesamtkunstwerk*'—the totality of the work of art—became the central focus, which Wagner made the basis for his compositions.

Wagner believed that, the Zersplitterung der Küste (the Split between the Arts) had happened during the times of Greek antiquity among music, word, and dance, which had been thought to originally exist in perfect harmony. Greek tragedy was believed to embody this harmony, but with the fall of the 'Athenian Polis,' the arts started to diverge. For Wagner (and this explains his youthful 'revolutionary' fervor during the revolutions of 1848) one should aspire to create a perfect society in which the perfect harmony of the work of art could again exist. (Wolfman, 2013)

Thus, the four operas that make up *The Ring Cycle* were designed musically with this approach, including the use of anvils as instruments. The premiere of his operatic masterpiece, *The Ring Cycle* was showcased in the Bayreuth Festspielhaus (Festival Theater), which was designed specifically for the presentation of *The Ring Cycle* operas.

A more recent example can be found in the creations of Walt Disney. Disney not only created and produced a rich body of iconic family content in the form of films and television, but he also went on to create Disneyland in 1955, a magical kingdom where all of his characters and storyworlds could come to life in a very different experiential way. The Disney Company pioneered this approach well before the digital age and it has allowed it to thrive over many decades.

The Franchise Licensing Versus Transmedia

The commercialization of feature films helped to popularize the "franchise," and a more traditional approach to the extension of storyworlds/films was done through licensing. One of the most successful examples of this is the *Star Wars* franchise. *Star Wars* actually holds a Guinness World Records title for the "Most successful film merchandising franchise." According to an article in Fortune magazine in 2015, the total value of the *Star Wars* empire was estimated at US $41.979 billion, one of the highest-grossing media franchises of all-time. Disney, the new owner of the *Star Wars* IP, expanded the world further by recently opening a new *Star Wars* world in their theme parks (Fortune, 2015).

Transmedia provides us with the ability to approach a more systematic, comprehensive and inclusive approach to including new media platforms and technologies in our creative development and design, rather than replacing existing media. It expands the opportunities for the audience to access new aspects of worlds and or information and has never been more relevant than now in learning how to incorporate new media.

Figure 2. The Harmony Channel.
Image courtesy of Ed Lantz

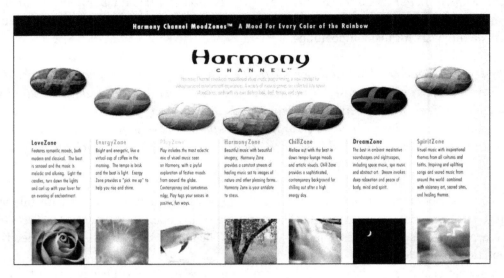

FORAYS INTO VISUAL MUSIC

After 20 years of working in traditional narrative storytelling in the studio system, I was hired as VP of Programming at Harmony Intermedia, Inc. to launch a Video on Demand (VoD) channel on Comcast called *The Harmony Channel*. *The Harmony Channel* featured hours of visual music content categorized into seven different mood zones: Energy Zone, Love Zone, Play Zone, Harmony Zone, Chill Zone, Dream Zone, and the Spirit Zone (Figure 2).

Unlike music videos, visual music focused more on art and music together versus featuring the artist or the band. Content such as *Koyaanisqatsi* (1983), *Chronos* (1985), or *Baraka* (1992) are good examples of longer form versions of this art form. In the role of VP of Programming, it was my responsibility to curate, view and program 100s of hours of visual music content submitted by artists around the world. I found this synesthetic art form combining visuals with music very compelling and especially appreciated the power it had to convey ideas, emotions, and experiences that transcend language to create a truly global art form.[1]

Note: For those interested in exploring more about this genre The Center for Visual Music is a non-profit organization and film archive dedicated to visual music and maintains historical documents, a content library, and reference materials should one be interested in researching this art form more deeply.

The Harmony Channel was founded by Ed Lantz, whose professional background includes working at science centers and planetariums, starting at a planetarium in Coco Beach Florida from 1991 to 1996, and then moving to Spitz, a planetarium manufacturer, from 1996 to 2004. While at Spitz, Lantz helped design and build planetariums in Alexandria, Egypt, Mexico City, Mexico and many other locations around the world.

Harmony Channel was one of the first VoD networks to launch on Comcast in 2006. The channel's first programming was MoodZones, visual musical experiences grouped according into seven programming zones as shown in Figure 2. Over 200 titles were licensed and broadcast to 9-14 million homes.

MoodZones is an example of "digital pharmacology" where selected nervous system states are intentionally evoked by programming designed for this purpose. While technically Harmony Channel was not an immersive technology, it demonstrates an attempt to use digital media to go beyond traditional cognitive and emotional storytelling, and to use a combination of music and visuals to evoke moods.

Lantz's ultimate goal was to launch the music channel as a resource for content creators. He also intended that the content could be repurposed and adapted for 360 fulldome venues. This aligned with his plans to fund and create a network of dome theaters to feature arts, entertainment and cultural content, going beyond the traditional scientific content focus for planetariums and science centers.

Harmony Channel launched and was on the air and accessible to over 11 million viewers, but unfortunately, the company was not funded in time with enough resources to advertise and market the channel. When people discovered it, they responded very positively to the programming and concept, but it wasn't getting strong enough viewership, so Comcast took it off the air.

THE OPERA

After Harmony Channel, I was offered a position at Los Angeles Opera and worked with the COO and Artistic Director, Maestro Placido Domingo. During the two and a half years I worked there we developed and produced an operatic version (story extension) of the feature film, *The Fly* (2008) with director David Cronnenberg, and music by composer Hans Zimmer. *Il Postino* (2010), another adaptation of the Oscar Award-winning feature film by the same name, was also in development at Los Angeles Opera, and on the slate was Richard Wagner's epic *The Ring Cycle* (2010), a $35M plus investment by the patrons of Los Angeles Opera to launch Los Angeles Opera's very first *Ring*. This is another fine example of the fluidity and value of IP to cross into other media and arts platforms.

THE FULLDOME CINETHEATER

The shift that has occurred in immersive media technologies can be considered as profound as the birth of cinema itself. From watching live theater and opera on a proscenium stage to viewing imagery on a screen—first peering into inventor Thomas Edison's Kinetoscope then into the Nickelodeon—cinema imagery was incorporated into vaudeville shows, and evolved its own cinematic language enable by wide distribution through dedicated screens and theaters. Early movie theaters grew to the magnificent movie palaces, multi-screen movie complexes, Cinerama theaters, then to the giant screen cinema such as IMAX, with new storytelling methods evolving in tandem. Immersive projected imagery and content were projected onto the fulldome planetarium theaters in the 1980s. In 1983, Evans & Sutherland installed the first planetarium projector displaying computer graphics (Handsen Planetarium, Salt Lake City, Utah) featuring the Digistar I projector and using a vector graphics system to display starfields as well as line art (E&S, 2018).

The newest generation of planetariums offer fully digital projection systems using the latest fulldome video technology. This gives the operator great flexibility in showing not only the modern night sky as visible from Earth, but any other image they wish (including the night sky as visible from points far distant in space and time). This technology allows creators to experiment with a new form of digital storytelling in the round: a 360/180 storyworld. To date, over 450 fulldome titles exist in the planetarium

Figure 3. The Vortex Dome at Los Angeles Center Studios installed 2010
Source: Kate McCallum

space. Some of these titles have been created from existing popular IP created from TV of feature films such as *Zulu Patrol: Down to Earth* (2010), or *One World, One Sky: Big Bird's Adventure* (2008) from the popular television series *Sesame Street*. And—fulldome festivals are growing in popularity around the world as detailed by contributing author and producer, Kelly Francis and Mickey Renman, the founder and producer of the Jena, Germany fulldome festival which takes place in the world's first planetarium (built 1922) located in Jena and soon to celebrate its 100-year anniversary.

Following the Harmony Channel, in 2008, scientist, inventor and producer, Ed Lantz founded Vortex Immersion Media. A thought leader and visionary in the planetarium field, Lantz's original vision was to bring the immersive power of the planetarium into arts, entertainment and mainstream culture. In 2010, Vortex invested in The Vortex Dome, a 50-foot dome theater installed on the roof of a building at a working production studio lot at Los Angeles Center Studios located in downtown Los Angeles (Figure 3). With an actual dome to showcase and demo to potential clients, the company's business took off. Individuals could experience the power of the immersive format on site, versus PowerPoint presentations, brochures, or on websites. Soon Vortex was being hired to install portable domes on location almost exclusively for marketing purposes, with clients and venues such as X-box at the Super Bowl, Adult Swim and NBC Universal at ComicCon, Pepsi at Times Square, Nike at Hollywood and Vine, Nike in Malaysia, EMC at Las Vegas, and many more. People loved the immersive experience that the domes provided.

Figure 4. "The Blue Apple," a 360 immersive ballet premieres in The Vortex Dome, Art by Audri Phillips
Source: Image Credit: Kate McCallum

Meanwhile, artists and creators were very interested in exploring the exciting new creative platform of the dome format so our team at Vortex worked to create The Vortex AIR: Artist-In-Residence program for The Vortex Dome theater that could be accessed through sponsorship from Vortex Immersion Media. Artists could also partner under a fiscal sponsor support program with the 501c3 non-profit founded in 2004, called the c3: Center for Conscious Creativity.[2] The c3 is an all-volunteer arts organization dedicated to supporting artists and creators to explore the power of storytelling, arts and media to create a better future and thus a better world. The c3 is also partnered with The Millennium Project, a global futurist think-tank made up of futurists and futures-oriented professionals focused on the solutions to 15 global challenges and each year they generate a report called *State of the Future*. The c3 serves as the Arts and Media Node of The Millennium Project and has collaborated with the organization to create an annual event called *State of the Arts*, an event that features creators, educators, and other professionals involved in new media tech and SIE. Topics have included *The Transformational Power of Music, AI for Good, VR for Good, Mindfulness in Virtual Worlds*, and a *FutureVision Award* has been given out annually that honors work being done in new media that has special impact.

IMMERSION IN MUSIC AND ART

Shortly after the stint at The Harmony Channel, I was inspired by the emotional power of visual music content to launch a unique art+music label I created called *The Art of Sound*. The goal was to pair up a musical artist with a visual artist, create a beautiful album package and also have them perform together live. The Vortex Dome was a perfect venue for this vision, and we hosted our first immersive art+music concert in the dome in 2011 featuring the visual art of animator and VFX artist, Audri Phillips and the music of Winter Lazarus, a collaborator in the label. The concert, *Migrations*, was sold out and was the first of many to come. Audri went on to create a 360 ballet with choreographer Stephen Wenta called

Figure 5. Eye Q Production's Jenni Ogden, Jeff Klein, and Maria Torres's "Pasion" a 360 immersive musical showcase in The Vortex Dome.
Source: Kate McCallum

Blue Apple featured in (Figure 4). *Blue Apple* touched upon the theme and issues of mental health. *Blue Apple* was also the first project that catalyzed the actualization of the dome space as a true CineTheater™, blending cinema with live performances in which the audience could be immersed in the storyworld.

Another mixed media musical project developed in The Vortex Dome was *Bollydoll*, created by visual artist, musician, and Harvard MBA grad, Amrita Sen and Anthony Marinelli who workshopped and presented it to the public. *Bollydoll*, is a 360 Bollywood style musical using Amrita's original art as the background.

These were the first of many immersive experiments to launch under the Vortex Artist-in-Residence (AIR) program. Other experiences have included experiences such as Aaron Axelrod's *Melting Rainbows*, a live performance piece with Aaron painting on a Lucite half-dome with a Canon 5D camera and a fisheye lens mounted under it. *Pasion* (2015), a mixed-media 360 dome musical about the origin of Latino history and culture was created by Eye Q Productions and producers Jenni Ogden and Jeff Klein, with choreographer Maria Torres (Figure 5). *Robot Prayers* (2016), is a multi-media interactive music and arts piece addressing AI and ethics by Audri Phillips (Figure 6). *The Everything Nothing* (2018) presented an immersive live performance concert and dome show by IamEve (Tiff Randol) (Figure 7). Other works include *Refractor Piano* (2017) with pianist and composer Peter Manning Robinson (Figure 8), and *Ceremony* (2014) and *Mesmerica* (2018) (Figure 9) both created by musician James Hood.

Figure 6. "Robot Prayers," a mixed-media XR 'technopera' developed in The Vortex Dome by artist, Audri Phillips and Winter Lazarus, composer
Source: Kate McCallum

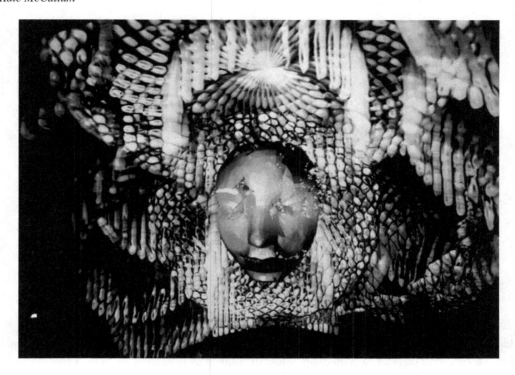

Figure 7. "The Everything Nothing" immersive mixed-media showcase by musician, composer and creator, IamEve (Tiff Randol) in The Vortex Dome
Source: Kate McCallum

Figure 8. Pianist and composer, Peter Manning Robinson performed "Refractor Piano" in The Vortex Dome with visuals by animation artist, Hana Kim and director, Klaus Hoch. The concert was captured and live streamed in 360 video
Source: Kate McCallum

CASE STUDY: MESMERICA

Mesmerica is actually a unique case study in the emerging business of immersive media. I served as the producer on this project created by James Hood and Moodswings, LLC in partnership with Vortex Immersion Media. The project, directed by Michael Saul, was designed as both a live music and 360 visual art performance piece and as a stand-alone one-hour fulldome film. As we developed the narrative concept, which we call "poetic narrative" we looked at theories found in the science of happiness and positive psychology as well as at relevant neuro-scientific data and included elements from this research into the film. The film thus became a poetic journey through these positive emotional states.

Because there were no commercial dome theaters for exhibiting fulldome productions or distributed fulldome films when *Mesmerica* premiered in July 2018, the piece opened at The Fleet Science Center planetarium in San Diego. James Hood performed live on a variety of hang drums with the film projected around him on the fulldome screen. The show sold out to two audiences and was very well received. We then took the show to the Chabot Science Center's planetarium in Oakland, California in September 2018, and experienced similar success. The only challenge to the production was that it was expensive to tour the crew, and to set up sound and lights to enhance the show. We decided to try booking just the film without James performing and did so in Oakland for another month. Afterwards we took the show back to San Diego in October 2018. The film experience again sold out and has been playing every weekend since then (over a year now) to robust audiences and will continue to play as long as it is profitable. After the success of San Diego and Oakland, we expanded our distribution efforts, and at the time of this writing the show has played in over 23 venues around the country and in Canada. *Mesmerica* will continue to open more venues and have had great success with showcasing the show in this manner.

Until there are more commercial dome venues built, either science center planetariums or portable pop-up domes are the main options for showcasing arts and entertainment dome content. That should change in the next few years.

Immersive Experience

Figure 9. Mesmerica poster (2019)
Source: Moodswings, LLC

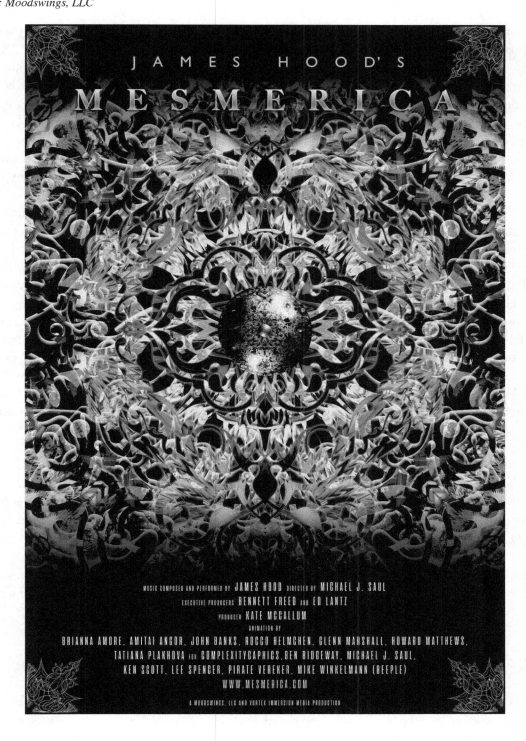

COMMERCIALIZED DOME THEATERS

As evidence of the move to commercial domes for entertainment, Madison Square Garden (MSG) in New York is funding and building a huge, arena-sized dome theater in Las Vegas called the MSG Sphere, which is set to open in 2021. This theater will seat 17,500 and will utilize LED screen technology.[3]

Another permanent dome theater called The Universal Sphere was recently constructed at the Comcast headquarters in Philadelphia, Pennsylvania. On the Comcast website Steven Spielberg is listed as executive director of the short film being shown there. Talent from DreamWorks Animation, Universal Creative, Universal Parks & Resorts and Comcast Labs also worked on production. The dome was designed and built by Mychael and Jeff Danna, who won Academy Awards for work on the feature film, *Life of Pi*, and composed the original score. Narration is by Peter Coyote, who some might remember for his role as the scientist/government agent in the 1982 Spielberg film, *E.T.*

The first permanent dome theater dedicated to arts and culture is located at in Montreal at the Society for Arts and Technology (SAT). SAT was founded in 1996, and is a non-profit organization recognized internationally for developing immersive technologies. As stated on its website SAT's double mission as a center for the arts and research, SAT was created to support a new generation of creators/researchers in the digital age (Science, Arts and Technology [SAT], n.d.). SAT is a gathering place for diverse intelligence, curiosity, knowledge and talent, the Society for Arts and Technology is a live creative laboratory whose unconventional experiences bring together the tangible and the unexpected. SAT also built and installed the Satosphère, a permanent dome theater, dedicated to the development and presentation of 360° immersive experiences. The dome venue serves to expand upon the studio creations and the educational workshops also hosted by SAT.

The AlloSphere, is located at the University of Santa Barbara, California and is a fulldome/spherical space. It was created by visionary music composer, researcher and educator, Professor JoAnn Kucher-Morin who serves as the Director of the AlloSphere:

The AlloSphere is a one-of-a-kind immersive instrument that is the culmination of 30 years of Professor JoAnn Kuchera-Morin's creativity and research efforts in media systems and studio design. It is differentiated from conventional virtual reality environments by its seamless surround-view capabilities, ability to accommodate 30 or more people simultaneously in a shared virtual world with no loss of self, and its focus on multiple sensory modalities and interaction. (AlloSphere, n.d.)

The AlloSphere is a 5-meter radius sphere, fitted with multiple projectors, and a walkway bridge that provides viewers the ability to observe the immersive space all around them and it is used primarily for scientific simulations, data visualization and also artistic content.

VR HEADSETS AS A CATALYST FOR IMMERSIVE MEDIA

VR headsets that provide immersion can be considered a compliment to the fulldome immersive space and the introduction of today's relatively low-cost devices has served to escalate the creation of immersive narrative worlds. When Oculus VR was purchased by Facebook in March 2014 for $2.3 billion in cash and stock the VR industry started to be taken seriously (Forbes, 2014). Big media companies, as well as manufacturers such as camera makers, jumped in and began developing headsets, 360 camera solutions, and the software and equipment needed to capture and showcase immersive experiences. The creative community also took up the challenge, and dozens, if not hundreds of VR production companies sprung up. The VRLA event evolved from a small meet-up group to one of the world's largest conference showcasing the latest in VR. Several trade conferences and associations have been formed to service the burgeoning industry such as Virtual Reality Augmented Reality Association (VRARA), the XR Association (XRA), Immersive Media Entertainment Research, Science and Arts (IMERSA), and EuroVR to name a few.

While the headsets for home consumer use haven't been as commercially successful as the industry had hoped, Location-Based Virtual Reality (LBVR), which uses the gear in a destination setting, is taking off. Companies like Dreamscape VR, The Void, and Hologate are thriving and attracting investors and consumers (Virtual Reality Pulse, 2019).

The Producers Guild of America New Media Council has produced several educational events featuring visits to these venues under the moniker of PGA *Special Venue Deep Dive*. Members get to experience the content the venue provides and then a company representative presents and speaks about the business and creation of their tech and content. These experiences are typically coordinated to serve groups of four to six attendees and participants "step into" an avatar character and take a 360 virtual journey into the immersive worlds. This is not passive entertainment where a viewer is just wearing a headset and watching content unfold. In the case of The Void and Dreamscape experiences, the viewer becomes part of the story narrative, suits up and then is in the storyworld as a character avatar that moves and interacts with others and the environment in real time. Personally, I found the experiences of these VR venues very profound and visceral, and one can understand the power and potential of this medium when produced well. Destination-based LBVR has tremendous potential for entertainment, training, and educational experiences.

THE CHALLENGES OF MODERN CINEMA-GOING

Movie theaters are faced with increasing competition and have been working to find ways to attract audiences to the theaters for unique experiences they can't get at home. This has resulted in experiments with new novel format offerings such as Barco's multiscreen Escape format, CJ's ScreenX out of Korea, and also CJ's 4DX theaters with movable seats, smells, and water effects. How long lived these venues will be is a question, as they tend to be either too expensive or not compelling enough to bear repeat visits. And the size of the audience for these experiences may be small outside of large cities. The Barco Escape system even after inking numerous content deals and installing the technology in 23 theaters since its 2015 launch, was closed down in February 2018 (Dager, 2018).

The Regal Los Angeles Live Cinema, which also houses the Barco Innovation Center, recently announced that it would be installing ICE (Immersive Cinema Experience) in partnership with a company called CGR based in France. According to an article in the Hollywood Reporter, the initiative has been successful, and ICE Immersive accounted for 75% of CGR's box office revenue in 2018. Thirty-two of CGR's 680 auditoriums are now ICE theaters (Giardina, 2019).

D-BOX is another technology that has been introduced into movie theaters and was first installed at Hollywood's iconic TCL Chinese Theatre in 2009 and premiered the experience with Justin Lin's feature film *Fast & Furious* (Coates, 2009). D-BOX redefines and creates hyper-realistic, immersive entertainment experiences by moving the audience members' bodies via a motion device like those used in training simulators. Hundreds of D-Box systems have been installed globally as of 2019. With the continued growth and expansion of the D-BOX systems into theaters, one can assume that the D-BOX motion technology has been received successfully by audiences, resulting in the fact that moviegoers are willing to pay for a premium ticket in order to experience this new, innovative way to further "immerse" themselves in the movies.

It will be of great interest to see how Location-Based Entertainment (LBE), novel theater experiences, fulldome spaces and XR populate and continue to expand in the near future. How we consume stories and experiences immersively has advanced greatly. Now the venues and business models need to be created to support and profit from the content creation and venue investments.

ADDITIONAL TRENDS IN LBE AND SPATIAL IMMERSIVE EXPERIENCES

Location-based entertainment (LBE) and the term *immersive* have now crossed over into other types of experiences that may or may not include immersive media technologies. A selection of the most high-profile trends in this space from the arts, entertainment, societal and cultural landscapes are presented next as indicators of the potential and possibilities for all these media to learn from each other. Many of these experiences are based on actual physical locations rather than virtual or cinematic, and therefore are not confined to technology platforms. Starting with new forms of immersive entertainment and ending with meaningful human experiences to ease pain and suffering, the possibilities are vast and varied.

Immersive Live Theater

- **Sleep No More:** Many trends occurring in the immersive, experiential space have correlates in immersive theater space. Such projects as Punchdrunk's immersive interpretation of Macbeth called Sleep No More (March 7, 2011) has been showing since 2011 in a building in Chelsea in New York designed to look like a 1930s hotel, The McKittrick (McKittrick Hotel, n.d.).
- **Tamara:** An early predecessor to this was a theater piece called Tamara, a popular immersive theater experience presented in the American Legion Hall in Los Angeles in1985 (Lasley, P. & Harriman, E., 1985).
- **Secret Cinema:** Another immersive theater company is Secret Cinema, which was launched in London, England in 2007 by Fabien Riggall. This group started by hosting enhanced "film screenings" in warehouses, adding in thematic physical elements from the films and encouraging audiences to dress according to the film's motifs. Secret Cinema creates 360-degree participatory "Secret Worlds" blurring the boundaries between performer and audience, where the set and reality are constantly shifting. They fuse film, music, art, theatre, and dance to create unique spaces for social encounters, adventures and discoveries where films come to life (Secret Cinema, n.d.).
- **Little Cinema:** Similarly, Little Cinema out of Brooklyn, New York was founded by Jay Rinsky who collaborates with a collective of artists, musicians, dancers and circus performers to reimagine a film. A collective of artists screens a film and then enhance it by enacting experiences and aspects of the film live in front of the screen. For example, during an immersive screening of the 1996 biographical drama Basquiat by director, Julian Schnabel (which features David Bowie as Andy Warhol), actors dressed like Warhol and Marilyn Monroe swung from a trapeze. Artists stood at easels on the sides of the stage and painted along with the film (Little Cinema, 2017).

Immersive Amusement Arcades

- ***Two Bit Circus***: Two Bit Circus describes themselves the "World's 1st Micro-Amusement Park." It was founded by Brent Bushnell, the son of Nolan Bushnell who created Atari and the Chuck E Cheese chain of entertainment restaurants, and Eric Gradman, a highly-educated circus performer and businessman. The duo started the STEAM Carnival, a high-tech electronic learning festival that popped up in LA in 2014 and San Francisco in 2016. In an article written for *Forbes* magazine Charlie Fink describes Two Bit Circus as a multi-faceted celebration of the new wave of out-of-home entertainment: custom escape rooms called Story Rooms, VR Cabanas (private rooms), VRcades, reimagined arcade games, free roam VR, food, drink and live interactive game shows (Fink, 2018; Two Bit Circus, 2016).

Immersive Themed Attractions

- **Gepetto:** Gepetto is an award-winning technology that brings animated interactive characters to life. It was created by Los Angeles-based Super 78 founders, Dina Benadon and Brent Young, and has been utilized in theme park installations around the world. Gepetto allows an operator to voice an animated character and also manipulate its movements and responses in real time so that it can engage with an audience live. It is being utilized in such attractions as the *Shrek* 4D Show experience at Universal Studios, Singapore, and most recently, it's incorporated into the 20,000 Leagues Under the Sea Interactive Adventure at Moody Gardens in Galveston, Texas (Super 78, n.d.).

Immersive Arts Installations

- **teamLab:** teamLab (sic.) out of Tokyo was founded in 2001 as an art collective, interdisciplinary group of ultra-technologists whose collaborative practice seeks to navigate the confluence of art, science, technology, design and the natural world. Various specialists such as artists, programmers, engineers, CG animators, mathematicians and architects form teamLab. teamLab has done extraordinary installations and is expanding their presence internationally (teamLab, n.d.).
- **Meow Wolf:** Meow Wolf was formed in February 2008 as an artist collective by a number of local residents and creative hoping to bring alternative art and music venues to the city of Santa Fe. They initially leased commercial spaces to hold gallery shows and underground music events. However, in January 2015, author George R. R. Martin pledged $2.7 million to renovate and lease a vacant bowling alley to create a permanent facility for Meow Wolf. This was supplemented by additional funding, including $50,000 from the city of Santa Fe and $100,000 from a crowd-funding campaign. The Meow Wolf Art Complex opened March 17, 2016 in Santa Fe, New Mexico (Meow Wolf, n.d.). The building is also home to the group's first permanent installation, House of Eternal Return, which received a 2017 Themed Entertainment Association (THEA) Award for Outstanding Achievement – Connected Immersion on a Limited Budget (THEA, 2019). As described on their website, as a company, Meow Wolf focuses on sharing abilities and processes amongst their artists to create elaborate maximalist art installations with a focus on interactivity, narrative and immersive art (Meow Wolf, n.d.).

Figure 10. Vortex Immersion Media, Inc. installation, Toronto Canada
Source: Ed Lantz

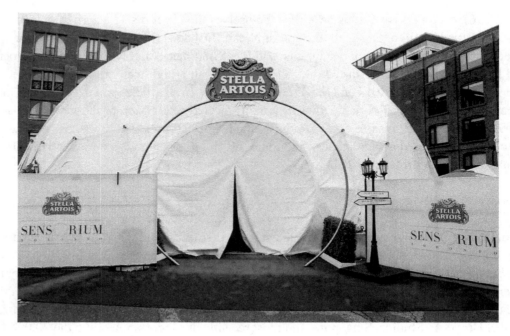

- **Atelier Des Lumieres:** The digitals arts museum, Atelier Des Lumieres, located in Paris, France is a fully immersive venue space that projects art and imagery on the floors and walls of a converted foundry (using 130 Barco projectors). It features the works of well-known artists such as Klimt or Van Gough projected on the walls and floors along with musical accompaniment that the visitor can experience as they walk through the venue. There isn't a cohesive story narrative; it presents more of a spectacular visual and musical environment that can be experienced for as long or as little as one chooses to stay in the space. Viewers sit on the ground and or walk through different sections of the venue, including an upper area where an exhibit offers information and biographies of the artists in involved (Atelier Lumieres, n.d.).

Immersive Dining Experiences

Immersive dining is increasingly becoming an actual category of immersive experiences. The diner is immersed in projected worlds and often interacts with the food and dining experience in unique ways.

- **Sensorium Dome:** In September 2015, Vortex Immersion Media was hired by client Stella Artois to create the Sensorium Dome (Figure 10) to host an immersive dining experience during the Toronto Film Festival in Canada (Figure 11). Tickets for this five-course meal, which included beer pairings, cost a hefty $125. In spite of this price tag, all seatings sold out. Marketing Mag described the brand activation as "part dinner series, part immersive theatre," and Stella brought in Michelin-starred chef Richie Farina, Toronto-based designer Jamie Webster and Canadian sound engineer Nyles Miszczyk—to bring their elevated dinner to life (Marketing Mag, 2015).

Figure 11. Interior Sensorium Dome Dining Experience
Source: Ed Lantz

- **Ultraviolet:** Other immersive dining experiences with a history of success include chef Paul Pairet's Ultraviolet restaurant out of Shanghai, China. Founded in 2012, Ultraviolet is the first experimental dining space of its kind. Guests are seated at a table for 10 in a fully immersive space that is projected upon during a 20 course meal (Ultraviolet, n.d.).
- **MoonFlower Sagaya Ginza:** MoonFlower Sgaya Ginza is a dining space born from a collaboration of Sagaya Ginza, a restaurant that specializes in seasonal dishes and the high quality brand of Wagyu beef "Saga Beef," and the art collective teamLab mentioned earlier. MoonFlower is an eight-seat restaurant, featuring a permanent digital art installation by teamLab, based on the theme of "Worlds Unleashed and then Connected." Similar to Ultraviolet, guests are seated in a fully immersive space while dining (Moonflower, n.d.).
- **Sublimotion by Paco Roncero:** Touted as "the world's most expensive restaurant" (Strause, 2015), Sublimotion by Paco Roncero features a 15 course, multi-sensory experience that includes unique molecular gastronomy and an innovative projected space that seats a group of 12 diners who experience "The Gastronomic Performance" of the meal along with fully immersive artistic scenes (Sublimotion Ibiza, n.d.).

These examples and the many you've read about in this book, are indicative of the rising awareness and popularity of immersive media and experiences. These are powerful experiences, powerful tools and new ways of entertaining, engaging, experiencing and educating that have deep impact. One of the considerations when designing transmedia and content strategy is to consider how Social Impact can be woven into these storyworlds and experiences.

CREATING IMPACT THROUGH MEDIA

It is not enough to simply create entertainment with immersive media, but to also recognize its use as a powerful communications tool. According to *Deepening Engagement for Lasting Impact*, a study commissioned by the Bill & Melinda Gates Foundation and the John S. and James L. Knight Foundation

All communications efforts are built by engaging individual people. If you want to create change at the group or systems level, it's important to recognize the difference between getting individuals who see your media to behave in a certain way, and having those behaviors integrated as norms, policies or shared practices. (Bill & Melinda Gates Foundation, 2013)

This philosophy is nowhere more evident than in efforts to recognize and promote Social Impact Entertainment, or SIE.

SOCIAL IMPACT ENTERTAINMENT

From 2013-2019, I was honored to sit on the Board of the Producers Guild of America's New Media Council (PGA), and I was also voted to serve on the PGA National board for three years. As a member of this council, it was one of our responsibilities to educate and inform members of trends in storytelling and new media technologies emerging in the entertainment landscape. I produced and or collaborated on presenting several educational workshops related to new media while in this role including a *Transmedia Storytelling and Strategy Design Workshop* for both the PGA and the TV Academy. Additionally, in 2018 a group of us from the PGA collaborated with Kate Folb and USC's Hollywood, Health and Society under the Norman Lear Center and produced an event called *Producing Social Impact Entertainment*.

The History of Hollywood, Health and Society

Hollywood has a 25-year history of helping in several health initiatives. In 1994, the Centers for Disease Control (CDC) convened an expert panel to consider how it could work with the entertainment industry to better inform the public about the devastating virus HIV. For two days, entertainment, public health, academic and advocacy organizations came together to discuss how this collaboration could work, and produced a final report with recommendations. In 1997, the director's office of CDC created a pilot program to provide experts on health matters to Hollywood creatives. As this effort proved to be well utilized, the CDC awarded the USC Annenberg School's Norman Lear Center a five-year cooperative agreement grant to lead this project staring in 2001. Since then, this program, known as Hollywood, Health & Society (HH&S) has received funding from a range of federal agencies, partner organizations and private foundations. It provides entertainment professionals accurate and up-to-date information on health, safety and national security for narratives they are developing. With generous support from funders including the CDC, the Bill & Melinda Gates Foundation, the SCAN Foundation, N Square, the California Health Care Foundation, Open Society Foundations, the Chan Zuckerberg Initiative, John Pritzker Family Fund, LUNGevity, and the Substance Abuse and Mental Health Services Administration, HH&S recognizes the profound impact that entertainment has on audience knowledge and behavior. (Hollywood, Health & Society, n.d.)

Through this support, HH&S offers many resources such as briefings and consultations with experts, case examples, panel discussions about timely health issues, a quarterly HH&S newsletter, and an expanding list of tip sheets written specifically for writers and producers."[4]

Supported by HH&S, the PGA created a new task effort called the *PGA Social Impact Entertainment Task Force.* The purpose of this task force is to provide resources and to educate members on how to implement SIE into their film, TV, and new media projects, thus bringing a greater social impact to Hollywood entertainment work in all media, including immersive media as it develops. (ibid., n.d.)

The Skoll Center for Social Impact Entertainment

Another important effort, The Skoll Center for Social Impact Entertainment at UCLA, was created by UCLA Dean Teri Schwartz in collaboration with Jeff Skoll, a visionary philanthropist, and social entrepreneur. In 2014, Skoll gave a $10 million gift to name and endow the Skoll Center SIE at UCLA. The purpose of the Center is to encourage and support the use entertainment and performing arts to inspire and drive social impact. Efforts encourage industry leaders, creative talent and scholars to create their works with social impact topics woven into their stories, the decisions they make in leadership, research and their careers. Research, education and public engagement are the pillars of the Skoll Center SIE, and as well as bringing together diverse groups that may not normally intersect around the topic of storytelling. The Center seeks to serve as a connector for foundations, social entrepreneurs, non-profits, philanthropists, corporations and the creative community, to promote new ways to connect and tell stories that make a difference (The Skoll Center for Social Impact Entertainment, n.d.).

Jeff Skoll also founded Participant Media, the leading media company which focuses on SIE and produces Academy Award-winning films such as: *Green Book* (2018) and *Roma* (2018), as well as acclaimed, award-winning documentaries *Inconvenient Truth* (2006), and *America to Me* (2018). Participant was founded on the belief that a well-told story has the power to inspire and engage audiences toward positive social action. Participant focuses on supporting artists and projects that contain social issues and engage audiences and consumers to help change the world. The synergy of telling stories that matter and then offering pro-active solutions is a great example of SIE (Participant, n.d.).

The Skoll Center for Social Impact in partnership with Participant Media has recently published their first annual report called *The State of SIE: Mapping the Landscape of Social Entertainment* (Skoll Center for Social Impact, 2019). This report includes categories like feature films, documentary films, television theater and emerging forms.

According to the report, social impact entertainment is an emergent space that is being shaped "not just by the content creators, but also the funders, nonprofits, and academics that help support them" (pg. 6). The path leading to the creation of social impact entertainment involves engagement, raising awareness, a change of attitude, mobilization and, ultimately, social change. Shifting demographics, ways of consuming media, changes in consumer taste (wanting/supporting media that also has a double bottom line) all point to a current climate that is ripe for social impact entertainment. This report will serve as a foundation for future research and collaboration, setting the stage for further reports exploring the growing power and potential of social impact entertainment.

Through data, research and commentary from experts across the field, the report breaks down key components of SIE including guidelines for engaging audiences on social issues, examples to confirm why SIE's financial potential is on a growth curve, metrics that reflect its impact, descriptions of theories of change and how these concepts can be effective when utilized by mainstream Hollywood.

The Skoll Center for Social Impact Entertainment also created the "Spark Change: Social Impact Entertainment" Summit in partnership with Creative Visions and Participant Media. The first Spark Summit in 2018, took place at UCLA Theater Film and Television's James Bridges' Theater, and featured award-winning producers, writers, directors and creatives—all focusing on entertainment that raises awareness, changes behavior, influences policy and catalyzes movements.

IMMERSIVE MEDIA AND SIE

Immersive media and experiences fall into the Skoll Center's category "emerging forms." There has much attention given to VR and headset experiences designed for SIE. One of the leading pioneers in this space is VR visionary and creator, Nonny de la Peña, Founder and CEO of Emblematic Group, whose notable works include; *After Solitary* (2017*), Project Force* (2014*), Project Syria* (2014).[5]

Other organizations have also realized the power of immersive media. As it states on their website, The **United Nations Virtual Reality (UNVR)**,[6] is a project implemented by the UN Sustainable Development Goals (SDGs) Action Campaign, to use the power of immersive storytelling to inspire viewers towards increased empathy, action and positive social change. The project supports the UN system with disseminating their content and expanding their impact in 360' video and virtual reality. The series provides a deeper understanding for those living in the most complex development challenges, catalyzing urgency for those most in danger of being left behind if the SDGs are not met.

In the corporate sector, Facebook's Oculus division, responsible for the VR Oculus Rift headset, has an initiative in their organization called VR for Good that supports the creation of content for social impact through various programs.[7] As noted on their website they have introduced a challenge to inspire students to use next-generation technologies for real-world projects. High school students create 360° video content to be used to connect with their communities, catalyze action for change, and motivate learning. High schools that participate receive 360° video production equipment and support from professional mentors. Students work together with these filmmaker mentors to create 3-5 minute 360 films to share what's special about their communities. Students learn new technology and production skills while they explore careers and higher education opportunities in STEM. The six-week challenge concludes with a film showcase to celebrate their efforts and highlight the top films.

IMMERSIVE MEDIA FOR MENTAL AND SPIRITUAL HEALTH

As humanity continues to evolve and explore the mind and other phenomena, immersive media provides powerful tools for exploring the greater mysteries of life. These tools have been proven to create healing experiences that can reduce stress, create altered states of awareness and instill feelings of awe and wonder.

When Apollo 14 astronaut, Edgar Mitchell first observed Earth from, space he experienced something so profound that it inspired him to found and create IONS: The Institute of Noetic Sciences (IONS, n.d.). That experience has been called the *Overview Effect* and has been described as a profound feeling of awe, oneness and global consciousness.

The planetariums were one of the first venues that gave audiences the ability to experience a similar view from space, and a software program originally created by Sciss called UNIVIEW (now owned by Zeiss) can take viewers on a real-time tour of space from Earth to the furthest reaches of the known Universe. (Zeiss, n.d.). Audiences members have reported deeply moving experiences, and I personally experienced this program and was profoundly touched by the beauty of our planet from space and how very small and fragile we are in the scheme of things.

Steven Pratscher, a psychologist with the University of Missouri has designed an experimental trial designed to recreate the 'Overview Effect' on Earth to test whether it can be replicated. Pratscher plans to recruit about 100 volunteers who will wear a VR headset while experiencing a dark, flotation tank. The experience is designed to re-create the sensation of floating in space, while the VR headset plays high-definition, 360-degree immersive video recorded by the Silicon Valley startup, SpaceVR. The volunteers will be assigned randomly to experience the full flotation tank VR experience, to float without VR, or to have VR while lying on a bed. The participants will complete a series of questionnaires before and after their sessions to assess whether they had any mystical experiences, felt more connected to others, or had what psychologists call an "emotional breakthrough" moment (Sample, 2019).

In the last few years, the medical community has been recognizing the healing power of the arts and more and more research and study is being done on this topic. In 2018, the UK implemented a new national imitative to provide its citizens with medically prescribed treatment using the arts for symptoms such as depression (Solly, 2018).

A Los Angeles company, Tripp, has an immersive application designed to keep you psychologically fit. It provides mood enhancing sound and visuals experienced via immersive VR. Eye tracking customizes the experience to your shifting gaze, and the visuals can be relaxing or stimulating, depending on where and for how long you look. Tipp founder Nanea Reeves hopes that people find Tripp to be a valuable daily habit that enhances their well-being (Stuart, 2018).

IMMERSIVE EXPERIENCES FOR THE DYING, LONELY OR INFIRMED

As we also evolve our understanding of the death process and how we can choose to die and transcend more consciously, one could envision the creation and implementation of domes and VR for the dying installed in hospice treatment centers, hospitals, and or in specially designed facilities for those undergoing palliative care. People undergoing the death process could choose to experience a variety of musical styles programmed along with visuals taking them places they would wish to be versus lying under the harsh glare of fluorescent and or sterile facilities lighting. This could be groundbreaking and offer a much more pleasant, humanistic, transcendent experience during the death process. The same immersive technology could be utilized by those patients who are desiring a mood-enhancing experience and or undergoing radical treatments such as chemotherapy.

IMMERSIVE FUTURES

In *The Spatial Web: How Web 3.0 Will Connect Humans, Machines, And AI to Transform the World*, authors Gabriel Rene and Dan Mapes make this powerful statement in their book section titled *Humanity is a Reality Engine*:

> The tools and technologies that we invented in the Agricultural, Industrial, and Information
> Age extended our hands and feet, then other muscles, then our senses, and finally our brains.
> The key technologies in the Spatial Web stack represent a continuation of the theme of
> Extension of our embodied abilities into the world, just as it has always been.

XR = Input/Output Senses
IoT = Body/Muscles/Cells/Senses
AI = Brain/Mind
Blockchain/Edge = Memory Storage/Sensory Neurons

Each of these exponential technologies is powerful in its own right. Each alone is capable of transforming our world and our realities in unprecedented ways. But the applications and implications of the convergence of these exponential technologies over the next few decades—especially with the inclusion of Biotech, Nano, and Quantum technologies—presents an opportunity far too important for our global society to ignore. Although we have used our tools to create an amazing world, filled with global communication, commerce, and content sharing, if we are being honest we know that we have also used them to drive ourselves and inhabitants of this planet to the very brink of survival. But there is hope because we are the species that makes and remakes its own reality, with the most powerful tools in the history of our species. These tools can make reality easier, more useful, safer and more enjoyable, not just for a small tribe, city-state, or nation, but for the world. With these tools we can build a Smart World. If we can imagine it in our own Private VR, we can create it as a shared Public AR. (Rene & Mapes, p. 211)

Immersive media has its own unique power and it is important for creators to realize the impact that experiences designed for these media might have. Just as fire can either burn and destroy or be used to bring warmth and create, our historical mass media—cinema, TV, print, radio—have brought both light and shadow in their wake. This next iteration of media—immersive media as experience—will impact the future to an equal, or even greater, degree. Immersive media and experiences, in actuality, are self-created reflections of the ways that we experience our normal waking world. Unlike traditional art and media, immersive is just that: it thoroughly surrounds us and shapes us. It will be fascinating to see how humankind moves from glancing through the window to stepping into these worlds.

CONCLUSION

Whether XR, VR, AR, MR, fulldomes, or holographic projections, the immersive media space has arrived and will be quickly evolving and creating experiences that free the viewer out of the constraints of the more traditional frame and into more realistic lived perspectives. Immersive creation tools offer makers and distributors ever-increasing platforms through which to extend their storyworlds and to reach both existing and new audiences and consumers.

From years of looking through windows or doorways into stories and other worlds, we can now enter these worlds, and also experience the inner world of the mind and the self. Not only are these technologies evolving into more commercial applications, but the opportunity to use these platforms for SIE is obvious. VR and immersive experiences have been known to create more powerful empathetic experiences in the viewer as they can literally take one into a world of lived experience as a participant (Stanford, 2018). This power can be used to create profound social impact.

As the world grows more and more connected and we realize our connectedness and our challenges, powerfully designed storytelling, arts and media can truly assist in advancing and evolving human consciousness. Just as traditional film and TV has been extremely instrumental in advancing humanity, immersive media and emerging art forms can assist in further catalyzing deep transformation, resulting in a more peaceful and sustainable world.

As Peter Drucker says in a favorite quote, "The best way to predict the future is to create it." Immersive media gives us the tools to visualize and explore our future in whole new and exciting ways.

REFERENCES

AlloSphere. (n.d.). Retrieved from http://www.allosphere.ucsb.edu/about

Atelier Lumiéres. (n.d.). *The Atelier Des Lumieres From Yesterday to Today*. Retrieved from https://www.atelier-lumieres.com/en/atelier-lumieres-yesterday-today

Bill & Melinda Gates Foundation and the John S. and James L. Knight Foundation. (2013). *Deepening Engagement for Lasting Impact: A Framework For Measuring Media Performance And Results*. Retrieved from https://dl.orangedox.com/Media-Measurement-Framework

Bonasio, A. (2019). Exploring Location-Based VR. *Tech Trends*. Retrieved from https://techtrends.tech/tech-trends/exploring-location-based-vr

Center for Visual Music. (n.d.). Retrieved from http://www.centerforvisualmusic.org

Chew, J. (2015). Star Wars Franchise Worth More Than Harry Potter and James Bond, Combined. *Fortune*. Retrieved from https://fortune.com/2015/12/24/star-wars-value-worth

Coates, C. (2017, July 1). D-BOX Celebrates Release of Hobbs & Shaw on 10th Anniversary. *Blooloop. com Website*. Retrieved from https://blooloop.com/news/d-box-celebrates-hobbs-shaw-10th-anniversary

Dager, N. (2018, February). Barco Escape Ceases Operation. *Digital Cinema Report*. Retrieved from http://www.digitalcinemareport.com/article/barco-escape-ceases-operations

Encyclopedia Britannica. (2019). Retrieved from https://www.britannica.com/topic/Motion-Picture-Association-of-America

Fink, C. (2018). Two Bit Circus: The Carnival Painted with Pictures. *Forbes Magazine.* Retrieved from https://www.forbes.com/sites/charliefink/2018/08/22/two-bit-circus-the-carnival-painted-with-pixels/

Giardina, C. (2019). CGR Cinemas' First ICE Theater in the U.S. to Open at Regal's L.A. Live. *Hollywood Reporter.* Retrieved from https://www.hollywoodreporter.com/behind-screen/cgr-cinemas-first-ice-theater-us-open-at-regals-la-live-1224871

Hollywood, Health & Society. (n.d.). Retrieved from https://hollywoodhealthandsociety.org/about-us/history-hhs-numbers

IONS. (n.d.). *IONS Our Origins.* Retrieved from https://noetic.org/about/origins

Jenkins, H. (2008). *Convergence Culture: Where Old and New Media Collide.* New York: NYU Press.

Lasley, P., & Harriman, E. (1985). *Tamara*: Audience Follows Cast from Room to Room. *Christian Science Monitor.* Retrieved from https://www.csmonitor.com/1985/0709/ltama-f.html

Little Cinema. (n.d.). *About Little Cinema.* Retrieved from http://littlecinema.net/about

Martin, R. (2015). Stella Takes Torotonians on a Journey of the Senses. *Marketing Magazine.* Retrieved from: http://marketingmag.ca/advertising/stella-takes-torontonians-on-a-journey-of-the-senses-153882

Moon Flower. (n.d.). *About Moon Flower Sagaya Ginza Art by Team Lab.* Retrieved from: https://moonflower-sagaya.com/en

Participant. (n.d.). *About Participant.* Retrieved from https://participant.com/about-us

PGA. (2010). PGA Board of Directors Approves Addition of Transmedia Producer to Guild's Producers Code of Credits. April 6, 2010. *Producers Guild of America.* Retrieved from https://www.producersguild.org/news/news.asp?id=39637

Rene, G. & Mapes, D. (2019). *The Spatial Web How Web 3.0 Will Connect Humans, Machine and AI to Transform the World.* Amazon.com.

Sample, I. (2019). Scientists Attempt to Recreate 'Overview effect' from Earth. *The Guardian.* Retrieved from https://www.theguardian.com/science/2019/dec/26/scientists-attempt-to-recreate-overview-effect-from-earth

Science, Arts and Technology. (n.d.). *Discover the SAT.* Retrieved from https://sat.qc.ca/en/sat#section

Secret Cinema. (n.d.). *History of Secret Cinema.* Retrieved from https://www.secretcinema.org/history

Shashkevich, A. (2018). Virtual reality can help make people more compassionate compared to other media, new Stanford study finds. *Stanford News.* Retrieved from https://news.stanford.edu/2018/10/17/virtual-reality-can-help-make-people-empathetic

Silver, S. (2018). The story of the original iPhone, that nobody thought was possible. *Apple Insider.* Retrieved from https://appleinsider.com/articles/18/06/29/the-story-of-the-original-iphone-that-nobody-thought-was-possible

Solly, M. (2018). British Doctors May Soon Prescribe Art, Music, Dance and Singing Lessons. *Smithsonian Magazine*. Retrieved from https://www.smithsonianmag.com/smart-news/british-doctors-may-soon-prescribe-art-music-dance-singing-lessons-180970750

Solomon, B. (2014). Facebook Buys Oculus, Virtual Reality Gaming Startup, for $2 Billion. *Forbes*. Retrieved from https://www.forbes.com/sites/briansolomon/2014/03/25/facebook-buys-oculus-virtual-reality-gaming-startup-for-2-billion

Strause, J. (2015). Inside the World's Most Expensive Restaurant. *News.Com.AU*. Retrieved from https://www.news.com.au/travel/travel-ideas/luxury/inside-the-worlds-most-expensive-restaurant/news-story/f1502c6c2985beeb56993f3ebf052b59

Stuart, S. C. (2018). TRIPP Wants to Be Your Daily Rest and Relaxation Fix. *PC Reviews*. Retrieved from https://www.pcmag.com/news/362814/tripp-wants-to-be-your-daily-rest-and-relaxation-fix

Sublimoton Ibiza. (n.d.). *Concept Sublimotion Ibiza*. Retrieved from https://www.sublimotionibiza.com/main.html

Super78. (n.d.). *About Super78*. Retrieved from Website: https://www.super78.com/process

teamLAB, (n.d.). *Concept teamLab*. Retrieved from https://www.teamlab.art/concept/

The Skoll Center for SIE at UCLA. (2019). *The State of SIE Mapping the Landscape of Social Impact Entertainment Report*. Retrieved from https://thestateofsie.com/skoll-center-for-sie/home/

The Skoll Center for Social Impact Entertainment. (n.d.) Retrieved from http://www.tft.ucla.edu/skoll-center-for-social-impact-entertainment/

THEA Award 2017. (2017). Retrieved from http://www.teaconnect.org/Thea-Awards/Past-Awards/index.cfm?id=6889&redirect=y

Trahndorff, K. F. E. (1827). *Ästhetik oder Lehre von Weltanschauung und Kunst*. Berlin: Maurer.

Two Bit Circus. (n.d.). *About Two Bit Circus*. Retrieved from https://twobitcircus.com/about/

Ultra Violet. (n.d.). *Ultra Violet by Paul Pairet*. Retrieved from https://uvbypp.cc

Wagner, R. (1849). *Die Kunst und die Religion (Art and Religion)*. Leipzig: Otto Wigand Verlag. Retrieved from https://spinnet.humanities.uva.nl/images/2013-10/wagnerkunstundrevolution_2.pdf

Wagner, R. (1849). *Das Kunstwerk der Zukunft [Artwork of the Future]*. Leipzig: Wigand.

Wagner, R. (1995). *Opera and Drama* (W. A. Ellis, Trans.). University of Nebraska Press. (Originally published 1852)

Wolfman, U. R. (2013). Richard Wagner's Concept of the 'Gesamtkunstwerk.' *Interlude*. Retrieved from https://interlude.hk/richard-wagners-concept-of-the-gesamtkunstwerk/

ADDITIONAL READING

Berendo, N., (2014). *Transmedia 2.0: How to Create an Entertainment Brand Using a Transmedia Approach to Storytelling*. Lisbon, Portugal: beActive books.

Csathy, P. (2018). FEARLESS MEDIA: Survival of the Fittest. In *Today's Media 2.0 World, CREATV Media*. New Providence, New Jersey: Bowker.

Dowd, T., Fry, M., Niederman, M., & Steiff, J. (2013). *Storytelling Across Worlds, Transmedia for Creatives and Producers*. New York, London: Focal Press, Taylor & Francis Group.

Glenn, J. (2018). *2018 State of the Future Report*. Washington, D.C.: The Millennium Project.

McCallum, K. (2011). State of the Future Report, Chapter 4: Future Arts, Media, and Entertainment: Seeds for 2020. Washington D.C., The Millennium Project.

McCallum, K. (2012). *Transmedia: A Merger of Story, Technology and Marketing Transmedia Coalition*, Createasphere. Retrieved from http://bridgeartsmedia.com/wp-content/uploads/2012/05/Transmedia-Final-050412.pdf

Rose, F. (2012). *The Arts of Immersion: How the Digital Generation is Remaking Hollywood, Madison Avenue, and the Way We Tell Stories New York*. New York: W.W. Norton & Company.

The State of SIE: Mapping the Landscape of Social Impact Entertainment Report. (2019). Los Angeles, California: The Skoll Center for Social Impact Entertainment, UCLA.

Vandermeer, J. (2013). *Wonderbook: The Illustrative Guide to Creative Imaginative Fiction New York*. New York: Abrams.

KEY TERMS AND DEFINITIONS

Convergence: Convergence is the merging of communication platforms such as; feature films, print, television, radio, live experiences, theme parks, games, the Internet along with portable and interactive technologies through various digital media platforms. Media convergence is the use of multiple media formats extending from one storyworld or platform to deliver a more expanded or enhanced experience.

Fulldome: Fulldome is often referred to when describing a 360, 180 degree theater venue or content designed for the venue. The fulldome theater can be found most often in digital planetariums found in and science centers and universities, there are now fulldome theaters emerging in mainstream culture and entertainment, arts and culture. Most typically in the form of a temporary pop up dome. Cinema content created for these spaces is typically done with live-action captured film or video, pre-rendered animation, real-time visuals mixed live, or a with a mix of formats.

Intellectual Property (IP): An original work or invention that is the result of creativity, such as a manuscript or a design, to which one has rights and for which one may apply for a patent, copyright, trademark, etc.

Producers Guild of America: The Producers Guild of America is a non-profit trade organization that represents, protects and promotes the interests of all members of the producing team in film, television and new media. The Producers Guild works to protect the careers of producers and improve the producing community at large by facilitating health benefits for members, encouraging the enforcement of workplace labor laws and sustainable practices, creating fair and impartial standards for the awarding of producing credits, and hosting educational opportunities for new and experienced producers alike.

Social Impact Entertainment (SIE): Defines a type of entertainment format, primarily feature films, television, and streaming content designed to embed a topic or action that inspires social impact.

Storyworlds: The term storyworld refers to the whole of the "narrative universe" that a story and or stories emerge from. It contains the characters, settings, the time periods (backstories and future stories), props, and events and actions that take place in the storyworld. A storyworld can contain a "canon" which defines the "rules" of the storyworld universe as well.

Television Academy: The Television Academy, the only major organization devoted to the television and broadband screen entertainment industry, is made up of over 24,000 members, representing 30 professional peer groups, including performers, directors, producers, art directors and various other artisans, technicians and executives.

Transmedia Media: Similar to convergence, transmedia is the results of utilizing a variety of media platforms and or designed experiences to extend a storyworld or IP into a variety of cohesively executed unique experiences or narratives that offers the viewer or participant to access aspects of the storyworld for alternative experiences of that storyworld.

ENDNOTES

[1] For those interested in exploring more about this genre, The Center for Visual Music is a non-profit organization and film archive dedicated to visual music and maintains historical documents, a content library, and reference materials should one be interested in researching this art form more deeply. www.centerforvisualmusic.org

[2] For more information on c3 please visit www.consciouscreativity.org

[3] https://msgsphere.com

[4] https://hollywoodhealthandsociety.org

[5] Note: The c3 awarded Nonny a *FutureVision Award* in 2015.

[6] http://unvr.sdgactioncampaign.org/home/#.XVbDWaeZMWo

[7] https://www.oculus.com/vr-for-good/high-school-360-challenge/

APPENDIX A: IMMERSIVE DESIGN RESOURCES

The *No Proscenium* blog site founded by Noah J. Nelson serves as a resource for the latest in immersive experiences.
https://noproscenium.com/about
And the *Immersive Design Summit* was founded in 2018 by Mikhael Tara Garver to bring together leading creators in the immersive arts to share ideas and network.
https://immersivedesignsummit.com

APPENDIX B: TECHNIQUES FOR SIE INCLUSION

As we approach storytelling and experience design for immersive media one can consider inclusion of social impact entertainment. So when we ask what is social impact entertainment and how to do it well? The Skoll Center for SIE UCLA Report (2019) mentions these Five Key Considerations that were continually cited by the contributors:

1. **Focus on Story:** Discover and tell the best story you can to reach your audience. It starts with story.
2. **Know the Issue:** Take time to fully understand the world of the story and determine the impact you want to make.
3. **Find the Best Partner:** Identify and partner with leading organization and people already working on the issues you've chosen to address. Building the social impact campaign in conjunction with these experts can maximize your potential impact.
4. **Rethink Distribution:** Create a distribution plan that surround your work and activates all relevant shareholders, stakeholders and communities of action.
5. **Evaluate, Learn and Share:** Assess what you have done and pass on key learnings. Doc Society's *Impact Field Guide & Toolkit* and the Center for Media & Social Impact's *Assessing the Impact of Issues-Focused Documentaries* are just two best-in-class resources. (See Skoll, 2019) in the References section.

Compilation of References

(n.d.). InBauder, H., & Engel-Di Mauro, S. (Eds.), *Critical Geographies. A Collection of Readings. Praxis (e)*. Press.

Aaronson, X. (2014). The Exquisite Sounds of Plants. *Motherboard, Soundbuilders*. Retrieved from www.vice.com/en_us/article/4x3nmb/the-exquisite-sounds-of-plants

Abate, A. F., Nappi, M., Riccio, D., & Sabatino, G. (2007). 2D and 3D face recognition: A survey. *Pattern Recognition Letters*, *28*(14), 1885–1906. doi:10.1016/j.patrec.2006.12.018

Abdalla, M. (2018). *Make Noise* [interactive VR installation]. United Kingdom.

Abdalla, M., & Rose, A. (2018). *The Collider* [interactive VR installation]. United Kingdom.

Accenture. (2017). *Accenture and Specular Theory Create Interactive Vcommerce Experience "Behind the Style."* Retrieved from https://newsroom.accenture.com/news/accenture-and-specular-theory-create-interactive-vcommerce-experience-behind-the-style.htm

Adams, P. (2016). Report: VR delivers big on engagement, emotional response. *Marketing Dive*. Retrieved from https://www.marketingdive.com/news/report-vr-delivers-big-on-engagement-emotional-response/430113/

Adobe Communications Team. (2018). *Using VR as a Force for Social Good*. Retrieved from https://theblog.adobe.com/using-vr-force-social-good

Aguilera, J. (2019a). *Mindfulness and Embodiment in the Design of a Synthetic Experience* (Doctoral dissertation). University of Plymouth.

Aguilera, J., Goebel, J., & Mann, M. (2017). 3D across media: ceramics, print and VR. *ACM SIGGRAPH 2017 Educator's Forum*, 1.

Aguilera, J., Roberts, D., SubbaRao, M., Minerva, C., Nichols, M., Salgado, J.F., & Kooima, R. (2008). The SVL, a Working Laboratory Inside a Museum. *Proceedings of IPS 2008, 19th Biennial Conference of the International Planetarium Society*.

Aguilera, J., Tsoupikova, D., Sandin, D., Plepys, D., & Kauffman, L. (2006). Unfolding Space (Unpublished Doctoral dissertation). Electronic Visualization Laboratory, University of Illinois at Chicago.

Aguilera, J. (2013). The perceptual world of a virtual Umwelt. *Technoetic Arts: a Journal of Speculative Research*, *11*(3), 193–198. doi:10.1386/tear.11.3.193_1

Aguilera, J. (2015). Senses in space: Mapping the Universe to the human body. In *International Conference on Universal Access in Human-Computer Interaction* (pp. 177-185). Springer. 10.1007/978-3-319-20681-3_16

Aguilera, J. (2019b, July). Point of View When Designing Around Behavior. In *International Conference on Human-Computer Interaction*, (pp. 3-13). Springer. 10.1007/978-3-030-23570-3_1

Aguilera, J. C. (2014). Museum as spacecraft: a building in virtual space. In *The Engineering Reality of Virtual Reality 2014, 9012* (p. 90120D). International Society for Optics and Photonics.

Ah-young, C. (2013). Can holograms replace real K-pop stars? *The Korea Times*. Retrieved from http://koreatimes.co.kr/www/news/culture/2013/07/135_139321.html

Aitoro, J. (2016). 30 Years: Virtual Reality—Training Transformation. *Defense News*. Retrieved from https://www.defensenews.com/30th-annivesary/2016/10/25/30-years-virtual-reality-training-transformation/

Albers, J. (1963). *Interaction of Color*. New Haven, CT: Yale University Press.

Alberti, L. B. (1966). On Painting, Book II (J. R. Spencer, Trans.). Yale University Press.

Alchemy, V. R. (2017). *Munduruku: The fight to defend the heart of the Amazon* [interactive VR installation]. Retrieved from http://alchemyvr.com/productions/munduruku/

Alejandro, G. I. (Producer & Director). (2006). *Babel* [Motion Picture]. United States: Paramount Pictures & France: Mars Distribution.

Alejandro, G. I. (Producer & Director). (2014). *Birdman* [Motion Picture]. United States: Fox Searchlight Pictures.

All Seeing Eye. (2018). *Immersive Histories: Dam Busters* [VR installation]. Retrieved from http://allseeingeye.co/projects/immersive-histories-dam-busters/

AlloSphere. (n.d.). Retrieved from http://www.allosphere.ucsb.edu/about

Almaas, A. H. (1986). *The void: Inner spaciousness and ego structure*. Boulder, CO: Shambhala.

Almaas, A. H. (2000). *Diamond heart book three: Being and the meaning of life*. Boulder, CO: Shambhala.

Amaral, C. P., Simões, M. A., Mouga, S., Andrade, J., & Castelo-Branco, M. (2017). A novel brain computer interface for classification of social joint attention in autism and comparison of 3 experimental setups: A feasibility study. *Journal of Neuroscience Methods*, *290*, 105–115. doi:10.1016/j.jneumeth.2017.07.029 PMID:28760486

Anagram. (n.d.). Retrieved from http://weareanagram.co.uk/project/the-collider/

Anderson, R. (1998a). Intuitive inquiry: Exploring the mirroring discourse of disease. In F. Wertz, K. Charmaz, L. McMullen, R. Josselson, & R. Anderson (Eds.), *Five ways of doing qualitative analysis: Phenomenological psychology, grounded theory, discourse analysis, narrative research, and intuitive inquiry* (Kindle version). New York, NY: Guilford. Retrieved from www.amazon.com

Anderson, P. L., Rothbaum, B. O., & Hodges, L. (2000). Virtual reality: Using the virtual world to improve quality of life in the real world. *Bulletin of the Menninger Clinic*, *65*(1), 78–91. doi:10.1521/bumc.65.1.78.18713 PMID:11280960

Anderson, R. (1998b). Intuitive inquiry: A transpersonal approach. In W. Braud & R. Anderson (Eds.), *Transpersonal research methods for the social sciences: Honoring human experience* (pp. 69–94). Thousand Oaks, CA: Sage.

Andrew, E. (2019). These Virtual Reality Headsets Make Farmed Chickens Believe They Roam Free. *IFLScience*. Retrieved from https://www.iflscience.com/plants-and-animals/these-virtual-reality-headsets-make-farmed-chickens-believe-they-roam-free/

Ansuini, C., Pierno, A. C., Lusher, D., & Castiello, U. (2006). Virtual reality applications for the remapping of space in neglect patients. *Restorative Neurology and Neuroscience*, *24*, 431–441. PMID:17119316

Area15. (2018). *AREA15, A First-of-Its-Kind Experiential and Interactive Entertainment, Retail, Dining and Night-life Complex, Opening in Las Vegas Mid-2019.* Area15 Press Release. Retrieved from https://www.prnewswire.com/news-releases/area15-a-first-of-its-kind-experiential-and-interactive-entertainment-retail-dining-and-nightlife-complex-opening-in-las-vegas-mid-2019-300584326.html

Artnet News. (2019). What Was the Most Influential Work of the Decade? We Surveyed Dozens of Art-World Experts to Find Out. *Artnet News*. Retrieved from https://news.artnet.com/art-world/what-was-the-most-influential-work-of-the-decade-we-surveyed-dozens-of-art-world-experts-to-find-out-1736172

Ashbach, H. (2019). *The case against reality: School of Social Sciences: UCI Social Sciences. Interview with D. Hoffman.* Retrieved from https://www.socsci.uci.edu/newsevents/news/2019/2019-07-22-hoffman-reality.php

Asimov, I. (1950). Runaround. In I, Robot (The Isaac Asimov Collection ed.). New York: Doubleday.

Asimov, I. (1942). *Runabout. Astounding Science Fiction Magazine.*

Aslam, S. (2019). Snapchat by the Numbers: Stats, Demographics & Fun Facts. *Omnicore*. Retrieved from www.omnicoreagency.com/snapchat-statistics

Assagioli, R. (1965). *Psychosynthesis: A Manual of Principles and Techniques.* New York: Hobbs, Dorman & Company.

Atelier Lumiéres. (n.d.). *The Atelier Des Lumieres From Yesterday to Today.* Retrieved from https://www.atelier-lumieres.com/en/atelier-lumieres-yesterday-today

Axon, S. (2017). Returning to Second Life. *Ars Technica*. Retrieved from https://arstechnica.com/gaming/2017/10/returning-to-second-life

Babu, S. K., Krishna, S., Unnikrishnan, R., & Bhavani, R. R. (2018). Virtual reality learning environments for vocational education: A comparison study with conventional instructional media on knowledge retention. In *2018 IEEE 18th International Conference on Advanced Learning Technologies (ICALT)* (pp. 385-389). IEEE. 10.1109/ICALT.2018.00094

Badler, N. I. (1975). *Temporal Scene Analysis: Conceptual Descriptions of Object Movements* (PhD Thesis). Retrieved from https://repository.upenn.edu/cgi/viewcontent.cgi?article=1247&context=hms

Baer, J. (2016). *Domain Specificity of Creativity.* Amsterdam: Elsevier Academic Press.

Bagozzi, R. P., & Yi, Y. (1988). On the evaluation of structural equation models. *Journal of the Academy of Marketing Science, 16*(1), 74–94. doi:10.1007/BF02723327

Bailenson, J. (2018). *Experience on demand: what virtual reality is, how it works, and what it can do.* New York, NY: W. W. Norton & Company.

Bailenson, J. N. (2018). *Experience on Demand: What Virtual Reality Is, How It Works, and What It Can Do.* New York: W.W. Norton.

Bailenson, J. N., & Yee, N. (2007). Virtual interpersonal touch and digital chameleons. *Journal of Nonverbal Behavior, 31*(4), 225–242. doi:10.100710919-007-0034-6

Bailenson, J., Yee, N., Blascovitch, J., Beall, A. C., Lundblad, M., & Jin, M. (2008). The Use of Immersive Virtual Reality in the Learning Sciences: Digital Transformations of Teachers, Students, and Social Context. *Journal of the Learning Sciences, 17*(1), 102–141. doi:10.1080/10508400701793141

Baldwin, M., & Landau, M. J. (2014). Exploring nostalgia's influence on psychological growth. *Self and Identity, 13*(2), 162–177. doi:10.1080/15298868.2013.772320

Bal, M. (1997). *Narratology: Introduction to the Theory of Narrative*. Toronto, Canada: University of Toronto Press.

Banas, J. A., Dunbar, N., Rodriguez, D., & Liu, S. (2010). A review of humor in educational settings: Four decades of research. *Communication Education*, (60): 115–144.

Barker, S. (2019). What is the Future of CGI Influencers in the Marketing World? *Shane Barker Blog*. Retrieved from https://shanebarker.com/blog/cgi-influencers

Barlow, S. (2015). *Her Story* [Computer software]. Sam Barlow.

Barmann, J. (2019). Former Bisou Chef Now Cooking for Instagram Centric Mid-Market Pop-Up Called F.E.A.S.T. *SFIST*. Retrieved from https://sfist.com/2019/03/21/former-bisou-chef-now-cooking-for-instagram-centric-mid-market-pop-up-called-f-e-a-s-t/

Barrett, S. (2019). BWW Review: SAMSKARA at Wisdome: Immersive Art Park Dazzles Audiences with Digital Artwork by Android Jones. *Broadway World*. Retrieved from https://www.broadwayworld.com/los-angeles/article/BWW-Review-SAMSKARA-at-Wisdome-Immersive-Art-Park-Dazzles-Audiences-With-Digital-Artwork-by-Android-Jones-20190502

Barrett, F. S., Grimm, K. J., Robins, R. W., Wildschut, T., Sedikides, C., & Janata, P. (2010). Music-evoked nostalgia: Affect, memory, and personality. *Emotion (Washington, D.C.)*, *10*(3), 390–403. doi:10.1037/a0019006 PMID:20515227

Barr, P. (2014). Baby Boomers Will Transform Health Care as They Age. *Hospitals & Health Networks*, *14*. Retrieved from https://www.hhnmag.com/articles/5298-Boomers-Will-Transform-Health-Care-as-They-Age

Barthes, R. (1981). *Camera Lucida: Reflections on photography*. New York: Hill and Wang.

Batcho, K. I. (2013). Nostalgia: The bittersweet history of a psychological concept. *History of Psychology*, *16*(3), 165–176. doi:10.1037/a0032427 PMID:23646885

Baumann, S., Neff, C., Fetzick, S., Stangl, G., Basler, L., Vereneck, R., & Schneider, W. (2003). A virtual reality system for neurobehavioral and functional MRI studies. *Cyberpsychology & Behavior*, *6*(3), 259–266. doi:10.1089/109493103322011542 PMID:12855081

Bazin, A. (2004). *What is Cinema* (2nd ed., Vol. 1). Berkeley, CA: University of California Press.

BBC Media Applications Technologies Ltd. (2017). *Easter Rising: The Voice of Rebel* [Video file]. Retrieved from https://www.youtube.com/watch?v=Nyc2F3evi-Y

Beard, J. J. (1993). Casting Call at Forest Lawn: The Digital Resurrection of Deceased Entertainers-A 21st Century Challenge for Intellectual Property Law. *J. Copyright Soc'y USA*, *41*, 19.

Beard, J. J. (1997). Will the Reel, er, Real Bill Clinton Please Stand Up-The Unauthorized Use of the President's Image-A New Contact. *Sport. Ent. & Sports Law*, *15*, 3.

Beard, J. J. (1999). Fresh Flowers for Forest Lawn: Amendment of the California Post-Mortem Right of Publicity Statute. *Ent. & Sports Law*, *17*, 1.

Beard, J. J. (2000). Digital Replicas of Celebrities: Copyright, Trademark, and Right of Publicity Issues. *UALR L. Rev*, *23*, 197.

Beard, J. J. (2001). Clones, bones and twilight zones: Protecting the digital persona of the quick, the dead and the imaginary. *J. Copyright Soc'y USA*, *49*, 441.

Beard, J. J. (2003). Is Virtual Kiddie Porn a Crime. *Ent. & Sports Law*, *21*, 1.

Beard, J. J. (2003). Virtual Kiddie Porn: A Real Crime-An Analysis of the PROTECT Act. *Ent. & Sports Law.*, *21*, 3.

Beard, J. J. (2004). Everything old is new again: Dickens to digital. *Loy. LAL REV*, *38*, 19.

Beck, A. T., & Weishaar, M. E. (1995). Cognitive therapy. In R. J. Corsini & D. Wedding (Eds.), *Current psychotherapies* (pp. 229–261). Itasca, IL: Peacock.

Becker, E. (1973). *The denial of death*. New York, NY: Free Press.

Belew, A. (2017, September 24). Retrieved July 3, 2019, from https://www.facebook.com/AdrianBelew/posts/10150895474944995

Beltran, D., & Basañez, L. (2014). A comparison between active and passive 3d vision sensors: Bumblebeexb3 and Microsoft Kinect. In *Proceedings of Robot2013: First Iberian Robotics Conference* (pp. 725-734). Springer.

Berger, K. (2018). We Are All Bewildered Machines. *The Nautilus*. Retrieved from http://nautil.us/issue/66/clockwork/we-are-all-bewildered-machines

Bernard, F. D. (2009). *Anatomy of Film* (6th ed.). New York, NY: St. Martins Press.

Bertin, K. (2018). *Manic VR* [VR installation]. Retrieved from http://kalinabertin.com/manic-vr/

Bill & Melinda Gates Foundation and the John S. and James L. Knight Foundation. (2013). *Deepening Engagement for Lasting Impact: A Framework For Measuring Media Performance And Results*. Retrieved from https://dl.orangedox.com/Media-Measurement-Framework

Bimber, O., Grundhofer, A., Zeidler, T., Danch, D., & Kapakos, P. (2006). Compensating Indirect Scattering for Immersive and Semi-Immersive Projection Displays. *IEEE Virtual Reality Conference (VR 2006)*. 10.1109/VR.2006.34

Biocca, F., Harms, C., & Burgoon, J. K. (2003). Toward a more robust theory and measure of social presence: Review and suggested criteria. *Presence (Cambridge, Mass.)*, *12*(5), 456–480. doi:10.1162/105474603322761270

Black, E. R. (2017). *Learning then and there: An exploration of virtual reality in K-12 history education* (doctoral dissertation). Accessed on August 23, 2019 at https://repositories.lib.utexas.edu/handle/2152/63616

Blair, K., & Hoy, C. (2006). Paying attention to adult learning online: The pedagogy and politics of community. *Computers and Composition*, *23*(1), 32–48. doi:10.1016/j.compcom.2005.12.006

Blascovich, J., & Bailenson, J. (2005). Immersive virtual environments and education simulations. In P. Cohen & T. Rehberger (Eds.), *Virtual decisions: digital simulations for teaching reasoning in the social sciences and humanities*. Mahwah, NJ: Lawrence Earlbaum Associates, Inc.

Bleus, G. (1978). *The Thrill of Working with Odours, A Smell Manifesto* [Mail Art Archive]. Retrieved from http://www.mailart.be/thrill.html

Bloom, P. (2011). *The New Science of Why We Like What We Like*. W. W. Norton & Company.

Bode, L. (2007). 'Grave Robbing' or 'Career Comeback'? On the Digital Resurrection of Dead Screen Stars. *History of Stardom Reconsidered*, 36-40.

Boger, Y. (2018). Understanding Pixel Density & Retinal Resolution, and Why It's Important for AR/VR Headsets. *Road to VR*. Retrieved from https://www.roadtovr.com/understanding-pixel-density-retinal-resolution-and-why-its-important-for-vr-and-ar-headsets/

Bojanova, I., & Pang, L. (2011). Enhancing Graduate Courses through Educational Virtual Tours. In C. Wankel & R. Hinrichs (Eds.), *Transforming Virtual World Learning* (pp. 215–240). Bingley, UK: Emerald Group Publishing Limited. doi:10.1108/S2044-9968(2011)0000004013

Bojic, Z. (2019). Come fly with MRI. Spotlight Quality and Safety. *SickKids Diagnostic Imaging, 3*(1), 2-3. Retrieved from https://www.researchgate.net/publication/334249355_Come_fly_with_MRI_Spotlight_Quality_and_Safety_Sick-Kids_Diagnostic_Imaging_Toronto_Ontario

Bolin, G. (2016). Passion and nostalgia in generational media experiences. *European Journal of Cultural Studies, 19*(3), 250–264. doi:10.1177/1367549415609327

Bonasio, A. (2019). Exploring Location-Based VR. *Tech Trends*. Retrieved from https://techtrends.tech/tech-trends/exploring-location-based-vr

Bond, J. R., Kofman, L., & Pogosyan, D. (1996). How filaments of galaxies are woven into the cosmic web. *Nature, 380*(6575), 603–606. doi:10.1038/380603a0

Bonus, J. A., Peebles, A., Mares, M.-L., & Sarmiento, I. G. (2018). Look on the bright side (of media effects): Pokémon Go as a catalyst for positive life experiences. *Media Psychology, 21*(2), 263–287. doi:10.1080/15213269.2017.1305280

Boréales, R. (2019). *Résonances Boréales*. Retrieved from www.resonancesboreales.com

Bostrom, N. (2003). Are We Living in a Computer Simulation? *The Philosophical Quarterly, 53*(211), 243–255. doi:10.1111/1467-9213.00309

Botterill, J. (1997). *The Fairest of the Fairs: a History of Fairs, Amusement Parks, and Theme Parks* (Doctoral dissertation Theses). School of Communication, Simon Fraser University.

Bouchard, S., Baus, O., Bernier, F., & McCreary, D. R. (2010). Selection of key stressors to develop virtual environments for practicing stress management skills with military personnel prior to deployment. *Cyberpsychology, Behavior, and Social Networking, 13*(1), 83–94. doi:10.1089/cyber.2009.0336 PMID:20528298

Bowlby, J. (1982). Attachment and loss: Retrospect and prospect. *The American Journal of Orthopsychiatry, 52*(4), 664–678. doi:10.1111/j.1939-0025.1982.tb01456.x PMID:7148988

Bowlby, J. (1988). *A secure base: Parent-child attachment and healthy human development*. New York, NY: Basic Books.

Boym, S. (2008). *The future of nostalgia*. New York: Basic Books.

Bozorgzadeh, A. (2019). The future of immersive education will be live, social, and personalized. *Venture Beat*. Retrieved from https://venturebeat.com/2019/07/26/the-future-of-immersive-education-will-be-live-social-and-personalized/

Bradbury, A. (2018). *Vestige VR* [interactive VR]. Retrieved from http://vestige-vr.com/

Bradstreet, C. (2016). A Trip to Japan in Sixteen Minutes: Sadakichi Hartmann's Perfume Concert and the Aesthetics of Scent. In P. di Bello & G. Koureas (Eds.), *Art, History and the Senses: 1830 to the Present*. Oxfordshire, UK: Routledge, Taylor & Francis Group.

Brennesholtz, M. (2019). NAB's 2019 Display Awards: DesignLED Technology. *Display Daily*. Retrieved from https://www.displaydaily.com/article/display-daily/nab-s-2019-display-awards

Bricken, M. (1991). Virtual reality learning environments: Potentials and challenges. *Computer Graphics, 25*(3), 178–184. doi:10.1145/126640.126657

Bricken, M. (1994). *Virtual Worlds: No Interface to Design. Technical Report R-90-2. Human Interface Technology Laboratory (HITL)*. Seattle, WA: Washington Technology Center University of Washington. Retrieved from http://papers.cumincad.org/data/works/att/5dff.content.pdf

Broderick, D. (1982). *The Judas Mandala*. New York: Pocket Books.

Brooks, B., & Rose, F. (2003). The use of virtual reality in memory rehabilitation: Current findings and future directions. *NeuroRehabilitation, 18*, 147–157. PMID:12867677

Brown Institute for Media Innovation. (2018). *NeverEnding 360*. Retrieved from https://brown.columbia.edu/portfolio/neverending-360/

Brown, A. D., & Humphreys, M. (2002). Nostalgia and the narrativization of identity: A Turkish case study. *British Journal of Management, 13*(2), 141–159. doi:10.1111/1467-8551.00228

Brown, A., & Green, T. (2016). Virtual reality: Low-cost tools and resources for the classroom. *TechTrends, 60*(5), 517–519. doi:10.100711528-016-0102-z

Brown, E., & Cairns, P. (2004). A grounded investigation of game immersion. *Proceedings of CHI 2004*, 1279–1300.

Bryanton, C., Bosse, J., Brien, M., McLean, J., McCormick, A., & Sveistrup, H. (2006). Feasibility, motivation, and selective motor control: Virtual reality compared to conventional home exercise in children with cerebral palsy. *Cyberpsychology & Behavior, 9*(2), 123–128. doi:10.1089/cpb.2006.9.123 PMID:16640463

Bublitz, D. (2011). *Projektionsfläche zur Frontprojektion*. Patent Disclosure Document DE 10 2011 008471 A1.

Bui, H.-T. (2019). De-Aging Technology and Fully CGI Characters "Raises Some Serious Issues," Andy Serkis Says. *Slashfilm*. Retrieved from https://www.slashfilm.com/digital-actors-de-aging-tech-andy-serkis

Burkard, K. (2018, July 13). *The Top 10 Best Customer Experiences (and What You Can Learn From Them)*. Retrieved from https://blog.smile.io/top-10-best-customer-experiences

Büscher, M., & Urry, J. (2009). Mobile methods and the empirical. *European Journal of Social Theory, 12*(1), 99–116. doi:10.1177/1368431008099642

Calbee. (2019). *Talking about the Narrative Structure Design of Games*. Retrieved from https://indienova.com/indie-game-development/narrative-structure-design-of-game/

California Academy of Sciences. (Producer), & Wyatt, R. (Director). (2018). Expedition Reef [Fulldome Film]. United States: California Academy of Sciences.

Call of Duty: Modern Warfare. (2019). [Computer software]. Activision Publishing, Inc.

Calleja, G. (2007). Digital game involvement: A conceptual model. *Games and Culture, 2*(3), 236–260. doi:10.1177/1555412007306206

Cambridge English Dictionary. (n.d.). *Creativity*. Retrieved from https://dictionary.cambridge.org/dictionary/english/creativity?q=creativity

Cameron, J. (Producer and Director). (2009). *Avatar* [Motion Picture]. United States: 20th Century Fox & Lightstorm Entertainment.

Campos-Castillo, C., & Hitlin, S. (2013). Copresence: Revisiting a building block for social interaction theories. *Sociological Theory, 31*(2), 168–192. doi:10.1177/0735275113489811

Campos, G. (2019). Kraftwerk Living Technologies launches LED dome solution. *AV Magazine*. Retrieved from https://www.avinteractive.com/news/products/kraftwerk-living-technologies-launches-led-dome-solution-04-04-2019/

Cardinal, D. (2015). *Lytro's Immerge aims to make virtual reality video more realistic*. Retrieved from https://www.extremetech.com/extreme/217536-lytros-immerge-aims-to-make-virtual-reality-video-more-realistic

Carrieri, M., Petracca, A., Lancia, S., Basso Moro, S., Brigadoi, S., Spezialetti, M., & Quaresima, V. (2016). Prefrontal cortex activation upon a demanding virtual hand controlled task: A new frontier for neuroergonomics. *Frontiers in Human Neuroscience*, *10*, 53. doi:10.3389/fnhum.2016.00053 PMID:26909033

Carson, E. (2015). How NASA uses virtual reality to train astronauts. *TechRepublic*. Retrieved from https://www.yahoo.com/news/nasa-uses-virtual-reality-train-151645861.html

Carvalho, M., Freire, R. C., & Nardi, A. (2010). Virtual reality as a mechanism for exposure therapy. *World Journal of Biological Psychiatry*, *11*(2_2), 220-230.

Casey, E. S. (1987). *Remembering: A phenomenological study*. Bloomington, IN: Indiana University Press.

Cavanna, A. E., & Trimble, M. R. (2006). The precuneus: A review of its functional anatomy and behavioural correlates. *Brain*, *129*(Pt 3), 564–583. doi:10.1093/brain/awl004 PMID:16399806

Cavendish, R. (2005). London's Last Bartholomew Fair: September 3rd, 1855. *History Today*, *55*(9), 52.

CBC News. (2016). Diefenbunker Museum escape room promises interactive Cold War history lesson. *CBC News*. Retrieved from https://www.cbc.ca/news/canada/ottawa/diefenbunker-escape-room-cold-war-1.3445576

Center for Visual Music. (n.d.). Retrieved from http://www.centerforvisualmusic.org

Cheung, W.-Y., Sedikides, C., Wildschut, T., Tausch, N., & Ayanian, A. H. (2017). Collective nostalgia is associated with stronger outgroup-directed anger and participation in ingroup-favoring collective action. *Journal of Social and Political Psychology*, *5*(2), 301–319. doi:10.5964/jspp.v5i2.697

Chew, J. (2015). Star Wars Franchise Worth More Than Harry Potter and James Bond, Combined. *Fortune*. Retrieved from https://fortune.com/2015/12/24/star-wars-value-worth

Chirico, A., Lucidi, F., De Laurentiis, M., Milanese, C., Napoli, A., & Giordano, A. (2016). Virtual reality in health system: Beyond entertainment. A mini-review on the efficacy of VR during cancer treatment. *Journal of Cellular Physiology*, *231*(2), 275–287. doi:10.1002/jcp.25117 PMID:26238976

Chouinard, H. (2019). Is virtual reality the end of the physical showroom? *Business of Home*. Retrieved from www.businessofhome.com/articles/is-virtual-reality-the-end-of-the-physical-showroom

Cho, Y., Biocca, F., & Biocca, H. (2018). *How Spatial Presence in Virtual Reality Affects Memory Retention and Motivation on Second Language Learning*. Syracuse University.

Christopher, N. (Producer & Director), & Emma, T. (Producer) (2010). *Inception* [Motion Picture]. United States: Warner Bros Pictures.

Cizek, K. (2016). Towards a VR Manifesto. *Immerse*. Retrieved from https://immerse.news/towards-a-vr-manifesto-b97aca901192

Clement, J. (2019a). Number of monthly active Facebook users worldwide as of 2nd quarter 2019 (in millions). *Statistica*. Retrieved from www.statista.com/statistics/264810/number-of-monthly-active-facebook-users-worldwide

Clement, J. (2019b). Number of monthly active Twitter users worldwide from 1st quarter 2010 to 1st quarter 2019 (in millions). *Statistica*. Retrieved from www.statista.com/statistics/282087/number-of-monthly-active-twitter-users

Clements, J. (2004). Organic inquiry: Toward research in partnership with spirit. *Journal of Transpersonal Psychology*, *36*, 26–49.

Cline, E. (2012). *Ready Player One: A Novel*. New York: Broadway Books.

Coates, C. (2017, July 1). D-BOX Celebrates Release of Hobbs & Shaw on 10th Anniversary. *Blooloop.com Website*. Retrieved from https://blooloop.com/news/d-box-celebrates-hobbs-shaw-10th-anniversary

Cohen, K. (1979). *Film and Fiction: The Dynamics of Exchange* (1st ed.). New Haven, CT: Yale University Press.

Collodi, D., & Brundage, F. (1924). *Pinocchio*. Mineola, NY: Saalfield Publishing Company.

Conrads, U., & Bullock, M. (1975). *Programs and Manifestoes on 20th-Century Architecture*. Boston: MIT Press.

Constantine, J. (2014). Facebook's $2Billion Acquisition of Oculus Closes, Now Official. *Techcrunch.com*. Retrieved from https://techcrunch.com/2014/07/21/facebooks-acquisition-of-oculus-closes-now-official/

Corbett-Drummond, T., Carole, N. R., & Strum, B. (2017). The Future of Immersive Branding and Retail According to the AT&T Foundry. *AT&T Foundry*. Retrieved from https://foundry.att.com/media/The-Future-of-Immersive-Branding-and-Retail.pdf

Corkill, E. (2009). Real Escape Game brings its creator's wonderment to life. *The Japan Times*. Retrieved from https://www.japantimes.co.jp/life/2009/12/20/general/real-escape-game-brings-its-creators-wonderment-to-life/

Corrigan, F. (2019). *Flash Lidar Time of Flight (ToF) Camera Sensors On Drones And 10 Terrific Uses*. Retrieved from https://www.dronezon.com/learn-about-drones-quadcopters/best-uses-for-time-of-flight-tof-camera-depth-sensor-technology-in-drones-or-ground-based/

Côté, S., & Bouchard, S. (2008). Virtual reality exposure for phobias: A critical review. *Journal of Cyber Therapy and Rehabilitation*, *1*(1), 75–91.

Courtney, C. (2017). Edwin Albert Link: Inventor of the First Flight Simulator. *Disciples of Flight*. Retrieved August 24, 2019 from: https://disciplesofflight.com/edwin-albert-link-flight-simulator/

Crowther, B. (1959, Dec. 10). Smells of China; Behind Great Wall Uses AromaRama. *The New York Times*.

Crowther, B. (1960, Feb. 9). Screen: Olfactory Debut: Scent of Mystery Opens at Warner. *The New York Times*.

Cruz-Neira, C., Sandin, D. J., & DeFanti, T. A. (1993, September). Surround-screen projection-based virtual reality: the design and implementation of the CAVE. In *Proceedings of the 20th annual conference on computer graphics and interactive techniques* (pp. 135-142). ACM. 10.1145/166117.166134

Csathy, P. (2018). Fearless Media 2.0: An insider's guide & call to action for today's media 2.0 world & where it's going. *CREATV Media, Ch.*, *3*(Part III), 269–271.

Cuarón, A., & Heyman, D. (Producers), & Cuarón, A. (Director). (2013). *Gravity* [Motion Picture]. United Kingdom, United States: Warner Bros. Pictures.

Cukor, J., Spitalnick, J. S., Difede, J., Rizzo, A. A., & Rothbaum, B. O. (2009). Emerging treatments for PTSD. *Clinical Psychology Review*, *29*(8), 715–726. doi:10.1016/j.cpr.2009.09.001 PMID:19800725

Cummings, C. (2016, July 24). Infographic: Pokemon Go Could Be What Farmville Never Was—Successful: Here's how brands can catch 'em all. *ADWEEK*. Retrieved from http://www.adweek.com/digital/infographic-pokemon-go-could-be-what-farmville-never-was-successful-172626/

Cummins, E. (2018). *The surprising politics of Sidewalks*. Retrieved from https://www.popsci.com/politics-versus-sidewalks/

Cupchik, G. (2016). The Aesthetics of Emotion: Up the Down Staircase of the Mind Body. *Empirical Studies of the Arts*, *36*(1), 114–121.

Dachis, A. (2016). How Snapchat Quietly Became the First Social AR Platform. *Next Reality*. Retrieved from https://mobile-ar.reality.news/news/snapchat-quietly-became-first-social-ar-platform-0171923

Dager, N. (2018, February). Barco Escape Ceases Operation. *Digital Cinema Report*. Retrieved from http://www.digitalcinemareport.com/article/barco-escape-ceases-operations

Daily Mail. (2007). Warning over cyber-bullying in Second Life. *The Daily Mail*. Retrieved from www.dailymail.co.uk/sciencetech/article-458743/Warning-cyber-bullying-Second-Life.html

Dainer-Best J., Lee H.Y., Shumake J., Yeager D. S. & Beevers C.G. (2018). Determining optimal parameters of the self-referent encoding task: A large-scale examination of self referent cognition and depression *Psychological Assessment*, Advanced Online Publication.

Daley, J. (2019). 'Mona Lisa' Comes to Life in Computer-Generated 'Living Portrait.' *Smithsonian Institution*. Retrieved from www.smithsonianmag.com/smart-news/mona-lisa-comes-life-computer-generated-living-portrait-180972296/

Damasio, A. (2010). *Self comes to mind: Constructing the conscious brain* (Kindle version). Knopf Doubleday. Retrieved from www.Amazon.com

Damasio, A. (1999). *The feeling of what happens: Body and emotion in the making of consciousness*. Fort Worth, TX: Harcourt College.

Damasio, A. R. (1996). The somatic marker hypothesis and the possible functions of the prefrontal cortex. *Philosophical Transactions of the Royal Society of London. Series B, Biological Sciences*, *351*(1346), 1413–1420. doi:10.1098/rstb.1996.0125 PMID:8941953

Damasio, A. R., & Damasio, H. (1996). Making images and creating subjectivity. The mindbrain continuum. *Sensory Processes*, 19–27.

Damiani, J. (2019). Jessica Brillhart Named Director of USCICT Mixed Reality Lab (Exclusive). *Forbes*. Retrieved from https://www.forbes.com/sites/jessedamiani/2019/06/25/jessica-brillhart-named-director-of-usc-ict-mixed-reality-lab-exclusive/#65bb01a07cb2

Daniel, E. (2019). We Live in an Ocean of Air: How VR art is capturing the hearts and minds of audiences. *The Verdict Podcast*. Retrieved from https://www.verdict.co.uk/vr-art/

Davidson, R., Kabat–Zinn, J., Schumacher, J., Rosenkranz, M., Muller, D., Santorelli, S. F., ... Sheridan, J. F. (2003). Alterations in Brain and Immune Function Produced by Mindfulness Meditation. *Psychosomatic Medicine*, *65*(4), 564–570. doi:10.1097/01.PSY.0000077505.67574.E3 PMID:12883106

Davidson, R., & Lutz, A. (2008). Buddha's Brain: Neuroplasticity and Meditation. *IEEE Signal Processing Magazine*, *25*(1), 176–174. doi:10.1109/MSP.2008.4431873 PMID:20871742

Davis, B. (2016). Is This Art Space Backed by 'Game of Thrones' Author George R. R. Martin a Force of Good or Evil? *Artnet News*. Retrieved from https://news.artnet.com/art-world/george-r-r-martin-backed-art-collective-556880

Davis, F. (1979). *Yearning for yesterday: A sociology of nostalgia*. New York: Free Press.

Davis, S. G. (1996). The theme park: Global industry and cultural form. *Media Culture & Society*, *18*(3), 399–422. doi:10.1177/016344396018003003

Dawes, M., Summerskill, W., Glasziou, P., Cartabellotta, A., Martin, J., Hopayian, K., & Osborne, J. (2005). Sicily statement on evidence-based practice. *BMC Medical Education*, *5*(1), 1. doi:10.1186/1472-6920-5-1 PMID:15634359

de Feydeau, E. (2006). A Scented Palace (J. Lizop, Trans.). London, UK: I.B. Tauris & Co., Ltd.

De Freitas, S., Rebolledo-Mendez, G., Liarokapis, F., Magoulas, G., & Poulovassilis, A. (2010). Learning as immersive experiences: Using the four-dimensional framework for designing and evaluating immersive learning experiences in a virtual world. *British Journal of Educational Technology, 41*(1), 69–85. doi:10.1111/j.1467-8535.2009.01024.x

De la Rosa, A., & Cárdernas-López, G. (2012). Posttraumatic stress disorder: Efficacy of a treatment program using virtual reality for victims of criminal violence in Mexican population. *Anuario de Psicología, 42*, 377–391.

de Tommaso, M., Ricci, K., Delussi, M., Montemurno, A., Vecchio, E., Brunetti, A., & Bevilacqua, V. (2016). Testing a novel method for improving way finding by means of a P3b virtual reality visual paradigm in normal aging. *SpringerPlus, 5*(1), 1297. doi:10.118640064-016-2978-7 PMID:27547671

Debord, G. (1955). Introduction to a Critique of Urban Geography. *Les Lèvres Nues, 6*, 23–27.

Dede, C. (2009). Immersive interfaces for engagement and learning. *Science, 323*(5910), 66–69. doi:10.1126cience.1167311 PMID:19119219

Dede, C., Salzman, M., Loftin, R. B., & Ash, K. (1997). *Using virtual reality technology to convey abstract scientific concepts. Learning the Sciences of the 21st Century: Research, Design, and Implementing Advanced Technology Learning Environments*. Hillsdale, NJ: Lawrence Erlbaum.

Dent, S. (2014). *What you need to know about 3D motion capture*. Retrieved from https://www.engadget.com/2014/07/14/motion-capture-explainer/

Dickson, B. (2017). *Unlocking the potential of eye tracking technology*. Retrieved from https://techcrunch.com/2017/02/19/unlocking-the-potential-of-eye-tracking-technology/

Diers, M., Kamping, S., Kirsch, P., Rance, M., Bekrater-Bodmann, R., Foell, J., ... Flor, H. (2015). Illusion-related brain activations: A new virtual reality mirror box system for use during functional magnetic resonance imaging. *Brain Research, 1594*, 173–182. doi:10.1016/j.brainres.2014.11.001 PMID:25446453

DIGSS. (2018). *Digital Immersive Giant Screen Specifications 2.0 (DIGSS)*. Giant Screen Cinema Association. Retrieved from https://www.giantscreencinema.com/Member-Center/DIGSS

Doctor, R. J. (2019). The slow death of the American mall and the social imperfections it exhibited. *Daily Kos*. Retrieved from https://www.dailykos.com/stories/2019/11/27/1901730/-The-slow-death-of-the-American-mall-and-the-social-imperfections-it-exhibited

Don, C., Paul, H., Mark, R. H., Bobby, M., Cathy, S., & Bob, Y. (Producer) & Paul, H. (Director). (2004), *Crash* [Motion Picture]. United States: Lionsgate Films.

Donati, A. R., Shokur, S., Morya, E., Campos, D. S., Moioli, R. C., Gitti, C. M., ... Nicolelis, M. A. (2016). Longterm training with a brain-machine interface-based gait protocol induces partial neurological recovery in paraplegic patients. *Scientific Reports, 6*(30383). PMID:27513629

Dotson, K. (2019). Amazon Prime releases streaming VR shows and movies for Oculus headsets. In *SiliconAngle: The Voice of Enterprise and Emerging Tech*. Retrieved from https://siliconangle.com/2019/07/25/amazon-prime-releases-streaming-vr-shows-movies-oculus-headsets/

Dronsfield, J. L. (2018). Immediacy. In *Immersion - Design - Art: Revisited*. Marburg, Germany: Buechner Verlag.

Dunham, E. (2017). Facebook of the Dead. *What if*. Retrieved from what-if.xkcd.com/69/

Dunn, A., Patterson, J. F., Biega, C., Grishchenko, A., Luna, J., Stanek, J. R., & Strouse, R. (2018). A Novel Clinician-Orchestrated Virtual Reality Platform for Distraction During Pediatric Intravenous Procedures in Children with Hemophilia: A Randomized Clinical Trial (Preprint). JMIR Serious Games, 7(1).

Earnshaw, R., & Vince, J. A. (1995). *Computer Graphics: Developments in Virtual Environments*. Academic Press.

Ehrman, M. (2002). The Last Laser Show Laserium, once playing at an observatory near you, has gone the way of the pet rock. Mark Ehrman tracks the history—and future? —of the light fantastic. *CNN Money*. Retrieved from https://money.cnn.com/magazines/fortune/fortune_archive/2002/02/18/318144/index.htm

Einstein, A. (1952). *Relativity: Relativity. The special and the general theory*. New York: Crown Publishers.

Elias, J. (2006). *Finding true magic: Transpersonal hypnosis and hypnotherapy/NLP (Kindle version)*. Seattle, WA: Five Wisdom Press. Retrieved from www.Amazon.com

Ellard, C. (2015). *Places of the heart: The psychogeography of everyday life*. New York: Bellevue Literary Press.

Encyclopaedia Britannica. (2012). *Gestalt therapy*. Retrieved from https://www.britannica.com/science/Gestalt-therapy

Encyclopedia Britannica. (2019). Retrieved from https://www.britannica.com/topic/Motion-Picture-Association-of-America

Enklu. (2019). Success for The Unreal Garden at E3. *Enklu in the News*. Retrieved from https://www.enklu.com/

Eroglu, S. A., Machleit, K., & Barr, T. F. (2005). Perceived retail crowding and shopping satisfaction: The role of shopping values. *Journal of Business Research*, 58(8), 1146–1153. doi:10.1016/j.jbusres.2004.01.005

Evans, N. (2018). Lucasfilm Actually Scans All of Its Lead Actors for Later Use. *CinemaBlend*. Retrieved from https://www.cinemablend.com/news/2400072/lucasfilm-actually-scans-all-of-its-lead-actors-for-later-use

Eventbrite. (2017). *The Experience Movement: Research Report: How Millennials are Bridging Cultural & Political Divides Offline*. Retrieved from https://www.eventbrite.com/l/millennialsreport-2017/

Fahey, R. (2018, November 16). *Pokémon's strategy is cross-generational: By balancing nostalgia for parents with appeal to children*. Retrieved from https://www.gamesindustry.biz/articles/2018-11-16-pokemons-strategy-is-cross-generational

Faidit, J. M. (2009). Planetariums in the world. *Proceedings of the International Astronomical Union*, 5(S260), E9. doi:10.1017/S1743921311003292

Fairley, S. (2003). In search of relived social experience: Group-based nostalgia sport tourism. *Journal of Sport Management*, 17(3), 284–304. doi:10.1123/jsm.17.3.284

Faraone, C. A. (1999). *Ancient Greek Love Magic*. Boston, MA: Harvard University Press.

Farb, N., Anderson, A., & Segal, Z. (2012). The Mindful Brain and Emotion Regulation in Mood Disorders. *Canadian Journal of Psychiatry*, 57(2), 70–77. doi:10.1177/070674371205700203 PMID:22340146

Farkas, J. (2019a). Inside the innovative Disney ride that's key to its *Star Wars* strategy. *CNN Business*. Retrieved from https://www.cnn.com/2019/12/03/tech/star-wars-rise-of-the-resistance-ride

Farkas, J. (2019b). Disney's Star Wars hotel is a cruise ship in space. *CNN Travel*. Retrieved from https://www.cnn.com/travel/article/disney-star-wars-epcot-d23

Feige, K. (Producer), & Coogler, R. (Director). (2018). *Black Panther* [Motion Picture]. United States. Marvel Studios.

Félix and Paul Studios. (2016). Introduction to Virtual Reality. 360 degree video for the Oculus Rift platform. Montreal, Canada: Author.

Fendt, M., & Fanselow, M. S. (1999). The neuroanatomical and neurochemical basis of conditioned fear. *Neuroscience and Biobehavioral Reviews*, *23*(5), 743–760. doi:10.1016/S0149-7634(99)00016-0 PMID:10392663

Ferrer, J.N., & Sherman. (2000). Transpersonal Knowledge: A Participatory Approach to Transpersonal Phenomena. In T. Hart, P. Nelson, & K. Puhakka (Eds.), *Transpersonal Knowing: Exploring the Farther Reaches of Consciousness*, (pp. 213-252). Albany, NY: State University of New York Press.

Ferrer, J. N. (2017). *Participation and the mystery: Transpersonal essays in psychology education, and religion (Kindle version)*. Albany, NY: State University Press. doi:10.1215/08879982-4252974

Filmsite. (2019). Academy Awards Best Picture: Genre Biases. *AMC Filmsite*. Retrieved from https://www.filmsite.org/bestpics2.html

Fink, C. (2018). Two Bit Circus: The Carnival Painted with Pictures. *Forbes Magazine*. Retrieved from https://www.forbes.com/sites/charliefink/2018/08/22/two-bit-circus-the-carnival-painted-with-pixels/

Fink, J. (2004). Cirque du Soleil spares no cost with 'KA.' *Las Vegas Sun*. Retrieved from https://lasvegassun.com/news/2004/sep/16/cirque-du-soleil-spares-no-cost-with-ka/

Firebrace, W. (2017). *Star Theatre: The Story of the Planetarium*. London: Reaktion Books.

Fischer, M. H., & Coello, Y. (Eds.). (2016). *Foundations of embodied cognition: Conceptual and interactive embodiment*. Routledge/Taylor & Francis Group.

Formosa, N. J., Morrison, B. W., Hill, G., & Stone, D. (2018). Testing the efficacy of a virtual reality-based simulation in enhancing users' knowledge, attitudes, and empathy relating to psychosis. *Australian Journal of Psychology*, *70*(1), 57–65. doi:10.1111/ajpy.12167

Fornell, C., & Larcker, D. F. (1981). *Structural equation models with unobservable variables and measurement error: Algebra and statistics*. Los Angeles, CA: SAGE Publications Sage CA.

Frank, P. (2016). An Art Museum in Los Angeles Is Killing the Snapchat Game. *Huffpost*. Retrieved from https://www.huffpost.com/entry/you-need-to-start-following-lacma-on-snapchat_n_55b136afe4b08f57d5d3fdf7

Frankenfield, J. (2019). What is the General Data Protection Regulation (GDPR)? *Investopedia*. Retrieved from www.investopedia.com/terms/g/general-data-protection-regulation-gdpr.asp

Fraser, P. (2018, Feb.). Giant-Screen Biz Meets Themed Entertainment...and They Get Along Just Fine! *LF Examiner*.

Fredrickson, B. L., & Branigan, C. (2005). Positive emotions broaden the scope of attention and thought-action repertoires. *Cognition and Emotion*, *19*(3), 313–332. doi:10.1080/02699930441000238 PMID:21852891

Fredrickson, B. L., & Levenson, R. W. (1998). Positive emotions speed recovery from the cardiovascular sequelae of negative emotions. *Cognition and Emotion*, *12*(2), 191–220. doi:10.1080/026999398379718 PMID:21852890

Fredrickson, B. L., Mancuso, R. A., Branigan, C., & Tugade, M. M. (2000). The undoing effect of positive emotions. *Motivation and Emotion*, *24*(4), 237–258. doi:10.1023/A:1010796329158 PMID:21731120

Freedberg, D., & Gallese, V. (2007). Motion, emotion and empathy in esthetic experience. *Trends in Cognitive Sciences*, *11*(5), 197–203. doi:10.1016/j.tics.2007.02.003 PMID:17347026

Freedom du Lac, J. (2010). Guidebook that aided black travelers during segregation reveals vastly different D.C. *Washington Post*. Retrieved from http://www.washingtonpost.com/wp-dyn/content/article/2010/09/11/AR2010091105358.html

Freud, S. (2005). Massenpsychologie und Ich-Analyse. Die Zukunft einer Illusion [Group psychology and the analysis of the ego: The future of an illusion]. Frankfurt-on-Main, Germany: Fischer Verlag. (Original work published 1921)

Fried, I. (2011). Meet the stealthy start-up that aims to sharpen focus of entire camera industry. *All Things D*. Retrieved from http://allthingsd.com/20110621/meet-the-stealthy-start-up-that-aims-to-sharpen-focus-of-entire-camera-industry/

Friedhoff, J. (2018). *Playful Possibilities*. Talk presented at Eyeo Festival. Retrieved from https://vimeo.com/287093861

Friedman, J. (2011). *Robots Through History*. Rosen Central.

Fry, W. F. (1994). The biology of humor. *Humor: International Journal of Humor Research*, 7(2), 111–126. doi:10.1515/humr.1994.7.2.111

FullDome Festival. (2015). *Program Brochure of the 10th FullDome Festival*. Program Brochure of the 10th FullDome Festival.

Funk, D. C., Ridinger, L. L., & Moorman, A. M. (2004). Exploring origins of involvement: Understanding the relationship between consumer motives and involvement with professional sport teams. *Leisure Sciences*, 26(1), 35–61. doi:10.1080/01490400490272440

Gajadhar, B. J., De Kort, Y. A., & Ijsselsteijn, W. A. (2008). *Shared fun is doubled fun: player enjoyment as a function of social setting. In Fun and games* (pp. 106–111). Berlin: Springer-Verlag.

Ganter, C. (2012). Projectors and Dome Effective Contrast. *IPS 2012 Conference Proceedings*. Retrieved from http://media.definititheaters.com/node/43

Gardner, E. (2019). Deepfakes Pose Increasing Legal and Ethical Issues for Hollywood. *Hollywood Reporter*. Retrieved from https://www.hollywoodreporter.com/thr-esq/deepfakes-pose-increasing-legal-ethical-issues-hollywood-1222978

Garland, E. L., & Howard, M. O. (2018). Mindfulness-based treatment of addiction: Current state of the field and envisioning the next wave of research. *Addiction Science & Clinical Practice*, 13(1), 14. doi:10.118613722-018-0115-3 PMID:29669599

Gaston, L., Dougall, P., & Thompson, E. D. (2008). Methods for Sharing Stereo and Multichannel Recordings among Planetariums. *Proceedings of the AES 124th Convention*.

Gefter, A. (2009). Green Aria: An opera for your nose. *New Scientist*, 5. Retrieved from https://www.newscientist.com/article/dn17236-green-aria-an-opera-for-your-nose/

Gelernter, D. (1992). *Mirror worlds - or the day software puts the universe in a shoebox: how it will happen and what it will mean*. Oxford, UK: Oxford University Press.

Gendlin, E. T. (1994). *The primacy of perception: An ancient and modern mistake*. Unpublished manuscript.

Gendlin, E. T. (1992). The wider role of bodily sense in thought and language. In M. Sheets Johnstone (Ed.), *Giving the body its due* (pp. 192–207). Albany, NY: State University of New York Press.

Genette, G. (1983). *Narrative Discourse: An Essay in Method*. Ithaca, NY: Cornell University Press.

Gent, E. (2018, February). Baidu can clone your voice after hearing just a minute of audio. *New Scientist*, 26. Retrieved from https://www.newscientist.com/article/2162177-baidu-can-clone-your-voice-after-hearing-just-a-minute-of-audio/

Gentsch, P. (2019). Conversational AI: How (Chat) Bots Will Reshape the Digital Experience. In *AI in Marketing, Sales and Service* (pp. 81–125). Cham: Palgrave Macmillan. doi:10.1007/978-3-319-89957-2_4

Giardina, C. (2017) How Artificial Intelligence Will Make Digital Humans Hollywood's New Stars August 25, 2017. *The Hollywood Reporter*. Retrieved from https://www.hollywoodreporter.com/behind-screen/how-artificial-intelligence-will-make-digital-humans-hollywoods-new-stars-1031553

Giardina, C. (2018). NAB: Location-Based Entertainment Could Be $12 Billion Industry in Five Years. *Hollywood Reporter*. Retrieved from https://www.hollywoodreporter.com/behind-screen/nab-location-based-entertainment-could-be-12-billion-industry-five-years-1100772

Giardina, C. (2019). CGR Cinemas' First ICE Theater in the U.S. to Open at Regal's L.A. Live. *Hollywood Reporter*. Retrieved from https://www.hollywoodreporter.com/behind-screen/cgr-cinemas-first-ice-theater-us-open-at-regals-la-live-1224871

Giard, M. H., & Peronnet, F. (1999). Auditory-visual integration during multimodal object recognition in humans: A behavioral and electrophysiological study. *Journal of Cognitive Neuroscience*, *11*(5), 473–490. doi:10.1162/089892999563544 PMID:10511637

Gilliam, T. (Director), & Gilliam, T., Stoppard, T., & McKeown, C. (Writers). (1985). *Brazil* [Motion picture]. US/UK: 20th Century Fox.

Gillies, M. (2018). Purposeful Practice for Learning Social Skills in VR. *Medium*. Retrieved from https://medium.com/virtual-reality-virtual-people/purposeful-practice-for-learning-social-skills-in-vr-362657cbfc88

Ginsburg, C. (1999). Body-Image, Movement and Consciousness. In J. Shear & F. J. Varela (Eds.), *The view from within: First-person approaches to the study of consciousness*. Imprint Academic.

Glanz, K., Rizzo, A., & Graap, K. (2003). Virtual reality for psychotherapy: Current reality and future possibilities. *Psychotherapy (Chicago, Ill.)*, *40*(1-2), 55–67. doi:10.1037/0033-3204.40.1-2.55

God of War. (2018). [Computer software]. SIE.

Goel, V., & Dolan, R. J. (2001). The functional anatomy of humor: Segregating cognitive and affective components. *Nature Neuroscience*, *4*(4), 237–238. doi:10.1038/85076 PMID:11224538

Google Patents. (2017). *Combination training device for student aviators and entertainment apparatus*. Retrieved from https://patents.google.com/patent/US1825462

Google Spotlight Stories. (2013). *Windy Day* [Video file]. Retrieved from https://www.youtube.com/watch?v=VG4FlT7c-AY

Google Spotlight Stories. (2014). *Duet* [Video file]. Retrieved from https://www.youtube.com/watch?v=x0Y35XLBY8A

Google Spotlight Stories. (2016a). *Buggy Night* [Video file]. Retrieved from https://www.youtube.com/watch?v=sk8hm7DXD5w

Google Spotlight Stories. (2016b). *Rain or Shine* [Video file]. Retrieved from https://www.youtube.com/watch?v=QXF7uGfopnY

Google Spotlight Stories. (2017). *Pearl* [Video file]. Retrieved from https://www.youtube.com/watch?v=WqCH4DNQBUA

Google Spotlight Stories. (2018). *Age of Sail* [Video file]. Retrieved from https://www.youtube.com/watch?v=TH3HOcRayC8

Gorini, A., Pallavicini, F., Algeri, D., Repetto, C., Gaggioli, A., & Riva, G. (2010).. . *Studies in Health Technology and Informatics*, *154*, 39–43. PMID:20543266

Gorisse, G., Christmann, O., Amato, E., & Richir, S. (2017). First-and third-person perspectives in immersive virtual environments: Presence and performance analysis of embodied users. *Frontiers in Robotics and AI, 4*(33).

GOTO, Inc. (2016). *Second full-sphere projection system installed at Fukushima Prefectural Government Environmental Creation Center*. Retrieved from http://www.goto.co.jp/english/news/20160908/

Gotter, A. (2017). What Your Brand Can Learn from Warby Parker's Massive Success. *Pixlee*. Retrieved from www.pixlee.com/blog/what-your-brand-can-learn-from-warby-parkers-massive-success

Greenberg, J., & Mitchell, S. (1983). *Object relations in psychoanalytic theory (Kindle version)*. Cambridge, MA: Harvard University Press. doi:10.2307/j.ctvjk2xv6

Greenwald, S. W., Corning, W., Funk, M., & Maes, P. (2018). Comparing Learning in Virtual Reality with Learning on a 2D Screen Using Electrostatics Activities. *J. UCS*, *24*(2), 220–245.

Greenwell, L., Jones, A., Panetta, F., Oppermann, H., Kranot, U., Andersen, M., & von Bubnoff, A. (2018). *Songbird* [interactive VR]. Retrieved from https://www.theguardian.com/technology/video/2018/jul/30/songbird-a-virtual-moment-of-extinction-in-hawaii-360-video

Gromala, D. J., & Sharir, Y. (1996). Dancing with the virtual dervish: virtual bodies. In M. A. Moser & D. MacLeod (Eds.), *Immersed in technology* (pp. 281–285). Cambridge, MA: MIT Press.

Gropius, W. (1935). *Die Neue Architektur Und Das Bauhaus. Grundzüge Und Entwicklung Einer Konzeption*. Faber & Faber.

Gross, M. J., & Brown, G. (2008). An empirical structural model of tourists and places: Progressing involvement and place attachment into tourism. *Tourism Management*, *29*(6), 1141–1151. doi:10.1016/j.tourman.2008.02.009

Grow, K. (2017). Frank Zappa Hologram to Perform with Steve Vai, Ex-Mothers of Invention. *Rolling Stone*. Retrieved from https://www.rollingstone.com/music/music-news/frank-zappa-hologram-to-perform-with-steve-vai-ex-mothers-of-invention-199881/

Grybko, M. (2016). *Quote from Podcast and blog by Damien Farnworth*. Retrieved from https://www.copyblogger.com/define-creativity/

Guarino, B. (2016). Edge of Nowhere, Lucky's Tale, and the case for third person VR. *Inverse*. Retrieved from https://www.inverse.com/article/9996-edge-of-nowhere-lucky-s-tale-and-the-case-for-third-person-vr

Haahr, M. (2015). Everting the Holodeck: Games and Storytelling in physical Space. In H. Koenitz, G. Ferri, M. Haahr, D. Sezen, & I. T. Sezen (Eds.), *Interactive digital narrative: History, Theory and Practice* (pp. 212–226). Oxfordshire, UK: Routledge Co. doi:10.4324/9781315769189-17

Haahr, M. (2018). Playing with Vision: Sight and Seeing as Narrative and Game Mechanics in Survival Horror. *11th International Conference on Interactive Digital Storytelling. ICIDS 2018*, 11318, 193-205. 10.1007/978-3-030-04028-4_20

Habe, H., Saeki, N., & Matsuyama, T. (2007). Inter-reflection compensation for immersive projection display. *Proceedings of the IEEE International Workshop on Projector-Camera Systems (ProCams)*.

Hagenback, D., & Wertmüller, L. (2013). *Mystic Chemist: The Life of Albert Hofmann and His Discovery of LSD*. Santa Fe, NM: Synergetic Press.

Hair, J. F., Black, W. C., Babin, B. J., Anderson, R. E., & Tatham, R. L. (2006). *Multivariate data analysis*. Upper Saddle River, NJ: Pearson Prentice Hall.

Hallema, S. (2018). *The Social Sorting Experiment* [interactive performance]. The Smartphone Orchestra. Retrieved from https://www.doclab.org/2018/the-social-sorting-experiment/

Halls, A. (2018). *A Brief History of Immersive Theater*. Retrieved from https://www.postandcourier.com/spoleto/a-brief-history-of-immersive-theater/article_baf19760-637c-11e8-b8ad-3b7339b572ac.html

Harari, Y. N. (2017). *Power and Imagination*. Retrieved from https://www.ynharari.com/topic/power-and-imagination/

Haridy, R. (2017). New face-aging technique could help locate missing persons. *New Atlas*. Retrieved from https://newatlas.com/facial-aging-software-missing-persons/50051/

Harms, C., & Biocca, F. (2004). Internal Consistency and Reliability of the Networked Minds Measure of Social Presence. In M. Alcaniz & B. Rey (Eds.), *Seventh Annual International Workshop: Presence 2004*. Valencia: Universidad Politecnica de Valencia.

Harris, B. J. (2019). *The History of the Future: How a Bunch of Misfits, Makers, and Mavericks Cracked the Code of Virtual Reality*. New York: HarperCollins Publishers.

Harrison, J. E. (1951). *Ancient Art and Ritual*. New York: Greenwood Press.

Harris, S. R., Kemmerling, R. L., & North, M. M. (2002). Brief virtual reality therapy for public speaking anxiety. *Cyberpsychology & Behavior*, 5(6), 534–550. doi:10.1089/109493102321018187 PMID:12556117

Hartmann, S. (1913, July). In Perfume Land. *Forum*, 50(1), I-1.

Hashkes, S., Ho, M., & Bye, K. (2019, June 23). #780: Invoking Psychedelic Embodiment Experiences in VR. *Voices of VR Podcast*. Retrieved from https://voicesofvr.com/780-invoking-psychedelic-embodiment-experiences-vr-radix-motion-meu/

Hasson, U., Landesman, O., Knappmeyer, B., Vallines, I., Rubin, N., & Heeger, D. (2008). Neurocinematics: The neuroscience of film. *Projections: Journal for Movies and Mind*, 2(1), 1–26. doi:10.3167/proj.2008.020102

Havens, J. (2011). Who Owns the Advertising Space in an Augmented Reality World? *Mashable*. Retrieved from www.mashable.com/2011/06/06/virtual-air-rights-augmented-reality

Hayden, S. (2016). 'Sequenced' creates truly reactive storytelling in VR. *Road to VR*. Retrieved from https://www.roadtovr.com/vr-animated-series-sequenced-creates-truly-reactive-storytelling-vr/

Hazleton, A. (2016). *CrossBounce Simulation*. GitHub, Inc. Retrieved from https://github.com/zicher3d-org/domemaster-stereo-shader/wiki/CrossBounce-Simulation

Heavens of Copernicus Productions (Producer), Majda, P. (Director). (2013). *Dream to Fly* [Fulldome Film]. Poland: Heavens of Copernicus Productions.

Heavy Rain. (2010). [Computer software]. SCE.

Hebb, D. O. (1946). Emotion in man and animal: An analysis of the intuitive processes of recognition. *Psychological Review*, 53(2), 88–106. doi:10.1037/h0063033 PMID:21023321

Hedman, P., Alsisan, S., Szeliski, R., & Kopf, J. (2017). Casual 3D photography. *ACM Transactions on Graphics*, 36(6), 234. doi:10.1145/3130800.3130828

Heim, M. (1993). *The metaphysics of virtual reality*. New York: Oxford University Press.

Heinlein, R. (1950). *Waldo and Magic, Inc.* Doubleday.

Hill, S. (2016). Is VR too dangerous for kids? We asked the experts. *Digital Trends*. Retrieved from https://www.digitaltrends.com/virtual-reality/is-vr-safe-for-kids-we-asked-the-experts/

Hodgson, P., Lee, V. W. Y., Chan, J. C. S., Fong, A., Tang, C. S. Y., Chan, L., & Wong, C. (2019). Immersive Virtual Reality (IVR) in Higher Education: Development and Implementation. In Augmented Reality and Virtual Reality: The Power of AR and VR for Business. New York: Springer International Publishing.

Hoffman, H. G., Patterson, D. R., & Carrougher, G. J. (2000, September 16). Use of virtual reality for adjunctive treatment of adult burn pain during physical therapy: A controlled study. *The Clinical Journal of Pain*, *16*(3), 244–250. doi:10.1097/00002508-200009000-00010 PMID:11014398

Hoium, T. (2018). Why Facebook's Oculus Acquisition Hasn't Paid Off... Yet Facebook has a lot of work to do growing its virtual reality business. *The Motely Fool*. Retrieved from https://www.fool.com/investing/2018/08/31/why-facebooks-oculus-acquisition-hasnt-paid-off-ye.aspx

Holak, S. L., & Havlena, W. J. (1992). *Nostalgia: An exploratory study of themes and emotions in the nostalgic experience*. ACR North American Advances.

Hollywood, Health & Society. (n.d.). Retrieved from https://hollywoodhealthandsociety.org/about-us/history-hhs-numbers

Hölzel, B., Carmody, J., Vangel, M., Congleton, C., Yerramsetti, S. M., Gard, T., & Lazar, S. W. (2011). Mindfulness Practice Leads to Increases in Regional Brain Gray Matter Density. *Psychiatry Research*, *191*(1), 36–43. doi:10.1016/j.pscychresns.2010.08.006 PMID:21071182

Houghton, R. (2019). Will Smith clone movie Gemini Man praised as "breathtaking" in first reactions. *DigitalSpy*. Retrieved from https://www.digitalspy.com/movies/a29117708/will-smith-clone-movie-gemini-man-first-reactions-ang-lee/

House, P. (2016). *Werner Herzog Talks Virtual Reality*. Retrieved from https://www.newyorker.com/tech/annals-of-technology/werner-herzog-talks-virtual-reality

Howard, A. (2016). *A Short History of Ancient Theatre*. Retrieved from https://www.newhistorian.com/2016/09/19/short-history-ancient-theatre/

Hsu, T. (2017). These Influencers Aren't Flesh and Blood, Yet Millions Follow Them. *New York Times*. Retrieved from www.nytimes.com/2019/06/17/business/media/miquela-virtual-influencer.html

Hsu, C. T., Conrad, M., & Jacobs, A. M. (2014). Fiction feelings in Harry Potter: Haemodynamic response in the mid cingulate cortex correlates with immersive reading experience. *Neuroreport*, *25*(17), 1356–1361. doi:10.1097/WNR.0000000000000272 PMID:25304498

Humphreys, L. (2018). *The Qualified Self: Social Media and the Accounting of Everyday Life*. The MIT Press. doi:10.7551/mitpress/9990.001.0001

Husband, J., & Barsalo, R. (2005). *The SAT Urban Hub. Vision, issues and opportunities and future directions*. SAT Metalab White Paper. Retrieved from https://bibbase.org/network/publication/husband-barsalo-thesaturbanhubvisionissuesandopportunitiesandfuturedirection-2005

Hutchinson, L. (2018) *Pilgrim* [interactive augmented audio walk]. Retrieved from https://www.doclab.org/2018/pilgrim/

Iacoboni, M., Woods, R. P., Brass, M., Bekkering, H., Mazziotta, J. C., & Rizzolatti, G. (1999). Cortical mechanisms of human imitation. *Science*, *286*(5449), 2526–2528. doi:10.1126cience.286.5449.2526 PMID:10617472

i. Badia, S. B., Morgade, A. G., Samaha, H., & Verschure, P. F. (2013). Using a hybrid brain computer interface and virtual reality system to monitor and promote cortical reorganization through motor activity and motor imagery training. *IEEE Transactions on Neural Systems and Rehabilitation Engineering*, *21*(2), 174–181. doi:10.1109/TNSRE.2012.2229295 PMID:23204287

IMDB. (2019). *Eve Weston*. Retrieved from https://www.imdb.com/name/nm2542598/?ref_=fn_al_nm_1

IMERSA. (2014). *IMERSA/AFDI Dome Standards Group, Dome Master Standards*. Retrieved from https://www.imersa.org/standards

Immersive Design Industry. (2019). Interactive, Intimate, Experiential: The Impact of Immersive Design. *2019 Immersive Design Industry Annual Report*. Retrieved from https://immersivedesignsummit.com/2019industryreport.pdf

Iñárritu, A. G., Lesher, J., Milchan, A., & Skotchdopole, J. W. (Producers), Iñárritu, A. G., (Director). (2014). *Birdman* [Motion Picture]. United States. Fox Searchlight Pictures.

Innerspace, V. R. (2017). *Firebird: The Unfinished* [Video file]. Retrieved from https://www.youtube.com/watch?v=2QPMbkQEOks

IONS. (n.d.). *IONS Our Origins*. Retrieved from https://noetic.org/about/origins

Irving, T. (2019). From quality control to deepfakes: How one U of T Engineering team is advancing VR technology. *University of Toronto Engineering News*. Retrieved October 3, 2019, from https://news.engineering.utoronto.ca/from-quality-control-to-deepfakes-how-one-u-of-t-engineering-team-is-advancing-vr-technology/

Isen, A. M. (1993). Positive affect and decision making. In M. Lewis & J. M. Haviland (Eds.), *Handbook of emotions* (pp. 261–277). New York: Guilford.

Isenberg, B. (1989). Secrets of the Play that Refuses to Close. *Los Angeles Times*. Retrieved from https://www.latimes.com/archives/la-xpm-1989-02-12-ca-3037-story.html

Itin, C. M. (1999). Reasserting the philosophy of experiential education as a vehicle for change in the 21st century. *Journal of Experiential Education*, *22*(2), 91–98. doi:10.1177/105382599902200206

Ivens, G. (2018). *Leaked Recipes* [interactive installation/performance]. Retrieved from https://www.doclab.org/2018/leaked-recipes/

Jackson, L., & Borrett, M. (2018). *Biidaaban: First Light* [VR installation]. Canada: Jam3 & National Film Board of Canada. Retrieved from https://www.nfb.ca/interactive/biidaaban_first_light/

James, C. (Producer & Director), & Jon, L. (Producer). (1997). *Titanic* [Motion Picture]. United States: Paramount Pictures & 20th Century Fox Film.

Jenkins, A. (2019). The Fall and Rise of VR: The Struggle to Make Virtual Reality Get Real. *Fortune*. Retrieved from https://fortune.com/longform/virtual-reality-struggle-hope-vr/

Jenkins, H. (2008). *Convergence Culture: Where Old and New Media Collide*. New York: NYU Press.

Johnson, K. (2019, May 23). *Samsung's AI animates paintings and photos without 3D modeling*. Retrieved August 20, 2019, from https://venturebeat.com/2019/05/22/samsungs-ai-animates-paintings-and-photos-without-3d-modeling/

Johnson, M. (1987). *The Body in the Mind*. Chicago, IL: University of Chicago Press. doi:10.7208/chicago/9780226177847.001.0001

Johnson, M., & Ryan, T. (2005). *Sexuality in Greek and Roman Society and Literature*. London, UK: Routledge.

Jonze, S. (Dir.) (2013). *Her* [motion picture]. United States: Warner Bros.

Joseph, T. (2019). How Is Augmented Reality Reshaping Travel and Tourism? *Fingent*. Retrieved from www.fingent.com/blog/how-is-augmented-reality-reshaping-travel-and-tourism

Joshi, N. (2019). AR and VR in the Utility Sector. *Forbes*. Retrieved from https://www.forbes.com/sites/cognitive-world/2019/09/29/ar-and-vr-in-the-utility-sector

Joyce, K. (2017). Review: Lucky's Tale: Playful Corp.'s Lucky's Tale defines what it means to be a platform videogame in VR. *VR Focus*. Retrieved from https://www.vrfocus.com/2016/03/review-luckys-tale/

Jung, C. G. (1959). *The archetypes and the collective unconscious* (R. F. C. Hull, Trans.). Princeton, NJ: Princeton University Press.

Jung, C. G. (1965). *Memories, dreams, reflections.* New York, NY: Vintage Books.

Kalawsky, R. S. (1993). *The Science of Virtual Reality and Virtual Environments: A Technical, Scientific and Engineering Reference on Virtual Environments.* Wokingham, UK: Addison-Wesley.

Kalpana. (2017). *Injustice* [interactive VR]. Retrieved from http://www.etc.cmu.edu/projects/kalpana/

Kant, I. (2018). *Critique of Pure Reason* (J. M. Meiklejohn, Trans.). Mineola, NY: Dover Publications. (Original work published 1781)

Karras, T., Laine, S., Aittala, M., Hellsten, J., Lehtinen, J., & Aila, T. (2019). *Analyzing and Improving the Image Quality of StyleGAN.* arXiv preprint arXiv:1912.04958

Katz, M. (2018). CGI 'Influencers' Like Lil Miquela Are About to Flood Your Feeds. *Wired*. Retrieved from www.wired.com/story/lil-miquela-digital-humans/

Keith, C. (1979). *Film and fiction: The dynamics of exchange* (1st ed.). New Haven, CT: Yale University Press.

Keller, G. B., Bonhoeffer, T., & Hübener, M. (2012). Sensorimotor mismatch signals in primary visual cortex of the behaving mouse. *Neuron*, *74*(5), 809–815. doi:10.1016/j.neuron.2012.03.040 PMID:22681686

Kelly, K. (2019). AR Will Spark the Next Big Tech Platform—call It Mirrorworld. *Wired*. Retrieved from https://www.wired.com/story/mirrorworld-ar-next-big-tech-platform/

Keltner, D., & Haidt, J. (2003). Approaching awe, a moral, spiritual, and aesthetic emotion. *Cognition and Emotion*, *17*(2), 297–314. doi:10.1080/02699930302297 PMID:29715721

Keogh, B. (2017). Pokémon Go, the novelty of nostalgia, and the ubiquity of the smartphone. *Mobile Media & Communication*, *5*(1), 38–41. doi:10.1177/2050157916678025

Kim, K., Kim, C. H., Cha, K. R., Park, J., Han, K., Kim, Y. K., ... Kim, S. I. (2008). Anxiety provocation and measurement using virtual reality in patients with obsessive compulsive disorder. *Cyberpsychology & Behavior*, *11*(6), 637–641. doi:10.1089/cpb.2008.0003 PMID:18991527

King, D. (2018). *Spend A Night at The McKittrick Hotel, A Damned Good Spot.* Retrieved from https://www.forbes.com/sites/darrynking/2018/07/19/spend-a-night-at-the-mckittrick-hotel-a-damned-good-spot/#7d5e04df126d

Kleiman, J. (2019). Evans & Sutherland launches DomeX LED display for fulldome planetariums and giant screen theaters. *InPark Magazine*. Retrieved from http://www.inparkmagazine.com/about/

Kline, R. B. (2015). *Principles and practice of structural equation modeling.* Guilford publications.

Klinger, E., Bouchard, S., Légeron, P., Roy, S., Lauer, F., Chemin, I., & Nugues, P. (2005). *CyberPsychology & Behavior*. Preprint. doi:10.1089/cpb.2005.8.76

Klinger, E., Chemin, I., Lebreton, S., & Marié, R. M. (2006). Virtual action planning in Parkinson's disease: A control study. *Cyberpsychology & Behavior*, *9*(3), 342–347. doi:10.1089/cpb.2006.9.342 PMID:16780402

Knickman, J. R., & Snell, E. K. (2002). The 2030 problem: Caring for aging baby boomers. *Health Services Research*, *37*(4), 849–884. doi:10.1034/j.1600-0560.2002.56.x PMID:12236388

Koetz, C., & Tankersley, J. D. (2016). Nostalgia in online brand communities. *The Journal of Business Strategy*, *37*(3), 22–29. doi:10.1108/JBS-03-2015-0025

Koster, F., & Oosterhoff, M. (2004). *Liberating Insight: Introduction to Buddhist Psychology and Insight Meditation*. Chiang Mai: Silkworm Books.

Koutny, D., Palousek, D., Koutecky, T., Zatocilova, A., Rosicky, J., & Janda, M. (2012). 3D digitalization of the human body for use in orthotics and prosthetics. In Proceedings of World Academy of Science, Engineering and Technology (No. 72, p. 1628). World Academy of Science, Engineering and Technology (WASET).

Krueger, M. W. (1977, June). Responsive environments. In *Proceedings of the June 13-16, 1977, national computer conference* (pp. 423-433). ACM. 10.1145/1499402.1499476

Kruse, J. (2006). Architektur Aus Dem Geist Der Projektion: Das Zeiss-Planetarium. Wissen in Bewegung. 80 Jahre Zeiss-Planetarium Jena, 51-78.

Kubrick, S. (Director). (1999). *Eyes Wide Shut* [Motion Picture]. UK: Stanley Kubrick Productions. Distributed by Warner Bros.

Kuchera-Morin, J., Wright, M., Wakefield, G., Roberts, C., Adderton, D., Sajadi, B., ... Majumder, A. (2014). Immersive full-surround multi-user system design. *Computers & Graphics*, *40*, 10–21. doi:10.1016/j.cag.2013.12.004

Kudsk Steensen, J. (2018). *Re-Animated* [interactive VR - 15 min]. Retrieved from https://cphdox.dk/en/programme/film/?id=1207

Kukula, M. (2017). Planetariums and the rise of spectacular science. *Nature Magazine*. Retrieved from https://www.nature.com/articles/d41586-017-08441-9

Kulp, P. (2019). A Small But Growing Startup Scene Is Exploring Uses for Digital Human Avatars. *Adweek*. Retrieved from www.adweek.com/digital/a-small-but-growing-startup-scene-is-exploring-uses-for-digital-human-avatars

Kurzweil, R. (2009). Get ready for hybrid thinking. *Ted Talk*. Retrieved from https://www.ted.com/talks/ray_kurzweil_get_ready_for_hybrid_thinking

Kushins, J. (2016). *A brief history of sound in cinema*. Retrieved from https://www.popularmechanics.com/culture/movies/a19566/a-brief-history-of-sound-in-cinema/

Kwon, J. H., Chalmers, A., Czanner, S., Czanner, G., & Powell, J. (2009). A study of visual perception: social anxiety and virtual realism. *Proceedings of the 25th Spring Conference on Computer Graphics*, 167-172. 10.1145/1980462.1980495

Kyle, G., & Chick, G. (2002). The social nature of leisure involvement. *Journal of Leisure Research*, *34*(4), 426–448. doi:10.1080/00222216.2002.11949980

Kyodo News. (2017, July 15). One year after release, Pokemon Go is fitness tool for older people. *Kyodo News*. Retrieved from https://english.kyodonews.net/

Lacher, I. (1997). Fred Is Her Co-Pilot. *Los Angeles Times*. Retrieved from www.latimes.com/archives/la-xpm-1997-aug-17-ca-23118-story.html

LaFrance, A. (2017). An Artificial Intelligence Developed Its Own Non-Human Language. *Atlantic (Boston, Mass.)*, *21*. Retrieved from https://www.theatlantic.com/technology/archive/2017/06/artificial-intelligence-develops-its-own-non-human-language/530436/

Lakoff, G., & Johnson, M. (1980). *Metaphors we live by*. Chicago: University of Chicago Press.

Lakoff, G., & Johnson, M. (1980). *Metaphors We Live By*. Chicago: University of Chicago Press.

Lambert, N., & Phillips, M. (2012). Introduction: Fulldome. *Digital Creativity*, *23*(1), 1–4. doi:10.1080/14626268.2012.666980

Lampton, D. R., Knerr, B. W., Goldberg, S. L., Bliss, J. P., Moshell, J. M., & Blau, B. S. (1994). The Virtual Environment Performance Assessment Battery (VEPAB): Development and Evaluation. *Presence (Cambridge, Mass.)*, *3*(2), 145–157. doi:10.1162/pres.1994.3.2.145

Lan, L. (2019). China's virtual reality arcades aim for real-world success. *The Jakarta Post*. Retrieved from https://www.thejakartapost.com/life/2019/04/07/chinas-virtual-reality-arcades-aim-for-real-world-success.html

Lancaster, L. (2011). The cognitive neuroscience of consciousness, mysticism and psi. *International Journal of Transpersonal Studies*, *30*(1-2), 11–22. doi:10.24972/ijts.2011.30.1-2.11

Lange, P. G. (2011). Video-mediated nostalgia and the aesthetics of technical competencies. *Visual Communication*, *10*(1), 25–44. doi:10.1177/1470357210389533

Lanier, J. (2010). On the Threshold of the Avatar Era. *Wall Street Journal*. Retrieved from: https://www.wsj.com/articles/SB10001424052702303738504575568410584865010

Lansard, M. (2019). The 16 Best 3D Body Scanners in 2019. *Aniwaa*. Retrieved from https://www.aniwaa.com/best-3d-body-scanners/

Lantz, E. (2004). Fulldome Display Specifications: A Proposal. IPS 2004 Fulldome Standards Summit, Valencia, Spain.

Lantz, E., Wyatt, R., Bruno, M., & Neafus, D. (2004). *Proceedings of the IPS 2004 Fulldome Standards Summit, Valencia, Spain, 7 July 2004*. Retrieved from http://extranet.spitzinc.com/reference/IPS2004/default.aspx

Lantz, E. (1997). Future Directions in Visual Display Systems. Guest Editor. *Computer Graphics*, *31*(2), 38–45. doi:10.1145/271283.271301

Lantz, E. (2009, June). The Planetarium: A Transitional Animal. *Planetarian*, *38*(2), 6–12.

Lantz, E. (2011, July). Planetarium of the Future. *Curator*, *54*(3), 293–312. doi:10.1111/j.2151-6952.2011.00093.x

Lantz, E. (2018). From space to the stars: Ten years of arts and entertainment at The Vortex Dome-Los Angeles. *Planetarian*, *47*(2), 22–28.

Lasley, P., & Harriman, E. (1985). *Tamara*: Audience Follows Cast from Room to Room. *Christian Science Monitor*. Retrieved from https://www.csmonitor.com/1985/0709/ltama-f.html

LaValle, S. (2016, January 24). Goals and VR definitions [Video file]. *Retrieved from*, *14*, 40m.

Lazarus, A. A. (1997). *Brief but comprehensive psychotherapy: The multimodal way*. New York, NY: Springer.

Leaver, T. (2019). Posthumous Performance and Digital Resurrection: From Science Fiction to Startups. In T. Kohn, M. Gibbs, B. Nansen, & L. van Ryn (Eds.), *Residues of Death: Disposal Refigured*. London: Routledge. doi:10.4324/9780429456404-7

Lebowitz, J., & Klug, C. (2011). *Interactive storytelling for video games*. Waltham, MA: Focal Press.

Lechner, A., Ortner, R., & Guger, C. (2014). Feedback strategies for BCI based stroke rehabilitation: Evaluation of different approaches. In W. Jensen, O. K. Andersen, & M. Akay (Eds.), *2nd International Conference on NeuroRehabilitation (ICNR)*. 10.1007/978-3-319-08072-7_75

Leclerc, F. (2012). 3D Scanning for Post-Mastectomy Custom Breast Prosthesis. *Medical Design Briefs*. Retrieved from medicaldesignbriefs.com/component/content/article/mdb/tech-briefs/15287

LeDoux, J. (2014). Coming to terms with fear. *Proceedings of the National Academy of Sciences of the United States of America*, *111*(8), 2871–2878. doi:10.1073/pnas.1400335111 PMID:24501122

Lee, M., & Faber, R. J. (2007). Effects of product placement in on-line games on brand memory: A perspective of the limited-capacity model of attention. *Journal of Advertising*, *36*(4), 75–90. doi:10.2753/JOA0091-3367360406

Legault, J., Zhao, J., Chi, Y. A., Chen, W., Klippel, A., & Li, P. (2019). Immersive Virtual Reality as an Effective Tool for Second Language Vocabulary Learning. *Languages*, *4*(1), 13. doi:10.3390/languages4010013

Lerch, T., MacGillivray, M., & Domina, T. (2007). 3D Laser Scanning: A Model of multidisciplinary research. *Journal of Textile and Apparel. Technology and Management*, *5*(4), 1–8.

Levinas, E. (1969). *Totality and Infinity: An Essay on Exteriority* (A. Lingis, Trans.). Pittsburgh, PA: Duquesne University Press.

Lewis, T. (2013). Incredible Technology: How to Explore the Microscopic World. *Live Science*. Retrieved from https://www.livescience.com/38470-how-to-explore-microscopic-world.html

Lewis, A. M. (2014). Terror Management Theory applied clinically: Implications for existential integrative psychotherapy. *Death Studies*, *38*(6), 412–417. doi:10.1080/07481187.2012.753557 PMID:24666148

Lewis, W. H. (1997). *The Splendid Century: Life in the France of Louis XIV*. Long Grove, IL: Waveland Press Inc.

Li, X. J. (2000). Film Narratology: Theories and Examples, Beijing, China: China Film Press.

Libby, K. (2019). This Bill Hader Deepfake Video Is Amazing. It's Also Terrifying for Our Future. *Popular Mechanics*. Retrieved from https://www.popularmechanics.com/technology/security/a28691128/deepfake-technology/

Library of Congress. (n.d.). *Early Motion Picture Productions*. Retrieved from https://www.loc.gov/collections/edison-company-motion-pictures-and-sound-recordings/articles-and-essays/history-of-edison-motion-pictures/early-motion-picture-productions/

Lieberman, M. (2013). *Social: Why Our Brains Are Wired to Connect*. New York: Crown Publisher.

Lifshitz, M., Cusumano, E. P., & Raz, A. (2013). Hypnosis as neurophenomenology. *Frontiers in Human Neuroscience*, *7*, 469. doi:10.3389/fnhum.2013.00469 PMID:23966930

Li, J. L. (2018). Challenges and Revolutions of VR Film Narration. *Advanced Motion Picture Technology*, *12/2018*, 4–7.

Lin, C.-T., Lin, H.-Z., Chiu, T.-W., Chao, C.-F., Chen, Y.-C., & Liang, S.-F. (2008). Distraction related EEG dynamics in virtual reality driving simulation. In *IEEE International Symposium on Circuits and Systems,* (pp. 1088-1091). Seattle, WA: IEEE.

Lindberg, E. (2019). Personal stories of surviving the Holocaust unveiled at powerful art exhibition. *USC News*. Retrieved from https://news.usc.edu/160806/holocaust-survivors-art-exhibition-usc-shoah-foundation-fisher-museum

Little Cinema. (n.d.). *About Little Cinema*. Retrieved from http://littlecinema.net/about

Liu, Y., & Berger, P. D. (2018). The Sephora Mobile-App and Its Relationship to Customer Loyalty. *Business and Management Horizons, 6*(1). Retrieved from: www.macrothink.org/journal/index.php/bmh/article/view/13005/10285

Liu, F. (2011). Analysis on the Narrative Structure of Films: Linear and Non-linear. *Movie Literature, 15/2011*, 18–19.

Löfgren, K. (2013). *What is ontology? Introduction to the word and the concept*. Talk given in Sweden. Retrieved from https://youtu.be/XTsaZWzVJ4c

Loften, A., & Vaughan-Lee, E. (2018). *Sanctuaries of Silence* [VR experience]. Go Project Films. Retrieved from https://sanctuariesofsilence.com/

Lonsway, B. (2016). Complicated Agency. In S. A. Lukas (Ed.), *A reader in themed and immersive spaces* (pp. 239–248). Pittsburgh, PA: Carnegie Mellon/ETC Press.

Lorenzo, B., Tom, D., Don, M., & Ian, B. (Producer), & Michael, B. & Travis, K. (Director). (2007). *Transformers* [Motion Picture]. United States: DreamWorks Pictures & Paramount Pictures.

Loveday, P., & Burgess, J. (2017). Flow and Pokémon GO: The Contribution of Game Level, Playing Alone, and Nostalgia to the Flow State. *E-Journal of Social & Behavioural Research in Business, 8*(2), 16–28.

Low, A. (2017, July 10). These seniors are kicking ass in Pokemon Go: And staying healthy while doing so. *CNET*. Retrieved from https://www.cnet.com/

Luckel, M. (2016). Yes, There's a Museum of Ice Cream. And It's Everything You'd Imagine. *Vogue Daily*. Retrieved from https://www.vogue.com/article/museum-of-ice-cream-august-2016-nyc

Lyubomirsky, S., King, L., & Diener, E. (2005). The benefits of frequent positive affect: Does happiness lead to success? *Psychological Bulletin, 131*(6), 803–855. doi:10.1037/0033-2909.131.6.803 PMID:16351326

Maceda, C. (2015). Take a tour of Dubai in 3.5 minutes: 'The Sphere'-a first of its kind in the Middle East-offers virtual tour to visitors. *Gulf News*. Retrieved from https://gulfnews.com/travel/destinations/take-a-tour-of-dubai-in-35-minutes-1.1469766

Malicki-Sanchez, K. (2017). *Virtual Reality: ideacity 2017*. Retrieved from https://ideacity.ca/video/keram-malicki-sanchez-virtual-reality-toronto/

Malik, A. J. (2017). *Terminal 3* [interactive augmented reality experience]. United States: RYOT. Retrieved from https://www.tribecafilm.com/filmguide/terminal-3-2018

Mallenbaum, C. (2018). Why Escape Rooms Have a Lock on the U.S. *USA Today*. Retrieved from https://www.usatoday.com/story/life/people/2018/04/25/escape-rooms-trend-us/468181002/

Mallet, C. (2018). Is Kylie Jenner going to save VR? *VR Influencer Marketing*. Retrieved from www.somewhereelse.co/vr-influencer-marketing

Manninen, S., Tuominen, L, Dunbar, R., Karjalainen, T., Hirvonen, J., Arponen, E., … Nummenmaa, L. (2017). Social Laughter Triggers Endogenous Opioid Release in Humans. *The Journal of Neuroscience*.

Maples-Keller, J., Bunnell, B., Kim, S. J., & Rothbaum, B. (2017). The use of virtual reality technology in the treatment of anxiety and other psychiatric disorders. *Harvard Review of Psychiatry*, *25*(3), 103–113. doi:10.1097/HRP.0000000000000138 PMID:28475502

Marche, J. (2005). *Theaters of Time and Space: American Planetaria, 1930-1970*. New Brunswick, NJ: Rutgers University Press.

Mardia, K. V. (1970). Measures of multivariate skewness and kurtosis with applications. *Biometrika*, *57*(3), 519–530. doi:10.1093/biomet/57.3.519

Maren, S., & Holt, W. (2000). The hippocampus and contextual memory retrieval in Pavlovian conditioning. *Behavioural Brain Research*, *110*(1-2), 97–108. doi:10.1016/S0166-4328(99)00188-6 PMID:10802307

Martin, R. (2015). Stella Takes Torotonians on a Journey of the Senses. *Marketing Magazine*. Retrieved from: http://marketingmag.ca/advertising/stella-takes-torontonians-on-a-journey-of-the-senses-153882

Martineau, P. (2019). Facebook Removes Accounts With AI-Generated Profile Photos. *Wired*. Retrieved from https://www.wired.com/story/facebook-removes-accounts-ai-generated-photos/

Martin, R. A. (2006). *The Psychology of Humor: An Integrative Approach*. Cambridge, MA: Academic Press.

Mateo, D. J. (2017). Pokémon GO May Increase Physical Activity and Decrease Sedentary Behaviors Regular physical. *American Journal of Public Health*, *107*(1), 37–38. doi:10.2105/AJPH.2016.303532 PMID:27854536

Matthew, V. (Producer), & Guy, R. (Director). (1998). *Lock, Stock and Two Smoking Barrels* [Motion Picture]. United Kingdom & United States: Gramercy Pictures.

Maunsell, J. H., & Treue, S. (2006). Feature-based attention in visual cortex. *Trends in Neurosciences*, *29*(6), 317–322. doi:10.1016/j.tins.2006.04.001 PMID:16697058

McClure, R., & McGonagle, C. (2018). *Spotlight talk*. Expanded Realities Symposium—Open City Documentary Festival, London, UK.

McClure, R., & McGonagle, C. (2018). *VVVR* [interactive VR installation]. Retrieved from https://plusfour.io/vvvr/

McConnon, A. (2018). Breaking into the boom in escape rooms: what entrepreneurs need to know. *The New York Times*. Retrieved from https://www.nytimes.com/2018/04/11/business/escape-room-small-business.html?

McCormick, B. H., Defanti, T. A., & Brown, M. D. (1987). *Visualization in scientific computing: Report of the NSF Advisory Panel on Graphics*. Image Processing and Workstations.

McGregor, L. (2016). The Surprisingly Fascinating World of Frame Rates. *The Beat*. Retrieved from https://www.premiumbeat.com/blog/advanced-look-into-frame-rates/

McNeill, D. (1992). *Hand and mind: What gestures reveal about thought*. Chicago, IL: University of Chicago Press.

Mednick, S. A. (1968). The Remote Associates Test. *The Journal of Creative Behavior*, *2*(3), 213–214. doi:10.1002/j.2162-6057.1968.tb00104.x

mei.pi [Username]. (2014, June 25). *Real World Third Person Perspective VR/AR Experiment* [Video file]. Retrieved from https://www.youtube.com/watch?v=RgBeRP4dUGo

Melville, H. (1902). *Moby Dick*. New York: Charles Scribner's Sons.

Meyers, S. (2018). Capturing depth: Structured light, Time-of-Flight, and the Future of 3D Imaging. *Android Authority Features*. Retrieved from https://www.androidauthority.com/structured-light-3d-imaging-870016/

Michael, D. *(Producer), & Michael, D. (Director). (2002). Microcosm: The Adventure Within* [Fulldome Film]. United States: Evans & Sutherland.

Miley, J. (2018). Amazon Wants to Scan Your Body So You'll Never Return Your Online Shopping Again. *Interesting Engineering.* Retrieved from https://interestingengineering.com/amazon-wants-to-scan-your-body-so-youll-never-return-your-online-shopping-again

Miller, D. C. (2015). *SIMNET and Beyond: A History of the Development of Distributed Simulation.* Interservice/Industry Training, Simulation, and Education (IITSEC) Fellows Paper. Retrieved from https://www.iitsec.org/-/media/sites/iitsec/link-attachments/iitsec-fellows/2015_fellowpaper_miller.ashx

Miller, L. (2018). Hulu tests whether VR can be funny with new interactive 360 experience 'Door No. 1.' *IndieWire.* Retrieved from https://www.indiewire.com/2018/05/hulu-door-no-1-interactive-video-nora-kirkpatrick-1201968459/

Minocha, S., Tudor, A., & Tilling, S. (2017). Affordances of Mobile Virtual Reality and their Role in Learning and Teaching. *Proceedings of the 31st British Human Computer Interaction Conference.* 10.14236/ewic/HCI2017.44

Minoru, J. (Producer), & Akira, K. (Director). (1950). *Rashomon* [Motion Picture]. Japan: Daiei Film.

Miodownik, M. (2019). *Liquid Rules: The delightful and dangerous substances that flow through our lives.* Rancho Cucamonga, CA: Houghton Mifflin Harcourt.

Mitham, N. (2014). Virtual Worlds: Industry and User Data: Universe Chart for Q2 2014. *KZERO, Worldswide.* Retrieved from https://www.slideshare.net/nicmitham/kzero-universe-q2-2014

Mitry, J. (2000). *The Aesthetics and Psychology of the Cinema.* Bloomington, IN: Indiana University Press.

Mok, K. (2014). Sonic artist derives captivating "organic electronic" sounds from plants. *Treehugger webite.* Retrieved from https://www.treehugger.com/culture/organic-electronic-sounds-from-plants-sonic-artist-mileece.html

Montgomery, R. A. (2011). *The Trail of Lost Time.* Chooseco, LLC.

Montgomery, S. (2016). *The soul of an octopus: A surprising exploration into the wonder of consciousness.* New York: Atria Paperback.

Moon Flower. (n.d.). *About Moon Flower Sagaya Ginza Art by Team Lab.* Retrieved from: https://moonflower-sagaya.com/en

Mordor Intelligence. (2019). Location-Based Virtual Reality (VR) Market: Growth, Trends, and Forecast (2020-2025). *Mordor Intelligence.* Retrieved from https://www.mordorintelligence.com/industry-reports/location-based-virtual-reality-vr-market

Morency, C. (2018). Meet Fashion's First Computer-Generated Influencer. *Business of Fashion.* Retrieved from http://www.businessoffashion.com/articles/intelligence/meeting-fashions-first-computer-generated-influencer-lil-miquela-sousa

Mori, M., MacDorman, K. F., & Kageki, N. (2012). The uncanny valley: The original essay by Masahiro Mori. IEEE Spectrum, 98-100.

Moura, G. (2016). *Mise-En-Scène.* Retrieved from http://www.elementsofcinema.com/directing/mise-en-scene-in-films/

Mu, C. J. (2018). A Research on Storytelling of Interactive Documentary: Towards a New Storytelling Theory Model. *11th International Conference on Interactive Digital Storytelling. ICIDS 2018,* 11318, 181-184. 10.1007/978-3-030-04028-4_18

Muehling, D. D., & Pascal, V. J. (2012). An involvement explanation for nostalgia advertising effects. *Journal of Promotion Management, 18*(1), 100–118. doi:10.1080/10496491.2012.646222

Murray, J. H. (2016). Not a Film and Not an Empathy Machine. *Immerse*. Retrieved from https://immerse.news/not-a-film-and-not-an-empathy-machine-48b63b0eda93

Murray, J. H. (1997). *Hamlet on the Holodeck: The Future of Narrative in Cyberspace*. New York: The Free Press.

Murtagh, T., & Daut, M. (Producers & Directors). (2004). Stars of the Pharaohs [Fulldome Film]. United States: Evans & Sutherland.

Museum Hack. (2016). Snapchat Filters for Museums: Our Paid Results at AAM 2016. *Museum Hack*. Retrieved from www.museumhack.com/snapchat-filters

Muybridge, E. (1955). *Eadweard Muybridge: The Human Figure in Motion*. New York: Dover.

Nabi, R. L., & Krcmar, M. (2004). Conceptualizing media enjoyment as attitude: Implications for mass media effects research. *Communication Theory*, *14*(4), 288–310. doi:10.1111/j.1468-2885.2004.tb00316.x

Nadworny, E., & Anderson, M. (2017). Relics of The Space Race, School Planetariums Are an Endangered Species. *NPREd: How Learning Happens*. Retrieved from https://www.npr.org/sections/ed/2017/01/03/504715174/relics-of-the-space-race-school-planetariums-are-an-endangered-species

Nafarrete, J. (2015). Tom's Brings Virtual Reality Giving Trips to Retail Customers. *VR Scout*. Retrieved from https://vrscout.com/news/toms-virtual-reality-giving-trips

NASA. (n. d.). *The Golden Record*. Retrieved from voyager.jpl.nasa.gov/golden-record/

Nash Information Services. (2019) Domestic Movie Theatrical Market Summary 1995 to 2019. The Numbers: Where Data and Business Meet. *Nash Information Services*. Retrieved from https://www.the-numbers.com/market/

Nash, K. (2018). Virtual reality witness: Exploring the ethics of mediated presence. *Studies in Documentary Film*, *12*(2), 119–131. doi:10.1080/17503280.2017.1340796

NASSCOM. (2019). *Growth of Immersive Media: A Reality Check*. Retrieved from https://www.nasscom.in/knowledge-center/publications/growth-immersive-media-reality-check

Nat. Geo. (2017). *National Geographic Press release*. Retrieved from https://www.nationalgeographicpartners.com/press/2017/09/national-geographic-encounter-ocean-odyssey-opens/

National Academy Press. (1999). Funding a Revolution: Government Support for Computing Research. Committee on Innovations in Computing and Communications: Lessons from History. Washington, DC: Author.

Navajo, T. I. M. E. (Temporary Installations Made for the Environment) 2014 Inaugural Biennale. (2014). *New Mexico Arts*. Retrieved from www.nmarts.org/Navajo-Time-Pull-of-the-Moon.html

Navarro-Haro, M. V., López-del-Hoyo, Y., Campos, D., Linehan, M. M., Hoffman, H. G., García-Palacios, A., ... García-Campayo, J. (2017). Meditation experts try Virtual Reality Mindfulness: A pilot study evaluation of the feasibility and acceptability of Virtual Reality to facilitate mindfulness practice in people attending a Mindfulness conference. *PLoS One*, *12*(11), e0187777. doi:10.1371/journal.pone.0187777 PMID:29166665

Navitar. (2019). HemiStar™ Application Notes. *Navitar*. Retrieved from https://navitar.com/products/download-document/2359/

Nelson, R. (2018). *Pokémon GO revenue hits $1.8 billion on its two year launch anniversary*. Retrieved from https://sensortower.com/blog/pokemon-go-revenue-year-two

News, B. B. C. (2016). Adobe Voco 'Photoshop-for-voice' causes concern. *BBC News*. Retrieved from https://www.bbc.com/news/technology-37899902

Niemeyer, K., & Wentz, D. (2014). Nostalgia is not what it used to be: Serial nostalgia and nostalgic television series. In K. Niemeyer (Ed.), *Media and Nostalgia: Yearning for the Past, the Present and the Future* (pp. 129–138). London: Palgrave McMillan. doi:10.1057/9781137375889_10

Nir, Y., & Tononi, G. (2010). Dreaming and the brain: From phenomenology to neurophysiology. *Trends in Cognitive Sciences*, *14*(2), 88–100. doi:10.1016/j.tics.2009.12.001 PMID:20079677

Noë, A. (2004). *Action in perception*. Boston, MA: MIT Press.

North, D. (2005). Virtual Actors, Spectacle and Special Effects: Kung Fu Meets 'All That CGI Bullshit.' *The Matrix Trilogy: Cyberpunk Reloaded*, 48-61.

Nowak, K. (2001). *Defining and differentiating copresence, social presence and presence as transportation*. Paper presented at the Presence 2001 Conference, Philadelphia, PA.

O'Keeffe, H. (2013). Mystery of preserved T Rex tissue solved: High levels of iron in dinosaur's body kept it intact. *Daily Mail*. Retrieved from https://www.dailymail.co.uk/news/article-2515769/How-T-Rex-tissue-preserved-68million-years.html

O'Leary, E. (Ed.). (2013). *Gestalt therapy around the world*. Hoboken, NJ: John Wiley & Sons. doi:10.1002/9781118323410

O'Shannon, D. (2012). *What are you laughing at? A comprehensive guide to the comedic event*. Continuum International Publishing Group.

O'Shea, D. (2018). Macy's expanding VR furniture shopping to 90 stores by January. *Retail Dive*. Retrieved from www.retaildive.com/news/macys-expanding-vr-furniture-shopping-to-90-stores-by-january/539873

O'Sullivan, D. (2019). When seeing is no longer believing: Inside the Pentagon's race against Deepfake videos. *CNN Business*. Retrieved from https://www.cnn.com/videos/business/2019/01/28/deepfakes-interactive-social-cut-orig.cnn

Oculus Story Studio. (2015). *Henry* [Video file]. Retrieved from https://www.youtube.com/watch?v=IUY2yI5F16U

Oculus Story Studio. (2016). *Lost* [Video file]. Retrieved from https://www.youtube.com/watch?v=_gkcLuAGzLw

Oculus. (2015). *Strangers with Patrick Watson*. Felix and Paul Studios, Developers.

Oleksy, T., & Wnuk, A. (2017). Catch them all and increase your place attachment! The role of location-based augmented reality games in changing people-place relations. *Computers in Human Behavior*, *76*, 3–8. doi:10.1016/j.chb.2017.06.008

Orson, W. (Producer & Director). (1941). *Citizen Kane* [Motion Picture]. United States: RKO Radio Pictures.

Osburn, L. (2017). *Storytelling, Central to Human Experience*. Retrieved from https://500womenscientists.org/updates/2017/7/31/storytelling-human-experience

Ottens, A. J., & Hanna, F. J. (1998). Cognitive and existential therapies: Toward an integration. *Psychotherapy (Chicago, Ill.)*, *35*(3), 312–324. doi:10.1037/h0087832

Overbeck, R. S., Erickson, D., Evangelakos, D., Pharr, M., & Debevec, P. (2018). A system for acquiring, processing, and rendering panoramic light field stills for virtual reality. *ACM Transactions on Graphics*, *37*(6), 197. doi:10.1145/3272127.3275031

Page-Kirby, K. (2015). 'he D Train' isn't actually about trains. But these 5 movies are. *Nearly done final edits*. Retrieved from https://www.washingtonpost.com/express/wp/2015/05/07/the-d-train-isnt-actually-about-trains-but-these-5-movies-are/

Pallasmaa, J. (2012). *The eyes of the skin: architecture and the senses*. Hoboken, NJ: John Wiley & Sons.

Palmer, S. E. (1999). *Vision science: Photons to Phenomenology*. Boston: MIT press.

Panksepp, J. (1993). Neurochemical control of moods and emotions: Amino acids to neuropeptides. In M. Lewis & J. M. Haviland (Eds.), *Handbook of emotions* (pp. 87–107). New York: Guilford.

Panofsky, E., Wood, C. S., & Wood, C. (1991). Perspective as symbolic form. New York: Zone Books.

Papert, S. (1980). *Mindstorms: Children, Computers, and Powerful Ideas*. New York: Basic Books.

Parke, F. (1972). Computer generated animation of faces. *Proceedings of the ACM Annual Conference, 1*, 451–457. 10.1145/800193.569955

Parkes, W. F., & Valdes, D. (Producers), & Wells, S. (Director). (2002). *The Time Machine* [Motion Picture]. United States: Dreamworks Pictures.

Parkhomenko, E., O'Leary, M., Safiullah, S., Walia, S., Owyong, M., Lin, C., ... Clayman, R. (2018). Pilot Assessment of Immersive Virtual Reality Renal Models as an Educational and Preoperative Planning Tool for Percutaneous Nephrolithotomy. *Journal of Endourology, 33*(4), 283–288. doi:10.1089/end.2018.0626 PMID:30460860

Participant. (n.d.). *About Participant*. Retrieved from https://participant.com/about-us

Passy, C. (2013, June 10). How to invest in a Broadway show. *Market Watch*.

Pearce, C. (2011). *Communities of Play: Emergent Cultures in Multiplayer Games and Virtual Worlds*. Boston, MA: MIT Press.

Pelowski, M., Markey, P. S., Forster, M., Gerger, G., & Leder, H. (2017). Move me, astonish me... delight my eyes and brain: The Vienna Integrated Model of top-down and bottom up processes in Art Perception (VIMAP) and corresponding affective, evaluative and neurophysiological correlates. *Physics of Life Reviews, 21*, 80–125. doi:10.1016/j.plrev.2017.02.003 PMID:28347673

Pendleton-Jullian, A. M. (1996). *The road that is not a road and the open city, Ritoque, Chile*. Boston, MA: MIT Press.

Perls, F., Hefferline, G., & Goodman, P. (1951). *Gestalt therapy*. New York.

Petersen, M. (2019). *Fulldome Theater Compendium*. Lochness Productions. Retrieved from http://lochnessproductions.com/lfco/lfco.html

Petitmengin, C. (2017). Enaction as a Lived Experience. *Constructivist Foundations, 12*(2).

Petitmengin-Peugeot, C. (1999). The intuitive experience. In F. Varela & J. Shear (Eds.), *The view from within* (pp. 43–77). Exeter, UK: Academic-Imprint.

PGA. (2010). PGA Board of Directors Approves Addition of Transmedia Producer to Guild's Producers Code of Credits. April 6, 2010. *Producers Guild of America*. Retrieved from https://www.producersguild.org/news/news.asp?id=39637

Phase Core Technology. (n.d.). *Professional avatar and beauty solutions*. Retrieved August 20, 2019, from http://faceunity.com/#/faceswipe

Pivec, M. (2007). Play and learn: Potentials of game-based learning. *British Journal of Educational Technology, 38*(3), 387–393. doi:10.1111/j.1467-8535.2007.00722.x

Poling, C. V. (1986). *Kandinski's Teaching at the Bauhaus*. New York: Rizzoli.

Popova, M. (2014). A Wave in the Mind: Virginia Wolf on Writing and Consciousness. *Brainpickings*. Retrieved from www.brainpickings.org/2014/10/23/virginia-woolf-a-wave-in-the-mind

Porges S. W. (2009). The polyvagal theory: new insights into adaptive reactions of the autonomic nervous system. *Cleveland Clinic Journal of Medicine, 76*(Suppl 2), S86–S90.

Porges, J. (1995). Orienting in a defensive world: Mammalian modifications of our evolutionary heritage. A polyvagal theory. *Psychophysiology, 32*(4), 301–318. doi:10.1111/j.1469-8986.1995.tb01213.x PMID:7652107

Porges, S. (2019). The Future of VR? Site-Specific Art Installations. *Forbes*. Retrieved from https://www.forbes.com/sites/sethporges/2019/11/04/the-future-of-vr-site-specific-art-installations

Preston, T. (1890). *The Theory of Light*. London: Macmillan and Co.

Proctor, D. (2017). Inside South Korea's first spherical projection theatre. *AV Technology Europ*. Retrieved from https://www.installation-international.com/technology/inside-south-koreas-first-spherical-projection-theatre

Proietti, M., Pickston, A., Graffitti, F., Barrow, P., Kundys, D., Branciard, C., ... Fedrizzi, A. (2019). Experimental test of local observer independence. *Science Advances, 5*(9), eaaw9832. doi:10.1126ciadv.aaw9832 PMID:31555731

Pulijala, Y., Ma, M., Pears, M., Peebles, D., & Ayoub, A. (2018). Effectiveness of Immersive Virtual Reality in Surgical Training: A Randomized Control Trial. *International Journal of Oral and Maxillofacial Surgery, 76*(5), 1065–1072. doi:10.1016/j.joms.2017.10.002 PMID:29104028

Puschmann, M. (2016). Notes on Blindness, a virtual reality journey into the world of blindness. *The Drum*. Retrieved from https://www.thedrum.com/news/2016/10/21/notes-blindness-virtual-reality-journey-the-world-blindness

PYMNTS. (2019). *L'Oréal To Partner with Amazon On Makeup Tech*. Retrieved from www.pymnts.com/news/retail/2019/loreal-amazon-makeup-augmented-reality-tech

Raessens, J. (2019). Virtually Present, Physically Invisible: Alejandro G. Iñárritu's Mixed Reality Installation Carne y Arena. *Television & New Media, 20*(6), 634–648. doi:10.1177/1527476419857696

Rake, R. (2019). Family Entertainment Centers Market Overview. *Allied Market Research*. Retrieved from https://www.alliedmarketresearch.com/family-entertainment-centers-market

Rathbone, O. (2019). Ahmet Zappa And Eyellusion Talk The Bizarre World Of Frank Zappa. *UDiscover Music*. Retrieved from www.udiscovermusic.com/stories/ahmet-zappa-bizarre-world-frank-interview

Ravassard, P., Kees, A., Willers, B., Ho, D., Aharoni, D. A., Cushman, J., ... Mehta, M. R. (2013). Multisensory control of hippocampal spatiotemporal selectivity. *Science, 340*(6138), 1342–1346. doi:10.1126cience.1232655 PMID:23641063

Recalled by Robert Sproull. (2006). *In DARPA Case No. 13-01968.000048 Interview: December 7, 2006*. Retrieved August 23, 2019 from https://www.esd.whs.mil/Portals/54/Documents/FOID/Reading%20Room/DARPA/15-F-0751_DARPA_Director_Robert_Sproull.pdf

Red Accent Studios. (2017). *Little Prince VR* [Video file]. Retrieved from https://www.youtube.com/watch?v=k7qoZOpJRLU

Reichard, K. (2019). Closer Chainsmokers 5G Experience on Tap at Chase Center. *Arena Digest*. Retrieved from https://arenadigest.com/2019/11/27/closer-chainsmokers-5g-experience-on-tap-at-chase-center/

Reid, J. (2014, March 26). *The power of animism: John Reid at TEDxQueenstown* [Video]. Retrieved from https://www.youtube.com/watch?v=lmhFRarkw8E

Reid, L. F., Vignali, G., Barker, K., Chrimes, C., & Vieira, R. (2020). Three-dimensional Body Scanning in Sustainable Product Development: An exploration of the use of body scanning in the production and consumption of female apparel. In *Technology-Driven Sustainability* (pp. 173–194). Cham: Palgrave Macmillan. doi:10.1007/978-3-030-15483-7_10

Rene, G. & Mapes, D. (2019). *The Spatial Web How Web 3.0 Will Connect Humans, Machine and AI to Transform the World*. Amazon.com.

Repetto, C., & Riva, G. (2011). From virtual reality to interreality in the treatment of anxiety disorders. *Neuropsychiatry*, *1*(1), 31–43. doi:10.2217/npy.11.5

Rice, V. J., Houston, F. S., & Schroeder, P. J. (2017, September). The Relationship between Mindful Awareness and Cognitive Performance among US Military Service Members and Veterans. *Proceedings of the Human Factors and Ergonomics Society Annual Meeting*, *61*(1), 843–847. doi:10.1177/1541931213601684

Riva, G., Raspelli, S., Algeri, D., Pallavicini, F., Gorini, A., Wiederhold, B. K., & Gaggioli, A. (2006). Interreality in practice: Bridging virtual and real worlds in the treatment of posttraumatic stress disorders. *Cyberpsychology, Behavior, and Social Networking*, *13*(1), 55–65. doi:10.1089/cyber.2009.0320 PMID:20528294

Rizzo, A. A., Lange, B., Buckwalter, J. G., Forbell, E., Kim, J., Sagae, K., & Parsons, T. (2011). *An intelligent virtual human system for providing healthcare information and support*. Madigan Army Medical Center. doi:10.1515/IJDHD.2011.046

Rizzo, A., Cukor, J., Gerardi, M., Alley, S., Reist, C., Roy, M., ... Difede, J. (2015). Virtual reality exposure for PTSD due to military combat and terrorist attacks. *Journal of Contemporary Psychotherapy*, *45*(4), 255–264. doi:10.100710879-015-9306-3

Rizzo, A., Difede, J., Rothbaum, B. O., Reger, G., Spitalnick, J., Cukor, J., & Mclay, R. (2010). Development and early evaluation of the virtual Iraq/Afghanistan exposure therapy system for combat-related PTSD. *Annals of the New York Academy of Sciences*, *1208*(1), 114–125. doi:10.1111/j.1749-6632.2010.05755.x PMID:20955333

Rizzo, A., Reger, G., Gahm, G., Difede, J., & Rothbaum, B. O. (2009). Virtual reality exposure therapy for combat-related PTSD. In *Post-traumatic stress disorder* (pp. 375–399). Humana Press. doi:10.1007/978-1-60327-329-9_18

Rizzotto, L. (2019). Why Deepfakes Will Change Advertising Forever. *Medium*. Retrieved from https://medium.com/futurepi/why-deepfakes-will-change-advertising-forever-2949ec3f87ee

Roettgers, J. (2018). Netflix Takes Interactive Storytelling to the Next Level With 'Black Mirror: Bandersnatch. *Variety*. Retrieved from https://variety.com/2018/digital/news/netflix-black-mirror-bandersnatch-interactive-1203096171/

Roettgers, J. (2019). Vortex Plans to Open 2,500-Seat Dome Multiplex for Headset-Free VR Experiences. *Variety*. February 12, 2019. Retrieved from https://variety.com/2019/digital/news/vortex-domeplex-arizona-headse-free-vr-1203136609/

Rohani, D. A., & Puthusserypady, S. (2015). BCI inside a virtual reality classroom: A potential training tool for attention. *EPJ Nonlinear Biomedical Physiology*, *3*(1), 12. doi:10.1140/epjnbp40366-015-0027-z

Roland, C. (2018). The Future of Immersive Branding and Retail. *AT&T Shape*. Retrieved from https://shape.att.com/blog/future-of-immersive-branding-and-retail

Roof, K. (2019). Museum of Ice Cream Valued at $200 Million. *The Wall Street Journal*. Retrieved from https://www.wsj.com/articles/museum-of-ice-cream-valued-at-200-million-11565782201

Rößner, M., Christensen, L., & Ganter, C. (2016). Characterising Fulldome Planetarium Projection Systems: The Limitations Imposed by Physics, and Suggestions on How to Mitigate, In IPS 2016 Proceedings. Retrieved from https://www.semanticscholar.org/paper/Characterising-Fulldome-Planetarium-Projection-%3A-by-R%C3%B6%C3%9Fner-Christensen/eddb673f09666d9468e04c9cd0d1ab5dfc93e9fb

Rowling, J. K. (2007). *Harry Potter and the Deathly Hallows*. Bloomsbury.

Rubin, P. (2017). VR's First Major Casuality Was One of Its Smartest Startups. *Wired Magazine*. Retrieved from https://www.wired.com/story/altspace-vr-closes/

Runco, M. (2013). *Divergent Thinking and Creative Potential Creativity*. New York: Hampton Press.

Rushkoff, D. (2019). *Team Human*. New York: W. W. Norton & Co.

Russell, M. (Producer), & David, S. (Director). (2018). *Black Mirror: Bandersnatch* [Motion Picture]. Netflix, Inc.

Russell, J. A., & Ward, L. M. (1982). Environmental psychology. *Annual Review of Psychology*, *33*(1), 651–689. doi:10.1146/annurev.ps.33.020182.003251

Rylaf, J. B. (2018). House of Secrets: A Night With 'The Willows' (REVIEW). *Noproscenium*. Retrieved from https://noproscenium.com/house-of-secrets-a-night-with-the-willows-review-a3e13bc3e0e1

Sahar, T., Shalev, A. Y., & Porges, S. W. (2001). Vagal modulation of responses to mental challenge in posttraumatic stress disorder. *Biological Psychiatry*, *49*(7), 637–643. doi:10.1016/S0006-3223(00)01045-3 PMID:11297721

Salimpoor, V. N., Benovoy, M., Larcher, K., Dagher, A., & Zatorre, R. (2011). Anatomically distinct dopamine release during anticipation and experience of peak emotion to music. *Nature Neuroscience*, *14*(2), 257–262. Retrieved from https://www.academia.edu/5008150/Anatomically_distinct_dopamine_release_during_anticipation_and_experience_of_peak_emotion_to_music. doi:10.1038/nn.2726 PMID:21217764

Salzman, M. C., Dede, C., Loftin, R. B., & Chen, J. (1999). A model for understanding how virtual reality aids complex conceptual learning. *Presence (Cambridge, Mass.)*, *8*(3), 293–316. doi:10.1162/105474699566242

Sample, I. (2019). Scientists Attempt to Recreate 'Overview effect' from Earth. *The Guardian*. Retrieved from https://www.theguardian.com/science/2019/dec/26/scientists-attempt-to-recreate-overview-effect-from-earth

Sandler, E. (2007). *The tv writer's workbook: a creative approach to television scripts*. New York, NY: Bantam Dell.

Sankaranarayanan, G., Wooley, L., Hogg, D., Dorozhkin, D., Olasky, J., Chauhan, S., ... Jones, D. B. (2018). Immersive virtual reality-based training improves response in a simulated operating room fire scenario. *Surgical Endoscopy*, *32*(8), 3439–3449. doi:10.100700464-018-6063-x PMID:29372313

Sapolsky, R. M. (2001). Depression, antidepressants, and the shrinking hippocampus. *Proceedings of the National Academy of Sciences of the United States of America*, *98*(22), 12320–12322. doi:10.1073/pnas.231475998 PMID:11675480

Scannell, L., & Gifford, R. (2010). Defining place attachment: A tripartite organizing framework. *Journal of Environmental Psychology*, *30*(1), 1–10. doi:10.1016/j.jenvp.2009.09.006

Scargill, J. H. C. (2019). *Can Life Exist in 2+1 Dimensions?* arXiv preprint arXiv:1906.05336

Schedlbauer, A. M., Copara, M. S., Watrous, A. J., & Ekstrom, A. D. (2014). Multiple interacting brain areas underlie successful spatiotemporal memory retrieval in humans. *Scientific Reports*, *4*(1), 6431. doi:10.1038rep06431 PMID:25234342

Scherer, K. R. (2005). What are emotions? And how can they be measured? *Social Sciences Information. Information Sur les Sciences Sociales*, *44*(4), 695–729. doi:10.1177/0539018405058216

Schindler, A., & Bartels, A. (2013). Parietal cortex codes for egocentric space beyond the field of view. *Current Biology*, *23*(2), 177–182. doi:10.1016/j.cub.2012.11.060 PMID:23260468

Schindler, R. M., & Holbrook, M. B. (2003). Nostalgia for early experience as a determinant of consumer preferences. *Psychology and Marketing*, *20*(4), 275–302. doi:10.1002/mar.10074

Schlitz, M. (2015). *Death makes life possible: Revolutionary insights on living, dying, and the continuation of consciousness*. Boulder, CO: Sounds True.

Schlitz, M., Vieten, C., & Amorok, T. (2007). *Living deeply: The art and science of transformation in everyday life*. Berkeley, CA: New Harbinger.

Schott, G. D. (2015). Neuroaesthetics: Exploring beauty and the brain. *Brain*, *138*(8), 2451–2454. doi:10.1093/brain/awv163

Schroeder, R., Steed, A., Axelsson, A.-S., Heldal, I., Abelin, Å., Wideström, J., ... Slater, M. (2001). Collaborating in networked immersive spaces: As good as being there together? *Computers & Graphics*, *25*(5), 781–788. doi:10.1016/S0097-8493(01)00120-0

Science, Arts and Technology. (n.d.). *Discover the SAT*. Retrieved from https://sat.qc.ca/en/sat#section

Sciutteri, M. (2018). Interactive Storytelling: Non-Linear. Retrieved from https://gamedevelopment.tutsplus.com/articles/interactive-storytelling-part-2--cms-30273

Secret Cinema. (n.d.). *History of Secret Cinema*. Retrieved from https://www.secretcinema.org/history

Sedikides, C., & Wildschut, T. (2016). Past forward: Nostalgia as a motivational force. *Trends in Cognitive Sciences*, *20*(5), 319–321. doi:10.1016/j.tics.2016.01.008 PMID:26905661

Segovia, K. Y., & Bailenson, J. (2019). Memory versus media: creating false memories with virtual reality. *Brain World*. Retrieved from https://brainworldmagazine.com/memory-versus-media-creating-false-memory-virtual-reality

Segovia, K. Y., & Bailenson, J. N. (2009). Virtually true: Children's acquisition of false memories in virtual reality. *Media Psychology*, *12*(4), 371–393. doi:10.1080/15213260903287267

Sellars, W. (2003). *Empiricism and the philosophy of mind*. Cambridge, MA: Harvard University Press.

Septimus Piesse, G. W. (1857). The Art of Perfumery And Methods of Obtaining the Odors of Plants. Philadelphia: Lindsay and Blakiston.

Shaefer, K. (2019). Malls Have a Future: Location-Based Entertainment. *VentureBeat*. Retrieved from https://venturebeat.com/2019/09/25/malls-have-a-future-location-based-entertainment/

Shafer, D. M., & Carbonara, C. P. (2015). Examining enjoyment of casual videogames. *Games for Health Journal*, *4*(6), 452–459. doi:10.1089/g4h.2015.0012 PMID:26509941

Shapiro, F. (2014). The role of eye movement desensitization and reprocessing (EMDR) therapy in medicine: Addressing the psychological and physical symptoms stemming from adverse life experiences. *The Permanente Journal*, *18*(1), 71–77. doi:10.7812/TPP/13-098 PMID:24626074

Sharir, Y., & Gromala, D. J. (1997). Dancing with the Virtual Dervish: Virtual Bodies. In M. A. Moser & D. MacLeod (Eds.), *Immersed in technology: Art and virtual environments* (pp. 281–286). Cambridge, MA: MIT.

Shashkevich, A. (2018). Virtual reality can help make people more compassionate compared to other media, new Stanford study finds. *Stanford News*. Retrieved from https://news.stanford.edu/2018/10/17/virtual-reality-can-help-make-people-empathetic

Shaw, A. (2019). Marina Abramovic's *The Life* to become first mixed reality work ever auctioned. *The Art Newspaper*. Retrieved from https://www.theartnewspaper.com/news/marina-abramovic-s-the-life-to-become-first-mixed-reality-work-ever-auctioned

Shayon, S. (2018). Macy's Rolls Out VR to Sell More Furniture in Less Space. *Brand Channel*. Retrieved from www.brandchannel.com/2018/10/19/macys-vr-furniture

Shelby, B., Vaske, J. J., & Donnelly, M. P. (1996). Norms, standards, and natural resources. *Leisure Sciences*, *18*(2), 103–123. doi:10.1080/01490409609513276

Siegel, D. J. (2006). An interpersonal neurobiology approach to psychotherapy. *Psychiatric Annals*, *36*, 248–256.

Siegel, D. J. (2012). *The developing mind: How relationships and the brain interact to shape who we are* (2nd ed.). New York, NY: Guilford Press.

Silver, S. (2018). The story of the original iPhone, that nobody thought was possible. *Apple Insider*. Retrieved from https://appleinsider.com/articles/18/06/29/the-story-of-the-original-iphone-that-nobody-thought-was-possible

Silverstein, S. (2004). *Where the sidewalk ends: the poems & drawings of Shel Silverstein*. New York: Harper Collins.

Sip, R. (Producer & Director). (2007). *Dawn of the Space Age* [Fulldome Film]. Netherlands: Mirage3D.

Sivitilli, D., & Gire, D. H. (2019). *Researchers model how octopus arms make decisions*. Retrieved from https://phys.org/news/2019-06-octopus-arms-decisions.html

Skalski, P., Tamborini, R., Shelton, A., Buncher, M., & Lindmark, P. (2011). Mapping the road to fun: Natural video game controllers, presence, and game enjoyment. *New Media & Society*, *13*(2), 224–242. doi:10.1177/1461444810370949

Sklar, R., & Cook, D. A. (2019). *History of the Motion Picture*. Retrieved from https://www.britannica.com/art/history-of-the-motion-picture

SklarR.CookD. (2019). *Edwin S. Porter*. Retrieved from https://www.britannica.com/biography/Edwin-S-Porter

Skwigly. (2004). The Rotoscope of Max Fleischer. *Skwigly Online Animation Magazine*. Retrieved from https://www.skwigly.co.uk/the-rotoscope-of-max-fleischer/

Slater, M. (2009). Place Illusion and Plausibility Can Lead to Realistic Behaviour in Immersive Virtual Environments. *Philosophical Transactions of the Royal Society of London. Series B, Biological Sciences*, *364*(1535), 3549–3557. doi:10.1098/rstb.2009.0138 PMID:19884149

Slater, M., Sadagic, A., Usoh, M., & Schroeder, R. (2000). Small-group behavior in a virtual and real environment: A comparative study. *Presence (Cambridge, Mass.)*, *9*(1), 37–51. doi:10.1162/105474600566600

Slater, M., Spanlang, B., Sanchez-Vives, M. V., & Blanke, O. (2010). First Person Experience of Body Transfer in Virtual Reality. *PLoS One*, *5*(5), e10564. doi:10.1371/journal.pone.0010564 PMID:20485681

Slater, M., & Usoh, M. (1994). Representation systems, perceptual position, and presence in immersive virtual environments. *Presence (Cambridge, Mass.)*, *2*(3), 221–233. doi:10.1162/pres.1993.2.3.221

Sloane, G. (2016). Gatorade's Super Bowl Snapchat filter got 160 million impressions. *Digiday.com*. Retrieved from https://digiday.com/marketing/inside-gatorades-digital-ad-playbook-snapchat-facebook

Smith, D., Schlaepfer, P., Major, K., Dyble, M., Page, A. E., Thompson, J., . . . Migliano, A. B. (2017). Cooperation and the evolution of hunter gatherer storytelling. *Nature Communications*, *8*, 1853. Retrieved from https://www.nature.com/articles/s41467-017-02036-8

Smith, P. (2018). *Homestay VR* [animated VR]. National Film Board of Canada. Retrieved from https://www.jam3.com/work/#homestay-vr

Smith, P. (2018). *Spotlight talk*. Expanded Realities Symposium—Open City Documentary Festival, London, UK.

Smolenski, D. J., Pruitt, L. D., Vuletic, S., Luxton, D. D., & Gahm, G. (2017). Unobserved heterogeneity in response to treatment for depression through videoconference. *Psychiatric Rehabilitation Journal*, *40*(3), 303–308; Advance online publication. doi:10.1037/prj0000273 PMID:28604014

SMPTE. (2006). SMPTE Standard-D-Cinema Quality—Screen Luminance Level, Chromaticity and Uniformity. In ST 431-1:2006. 18 April 2006. pp.1-5. Retrieved from http://ieeexplore.ieee.org/stamp/stamp.jsp?tp=&arnumber=72921 24&isnumber=7292123

Sobel, K. (2019). *Immersive media and child development: Synthesis of a cross-sectoral meeting on virtual, augmented, and mixed reality and young children*. New York: The Joan Ganz Cooney Center at Sesame Workshop.

Sofroniew, N. J., Vlasov, Y. A., Hires, S. A., Freeman, J., & Svoboda, K. (2015). Neural coding in barrel cortex during whisker-guided locomotion. *eLife*, *4*, e12559. doi:10.7554/eLife.12559 PMID:26701910

Solly, M. (2018). British Doctors May Soon Prescribe Art, Music, Dance and Singing Lessons. *Smithsonian Magazine*. Retrieved from https://www.smithsonianmag.com/smart-news/british-doctors-may-soon-prescribe-art-music-dance-singing-lessons-180970750

Solomon, B. (2014). Facebook Buys Oculus, Virtual Reality Gaming Startup, for $2 Billion. *Forbes*. Retrieved from https://www.forbes.com/sites/briansolomon/2014/03/25/facebook-buys-oculus-virtual-reality-gaming-startup-for-2-billion

Solomon, S., Greenberg, J., & Pyszczynski, T. (1991). A terror management theory of social behavior: The psychological functions of self-esteem and cultural worldviews. *Advances in Experimental Social Psychology*, *24*, 93–159. doi:10.1016/S0065-2601(08)60328-7

Solomon, S., Greenberg, J., & Pyszczynski, T. (2015). *The worm at the core: On the role of death in life (Kindle version)*. New York, NY: Random House. Retrieved from www.Amazon.com

Sonsev, V. (2017). How Augmented Reality Is Giving Furniture A Boost in Sales. *Forbes*. Retrieved from www.forbes.com/sites/veronikasonsev/2017/12/20/how-ar-is-giving-furniture-a-boost-in-sales/#7e2cd2d21d3a

Sovie, D. R. G., Murdoch, R., McMahon, L., & Schoelwer, M. (2018). Time to Navigate the Super MyWay. *Accenture 2018 Digital Consumer Survey Findings*. Retrieved www.accenture.com/us-en/_acnmedia/PDF-69/Accenture-2018-Digital-Consumer-Survey-Findings.pdf

Spark, C. G. I. (2019). World First: Virtual Female Model Signs to Top US Agency. *Cision PR Newswire*. Retrieved from www.prnewswire.com/news-releases/world-first-virtual-female-model-signs-to-top-us-agency-300871973.html

Speakman, D. (2017). *It Must Have Been Dark By Then* [interactive augmented audio walk]. Retrieved from http://duncanspeakman.net/darkbythen/

Squiers, A. (2015). A Critical Response to Heidi M. Silcox's 'What's Wrong with Alienation?'. *Philosophy and Literature*, *39*(1), 243–247. doi:10.1353/phl.2015.0016

Stanley, K. (Producer & Director). (1964). *Dr. Strangelove* [Motion Picture]. United States: Columbia Pictures.

Stanley, K. (Producer &Director). (1968). *2001: A Space Odyssey* [Motion Picture]. United States: MGM.

Staugaitis, L. (2018). Meow Wolf Explains their Origin Story in a Feature-Length Documentary. *Colossal*. Retrieved from https://www.thisiscolossal.com/2018/11/meow-wolf-documentary/

Steele, J. (2019). Multifamily Marketers Using Virtual Staging to Make Real Impact. *Forbes*. Retrieved from www.forbes.com/sites/jeffsteele/2019/06/28/multifamily-marketers-using-virtual-staging-to-make-real-impact/

Stefan, A. (Producer), & Tom, T. (Director). (1998). *Run Lola Run* [Motion Picture]. Germany: Prokino Filmverleih.

Steiner, R. (1995). Intuitive Thinking as a Spiritual Path: A Philosophy of Freedom (M. Lipson, Trans.). Hudson, NY: Anthroposophic Press.

Stenson, B. (2019). Immersive Van Gogh show opens in Paris – in pictures. *The Guardian*. Retrieved from https://www.theguardian.com/travel/gallery/2019/mar/04/immersive-vincent-van-gogh-show-opens-paris-digital-art

Stepan, K., Zeiger, J., Hanchuk, S., Del Signore, A., Shrivastava, R., Govindaraj, S., & Iloreta, A. (2017). Immersive virtual reality as a teaching tool for neuroanatomy. *International Forum of Allergy & Rhinology*, 7(10), 1006–1013. doi:10.1002/alr.21986 PMID:28719062

Stephens, R. (2019). You'll Be Surprised by Steven Spielberg's Latest Project. *Fortune*, July 27, 2019. Retrieved from https://fortune.com/2019/07/27/steven-spielberg-universal-sphere-comcast/

Stokols, D., Rall, M., Pinner, B., & Schopler, J. (1973). Physical, social, and personal determinants of the perception of crowding. *Environment and Behavior*, 5(1), 87–115. doi:10.1177/001391657300500106

Stowers, J. R., Hofbauer, M., Bastien, R., Griessner, J., Higgins, P., Farooqui, S., ... Straw, A. D. (2017). Virtual reality for freely moving animals. *Nature Methods*, 14(10), 995–1002. doi:10.1038/nmeth.4399 PMID:28825703

Strause, J. (2015). Inside the World's Most Expensive Restaurant. *News.Com.AU*. Retrieved from https://www.news.com.au/travel/travel-ideas/luxury/inside-the-worlds-most-expensive-restaurant/news-story/f1502c6c2985beeb56993f3ebf052b59

Stuart, S. C. (2018). TRIPP Wants to Be Your Daily Rest and Relaxation Fix. *PC Reviews*. Retrieved from https://www.pcmag.com/news/362814/tripp-wants-to-be-your-daily-rest-and-relaxation-fix

Studio, S. (2018). *Fresh Out* [Video file]. Retrieved from https://www.with.in/watch/fresh-out

Sturman, D. J. (1998). Computer Puppetry. *IEEE Computer Graphics and Applications*, 18(1), 38–45. doi:10.1109/38.637269

Sublimoton Ibiza. (n.d.). *Concept Sublimotion Ibiza*. Retrieved from https://www.sublimotionibiza.com/main.html

Sundance Institute. (2016). Notes on Blindness. *Sundance Institute Projects*. Retrieved from https://www.sundance.org/projects/notes-on-blindness

Super78. (n.d.). *About Super78*. Retrieved from Website: https://www.super78.com/process

Sutherland, I. E. (1965). The Ultimate Display. *Proceedings of IFIP*, 65(2), 506–508.

Sutton, R. (2018). *Investing in Creativity*. Retrieved from https://www.arts.gov/NEARTS/2018v3-pushing-boundaries-look-visionary-approaches-arts/investing-creativity

Suzanne, T., & Jennifer, T. (Producer), & Christopher, N. (Director). (2000). *Memento* [Motion Picture]. United States: Newmarket Films.

Symposium, I. X. (2001). Excerpt Medica. *Stratosphere Dome*. Retrieved from ix.sat.qc.ca

Takahasi, D. (2018). VRstudios launches Jurassic World VR attraction at Dave & Buster's restaurants. *Venture Beat*. Retrieved from https://venturebeat.com/2018/06/06/vrstudios-launches-jurassic-world-vr-attraction-at-dave-busters-restaurants/

Takatalo, J., Häkkinen, J., Kaistinen, J., & Nyman, G. (2010). Presence, involvement, and flow in digital games. In R. Bernhaupt (Ed.), *Evaluating User Experience in Games. Human-Computer Interaction Series* (pp. 23–46). London, UK: Springer. doi:10.1007/978-1-84882-963-3_3

Takeda, S., Iwai, D., & Sato, K. (2016). Inter-reflection Compensation of Immersive Projection Display by Spatio-Temporal Screen Reflectance Modulation. *IEEE Transactions on Visualization and Computer Graphics*, 22(4), 1424–1431. doi:10.1109/TVCG.2016.2518136 PMID:26780805

Tamborini, R., & Bowman, N. D. (2010). Presence in video games. In C. Campanella Bracken & P. D. Skalski (Eds.), Immersed in media: Telepresence in everyday life (pp. 87–109). Academic Press.

Tapely, K. (2017). Oscars: Alejandro G. Inarritu's Virtual Reality Installation 'Carne y Arena' to Receive Special Award. *Variety*. Retrieved from https://variety.com/2017/film/awards/oscars-alejandro-g-inarritus-virtual-reality-installation-carne-y-arena-to-receive-special-award-1202601265/

Tarrant, J., Viczko, J., & Cope, C. (2018). Virtual reality for anxiety reduction demonstrated by quantitative EEG: A pilot study. *Frontiers in Psychology*, 9(1280). PMID:30087642

Tassi, P. (2019). How on earth did 'Pokémon GO' make almost $800 million in 2018? *Forbes*. Retrieved from https://www.forbes.com/

Tassi, P. (2019). 'Fortnite' Had 10 Million Concurrent Players in The Marshmello Concert Event. *Forbes*. Retrieved from www.forbes.com/sites/insertcoin/2019/02/03/fortnite-had-10-million-concurrent-players-in-the-marshmello-concert-event/

teamLAB, (n.d.). *Concept teamLab*. Retrieved from https://www.teamlab.art/concept/

Terrell, K. (2016). *The History of Social Media: Social Networking Evolution!* Retrieved from https://historycooperative.org/the-history-of-social-media

Thaddeus-Johns, J. (2019). Welcome to the Cinema of Smells, where Movies are a Different Kind of Cheesy. *The Outline*. Retrieved from https://theoutline.com/post/7044/wolfgang-georgsdorf-the-smeller-osmodrama

The Communist Manifesto. (n.d.). Retrieved from en.wikipedia.org/wiki/The_Communist_Manifesto

The National Association of Realtors Research Department. (2017). *2017 Profile of Home Staging*. Retrieved from www.nar.realtor/sites/default/files/migration_files/reports/2017/2017-profile-of-home-staging-07-06-2017.pdf

The Sims. (2000). [Computer software]. Electronic Arts.

The Skoll Center for SIE at UCLA. (2019). *The State of SIE Mapping the Landscape of Social Impact Entertainment Report*. Retrieved from https://thestateofsie.com/skoll-center-for-sie/home/

The Skoll Center for Social Impact Entertainment. (n.d.) Retrieved from http://www.tft.ucla.edu/skoll-center-for-social-impact-entertainment/

The Witcher 3: Wild Hunt. (2015). [Computer software]. CD Projekt Red.

THEA Award 2017. (2017). Retrieved from http://www.teaconnect.org/Thea-Awards/Past-Awards/index.cfm?id=6889&redirect=y

Thompson, S. (2019). VR for Corporate Training: Examples of VR already Being Used. *Virtual Speech*. Retrieved from https://virtualspeech.com/blog/how-is-vr-changing-corporate-training

Thorpe, J. A. (2010). Trends in Modeling, Simulation & Gaming: Personal Observations About the Last Thirty Years and Speculation About the Next Ten. *Interservice/Industry Training, Simulation, and Education Conference (I/ITSEC)*.

Tidy, J., & Aarabi, P. (2010). Visual modeling of faces for security applications. *Government Security News*. Retrieved from https://www.gsnmagazine.com/node/20213?c=cbrne_detection

Tommasini, A. (2009, June 1). Opera to Sniff at: A Score Offers Uncommon Scents. *The New York Times*.

Torrance, E. P. (1977). *Creativity in the Classroom; What Research Says to the Teacher*. National Education Association.

Trafton, A. (2014). In the Blink of an Eye. *MIT News*. Retrieved from http://news.mit.edu/2014/in-the-blink-of-an-eye-0116

Trahndorff, K. F. E. (1827). *Ästhetik oder Lehre von Weltanschauung und Kunst*. Berlin: Maurer.

Travelogues. (2018). Borderless: Tokyo's New Digital Art Museum is a Creative Paradigm Shift. *Travelogues*. Retrieved from https://www.remotelands.com/travelogues/tokyos-new-digital-art-museum-is-simply-stunning/

Trip, H. M., & Gillette, J. M. (2015). *Stagecraft*. Retrieved from https://www.britannica.com/art/stagecraft

Troche, J., & Weston, E. (forthcoming). Virtual Reality Storytelling: Pedagogy and Applications. In *Proceedings of the Ancient Egypt – New Technology Conference*. Leiden, The Netherlands: Brill.

Turner, N. K. (2017). Virtual Reality + Digitizing Scent with Simon Niedenthal and Jacki Morie. *Art and Cake*. Retrieved from https://artandcakela.com/2017/07/18/virtual-reality-digitizing-scent-with-simon-niedenthal-and-jacki-morie/

Turner, R., & Whitehead, C. (2008). How collective representations can change the structure of the brain. *Journal of Consciousness Studies, 15*(10-1), 43-57.

Two Bit Circus. (n.d.). *About Two Bit Circus*. Retrieved from https://twobitcircus.com/about/

Ultra Violet. (n.d.). *Ultra Violet by Paul Pairet*. Retrieved from https://uvbypp.cc

Uncharted 2: Among Thieves. (2009). [Computer software]. SCE.

Universal Creative. (2016). *Harry Potter and the Forbidden Journey motion simulator ride*. Author.

Universal Creative. (2019). *Godzilla: King of the Monsters 3D theme park film*. Author.

Van Bavel, J. J., Hackel, L. M., & Xiao, Y. J. (2014). The group mind: The pervasive influence of social identity on cognition. In *New frontiers in social neuroscience* (pp. 41–56). Cham: Springer. doi:10.1007/978-3-319-02904-7_4

Van Gordon, W., Shonin, E., Dunn, T. J., Sheffield, D., Garcia-Campayo, J., & Griffiths, M. D. (2018). Meditation-Induced Near-Death Experiences: A 3-Year Longitudinal Study. *Mindfulness, 9*(6), 1794–1806. doi:10.100712671-018-0922-3 PMID:30524512

Van Tilburg, W. A., Igou, E. R., & Sedikides, C. (2013). In search of meaningfulness: Nostalgia as an antidote to boredom. *Emotion (Washington, D.C.), 13*(3), 450–461. doi:10.1037/a0030442 PMID:23163710

Varela, F. (1995). The emergent self. In J. Brockman (Ed.), *The third culture: Beyond the scientific revolution* (p. 209). New York, NY: Touchstone.

Varela, F. J., Thompson, E., & Rosch, E. (1991). *The embodied mind: Cognitive science and human experience*. Boston, MA: MIT Press. doi:10.7551/mitpress/6730.001.0001

Variety Staff. (1980, Dec. 31). Polyester [film review]. *Variety*.

Videos, C. (2019, December 12), *Leonardo DiCaprio as Anakin Skywalker in the Star Wars Saga - Deepfake Theater* [Video File]. Retrieved from https://www.youtube.com/watch?v=pVW6cdpEirU

Vieten, C., Amorok, T., & Schlitz, M. M. (2006). I to we: The role of consciousness transformation in compassion and altruism. *Zygon, 41*(4), 915–932. doi:10.1111/j.1467-9744.2006.00788.x

Villani, D., Preziosa, A., & Riva, G. (2006). Coping with stress using Virtual Reality: A new perspective. *Annual Review of Cybertherapy and Telemedicine*, *4*, 25–32.

Virtual Reality Oasis [Username]. (2018, October 11). *The Great C: The first 5 minutes of this cinematic virtual reality movie* [Video File]. Retrieved from https://youtu.be/lwL9FpnSlrk

Volino, P., Thalmann, N. M., Jianhua, S., & Thalmann, D. (1996). An evolving system for simulating clothes on virtual actors. *IEEE Computer Graphics and Applications*, *16*(5), 42–51. doi:10.1109/38.536274

Von Uexküll, J. (1957). A stroll through the worlds of animals and men. In C. Schiller (Ed.), *Instinctive behavior: The development of a modern concept*. Madison, CT: International Universities Press, Inc.

Vosmeer, M., & Schouten, B. (2014). Interactive Cinema: Engagement and Interaction. *7th International Conference on Interactive Digital Storytelling. ICIDS 2014*, 8832, 140-147.

Wagner, R. (1849). *Die Kunst und die Religion (Art and Religion)*. Leipzig: Otto Wigand Verlag. Retrieved from https://spinnet.humanities.uva.nl/images/2013-10/wagnerkunstundrevolution_2.pdf

Wagner, R. (1995). *Opera and Drama* (W. A. Ellis, Trans.). University of Nebraska Press. (Originally published 1852)

Wagner, R. (1849). *Das Kunstwerk der Zukunft [Artwork of the Future]*. Leipzig: Wigand.

Waldrop, M. M. (2018). Free Agents. *Science*, *360*(6385), 144–147. doi:10.1126cience.360.6385.144 PMID:29650655

Walikainen, D. (2014, Feb. 11). Scents that are Sent: oPhone Delivers Aromas. *Michigan Tec News*. Retrieved from https://www.mtu.edu/news/stories/2014/february/scents-sent-ophone-delivers-aromas.html

Wallace-Wells, D. (2019). Time to Panic. *The New York Times*. Retrieved from https://www.nytimes.com/2019/02/16/opinion/sunday/fear-panic-climate-change-warming.html

Wallworth, L. (2017). *Collisions* [interactive VR]. Retrieved from http://www.collisionsvr.com/

Wallworth, L. (2018). *Awavena* [interactive VR]. Retrieved from http://www.awavenavr.com/

Walsh, R. (1979). Meditation research: An introduction and review. *Journal of Transpersonal Psychology*, *11*(2).

Walsh, R., & Shapiro, S. L. (2006). The meeting of meditative disciplines and western psychology: A mutually enriching dialogue. *The American Psychologist*, *61*(3), 227–239. doi:10.1037/0003-066X.61.3.227 PMID:16594839

Walt Disney Imagineering with Industrial Light and Magic. (1986). *Captain Eo, 3D theme park film*. Author.

Walt Disney Imagineering with Industrial Light and Magic. (1987). *Star War's Star Tours motion simulator ride*. Author.

Wankle, C., & Hinrichs, R. (2011). Introduction. In C. Wankle & R. Hinrichs (Eds.), *Transforming Virtual World Learning*. Bingley, UK: Emerald Group Publishing Limited.

Watson, J. B., & Rayner, R. (1920). Conditioned emotional reactions. *Journal of Experimental Psychology*, *3*(1), 1–14. doi:10.1037/h0069608

Watts, A. (1936). *The Spirit of Zen: A Way of Life, Work and Art in the Far East*. New York: E. P. Dutton and Co.

Watts, A. (1995). *Om: On Creative Meditations*. Anaheim, CA: Creative Press.

Waugh, A. (1999). *Time*. Terra Alta, WV: Headline Books.

Weiler, L. (2018) *Frankenstein AI* [interactive installation/experience]. Columbia University Digital Storytelling Lab. Retrieved from http://frankenstein.ai/

Wesch, M. (2008, July 26). *An Anthroplogical Introduction to YouTube* [Video file]. YouTube.

Westmas, R. (2018). *This AI-Assisted Aging Software Looks Spookily Realistic.* Retrieved from https://curiosity.com/topics/this-ai-assisted-aging-software-looks-spookily-realistic-curiosity/

Weyers-Lucci, D. (2016). *The impact of an 8 week daily exposure to a VR experience for anxiety and depression.* Unpublished study. Palo Alto, CA: Institute of Transpersonal Psychology at Sofia U.

Wheeler, B. (2005). Reality is What You Can Get Away With: Fantastic Imaginings, Rebellion and Control in Terry Gilliam's Brazil. Critical Survey, (17), 95-108.

White Hutchinson. (n.d.). What is a Family Entertainment Center? *White Hutchinson Leisure and Learning Group.* Retrieved from https://www.whitehutchinson.com/leisure/familyctr.shtml

White, C. (2014). *The science delusion: Asking the big questions in a culture of easy answers.* Brooklyn, NY: Melville House.

Whitehead, A. N. (1929). *Process and reality: An essay in cosmology: Gifford lectures delivered in the University of Edinburg during the session 1927-1928.* New York: Macmillian Company.

Whitney, L. (2017). How to Use Google's Translate App. *PC Magazine.* Retrieved from www.pcmag.com/news/352206/how-to-use-googles-translate-app

Wiederhold, B. K., Jang, D. P., Gevirtz, R. G., Kim, S. I., Kim, I. Y., & Wiederhold, M. D. (2002). The treatment of fear of flying: A controlled study of imaginal and virtual reality graded exposure therapy. *IEEE Transactions on Information Technology in Biomedicine*, 6(3), 218–223. doi:10.1109/TITB.2002.802378 PMID:12381038

Wiggers, K. (2019). Generative adversarial networks: What GANs are and how they've evolved. *Venture Beat.* Retrieved from https://venturebeat.com/2019/12/26/gan-generative-adversarial-network-explainer-ai-machine-learning/

Wilber, K. (2006). *Integral spirituality: A startling new role for religion in the modern and postmodern world.* Boston, MA: Shambhala.

Wilde, O., & Wilde, O. (1925). *The writings of Oscar Wilde. Intentions.* New York: Wells.

Wilhelm, F. H., & Roth, W. T. (2001). The somatic symptom paradox in DSM-IV anxiety disorders: Suggestions for a clinical focus in psychophysiology. *Biological Psychology*, 57(1-3), 105–140. doi:10.1016/S0301-0511(01)00091-6 PMID:11454436

Wilkins, C. (2015). *Let's Talk About: The Polar Express.* Retrieved from http://laurawilkens.com/thoughts/2015/12/14/lets-talk-about-the-polar-express

Williams, M. (2014). A Universe of 10 Dimensions. *Universe Today.* Retrieved from https://phys.org/news/2014-12-universe-dimensions.html

Williams, R. (2017). Estée Lauder's AR chatbot offers advice on lipstick colors. *MobileMarketer.* Retrieved from http://www.mobilemarketer.com/news/estee-lauders-ar-chatbot-offers-advice-on-lipstick-colors/447096

Williams, D. R., & Vaske, J. J. (2003). The measurement of place attachment: Validity and generalizability of a psychometric approach. *Forest Science*, 49(6), 830–840.

Williamson, C. (2018). "An Escape Into Reality": Computers, Special Effects, and the Haunting Optics of Westworld (1973). *Imaginations: Journal of Cross-Cultural Image Studies*, 9(1), 19–39.

Willmott, P. (2019). Review: The War of the Worlds Immersive Experience at 56 Leadenhall Street. *London Box Office*. Retrieved from https://www.londonboxoffice.co.uk/news/post/review-war-of-the-worlds-immersive-experience

Wilson, J. A., Onorati, K., Mishkind, M., Reger, M. A., & Gahm, G. A. (2008). Soldier attitudes about technology-based approaches to mental health care. *Cyberpsychology & Behavior*, *11*(6), 767–769. doi:10.1089/cpb.2008.0071 PMID:18991533

Winkler, I., Chartoff, B., Winkler, C., Winkler, D., King-Templeton, K., & Stallone, S. (Producers), & Coogler, R. (Director). (2015). *Creed*. [Motion Picture]. United States: Warner Bros. Pictures.

Wolfman, U. R. (2013). Richard Wagner's Concept of the 'Gesamtkunstwerk.' *Interlude*. Retrieved from https://interlude.hk/richard-wagners-concept-of-the-gesamtkunstwerk/

Wolf, V. (1931). *The Waves*. London: Hogarth Press.

World Health Organization (WHO). (2017). *World mental health atlas*. Geneva, Switzerland: WHO.

Worsley, R. (Producer, Director). (2017). *How Radio Isn't Done* [Motion Picture]. USA: Independent.

Wulf, T., Rieger, D., & Schmitt, J. B. (2018). Blissed by the past: Theorizing media-induced nostalgia as an audience response factor for entertainment and well-being. *Poetics*, *69*, 70–80. doi:10.1016/j.poetic.2018.04.001

Yalom, I. (1980). *Existential psychotherapy (Kindle version)*. New York, NY: Basic Books. Retrieved from www.amazon.com

Yalom, I. (2009b). *Staring at the sun: Overcoming the terror of death (Kindle version)*. San Francisco, CA: Jossey Bass. Retrieved from www.amazon.com

Yalom, I. D. (2009). *The gift of therapy: An open letter to a new generation of therapists and their patients*. New York, NY: Harper Perennial.

Yamamoto, N., & Philbeck, J. W. (2013). Peripheral vision benefits spatial learning by guiding eye movements. *Mem Cogn 41*: pp. 109-121. Retrieved from https://link.springer.com/content/pdf/10.3758%2Fs13421-012-0240-2.pdf

Yang, C., & Liu, D. (2017). Motives matter: Motives for playing Pokémon Go and implications for well-being. *Cyberpsychology, Behavior, and Social Networking*, *20*(1), 52–57. doi:10.1089/cyber.2016.0562 PMID:28080150

Yildirim, K., & Akalin-Baskaya, A. (2007). Perceived crowding in a café/restaurant with different seating densities. *Building and Environment*, *42*(9), 3410–3417. doi:10.1016/j.buildenv.2006.08.014

Yirka, B. (2019). Researcher shows physics suggests life could exist in a 2-D universe. *PhysOrg*. Retrieved from https://phys.org/news/2019-06-physics-life-d-universe.html

Youngblood, G. (1970). *Expanded Cinema*. Boston: P. Dutton & Co.

Yu, K. (2019). How Immersive Virtual Reality Theatre Pushes the Limits of Storytelling. *No Proscenium*. Retrieved from https://noproscenium.com/how-immersive-virtual-reality-theatre-pushes-the-limits-of-storytelling-8265b198bfc7

Zehrer, A., & Raich, F. (2016). The impact of perceived crowding on customer satisfaction. *Journal of Hospitality and Tourism Management*, *29*, 88–98. doi:10.1016/j.jhtm.2016.06.007

Zeiss (n.d.). *History of ZEISS Planetariums: How it all began*. Retrieved from https://www.zeiss.com/corporate/int/about-zeiss/history/technological-milestones/planetariums.html

Zemekis, R., Starky, S., & Geotzman, G. &Teitler, W. (Producers) & Zemekis, R. (Producer). (2004). *The Polar Express* [Motion Picture]. United States: Warner Brothers.

Zhang, J. (2019). *Immersive Virtual Reality Training to Enhance Procedural Knowledge Retention* (Doctoral dissertation). Purdue University.

Zhang, Y., Shen, Y., Zhang, W., Zhu, Z., & Ma, P. (2019). Interactive spatial augmented reality system for Chinese opera. In Proceedings of SIGGRAPH 2019. Article 14. pp. 1-2. Retrieved from https://dl.acm.org/citation.cfm?id=3338566

Zhao, S. (2003). Toward a taxonomy of copresence. *Presence (Cambridge, Mass.)*, *12*(5), 445–455. doi:10.1162/105474603322761261

Zhen, Y. Z. (Producer), & Yi, M. Z. (Director). (2002). *Hero* [Motion Picture]. China: Beijing New Picture Film Co.

Zuidhoek, S., Visser, A., Bredero, M. E., & Postma, A. (2004). Multisensory integration mechanisms in haptic space perception. *Experimental Brain Research*, *157*(2), 265–268. doi:10.100700221-004-1938-6 PMID:15197527

Zyber, J. (2012). Douglas Trumbull May Have This Frame Rate Thing Figured Out. *High Def Digest: The Bonus View*. Retrieved from https://www.highdefdigest.com/blog/douglas-trumbull-showscan-digital/

About the Contributors

Jacquelyn Morie's 30 years of researching & creating meaningful VR experiences combines multi-sensory and perceptual techniques for VR that predictably elicit emotional responses from participants. Her company All These Worlds, LLC is active in social VR, Mindfulness applications, storytelling, stress relief experiences, avatars and immersive education & training. In 2016 she concluded a special project for NASA called ANSIBLE, a full virtual world ecosystem designed to provide psychological benefits for future astronauts who will undertake extremely long isolated missions to Mars. ANSIBLE was tested in an analog facility called HISEAS in Hawaii, where a team of six scientists was sequestered for a full year to simulate the conditions of isolation on Mars, including long communications delays. Dr. Morie also investigates the use of personal avatars for how we use them and how they affect our human selves. In 2004 she invented a novel scent release device for VR (now called called RemniScent), to aid in the evocative power of VR experiences. Her education includes advanced degrees in Fine Arts and Computer Science (MFA, 1984 & MS, 1988 from the University of Florida) and a PhD in Computer and Information Systems from Smartlab, University of East London in 2007. Morie lives on a tiny urban farm with her extended family in a 110 year old house near downtown Los Angeles, CA.

Kate McCallum is a forward-thinking multi-media producer, writer, and digital arts and media strategist with an emphasis in IP development, transmedia, and new media technology platforms. Kate served as a Board Delegate on the Producers Guild of America New Media Council for six years and on the PGA National Board for three years. She was the recipient of the 2019 Marc A. Levey Award for Distinguished Service, and as a Co-Chair, Kate helped to spearhead the creation of the PGA Social Impact Entertainment Task Force. She is a member of the TV Academy, the WFSF: World Future Studies Federation, and is Chair of the Arts & Media Node for The Millennium Project, a global futurist think tank. In 2004, Kate founded her own development and multi-media production company, Bridge Arts Media, LLC, and consults and produces for a variety of clients including Vortex Immersion Media, a company specializing in fulldome 360/VR immersive content and experience design, immersive brand experiences, VR, interactive, live mixed-media performances, and projection mapping. In 2010, Kate established the Vortex AIR: Artist-in-Residence program and innovation lab in The Vortex Dome CineTheater at Los Angeles Center Studios. Prior, Kate spent 20 years at NBCUniversal and Paramount Studios working in development and production of feature films, and broadcast and cable episodic television with some of the top showrunners and writers in the industry on such shows as; Miami Vice, Law & Order, Equalizer, Gimme a Break, Charles in Charge and The Marshal to name a few. She produced a TV Movie for NBC called What Kind of Mother Are You? and as VP of Creative for Western Sandblast at Paramount, Kate developed and sold TV movies and off-net series concepts to outlets such as Showtime and UPN.

She has produced and/or written for traditional, digital and immersive media, produced live events, industry conferences, educational workshops, concerts, currently serves as the Managing Editor for the SOC: Society of Camera Operators' quarterly magazine, Camera Operator, and is the producer and co-designer of an innovative distribution model for James Hood's MESMERICA 360, a fulldome visual music production and upcoming sequel. Kate's also been an international guest speaker and instructor on the topics of future trends in media and entertainment, and transmedia storytelling at the Hong Kong Design Institute, Singapore Media Academy, the Asian Childrens' Content Conference, XMedia LAB in Australia, the China Science Film and Video Association in Shenzhen, China, TiE Global Summit in Mumbai, India, and InventureS, Calgary, Canada to name a few. She co-produced and presented "Transmedia Storytelling and Strategy Design" for the PGA and the TV Academy, and was a featured speaker at the Global Leaders Forum in Seoul, Korea addressing the "Future of Entertainment and Media." Kate has pursued a lifelong interest in human potential and in 2004, earned an MA in Consciousness Studies from the University of Philosophical Research in Los Angeles. Kate was awarded an Alumni Achievement Award from Western Michigan University, was appointed as an honorary fellow at SNCR: Society for New Communication Research, and serves on the Advisory Board of The Studio School, Los Angeles.

* * *

Julieta Christina Aguilera studied Design at the School of Architecture, Catholic University of Valparaíso, Chile. She holds two Masters of Fine Arts: in Design from the University of Notre Dame, and in Electronic Visualization from the Electronic Visualization Laboratory at the University of Illinois at Chicago, with an emphasis on Virtual Reality and a focus on shared spaces. Because of these research interests, Julieta took a job at the Adler Planetarium's Space Visualization Laboratory where she created or contributed to scientific visualizations for exhibitions and planetarium shows. Julieta eventually became the Associate Director of the Laboratory, working alongside Adler astrophysicists, educators and administration staff, as well as astrophysicists from the University of Chicago, Northwestern University and University of Illinois at Chicago. She handled weekly presentations on how scientific visualization and current technologies are used to explore, study and communicate scientific discoveries and theories. While at Adler she also spearheaded events geared to advance the understanding and integration of immersive, collaborative and interactive media. She has taught the full Design curriculum, as well as Graphical Interfaces, Immersive Environments and Scientific Visualization (with scientist colleagues). While completing her Doctoral disertation with the Planetary Collegium at Plymouth University in the United Kingdom, Julieta worked for a year at the University of Hawai'i in Hilo, sponsored by the Academia of Creative Media and hosted by the 'Imiloa Planetarium. Julieta has participated in various conferences related to Art, Science, and Planetariums.

Leila Amirsadeghi has over 20 years of experience in entertainment, technology and live event production; designing, building and producing integrated marketing campaigns, experiential activations, brand events, festivals and digital products for some of the world's most notable brands. Leila's experience in digital product development spans AR/MR/XR, OTT, mobile & web for art, entertainment and video games, and she has created and helped launch award-winning campaigns for a number of TV and movie titles including The Walking Dead, Jurassic World and Ready Player One. Leila co-founded and launched the 20,000 sq.ft. LBE, Onedome, in San Francisco in 2018, featuring three immersive entertainment experiences (F.E.A.S.T, LMNL and The Unreal Garden); including the world's first mass-consumer, AR multiplayer mixed reality experience. Leila has worked with some of the world's largest brands including Disney, Microsoft, Warner Bros, Google, DreamWorks and Adobe, and with some of the world's most successful location-based entertainment startups including Two Bit Circus, the VOID and Electric Playhouse. Leila currently consults within the XR world under her own brand, MESH, and is an advisor to a number of XR & LBE startups including Enklu, Portals, Vibiana Immersive, Otherside and WeHOWL.

Michael Daut is an immersive media specialist, working as an independent writer/producer/director in Los Angeles, CA. Michael brings a wealth of experience within the giant screen cinema and digital fulldome industries. He is an award-winning writer, producer, and director for fulldome videos, theatrical productions, music videos, live concert videos, commercials, documentaries, corporate videos, and trade show presentations. He most recently served as the Director of New Business Development for Mouse-trappe, an experience design and production studio in Burbank. Previously he worked for over 20 years at Evans & Sutherland, where he was instrumental in acquiring numerous large accounts, expanding the product line, and developing a library of shows for the digital fulldome community. Michael's current clients include K2 Studios, a giant screen film production and distribution company, and Moodswings, LLC, creators of the visual music show Mesmerica, currently playing in digital dome theaters across North America. He has a BA in Media Communications with a video/film emphasis from Webster University, where he also served as an adjunct professor. He created the world's first digital fulldome film for SIGGRAPH '99 in Los Angeles. He also helped create the world's first digital fulldome transfer of a giant screen film, Africa the Serengeti, in 2007. Because of this groundbreaking first step, there are now over 60 giant screen films converted to fulldome digital. He also produced the first two 8K Digital Dome Demos for Giant Screen Cinema Association and co-produced 2016's True8K digital dome event and 2018's HD Digital Camera Comparison with members of the GSCA Technical Committee. Michael is a member of the Producer's Guild of America, the Themed Entertainment Association, a founding member of the Association of Fulldome Innovators, a member of the Telly Awards' Silver Council, a board member of the Giant Screen Cinema Association, and a board member of IMERSA.org, the Immersive Media Entertainment, Research, Science and Arts organization dedicated to raising the visibility of immersive media across a variety of disciplines throughout the world.

Kelley Francis, as a producer and pioneer in immersive media art and fulldome cinema, works to combine the arts, technology, entertainment and big ideas for installations that provoke a lasting experience among audiences. Culling from inspiration which includes the sciences, wellness, storytelling, and play— her works are interactive, immersive, and cross-disciplinary.

Christina Heller is the CEO of Metastage, an XR studio that brings real people and performances into digital worlds through volumetric capture and complementary tools. Metastage uses the Microsoft Mixed Reality Capture system and is located in Los Angeles. Prior to leading Metastage, Christina was the CEO of VR Playhouse, an immersive content company based out of Los Angeles. She is a recipient of the Advanced Imaging Society's Distinguished Leadership in Technology Award and was named in the Huffington Post as one of five women changing the virtual reality scene. She has contributed to over 80 immersive projects and comes from the world of journalism, radio and television.

Brian Hurst, a multi-disciplinary producer, writer and strategist, has spent his career at the forefront of innovation and storytelling. His work in theater, television, emerging and new media and now immersive media has enabled the building and extension of storyworlds and brands. He has also held leadership positions in the Academy of Television Arts & Sciences (Board of Governors and Second Vice Chair), the Producers Guild of America (Board Member and Chairman of the New Media Council) and the International Academy of Television Arts & Sciences (Digital Ambassador). As President and Chief Storyteller of StoryTech® Immersive, Hurst leads the company's work in cinematic and Live VR as well as immersive event production. Credits include My Brother's Keeper (VR, PBS, Digital Studios), The Circus: Inside the Greatest Political Show on Earth 360 (VR, Showtime) Gettysburg: A National Divided (MR, QuantumERA), The Rolling Loud Hip Hop Festival (Live 360 broadcast, LivexLive, SamsungVR) Super Splat Brothers E-sports Tournament (Live 360 broadcast, E-Sports Arena, SamsungVR), Passport to Philadelphia (AR, QuantumERA).The company produces, curates and manages the competition for the Vancouver International Film Festival VIFF Immersed program. Recipient of the Interactive TV Today Award for Leadership in Interactive Television, Hurst was profiled in emmy magazine as one of the 10 media executives leading the industry's digital drive and was named two years running to the Hollywood Reporter/PGA Digital 50. He was awarded the Television Academy Interactive Media Peer Group Digertati Award for his contributions to the industry and the Emmy® organization; and was named one of the AlwaysOn Power Players in Digital Entertainment. He has received the Producers Guild of America Marc A. Levey Award for Distinguished Service in recognition of his service to the PGA and the new media industry. He also received a Lifetime Achievement Award from the Television of Tomorrow Show. Hurst is also co-author with Olivia Newton-John of the best selling children's book "A Pig Tale" from Simon & Schuster and the book "WHOLE," a collection of essays on life's challenges.

Jessica Kantor is highly sought after for her work in virtual and augmented reality, having developed a unique perspective of place, movement, and worldbuilding she now brings to traditional filmmaking. She has made 100s of branded videos, op-docs and short films including the recent Alcoholocaust which premiered at the LA Shorts Fest 2018, a music video for rising artist Rebecca Perl and a branded series for Vox/ Microsoft. Jessica's VR work has premiered at Film Festivals all over the world. Most recently, Together as One made for Oculus as part of their VR for Good Program which premieres October 2018 at San Francisco Dance Film Festival and on the Oculus store. In the 360/VR space, she's made work for pride.com, Miller Lite, Wiser Distillery, Youtube/ Vsauce, and Music Artist Hunter Hays. Additionally, Jessica is asked to speak about her take on immersive storytelling at film schools and film festivals including USC, North Carolina School of the Arts, Sundance Film Festival and New Orleans Film Festival.

Ed Lantz is an entertainment technology engineer, immersive experience designer and innovator in giant-screen digital cinema and large-scale immersive environments. He left aerospace engineering in 1990 to transform traditional planetariums into 360-degree immersive visualization environments, designing over a dozen dome theaters worldwide including the Library of Alexandria in Egypt, National Space Center in Leicester, UK and Papalote Museo del Nino in Mexico City. Ed founded Vortex Immersion Media in 2007 to bring 360-degree immersive and interactive experiences into mainstream arts and entertainment markets. Vortex has produced 360 venues and programming for concerts, EDM festivals, VR Cinemas and experiential marketing for numerous brands including AT&T, CAA, Condé Nast, EMC2, IBM, Live Nation, Microsoft, NBC Universal, Nestle, NFL, Nike, Nokia, Sprint and Turner Broadcast. Artists supported include Childish Gambino (Donald Glover), Skrillex, Diplo, Braves, Kaleo,

JZ/Beyoncé and more. The company operates the Vortex Dome, the first commercial immersive media studio and events venue in downtown Los Angeles which has hosted a wide range of arts, entertainment, cultural and special event productions. Vortex Immersion's studio is focused on partnering with top talent to produce transformative immersive experiences for mainstream audiences. VIM's latest collaborative production, James Hood's MESMERICA, has currently presented over 1,000 shows to sell-out crowds in digital domes across North America. The company recently announced plans to build a network of DomePlex immersive location-based attractions with their initial venue opening in Phoenix, Arizona in 2020. The DomePlex features a central 2500-seat CineTheater and a cluster of smaller dome venues featuring the world's best immersive arts and entertainment experiences. Ed holds a Master's Degree in Electrical Engineering, is a Board Delegate of the Producer's Guild of America's New Media Council, and he Chairs the LA Chapter of ACM SIGGRAPH.

Brett Leonard, for over 25 years, has been at the forefront of the digital media revolution—whether it be as Director/ Writer of the groundbreaking cult-classic film Lawnmower Man, which introduced the concept of Virtual Reality to popular culture—or being the first to pioneer modern stereoscopic techniques and photo-realistic CGI in his hit IMAX 3D film "T-Rex"—or introducing American audiences to Russell Crowe and many other talents both in front of and behind the camera, Brett's work as a visionary Director/Producer/Futurist has always pushed the edge of innovation in the entertainment industry, and continues to do so with a project slate at his company Studio Lightship, focused on creation of VX (Virtual eXperience) executed in a hybrid approach with Film and Television. Studio Lightship is dedicated to defining a process and platform for truly interactive narrative VX StoryWorlds for the emerging era of Immersive Entertainment.

Keram Malick-Sanchez founded both the VRTO World Conference and the FIVARS Festival in 2015. A graduate of UCLA's certification programs in Cinematography, Producing, and Digital Media, he is also an alumnus of Werner Herzog's Rogue Film School, was a student in Ryerson University's inaugural New Media Studies program, a business and creative consultant to a wide variety of tech companies, and has over 30 years of experience as an actor in Hollywood.

Gregory Peter Panos is an American writer, futurist, educator, strategic planning consultant, conference/event producer, and technology evangelist in Augmented Reality, virtual reality, human simulation, motion capture, performance animation, 3D character animation, human-computer interaction and user experience design. Greg has worked as an engineer with Rockwell International Space Station Systems Division visualizing real-time, computer generated Space Station designs. As a Chairman of Siggraph - Los Angeles Chapter, he has led the entertainment industry in the adoption of computer-generated visuals and animation. As a consultant and industry expert, Greg is often invited to speak at events and conferences on Human Simulation, Virtual Reality and 3D Scanning.

Audri Phillips, director/3D animator, content creator, immersive media specialist. She is based in Los Angeles and has a wide range of experience that includes over 25 years working in the visual effects/entertainment industry in studios such as Sony, Rhythm and Hues, Digital Domain, Disney and Dream Works feature animation. Starting out as a painter she was quickly drawn to time-based art and visual poetry. An interest in science and technology has always played a part in her work. She is a pioneer of using cutting-edge technology in immersive media performances, fulldome and mixed reality.

As a member of the Intel Innovators Group, she writes online articles for Intel, is a member of ADN (Autodesk Developers Network), a resident artist at The Vortex Dome/Vortex Immersion Media, and is a consultant/researcher for a technology company, Stratus Systems. Audri is co-founder and director of Robot Prayers, an immersive transmedia project which explores AI and our hybrid identities in a world where man and machine are melding. Over the past six years she directed/animated/designed over six fulldome shows, one with composer/musician Steve Roach. She created animations for dance companies as well as a number of cinematic and interactive VR pieces using Autodesk Maya, Touch Designer and Unreal Engine. One of the VR pieces, "Migrations" is on the Samsung Indie channel and the fulldome piece, "Migrations" was chosen to be shown in the 2019 DTLAFF. All of the fulldome pieces as well as her animations and paintings have been shown in festivals and conferences around the world some of which she has spoken at and given master classes. She holds a BFA from Carnegie Mellon University and has been an adjunct professor at a number of Universities in Los Angeles. BFA from Carnegie Mellon University.

Micky Remann is a German born media artist and producer of media events. He is Professor for Immersive Media at the Bauhaus-Universität Weimar, where he has been teaching the art of fulldome since 2007. In the same year, Micky Remann initiated the FullDome Festival at the Zeiss-Planetarium Jena, which he continues to direct until today. The international festival showcases and awards innovative productions in the genre of 360-degree audio-visual media and fulldome theatre performance. As the inventor of "Liquid Sound," Micky Remann is also connected to another experience of immersion: floating in body temperature salt water, immersed in underwater sounds, lights and video images. The concept and media technology of "Liquid Sound" is installed in three major Spa venues in Germany, operated by Toskanaworld, where it has become the key attraction, featuring regular underwater live concerts, DJ nights and an annual all night Liquid Sound Festival. As a travelling author, Micky Remann also published articles, books and travelogues, he hosts TV-Dome shows with the network Salve.tv, he presents at scientific conferences and performs at cultural events. One of his international media projects is the "Apolda World Bell Concert", which connects sounds and stories of bells from around the world with music via livestream. www.fulldome-festival.de www.liquidsound.com.

Linda Ricci is senior professional with successful international consulting and management experience delivering thought leadership and strategic solutions to clients in industries where technologies are transforming consumer behavior.

Julia Scott-Stevenson is a research fellow in interactive factual media with the Digital Cultures Research Centre at the University of the West of England, Bristol. She works with researchers and industry to explore the potential of interactive and immersive factual media, and produces the biennial i-Docs Symposium. Julia holds a PhD in i-docs and social impact, for which she created the i-doc Giving Time. Julia received an academic immersion fellowship on the South West Creative Technology Network, to explore whether immersive media experiences might offer ways of imagining a preferred future, and her other research interests include digital rights, surveillance and data storytelling.

Mei Si is an associate professor in the Cognitive Science Department, Rensselaer Polytechnic Institute (RPI). She is also part of the Games and Simulation Arts and Sciences (GSAS) Program at RPI. Mei Si received a Ph.D. in Computer Science from the University of Southern California and an M.A. in

Psychology from the University of Cincinnati. Her primary research interest is embodied conversational agents and cognitive robots. Mei has more than ten years of experience developing virtual environments, intelligent conversational agents, and serious games. Her work is supported by NSF, DOD, NIH, Amazon, Disney, IBM, Tencent and the ESA Foundation.

Shaojung Sharon Wang, PhD, is an associate professor of Institute of Marketing Communication at National Sun Yat-sen University, Taiwan. She received her Ph.D. from the Department of Communication, University at Buffalo, State University of New York. Her research span both communication technologies and media entertainments. Much of her work has been focusing on the social and psychologial implications of new media use on human behaviors and how these behaviors interact with the environment and technologies. Her work can be found in numerous academic journals such as Social Science Computer Review, Cyberpsychology, Behavior, and Social Networking, Electronic Commerce Research and Applications, and Computers in Human Behavior.

Eve Weston believes in storytelling as a force for positive change. She is CEO and Creator of Realities at Exelauno (www.exelauno.co) and writer/director of the first immersive 360VR sitcom, The BizNest. Featuring actors from Marvel's Legion, FX's The Bridge and YouTube's Emmy-nominated Epic Rap Battles of History, The BizNest was one of six finalists for the Auggie Award for Best Art or Film at the 10th annual Augmented World Expo. Weston's VR art has shown at galleries in LA, Miami and NYC and at Disney Concert Hall as a prelude to LA Phil's Yoko Ono Tribute Concert. Weston is adjunct professor of 360VR filmmaking at Emerson College LA. Her speaking engagements as a VR storytelling expert include the National Conference of Science Writers' in Washington, DC, Samsung's Harman University, Stanford University, Stanford's Brown Institute of Media Innovation, the Academy of Television Arts and Sciences of Emmy's fame, and Silicon Valley's Augmented World Expo. Weston began her creative career writing jokes on Will & Grace and Better Off Ted. She's since written television episodes for ABC's Better With You, Disney XD's Randy Cunningham: 9th Grade Ninja, and Disney's Wizards of Waverly Place, where she also wrote and choreographed the song "Funky Hat Dance," which became a YouTube sensation with more than a million views and girls internationally uploading videos of themselves and their best friend doing the dance. Weston developed a musical web series for AwesomenessTV and wrote the multi-cam pilot The Fast Track for ABC Family. Weston is also an award-winning journalist, having written about VR for Ms. Magazine and The New York Post. She earned her MFA in screenwriting from USC and her BA in classics cum laude from Princeton. Weston is also a Goldman Sachs alumna, honored to have had both a deal written up in The Wall Street Journal and a joke praised in The New York Times. She can be followed on Twitter at @eveweston.

Dorote Weyers-Lucci helps people manage and heal their anxiety and chronic stress symptoms with mindfulness-based approaches. She is focused on innovative and lasting habit transformation. She facilitates workshops and support groups, and is involved in research focused on immersive experiences, both digital and nondigital for wellness and mental health. Having noticed a need in her clients for gentle support in addition to therapy and healing work she had co-founded Embodied Inc. in 2014. The first app for reprogramming habit patterns was called Worry Bubble (Apple app store) and was born in the same year. In 2015, she created Corereboot and brought out StarflightVR, a mobile Virtual Reality experience to support deep and lasting habit change. FlowforbreathVR the next VR experience she created supports meditative breath training and its benefits for stress relief and mental health. Both apps focus on a gentle, non invasive and intuitive approach to transformation and habit change and are used as psychotherapeutic support tools. Her background includes complementary medicine practices, interpersonal neurobiology, a Master of Clinical Hypnosis, spiritual practices and psychology as well as a Master in International Management. She is currently doing her PhD in Psychology and researches the most efficacious links for psychophysiological transformation. She loves the connection between neuroplasticity, human behavior, spiritual transformation and the possibilities available for us to change our patterning and habits through somatic and visual experiences. She is fluent in English, German, French and Spanish. She believes in the healing rhythms of poetry and the power of neuroaesthetics.

Saskia Wilson-Brown co-directed the Silver Lake Film Festival and ran international filmmaker outreach at Al Gore's Current TV while producing initiatives around new models in the arts. In 2012, her interest in transmedia practices led her to create The Institute for Art and Olfaction, a non-profit devoted to experimentation and access in perfumery. Through the IAO, she has launched projects with institutions such as Pulitzer Foundation, Getty Institute, Danish Film Institute, National Media Museum UK, Hammer Museum, Wallace Collection, New Mexico Highlands University, and many more. In 2013, she launched the Art and Olfaction Awards, an international awards mechanism for independent perfumers. She recently served as a visiting lecturer at the Royal College of Art in London. Her current interests relate to the creation of open source mechanisms for the perfume industry.

Li Zheng is an associate professor in the Animation department, Shandong University of Arts, P. R. China. She is also a visiting scholar at Rensselaer Polytechnic Institute between Feb 2018 and Sep 2019. Li Zheng received an M.A. in Visual Communication from Birmingham City University, United Kingdom. Her primary research interest is game design and interactive narrative.

Index

360 cinema 333, 339
360 video 142-143, 150, 201, 203, 205-206, 225, 271, 289-291, 325, 340, 342, 466
3D Digitizing Rig 41, 57

A

a story 5, 60, 64-69, 72, 88, 130, 142, 145-146, 148-150, 152-155, 167-168, 180, 188-189, 222, 231, 235, 267-268, 338, 396-397, 404, 456, 483
Accord 118, 121
aesthetics 11, 419, 422
agency 4-7, 18-19, 25, 67, 73, 117, 142-143, 147-150, 154-155, 170, 194, 203, 215, 217, 238, 271-272, 302, 315, 353, 355, 406, 423-426
Alan Smithson 408, 411
Alex McDowell 203
Alex Meader 225
ambisonics 35, 331
Animism 35
anosmia 119, 121
Anthropocentrism 35
Antietam 225, 227, 230
artificial intelligence 3, 11, 13, 35, 45, 50, 57, 62, 92, 106, 123, 132-133, 138, 171, 362, 374, 393-394, 402, 405-406, 415
Augmented-Reality 7, 10, 25, 54, 57-58, 119, 124, 126, 142-143, 150-151, 165, 169, 223, 237, 275, 291, 297, 300, 307, 314, 352-353, 371, 387, 393, 395-400, 424, 456, 469
Avant-Immersive 81, 106
Avatarism 37, 57
avatars 18, 20, 24, 35, 37, 50, 52, 179, 196, 218, 334, 362-363, 365, 374, 393, 404-406, 408, 443

B

bewilderment 1, 3-4, 6-7
Bokeh 231-232

C

CamBLOCK 231, 236
care 1, 6-7, 12, 17, 23, 116, 166, 203, 234, 285, 431, 443, 475, 477
CEEK VR 207, 212
Chatbot(s) 11, 35, 398, 405, 407
Chemophobia 119, 121
Choose Your Own Attention 188, 198
cinematic 130, 142, 163, 166, 201-204, 206, 209-211, 215, 221, 224-225, 227, 232-233, 237-239, 242, 245, 250, 252, 255, 257-258, 267, 274, 286, 299, 301-302, 310, 314-316, 318, 329-330, 333, 461, 470
Civil War 225, 227, 231
climate change 3, 416, 424-426
codec 165, 174
computer vision 45-46, 123, 133, 137
construct 17, 21, 26-27, 35, 38-40, 44, 49-50, 53, 57-58, 82, 129, 269, 353, 357, 416-417
convergence 224, 453, 457-458, 478, 482-483
convergent thinking 124-125
co-presence 371-372, 374-377, 380, 382, 384, 386-387
Cortney Harding 411
crossbounce 328-330
crowding 373, 376, 380, 382, 384, 386

D

dark ride 223, 236, 302, 320
Deep Fakery (aka Deep Fake) 57
Deepfake(s) 19-23, 35, 57
deity 85, 274-276, 278-279
Depth-Sensing Camera 43, 57
Digital Dome(s) 94, 237, 239, 242, 251, 314-316, 324-326, 330-333, 340, 343-344
directing 70, 125, 127, 149, 176-177, 183, 188, 192, 224-225
disembodied 16, 269, 279-280

divergent thinking 124-125

dome 26, 79-81, 83-84, 87-88, 91-98, 100-103, 106, 128, 206-208, 237-238, 242-247, 249-253, 256-257, 259-262, 290, 314-344, 354-355, 361, 417, 423-424, 461-466, 468, 473, 482

Don R. Wilcox 225, 228, 235

E

Eadweard Muybridge 136

edge-blend 322

education 3, 39, 52, 103, 242, 244, 262, 284, 289, 298, 307-308, 348-351, 353-354, 360, 363, 365-366, 395-396, 400, 454, 475-476

effectual POV 271-272, 274

Ellie Araiza 193

embodied 5, 10, 12, 14-15, 17, 25-26, 69, 117, 217, 269, 278-281, 348-350, 352-353, 374-375, 377, 395, 400, 406, 418-419, 422, 434, 453, 478

embodied cognition 350

embodiment 2, 5-7, 10, 23, 26, 57, 350, 353-354, 386, 406, 435, 440

encounter 1-3, 6-7, 53, 100, 117, 297, 308, 356-357, 376, 387

entity 163, 217, 271, 278-279, 374

escape room 217, 220, 291, 303

essentialism 11, 15-16, 35

existential fears 432, 440

Existential psychotherapy 441

Expanded cinema 82

experiential 81, 100, 125, 127, 130, 194, 227, 264-265, 274-277, 285, 293, 297, 303, 308, 334, 336, 342, 348-349, 360, 365, 393, 395-396, 401, 411, 421, 424, 457, 459

experiential POV 274-276

expression 18, 20, 37-38, 43-44, 47, 49, 51, 61, 109, 123, 129, 150, 212, 238, 340, 362, 437, 439, 444

F

Facebook 11, 21-22, 25, 62, 65, 113, 176, 200-201, 224, 351, 379-380, 398-399, 407, 456, 468, 476

Fiducial Markers 46, 57

filmmaking 61, 83, 114, 130, 133, 149, 154, 167, 169, 203-204, 221, 223-224, 228-229, 231-234, 249, 262, 274

first person 18, 25, 151, 215, 221, 227, 258, 265, 267-270

Flatie 207, 220

Foveated rendering 131

Frag Film 212, 220

frameless medium 246

fulldome 79-95, 97-103, 105-106, 124, 135, 137-138, 237-239, 243-252, 254-262, 290, 314, 316, 322, 341, 354-355, 456, 461-462, 466, 468, 470, 482

Fulldome Festival 80, 82, 85-87, 92-95, 99-100, 105-106, 462

G

game enjoyment 371, 375-378, 380, 382-386

Generative Adversarial Networks (GANs) 19, 35

Generative systems 106

Gesamtkunstwerk 82, 458-459

gestalt 16, 432, 436-444

Globbing 174

Gregg Leonard 211

H

Healthmap 39, 57

Hollywood Rooftop 201, 204-206, 208, 210-212, 215

holographic capture 159

Holographic Recordings 57

Holoportation 51, 57

HTC 224-225, 227, 358

I

IMAX 249, 252, 315-316, 321-322, 330, 333, 341, 461

IMERSA 94, 102, 316, 469

Immanuel Kant 11, 81, 127

IMMERSIVE BRANDING 393-395, 400, 415

immersive entertainment 223, 284-289, 291, 293, 300, 305-306, 469-470

immersive experience 5, 27, 125-126, 144, 147, 151, 154, 177, 193, 198, 203, 205, 212-213, 215, 245, 269, 272, 275-276, 289, 295-296, 300, 307-308, 353, 365, 387, 418, 423, 433, 436-437, 442, 453, 462

immersive media 1-3, 11, 13, 22-27, 63, 79, 94, 109, 123-125, 127, 129-130, 139, 142-155, 158, 185, 187, 200-201, 205, 212-217, 219, 237, 257, 264, 287-288, 299, 305-306, 314, 316, 335-336, 338-339, 343-344, 348, 351, 364-365, 393, 416, 418-421, 424-426, 453-454, 461, 466, 468-470, 474-479, 484

immersive storytelling 87, 115, 142, 163, 179, 198, 203, 206, 222-225, 237-238, 246, 259, 284, 304, 476

immersive theatre 106, 147, 178

immersivists 84, 101

Integrity Test 174

Intellectual Property (IP) 482

interactive art 286, 288, 292-293, 296, 306, 334
interactivity 4, 63, 103, 133, 135, 137, 143, 149, 155,
  166-167, 169-171, 189, 192, 224, 272, 288, 295,
  300, 307, 355, 386

J

Jaunt 224, 228, 230, 235

K

keyframing 165, 174

L

Laughter of Knowledge 190, 198
Laughter of Surprise 190, 198
Laura Osburn 143
Lawnmower Man 176, 202-203, 214
LBE 284-290, 296-298, 300, 302-303, 305-306, 308-
  310, 470
learning 11, 19-20, 22, 35, 40, 45-46, 57, 101, 129,
  132-133, 138, 144, 148, 155, 178, 223-224, 268,
  277, 302-303, 307-308, 315, 343, 348-351, 354-
  360, 362-363, 365-366, 378, 398, 459, 476
LIDAR 24, 134
Light field 25
Light-Field Capture 35
lighting 42, 45, 149-150, 153, 207, 256, 296, 325-326,
  331, 333, 337, 342-343, 477
Liquid Sound 102-103
location-based entertainment 179, 284-290, 299-301,
  305, 309-310, 470

M

MacGyver 217-218
machine learning 19-20, 35, 40, 45-46, 57, 132-133, 303
Mary Spio 207
mass market 113, 200, 216-217
Max Fleisher 136
mental health 98, 299, 430-432, 435, 442-444, 456,
  464, 475
Metaphors 126-127
Metastage 158-164, 166, 169-171, 174
Mixed Reality 37, 126, 133, 135, 143, 149, 163-164,
  223-224, 237, 289-290, 300, 306, 315, 393, 395,
  403, 456
mocap 135, 137, 159, 161, 167, 169
Mona Lisa Moru 204-205
montage 61, 63, 70-71

mortal 274-276, 279-281
multi-camera 42, 46, 177, 180, 183, 185, 192, 198, 252
multi-projector 323-324, 330

N

narrative games 59-60, 62, 64, 71
narrative POV 265-269
narrative structure 61-63, 68-69, 71-73, 75, 155, 170
non-entity 271, 274, 279
nostalgia 371-372, 374-375, 377-380, 382-387

O

Oculus Rift 62, 200-201, 476
Olfaction 113, 116
olfactory art 109, 112, 114

P

participant 2, 4-6, 10, 67, 125, 130, 143-144, 147-148,
  151, 173, 201, 212, 246, 268-269, 271-272, 279-
  281, 295, 298, 301, 353, 380, 395, 400, 433, 437,
  475-476, 479, 483
Path-Mapping 198
Paul Debevec 42
Performance Animation 47-49, 57
perfume 84, 110-113, 115, 120
persona 38, 40, 89, 143, 406
Phenomenology 24, 35, 131
photogrammetry 24, 43-44, 58, 133, 135
place attachment 371, 373, 378, 381, 383-384
planetarium 83, 88, 94-97, 103, 238, 242-244, 316,
  321, 341, 354-355, 416-417, 422-424, 426, 460-
  462, 466
play 4, 20, 37, 63, 69, 83, 88, 118, 123, 127, 129-130,
  134-135, 146-148, 150-153, 159-161, 164, 167,
  178, 180, 185, 192-193, 209, 218, 222, 227, 233,
  246-248, 255, 269, 284-286, 292, 294, 303, 308-
  310, 316, 350, 363, 371-374, 376-377, 379, 381,
  384-385, 405, 423, 439, 460, 466
point cloud 44, 57, 135, 137, 161, 164
procedural 215, 220, 360
Producers Guild of America 458, 469, 474, 483
production design 150-151, 153
projection mapping 135, 299, 305, 314, 331, 334, 338
psychogeography 16, 24, 35

R

Rachel Shanblatt 183, 187, 268

Radiant Images 228-229, 235, 252

Ray Kurzweil 128

real time 19, 22, 48, 103, 130, 135, 160, 173, 208, 215-220, 223, 246-247, 260, 268, 299, 304, 353-355, 363, 395, 400, 469

Real-Time Computing 106

Richard Cray 48

Rick Lazzarini 47

Robot 66, 123-124, 127-129, 134-139, 163, 169, 229, 271, 274-275, 339, 464-465

Runner 100, 130, 180, 182, 198

S

Samantha Wolfe 406, 411

scale 6, 11, 52, 79-80, 94, 119, 129, 147, 249, 251, 289, 292, 304-305, 314-316, 326-327, 330, 350, 365, 405, 416-425, 442

scene switch 62, 70

scientific visualization 416-420, 422-426

screen time 159

second person 265, 267, 270, 277

SimGraphics 47-48

Simulation Hypothesis 13, 35

Simul-Story 181, 198

Smell-O-Vision 114-117

SMPTE 325

Social Impact Entertainment (SIE) 453-454, 474-476, 483-484

solve 49, 53, 101, 125, 127, 174, 215, 218, 291, 306, 308, 328

sound design 150, 152-153, 211-212, 234, 257

Spatial augmented reality 314

spatial computing 26, 126, 158, 200, 213-217, 219, 224, 393-394, 407, 415

springline 317, 321-322, 326, 332

Starbright Foundation 48

Stella Adler 205, 209

stereoscopic 22, 24, 44-45, 59, 131, 206, 209-210, 221, 228, 230-231, 234, 324, 423

Story-Organic Immersive Marketing 194, 198

storytelling 3, 5, 48, 50, 60, 62-63, 71, 81, 84, 87-88, 90, 92, 98, 115-117, 127, 142-146, 148, 150, 152-153, 155, 163, 166-167, 169, 171, 176-177, 179, 196, 198, 201-203, 205-206, 221-225, 233-234, 237-239, 245-246, 248-249, 254, 258-259, 261-262, 264, 277, 284-285, 289, 293-295, 298, 304, 309, 314, 316, 318, 338, 342-343, 362, 375, 396, 399, 406, 411, 453-454, 456, 458, 460-461, 463, 474-476, 479, 484

storyworlds 88, 119, 203, 219, 221-222, 288, 453, 457, 459, 474, 479, 483

Structure From Motion 44, 57

structured light 25, 44-45, 58, 134, 323-324

surface model 218, 220

synthetic 40, 83, 109, 112, 119, 121, 169, 416

T

Technicolor 207, 225, 228, 231, 233-235

Television Academy 483

third person 18, 61, 215, 258, 264-265, 267, 269-270, 277

Three Foot Rule 192, 198

Time-of-Flight 44-45, 58

training 52, 57, 117, 222, 315, 348, 350-357, 361, 363-365, 395, 400, 431-432, 435, 437, 469-470

transmedia 123, 213, 223, 453, 457-459, 474, 483

Transmedia Media 483

transpersonal psychology 430, 435, 438-439

TV Academy 474

U

umwelt 416-422, 425-426

uncanny valley 163-164

V

Vactor 47-48, 58

Virtual Assistant(s) 35

virtual beings 124, 132-133, 405, 415

virtual human 39, 41

Virtual Influencer(s) 19, 393, 405-406, 415

virtual reality 1, 10, 12, 16-18, 27-28, 37, 59-60, 70, 82, 101, 119, 124, 128, 142-143, 146-149, 151, 153, 176, 178, 188, 194, 200, 202, 204, 221-225, 227-228, 230-234, 237, 251, 264-265, 267-268, 274, 281, 286-288, 292, 298, 300-301, 306, 349-351, 353-354, 357-358, 393, 400-401, 416, 419, 430, 434, 438, 442-443, 456, 468-469, 476

Virtuosity 202

Visual Effects (VFX) 174

visual POV 266-267, 269-270, 277

volcap 159, 161

volumetric 11, 14, 23-25, 35, 40, 51, 54, 57-58, 133, 135, 137, 150-151, 158-171, 173, 179, 228, 307

volumetric capture 23-25, 40, 57, 150, 158-161, 163-167, 169, 171, 307

Volumetric Effigy 35

volumetric video 51, 58, 159

Vortex Immersion Media 330, 332-333, 335-339, 342,

462-463, 466, 472
voxel 164, 220
VR films 61-62, 64-73, 75-76, 232

W

Waldo 47, 58
Walking Simulator 35
WebXR 159
wellness 39, 52, 80, 320, 430, 436

X

XR 10, 109, 116-117, 126, 158, 160, 169, 176, 179, 181, 213, 223, 264-265, 270, 272, 275, 277-278, 288-290, 293, 314, 343, 393, 411, 456, 465, 469-470, 479

Y

Yuval Harari 143

Recommended Reference Books

ISBN: 978-1-5225-8491-9
© 2019; 454 pp.
List Price: $295

ISBN: 978-1-5225-7458-3
© 2019; 356 pp.
List Price: $195

ISBN: 978-1-5225-6023-4
© 2019; 384 pp.
List Price: $195

ISBN: 978-1-5225-5715-9
© 2019; 273 pp.
List Price: $175

ISBN: 978-1-5225-5696-1
© 2019; 277 pp.
List Price: $185

ISBN: 978-1-5225-9369-0
© 2019; 358 pp.
List Price: $205

Do you want to stay current on the latest research trends, product announcements, news and special offers?
Join IGI Global's mailing list today and start enjoying exclusive perks sent only to IGI Global members.
Add your name to the list at **www.igi-global.com/newsletters.**

Publisher of Peer-Reviewed, Timely, and Innovative Academic Research

IGI Global
DISSEMINATOR OF KNOWLEDGE

www.igi-global.com　　✉ Sign up at www.igi-global.com/newsletters　　f facebook.com/igiglobal　　t twitter.com/igiglobal　　in linkedin.com/igiglobal

Ensure Quality Research is Introduced to the Academic Community

Become an IGI Global Reviewer for Authored Book Projects

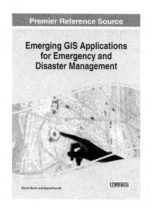
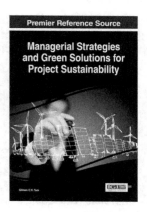

The overall success of an authored book project is dependent on quality and timely reviews.

In this competitive age of scholarly publishing, constructive and timely feedback significantly expedites the turnaround time of manuscripts from submission to acceptance, allowing the publication and discovery of forward-thinking research at a much more expeditious rate. Several IGI Global authored book projects are currently seeking highly-qualified experts in the field to fill vacancies on their respective editorial review boards:

Applications and Inquiries may be sent to:
development@igi-global.com

Applicants must have a doctorate (or an equivalent degree) as well as publishing and reviewing experience. Reviewers are asked to complete the open-ended evaluation questions with as much detail as possible in a timely, collegial, and constructive manner. All reviewers' tenures run for one-year terms on the editorial review boards and are expected to complete at least three reviews per term. Upon successful completion of this term, reviewers can be considered for an additional term.

If you have a colleague that may be interested in this opportunity,
we encourage you to share this information with them.

IGI Global Proudly Partners With eContent Pro International

Receive a 25% Discount on all Editorial Services

Editorial Services

IGI Global expects all final manuscripts submitted for publication to be in their final form. This means they must be reviewed, revised, and professionally copy edited prior to their final submission. Not only does this support with accelerating the publication process, but it also ensures that the highest quality scholarly work can be disseminated.

English Language Copy Editing

Let eContent Pro International's expert copy editors perform edits on your manuscript to resolve spelling, punctuaion, grammar, syntax, flow, formatting issues and more.

Scientific and Scholarly Editing

Allow colleagues in your research area to examine the content of your manuscript and provide you with valuable feedback and suggestions before submission.

Figure, Table, Chart & Equation Conversions

Do you have poor quality figures? Do you need visual elements in your manuscript created or converted? A design expert can help!

Translation

Need your documjent translated into English? eContent Pro International's expert translators are fluent in English and more than 40 different languages.

Email: customerservice@econtentpro.com   **www.igi-global.com/editorial-service-partners**

www.igi-global.com

Celebrating Over 30 Years of Scholarly
Knowledge Creation & Dissemination

InfoSci®-Books

A Database of Over 5,300+ Reference Books Containing Over 100,000+ Chapters Focusing on Emerging Research

GAIN ACCESS TO **THOUSANDS** OF REFERENCE BOOKS AT **A FRACTION** OF THEIR INDIVIDUAL LIST **PRICE**.

InfoSci®-Books Database

The **InfoSci®-Books** database is a collection of over 5,300+ IGI Global single and multi-volume reference books, handbooks of research, and encyclopedias, encompassing groundbreaking research from prominent experts worldwide that span over 350+ topics in 11 core subject areas including business, computer science, education, science and engineering, social sciences and more.

Open Access Fee Waiver (Offset Model) Initiative

For any library that invests in IGI Global's InfoSci-Journals and/ or InfoSci-Books databases, IGI Global will match the library's investment with a fund of equal value to go toward **subsidizing the OA article processing charges (APCs) for their students, faculty, and staff** at that institution when their work is submitted and accepted under OA into an IGI Global journal.*

INFOSCI® PLATFORM FEATURES

- No DRM
- No Set-Up or Maintenance Fees
- A Guarantee of No More Than a 5% Annual Increase
- Full-Text HTML and PDF Viewing Options
- Downloadable MARC Records
- Unlimited Simultaneous Access
- COUNTER 5 Compliant Reports
- Formatted Citations With Ability to Export to RefWorks and EasyBib
- No Embargo of Content (Research is Available Months in Advance of the Print Release)

*The fund will be offered on an annual basis and expire at the end of the subscription period. The fund would renew as the subscription is renewed for each year thereafter. The open access fees will be waived after the student, faculty, or staff's paper has been vetted and accepted into an IGI Global journal and the fund can only be used toward publishing OA in an IGI Global journal. Libraries in developing countries will have the match on their investment doubled.

To Learn More or To Purchase This Database:
www.igi-global.com/infosci-books

eresources@igi-global.com • Toll Free: 1-866-342-6657 ext. 100 • Phone: 717-533-8845 x100

www.igi-global.com

www.igi-global.com

Publisher of Peer-Reviewed, Timely, and
Innovative Academic Research Since 1988

IGI Global's Transformative Open Access (OA) Model:
How to Turn Your University Library's Database Acquisitions Into a Source of OA Funding

In response to the OA movement and well in advance of Plan S, IGI Global, early last year, unveiled their OA Fee Waiver (Offset Model) Initiative.

Under this initiative, librarians who invest in IGI Global's InfoSci-Books (5,300+ reference books) and/or InfoSci-Journals (185+ scholarly journals) databases will be able to subsidize their patron's OA article processing charges (APC) when their work is submitted and accepted (after the peer review process) into an IGI Global journal.*

How Does it Work?

1. When a library subscribes or perpetually purchases IGI Global's InfoSci-Databases including InfoSci-Books (5,300+ e-books), InfoSci-Journals (185+ e-journals), and/or their discipline/subject-focused subsets, IGI Global will match the library's investment with a fund of equal value to go toward subsidizing the OA article processing charges (APCs) for their patrons.

   Researchers: Be sure to recommend the InfoSci-Books and InfoSci-Journals to take advantage of this initiative.

2. When a student, faculty, or staff member submits a paper and it is accepted (following the peer review) into one of IGI Global's 185+ scholarly journals, the author will have the option to have their paper published under a traditional publishing model or as OA.

3. When the author chooses to have their paper published under OA, IGI Global will notify them of the OA Fee Waiver (Offset Model) Initiative. If the author decides they would like to take advantage of this initiative, IGI Global will deduct the US$ 1,500 APC from the created fund.

4. This fund will be offered on an annual basis and will renew as the subscription is renewed for each year thereafter. IGI Global will manage the fund and award the APC waivers unless the librarian has a preference as to how the funds should be managed.

Hear From the Experts on This Initiative:

"I'm very happy to have been able to make one of my recent research contributions, 'Visualizing the Social Media Conversations of a National Information Technology Professional Association' featured in the *International Journal of Human Capital and Information Technology Professionals*, freely available along with having access to the valuable resources found within IGI Global's InfoSci-Journals database."

– **Prof. Stuart Palmer,**
Deakin University, Australia

For More Information, Visit: www.igi-global.com/publish/contributor-resources/open-access or contact IGI Global's Database Team at eresources@igi-global.com.

CPSIA information can be obtained
at www.ICGtesting.com
Printed in the USA
BVHW010743260220
573205BV00007B/2

9 781799 824336